LENNON

LENNON

RAY COLEMAN

McGraw-Hill Book Company

New York   St. Louis   San Francisco
Hamburg   Toronto   Mexico

The author and publisher gratefully acknowledge permission to reproduce lyrics from the following songs:

The songs "Help!" (1965), "I'm Only Sleeping" (1966), "Getting Better" (1967), "Revolution" (1968), "Cold Turkey" (1969), and "How Do You Sleep?" (1971) are copyright © Northern Songs. All rights for the United States and Mexico are controlled and administered by Blackwood Music, Inc., under license from ATV Music [Maden]. All rights reserved. International copyright secured. Used by permission.

1 2 3 4 5 6 7 8 9 A R G A R G 8 7 6

First paperback edition, 1986

ISBN 0-07-011788-8

First American edition published in 1985 by the McGraw-Hill Book Company

LIBRARY OF CONGRESS CATALOGING IN PUBLICATION DATA

Coleman, Ray.
  Lennon.
  Original title: John Winston Lennon.
  Includes index.
  1. Lennon, John, 1940–   . 2. Rock musicians—
England—Biography. I. Title.
ML420.L38C64 1985   784.5'4'00924 [B]   85–71
ISBN 0-07-011788-8 (pbk.)

For Julian and Sean Lennon

ACKNOWLEDGEMENTS

The author and publishers gratefully acknowledge the permission of David Sheff and G. Barry Golson at *Playboy* magazine for reproduction of parts of their 1980 interview with John Lennon and Yoko Ono; Bill Harry, editor and publisher of *Mersey Beat* in Liverpool, for the right to reproduce John Lennon's first published writings; *Melody Maker* in London for permission to reproduce parts of several interviews conducted with the Lennons; Patrick Humphries, who collaborated with the author on the chapter on John's music; Capital Radio, London, and interviewer Roger Scott for the statements by Paul McCartney on the break-up of the Beatles and on John's relationship with Brian Epstein; and L. G. Wood, former managing director of EMI Records, London, for the loan of John's letter and a list of his songs.

CONTENTS

INTRODUCTION

When John Lennon's dearest friend, Stuart Sutcliffe, died at the appallingly premature age of twenty-one, John told Stuart's distraught fiancée, Astrid Kirchherr: 'Make your decision. You either die with him or you go on living your life.' John would want *his* survivors to heed that same sentence: he loathed martyrdom or too much accent on history. He preferred to look ahead rather than over his shoulder.

Yet since the murder of John Lennon on 8 December 1980, millions of people have felt enriched by looking back on his life and his music. He continues to touch us with the power of his songs that will stand for ever, and with the continuing evidence of his searing honesty.

History will record him as one of the great pacemakers of the twentieth century. Teddy boy, pop star, rebel student, propagandist for peace, poet, artist, songwriter, musician, bandleader, sloganeer, philosopher, wit, loving husband, doting father—Lennon was all these things and more. The founder, the powerhouse, the engine room of the Beatles, he became a catalyst and a dream-weaver for a generation's ideals.

Without him, the Beatles would never have existed, still less have become popular music's finest group; without him, they would have had no cutting edge, conscience or originality. And without him, the 1960s and its people would have been very different, much colder, much poorer.

I knew John Lennon for eighteen years but no one ever knew the complete person. He slipped through our fingers as a questing, restless spirit. We all snatched at parts of him.

'He was a simple, complex man,' says his widow, Yoko Ono. As in any biography, the blemishes as well as the strength in the man's behaviour and character are reported here. He was brilliant, warm, tender, sensitive, generous. He was also infuriating, tough, aggressive, naive and woundingly abrasive. He bruised many victims, often verbally, sometimes physically. But even to have been attacked, in any way, by John Lennon brought fame of a kind.

I saw him in Liverpool, a young man in a hurry before the Beatles achieved anything; and then in dressing rooms, recording studios, hotel rooms, cars and planes and trains all over the world. I saw him at his home during his first marriage to Cynthia when he was wary of fatherhood and fame; and I saw him from 1966 with Yoko, indivisible, interdependent. John Lennon's music, a rich legacy, testifies to his enjoyment of the highest of highs and his introspection during the lowest of lows. He was both a butterfly and a bee. Yet it's an extraordinary fact that all the many women who passed through his life, whether rejected girlfriend or divorced wife, or grieving widow or aunt, still love him madly. The paradox of this achievement is that he remains very much a man's man.

There were many facets to his character, and although he enjoyed the Beatles, he quickly tired of the emptiness of life as a pop star. 'Here I am, rich and famous as I always wanted to be, and *nothing's happening*,' he said to me at his home in Weybridge, Surrey, England, in 1965. Hundreds of superficial pop idols have been satisfied with fame and fortune, but ephemeral success would never satisfy John Lennon. Part of his philosophy was, ironically, voiced on his penultimate album, *Double Fantasy*, when he sang: 'Life is what happens to you when you're busy making other plans.' John wrote these words for 'Beautiful Boy', the song to his son Sean. He wrote the song fifteen full years after talking about his disaffection with life as a Beatle, when as a pop star he had been gaining weight, gaining money, gaining the adulation of millions, but losing himself.

He did not have to wait long for his life, and particularly his art, to change dramatically. Within a year of his restlessness, the Beatles stopped touring and he met Yoko Ono. As man and woman, husband and wife, and artists who were both competitive and compatible, they began a journey unheard of for a pop star. Eventually, they captivated millions, but it was a long, hard road. At first reviled as 'the woman who broke up the Beatles', taking cuddly John from the world, Yoko Ono, with John's help, confounded the bigots with her patience, her grace, her imagination, and by propounding a message that everyone understood but few articulated so well: peace and love. John, understandably, was intensely angry at the hatred poured on his wife. It was, he said, an insult to him as well as to Yoko. John's first wife, Cynthia, graphically describing in this book the sequence of events leading up to their divorce, says of John and Yoko: 'It was a meeting of the minds . . . I knew immediately I saw them together that they were right for each other. I knew I'd lost him.'

Many of us who knew John Lennon in Liverpool, London and New York, during three key phases of an exceptionally rich life, saw his extraordinary evolution from ambitious student, through the years of desperate, embryonic pop stardom, to millionaire, mature artist, and family man and philosopher. Few have achieved that sort of transformation with such distinction or with such heartfelt affection from the people. This book aims to capture the frenzy, the turbulence, the achievements and the joy of John's forty years. The people who helped me shape it, John's relatives and friends, as well as detached observers, had a unique perspective of Lennon and have been a tremendous source of inspiration, observation, information and illustrative material. Together with my own interviews with the man, these people have helped me portray John Lennon in his truest and most human light; their memories will allow readers to form their own views of an often misinterpreted artist.

My special thanks to John's indomitable, ever-loving Aunt Mimi for hours of patient conversation and memories; to John's first wife Cynthia for her total, often painful honesty, and for allowing me to reproduce for the first time her insightful, precious letters from John, as well as photographs; and to Astrid

Kirchherr for setting the scene in Hamburg and for the loan of Stuart Sutcliffe's drawings of John, published here for the first time.

I thank my wife Pamela and my sons Miles and Mark for their tolerance and for enduring and sustaining me in more than two years of research.

Yoko Ono Lennon's continual encouragement and unending patience have been an inspiration as well as a great practical help in recapturing the essence of their work, their marriage and their extraordinary chemistry. In Los Angeles, Elliot Mintz, John's closest male friend in America since 1971, gave, unstintingly, hours of his time, contributing perceptive insights into John's moods and movements, particularly during his years of seclusion. In New York, Leon Wildes, John's lawyer during his four-year immigration battle, was an irreplaceable help in describing those harrowing years, and photographer Bob Gruen and cafe owner Vincent Urwand, who both had unique friendships with John, provided important recollections.

Julian Lennon's enthusiastic interest has been infectious and I thank him particularly for his time and for the loan of illuminating postcards from his father.

The chronology of John's life at the end of the book was compiled by Britain's most knowledgeable, indefatigable researcher on all things Beatle: Mark Lewisohn, who also undertook most of the picture research. Mark's suggestions, and his assurance of the accuracy of all the facts in this book, have been invaluable since its inception and I thank him warmly.

My gratitude is due to many people, particularly in Liverpool, for their generous help: to Helen Anderson for great practical assistance and inspiration; Uncle Charles Lennon for remembering; Michael Isaacson for a memorable, informative night; Tony Barrow; Don Short; Brian Southall at EMI Records in London; William Pobjoy, John's headmaster at Quarry Bank High School, Liverpool, and his housemaster, Eric Oldman; Dick and Stephen James in London; George Martin; George Melly; Victor Spinetti; Rod Davis; Ron King; Helen Shapiro; Arthur Howes; Johnny Beerling; Billy J. Kramer; Richard Lester; Clive Epstein; Kenny Lynch; Gerry Marsden; Cilla Black; Hilary Williams; Liz and Jim Hughes at the fondly remembered Cavern Mecca in Liverpool; Bob Wooler, the superb Cavern compère with a fund of memories and a lifelong love of the 1960s; Bill Harry; Joe Flannery; Michael McCartney; Janet Webb; June Furlong; Ann Mason; Thelma Pickles; Phyllis McKenzie; Derek Taylor and Neil Aspinall.

I thank my agents David Grossman (in London) for his constant encouragement and wisdom and Merrilee Heifetz (New York) for her assid<u>i</u>ty and enthusiasm at all times. And without the shrewd editing of Jane Birdsell in London and Tom Miller in New York, the book would be poorer; their guidance and marshalling of the project through its many stages have been vital.

In a life that touched millions with its honesty and style, John Lennon became the victim of many myths. Chief among these was that he was an uncaring, rumbustious rock 'n' roller with little compassion. The reverse is true, as his music demonstrated from 'If I Fell', which he wrote in 1964, right through to 'Imagine' (1971), 'Woman' (1980) and 'Nobody Told Me', a record of extraordinary prescience released three years after his death. His anthems, 'Imagine', 'All You Need Is Love', 'Give Peace A Chance' and 'Jealous Guy', testify to his heart, his sincerity and his search for his own truths.

As an artist, he understood the full range of human emotions; as a man he displayed great bravery. To know him was to love him.

Ray Coleman
London, England

PROLOGUE

Aunt Mimi, who brought him up, never smacked him; but she long ago lost count of their arguments. They were usually about his studies or homework or the trouble he was getting into because of his terrible discipline at grammar school. Two or three days a week, at about ten o'clock, the phone would ring in her house, Mendips, 251 Menlove Avenue, Woolton, Liverpool.

'Oh Lord,' she'd say under her breath, knowing it was another call from the secretary at Quarry Bank High School. 'What's he done *now*?' John would have been disruptive, or involved in mocking teachers. He was often caned.

'And yet, you know,' says Mimi, 'the main reason he was such a worry to me while he was growing up was because I knew he had *something*. *He* knew he had it too. But he didn't know where exactly to put this talent he had, or where it might lead him.'

Day after day, Mimi would berate him. The reports coming from school told of his indolence, his troublemaking and his potential expulsion unless he changed. And every time she scolded him, Lennon would say something like: 'I know what I want to do, and it's not coming from the teachers. It's in *here*.' And he would bang his chest.

'That's all right, dear,' said Mimi, 'but don't neglect your work.' She knew he was right, but she was worried that he would end his schooldays with no qualifications. She was right about that too.

But young Lennon, even from the age of ten, confronted authority. He was simply not interested in orthodox schooling. 'I'm not having people bending over my shoulder, rubbing my work out and telling me it's no good,' he would tell his aunt. But in Mimi Smith he met a dead end. She offered more resistance than any schoolteacher. She loved and cared for John Lennon with a passion and determination that he was not to understand until much later in his life. But she wasn't having her nephew playing a dangerous game with his future.

'The school reports are bad, John. I won't have it. How are you going to get yourself a job if you don't do well at school?'

'But the teachers are so boring, Mimi.' He was good at English, art and French, awful at arithmetic, and made little effort at anything.

'Go to your room. Go on. Go, John. Do some homework.'

John stood for as long as he dared by the door of the morning-room at Mendips, a semi-detached house in a respectable suburb. Mimi kept it immaculately clean and well furnished. 'You wait,' he said. 'One of these days, I'm going to be famous and then you'll be sorry you were like this to me.'

'All right then, John. Until that day when you are, get upstairs. Elvis Presley may be a very nice man but I don't want him for breakfast, dinner, and supper.'

Eight years later and after scores of similar scenes with Mimi, John Lennon went back to Mendips, a successful Beatle, his face, his music, and his personality celebrated throughout the world. She cooked him his favourite: egg and chips and tea.

'He reminded me,' says Mimi, 'of what he'd said at that doorway when he was about sixteen.'

'Remember I said I'd be famous?' he said.

'Well,' said Mimi, thrilled but totally unimpressed. 'What always worried me, John, was that you wouldn't be so much famous as *notorious*. You were certainly *that* as a child. Think of the worries I had. If the Beatles hadn't come along, you could have ended up on the scrap heap without any school qualifications, and you'd soon have got through the bit of money I had. . . . '

'Oh Mimi, if the Beatles hadn't happened I'd always have been able to write or paint or draw.'

She reminded him of her favourite phrase, when she would banish him to the front porch with the £17 guitar she had reluctantly bought him from Hessy's store in Liverpool. He had nagged her when he was sixteen to 'let me get the music bug out of my system'.

'The guitar's all right as a hobby, John, but you'll never make a living from it.'

John replied, 'Well, I can always be an illustrator.'

The castigation, so typical of Mimi in its opinionated certainty, reverberated around the world as the Beatles story gained speed and the legend of Lennon's tough but caring aunt grew stronger.

'He was a worry to educate at school, and he kept telling me he was bored at college. I'd have to lay down the law: ''Get on that eight-thirty bus until your time as a student is up, John. *Then* you can mess about with the guitar.'' '

When he became a pop star and laughed at his aunt's reprimands, John said to her: 'Actually, Mimi, you were quite right. I'd never have made it as a single performer as a guitarist. I was never good enough. But, y'know, I always guessed something would happen. And I met Paul and we met George and —well, it turned out great, didn't it, Mimi?'

1
THE REBEL

'Oh God, Buddy Holly's dead'

She loved him but the smell of scallops in his hair and on his body drove her crazy. Liverpool scallops were slices of potato surrounded by a greasy, thick batter, dipped into fat and deep-fried. John Lennon was addicted to them. Most lunchtimes, as a student at Liverpool College of Art, he crossed the road to the chip shop in Falkner Street and piled himself up with a bag of chips and a bag of scallops. He would take them back to one of the classrooms, perhaps play the guitar while eating, and enthral a few students. The gentleness of his playing contrasted vividly with his hell-raising personality. To many students this reprobate seventeen-year-old was absolutely magnetic.

But he stank. 'It permeated from his head, through his clothes, and his entire body reeked of greasy scallops,' recalls Helen Anderson, one of the students who adored the 'lovable swine' who dressed like a teddy boy. She nagged him to wash the grease out of his hair and get rid of the DA ('duck's arse') style at the back. 'Get lost,' Lennon would snap. The greased-back hair, DA at the rear, sideburns, drape jackets, crepe-soled shoes, tatty checked shirt, and drainpipe trousers, all based on Elvis Presley whom he regarded as the king, were central to Lennon's personality. For they made him stand out from the rest of the students. Nothing was more important to him than individuality.

Helen Anderson had a unique, direct line to John Lennon's

thoughts: he would confide in her about his love affairs. She
was a patient listener and admirer of his wit, and since there
was never any suggestion that they would become lovers she
became a platonic friend and confidante.

She possessed a major attraction for John Lennon. At sixteen, she had actually *met* a pop star of the day, Lonnie Donegan, whom she had painted in oils for the astronomical fee of
forty dollars. There had been stories in the newspapers about
her artistic talent. 'Hey, are you that bird who painted Lonnie
Donegan?' John asked her on her first day at art school. He
was impressed.

As John's undisciplined, hilarious behaviour made more of
an impact on her, Helen would go home and tell her mother
every day about John's crazy antics that had broken up the
class. She demonstrated how John crept up behind people and
suddenly boomed one of his favourite songs into their ear. It
was Screaming Jay Hawkins' hit, 'I Put A Spell On You'.
Helen and John's special friendship was sealed when he regularly gave her his trousers to narrow the legs into drainpipe
style. 'Take these in for me, would you, Heloon,' he would
say. 'They're too bloody wide.' (Heloon was his nickname for
her because she always laughed uproariously at his outrageous
behaviour.) Dutifully, she often took John's black trousers home
and returned them next morning tapered. The 'drainies' were
worn *underneath* his 'regulation shape' trousers until he reached
the bus stop on his way to college, where he slipped them off.
That way, his Aunt Mimi would not see over breakfast that he
was a latent 'ted'. He had to find many similar methods of
fending off her wrath about his untidy appearance.

Those who were at art college with John Lennon are unanimous: he was destined either to be a great public figure, a
triumphant star with unique gifts, or he would be a layabout,
a burden on society who achieved nothing. There would be no
halfway for this extraordinary teenager who roared through
Liverpool, making an impact on everybody who was willing
to be touched by him.

'Even at sixteen I knew he was destined to some sort of
grandeur and greatness,' says Helen Anderson. 'In his first six
months at college, his paintings were very wild and aggressive.
Every one he did incorporated the interior of a night club and

they were very strongly drawn, very dark, and there was always a blonde girl sitting at the bar looking like Brigitte Bardot. There were always musicians in John's early drawings, a band on a bandstand, dim lights, something sleazy. I always liked them. But very few people noticed his work in his early days at college.'

To the teachers Lennon was a pest, a danger. His work, erratically presented, was the last thing they worried about. It was his behaviour as a catalyst for trouble in every classroom that they outlawed in unison. Eventually, Lennon and the masters became polarized, just as they had done at his previous school, Quarry Bank High School, Woolton. The more they bored him with their orthodox, predictable, unyielding methods of education which he abhorred, the more he would seek his own route. 'The masters were not interested in him,' says Helen Anderson. 'He was a nuisance to the entire college, distracting everybody else who wanted to learn.'

Lennon didn't care. He had his gang, camp followers like the laconically funny Geoff Mohammed, who was a perfect foil for John's pungent humour. There was Tony Carricker, who joined in the crowd who laughed almost non-stop at John's ribaldry. And there was even June Furlong, the twenty-seven-year-old model who was the subject of the life class in which they would all have to draw her body. Even she became convulsed with laughter on many days when she was supposed to be a serious art subject. Lennon discovered early in his teen years what was to be one of his most endearing characteristics when he was in deep trouble; he could always make people laugh with his very distinctive, cruel, exploitative sense of humour.

In the very warm life class of room 71 at the college, fifteen students were set their weekly task of drawing June. Some would doze off when the teacher left the room. Suddenly Lennon would give out a little giggle. Nobody would take much notice. Two or three minutes later, his giggle would be louder. That would disturb people, especially those trying to concentrate on drawing. A real laugh followed, and a few minutes later his loud, hyena-like cackle totally broke up the class. By then everyone was hysterical at John's calculated disruption. To top it off, Lennon then jumped out from behind his easel, ran into the middle of the room where June was sitting, naked, rocking with laughter and trying to stop her body from shaking for the benefit of the students who wanted to continue to draw it. Finally, for his *pièce de résistance*, Lennon brought laughter to the entire class by leaping around the room where silence and decorum were the rule.

During another life class session, the whole class produced proper drawings of the nude which were soberly dissected by the teacher, Teddy Griffiths. When John came to hand in his effort, he had perversely drawn nothing of June. He produced a drawing of the only item on June's body—her wristwatch. Students were aghast at his nerve—and originality.

While John's eccentric behaviour, non-conformist dress and swearing in front of the teachers were enough to make him prominent, a less rational, disturbing side to his character emerged soon after he joined the art college. He quickly developed a bizarre obsession for cripples, spastics, any human deformities, and people on crutches. He had a particular fascination for warts. It was a subject that was to manifest itself throughout John Lennon's years of fame. It took root, firmly and with a gaggle of students embarrassed at their own sick sense of humour in laughing at him, here at art college.

Deformities cropped up in his drawings all the time. So did his dry wit, the quality that dominated his personality. For a seventeen-year-old he had a subtle sense of humour way ahead of his time. There was always life and movement in his drawings, to redeem that streak of cruelty. Every person he portrayed had a physical affliction, usually a wart sticking out of the side of the head. Asked why, John would shrug it off, with the implication that if you had to ask, you weren't on his wavelength, so there was no point in discussing it.

By 1958, in his eighteenth year, with all the guns blazing at the art college which bestowed upon him lots of freedom in dress, and demeanour, but which was unsuccessfully grappling on all fronts with his wildness, John Lennon could not be missed. He was desperately short-sighted, which somehow added to his mystique among the girls. He wore teddy boy clothes and his black horn-rimmed spectacles, worn only under the greatest pressure, for he had an ego, were held together at the joints by Elastoplast. He rarely had any money, and borrowed it permanently from his gang. He scrounged ciggies all the time, somehow managing to get through between ten and twenty Woodbines a day. He drank too many pints, usually black velvets, in Ye Cracke, the students' pub in Rice Street near the college, and since he could not take much beer without feeling its effects, he frequently behaved either obnoxiously or violently. He kept losing his artist's materials and would constantly ask his Aunt Mimi, with whom he lived, for more money on the pretext of needing a new pen or other equipment.

He was a startlingly talented, non-conforming artist, but so lazy that even his close college friend, the serious intellectual Stuart Sutcliffe, could not drag John's attributes into line and get him properly on course. Music, rock 'n' roll, Elvis Presley, Chuck Berry, Little Richard—it was all too much of a pull for Lennon, who would stalk the college with a guitar strapped to his back, ready for the lunchtime sessions over scallops and chips in Arthur Ballard's classroom with two other kids from the more academic Liverpool Institute next door. Their names were Paul McCartney and George Harrison.

On 4 February 1959 John walked solemnly into the classroom, visibly shaken. It was not often that students saw John Lennon vulnerable, broken, unhappy. 'Oh God, Buddy Holly's dead,' he muttered. Holly, a vital pioneer of early rock 'n' roll, a singer of plaintive love songs wedded to jerky, haunting melodies, was one of John's idols. He had died in a plane crash in America. Unlike many of the students John did not cry over the news, but went silent for the day and took some time to snap out of the shock. Lennon always buried his feelings deeply.

It was the third great emotional death to mark John's life, and he was still only eighteen. Seven months before Buddy Holly's death John's mother, Julia Lennon, had died instantly at the age of forty-four after being knocked down by a car when leaving the home of John's Aunt Mimi, with whom John was living. The death of Uncle George, Mimi's husband, who doted on John and had bathed him, protected him and been a warm and loving father-figure during his childhood, had rocked John at the age of eleven. And now, just as John was getting inspiration from Buddy Holly, and totally absorbing the wonderful, embryonic sounds of American rock 'n' roll music, it was like another death in the family.

For the teenager who had come from a broken home, despite all his natural inner orthodoxy, respect, and sentimentality, there seemed only one way to get through his early life after eighteen years punctuated by physical fights and emotional scars. That was to erect a cocoon of belligerence, aggression, sick or vicious wit, and castigation. The real John Lennon, from his birth until his death, was a vastly misunderstood man. His drawings and his spoken word may have injured or hurt, and he was capable of wounding with pertinent jibes that shot straight through the heart of the victim. But he always aimed his arrows at people he could not respect, and beneath that abrasive exterior beat a heart of pure gold. Eventually, it was to come out in his music as he mushroomed into one of popular music's most beloved, searingly honest artists who, more than anyone else in his field, wore his heart, as well as his art, on his sleeve. In 1959 the personality of John Lennon was changing quickly, but the world had not heard of him. A few were privileged to see the man shaped by his own grit as he rampaged through first Quarry Bank High School and then made an indelible mark on Liverpool College of Art before becoming an emblem for youth: artist, poet, and philosopher. The family, students, and friends who saw John Lennon as a schoolboy and teenager testify to one undeniable fact that marked him then as it marked his entire life: you could loathe him or like him. But you could never feel neutral about him. And you certainly could not ignore him.

Cynthia Powell knew that she had fallen helplessly in love with John Lennon when, one day in the art college lecture hall, she noticed one of her closest friends, Helen Anderson, apparently stroking John's hair. Helen was sitting immediately behind John; Cynthia, a few seats away, began trembling with jealousy at the sight of another girl touching him.

To this day Cynthia believes that Helen and John were romantically linked, at the very least. Helen denies it. She was part of a coterie of Lennon college friends who formed his essential audience. Helen says she was not fondling John. Instead she was trying to straighten out his DA hairstyle which she hated. But the fact that Helen cared enough to make her presence known to John, and the banter between them, was enough to arouse Cynthia's envy.

A year older than John, and a serious, formal art student, Cynthia Powell seemed theoretically, to other students, the unlikeliest choice for a loud-mouthed, troublemaking teddy boy who was roaring through art college in the days when words like beatnik and bohemian evoked images of dangerous living. She lived her life, particularly at college, 'by the book', as a conscientious, ambitious student. But Cynthia had four key attractions that were to attract John. Firstly, she had the potential in his eyes to look like Brigitte Bardot, his strongest fancy. Many of his previous girlfriends had to bow to his demand: 'Grow your hair long, like Brigitte.' He would do drawings for them of how they were expected to look. One student, Joni Crosby, looked even more like Bardot, and Lennon drooled over her in the canteen. During tea break he said to Helen Anderson, day after day: 'Bloody hell—she's fantastic—just like Brigitte Bardot.' Secondly, Cynthia came from snooty Hoylake, 'over the water' on the Wirral, and 'spoke posh, talked proper', which he believed made her unattainable to a lad from Woolton. Thirdly, she was plainly besotted over him and would do anything to please him, even dye her brown hair blonde and grow it long. Fourthly, and crucially, she was serene. As an eighteen-year-old art student Cynthia had a composure that marked her out from the others in college. Lennon, the college performer who strove to make an impression by cackling in class, smoking when it was against the rules, and bucking the system at every twist and turn, was chemically attracted to Cynthia because she was supercool and different. *Vive la différence* was a characteristic that was to *drive* Lennon all his life. The orthodox and the predictable usually bored him, although he always clung strongly to traditional values in human relationships and family life.

Cynthia and John had two other important things in common. Cynthia was fatherless, her commercial traveller father having died when she was seventeen, so, like John, she knew the burdens of being a teenager with one parent; and Cynthia was, like John, hopelessly short-sighted and wore spectacles.

But in his earliest days at college, he played her attractiveness to him very cool and hung around with other girl students on a platonic basis.

In the tradition of the busking art student, John and two college girls, Helen Anderson and Ann Sherwood, spent afternoons drifting across the ferry from Pier Head to Seacombe. This route was chosen because it was the cheapest boat; when they arrived they would walk the three miles down the promenade or along the sands to New Brighton, with John playing the role of entertainer. 'Be funny, John!' 'Sing us a song, John!' they asked him. And John, his guitar slung across his black jacket, would love being the clown, the star of the show, for Helen and Ann. The girls had dutifully done the work Arthur Ballard had set them, and the afternoons were free for them. John told them he could not be bothered to do his work, so needed no persuading to have a musical day at the seaside.

Musically, his repertoire was funny but thin. 'He only strummed his guitar. It was obvious he wasn't much of a player then,' says Helen Anderson. His songs included Buddy Holly and Little Richard with a little Elvis Presley thrown in. He'd ad lib with everyday phrases and extemporize on the songs which he was to be heard jokingly playing around with in classes: he'd wander around looking over people's shoulders at their work, mumbling 'Sugar In The Morning, Sugar In The Evening, Sugar At Suppertime', 'When You're Smiling', and the one everyone laughed at:

> I like New York in June, how about you?
> I like a Lennon tune, how about you?
> Holding Rabbis in the movie show, when all the
> Lights are low, may not be new, but I like it,
> How about you?

Says Helen Anderson: 'He definitely had a thing about Jews and loved taking the mickey out of them. The slightest chance to work them into a song and make it funny, he'd take it. But it wasn't nearly so cruel as his thing about cripples and afflicted people.'

In 1958, as John Lennon swept through art college, world events that were changing a post-war Britain from uncertainty into prosperity were making an enormous impact on young people. Khrushchev became Russia's premier, marking the start of a cold war; the first transatlantic commercial jet service began; and an aeroplane crashed on take-off in Munich, Germany, killing twenty-three passengers including eight Manchester United footballers. There were terrible race riots in London's Notting Hill, the first serious riots of their kind; General de Gaulle was forming his first French government; and magical, influential pop music names like Elvis Presley ('Jailhouse Rock'), Jerry Lee Lewis ('Great Balls of Fire'), the Everly Brothers ('All I Have To Do Is Dream'), The Coasters ('Yakety Yak'), and the Teddy Bears ('To Know Him Is To Love Him') were forging a vital new impact for British popular music fans who listened to it in bed under their blankets on the barely audible, but adventurously hip, Radio Luxembourg.

The following year the M1 became Britain's first motorway, to presage a new era of speed and travel; the giant E.M.I. Records discontinued the use of 78 r.p.m. records in favour of 45 r.p.m. singles; and history was made by ten thousand members of the Campaign for Nuclear Disarmament marching from Aldermaston to London, the biggest demonstration of its kind until then. Musically, there were lots for Lennon and his friends to drool over, including Buddy Holly's 'It Doesn't Matter Any More', and Elvis Presley's 'I Got Stung'. Against all the good sounds that were grasped by Lennon, he developed an instinctive hatred for what he regarded as the bland, antiseptic music of new British stars like Cliff Richard, Adam Faith, and Craig Douglas.

The Lennon of these years, torn inside by a fractured family life, did not suffer fools. He was a young man in a hurry. But he did not know his destination. What he did recognize, immediately he felt it, was love. He had had torrid relationships with girls before he met Cynthia Powell. But with her, something else gelled to make her his automatic and serious partner. With the arrogance that characterized him he accepted that she was, in the words of Helen Anderson, nutty about him and prepared to be used as a doormat, to please John's every whim and lend him her art materials. But no, to John that wasn't all: many girls were ready to be servile towards him, to laugh at his weakest jokes and physically titillate him in his quest to learn everything about sex during an era when it was taboo among teenagers. Cynthia offered much, much more than those attractions to which he had become accustomed. From Cynthia came also intelligence and the great, unspoken heatwave that was to make them inseparable for about eight years: love, understanding, care, and devotion. John returned it, for, with the death of his mother and the desertion of his father, the need for an anchor to his life was much more real than might have been apparent to the students who saw him as a court jester. All he needed was love, music, an escape route from the hum-drum, routine, wage-earning future that many of his contemporaries seemed to regard as inevitable. To John Lennon, even at seventeen, nothing was inevitable. Deep down inside, he saw himself as special. His method of saying so was to project a rough and tough exterior, because he had no platform or power to do anything about it. Yet physically, mentally, and because her tranquillity offered a useful antidote to his excesses, Cynthia was his perfect partner.

Reflecting on those years, Cynthia is in love not merely with John—whom she will love to distraction until the day she dies—but with the sweet, innocent, yet passionate romance of the college years together. 'He had a strange fascination for many of the girls, like Helen Anderson and Thelma Pickles,' says Cynthia. 'He wasn't the sort of chap you'd swoon over. What concerned me, and drew me to him at first, was that he was so lazy about his work. He didn't give a damn and I got worried, being a conscientious type, that he would get into trouble and get kicked out of college. Everyone knew that he was in art college on sufferance. No teachers wanted him there, except Arthur Ballard, who was a similarly artistic type and saw some potential in John. I cared more about his future and his work than he did. I saw in John so much talent, as an artist, but if he got chucked out of college, which was likely, where would he go? I was a lot older than him, mentally.'

The story of their first encounters sounds like fiction but is fact. Cynthia, in her second year at art college, was among a dozen students who had chosen to attend lettering class twice a week. Everyone there felt positive about the subject, except John Winston Lennon. He quickly became the talk of the class because he had been shoved there through a series of rejections by teachers who had grown tired of his disruptiveness in other classes. Lennon was not a candidate for the lettering class, either; his natural style was to draw cartoons of whatever his teachers had ordered.

Cynthia remembers that the two lettering class days, on which she would study John, became her 'fix'. For the rest of the week they were separated during studying hours and she would roam the corridors of the college hoping for a glimpse of the boy who was the unruly focal point of the students but had become her obsession. It was all too much for a conventional girl from Hoylake who already had a steady boyfriend who was saving for their future in a building society.

To be hooked on Lennon was also slightly dangerous because of his notoriety. 'On lettering days he always arrived late, anything up to half an hour,' says Cynthia. 'He looked a mess. He had scruffy black trousers, quiffed hair with a slight DA at the back, and it was an attempt to look like a teddy boy. But often, even though he was late, he'd have a screwed-up drawing under his arm to present to the teacher. And it would get him off the hook, in a way. Arthur Ballard would hold it up to the class and say: "Now look, this is the kind of original idea and inspiration we're looking for." ' The fact that it was unrelated to lettering didn't matter. Lennon had quickly found a way to buck the system.

'After I'd first experienced John in lettering,' says Cynthia, 'I couldn't get him out of my mind.' On lettering days she would arrive in the classroom earlier than anyone else to sit near where he had been sitting in the previous lesson. What finally drove them together was a playful test, among all the students one morning, of each other's eyesight. 'We had identical short-sightedness, and when we started talking about what we couldn't see—like when the bus was coming—we took off,' says Cynthia. Major romances have been built on stranger events, but for Cynthia Powell the moment of that discovery was magical. She blessed her disability, for her passion for the wild one was now all-consuming.

Still, she thought that she, with her short, permed brown hair, tweedy skirt, twinset and Hoylake image, was too proper for Lennon. Cynthia could not see her attractiveness to him adding up to much. She loaned him materials during lettering, she had similarly bad eyesight, and he was always a fraction more polite to her than he was to the other students. But that was all. Her teenage crush seemed to offer no way out.

But fate smiled on her. As the college's vacation loomed for the summer of 1958, one of the students thought it would be fun to have a lunchtime end-of-term party. They got permission to use the smallest room in the college and one of them brought a record player. That year's hits were the Everly Brothers' 'All I Have To Do Is Dream', Conway Twitty's 'It's Only Make Believe' and 'Tom Dooley' by the Kingston Trio. Cynthia's eyes rarely left Lennon at that party, but she had teenage blushes of embarrassment at herself, too. When John walked over and asked her to dance, slowly, to the song 'To Know Him Is To Love Him' by the Teddy Bears, she nearly collapsed with excitement. 'I think John was slightly embarrassed too, which was unusual for him,' she says. 'Perhaps he knew what was happening to us. It was painful and beautiful.' The other students looked on amazed at the unlikely combination.

As the party began to break up, John asked Cynthia if she was involved with another man. He said he'd like to meet her, out of college.

'I'm awfully sorry,' Cynthia said. 'I'm engaged to this fellow in Hoylake.'

John's retort to this was: 'I didn't ask you to marry me, did I?'

Cynthia, flustered, thought she had let him slip through her fingers, for the Lennon reply seemed cutting and final. But he wasn't as dismissive as she feared. He said to Cynthia and her best friend, Phyllis McKenzie: 'Let's go and have a drink.'

Cynthia and Phyllis had never before been to the college boozer, Ye Cracke. Here, black velvets were drunk and Woodbines smoked most lunchtimes by hard-up Lennon, surrounded by his cronies. To Cynthia and Phyllis, adjourning from college to anything other than the train and bus home wasn't done; but suddenly Cynthia understood what college life was supposed to be like. Lennon was, however, still far away in the crowd of men and made no attempt to chat her up in the bar, so she began to leave. She thought the dance with John, and the drink, probably marked the start and end of their relationship.

As she neared the door, Lennon's voice boomed out above

the pub chat: 'Didn't you know Miss Powell was a nun, then?' It was a typically Lennonesque dig at her propriety. She spun round, their eyes met, and she walked over to his side. He persuaded her to stay. Both had had a few too many drinks and little to eat during the day when so much had happened. As the drinking session continued, it was obvious that John Lennon and Cynthia Powell were going to be together.

That night, they left the pub and spent all night together at the rented bedsitter in Gambier Terrace, a convenient two-minute walk from college, of John's best college friend, the serious-minded Stuart Sutcliffe, to whom Lennon turned when he tired of the audience of students who simply wanted him to act funny. Increasingly, John and Stuart became very close. There was never any discussion about what they had in common: it was intuitive. Sutcliffe and Lennon bounced off each other because they had the same speed of thought, restlessness, and a natural talent. In Stuart's case, though, it was a talent he marshalled and nursed.

Three months older than John, Stuart was a model student, a star pupil, and he wanted to become a famous painter. His drawings of skulls and skeletons, particularly, were outstanding and appealed to Lennon's interest in the macabre. A year ahead of John in college, Stuart was concentrating on painting and sculpture and worked long, arduous hours. 'He was very spotty with horn-rimmed glasses and, just like John's, they were taped up at the edges,' recalls Cynthia. 'As a student, he was precisely the opposite of John, because he was working himself to death, totally dedicated. He wasn't eating properly and didn't have much to do with girls. His work was all-important to him.'

As Stuart and John became more friendly, Sutcliffe became more of a leveller to Lennon. 'John needed Stuart really badly,' says Cynthia. 'He was going down the wrong road with these two characters, Tony Carricker and Geoff Mohammed, and he probably realized it because John wasn't stupid. It was Stuart who persuaded John to concentrate more on his art and less on messing about,' says Cynthia. 'When John saw Stuart's work, he was inspired by it. He started painting a lot more seriously himself, slapping great canvases around. Before, he had been working too tightly on little cartoons and on smaller areas. Suddenly, Stuart drew him into the painting rooms often and

John at last had a mate to help show him the way. After college, Stuart would stay on and say to John: "Don't worry about it. Just slap it on, a bit here, a bit there," whereas John had always been very wary and careful and detailed. Stuart was great fun in art and their minds were right for each other. John obviously looked up to him, and he was bringing John out as an artist.'

But it was too late to hold John back from what was becoming his major interest: music.

Strong though Stuart was in trying to pull John towards serious work, Lennon had by now reached the point of no return. If a lesson or a day went by without his causing mirth in the classroom, he would have been diagnosed ill by those who were expecting him to perform.

'He was the biggest mickey-taker I've met,' says Helen Anderson. 'He picked on all kinds of characters in school, whatever their backgrounds, and tried to find some way of laughing at them. There was one, awfully nice well brought-up fellow with frizzy red hair, whom John persisted in annoying by calling him Snodgrass and making everyone laugh. John wouldn't let go of something once it stuck with him: "Snoddy" this and "Snoddy" that, to the annoyance of this very straight student. Another poor student named Derek had the habit of picking his nose in front of everybody and didn't realize he was doing it. We'd be in the middle of a lesson, with everybody silent, and suddenly John would scream out at the top of his voice: "Dirty picky nosey, Derek!" Of course it broke up the class. We all fell about laughing.

'He used to make horrible jokes against the singer Alma Cogan, impersonating her singing "Sugar In The Morning, Sugar In The Evening, Sugar At Suppertime". He'd pull crazy expressions on his face to try to imitate her expressions. We all had hysterics. He was a real comedian.'

Curiously, when the Beatles became famous, John was to become friendly with Alma Cogan and visit her home.

'We could always tell when he was about to come out with a gem of a joke or a phrase,' says Helen Anderson. 'His nostrils and cheeks would swell up. He was such a wit, he made an impression on everybody in the whole college. But contrary to what Cynthia believed, I loved him and adored him but never fancied him.' He was a natural comic, but in a style that wasn't expected. When students asked his name, when he first arrived at art college, he would say: 'Simply Simple Pimple. John Wimple Lennon.' He would preen a little when he gave his real middle name of Winston—not because he felt nationalistic about having been named after Britain's great wartime prime minister, Winston Churchill, but because it sounded posh and was different and unexpected.

Stories of his outlandish college behaviour abound. One panto day, the annual event for which the students dressed up and went around the city shaking collection boxes for charities, seven students got together to dress up. John roped in Paul McCartney and George Harrison from the Liverpool Institute next door, together with Ann Preece, Rod Murray, Helen Anderson, and Mona Harris. At John's instigation, he and Paul and George were to dress up as vicars. They found yellow sweatshirts which they wore upside-down with their legs inside the sleeves, and dog collars with black tailcoats. The Lennon plan was to 'raid' every café in every department store in Liverpool. They marched in shaking their tins and everybody would turn round to look. Within a few minutes John would stand up on a table and shout: 'My lords, ladies and gentlemen. On my right, in the red corner . . .' and Paul would jump up. 'And on my left, in the blue corner . . .' and George would come out. The two would start fighting on restaurant tables, in every chain store, to attract attention. And they were ceremonially thrown out of every place they entered—but not before raising a few pounds by the sheer noise and audacity of their stunt.

Later that day the students went to the city's Adelphi Hotel, where John persuaded the staff to lend him a bucket and a mop. A crowd of several hundred gathered outside the hotel to watch Lennon, still dressed as a vicar, singing loudly and mopping the zebra crossing. He was the star turn; the others were giving him moral support, loudly and successfully, and shaking their tins.

The light, undisciplined attraction of college life greatly appealed to John. After the formality of his previous school, where he had trouble fighting the system and had been an academic disaster, art college at least seemed to give him the chance to behave as a young adult. There was the array of pretty girls, many of whom looked on him as a card as well as a tearaway; there was encouragement from Arthur Ballard, who, even though he didn't care for John's refractory style, knew the boy had something and did his utmost to encourage him; there was the security of the gang of Geoff Mohammed and Tony Carricker and Jeff Cane. There was, eventually, Cynthia with whom he had a fast-moving love affair.

'Before me,' says Cynthia, 'there was another girl he mentioned to me named Beth whom he was pretty serious about. But her parents couldn't stand John. He kept saying to me: "Don't worry, they've banned me from seeing her anyway, they think I'm a ruffian. They won't have me round." ' Lennon had met her when he was fifteen and a pupil of Quarry Bank High School. The fact that he talked openly about her infuriated Cynthia during their early romance, and reached breaking-point when, one night, he did not arrive for their nightly meeting. 'He quickly admitted he'd been to see Beth, to see if it was finished between them, and it was definitely all over and we were together.'

Unknown to Cynthia there were other girls in John's life before their romance blossomed, and during their love match John would vanish from the college on some afternoons and go off with them. One of his gang would support him by spinning a story about where John had gone. Lennon frequently found himself arm in arm with a casual girlfriend walking back to college, and suddenly went into a panic at the sight of Cynthia. He would flee round the corner in case she saw him. Outwardly sharp-tongued and tough though he was, even at that age Lennon did not want to hurt Cynthia, whom he quickly christened Cyn. She was on a pedestal, classier than any of the other girls with whom he had quickie affairs, and the last thing that could be risked was Cynthia discovering his unfaithfulness. Cynthia, to this day, is blissfully unaware that there was any other heavy romance for John in his college days . . . which is exactly what John wanted her to believe.

With Stuart fast emerging as his bosom mate, and trying in vain to pull him solidly into art as a career; Cynthia having a powerful love affair with him and meeting him whenever she could; and the teachers throwing up their hands in dismay at the eighteen-year-old who wouldn't listen, John Lennon in 1958 was a complex, talented young man. His restless mood was partly summed up by the way he moved around. 'He gave off this feeling that he was already battling through life, even at eighteen,' says Cynthia. 'Whenever he was going anywhere or doing anything, he walked like lightning, as if he was being shot from an arrow. It was a kind of panic. He would look round as if someone was chasing him. He staggered, quickly, as though he believed that if he moved quickly, people might miss him.

'Those of us who loved him for his lunacy and his cutting remarks realized that inside John was a lot more than he was showing. It was trying to get out and hadn't found the right way. The teachers couldn't care less because they just judged his appearance and his track record, which wasn't very good. And they feared him because they didn't understand him. Stuart was intelligent enough to see something special in John. I did, and so did just a few of the girls at college. But the people who realized he was destined to be either a giant or a bum were few and far between in those days. Most people thought he was a dangerous, loud-mouthed, troublemaking layabout. He really needed his friends. . . .'

The key to understanding the psyche of the errant teenager who arrived at Liverpool College of Art lies in his wounded childhood. Years later, he was to recapture the pain of those years with songs that spine-chillingly re-enacted the tensions of his early agonies. But the real pressure of nursing John Winston Lennon through his first twenty-two years of problems, while all the time believing that he had a special talent and ought eventually to 'go places', fell to one woman, Mary Elizabeth Smith, John's Aunt Mimi.

John's father, Alfred Lennon, was away from Liverpool at the time of his son's birth. He worked as a ship's steward, and his adventurous, romantic work, coupled with his carefree attitude to life which took him on passenger liners to otherwise unattainable places like New York, is what attracted John's mother to him. The son of a freight clerk, Alfred Lennon—

Freddy to his friends—was born at 57 Copperfield Street, Tox-teth Park, on 14 December 1912. He was one of five brothers and had one sister.

John's mother, Julia—known in her family as Juliet—was born on 12 March 1914, the youngest of five daughters of George Ernest Stanley, and Annie (née Millward). Julia was a cinema usherette before she married Freddy on 3 December 1938.

Named John after his paternal grandfather, he had a decid-edly Irish heritage. Lennon is the anglicized version of O'Lean-nain, a clan strong in the Galway, Fermanagh and Cork areas of southern Ireland. John's grandfather went to Liverpool from Ireland, as many did in the mid-nineteenth century, to seek better prospects of work in an England that was becoming industrialized faster than their own country. Born in Dublin in the 1850s, grandfather John Lennon—nicknamed Jack—was an occasional singer who spent some years singing in a group in America. At the age of nine, in 1921, Freddy Lennon became an orphan when his father died of a diseased liver. Freddy went to the Bluecoat orphanage in Liverpool.

Julia and Mimi's father was an official with the Glasgow and Liverpool Salvage Company, and often travelled on salvage work, retrieving submarines from the bottom of the Atlantic. His father had been a musician. Julia's mother, Annie, was the daughter of a solicitor's clerk; in the jobless Liverpool of the 1930s, a family like this was, for Julia and Mimi, something to be treasured, to be proud of, to mark out your values and aspirations. Compared with thousands of Merseyside people, they came from a privileged background.

Auburn-haired, slim and vivacious, Julia was attracted to Freddy by one major characteristic their personalities had in common: they were both fun-loving and carefree. A year after their marriage at Mount Pleasant Register Office, Freddy was on the high seas as a head waiter, eventually berthing at New York. 'Freddy was a ship's steward on troop ships carrying soldiers between Liverpool and Southampton and France,' says Charles Lennon, his brother and John's uncle. 'They also went over to Canada to bring troops back.' He returned home for the Christmas of that year but was soon off again, and was jailed when one boat on which he sailed reached North Africa and he was accused of stealing a bottle of vodka. Erratically, he wrote home to Julia from his ships saying he was doing well, singing songs like 'Begin The Beguine' during crew concerts; but his absence, during these dark war years, was placing an impossible strain on their marriage. In one letter, he wrote to Julia saying his date of return was uncertain and he suggested she should get out and enjoy herself and not sit around and mope.

Julia did just that, for she saw the marital storm clouds looming. By 1942 she considered Freddy to have left her for good, and she moved in with a new man, a hotel waiter called John Dykins. He was later to be nicknamed Twitchy by John because he had a pronounced facial tic. Julia wrote to Freddy asking for a divorce, and later asked for one when they met, but Freddy always refused. They were never divorced.

Julia had three illegitimate children outside her marriage, and John Dykins was the father of two who were John's half-sisters: Julia Dykins, born in Liverpool between January and March 1947 and Jacqueline Dykins, born in Liverpool between October and December 1949. Another child was fathered by a Norwegian ship's captain. John met his two half-sisters on his occasional visits to Twitchy's house.

Charles Lennon says, 'Fred worshipped Julia and told me he'd never give her the satisfaction of a divorce. He was broken-hearted when their marriage collapsed. He would have done anything to have her back but kept saying their future was ruined when she met Dykins. When Fred and Julia were together, they were very keen on music: he would sing and she would play the ukelele. I can hear him now, serenading her with those Italian love songs in Newcastle Road.' The reason for their final parting is contentious. Some people say Fred genuinely hoped for a reunion when he returned from sea but half expected her to leave him. Charles Lennon maintains that Julia had got together with her new regular man, Twitchy, by the time Freddy returned, and there was no chance of a reunion. Freddy Lennon died in Brighton, England, in 1976.

From his first days on earth, Mimi treasured her nephew, and her husband, John's Uncle George, 'thought John had been put here entirely for his pleasure', says Mimi. With no children of their own and Julia isolated by the frequent absence of

Freddy, Mimi made John a welcome fit for a king at her house in Woolton, where Uncle George ran a dairy farm around the corner from their home. Mimi could offer a stable home and was much better placed to raise a child than her sister who, on her separation from Freddy, was no longer entitled to payments each week from the shipping line for which he worked. Julia continued to live with her parents in Wavertree, a short bus ride from Mimi. Increasingly John was left in the care of Mimi, who needed no encouragement to have him for days and weeks at a time. Her husband George, too, entertained him by occasionally taking him early in the morning to see his cows being milked. John's pre-school years were idyllic.

By the time Julia had moved in with Twitchy, and John was five, Freddy Lennon suddenly reappeared in an attempt to patch up his marriage and reclaim his son. One day he arrived at Mimi's house and, against her better judgement, persuaded her and John to let him take his son to Blackpool for the day. Walking John on the Blackpool sands, his father asked John what he wanted to be when he grew up. John answered: 'Prime minister, or on the stage.'

Freddy had a vague plan to take him to New Zealand and start a new life there, but it was a plan that went horribly wrong. When Freddy did not return to Mimi with John after several days, Julia found out where he was and arrived, unannounced, in Blackpool. She said bluntly that she wanted John back; she had set up a new home with a new man, and, she insisted, could offer John a better childhood than Freddy. The uncertainty of his father's life at sea was no substitute for what Mimi and she could offer.

The scene that followed in that Blackpool flat was traumatic for a five-year-old. By then he had got used to a comfortable family pattern: he lived with Mimi, who insisted on caring for him as Julia was involved with Twitchy, but every day Julia would visit her son at Menlove Avenue. Gradually, he started to understand and come to terms with the situation, developing a rapport with his exuberant mother as well as a deep mutual affection for Mimi. 'Mimi' and 'Mummy' ran well together as the two women in his life; Uncle George was there as a benevolent, kindly man, an anchor and something of a substitute father.

One day, John said to his aunt: 'Why can't I call you Mummy?'

She answered: 'Well you couldn't very well have *two* Mummies, could you?'

Now, with his real parents arguing before his eyes over who was to have him, young John Winston Lennon was emotionally wracked. He had always hoped for the return of his father from seafaring, and 'Pater', as he called him, had given him a good time in Blackpool, romping in the sands every day. But his mother had been more constant than his father in his young life. Here, now, was a hideous tug-of-war.

It was Freddy who put John in the most hopeless situation. 'You have to decide if you want to stay with me or with Mummy.'

A tearful John replied: 'I'll stay with you.'

Julia intervened: 'Now John, are you sure about that? Do you want to go to another country with him, or will you stay here with me?'

'With Daddy,' sobbed John, tears pouring down his cheeks.

Freddy was triumphant and said to his wife: 'That's enough, Julia, you've had your answer. Leave him alone.' Freddy had already unsuccessfully tried to woo Julia back from the happiness she was enjoying with her new man.

Despite all her inner torment, and with the tears welling up inside her, Julia decided it was all over. She turned round and walked out of the door of the flat. She had lost her son.

When the door closed, the finality of his mother's departure and the uncertainty of a future with his father were too much for John. He ran after his mother, crying uncontrollably, and eventually found her in the street. 'Mummy, Mummy, don't go, don't go.'

They hugged each other in the Blackpool street, and Julia delivered him back to Liverpool, safe into the loving arms of her sister Mimi, who was to care for him with conscientiousness, strictness—and passion. Julia was so excited at having her son back that she forgot to get a train ticket at Blackpool and was apprehended by police when she arrived back at Lime Street Station. She explained her predicament and returned the next day with the money. Mimi's life, and much of Uncle George's, now centred totally on the little lad who had survived so much and who, soon after she had sent him at the age of five to Dovedale Road Primary School, had been described to her by the headmaster, Mr Evans, as 'sharp as a needle'.

Even at this age, John's character was shaping quickly. Part of his resilience, reaction against authority, aggression, and fierce independence may be traced to that anguished parting of his parents in Blackpool, when they threw an impossible decision into his young face. A second facet of his character was formed by the warm sanctuary of Mimi's home life. She brought him up with a rod of iron and a heart of gold, which he was never to forget.

2
CHILDHOOD

'I was either a genius or a madman'

Even as a toddler John was defiant, determined, and a leader. When he played cowboys and Indians, in the garden of Mimi's home, she recalls: 'He had to be in charge. Always. The other boys had to be the cowboys and he *had* to be the Indian. And when he said they were dead, they were dead. "Pretend properly," he would tell them.'

Nostalgia hardly suits Aunt Mimi, a tall, bold woman with a striking, no-nonsense, uncompromising personality, but she will make an exception and enjoy reminiscing on her favourite topic: John Lennon. She sits in the bungalow at Sandbanks, Dorset, which John bought for her in 1965. That year it became obvious that she could not survive, with sanity, the gathering hordes of fans rounding on John and Mimi's beloved home in Liverpool. 'The fans were not only sleeping in the driveway all night, without me knowing. They were phoning me from all over the world . . . America, Australia, everywhere. We kept changing the phone number but the fans found the new number every time. The Post Office said they'd run out of new numbers for me.'

John said one day: 'You're going from here, where do you want to live?' Mimi was visiting him at his Beatle home in Weybridge, Surrey.

'Bournemouth would be nice,' said Mimi.

'Let's go,' said John.

He set off with her in his chauffeured Rolls-Royce, headed south, and made her choose the pretty bungalow overlooking Poole Harbour where, within months, the passing holiday launches would carry finger-pointing passengers on pleasure trips. And on the megaphone the guides would shout: 'Over there on the right, is where John Lennon's Aunt Mimi lives.'

Mimi, who went there seeking solitude and anonymity, groaned. 'Why can't they leave me alone?' In 1983, after an illness, Mimi moved back north temporarily to within a few miles of her former home: she wanted company and went to stay with her sister Anne.

In 1965, when he moved Mimi from north to south, John Lennon was considered to be generally at his most acid-tongued, and had a reputation as the 'hard man' of the Beatles. Yet Mimi had ample evidence that, underneath, he was unchanged. He disagreed with her on a major point of sentimentality; he wanted her to keep Mendips, even though she was leaving it.

'Mimi, I grew up there. Let's keep it,' he said, as they drove south.

'John, if I leave there, it has to be sold. Have you ever been back to an empty house? A gloom comes over it. Sell it.'

'Well,' said John, 'spend six months up in Mendips and six down here in Bournemouth. I don't want anyone else owning that house where I grew up.'

Mimi was adamant. She wanted a total break. Not for the first time, she won her point with John. He was never easily persuaded about anything, but Mimi was at least his equal at digging in. He loved and respected her for that, and even his 1965 status as a wealthy Beatle would not change either Mimi or him. Mendips was sold, initially to doctors. Today a sign outside the neat house reads: 'Official Notice, Private. No Admission, Merseyside County Council.'

The house is a major focal point on Liverpool's tourist route. At dead of night, cars bearing people on pilgrimages from all over the world pull up outside, and dreamy passengers of all ages sit and stare. This, they reflect, is where John and the Beatles were born. If the walls of that house could only talk. . . .

Mimi remembers everything. From his birth, she was utterly enraptured by everything about the baby who would become

world-famous. Because he was due to be born at the end of
September, doctors planned a Caesarean operation on Julia
Lennon. 'She was overdue and I was phoning the hospital every
five minutes,' says Mimi. 'The same question they got tired
of hearing: "Has Mrs Lennon had her baby yet?"

' "No, not yet."

'The Caesarean became unnecessary. At six-thirty on
9 October I phoned and they said: "Mrs Lennon has just had
a boy."

'Well, we were five girls as sister in my family, and I nearly
went off my nut. I said, "Mother, mother, a boy, a boy!" The
air raids used to start at that time, dusk, so I ran to the maternity
hospital to see her.'

That night, Hitler's Luftwaffe pounded Liverpool in one of
its fiercest raids on a major city and port. 'I was dodging in
doorways between running as fast as my legs would carry me,'
says Mimi. 'I was literally terrified. Transport had stopped
because the bombs began always at dusk. There was shrapnel
falling and gunfire and when there was a little lull I ran into
the hospital ward and there was this beautiful little baby. But
they had this rough blanket around him and I said immediately:
"Take this blanket off his face, it's too rough." Just as I lifted
him up, the warning sirens went off again and visitors were
told we could either go down into the cellars or go home but
we couldn't stay. John, like the other babies, was put underneath the bed for safety. I ran every step of the way home.

'When I got home, I said: "Mother, he's beautiful."

'My father said: "Oh hell, they always say that. He'd *have*
to be better than any other."

'I said: "He *is* better than all the others. You know, the
others are all wrinkled and he isn't." '

Within a week, Julia and baby John had left hospital and
went to live at 9 Newcastle Road, Wavertree. He was a model
child but there were early signs of determination: in his high
chair with his feeding table in front of it, he would prefer to
try to spoon feed himself rather than be fed. At ten months he
was toddling, unsteadily, but trying hard.

When Julia and Mimi decided that John would be brought
up by his aunt, Uncle George entered the picture very firmly.
A gentle soul, George Smith came from three generations of

farmers. 'They started in a very small way,' says Mimi. 'The great-grandfather had only one cow, and the next a bigger business, until George carried on as a big breeder, and the milk was supplied mostly to hospitals.'

At four and a half John was taught to read and write by George, who sat him on his knee and worked the lad through the *Liverpool Echo* every night. 'Syllable by syllable, George would work at him till he got it right. John couldn't spell at that age, of course, but he could get down what he wanted. My husband went through all the headlines in the newspaper with John every night.'

The habit may have accounted for John's avid newspaper-reading habit throughout his life. During the Beatles years, he told me he got many ideas for song lyrics from reading newspapers. He was always quick to identify the idiosyncrasies of each newspaper, and was almost obsessively interested in the news of the day. It was a rare earthquake indeed that escaped his attention.

There were no toys in John's early life—the nearest was a plastic duck which swam in the bath with him. Books were his passion, particularly the *Just William* series by Richmal Crompton, which mirrored his own personality as a naughty but humorous boy. *Alice in Wonderland* was another favourite: he would re-read it until he could recite passages by memory. 'He never showed the slightest interest in games or toys,' says Mimi. 'I had twenty volumes of the world's best short stories and we had a love of books in common. John used to go back and read them over and over again, particularly Balzac. I thought there was a lot of Balzac in his song writing later on. Anyway, he'd read most of the classics by the time he was ten. He had such imagination and built up the stories himself when he and I talked them over.'

John had no illnesses when he was a child—just chicken pox (which he called chicken pots) when he was eight. 'He was never really ill for one day in his life, except for the occasional cold,' says Mimi. She ran her house, and disciplined him, the way she had been brought up: 'No picturedromes. He never gave me any trouble when he was young, and he never asked for much. I don't believe in people giving children money to go to the cinema just to get rid of them. He had three interests: painting and drawing in bed, if he was down with a cold; having his friends of the same age round; and reading.'

In his bedroom haven above the porch, the studious little Lennon was quiet for hours, aided by an extension speaker from the lounge radio, with long electrical wires stretching down the stairs from his room. With his pencils and crayons and drawing books, he would be totally happy apart from the occasional shouts like: 'Change the programme on the wireless, Mimi.'

Two special favourites were *Dick Barton, Special Agent*, the thriller serial that came on every night at 6:45 p.m., and *The Goon Show*. Says Mimi: 'When Dick Barton was in trouble, his face used to go deathly white. He couldn't sit down for worry. While it was on, George and I had to be absolutely silent. And with the Goons, he imitated their accents all the time. "I'm the Famous Eccles," John would say, and he would drive me crazy with non-stop mimicry of the various accents. He loved that play on words.'

Late at night, Mimi would get her instructions from above when her nephew was ready to go to sleep. She had tried to instil in him the value of money. 'We weren't short but we weren't rich and I couldn't bear waste, particularly of electricity. This little voice would shout down on so many nights, "Turn landing light out, Mimi." '

On his children's post office set, he would write letters to his Uncle George, saying: 'Dear Gerge, will you wash me tonight, not Mimi?' Young John didn't take long to work out the benefits of living with his doting aunt and uncle: Mimi would forever be the staunch disciplinarian and he was destined to spend his entire life persuading her that he wasn't all that bad; George was easily won over, and, especially when he was in trouble with Mimi, the kind uncle would bail him out with an encouraging word, a pat on the head.

'I had no time to go playing ducks in the bath with him,' says Mimi, 'but George would do anything John wanted when he was little. They adored each other. George would see him to bed with a smile, most nights.'

Bedtimes were happy, with George usually having to recite

a nursery rhyme to John, traditional favourites like: 'Let Him
Go, Let Him Tarry' or 'Wee Willie Winkie'. Mimi, ever practical, would be more concerned with scrubbing his knees.

Mimi would berate her husband, in the kindest fashion:
'George, you're ruining him. We can't have two fools in the
house. One's enough.' No matter what he wanted, John could
get it out of her husband. Whenever John was being rebuked
or pulled into line by Mimi, George would give him the nod
and a wink to go upstairs and look under his pillow. George,
anticipating trouble, had put a sweet or a biscuit there for his
surrogate son.

When John reached the age of five and it was time for primary
school, Mimi applied her usual diligence to the task of choosing
'not just anywhere, but the best possible'. After inspecting
various state schools in the area she settled on Dovedale Primary, just down the road from Penny Lane. To get there, some
three miles from Mendips, John would be taken by bus past
the Salvation Army hostel in Strawberry Field, down to Penny
Lane.

From his first visits to the school, John was considered
bright. On his informal look around Dovedale, the school secretary asked the five-year-old to run an errand, to take a letter
to a nearby classroom for her while she and Mimi talked. 'She
remarked even then on his confidence and said: "What a smart
little boy," ' says Mimi.

At the first parents' meeting to discuss their children's progress, the headmaster, Mr Bolt, told Mimi: 'There's no need to
worry about him. He's as sharp as a needle. But he won't do
anything he doesn't want to.'

In his first school, Lennon's individuality rose quickly.
Doug Freeman, now a farmer in England's Lake District, went
to Dovedale with John. 'To me, he was always stuck out as
somebody different, even from the age of five or six. Whatever
he did, he was going to be unusual. If there was anything out
of the ordinary going on in the school it was centred on him.
You definitely noticed him, even at that age. He was on a
totally different wavelength from the others, and although he
was sometimes causing trouble and disagreements, as kids do,
no teachers could ever work out properly what it was about

him that was different. It stuck out a mile. The teachers could never tie him down to anything. He was always the centre of attention; he was different from anyone else in the school.'

Sliding in the snow or ice in the school playground slopes and playing marbles were favourite hobbies among all the boys, but Lennon would not join in the communal games: he was off on his own, leading a pack. 'Always on the borders of getting into trouble, but never quite going over the edge,' recalls Doug Freeman. 'We were all a little bit frightened of him, too, and it stuck out to parents then that he was different. The mothers had their eyes on him as if to say: "Keep away from that one." ' Rather like the notices he puts up around some of the fields near his farm, Freeman makes this analogy: 'Chemically treated—beware.' John, he avers, had to be treated similarly —with great caution.

Art quickly became John's special subject at Dovedale. He was getting on well in all subjects, though with a notable weakness in mathematics, but in art he excelled. In an exhibition in the school hall, when he was ten, John's drawing startled several pupils. He drew a picture of what several boys recognized as Jesus Christ, in itself an adventurous move. Twenty years later, John Lennon's bearded facial appearance, when he was not wearing the 'granny spectacles' which were to become his trademark for a time, exactly resembled that drawing of Jesus which he had done at Dovedale Primary School. 'It was certainly strange. The similarity of the drawing, and the John with very long hair we later saw, was uncanny,' says Doug Freeman.

Comedian Jimmy Tarbuck, who went to Dovedale with John, recalls: 'Even at the age of eight he stood out, and had his gang of admirers. He wasn't easily missed at school—he wasn't the sort of kid to stand in corners, studiously reading his books. Oh no, he had a load of energy even then. If there was a playground fight, he'd be involved in it. He could be quite aggressive and when I saw him out of the classroom he'd be making his opinions known, though he always talked very slowly.' Tarbuck remembers going on a school camping trip with John to the Isle of Man. 'It wasn't so much what he did that was special, but the way he spoke,' he reflects. 'You could register, even as a kid, that here was an oddball. Now I can see that he was a genius all along.' Tarbuck did not go to grammar school with John, but caught up with him when the Beatles emerged and the comedian was one of the regulars at Liverpool's Cavern. 'He was a bit of a teddy boy then, very sarcastic, but also very funny.' In later years, the two went round London together on club crawls into the early hours. 'By then I was a comic, but John made *me* laugh. He would put down people with one crushing sentence. Some artists don't suffer fools gladly. John never suffered them at all.'

As an embryonic Beatle Lennon said, looking back on his troubled childhood: 'I had a feeling I was either a genius or a madman. Now I know I wasn't a madman, so I must have been a genius.'

John was fourteen when Uncle George died from a haemorrhage. When he came home from holiday in Durness, Scotland, with Aunt Elizabeth to be told by Mimi of George's sudden death, John went red-faced and ran to his room. After the separation of his parents, this was the second bitter blow to his young life. In the recurring arguments with Mimi about his lack of discipline, lovely Uncle George had been his mate. They had gone for walks together. He adored the man's gentleness. Mimi, heartbroken by the death of her husband who had not suffered a day's illness, put a brave face on but was quiet for days. Coincidentally, John was now seeing more of his mother. With the new man in her life, Twitchy, Julia lived a short bus ride away at 1 Blomfield Road, Spring Wood, Allerton. Apart from her maternal attraction, John found in her a total contrast with the authoritarian Mimi. Julia was effervescent, smiling, full of *joie de vivre*. And she enjoyed practical jokes. Most importantly to John, she tended to look down on authority.

Three years before Uncle George's death, John had sailed effortlessly through the 11-plus examination. He arrived home from Dovedale one afternoon and casually told Mimi: 'I've got it—I'm through.' His primary school days, though showing early signs of his individuality, had not caused Mimi any disturbance, so she was hardly surprised.

Uncle George had prepared for the great day, anyway. 'It's outside, what you were promised if you passed the exam,' he said. John immediately went out for a ride across the golf course opposite Mendips, on his new emerald green Raleigh Lenton bicycle. He used to show it proudly to the other boys who went to the garden fetes in the grounds of the Salvation Army hostel at Strawberry Field in Woolton: Mimi took John to these often.

John was glad to be leaving Dovedale; even at eleven he felt he was outgrowing it, with its uniform of a black blazer, with a dove as the badge, and grey shorts. He had made his little stabs against school rules by often not wearing the blazer when he should have done, or by arriving at school assembly with his tie askew and top shirt button undone. Only a few boys were similarly careless in their dress. 'It was also a school where sport was encouraged, and John was totally uninterested in it,' says Michael Isaacson, today the boss of a highly successful London advertising agency. He had the totally unique experience of being a year older than John Lennon, and seeing him arrive at all three schools: Dovedale Road Primary, Quarry Bank High, and Liverpool College of Art.

'He didn't do particularly well, academically, at Dovedale. Certainly nobody talked of his prowess at any subject although there were often drawings by him on display, just as there were by other boys. I do remember him at Dovedale as not making a lot of effort. But he had obvious talent, because getting through the 11-plus in those days wasn't an easy task. Only the minority passed. He was a bright, alert boy and you could see from his face that he was no fool. If he'd decided to be an academic, I imagine he'd have made a very good one.'

Even at primary school, John and a few others found a way of bucking the system and making a profit: he would take his dinner money, payable for school lunches, and not hand it in to the teacher. Instead of eating school lunch, he and three or four others would go down to Penny Lane on some days and buy sweets and their own 'lunch'—custard tarts. But he was shrewd enough not to get found out.

Quarry Bank High School was a different matter. When he went there, in September 1952, the sharp-eyed Lennon quickly realized he was going to be up against much sterner authority, more strictness, and rules. It was a state grammar school with pretentions to being a public school; the masters wore caps and gowns and the headmaster, E.R. Taylor, a tall, rangy-looking man and a devout Methodist, used the cane.

Lennon got the measure of the school very quickly and decided there was only one route for him: to confront it. He had done well in any fights at Dovedale, but here at Quarry Bank there were bigger boys. Combined with the aura of academic and disciplined heaviness about the school, it was intimidating, but on entering this formidable school John had a major asset: his two friends from Dovedale had also passed the 11-plus. While one of them, Ivan Vaughan, had gone to the more prestigious city school, the Liverpool Institute, another from the 'gang of three', Pete Shotton, was joining John at Quarry Bank. Mimi was pleased to see that John was not going to a city school but was continuing his education at a suburban grammar school. She would be able to keep an eye on him more easily if he didn't have long bus journeys. She scarcely knew what awaited her.

Quarry Bank High School's motto was *Ex Hoc Metallo Virtutem* (From This Rough Metal We Forge Virtue). In his black blazer, with red and gold stag's head badge, John cycled there each day, up the long Harthill Road and passing the old sandstone quarries on one of which the school was said to be built. Like most schools, it divided its pupils into houses. These were named according to the district in which the boys lived. It followed that boys from the middle-class homes would be together and boys from the rougher areas would be together. In pecking order of poshness and toughness, Childwall was the number one house, Allerton number two, and Woolton (John's house) was number three. The 'harder' houses were Wavertree and Aigburth. John, in a middle-class house, was thus expected to behave, like most of the others, with reasonable decorum and discipline.

But he didn't. 'From day one, he roared through the school,' says Michael Isaacson. 'He set out to be a noise, aided and abetted by Pete Shotton who had the face of an angel but was exactly the opposite.' John was, however, the leader in any partnership, and Shotton became his lieutenant in the hundreds of misdeeds that became legendary in a school that was to deliver brilliant students to universities.

John soon decided that he had no respect for most of the teachers, and academically he plummeted. A bright boy from Dovedale when he arrived, he failed to concentrate in lessons, did not do much homework, and dropped to the B stream by the third year. By the final term of the fourth year he was twentieth in the bottom class of the C stream. His school reports told Mimi more than she needed to know: 'Certainly on the road to failure . . . hopeless . . . rather a clown in class . . . wasting other pupils' time.' Mimi, worried by one report, took him to have his eyes tested. John read a figure 5 as an 8. Mimi's eyes watered with sadness as she realized that her young boy needed glasses. 'But he had said he wouldn't wear National Health glasses, so I had to buy him thick black-rimmed ones —even then on condition that when he grew up he could have contact lenses,' says Mimi. John hated wearing the spectacles, and the fact that he couldn't see the blackboards properly without them may have contributed to his general despair about learning much at Quarry Bank.

Skiving, swearing, and smoking became the three key activities in John's life at Quarry Bank. Every morning and night, Mimi would try to instil in him that it was his future at stake, as he dressed in the smart blazer that Mimi had had made specially at Uncle George's tailor in Woolton village. ('It lasted longer that way—and it looked nicer than the school outfitter's,' she says.) By the time he reached school, invariably late for assembly, John's uniform was liberally arranged around his body so that he looked as if he'd just tumbled out of bed in it.

Since the Quarry Bank badge was a stag, Lennon must have taken this to mean he could cavort around the place as if it were a field. 'His uniform', says Michael Isaacson, 'looked as if it had survived World War One. He rarely wore a tie until he was admonished for looking dishevelled.'

Lennon was particularly harsh on student teachers. 'He and Shotton could virtually send a new teacher who was standing in or studying at Quarry Bank for three weeks, to a mental home. They'd take no notice of anything he said, and do no work, and the teacher's only route would be to send them to the headmaster,' says Isaacson.

Lennon was caned literally scores of times but the stick made no difference. He would receive it for rudeness to teachers, refusing or ignoring their instructions to do work to a set pattern, missing assembly, scoring a direct hit with a peashooter during a lesson, being late in class, looking slovenly, swearing,

or causing a disruption in the school. The punishments mounted
through a simple fact of schoolmasters' expediency; once a boy
became notorious, like John, he was picked on, whether he
was causing trouble or not. Caning had no effect: he got so
used to it that he emerged from the headmaster's study with a
smile afterwards. His view was: if *that* was the worst that could
happen to you for leading such a liberal school life, it was
worth suffering a raw hand. Pete Shotton, who often followed
Lennon into the caning session, saw John coming out with a
smirk on his face, smiled back, and was admonished even more
strongly for not treating the matter seriously.

In nearby Calderstones Park, Quarry Bank schoolboys did
cross-country runs. Michael Isaacson was captain of athletics,
and head of the Woolton house which included Lennon. 'John
and his bunch were the constant bane of my life. He would do
anything to make the cross-country runs a total and utter mess.
In sport Lennon was a total drop-out. Not only did I not want
him in any run, because my job was to get Woolton house as
high as possible; I didn't want him anywhere *near* the run,
because he'd do his best to screw up any effort we were making.
Half of the lads were running their hearts out, the bulk of them
did it because that's what they had to do, and half a dozen
boys were so tubby that running was an effort. And of course,
it was those fatties whom Lennon and Shotton would verbally
torture if they were anywhere near. They'd stand there looking
as if a dust cart had been dropped over them, smoking and
swearing, mocking the fatties, and—if I'd let them—tripping
them up as they ran. I saw they were dangerous to have around
during any athletics and told them to get out of my way, very
early on after a few experiences like that in Calderstones Park.
Lennon and Shotton were as thick as thieves and they went out
looking for trouble.'

Stealing became a habit too. In Woolton and Allerton sweet
shops he would ask shopkeepers for a quarter of sweets from
a jar that was behind the counter and difficult to reach. The
time needed to reach down the jar enabled Lennon to whip a
bar of chocolate from the counter, unseen.

'Every situation I remember John in,' says Michael Isaacson, 'he led. The guys who were frightened of him, which was

quite a lot, kept out of his way. He had a sharp tongue and didn't mind a fight. But those who adored him just followed.'

While the school curriculum was boring him increasingly, so that he plunged down in position in each form, John continued the flicker of interest in art which he'd shown at Dovedale. He hung around the art room, recognized Michael Isaacson as the older boy from Dovedale, and admired Isaacson's prowess which was to win him the title of Young Cartoonist of the Year, at the age of nineteen, in a national contest in the *New Statesman* newspaper.

'I was never a mate of John Lennon's but we always got on OK. He knew I wasn't a pushover and he never tried anything on me,' says Isaacson. 'Despite having no real encouragement, I got a feeling he was good at art, early on at Quarry Bank. So he'd come in and have a chat when I was in the art room drawing cartoons, which were my forte. I had a sense of humour rather like his. My drawings were satirical.

'Despite his troublemaking, I quite liked him and he was very, very funny. I was having plenty of my own trouble with the school, which was very anti-Jewish, so we had this much in common at Quarry Bank; my attitude was to outrun them all and to be the top athlete and captain of athletics, to prove a point; John's attitude towards the school was "To hell with the whole lot of them." I'd say I was constructive, he was destructive. We had lots of laughs about this and the worse he got, the more I enjoyed it—as long as he didn't interfere with my hopes to win the athletics cup for Woolton house. I knew there was no way I could get him to jump three inches or run three yards. So he was happy to be told forcefully to clear off at games time.' Sport simply bored his restless mind. Even dear Uncle George's attempts to teach him to bowl met a dead end.

The more he dug a trench for himself, the more aggressive he became. The more appalling his school results, the more he would incur the unflagging persistence of Mimi. She was particularly upset about this in John as she was conscientious beyond reproach. Long before the phrase 'latchkey children' was invented, Mimi believed firmly that her duty was to be in the house whenever John arrived home from school. 'Wherever

I was in the village, by early afternoon I'd watch the clock and make sure I was back home by about three to prepare his meal. He never came home to an empty house.'

But the decline in his school work coincided with his increased visits to see his mother, particularly at weekends. Julia could play the banjo a little and tried to teach him a few chords; even at the age of four, he had received from her a £4 guitar. Her playing was limited, but the fact that she chuncked along and smiled was good enough for John. He was getting closer to his mother, and her casual approach to life, combined with a prankish sense of humour, was marvellous for a boy living with an aunt who was loving and caring but strict.

At Mendips, there were three cats in John's life. Tich, the marmalade-coloured half-Persian, died when John was at college. Tim, the half-Persian, was a stray found in the snowy street by John and became a specially pitied favourite. Sam was another cat he loved. And there was Sally, the mongrel dog who died when John was at art college. John often walked the dog around Woolton. As a young boy, John doted on the cats. Every day, he would cycle to Mr Smith the fishmonger in Woolton village to buy pieces of hake for his pets. Later, as a Beatle on tour, he would phone Mimi to ask how the cats were getting on without him.

'Nothing but the finest', was Mimi's motto for John during his growing years.

The solid middle-class values which Mimi Smith instilled into John were to earn her his love and respect when he grew up. As a Beatle, he would often phone her during his travels and say: 'Remember the old days, Mimi, when you told me off?'

And she would reply, 'There was always a reason, John. You had no job to go to. I was worried.'

John would laugh, secure in the knowledge that all was well in music.

'He only became obstreperous between the ages of fourteen and seventeen,' says Mimi. 'When he moved from Dovedale to Quarry Bank, the school reports became worrying to me. He'd bring them in, and throw them through the window before I could get to them. I knew something was wrong. ''You've got a brain, be thankful and use it,'' I kept saying. He'd just

look at me, even then, and in that tired way say: "Oh . . .
Mimi." And then when he looked at me I couldn't go on any
more. He'd give me a "squeaker" of a kiss on the side of my
face and I'd say: "Don't soft soap me now," but he knew how
to get round me.' Mimi, a great collector of books herself,
remembers he could not get enough books to read; an ency-
clopaedia absorbed him at the age of twelve, particularly a
section on magic.

Mimi's chief memory of the child is that he was not one
to waste a minute. 'He was always looking for something to
do or read, a very active child. And he loved to talk, about
growing up and why I was so strong on discipline, and he
listened.' He seemed interested especially in why she made a
point of always being in the house when he came home from
school around four o'clock.

'Because it's my duty John, to be here,' Mimi answered.
John said, 'But you've no need to.'

'Ah,' said Mimi, 'but when you're older, you'll understand.' And he did, she says. 'He grew to appreciate that, and
often mentioned that he never returned from Quarry Bank to
an empty house.'

For all his general studiousness and interest in words, he was
careless and casual about his possessions and constantly needed
money to replace things. He always asked for it at the same
time—just before the bus left. That way he knew Mimi had
no time to argue. But Mimi confirms that he was not mean;
from early childhood he would buy her a bar of chocolate on
her birthday, and his card to her would carry his own piece of
poetry.

The first signs of John's enjoyment of being on stage came
when he was about twelve. During an argument with her over
discipline, he would pull funny faces and act out a part, recalls
Mimi. 'He'd say, in a funny voice, "You know my name,
doooon't you? Aim John *Winston* Lennon." ' Mimi's reaction
was 'Save that for the music hall.' But she had a quiet laugh
at John's talent.

St Peter's, the Woolton village church, had been the place
of worship for Mimi's family for generations. John was sent
to Sunday School there from the age of eight, and sang in the

choir. He was conscientious about ensuring that he had enough money from Mimi to give to the church collection each Sunday. And throughout his years of living with her, John said he was a believer. 'Somebody's listening up there,' he would say.

He was about eight or nine when he walked into Mimi's kitchen and informed her: 'I've just seen God.'

'Well,' said Mimi, 'what was he doing?'

'Oh, just sitting by the fire,' John replied.

'Oh,' Aunt Mimi said, nodding thoughtfully, 'I expect he was feeling a bit chilly.'

At that age, she recalls, he was 'really good looking with fair hair and beautiful brown eyes, but he was nobody's fool'. He was resolute in whatever he decided to do—such as sitting in puddles whenever he was wearing new trousers. 'He was a bohemian, even as a boy. He'd never work at anything he wasn't interested in.'

John marked the start of the Beatles years with his Aunt Mimi by inviting Brian Epstein to Mendips. Mimi was impressed with the 'charming, gentle man' who said that he had enormous hopes for the future of the group. He also assured her that John's talent was so special that, whatever the success level of the Beatles, her nephew would 'always do well'.

Brian stayed overnight at Mendips twice, talking of his grand plans to get a recording contract. 'It was his dream,' says Mimi. 'I said, "It's all very well for you, Mr Epstein, you have got your career. But these boys haven't. What happens if you can't get them on the road to a career? What happens then?" '

Epstein would allow no such dark thoughts. 'Don't worry, Mrs Smith. They are so talented. . . .' He sent Mimi a pot plant after each visit to thank her for tea. Such politeness went down well with her.

But when John came home in 1962 with a demonstration of their début single, 'Love Me Do', Mimi saw no reason to lose her scepticism. 'If you think you're going to make your fortune with that,' she said sharply, 'you've got another think coming.' She was proved right: it reached only seventeen in the bestseller lists. Next, John and Brian appeared with the demonstration of 'Please Please Me'. She was upstairs when they put it on. 'That's more like it,' she shouted down. 'That should do well.' She remembers clearly John's accurate prediction.

'Mimi,' he said, 'that is going to be number *one*.'

Mimi remembers John's Quarry Men friends visiting her home during their schooldays: 'When Paul first came to Mendips he had a buckle on his shoe. John had never seen anything like it. Then George Harrison came along, with his pink shirt and winklepicker shoes.' Mimi's disapproving stare spoke volumes. 'Mimi,' said John, 'can I have some clothes like Paul and George have—you know, shoes and shirts . . . ?'

'Certainly not,' said Mimi, ending the conversation.

When he eventually had to move to London, Mimi missed him terribly. 'But I never said as much when he came to visit me. I was determined that there would be no clinging vine stuff.' The tough guy image which the public saw as a Beatle cut no ice with her: she remembered the little boy whom she had sent for a holiday to Scotland every year to his Aunt Elizabeth, nicknamed Mater by the family. When he had left the house with his Uncle George, he would always return to kiss Mimi and say, 'Don't be lonely or sad while I'm away. Read a good book.'

During early Beatlemania, Mimi kept a low profile. 'I didn't think it was any of my business to be seen and give interviews,' she says. And later, on a visit to Mendips, John said how grateful he was that she never pushed herself.

The old sparring between them resumed one night at the height of the Beatles' fame. She was in their dressing-room at Glasgow. As the time neared for John to go on stage, he ushered her out, saying, 'You'll have to go Mimi, I've got to get changed.'

She rasped, 'Have you any idea how many times I've seen you naked in twenty-four years?'

He laughed. The reaction was typical of the woman who remained completely unintimidated by his fame, money, or egotism.

Mendips, during the Beatles years, was under siege from fans. 'I'd go out and tell them it was no use waiting, but they knew his movements and insisted he was going to turn up,' says Mimi. Some had hitch-hiked for hundreds of miles for a glimpse of John Lennon's childhood home, and stood taking pictures. Mimi, worried about some of them and their lack of cash, invited them in for tea and sandwiches. 'They'd beg me to give them John's cup. I'd tell them he'd used them all. They'd absolutely shriek with delight!'

If she went upstairs while playing 'open house' to the fans, she had to lock the kitchen door. 'Otherwise there wouldn't be a piece of crockery left in the kitchen by the time I came down.' She worried about the kids who stood outside in the pouring rain. She asked them in to dry out their clothes. 'Because I didn't have any girls' clothes in the house, I'd have to give them an old pullover of John's. They'd swoon on the spot.'

John's room above the porch was appallingly untidy. He left his clothes all over the place. Sometimes the girls would ask to see his room. She usually refused, but once, 'just to teach John a lesson', she took them up to see the mess he'd left. Instead of being horrified, they made a grab for things.

That same year, 1964, the Beatles played thirty-two concerts in nineteen days throughout Australia and New Zealand, before 200,000 fans. John phoned Mimi two weeks before departure saying: 'You're coming on holiday with me. Get your jabs.'

The whirlwind struck her when she was whisked for the best trip of her life: 'one long party,' she recalls. On the flight through the Far East, John made sure particular attention was paid to her. 'I kept saying: "No special treatment, John." ' When they arrived in Wellington, New Zealand, Mimi made sure an exhausted John said hello, amid the pandemonium, to two second cousins he had never met. Mimi's mother's sister's children, John and Ann, did get to meet the hero in the family. 'He was quite interested in his family's history and finding out that they emigrated to become farmers,' says Mimi.

Memories of John's witticisms will never leave Mimi Smith. When American magazines asked her to write her memoirs, John said: 'Tell them! Take the money, Mimi! Tell them I was a juvenile delinquent who used to knock down old women!'

She recalls a press conference at which he was asked how, if he had never been any good at arithmetic, he managed to count his money. 'I just weigh it,' he answered.

And she sees him forever in her mind's eye, sitting in the

lounge at Mendips writing poetry and lyrics. 'He never had a pencil out of his hand. He'd write something down, then screw up the bit of paper and throw it away and start again. And he'd say: ''You ought to pick these up, Mimi, because I'm going to be famous one day and they'll be worth something.'' '

And she recalls, with heavy irony, a conversation with John at the start of the Beatles frenzy. 'I told him off about his accent. I said: ''What's all this Scouse accent about, John? You weren't brought up as a little Scouser. You know how to speak properly.'' '

John just looked at her and rubbed his fingers together. 'It's about money,' he replied. 'The fans *expect* me to talk like that.'

3
SCHOOLDAYS

'Just let it roll'

For the first five years of John's education at Quarry Bank the headmaster was E.R. Taylor, whose memory of John is of 'an under-achiever who made no really positive contribution to the life of the school, either in sport or in attempting to improve academic standards'. Says the ex-head: 'He did not share in what we set out to do. When I joined the school in 1947, I took over from an ageing headmaster who had been ill, and most of the staff, like me, had returned from the war. There was a major job to do, in establishing *esprit de corps*, and building up the school's standards. While there was never any question of expulsion for John Lennon, I think he despised what we were trying to do in our traditional manner.' He was not a 'grievous troublemaker', but the school punishment records showed him to have been caned for offences which now seem minor, such as, in the military jargon that lingered from the teachers' army days, 'going AWOL' (absent without leave), a euphemism for playing truant; he also gambled on the sports field during a house cricket match—a travesty in a school that took sport seriously.

'Liverpool,' in the immortal words of the playwright Alun Owen, who wrote *A Hard Day's Night*, 'scars its children for life.' One of the endearing characteristics of the Liverpudlian is to bounce back, never to take a verbal knock or a swipe without retorting with something at least as sharp. At Quarry

Bank, part of the penal system entailed the distribution of marks whereby two bad marks resulted in an hour's detention. One teacher devised a way of alternating the marks system with one that had more effect.

'Do you want a bad mark or a very dirty look?' he would ask.

Lennon would lead the chorus saying: 'A dirty look.'

The master's leer would break up the class into laughter; and Lennon mocked the dirty look, for he always enjoyed mimicking. That kind of rapport, treating the pupils more as people than as inferiors, always pleased John, who spoke regularly about how he hated being 'talked down' to.

Rod Davis, a firm school friend of John and the banjoist in Lennon's first musical group, found himself poles apart from John in attitudes towards school. 'I never saw any point in getting punished for anything, so I toed the line. I was probably a goody goody.' He became head boy, a fact that provoked Lennon's incredulity at a fellow skiffle musician managing to be so orthodox.

William Ernest Pobjoy was an energetic thirty-five-year-old when he became headmaster of Quarry Bank, taking over from the portentous, authoritarian E.R. Taylor. Mr Pobjoy's first year at the school was Lennon's fifth and final year, so that by the time he took up office the mould of John's irreverence and the trouble-making Lennon–Shotton axis was difficult to break. 'I went in there as a disciplinarian,' says Pobjoy. 'I was determined to stand no nonsense.' But he faced a major thorn in John Lennon. 'I inherited an extremely disruptive boy, the legend of the school. He was presented to me as my most urgent problem, he and his friend Shotton,' recalls Mr Pobjoy, a palpably kind but firm man who tried hard to get to grips with John Lennon as a person rather than confront the problem with force.

'He didn't come my way until I'd been there a month. All the teachers tried again with him at the beginning of a new school year. Eventually he was brought to me as headmaster as a last resort. On that first and one occasion I gave three strokes of the cane, which was the ordinary thing to do in those days.' Shortly afterwards, Pobjoy abolished corporal punishment at Quarry Bank and it has never been reinstated. 'Caning never stops misbehaving. I quickly realized that. And with or without the cane, John didn't stop misbehaving.

'Missing detention and all the other things John did might be regarded now as ordinary schoolboy pranks, but there was another side to it all. He did take advantage of anybody who was weak. He was extremely cruel.' There were incidents between John and some teachers which horrified them all in the staff room. Lennon was often brutally tough on teachers who did not know how to handle him. He raised his fists and flatly refused to obey instructions.

'When I did cane him on that one occasion,' says Pobjoy, 'apart from the usual "This is going to hurt me more than it hurts you", I reasoned with him. But it did not make a lot of difference with John. He was set in his ways by the time I arrived, and changing his attitude in favour of his school work was an uphill task.

'I saw his guardian, Mrs Smith, frequently. She saw him as not her problem but the school's. I recall her saying: "The school should do something about it." Well, with John's early history and parental background it's not easy in difficult family circumstances to get a boy to behave well—or even to work well.'

Mr Pobjoy's worst moment came when he was at an afternoon football match at Goodison Park, home of Everton football club. An announced message called him to the telephone and a distressed deputy headmaster told him of yet another Lennon problem. 'I said: "Oh suspend him." John was suspended for a few days and I saw his aunt again, but he survived right through from that day in February until July, coming to the natural end of his five-year course at the school.

'I recall talking to him about his ability and saying he could achieve a great deal if he set his mind to it. But he was only a failure at school because he attached little importance to academic work. He failed each of his O-levels by a single grade, and could clearly have passed if he'd wanted to. It simply didn't matter to him. He was particularly fond of an English master, Philip Burnett, who was rather advanced in his approach, his ideas, and his own way of life. John was very interested in poetry and wrote it.

'Among the Quarry Bank staff, John was seen as a wayward

talent. John had been a thorn in everyone's side at school. As headmaster, I had the difficulty of beginning with him by dealing out a punishment, and that wasn't the best way to begin an acquaintance. But he accepted his punishment as the natural consequence of something he had chosen to do.

'He resented any kind of constraint or discipline. He had no intention, even at Dovedale junior school, of being organized by others. He set out to cock a snook at authority and discipline from early childhood.'

Eric Oldman, John's housemaster and chemistry teacher, says: 'He was awkward but there was something *in* him. It wasn't sheer wickedness, but more spirit. He took up my time more than the others because he wouldn't conform so well. On football afternoons, he would slope off and we wouldn't be able to find him. He seemed determined not to conform to the rules.

'But he had a wit and a humour and ability. In chemistry and mathematics, which I taught a little, there was simple lack of any wish to get on. I remember writing, as his senior housemaster when he left Quarry Bank for art college: "Might make nothing of his life or something, if he brings out something *in his own way* to make a success of it." '

Gloom struck when the O-level results came. Mimi was distraught. 'What *was* I going to do? He'd been good enough at English and history, and when he began he picked up French quickly. I couldn't believe the results.'

John's artistic talent had been quite a talking point at Quarry Bank. But, an original even at that age, his drawings did not follow convention and he did not respond to the art teacher's instructions about what he should draw. A regular method of disrupting the class would be for John to pass from desk to desk an exercise book in which he drew bizarre, outlandish caricatures of the teachers. The book was called the *Daily Howl*. Boys stifled their laughter during class as it was passed round, surreptitiously, under desks.

When the end of term neared, Mr Pobjoy discussed John's prospects with him. This was before his disastrous results in his O-level examinations, but the headmaster, with the knowledge that Lennon was a troublemaker, decided to try to plan his future. Pobjoy also had a long discussion with Mimi, whom he had come to regard, if not fear, as what he calls a 'determined, informed and concerned guardian'.

The conversation with her was as electric as ever. 'Well, Mrs Smith, what are your thoughts about John's future? What do you think should be considered?'

'Well,' rasped Mimi, 'what are *you* going to do? You've had him for five years. You should have his future all ready.'

Mr Pobjoy said his standards in English, literature and poetry, were well above average, but in art he seemed to have a particular talent which should be encouraged. If he tried to get him admitted into art college, would Mimi finance his first year there, after which he would qualify for a grant?

'Yes,' said Mimi. 'Any port in a storm.'

'It wasn't very unusual in those days to get into art college without any G.C.E. passes,' says Pobjoy. 'He produced a portfolio of samples of his work and I had to say that he was suitable, without doing too much violence to my conscience. I did believe that he had talent and should be encouraged as a lively intelligent boy. The question was: Would he behave any better at college? He didn't, of course.'

His talent for line drawing, his attention to detail, and, above all, his grotesque sense of humour were obvious in all these drawings. The targets, the teachers, were sitting ducks for his blistering satire when he was fifteen. Lennon had little respect for any of them. And as subjects for his drawings they were appropriately bizarre in their daily behaviour. One master sewed a golf ball into the hem of his gown: he was literally a cracking shot. His walks around the school corridors and classrooms were punctuated by his taking aim and hitting troublesome boys on the backs of their heads with the golf ball. Another teacher was the talk of the school because he stank all day, every day, and the boys would openly put two fingers to their nose whenever he came near them. Yet another had a fifteen-foot-long pole which he held throughout lessons and which he swept through the air when a boy wasn't listening. He had perfect aim so that the pole smacked the offending boy across the back of his neck.

So John did not need to use much of his fertile imagination to satirize the schoolteachers. But the pungency of his wit, and the devastating captions to his drawings, were uproarious. In one red-covered exercise book which he gave as a gift to a friend, he gave the teachers names: Psyche, complete with the school badge of a stag but with a face bearing warts and a caption 'Spare Us, Oh Psyche', a commentary on the teacher with the deadly aim with the ball in his gown. His fascination with deformities was rife throughout John's drawings. Psyche's mate, with bulging eyes and warts, was balding, while another drawing of the Psinging Psychies featured six men with deformities in their faces. 'The Wife' was captioned 'My Little Glad' and the woman had a deformed eye. There were wart-ridden features all over a character nicknamed Rigo. 'Typical Hairy Hairless Smell-Type Smith', a dig at the teacher who was notorious for his odour, had a teddy boy hairstyle and a desperate caption: 'Ooh, mate, HELP! Phew, mate.'

There was even a drawing of himself headed: 'Simply a Simple Pimple: short-sighted John Wimple Lennon'. He drew himself as learned, studious, and wearing his horn-rimmed spectacles, with thick bushy hair and holding a dripping candle. But the clincher of the drawing was that he had claws, not human hands, and drainpipe trousers. Nick O'Teen, described as an Irish madman, was drawn smoking with both hands and a cigarette in his mouth. A man and a woman were depicted in bed and in church, saying, 'I do', while another couple were wheeling a pram with seven deformed children.

John's grasp of word-play was imaginative even at fifteen. He was shaping his sense of the absurd, his lampooning of hapless victims, his keen awareness of the ridiculous and—always—a tilt at authority. This would become the hallmark of his character later, with his two books *In His Own Write* and *A Spaniard In The Works*, which were acclaimed by critics as signalling a great new literary wit. But at fifteen, students and teachers at Quarry Bank had to assess poems like this:

> Owl George ee be a farmer's lad
> With mucklekak and cow
> Ee be the son of 'is owl Dad
> But why I don't know how
>
> Ee tak a fork and bale the hay
> And stacking-stook he stock

And lived his loif from day to day
Dressed in a sweaty sock

One day maybe he marry be
To Nellie Nack the Lass
And we shall see what we shall see
A-fucking in the grass

Our Nellie be a gal so fine
All dimpled wart and blue
She herds the pigs, the rotten swine
It mak me wanna spew!

Somehaps perchance ee'll be a man
But now I will unfurl
Owl George is out of the frying pan
'Cos ee's a little girl.

Even the teachers, hard-pressed to smile at Lennon, laughed.
They passed John's *Daily Howl* around the staff room, and
enjoyed being lampooned. They admired John's spoof on the
weather forecast: 'Tomorrow will be Muggy, followed by Tuggy,
Wuggy and Thuggy', and his send-up of Davy Crockett, entitled 'The Story of Davy Crutch-Head'.

While John clearly defied grammar school, there was ample
evidence later in life that he reflected on those years at Quarry
Bank with a hint of affection. In 1967 a Quarry Bank pupil,
Stephen Bayley, wrote to John. This was at the height of the
controversy surrounding the Beatles and drug-taking and when
their milestone-making new album, *Sgt Pepper's Lonely Hearts
Club Band*, was released. Scarcely expecting a reply, the boy
asked a few questions about the songs and added a postscript
about John's old school and its innovations, like the addition
of Russian to the curriculum.

John's handwritten reply demonstrated his interest in the
school no matter what he said; his patience for anyone who
genuinely was inquisitive about his work and opinions; and his
waspish wit:

Dear Stephen,

As Quarry Bank was never a very *high* school, the changes

(?) sound OK. How about sending me a copy of that magazine? All my writing has always been for laughs or fun or whatever you call it. I do it for that first. Whatever people make of it afterwards is valid but it doesn't necessarily have to correspond to my thoughts about it. OK? This goes for any books, creations, art, poetry, songs, etc. The mystery and shit that is built around all forms of art needs smashing, anyway. It must be obvious by today's trends. Enough said.

The song of Mr Kite is taken almost word for word from an old theatrical poster including the Hendersons.

Is Mr Burton* (English) [sic] still there? If so say hello. He was one of the only teachers who dug me and vice versa.

Russian, eh? Not in my day. How we've progressed. Don't tell me they let you into Calder as well** for experience and lessons. I think they asked me years ago rather vaguely if I would like to go back and look but I saw enough of it when I was there. I have fond memories, not too fond though. I have the same trouble as you in writing, but the answer is: just let it roll.

Love
John Lennon

P.S. I don't want to start a rush of letters from little Quarrymen so play it a bit cool as they say in Swinging London. But do say hello to any of those teachers—not quite the right word. Even Pobjoy who got me into art school so I could fail there as well. I can never thank him enough.

Quarry Bank produced many eminent public figures, among them William Rodgers and Peter Shore, who went on to become British government ministers; trade union leader David Basnett; actor Derek Nimmo; and prominent industrialists including the chairman of Ford, Europe. William Pobjoy looks back on Lennon's days at Quarry Bank with a smile, but he was irritated by one aspect of John's perverse attitude to schooling. 'I think

* John meant Philip Burnett, the progressive English teacher with whom he had a good relationship.
**Calder (Calderstones Park) is the girls' school next door to Quarry Bank where Lennon often trespassed to chat up the girls.

he was against school, not Quarry Bank, because he said during the Beatles period: "Look at me now, I've travelled all over the world and done these interesting things. I'm so well off and there are people who taught me at Quarry Bank who are *still there*!" He seemed to think that to still be here in one place was a sign of failure. At that time it obviously didn't enter his head that there might be such a thing as vocation, where material matters were of little account. But I think he probably changed later on.'

The sentimentalist inside Lennon did change his over-the-shoulder look back at his old school. One day in 1965 Aunt Mimi, out walking in Woolton, met Mr Pobjoy, who asked how he was. The answer to the question was obvious, for Beatlemania was at its height: John was a world-famous star. But she astonished the former headmaster by saying: 'John's scared to come back to the school, but he sleeps with a picture of it over his bed.'

At Quarry Bank John travelled quickly from his earlier desire merely to emulate the cheeky Just William: he was titillating girls with obscenities when he went to hang out in Calderstones Park. Rose Lane School nearby had a fair proportion of belligerent pupils, and John would enjoy a confrontation with a few of them in a café, or on Allerton Road, where both he and his mob and the Rose Lane crowd skived off lessons. He was rarely involved in actual fights, mostly backing off when fisticuffs were near. 'He regarded fighting itself as a waste of time, but if anyone set on him he could take care of himself,' says Michael Isaacson, who left the school a year ahead of John to go to art college.

One day, Isaacson returned to Quarry Bank from art college to collect some of his old drawings. Bumping into John in the art room, Michael asked how he had fared in his O-levels and John told him the bad news.

'You should try to get into art school—I'm having a marvellous time drawing nudes,' said Isaacson.

'Cor, that sounds good,' said Lennon.

4
ELVIS!

'Let me get it out of my system, Mimi'

It cannot have been a coincidence: John's hell-raising final two years at Quarry Bank coincided with the arrival in his life of a force that was to be his *cause célèbre*, his saviour, his lifeline. To John Lennon at fifteen, the arrival of two films was virtually a mirror-image of his own outlook on life.

Rebel Without a Cause, starring the mumbling, sharp, resentful hero James Dean, was youth's first tilt at the establishment, its first statement against such cosy pictures as *Oklahoma* and *A Star Is Born*. And *Blackboard Jungle* was even more important, for it reflected schoolboy aggression and catapulted a new music into the world. The music was electrifyingly urgent; the message of the film might have been written for Lennon and his cronies at Quarry Bank. But the star, Bill Haley, wouldn't do. He had no real charisma and his personality totally lacked the tough directness of his driving songs like 'Rock Around The Clock'. Still, the die was cast; the old guard of what was then called the hit parade, including ballad singers Jimmy Young, Tony Bennett, Dickie Valentine, and Tennessee Ernie Ford, now had a deadly rival. The infant was called rock 'n' roll.

In 1956, when John Lennon was sixteen, the film which was dramatically to re-route pop music was shown in Britain. *Rock Around the Clock*, starring Bill Haley and the Comets, disc jockey Alan Freed, the Platters and Freddie Bell and the

Bellboys, was not a strong movie, even by those days' standards. It had no story line, and was merely a vehicle for the
bands to play this new music called rock 'n' roll. In America,
the film went unnoticed. In Britain, it began what is still called
the generation gap.

This new music, loud, irreverent rock 'n' roll, thundered
through the cinema halls of Britain. Parents looked on in horror
as their sons and daughters—but mostly sons—identified with
this clarion call to confrontation. The best news of all, for
young people, was that adults thought it wasn't 'music'. It
wasn't, indeed, mere music: it signalled a new approach to
growing up. Rock 'n' roll was the new international anthem
of youth.

American teenagers emulated their big heroes of the screen,
the mumbling Marlon Brando and the gaunt, haunted James
Dean, by adopting jeans and T-shirts. In Britain, a much more
definite uniform was adopted. It was called the teddy boy outfit,
so described because of its vague similarity to Edwardian fashions.

Greasy hair was one of the major requirements of a ted. It
had to be shaped like an elephant's trunk at the front, coming
down on to the forehead and—crucially—a DA (duck's arse)
at the back, with side whiskers extending well down the face.
Very tight trousers, called drainpipes, bright socks, perhaps
luminous, thick crepe-soled shoes (called 'brothel creepers')
and a long drape jacket were *de rigueur*.

Pop music may have been fey until this point, but it was
at least a little escape from the drudgery of school work. And
in a house with no television, the nightly listen to Radio Luxembourg, broadcast then as now on the difficult-to-tune 208
metres from deep inside Europe, was mandatory for school-
children. The BBC broadcast light music. Luxembourg was
well ahead of the game, playing non-stop pop. Its poor reception somehow added to its clandestine magic.

Lennon did not have to wait long for his Pied Piper. It was
from this station one night that he heard Elvis Presley's earth-
shaking new anthem for rock 'n' roll, 'Heartbreak Hotel'. 'After
that,' John told me in 1962, 'nothing was the same for me. He
did it for me, him and Lonnie Donegan.'

Elvis's weapon was a triple ace. His robust voice was powerful, virtually beyond plagiarism; his songs, with the world-

wide chart topper 'Heartbreak Hotel' quickly followed by 'Don't Be Cruel' and 'Hound Dog', were revolutionary. They grabbed every listener by the ears as well as the hips. And then there was the way he looked.

Elvis was an Americanized version of the teddy boy. For him, the uniform was not necessary but he was quickly christened King of Rock 'n' Roll because of his look, his leer, his loudness, and his rudeness: his hip swivelling was the talk of the critics who branded him as a danger to morality. Sexuality oozed from him. For anyone remotely concerned with teenagers at that time, Presley was the partisan demarcation line: make up your mind, whose side are you on? It was them and us, the kids and the adults. The more adults bemoaned Presley's arrival, the more the newspapers screeched about the new music of youth, the more Lennon and thousands of sixteen-year-olds like him loved it.

Aunt Mimi remembers the period well. 'It was Elvis Presley all day long. I got very tired of him talking about this new singer. I was particularly upset because suddenly he wouldn't let me into his bedroom. If I opened the door, he'd say: "Leave it, I'll tidy it up." He became a mess, almost overnight, and all because of Elvis Presley, I say. He had a poster of him in his bedroom. There was a pyjama top in the bathroom, the trousers in the bedroom, socks somewhere else, shirts flung on the floor.'

Mimi's voice would boom up the stairs: 'There's going to be a change in this house. We're going to have law and order.' Throughout his life John would use the same sentence to tease Mimi about the 'Elvis period' as he reflected on it. 'And of course,' says Mimi, 'when John said it, later on, we would just both burst out laughing about the past. He was lucky to get away with what he did. It was because I'm a book lover and a bit of an artist myself, so I understood his attitude. What he wouldn't come to terms with was that I had a house to run. Oh, he *was* a mess and a problem in those years. Elvis Presley! If John's Uncle George had been alive even he certainly wouldn't have understood the bohemian bit.'

The anchor of Elvis, his music and what he represented, marked John's life as significantly as Lennon was to mark millions of young lives only ten years later. There was to be one vast difference between Presley and Lennon: the American rock giant was a physical phenomenon who rarely spoke, and when he did it was an unimportant mumble. Elvis called nearly all strangers 'sir' as a mark of polite nervousness. John was to combine an intuitive grasp of fundamental rock 'n' roll ethics with highly cerebral leadership. He probably never called anyone 'sir' in his life.

But in the mid-fifties the personal pull of Presley, quickly followed by Little Richard, Jerry Lee Lewis, Buddy Holly, the Coasters, Carl Perkins, and the Everly Brothers, meant liberation for the academic flop that John Lennon had become. It also perfectly fuelled his inherent resentment of authority.

If Presley was John's clarion call to stand up and stand out, Lonnie Donegan was, in 1956 when John was sixteen, just as great a catalyst for his life. This time the hero was not just a distant, masculine figure propelling rock 'n' roll into millions of teenagers' brains. Donegan, clean-cut and formal, in suit and tie as befitted his jazzy background, was nobody's idea of high fashion. He was nasal-voiced, played guitar and banjo, but mesmerized a nation with a curiously British interpretation of the songs of the great American folk singers Woody Guthrie and Huddie 'Leadbelly' Ledbetter. Donegan, who emerged from the traditional jazz ranks of the Chris Barber band, galvanized British youth into his music, named skiffle, with a record called 'Rock Island Line'.

Donegan's influence on British pop music has been incalculable. He had a basic three-chord style, easy to copy, and the line-up of his group at the time (one other guitarist, upright double bass, and drums) inspired hundreds of thousands of young people to make do-it-yourself music. The sound was unimportant. What was crucial was that it wasn't difficult; the guitars were props, allowing the singers to be actors. Here was do-it-yourself rock 'n' roll for thousands of young people. Donegan's cute little songs, like 'Putting On The Style', 'Does Your Chewing Gum Lose Its Flavour (On The Bedpost Overnight)' and 'Cumberland Gap', became the anthems of sixteen-year-olds everywhere. Skiffle groups, formed in schools and clubs, played as much for fun as for money.

Lennon, then a bellicose schoolboy, went for skiffle like a homing pigeon. Jazz audiences already knew of skiffle, because splinter groups formed from the bands led by Chris Barber and Ken Colyer played mostly in London clubs and a few knowledgeable provincial clubs like Liverpool's Cavern and Iron Door. All Lennon knew initially was 'Rock Island Line', which even the B.B.C. was playing. He thought its acceptance by *that* bastion of respectability, which even Aunt Mimi acknowledged as tolerable listening, was the key to his breakthrough. 'All the boys of my age are getting guitars,' he told Mimi. 'Could you lend me the money to get one?'

John was seeing more of his mother and asked both Julia and Mimi to buy him a guitar. Every afternoon, on her daily visits to Mendips, Julia would be asked, but she did not want to override Mimi's authority by installing John with a guitar under her roof. John alone was enough of a responsibility for her sister. Julia could see, anyway, from his interest in her banjo playing, that with a guitar in his hand his studies at school, already a cause for concern, would plunge into irretrievable disaster.

John, faced with the two women in his life not helping him get a guitar, decided to send away for his first model himself. From a mail order advertisement in the *Daily Mail* he ordered a £5 10s model, 'guaranteed not to split', and was canny enough, at this stage, to have the guitar posted to Julia's address where he would run less risk of a scolding. His musically-minded mother was less of a risk than Mimi. He took it to Mendips eventually, telling Mimi that Julia had got it for him.

Armed with the cheap guitar, which he would occasionally leave at Julia's in order not to push his luck with Mimi, John concentrated heavily on all the pop music sounds he could hear on Radio Luxembourg. Buying records was generally out of the question: they cost six shillings. But he did invest in a 78 r.p.m. record of Donegan's 'Rock Island Line'.

The person to whom Lennon quickly sold that record, for two shillings and sixpence, once he had played it to death on Julia's old record player, was to be one of the players in the group that John formed at school. Rod Davis, a studious, successful, A-stream student at Quarry Bank, met Lennon only because he too lived in Woolton. At the forty-five-minute prep sessions after each day's classes, students got together in classrooms according to the house they were in. As Davis and

Lennon and his inseparable partner Pete Shotton were in Wool-ton, they met on most days. The record Lennon persuaded Rod Davis to buy had a damaged centre hole: Davis felt conned when he realized why John wanted to sell it.

Inspired by the Donegan craze, Rod Davis had bought a Windsor banjo for £5 from his uncle. Excited about his pur-chase, he said to a classmate, Eric Griffiths, 'I went and bought a banjo yesterday.' Rod Davis was surprised to be told that Lennon and Griffiths already had guitars, and that Pete Shotton was learning to play the washboard, an integral part of any skiffle band's line-up. 'Why don't we have a practice on Thurs-day?' said Griffiths. 'We're going to start a skiffle group.'

Rod Davis had known John Lennon and Pete Shotton since they were all about six. He remembered him as the scourge of St Peter's Sunday School classes. 'He arrived looking resentful at having to come on Sunday mornings,' says Rod Davis, 'and he chewed gum throughout the lessons. It just wasn't done to chew gum at the Sunday School.' Eventually John and Shotton were invited to leave, although Mimi says that he was con-firmed, at his own request, at the same church. 'Religion was never rammed down his throat, but he certainly believed in God, all through his childhood, and he asked to be confirmed,' she says.

But the only religion that seriously grabbed Lennon at the age of sixteen was music. Even William Pobjoy, headmaster of Quarry Bank, noticed the passion with which young Lennon, the terror of the school, was interesting himself in skiffle. It was, he reflects, good to see him feeling positive about *some-thing*.

Mr Pobjoy was also surprised, and pleased, that making music seemed to be encouraging a generous side to John's nature; some schoolboy entertainers, however amateur, would ask for money to play at school dances and other functions. 'But John would always be most polite, and certainly not ask for money, when he offered the services of his group,' says the ex-headmaster, who retired in 1982. '`Some boys asked outrageous fees but John was really grateful for the chance to play free.' Pobjoy pointed out this attribute to those teachers who were despairing of him.

Inevitably Lennon and Shotton were the pilots of the skiffle group. After a few weeks of practice, with John hammering out 'Rock Island Line' and 'Cumberland Gap' as his *tour de force* songs and Shotton playing the washboard with thimbles— the accepted percussion for all skiffle groups of that period— Lennon felt in full swing.

Now that this 'new music' of Lonnie Donegan and Elvis Presley was the talk of the school, particularly in the C stream into which Lennon had plunged, the official formation of a school skiffle group was the next move and John its obvious leader. When John told his mother of his group, she suggested practices were held at her house after school. The first line-up was John (guitar), Rod Davis (banjo), Eric Griffiths (guitar), and Colin Hanton (drums). The first rehearsal was in Eric Griffiths' house in Woolton. Later they would play in Julia's bathroom, with one player standing in the bath to get the tinny echoey sound of amplification. 'John's mother really enjoyed us playing and encouraged us a lot,' says Rod Davis. 'She obviously preferred the banjo to the guitar so I got on well with her. I was always impressed with the fact that she played banjo with the back of her nails.

'John was the undisputed leader for two reasons. First, he knew one more chord than the rest of us. His mother's banjo playing had given him the edge—she used to teach John some banjo chords, and they used to tune the top four strings of his guitar to banjo intervals, forget about the bottom two strings, and play banjo chords on the guitars! It was all right for me— Julia would help me tune my banjo properly. So I'd probably be the only one in tune. I think everything was in C—I remember having terrible trouble playing F chords on the banjo.

'Secondly John was keen on singing and the rest of us were never particularly good at vocals. We joined in choruses but he sang lead.' The earliest songs were 'Don't You Rock Me, Daddy-O', 'Love Is Strange', 'Rock Island Line', 'Cumberland Gap', 'Freight Train', the big hit made famous by Chas McDevitt and Nancy Whiskey, Johnny Duncan's 'Last Train to San Fernando', and 'Maggie May'.

'John used to belt the daylights out of his guitar and was forever breaking strings,' says Rod Davis. 'When this happened, he'd hand me his guitar and I'd have to change the string for him because I was better at it than him. While I was changing it, he'd borrow my banjo, so he's actually played my banjo quite a few times.' Today he guards the instrument as a priceless memento.

The first name for the group was the Blackjacks. They hit upon the uniform for their much-hoped-for public performances: black jeans, with green stitching and plain white shirts. Two new recruits to the band alternated on playing tea-chest bass; Ivan Vaughan, who had gone to Dovedale Primary School with John but went on to the posh Liverpool Institute when John joined Quarry Bank; and Nigel Whalley, who went to Bluecoats Grammar School, but who knew John from his Sunday School days. In a rare show of allegiance to his school, John quickly changed the name to the Quarry Men, the line-up of which was erratic, and at one time included a bass player, Bill Smith, who was in John's class. But he did not arrive regularly for rehearsals and soon left. Eventually, the bass-playing role fell to Len Garry.

The fact that Nigel Whalley and Ivan Vaughan were not at Quarry Bank made their regular inclusion in the line-up difficult to arrange, anyway; but Nigel, highly organized and ambitious for the group, said he would try to get them some bookings. He persuaded shopkeepers in Woolton to put notices, free, in their windows: 'Country, Western, Rock 'n' Roll, Skiffle, The Quarry Men, Open for Engagements.'

John named the group the Quarry Men partly as a tongue-in-cheek dig at the school in which they had been born, and partly because the name had a ring of skiffle about it, anyway. 'Quarry Men Strong Before Our Birth' was the school song, sung lustily by most boys at the end of term. Lennon and Shotton, when they were not smiling or making up rude words to the school song under their breath, quietly admired its sentiments. John saw the adoption of the school song within the name of the group as a means to an end; it gave them a stamp of credibility. And he was to foster the 'means to an end' rule throughout his life. It was Lennon who thought of the name and he told the others. That was that.

Slowly but encouragingly, occasional engagements were secured for the Quarry Men by Nigel Whalley. Childwall Golf Club, St Barnabas Church Hall at Penny Lane and St Peter's Youth Club were among the earliest. The group had made its public début playing on the back of a lorry at a carnival in Rosebery Street, Liverpool 8.

John's beer drinking had its beginnings during these days. Payments for Quarry Men concerts at Conservative dances and youth club parties were only a few pounds, but of equal attraction to John was the liberation of an evening out, the chance to chat up girls outside his normal Woolton beat, and drink, often 'on the house' as he was a performer.

The teddy boy movement was gaining ground by the time the Quarry Men secured some bookings. At dances, teds would ask the group to play some rock 'n' roll instead of the comparatively mild skiffle. The request hit a chord inside the ever-restless Lennon, who had adopted a bit of a teddy boy look with the beginnings of 'sidies' down his face and tight jeans which were as near as he could get to the obligatory drainpipe trousers. The Quarry Men entered several skiffle contests, failed to win or get a position at any one, and John was particularly taken aback by a group from Rhyl which won the Carroll Levis Discoveries night at the Liverpool Empire. 'They were really putting their act over, the guitarist was all over the stage and really full of a show,' recalls Rod Davis. 'We were really purist by comparison. John learned a lesson from that night. He said: "You've got to put it over a bit to do rock 'n' roll." In his mind, if not in the minds of the others, that was going to be the route to success. If Lonnie Donegan had provided the *will* to play, Elvis Presley was still the foundation upon which his musical attitude was based.

'None of us thought of it going any further than a good school lark that earned a few bob,' says Rod Davis. But Lennon thought differently and swung the songs towards rock 'n' roll. 'Jailhouse Rock' and 'Blue Suede Shoes', Lennon favourites, took him way beyond the purism of the early skiffle sounds, and gave full rein to his increasing stage personality. His mother taught him, in one week of solid tuition after school, the chords to a hot Lennon favourite, Buddy Holly's 'That'll Be The Day'. It was the first song John learned to play and sing accurately. There was growing dissent in the group about the increasing rock element from John. Nigel Whalley secured the Quarry Men a coveted booking at a jazz stronghold in Liverpool city centre, the Cavern in Mathew Street. Lennon disliked jazz fans because they were, he thought, elitist. Here, in a club which tolerated skiffle because it was a jazz offshoot but which banished rock 'n' roll as the trashy sound of youth, Lennon bit off more than he could chew.

Rod Davis argued on stage with him that the idea of doing rock songs would be unacceptable to the audience, and anyway that wasn't the original idea behind the Quarry Men. John maintained that as he was the only singer in the group, he had a right to decide what would be sung; anyway, the skiffle repertoire was restricting and boring. It was time to move on. And so the jazz crowd, dressed, as Lennon later sneeringly described them, in their 'G.C.E. sweaters', jeered and booed as Lennon went through his rockers. Davis said to him: 'We shouldn't be playing rock 'n' roll on stage at the Cavern of all places, John. It's a jazz place.' He was also concerned that John didn't know the words to many of the rockers he was putting forward. He was making up any words as he sang along. But Lennon totally ignored Davis's opinions and announced the songs as he wanted them: Presley's 'Jailhouse Rock', 'Don't Be Cruel' and 'Heartbreak Hotel' were more exciting than the restricting skiffle repeats.

The £5 guitar was not standing up to the strain of all these public performances. 'He kept bothering me for what he called a real one,' says Mimi. 'I wasn't too ready to provide it because I thought he should be getting on with his school work a little more seriously. But he kept on and on: "Let me get it out of my system, Mimi."

'I said: "All right, get it out of your system." '

One Saturday morning she took him along to the famous musical instrument shop, Hessy's, off Whitechapel in Liverpool. 'There were guitars hanging all around the room and John didn't know which one to choose for the best. Finally, he pointed to one and the man took it down and he played it and said, "I'll have that one." What I do remember is John nodding his head to me and me paying the £17 there and then for it. He was as happy as could be on the bus home.' The Spanish-styled guitar had steel strings which quickly made John's fingers sore from his many hours of strumming, in his bedroom, to the exclusion of homework and to the continuing irritation of Mimi.

Finally, when she could no longer stand his foot tapping on the ceiling, Mimi ordered him into the porch at Mendips. It was to become his refuge and where, coincidentally, he preferred the acoustics, with the echo. On one occasion when he was banished there by an impatient Mimi she boomed the words: 'The guitar's all very well, John, but you'll never make a *living* out of it.'

At sixteen, John Lennon stood out as no ordinary schoolboy or teenager. Within the Quarry Men, the only disagreements were about skiffle versus rock 'n' roll. He was getting used to using his fists in a fight: being in the C stream, the going was rougher than in the academically higher streams, and he would not hesitate to punch when there was a verbal battle that couldn't be resolved. At home, the tension between him and Mimi increased as she tired of the regular morning phone calls from the headmaster's secretary, relaying John's latest misdemeanour. He was getting used to the prospect that he would have to battle his way through life, a fact confirmed by the punch-ups he saw in boozy audiences when the Quarry Men played at dances, particularly in the rough area of Garston.

Strangely, the most crucial decision in his professional life was to happen as a result of one of the most genteel events the Quarry Men played. It was there that he first met Paul McCartney.

The group was drifting between engagements and had fared poorly in talent contests when they secured a booking for the afternoon of 6 July 1957, as the music attraction at St Peter's, Woolton, garden fete. The weather was sunny and perfect for the Quarry Men—on this occasion John Lennon, Pete Shotton, Eric Griffiths, Colin Hanton and Len Garry on tea-chest bass—to perform their limited repertoire on a raised platform in the furthest field from the church. John, seizing Woolton's big day as an occasion when he could 'come out' and make an impression, dressed in full teddy boy regalia for the first time: tight drainpipe trousers which left nothing to the imagination; a jacket with heavy padding at the shoulders; blue and white checked shirt and—vitally—greased-back hair.

The Elvis Presley imitation fell stonily on Mimi, who began his day with a scolding. She reminded him that his school reports were appalling and for a grammar school boy to be adopting such a personality was a repudiation of all the standards she had been trying to instil into him. Lennon, never rude to his aunt but intransigent and defiant when it came to asserting himself, simply walked out in mid-morning and teamed up with Pete Shotton, ready for the afternoon's big appearance. John, who realized that the big garden fete audience could mean an important day for the group, steeled himself by buying bottles of light ale from the Woolton off-licence and getting mildly inebriated, but not drunk. All his life, drink was to be a recurring problem. He enjoyed it to relax, or celebrate, but he could never take much before feeling the effects. And when John got merry, he became aggressive.

That fateful sunny Saturday Aunt Mimi did not know John was taking his Quarry Men to the Woolton fete, and John did not realize she would be going to the fete with her sister. 'It was a gorgeous day, with all the young women in their backless dresses and summer frocks,' says Mimi. The chief attraction was the band of the Cheshire Yeomanry; the Quarry Men had to walk the gauntlet of stalls selling home-made cakes and fruit and vegetables, past the children's sideshows, before they could take the stand. The vicar, the Rev. Maurice Pryce-Jones, was doing the rounds and welcomed the band that was to provide the afternoon's skiffle, a particularly trendy attraction for a church event.

'Well, when I got there and stood talking to young people over a cup of tea, there was suddenly this loud beat—bang, bang, coming from the bottom field. It shook everybody up,' says Mimi. 'All the young people left their stalls and proceeded down to the field. I said: "Where are they going?" and my sister said: "There must be a band, let's go." '

The sight that greeted Mimi as she neared the band platform transfixed her. 'I couldn't take my eyes off him,' she said. It was the first time she had seen, and heard, John in full cry with the Quarry Men. 'There was this grin all over John's face and then he spotted me walking towards him and his expression changed a bit. I don't know why—I was pleased as punch to see him up there.' But Lennon, in his mildly alcoholic haze remembering the row that morning about his teddy boy attire, feared the renewed wrath of Mimi. He began to busk the words to the song he was singing: 'And Mimi's coming down the path, oh oh.' The songs played that day included 'Cumberland Gap', 'Railroad Bill', 'Maggie May' and 'Come Go With Me'. On that song John characteristically—and irreverently, for a church affair—changed into the more suggestive: 'Come little darling, come and go with me.' It was a lyrical tactic he was to employ to devastating, often hilarious, effect later in his life, as a writer.

John's shock at seeing Mimi was softened when she led the applause as the group finished its set. But that was not to be the only significant part of the day. Among the audience, unknown to John, casting a keen fifteen-year-old's eye on the music which he regarded as very primitive, was a boy from neighbouring Allerton: Paul McCartney. He and John had a mutual friend, Ivan Vaughan, who lived in a house immediately behind Mendips and had attended Dovedale Primary School with him. When John went to Quarry Bank Ivan had gone to the Liverpool Institute, the posh grammar school alongside the art college. Ivan became friendly with McCartney who was another Institute student. Realizing Paul's interest in rock, Ivan thought it would be good if he heard the Quarry Men and met John. 'You've got to come and meet this guy John Lennon,' Ivan said to Paul. 'You'll get on well with him . . .'

Paul stood with Ivan watching and listening as John stood on the stage, even at the age of not quite seventeen a commanding figure, undeniably the leader. Musically, John and the Quarry Men exuded more energy and enthusiasm than talent, but it was infectious enough. What impressed McCartney as much as anything was that these schoolboys, only a little older than him, had actually got a group together. His talent as a guitarist, coming from a musical family, was prodigious compared with John's; still, it had no outlet.

Ivan Vaughan led Paul across to the church hall after the Quarry Men finished playing. There, introductions were made. As Paul recalled later in a warm and amusing foreword to John's first book, *In His Own Write*: 'At Woolton village fete I met him. I was a fat schoolboy and, as he leaned an arm on my shoulder, I realized that he was drunk. We were twelve then [*sic*] but in spite of his sideboards we went on to become teenage pals. Aunt Mimi, who had looked after him since he was so high, used to tell me he was much cleverer than he pretended. . . .'

But that day at Woolton fete it was the clever young McCartney who held the aces. First, John was floored by the fact that Paul could actually tune his guitar, thus correcting the banjo tuning that John had inherited from his mother. Secondly, McCartney was able to demonstrate a stunning knowledge of the words to a favourite of John's beloved rock 'n' roll: Paul wrote down the words to Eddie Cochran's 'Twenty Flight Rock' from the film *The Girl Can't Help It*. Next, he ran through other rockers and floored John with what, to the skiffler trying to become more adept in musicianship, was the performance of a virtuoso.

John Lennon had never had an inferiority complex. He was a sixteen-year-old schoolboy hell-raiser, a defiant challenge for his caring Aunt Mimi, and had so far not needed to project himself beyond a punch-up, always backing off when the going got really tough or dangerous. But that day in July 1957 was to prove a watershed for John. The meeting with Paul McCartney had come just before he left Quarry Bank School, sadly failing all his O-levels. John didn't show signs of worrying much about that. He had a chip on his shoulder about formal education and 'pieces of paper that say you're bright'.

But the Quarry Men, for all their amateurism, were important to John. With school success slipping away he desperately wanted to stamp his personality on something, anything that would mark him out as a success. The skiffle group was obviously going to have to grow or go. That night, as he sobered up after the evening performance at the village fete, long after Paul McCartney had cycled home to 20 Forthlin Road, Allerton, the leader of the Quarry Men was tortured by a question. Should he invite Paul McCartney to join the group? A better guitarist than John, and with a better knowledge of rock 'n' roll songs, he was going to be a formidable performer. Lennon's leadership might be threatened. The alternative was to shun competition and plod on with the Quarry Men, going the same aimless way as thousands of skiffle groups all around Britain.

At first the decision was tough, but eventually it proved logical that he should offer Paul McCartney the chance to join. First, he would have a powerful, talented ally in the swing to break away from skiffle and make it a rock 'n' roll band. Secondly, he had enough confidence in his own dominance to believe that he would have the edge over a boy two years younger. Thirdly, the group needed new blood.

It was Pete Shotton who passed the news to McCartney. 'John wants you in the group,' he said to Paul as they cycled one day over Allerton golf course. McCartney was pleased but cool. It would be two months before he could get into the Quarry Men, he said; he was going to scout camp.

5
THE ART
STUDENT

'I want to be rich and famous'

For the art college's vital day of judgement on him John's carefully groomed appearance and his sober demeanour complemented the kind recommendation of William Pobjoy. He was accepted as a student at Liverpool College of Art. The soot-blackened building was just around the corner from Liverpool Institute where Paul McCartney, his brother Michael, George Harrison, and John's old friend Ivan Vaughan were studying.

When he went for an interview John took an impressive portfolio of his Quarry Bank work. This corroborated Mr Pobjoy's generous description of Lennon, to the college principal, Mr Stevenson, that the boy deserved a chance. Mimi went to the college with him for the interview; as on all bus journeys with her, he travelled alone upstairs on the bus while she sat downstairs—a typical teenage embarrassment at being seen out 'in the care' of a relation. 'He'd hardly been into town before that, certainly not on his own,' says Mimi. John dressed soberly for the big day, wearing Uncle George's old brown jacket, plus a shirt and tie. 'He was himself, not nervous, quite confident,' says Mimi; 'he was never one to *show* his feelings, even then.'

The interview went successfully. John was told that he would be expected to work hard on his own initiative, and he started college in September 1957.

As John entered college the Quarry Men continued, but

with less momentum than when he was at Quarry Bank. The pace of things was reduced because Pete Shotton had left Quarry Bank to become a police cadet, with Nigel Whalley holding things together with regular bookings. But all of them were preoccupied with getting used to new daily environments; John had the additional distraction of girls at college. No more did he have to climb the walls of Calderstones Park Girls' School, near Quarry Bank, to eye the schoolgirls, chat them up, and make rude signs to them. At Liverpool College of Art, in the autumn of 1957, there were pretty girls in every room. The beatnik period was under way: it meant teenage assertiveness and individuality in tandem with the recent youth explosion that had come with Elvis Presley, Lonnie Donegan and skiffle, James Dean, and the surly style of a great new young film actor, Marlon Brando, in *The Wild One*. It was a perfect period for the individualism in John Lennon to grow.

One student who got to know John from his first days at college was Phyllis McKenzie. They travelled on the number 72 bus together every morning from Woolton to Canning Street, near the college in Liverpool 8. Although John didn't care much about it in the early days of these journeys, Phyllis was the closest friend of another student, Cynthia Powell, whom she had known since they went to the Secondary School of Art together at the age of twelve.

Lennon could not be ignored on that bus, recalls Phyllis. He was scruffy, often in a black leather jacket, and always travelled upstairs so that he could smoke. John held his Woodbine between his first two fingers, with all four fingers curling around it, using the thumb as a support. It struck Phyllis as strange.

'He might have been scruffy but he was always clean,' says Phyllis. 'And he was not mean—he'd usually offer to pay my fare, eight old pence, just because he knew I was, like him, a hard-up student at the college.' As the months went by and he realized Phyllis was Cynthia's best pal, he became wary of talking to her, lest whatever he said should be repeated. 'He used to say I was his rival for Cynthia's attention.'

Art college was legendary to any young person in Liverpool. 'You just knew you were in for a good time,' says Michael Isaacson, who left Quarry Bank a year before John and was installed at art college when Lennon arrived. 'But it was tricky going in and establishing yourself because a lot of people there were a lot older than grammar school boys like John and me. The Korean War was on at the time and there were a lot of older men who had returned from Korea and got a grant.' The procedure was for all new entrants to go into the painting school for their first year and then go into specialist areas like illustration, sculpture, graphic design, or lettering.

'John had a tremendous amount of confidence, even then,' says Isaacson. 'Most of us spent the first few months, or maybe the first year, wondering what we should do and trying to be industrious in our work. Not John—he went straight in, played his part to the limit, and gathered people around him, and looking at him, from almost day one.'

There was an unlikely rapport between Lennon and Michael Isaacson, just as they found at Quarry Bank. 'I wasn't a pushover and he knew that and probably liked it,' says Isaacson. 'He knew I was good at art, and I drew cartoons not unlike the doodles which he did whenever he had a spare moment. Also, I decided not to join his teddy boy or beatnik element but to stand apart. My trick was to be the cleanest guy there. I found a shop in London Road where they made incredible silk brocade waistcoats. I didn't have much money but I bought lots of these in different colours, and I looked like something out of Wyatt Earp. John looked totally the opposite. We used to eye one another and size each other up. He admired my individuality.' John always had respect for people who were different.

'When John was on his way to join art college, I knew things would happen when he got up to his tricks and I looked forward to the years ahead with Lennon. He was a terrible guy, actually, but I liked him.' Other students say Isaacson despised John and they clashed, but he denies that: 'Of course I frowned on everything he did, his work and his attitude, but his responses were always beautiful, so we did get along fine. When you look down on someone, you can do it with total disrespect, or with respect.'

Lennon's recognition of Isaacson rose when he realized Michael's prowess. A year older and demonstrably more ambitious, Isaacson quickly became the art college artist who 'got printed', extensively at first by the Liverpool University students' union magazine and later, at the age of eighteen, by the *Liverpool Daily Post*. 'John was certainly aware of me. He commented on my success and said, "You're successful because you bloody well want to be, aren't you?" '

Isaacson's most animated clash with Lennon came, not unexpectedly, on the subject of music. Isaacson, who coveted leadership whenever it was available, took it upon himself to run the art college music club and provided a staple diet of jazz, notably the trendy sounds of Miles Davis and the Modern Jazz Quartet.

Lennon, who by the time he entered college was deeply into all things Elvis, confronted Isaacson one day in the music room. Eyeing the records by artists whose names he had never heard of, John said: 'What a lot of fucking shit you play. Why don't you play something proper—like Little Richard, Chuck Berry, Elvis Presley?'

Isaacson's retort was a challenge: 'What do *you* know about it? Most of the people here like this. If you really want to do something, bring your group to the art school dance and prove yourselves. I'll put you on and give you a break.' The group did play, and Isaacson says they were a shambles, with a poor sound, and deservedly got a thin reception.

The dominating characteristic at college inside everyone with ambition was a burning desire to get out of Liverpool. 'Lennon told me quite candidly even at that age, that he wanted to be rich and famous. That was the drive inside all of us at that time and that's why Liverpool in the late 1950s and early 1960s was such an exciting place. We all wanted to get out of the city as soon as possible, and be wildly successful.' Isaacson went to London, became a successful political cartoonist for the national media, and eventually formed his own advertising agency.

Reflecting on Lennon, he says: 'I think if he had not become successful he may well have become more than just a wayward bum. He might well have become a really nasty piece of work. It's all hypothetical, but I fear the worst could have happened. If he hadn't become famous his anger could have been vented in another direction. Where his energy was channelled into creative music, it would have gone into something destructive instead of creative. He was strictly an all-or-nothing kind of guy.'

None of the students who attended college with John recalls him as a profound person. He was more physical than cerebral. He had little time for lengthy discourse on anything beyond music and girls, notably Cynthia Powell, who had the most electrifying effect on him once she had become as besotted with him as he was with her. Once John had secured her love, his possessiveness about her was overpowering. Although he followed his own roving eye, the slightest move towards another man by Cyn brought forth John's fury and cross-examination. 'She was very pretty, Bardot-like, and I enjoyed looking across the canteen at her,' says Michael Isaacson. Another student, Ann Mason, says Cynthia was attractive enough to have been the girlfriend of many others at the college, but her passion for Lennon was incredible. 'It was certainly surprising that a girl like Cynthia had been caught by this shit called Lennon,' says Isaacson. 'They looked at each other adoringly. They were totally fixated.'

Ann Mason's link with John was not romantic, but she was unique in having, as her boyfriend for one afternoon, another student named Stuart Sutcliffe, who came from Prescot Grammar School and was John's closest friend, and, for a much longer period, Geoff Mohammed. John recognized in Stuart's gentleness the reality of his own personality. The difference was that John's quiet studious nature was submerged beneath an outward veneer of ruggedness, which often manifested itself in raw aggression. Stuart was the opposite; quiet outside, tough inside. This tension was to lead to Stuart's blinding headaches which would later prove fatal. But when they were together Lennon and Sutcliffe found a rapport which neither, in their teenage simplicity, needed to explain.

At college, John was forging strong musical links with Paul by having daily lunchtime sessions in Arthur Ballard's room; John had also developed a good non-musical friendship with another student who found it hard to concentrate on his work.

Geoff Mohammed was five years older than John, of much bigger build, and came from Manchester. His father was Indian, his mother French–Italian. Geoff was dark-skinned, good-looking, and for most of the time clowned his way through the classes. It was his irreverence for orderly work, and failure to complete his work, together with his great sense of humour, that drew John to him.

'I never had much time for John,' says Ann Mason, Geoff's one-time girlfriend. 'I despised him because he didn't work hard. He was a terrific tearaway but he had this strange thing about him: he was either going to land up as a great, or in the gutter. It wasn't because of anything he actually did, because his art work was rather poor. But there was this strange destiny about him. Geoff Mohammed had the same quality.' Geoff died a few years before Lennon, having left college to become a security man at the Whitworth Art Gallery back in his home city of Manchester.

Ann remembers her ex-boyfriend as 'intelligent, philosophical and far more sensitive than John'. He also had a neat line in self-deprecating fun. Aunt Mimi remembers that John went home one day roaring with laughter at a story about himself and Geoff who had been in a café where there were a lot of black people. The dark-skinned Geoff had them all laughing uproariously as he opened the café door and shouted: 'Right, all foreigners OUT!' This sense of the ridiculous appealed to John: in 1959, on the day they both received some money from their college grant, they went out together into the city and returned dressed in identical clothing—dark green suede shoes, dark grey trousers, and fawn donkey jackets. They were also boasting about having been to the barber's for a shave, an unnecessary extravagance for hard-up students. It was an innocent example of doing anything to make an impact.

'I was afraid of John because he could be so caustic,' says Ann Mason. 'I was never on the receiving end of his sarcasm. Maybe I was protected by being Geoff's girlfriend. People found John very amusing at times, but there was always this underlying fear that he might turn his wit around and use it against them. What made the partnership interesting between Geoff and John was that John respected Geoff, but Geoff in turn wasn't afraid of John as some were.' He was keen on palmistry, which also fascinated Lennon.

When Geoff had a row with Ann Mason, he and John went out for the night and got drunk. Everyone at college knew by the sight that greeted them all in the college canteen next morning; the two of them had returned late at night and filled the canteen with stuff they had stolen from the trendy Bold Street area of the city—street nameplates, signposts, posters, and even parts of cars and bicycles. They were admonished by the college principal but both quietly laughed. The prank—and the emotional release it had given Geoff during a heavy row with his girlfriend—was well worth the rebuke, and the hangover.

At the art college some students were serious about their work, others there mostly for the enjoyment of it all, letting their career take its own direction. John enjoyed art and was talented in an unorthodox way, particularly as a caricaturist, but he was not prepared to let art get in the way of his determination to press on with his rock 'n' roll.

Most lunchtimes, in Arthur Ballard's room 21, guitarist Len Garry from the Quarry Men would join Paul McCartney and George Harrison from the Liverpool Institute next door. About twenty students would finish their canteen lunch and form the audience as the musicians spent an hour playing Buddy Holly and Everly Brothers songs, finishing off every day with Lennon singing the old British variety favourite, 'When You're Smiling'. He would inject the names of college teachers into several of the songs, in a sardonic send-up that amused all the students.

John eased himself into college life with a central characteristic that was to mark his life. He *used* every moment. He manipulated every minute he was given to make it work to his advantage. Even the teachers who riled him, like the strong, colourful Welshman Charles Burton, who regularly picked on Lennon for his artistic inadequacies, had their value to John. They would crop up in his songs, used as target practice.

'He was an original, and being one myself, I could single him out as a true individual,' says June Furlong, who enjoyed a strangely intuitive relationship with Lennon from his first weeks in the art college. 'I'd seen him sitting in life class, or outside the pub Ye Cracke, and I can remember saying to myself about this seventeen-year-old teenager: "Where will your original talent take you? This is no ordinary boy student . . . he's going to do something unusual." '

June Furlong was the art college model whose class in room 71 John attended twice weekly during the day, and occasionally in the evenings if he wanted to return with any of his friends like Stuart Sutcliffe, Geoff Mohammed, Tony Carricker, or Dave Davies. To some, drawing a model while still only a teenager might have been the source of much nudging and winking. Occasionally, John would say to his friends when drawing June: 'Christ, I wonder what Mimi would have to say about *this*.' But that light joke was merely to emphasize the stern background from which he came. Most of the time, John was an earnest and conscientious member of June's drawing class. 'He was a completely charming and one hundred per cent decent person. Nobody alive could pull a fast one over him, but if he realized you were genuine and interested in talking intelligently to him, about art or anything else, he would talk to you for hours. And we did,' says June Furlong. 'He had no time for flippancy in conversation.'

He fascinated her. Their friendship was purely platonic, but during the sessions when he would be drawing her, their conversation would strike the most personal chords. 'He hadn't got it all together, mentally, when I first met him, but there was this . . . well, originality is the word, there was this total originality about him. I could see some potential in his mind, although his drawings were just average. John could just hold his own in art, and that was that. He wasn't anywhere near his closest friend, Stuart Sutcliffe. Stuart was not just good, he was great, but he had a streak in him which appealed to John. He lived every day as if it was going to be his last. The teachers all knew he had a rare talent, but they had to hold him back and try to channel him. "Yes, OK, Stuart. It's excellent work, but take it easy. Less output and more plan of thought," Charles Burton told him.'

But it was precisely that non-stop drive that endeared Stuart to John. And they both had this in common: they were determined to capitalize on what they were good at—for Stuart art, for John music.

'I could see from the first few times I met him that here was a bloke who wasn't prepared to play life from the sidelines,' says June Furlong. She sits in her house in Liverpool, just five minutes' walk from the college, where she was born, where

John Lennon visited her, and remembers the college's most famous student with fondness. 'Always, he either wanted to be in the scrum half, or he wasn't going to be involved in the game. I'd say that when he entered a room, or started a class like the life class, his attitude to everyone was: "What's going on here, what's this, who's that?" And that's how he quickly got to know all the people around him, in his groups, their strengths and their weaknesses, their hang-ups, their difficulties and the obstacles. His sarcasm with the weak was very cutting.'

Lennon wanted his own way in most things and didn't relax his pressure until he got it. After the evening life class sessions he went through the phase of insisting that some students joined him in going to the Liverpool Empire to see comedy acts like Robb Wilton; Wilson, Keppel and Betty; Morecambe and Wise; and the famous drunk comic, Jimmy James. The more traditional the comedian, like Robb Wilton, the more John enjoyed mimicking them. He would roam about college next day repeating Wilton's famous phrase: 'The day war broke out, my missus, she says to me: "What are you going to do about it?" ' Despite his outlandish behaviour, and assertiveness as a rock 'n' roll trailblazer, John was quite normal in his taste for traditional British humour.

Stuart Sutcliffe was not among those who went to the variety shows with John and the other students. He was not particularly interested in the stage, a fact that might at first have ensured that John and Stuart would be able to sustain only a casual, art college friendship. 'But I've never seen two teenagers so close as those two,' says June Furlong. 'John, as an extrovert personality, used to attract a lot of blokes who were not extroverts. He didn't have to have a lot in common with his best friend to consider him his best friend.' He expected a vast amount of loyalty from his friends, but gave a lot in return. Underneath an exhibitionist exterior, Lennon had a fermenting brain. Stuart Sutcliffe was a quiet, intellectual thinker. With his spiky hair and lithe physique, he didn't have to make any effort to be vulnerably attractive to women, whereas John kept working on his looks. Stuart, a runaway artistic talent whom all the teachers reckoned would be a star student in the years ahead, possessed the brooding authenticity that John secretly yearned for. In John, Stuart saw a speedy brain and a demonstrative style that he could never summon. The pair were inseparable and whatever other male friendships John forged, nothing compared with Stuart. 'That was his only friend,' says Aunt Mimi. 'He was the only other boy he really enjoyed being with for long periods of time.'

Stuart's nude drawings of June were stunning. 'I wonder what happened to them,' muses June Furlong today. 'He liked me in one particular pose, and he did several.' Normally, she did not bother to inspect students' interpretations of her poses, but Stuart's were so good that she took a particular interest in all his work.

Lennon, fully heterosexual though he was, had taste and respect for her nudity. His twice-weekly sessions in the life class during the week were augmented by his wandering over from Stuart's nearby flat at Gambier Terrace in the evenings from seven o'clock until nine. 'I was his foil for a while,' says June. 'I was attracted to him, not in a physical way but in a Liverpool way. He was a positive Liverpudlian, and there was this streak of iron and steel in his character, every moment. Look at anybody who's made it, and if they came from Liverpool, it's partly *because* they came from Liverpool. John hadn't the artistic talent, but to speak to, whether he was joking about the strictness of his Aunt Mimi, or whether he was on about last night's show at Liverpool Pavilion, he had this *edge*.'

Lennon always reacted firmly to the person he faced or the treatment he was given. Confronted by a fool asking cretinous questions, as he often was during Beatlemania, John was the most scathing, often vitriolic, adversary. But treated sensibly, engaged in serious conversation by anyone who was genuine and an enthusiast about his own craft—which didn't necessarily mean enthusing over music—John was a powerful, discerning conversationalist. 'He was a great sender-upper of other students,' says June Furlong. 'If he came across one who was crude or stupid or a bit of an upstart, he'd play on that. But I've never met anyone who could move so fast in detecting what made people tick.'

6
ROCK 'N' ROLL

'Be careful of that John Lennon'

Always speedy at analysing situations, John realized that while art college might not be crucial to him as a place to learn art, it offered other tremendous benefits, such as his deep attachment to Cynthia and his friendship with Stuart; and the infectious atmosphere in the college's Liverpool 8 district, which made it equivalent to Paris's Left Bank, was a perfect escape route for John from the genteel middle-class environs of Aunt Mimi's Woolton. The pubs of the college area, Ye Cracke, and the Philharmonic and the Jacaranda coffee bar at 23 Slater Street, were places to hang out and become an adult. Mentally, Lennon was always ahead of his years and sought out people who would travel with him as speedily as possible. And a fourth benefit was the 'fix' he was to get at lunchtime from sessions with Paul in Arthur Ballard's room.

Pop music was steadily taking over his life. In the months that followed their first meeting at the Woolton church fete, a teenage empathy had developed between John and Paul. The reluctant art college student and the more studiously rounded, conscientious academic from the posher Liverpool Institute (the 'Inny') next door had a friendship based solely on music. Lennon was increasingly nervous about letting Paul into the Quarry Men, but it became a *fait accompli* in the light of Paul's runaway talent.

George Harrison was a different matter. Another Liverpool

Institute scholar, he was three years younger than John but a gifted and accurate guitarist considering his age. Paul would bring him occasionally to the lunchtime sessions at the art college, and John was impressed with his skill. George quickly decided that the older, irreverent, and altogether adult John Lennon was great. Lennon and Cynthia became irritated by George's constant presence as he waited for them to come out of college together at lunchtime. With the insensitivity of youth, George did not realize that a passionate love affair needed privacy.

'Hi John, hi Cyn,' George would say.

'Oh hi,' John would say, coolly turning right quickly and increasing his and Cynthia's pace towards Gambier Terrace.

The loving couple regarded George as a bit of a hanger-on but tolerated his youthful lack of understanding. Harrison hero-worshipped Lennon at this stage. John, who eventually invited him to Menlove Avenue when Mimi was in, eventually had good reason partly to reciprocate and respect the teddy boy taste of young George, the son of a bus driver. When George had left her house, Mimi told John she disapproved of his mode of dress. 'He had a *pink* shirt on! And *winklepicker* shoes!' recalls Mimi. 'I wasn't having any of *that*.' That rejection was enough to clinch the acceptance by John of George as a fully-fledged Quarry Man.

Paul's mother, Mary, a nurse, had died from breast cancer on 31 October 1956, nine months before he first met John Lennon; Paul was fourteen then. Paul's father, Jim, had two sisters, Auntie Jinny and Auntie Millie, who went into the McCartney family house at 20 Forthlin Road, Allerton, every Monday to cook the 'Sunday' roast dinner. Paul's background was similar to John's in that he was living without a mother, but his father was a major influence on his life. A cotton industry salesman, Jim McCartney was a kindly man of firm British values. He was also an accomplished pianist who once ran his own traditional jazz band, so that the McCartney home was full of the most fashionable sounds of the period. Jim's favourite song was 'Stairway To Paradise', and young Paul was weaned on a diversity of sounds ranging from musicals to hot jazz.

The major difference in Paul's and John's attitude to making music lay in McCartney's background. While Lennon had to fight every inch of the way to get Mimi to see he was serious about playing, eventually persuading her to buy him a guitar, McCartney was actively encouraged. Family parties became singalongs with Jim at the piano, and he also played trumpet in various bands. Paul and Michael were sent every week for piano lessons round the corner in Mather Avenue, and when Paul warmed to the sounds of pop on hearing the Everly Brothers, Lonnie Donegan, and Buddy Holly, he had no trouble whatsoever in getting a guitar from his Dad. 'He was only too pleased,' says Michael. 'He made it look hard because he had to pay for it, and that was his way of making Paul appreciate what he was doing. But really, he was knocked out that his eldest son was getting into music. The only thing that bothered him was Paul's partner, John the ted!'

Paul's background was much more working-class than John's; his father, a widower at fifty-three, had a tough time raising two young sons. In fact, of all the Beatles who eventually emerged, John was the one from the most affluently middle-class home. But McCartney—whose surname John perversely mis-spelled as McArtrey for several years—was such an asset to John's confidence in learning music that any differences in background quickly became submerged by the joy of musical togetherness. 'Paul was very serious about his guitar,' says his brother Michael. 'He demanded to know every facet of it, every conceivable variation. Chords he hadn't heard of, or couldn't learn from a book, he'd make up. He was heavily into rock 'n' roll, of course, but not to the exclusion of other music. He never turned away from a thing just because it wasn't Elvis Presley or Little Richard, much as he liked them.' That catholic taste was to be both the strength of the Beatles and the cauldron of the songwriting partnership of John and Paul, as well as an artistic contrast and melting pot for them in the years ahead.

John always conceded Paul's instrumental superiority, and never made any claim for his own ability as a guitarist. Paul had his own pressures at home; his father regarded Lennon as an undesirable influence on the life of his son, who, far from needing encouragement down the teddy boy road, 'ought to have his sights on a decent career, like entry into a teacher's training college, or accountancy.'

But to Paul, a kindred rock 'n' roll spirit like John was the catalyst he needed. To John, Paul deserved respect not just for his prowess but because he had also actually started writing his own songs. A few months after meeting, John and Paul had engineered a way to meet secretly together, with no interruptions from other students; when Jim McCartney was out at work, they would safely install themselves in the living-room at Paul's home and start playing and writing songs together, often daring to smoke tea from a pipe, and indulging in what became known as 'afternoon sagging off school'.

It was an electric partnership at the time between two personalities that at first sight looked destined to clash. John was, at seventeen, caustic, cynical, assertive, and brash. Paul was, even then, more quietly diplomatic and certainly more facially attractive to girls. He was an academic swot who lived an orderly life. He wanted to please his widower father. Theoretically, Lennon should have loathed him, but both realized that, at that moment in life, they needed each other for a mutual passion: making music.

Michael McCartney, two years younger than Paul, enjoyed observing the afternoons which were to give rise to the most significant songwriting partnership in modern popular music. Sitting in the McCartneys' home in Forthlin Road, he 'saw this extraordinary-looking ted coming down the road, with long sideburns and wearing skin-tight dark blue jeans with a polo neck sweater and winklepicker shoes'. The McCartneys, Michael avers, had such a conservative upbringing that within days of being introduced by Paul to John their father warned both his sons: 'Be careful of that John Lennon. He could get you into trouble.' For Paul and Mike, the warning had the effect that parents everywhere risk: 'Paul and I were immediately drawn to John like moths to a flame because of what Dad said.' It was a remarkable parallel with John's bond with George Harrison, fired by Mimi's condemnation.

Brotherly love was one thing, but the braggadocio of Lennon was quite another: Michael McCartney grew to hero-worship John, for all his outward spunk and all his inner softness. 'Young as I was, and certainly later during the Beatle years, I decided he was a "pretend hard" man. He was a performer, all his life, and from his toughness right through to his teddy boy looks, he wasn't really either. It was just that, whatever he adopted, John did it with more reality than anybody else.' The smouldering fire inside John's mind did not allow him to go the whole way in any direction for very long. Teddy boy, beatnik, peacenik, poet—all were mantles to be adopted for periods and then discarded, victims of his chameleon-like personality at various points in his life. But as an eighteen-year-old playing truant from college his intuition and desperation to convert the hobby of music into something worthwhile made him work feverishly on his partnership with Paul.

It was a matter of expediency. By the skin of his teeth he'd got into art college with no credentials from school, and now he was pretty sure that art would not offer him a career. With Mimi bearing down on him, and a bleak future pretty well assured, Lennon clung to music, and McCartney, like a life raft.

He had plenty to offer Paul, though. McCartney had a wider grasp of music, and particularly its variety of styles from ballads to jazz, but John compensated for his technical inferiority with an almost indefinable, animal quality that screamed rock 'n' roll. Paul was supremely talented; John was an unrepeatable original. If music had not pulled them together, there would have been no reason for John Lennon and McCartney to have developed any bond of friendship. But both realized, even as teenagers, that they needed each other if their music was to flourish.

'I saw it, but our Dad didn't want to know,' says Michael McCartney. 'When John came round to the house, as far as Dad was concerned it might just as well have been the Devil. Yet there would be a double-edge, because Dad would realize that, musically, there must be something there in John.' Sometimes he would verbally condemn John's appearance. 'John didn't dare reply, because he respected my Dad as a good bloke who was looking after Paul and me. But once, Paul said something in defence of John and my father said: ''Bloody hell, you will *not* have your trousers as tight as his. They're teddy boy trousers and not only will you not wear them in this house, you won't wear them, full stop. It's a bad thing.'' ' A diplomat, Paul knew when a boat should not be rocked. He took far fewer chances with his father than John took with Mimi. The afternoon meetings and the chance to sing and practise a few tunes and write a few lyrics, as well as hone hits made famous by Eddie Cochran and the Everly Brothers, were too precious to fritter away by alienating his father completely. George Harrison's council house at 25 Upton Green, Speke, was to prove an alternative refuge for the three of them, but Paul's Forthlin Road home was their favourite, partly because it was closer to Woolton and meant travelling a shorter distance with their guitars.

Mimi approved of Paul as a 'nice polite boy', but John knew that even asking permission to play rock 'n' roll there would be regarded as a heinous crime. The tactic adopted to arrange meetings was that Paul would coolly enquire of his father what time he would be home, most days, and strategically inform John that it was safe for him to arrive at a prescribed time for their two-hour 'sagging off school' sessions.

On some afternoons when plans had been laid by John and Paul, young Michael would be paid two shillings as the incentive to 'go to the pictures, see what's on at the Gaumont'. This was Paul's ploy to guarantee privacy for the songwriters, but not only to make music.

'Hold on,' said Michael, 'you never give me anything for nothing. What's happening?'

'Well,' said Paul, 'John's coming round and . . . girls, well, you know what girls are, don't you, Mike? But you're a bit young. You do things with them that you don't understand. It's big boys' stuff, this.'

'Oh,' said Michael, 'I think I'd better stay. I can't take the money off you!' Michael faced a dilemma: whether to stay and wait for the girls to arrive, or take the money from Paul and head for the cinema in Allerton. Paul always ended such a discussion by threatening to go elsewhere with John, which would have denied his young brother both the money *and* the chance to see the action. Michael took the money and vanished. On the whole Michael was happy enough just to be allowed to take photographs, a burgeoning hobby, when the two musicians got together.

One of the first songs written by John at these songwriting sessions was 'One After 909', and another was the unrecorded 'Winston's Walk'. Sometimes when he entered Forthlin Road he would wear the black horn-rimmed spectacles which he had managed to persuade Mimi to buy him, rather than be saddled with wire National Health-style glasses which ironically, later in his life, he was to make fashionable. 'He'd never be seen with specs on if he could avoid it,' says Michael McCartney. 'But without them he was as blind as a bat. He'd walk down the path to our house, squinting, and whenever I saw him walking outside art college he'd hardly be able to see you. People used to think he was being off-hand or rude, not saying "Hi", but it wasn't rudeness. He just couldn't see.' Glasses were too 'sissy', John would tell me years later when the Beatles story was at its height. He wore contact lenses and we would hunt for lost lenses together on bedroom carpets and in dressing-rooms from Cheltenham to Munich and New York.

Just as his friendship with Paul blossomed and bore creative fruit, with tentative songwriting and a style taking shape that merged ballads and music with a beat, another powerful relationship was fast developing in John's life. He was getting to see more of his mother. She lived only a short bus ride from Woolton, in Spring Wood, where she had set up home with John Dykins (Twitchy). Julia, often called Julie by neighbours and friends in the street, had a twinkle in her eye, and a style and vivacity, which was at odds with the seriousness of these post-war years. Her handing over to her sister Mimi of the raising of her son had been a painful but rational decision, based on her uncertain home life with John's father Fred away at sea. Vitally, Aunt Mimi and Uncle George were not short of money, but were not ostentatious with what George had earned through his hard work as the Woolton dairyman. Paul McCartney's exaggerated claim that John's family 'almost owned Woolton at one time' can be seen as a comparative judgement. Certainly Mimi and George were better off than any other Beatle's parents. 'John wanted for nothing,' says Mimi proudly. 'But he was never spoiled. I wanted him to learn the value of money.' She would make him mow the lawn at Mendips for five shillings. 'He'd do it when he came home from school or college, and do it quickly and not well. As soon as he'd finished a bit of lawn and he thought he could get away with it, he'd come in with his hand out,' says Mimi.

John's reunion meetings with his mother were becoming more and more frequent, but he had little time for her man. John spied a weak streak in him because he gave him too much pocket money for no reason. John viewed this as courting popularity with Julia's son. As a sign of weakness and insecurity, he despised it. But he took the money: it came in useful to upgrade the cigarettes he normally bought—when Twitchy gave him a windfall he would buy Senior Service instead of the lower-priced Park Drive or Woodbines.

Because she missed his company so much, Julia overcompensated John whenever they were together, at teatime after school *en route* to Mimi, and at weekends when he would spend whole days with her. She was more of a friend than a mother-figure, and had an infectious sense of fun. She dressed colourfully and was the first and only woman in her road to wear trousers—which in the early fifties was rare for women. Julia loved music and wanted to know every move John and the Quarry Men were making.

When John was waiting at her house in Spring Wood one warm July evening in 1958, Julia was paying a visit to Mimi for the traditional cup of tea and chat. The sisters had totally different temperaments, but Julia loved Mimi for her bookish intelligence and worldliness, while Julia's sense of humour and warm personality were adored by Mimi. Julia went to Mimi's on most days, and nodded knowingly at the catalogue of problems in bringing up John with which Mimi would regale her.

On some nights Mimi would walk Julia to the bus stop two hundred yards away. But that night Mimi said, 'I won't walk with you tonight, Julia—I'll see you tomorrow.'

Julia's words were to be prophetic: 'Don't worry.'

Julia crossed one side of the dual carriageway, stepped through the hedge to cross the second half towards her bus stop, and was sent spinning into the air by a car. She died instantly, aged forty-four.

A policeman broke the news of the accident to John and Twitchy at the house in Spring Wood. They went together to Sefton General Hospital which, ironically, five years later, John would joyfully re-visit to see his wife Cynthia with their son, Julian, who was born there. It wasn't until they reached the hospital that the horrifying truth was given to John by a doctor:

'I'm sorry, but your Mummy's dead.' Twitchy was no help: he broke down in tears.

John was appalled: the woman he was coming to discover as his best friend had been cruelly snatched from him when he was seventeen, and just as his life was becoming structured by the routine of college, its camaraderie, and the growing importance of the Quarry Men, Paul McCartney and Stuart Sutcliffe. His father's absence had been capped by his mother's death. His early tears were replaced by silence on the subject.

Mimi was distraught. 'It was a terrible, terrible shock to me. One minute she was sitting here, having a cup of tea with me, the next'—Mimi snaps her fingers—'she'd gone. I never told any of the family where she was knocked down, to save them the pain. They drove past the spot every day. It wasn't just a case of my sister dying in a car accident, either—I'd got her little boy, so our relationship was very special. We'd never quarrelled about John and who should have him. She found a new man and I wasn't interfering with her life. After all, she'd had a rotten deal with that other thing [John's father, Fred]. When she went with the new man, I said that to think of another man providing for him shoes, clothes and food and perhaps grudging it later on—it's not fair. Nobody was going to have the chance to look sideways at one of ours. And Julia agreed. So as John got older, he naturally got to know his mother better and everything was happy. He was broken-hearted for weeks. He just went to his room, into a shell. First his Uncle George, now his mother. I was in a state.' Julia was buried in Allerton Cemetery as Mrs Lennon.

The agony was prolonged by a court case. The car which knocked down Julia had been driven by an off-duty policeman who stood trial, but was acquitted. The scars in John's young life were beginning to mount: the Blackpool tug-of-war between his parents; the death of lovable Uncle George; the self-inflicted abysmal failure of his schooldays; and now, at the emotionally crucial age of seventeen, the loss of his mother, so suddenly, was crushing.

John's hurt ran deep but he did not allow it to be seen. He bottled up his sadness at Mimi's home, and at college there were only a few occasions when, sitting alone in class, students would notice him becoming uncharacteristically quiet or, shortly after Julia's death, the tears welling up. Ann Mason, girlfriend of John's friend Geoff Mohammed, says: 'Most of us knew his mother had died, but he shied away from talking about it. We knew it wasn't a subject to be discussed.' Twelve years later, John was to articulate the pain of his mother's loss with poignant songs called 'My Mummy's Dead', 'Mother' and 'Julia'. But the immediacy of the tragedy was too much for a teenager who had already absorbed enough traumas.

Lennon sought early refuge in drink. The atmosphere of the Liverpool 8 district dominated by the art college and the Institute was conducive to behaving like an artist, poet or writer. Lennon found comfort in the pubs of the area and on many afternoons returned to Arthur Ballard's classroom drunk, accompanied by Geoff Mohammed. Most students and teachers, knowing the reason behind John's behaviour, turned a blind eye to his wildness.

Only one person fully understood John's suffering. Paul McCartney had been similarly hit by the loss of his mother two years earlier. Few words were spoken between John and Paul about Julia's death. 'We didn't say anything about our mothers' deaths, but I did notice a quieter, more serious John for a while afterwards when he came round to our house,' says Michael McCartney. 'Suddenly, though, Paul and John had a bond that went beyond even the music.'

The Quarry Men—later briefly called Johnny and the Moondogs—continued throughout 1958 with a succession of line-ups, notably adding George Harrison on guitar. The rounds of youth club dances and social club events, particularly in the Woolton area where they had a name, kept them active. It was a useful diversion from college for John, still feeling desolate as the impact of his mother's death lingered. Later, during the Beatle years, John would muse on these uncomplicated years as a Quarry Man playing for a pint of light ale and a pie: 'We were doing it for fun then. Now it's a job.'

John's attitude to his college work was not endearing him to the teachers. Only Arthur Ballard, who supervised painting, saw him as having much potential, and developed a rapport with John partly through drinking with him in Ye Cracke at lunchtimes; this was the kind of language John understood, trading light ale for black velvet. John's poor punctuality in the morning, leaving for lunch with his eye more on making music with Paul and George in Arthur Ballard's room, or the canteen, than on college lectures, and erratic attendances in the afternoons, made him stand apart from most students and teachers. Dressed as a teddy boy, albeit a mild version, he was a marked man.

He added up to a dangerous ally for all but the brave, like the wild-eyed Geoff Mohammed, with his manic sense of humour and lightweight ability at art, and Stuart Sutcliffe, who could read John like a book. Indeed, Stuart was to write of John later, in a deadly accurate portrayal of the college Lennon:

> Sometimes a girl or boy would ask him about his sudden changes of mood, why he could be charming one minute and distasteful the next. His reply was always the same, if he bothered to reply. Usually when he did he felt no sympathy with his interrogator and would say: 'I hate you. Why should you like me, charm is only superficial and is easily exposed as having no concrete value.' Underneath the reserve that he piled upon himself at times like this, we knew there beat a human heart. A heart as kind and gentle as could be. He really hated hurting people and hated himself for doing so. He regarded people as conniving scoundrels, endeavouring to have a private view of his behaviour.

This was the cynicism of John Lennon stripped bare and placed in perspective by one who knew and loved him. Since the death of his mother there had been a few girl students with whom Lennon had a relationship—Annette and Thelma and Barbara and Beth. But now his character was firmly shaped. He would be a loner.

7
ROMANCE

'Don't blame me just because your mother's dead'

'Hey, John, I believe your mother got killed by a police car.'
The cold, clinical way in which a girl student greeted John in
art college on their return from a long summer holiday in 1958
stunned the crowd of students gathering to sign on in the foyer
for the start of a new term.

John was sitting across the 'signing in' table, his legs dan-
gling, his expression introspective. His reaction to the girl's
greeting was as impassive as the remark itself was tactlessly
stark. 'Yeah, that's right.' He remained insouciant.

Thelma Pickles was stunned. She was introduced to John
by another student, Helen Anderson, who was established as
a mate of John's. And Thelma did not know how to react to
the embarrassment that the girl had caused her by speaking so
brusquely about such a sensitive subject.

But Thelma need not have worried. 'I couldn't believe
John's reaction. He didn't register anything. He didn't choke
on it. It was as if someone had said, "You had your hair cut
yesterday," or something like that.'

In the next six months Thelma came to understand a little
more about the mind and emotions of John Lennon, to whom
she was immediately drawn that day. Tony Carricker, one of
John's pals, was sitting with him on the table in the college
foyer. 'But my eyes definitely set on John. Tony was prettier,
more handsome, with dark hair and dark eyes, but John was

so powerful. When he was in a group like that, the focus of attention went to him. He had a presence. I found him very striking from that moment on.'

A year younger than John, Thelma was to figure in one of his most torrid teenage love affairs before he met Cynthia. Their friendship blossomed in a spectacular conversation one day as they walked after college to the bus terminus in Castle Street. In no hurry to get home, they sat on the steps of the Queen Victoria monument for a talk. 'I knew his mother had been killed and asked if his father was alive,' says Thelma. 'Again, he said in this very impassive and objective way: "No, he pissed off and left me when I was a baby." I suddenly felt very nervous and strange. My father had left me when I was ten. Because of that, I had a huge chip on my shoulder. In those days, you never admitted you came from a broken home. You could never discuss it with anybody and people like me, who kept the shame of it secret, developed terrific anxieties. It was such a relief to me when he said that. For the first time, I could say to someone: "Well, so did mine." '

At first Thelma registered that he didn't care about his fatherless childhood. 'As I got to know him, he obviously cared. But what I realized quickly was that he and I had an aggression towards life that stemmed entirely from our messy home lives.'

Their friendship developed, not as a cosy love match but as teenage kids with chips on their shoulders. 'It was more a case of him carrying my things to the bus stop for me, or going to the cinema together, before we became physically involved.' John, when she knew him, would have laughed at people who were seen arm in arm. 'It wasn't love's young dream. We had a strong affinity through our backgrounds and we resented the strictures that were placed upon us. We were fighting against the rules of the day. If you were a girl of sixteen like me, you had to wear your beret to school, be home at a certain time, and you couldn't wear make-up. A bloke like John would have trouble wearing skin-tight trousers and generally pleasing himself, especially with his strict aunt. We were always being told what we couldn't do. He and I had a rebellious streak, so it was awful. We couldn't wait to grow up and tell everyone to get lost. Mimi hated his tight trousers and my mother hated my black stockings. It was a horrible time to be young!' Lennon's language was ripe and fruity for the 1950s, and so was his wounding tongue. In Ye Cracke, one night after college, John rounded on Thelma in front of several students, and was crushingly rude to her. She forgets exactly what he said, but remembers her blistering attack on him: 'Don't blame me,' said Thelma, 'just because your mother's dead.'

It was something of a turning point. John went quiet but now he had respect for the girl who would return his own viciousness with a sentence that was equally offensive. 'Most people stopped short,' says Thelma. 'They were probably frightened of him, and on occasions there were certainly fights. But with me, he met someone with almost the same background and edge. We got on well, but I wasn't taking any of his verbal cruelty.'

When they were together, though, the affinity was special, with a particular emphasis on sick humour. Thelma says categorically that John and she laughed at afflicted or elderly people 'as something to mock, a joke'. It was not anything deeply psychological like fear of them, or sympathy, she says. 'Not to be charitable to ourselves, we both actually disliked these people rather than sympathized,' says Thelma. 'Maybe it was related to being artistic and liking things to be aesthetic all the time. But it just wasn't sympathy. I really admired his directness, his ability to verbalize all the things I felt amusing.' He developed an instinctive ability to mock the weak, for whom he had no patience.

In the early 1950s Britain had National Service conscription for men aged eighteen and over who were medically fit. John seized on this as his way of ridiculing many people who were physically afflicted. 'Ah, you're just trying to get out of the army,' he jeered at men in wheelchairs being guided down Liverpool's fashionable Bold Street, or 'How did you lose your legs? Chasing the wife?' He ran up behind frail old women and made them jump with fright, screaming 'Boo' into their ears. 'Anyone limping, or crippled or hunchbacked, or deformed in any way, John laughed and ran up to them to make horrible faces. I laughed with him while feeling awful about it,' says Thelma. 'If a doddery old person had nearly fallen over because John had screamed at her, we'd be laughing. We knew it shouldn't be done. I was a good audience, but he didn't do it just for my benefit.' When a gang of art college students went to the cinema, John would shout out, to their horror, 'Bring on the dancing cripples.' 'Children often find that kind of sick humour amusing,' says Thelma. 'Perhaps we just hadn't grown out of it. He would pull the most grotesque faces and try to imitate his victims.'

Often, when he was with her, he would pass Thelma his latest drawings of grotesquely afflicted children with mis-shapen limbs. The satirical *Daily Howl* that he had ghoulishly passed around at Quarry Bank School was taken several stages beyond the gentle, prodding humour he doled out against his grammar school teachers. 'He was merciless,' says Thelma Pickles. 'He had no remorse or sadness for these people. He just thought it was funny.' He told her he felt bitter about people who had an easy life. 'I found him magnetic,' says Thelma, 'because he mirrored so much of what was inside me, but I was never bold enough to voice.'

'Thel', as John called her, became well aware of John's shortsightedness on their regular trips to the cinema. They would 'sag off' college in the afternoons to go to the Odeon in London Road or the Palais de Luxe, to see films like Elvis Presley in *Jailhouse Rock* and *Kid Creole*. 'He'd never pay,' says Thelma. 'He never had any money.'

Whether he had his horn-rimmed spectacles with him or not, John would not wear them in the cinema. He told her he didn't like them for the same reason that he hated deformity in people: wearing specs was a sign of weakness. Just as he did not want to see crutches or wheelchairs without laughing, John wouldn't want to be laughed at. So he very rarely wore his specs, even though the black horn-rimmed style was a copy of his beloved Buddy Holly.

'So in the cinema we sat near the front and it would be: "What's happening now, Thel?" "Who's that, Thel?" He couldn't follow the film but he wouldn't put his specs on, even if he had them.'

Even then she was attracted to his 'very straight, lovely, Romanesque nose' which was accentuated by his habit of tilting his head back. The stance became a crucial hallmark of John's stage posture as a Beatle; it was generally thought to be part of his arrogance, a defiant declaration of his domain. In fact, the stance was caused by his short-sightedness. 'He'd take ages to see things in a room,' recalls Thelma. 'He'd say: "Who's that in that corner?" when it was someone he should have recognized immediately.'

It was not a big step from cinema visits and mutual mocking of people for John and Thelma to go beyond the drinking sessions in Ye Cracke. 'It wasn't love's young dream, but I had no other boyfriends while I was going out with John and as far as I knew he was seeing nobody except me.'

On the nights that John's Aunt Mimi was due to go out for the evening to play bridge, Thelma and John met on a seat in a brick-built shelter on the golf course opposite the house in Menlove Avenue. When the coast was clear and they saw Mimi leaving, they would go into the house.

'He certainly didn't have a romantic attitude to sex,' says Thelma. 'He used to say that sex was equivalent to a five-mile run, which I'd never heard before. He had a very disparaging attitude to girls who wanted to be involved with him but wouldn't have sex with him.

' "They're edge-of-the-bed virgins," he said.

'I said: "What does that mean?"

'He said: "They get you to the edge of the bed and they'll not complete the act."

'He hated that. So if you weren't going to go to bed with him, you had to make damned sure you weren't going to go to the edge of the bed, either. If you did, he'd get very angry.

'If you were prepared to go to his bedroom, which was above the front porch, and start embarking on necking and holding hands, and you weren't prepared to sleep with him, then he didn't want to know you. You didn't do it. It wasn't worth losing his friendship. So if you said, "No", that was OK. He'd then play his guitar or an Everly Brothers record. Or we'd go to the pictures. He *would* try to persuade you to sleep with him, though.

'He was no different from any young bloke except that if you led him on and gave him the impression you would embark on any kind of sexual activity and then didn't, he'd be very abusive. It was entirely lust.'

The art college in the late 1950s was a hotbed of promiscuity. 'There was much weeping in the loo,' says Thelma. 'At sixteen we were very ignorant; it was very much hit and miss. Suddenly there was a pregnancy explosion, and five students were pregnant in one year. They had to leave college. It was a social stigma, no matter what circle you came from—working-class, middle-class, or whatever.'

John never talked about the dangers of pregnancy. 'He wouldn't care. It wouldn't enter his mind to think about it.'

Thelma was John's girlfriend for six months. 'It just petered out,' she says. 'I certainly didn't end it. He didn't either. We still stayed part of the same crowd of students. When we were no longer close, he was more vicious to me in company than before. I was equally offensive back. That way you got John's respect.'

Her memory of her former boyfriend is of a teenager 'very warm and thoughtful inside. Part of him was gentle and caring. He was softer and gentler when we were alone than when we were in a crowd. He was never physically violent with me—just verbally aggressive, and he knew how to hurt. There was a fight with him involved once, in the canteen, but he'd been drinking. He wasn't one to pick a fight. He often enraged someone with his tongue and he'd been on the edge of it, but he loathed physical violence really. He'd be scared. John avoided real trouble.'

One day in the lettering class at college the uncouth rebel who looked unkempt, who delighted in disruptive behaviour and acting the fool in class, and who needed nursing with loaned ruler or paintbrush, became a source of fascination for another girl—Cynthia Powell. The story of their unlikely mutual attraction has already been told. At home, over tea one day, John said of Cynthia: 'Do you know what, Mimi, there's a girl sending me chocolate biscuits and coffee in the canteen at college.'

Mimi said, 'You don't accept them, do you?'

'If she's fool enough to send them,' said John, 'I'll eat them.'

The girl from the posh side of the Mersey seemed at first sight the least likely partner for the college troublemaker. She spoke very softly, neither drank nor smoked, and behaved decorously. She had had a strict upbringing with her two older brothers. Like John, she lived with one parent, her strong-minded mother, Lilian. Her father had died of cancer two years before she met Lennon; also like John, she was seventeen when she lost a parent.

It would be easy to analyse their mutual attraction as Cynthia the mother substitute and John the swaggering teenage tough guy, Cynthia's concession to dangerous living. But from the time they got together, it was more than just another fling for them both. It wasn't long before John and Cynthia were spending afternoons and nights at Stuart Sutcliffe's flat. It was a dangerous affair, demanding lies of both John and Cynthia: she would tell her mother that she had stayed at a girlfriend's flat for the night, and John would concoct a story for Mimi about playing with the Quarry Men too far away to get home. Neither Lilian Powell nor Aunt Mimi was to know of the affair, still less the intensity of it, for many months.

Cynthia's memory of John during their earliest days together is of a 'rough diamond with a heart of gold'. There were only two problems about him, in her view: his ferocious temper and his incredible jealousy if any other man should go near her. In true chauvinistic style, he considered it all right for him to dabble with other girls, as long as Cynthia did not discover it. Today, she smiles at the fact that she was kept under strict surveillance by him while he had other girlfriends. 'But it didn't matter. What mattered, in my eyes at that time, was that while John was with me, I was blind to anything else. He gave me his everything when he was with me, and I didn't need any other assurance.' In a small community such as Liverpool 8 at that time, secrets were hard to keep but Lennon did pretty well. His absence from college lectures and the lack of interest by the tutors in disciplining him gave him *carte blanche* to vanish at all sorts of odd hours to consolidate his trysts.

Just as he scorned the physically afflicted, John mocked people who were conventional, toed the line, and didn't join in his flouting of authority. Cynthia Powell, the epitome of middle-class Hoylake, was in that category. She was among the smartest dressed of the girl students, with pale pink twinsets and fancy embroidered collars. She was as polite as John was aggressive, and was not among the girls who joined Lennon's table during lunch in the canteen. There were different camps. 'I was in his camp of boys,' says Thelma Pickles, 'because I was a bit of an arty beatnik. Cynthia was dainty and sweet. We used to take the mickey out of her, but John always said he fancied her. He called her Miss Prim, and he said to me: "It's a pity she's a bit posh", implying there was a gulf he would never be able to overcome. He was certainly always attracted to her from the first time he saw her in the canteen.

'It wasn't that John thought *she* had any feelings of superiority. He just recognized her different background, because she was from over the water. It was *our* inverted snobbery. When she walked into the room, he'd say: "Don't talk like that, 'cos Cynthia's here." He meant we had to be on our best behaviour.'

John was acutely aware of one other girl at college who was besotted with him. 'She sat weeping over him,' says Thelma, 'but instead of feeling sorry for her and giving her a kind word, he'd put her down verbally.' John could not tolerate such a public display of emotion. He despised the girl for *showing* what he considered as a weakness. What weaknesses *he* had he either kept well hidden or exploited, as in the case of cripples.

Thelma Pickles heard when she was temporarily away from college that John and Cynthia had become as closeasthis. 'I was startled but pleased. I thought she'd be good for him, temper his aggression. I knew she'd have to tailor herself into looking like Brigitte Bardot for him, and I remember reflecting on the fact that he'd teased her so much about being so proper. I remember thinking: "He's got what he wanted—again." '

Cynthia believes that most of the staff and tutors were frightened of John. This led to mutual disrespect, as John could not stand weakness. 'He was constantly being told off for coming in late. If it hadn't been for Arthur Ballard, who acted as his guardian, I think some terrible things might have happened between John and the teachers. I heard Arthur Ballard saying to the others: "Look, he's not a bad lad, he's going through a bad patch. He's talented." '

But his greasy, quiffed hair, with the DA at the back, contrasted with most of the other students' long hair. His scruffy black trousers, with tight 'drainies' altered by Helen Anderson, and his shiny black jacket, made him look utterly different from the traditional bohemian student look of casual jacket, with leather elbow pads, or duffle coat. Eventually John demurred and, in another change which surprised students, came to school regularly in his Uncle George's brown tweed jacket and grey trousers.

'All the changes in dress, and particularly that teddy boy period, were a throwback to his younger days,' says Cynthia. 'At Dovedale and Quarry Bank, he told me he felt he had to look tough and hard. It was his wall against the world, in case somebody picked a fight. So he dressed in a tough way. When he first went to college, he felt as if he had to be on guard. Most of the students weren't tough or aggressive, but he'd come from a tougher school background. Woolton was a genteel area but he didn't want to be regarded as a genteel lad, so he played a hard role. It was his friendship with Stuart and then with me that changed him and made him realize there was no need for that acting at all.'

Nothing could deter Cynthia. Her work suffered as she spent every minute at college thinking of him, or seeking him out. She had plenty of conventional reasons for saying 'enough is enough' and dumping John. He could not take his drink and once, when a fellow student was rude to him at a party at a tutor's house, Lennon dragged him out to the street and pinned him to the ground within seconds, thumping him. 'I was dancing with Stuart Sutcliffe upstairs when the row began. We wondered where John had gone but were soon told there was a fight,' says Cynthia. 'It was the drink again—he had a very small capacity before he became aggressive. The slightest thing would have him in a terrible temper.' To a prim girl from the Wirral, he was quite a visual spectacle as he slouched into lettering class twice weekly, battered guitar slung nonchalantly across his shoulders. His fingers were permanently stained by nicotine from the twenty cigarettes he got through most days, most of them scrounged tersely ('Gimme a fag?') from the nearest student. The profile of John as an undesirable was completed by big ugly callouses on his fingers, the effect of his guitar picking.

The effect Cynthia and John had on each other was immediate. Within about a year, John had dropped even his teddy boy posturing. He took to an 'arty' look, wearing scarves, ordinary black jackets and trousers, and combing his hair more traditionally. That was his concession to Cynthia's conventional appearance and also an indication that their love affair was giving him fewer reasons to make a dramatic visual impression. He was growing up. Cynthia's change, for John, was much more radical. Aware of his fanatical enthusiasm for Brigitte Bardot and Juliette Greco, and a more pouting expression than she naturally showed, 'Cyn' took to wearing black fishnet stockings with seams, tighter skirts, and suspender belts. All three features were requested by John. Crucially Cyn, who had arrived at art college with reddish-brown hair, gradually lightened it until she was dyed a beautiful golden blonde. The transformation was complete: John had secured his Brigitte Bardot look-alike. For Cynthia, it was not just a pleasure but a political move, too: no more would John be able to drool to others in the canteen at lunchtime, at the sight of another student named Joni Crosby: 'Cor, doesn't *she* look just like Brigitte Bardot?' Cynthia, infatuated or in love, was acutely aware of what she perceived as competition.

During these teenage pre-Beatle years, Cynthia was the only person in whom John would confide his deepest feelings. Three people figured in his conversations with her about his home life, besides the omnipresent discipline of Aunt Mimi. There was Uncle George, whom John missed terribly and said so. He would proudly tell Cynthia when he was wearing one of George's old jackets. They did not fit but he did not care. His father was a taboo subject: John had this vision, which he gave to Cynthia, of a great seafaring man, with a wonderful singing voice, 'a hero in the distance' whom he could not see because he had to go away for important work at sea. It clearly troubled John but he had closed his mind to his father's existence. Thirdly, of course, there was his mother and the pain of her recent accidental death.

'He didn't talk about his Mum to anybody but me,' says Cynthia. 'It shattered his life. He often said how terrible it was that he'd lost her just at the time she was becoming his best friend. I could see the feeling welling up deep inside him, then he would say something like that, and close down. I'd say: "Come on, John, I want to know all about you." And he'd shake his head as if to say no. It was obviously too painful for him to open up very much. I'm sure that's why he went completely crazy at college and why the combination of drink and anger made him so aggressive. It was a bitter rage. When he became successful as a Beatle he was a different person altogether. The aggravation was restrained. He became gentle. He still drank but he didn't get so aggressive.'

John's jealousy and possessiveness about Cynthia were almost overpowering. When she could not stay the night with him he insisted she stayed in Liverpool until the last train left Central Station at 11.20 for Hoylake, getting her home just before the critical midnight hour. 'He always made me get that last train home to make sure he was the only man I was seeing that night.' After college, they would adjourn either to Stuart's flat or the cinema, or go for drinks. 'He wanted total commitment and I was pleased to give it,' says Cynthia. 'If I as much as looked at another man, he would go mad and say: "Who's *he*?" in a moody voice.' With her daily allowance of eight shillings, Cynthia plied John with cigarettes—the cheapest varieties, Woodbines or Embassy—because he was usually broke. 'He wasn't mean, just always broke from spending his cash on black velvet, the mixture of Guinness and cider which was the students' cheap way of getting drunk quickly: four pints most lunchtimes. But he was very moral—he pooled his money.'

Cynthia is philosophical about affairs which John had before and during his college days. 'When John was with me, it was total commitment. Whatever he did outside our relationship didn't seem very important. We were together such a lot of the time that whatever other affairs he had once we met couldn't have amounted to much because I was with him most of the time. He kept me in Liverpool as late as I dared stay. It wasn't as if he wanted to get rid of me. Later on, during the Beatles' very busy period and when he was away a lot, it was a different matter. But love is blind.'

Once their betrothal was clinched, and they couldn't bear to be apart, John and Cynthia decided it was time they met each other's families. 'After a few months, I went up to Mendips and got on fine with Mimi. The only thing that was kept secret from her was that John and I spent some nights together in Stuart Sutcliffe's flat. She must have thought I was a nice

young girl. Little did she know.' After tea of eggs and chips
and bread and butter, John and Cynthia and Mimi would sit
talking before, eventually, Cynthia would go and stay with her
best friend, Phyllis McKenzie, who also lived in Woolton.

The trips by John to Trinity Road, Hoylake, were less
frequent: he clashed with Cynthia's mother on their first meeting. 'He ran out of the house after he and Mum hadn't got on
well. It was all very tense, that first meeting. I ran after him
and found him halfway between the house and the station. He
wanted to get back to Liverpool quickly. But I persuaded him
to return and patch up the argument for my sake. Mum wasn't
mad about his appearance and made it clear to him. She'd much
rather I'd chosen a clean-cut office type.' John only went across
to the Wirral three times. He was destined never to get on well
with Cynthia's mother, not even during the most joyful days
of Beatlemania. When she lived at his Weybridge mansion, he
regarded her as an intruder.

The year 1959 was a significant one for John. First, he made
a tentative move from Mimi and Woolton, and went to live
with Stuart in Gambier Terrace, in a house with an impressive
view of the Anglican Cathedral which was then being built.
To describe Stuart's home as a flat would be an exaggeration;
it was a room with a shared toilet in a large Georgian house.
There were mattresses on the floor as beds, paints and kettles
and all the trappings of student living spread chaotically around
the floor. Its appeal to John was its very disorderliness, and
also the fact that it was a haven for him and Cynthia to sleep
together. 'Even though both our families knew we were seeing
a lot of each other,' says Cynthia, 'in those days kids were not
as open about their lives together. John and I took the view
that with Mimi and my Mum, what the eye didn't see the heart
couldn't grieve over.' She made no move to leave her Hoylake
home, but her mother noticed an increased number of nights
when Cynthia said she was staying at Phyllis's home in Woolton. Cynthia's alibi was perfect. But Mimi was furious about
his departure to 'dirty' Gambier Terrace.

'Please Cynthia, try to get him to move out of that place.
It's filthy and it's unhealthy.'

'There's not a lot I can do, Mimi,' said Cynthia. 'He wants to be with Stuart.'

John rubbed salt in Mimi's wound by technically not leaving Mendips: he would return there every few days to collect and deliver dirty and clean shirts, underpants and socks. Mimi consoled herself that at least she saw him regularly and made sure he got a square meal.

Living with Stuart had another stabilizing effect on John; there was his company, and conversations long into the night with the male friend he admired more than anyone, plus Stuart's encouragement to John to try his hand with painting. In return for the casual art lessons, John tried to teach Stuart bass guitar. He was never a good player, but John loyally brought his mate into the Quarry Men and later into the early Beatles. Even if he couldn't play well, and disguised the fact by turning his back on the audience so they couldn't see his inadequacies on the guitar, Stuart had a major redeeming quality which John liked: he looked mean and moody, and the girls liked him, complete with his adolescent spots. Stuart's quiet vulnerability made him something of a heart-throb. Visually, if not musically, he was an asset to the group at a time when they needed all the fans they could get. To Stuart, the music was light relief from his intensive work as a painter: at college he was known as a workaholic.

Cynthia remembers that, at this stage, John was totally consumed with music. 'It was his complete conversation outside college and a lot of the time in college, too. He couldn't get enough rehearsal time in and he seemed genuinely keen on the partnership that was developing with Paul McCartney.' Locations for rehearsing the hits of the day, particularly the prophetically titled Buddy Holly hit 'It Doesn't Matter Anymore', were getting better. Despite his mother's death, John remained in touch with Twitchy, and he, Paul and Cynthia would use Twitchy's house in Spring Wood for jam sessions and songwriting when they wanted a change from Paul's home. 'If Twitchy was in, he'd let us in. If he wasn't, we'd break in through a window, raid the larder, and leave after a jam session lasting two or three hours in the afternoons and early evenings,' says Cynthia. 'John suffered Twitchy all right. They were polite to each other, that's all. But his house came in useful. That's the way John would have seen it.'

Paul—then, as now, highly organized with fine attention to detail—carried an exercise book in which he wrote down the words to the songs he and John were working on. This year, too, they formally shook hands on an agreement that was to inscribe their names together in the history books. They agreed that, from then on, whether a song was written individually or together, they would have both their names stuck on them as songwriters, thus: 'Lennon–McCartney'. It was a touching manifestation of togetherness at a time when neither knew how significant the partnership would become, or how much rancour would result ten years later.

'It was a beautiful period,' reflects Cynthia, looking back. 'It wasn't just a musical convenience that put them together. By the time I saw them playing at the college or at Twitchy's they were friends, at one with each other. They seemed to have been friends for many years. It was intuitive. George, being younger and not writing songs, didn't have the communication with them, but John and Paul couldn't stop playing together, practising the chords of the latest Elvis Presley song, the Everly Brothers, and getting the confidence to try writing their own words. I sat there, on these "away days" of rehearsals, absolutely mesmerized. Their harmonies were so beautiful. John had this image of being the toughest boy in college but his music showed what all of us knew was underneath. He had a gentleness that needed to come out, and it did in those songs.'

Cynthia saw music come to be Lennon's salvation. Mimi might have thought she was punishing him by banishing him to the porch when she tired of his guitar strumming; but John relished it, because the acoustics were better than inside the house. The college lunchtime sessions with Paul and George only once attracted a crowd of any size. In the canteen, students who saw him during lectures as the wild one were astonished at the music that came from him. A typical programme would be 'Peggy Sue', 'Good Golly Miss Molly', 'Rip It Up', 'All I Have To Do Is Dream', and always, as a finale, 'When You're Smiling', sung by John in a cackling, Goon-like voice.

'He didn't like an audience for these sessions with Paul,' says Cynthia. 'But luckily for the big audience he didn't have his glasses on so he couldn't see how many people had gathered round. I remember several of the students saying: "My goodness, this is a different John Lennon." They'd see him walking round with a battered guitar and thought he was trouble. Suddenly, at the sight of him playing soft melodic music, they realized that inside him was so much more.'

Money, fame and ambition for the Quarry Men were still secondary to John's love and lust for Cynthia and a rarely admitted desire to please Mimi. 'I don't think that at nineteen John had the faintest idea he would be rich or successful, or even hoped for it in the same way that some people hope to win the football pools,' says Cynthia. 'Paul was a keen schoolboy but John wasn't like that. He was just happy doing what he wanted. He was carefree.' Underneath that indifference, though, was a conventional wish. As the Quarry Men earned a few pounds from their engagements, John would love the pleasure of giving Mimi a bundle of notes, erratically. 'He'd give her £10 or so from time to time. I saw the expression on his face that almost said: "Look, we've *made* it!" Even though they hadn't made it at all, he wanted Mimi to think he was doing something well. "There's the money for my keep," he'd say to his Auntie.'

Every student who was with Lennon at art college has a different anecdote about him. But they all agree on one central point: if John had not emerged successfully with the Beatles, he could easily have gone seriously off the rails. Cynthia says that if he had not had Paul McCartney to cajole him, and their son Julian to motivate him to make some money, and still later Brian Epstein as Beatles manager to push him, 'he would have ended up a bum. . . . It's hard to say that now, after what happened, but he wouldn't have cared that much. I'd have gone out to work, he wouldn't have any qualifications whatsoever because he was falling foul of the art college, and Mimi would have pushed him in all sorts of directions. He would have needed to learn a trade, or go back to school again, and I can't see him concentrating. He'd have gone downhill.'

8
HAMBURG

'Have a drink. We've been chucked out of college'

Predictably Lennon failed his lettering examinations. Even the combined faked papers from Cynthia and Thelma could not save him. His disorderliness at college, his swearing and contempt for the teaching system had all but resulted in his being expelled. Arthur Ballard came to the rescue and gained a stay of execution for Lennon, partly because of John's association with the brilliant Stuart Sutcliffe: this, it was claimed, redeemed Lennon as far as his ambition was concerned. Geoff Mohammed was thrown out of college and John and he were to be seen celebrating in a city coffee bar. Michael McCartney walked in to find the pair in jubilant mood: 'Hey, Mike, come on in and have a coffee. We've been chucked out of college!' It was not technically true in John's case, but it might well have been. Lennon was not the sort of nineteen-year-old who returned confidences or even the compliments of Arthur Ballard. His attendance at college became more and more erratic. He regarded himself as a 'visitor' rather than a permanent student.

Luck came to John's rescue; within a few weeks of facing expulsion he would visit Germany as a musician, an event which was to mark his entire life.

Days were now spent mostly drinking coffee in the Jacaranda, a club not far from the college in Slater Street. The *Sunday People* newspaper focused on Stuart and John's shambles of a room—with its stolen Belisha beacon and macabre, empty coffin as part of the furniture—in an exposé entitled 'This is the Beatnik Horror'. John, free of the shackles of Mimi's home, felt physically and mentally liberated. He could now enact all the fantasies of the world to combine rock 'n' roll with all that being an art student meant, without producing much art.

The 'Jac' was a coffee bar run by Allan Williams, a Welsh-born hustler with a keen eye on the pop scene. He proved to be an important stepping stone in the Beatles' success story. Through his affinity with Stuart Sutcliffe, whom he admired, Williams found himself constantly harangued by Lennon for a few sessions for the Quarry Men in the basement of the 'Jac' when regular groups like Cass and the Casanovas, Derry and the Seniors, and Rory Storm and the Hurricanes (featuring Ringo Starr on drums) failed to show up or were not available.

Williams relented. John dragged Stuart into the group on bass guitar (he had bought the instrument with the money he had won in an art competition). Within days, Stuart's delicate artist's fingers were in shreds. Lennon now believed that rock 'n' roll was the only avenue open to him, for he started to look moderately tidy for the sessions that Williams fixed. The band wore black polo-necked Marks and Spencer's sweaters, dark blue jeans, and white plimsoll shoes.

It was against this background of a fading interest in art and increasingly bohemian living, accompanied by life with Stuart in a flat of their own, that John slowly became more aggressively ambitious for his group. He pestered Allan Williams for dates and eventually landed one at the Grosvenor Ballroom in Seacombe. It was a notorious local bloodbath where gangs went not for music or dancing, nor to find women partners, so much as 'have a scene' with rival groups: 'a scene' meant a punch-up. The band playing rock 'n' roll from the stage would have a tough job making itself heard and not getting involved in the trouble. Although he would be one of the first to run at the sight of real danger to himself, John enjoyed being on the precipice overlooking a battle. The rock 'n' roll music he loved was anyway full of assertiveness, and a spot of bother seemed appropriate to the combative stance and sound of Elvis Presley. In his mind, John was moving well away from skiffle and such soft music as the Everly Brothers' 'Cathy's Clown'

and mellow ballads like Cliff Richard's 'Travelling Light'.
(John was later to describe Cliff Richard to me as the epitome
of all he hated in British pop. 'He's so bloody Christian I can't
stand him and his lot.') Rock 'n' roll was a clarion call for
John, an act of such defiance that a change of name for his
group was now on the horizon.

The momentum of the group was now quickening. Paul
might have been the better musician, singing the more acceptable, poppier melodies ('You Are My Sunshine', 'Home',
and 'You Were Meant For Me') while John went for the slightly
more abrasive, beatier stuff like 'Ain't She Sweet'. But Lennon
remained firmly the leader. When name changes were discussed, to try to steer them away from Quarry Men which was
'too skiffly and restricting', said John, his own name would
invariably be mentioned as an alternative. Long John Silver, a
parody on his name and a character in a favourite childhood
story, *Treasure Island*, was quickly rejected. It was almost as
corny as the pop music of Cliff Richard and Frankie Vaughan
and Craig Douglas which John was now trying to debunk!

Stylistically, no pop act came near Buddy Holly in John
and Paul's affection at that time. The light beat of Buddy
Holly's distinctive songs was a perfect progression from skiffle.
John was attracted by the name of Holly's backing group, the
Crickets, and played around with names to emulate that. It was
Stuart who first came up with the Beetles, as a 'play' on Crickets. It appealed to John who, in a masterly example of his skill
in word-play which was to stay with him throughout his life,
later modified the spelling to Beatles, to incorporate the word
'beat' which was fast becoming conversational currency in
Liverpool, with its proliferation of rock groups that no other
city could match.

John continued to pester Allan Williams for more work.
They secured a drummer who, even though he was thirty-six,
was very competent on the instrument which all groups regarded
as vital. Tommy Moore, a fork-lift truck driver, was a fine
player and technically the best John, Paul, and George had in
those years. What he lacked in youthful exuberance he compensated for by improving the tightness of their sound. John
had little patience with the slow-moving personality of Moore

but saw him as a means to an end, of raising the group to a higher musical level than the other groups on Merseyside.

The Quarry Men's last performances under that name were at a club in the Liverpool suburb of West Derby run by Mona Best, mother of the Beatles' future drummer, Peter. In August 1959 they played at the opening of the club, and over the next three years were to play there about a hundred and twenty times, going through various name changes along the way until they finally reached the Beatles. The problem in filling the drum chair was not easily solved by John, Paul, George, and short-lived guitarist Ken Brown. So difficult was it that, when they entered a Carroll Levis talent contest in Manchester towards the end of 1959 under the skiffle-like name of Johnny and the Moondogs, John, Paul, and George were without a drummer at all. Their appearance was a failure.

The Allan Williams and Jacaranda connection, as well as Williams' control of another club where the Beatles played, the Wyvern Social Club, later called the Blue Angel, at 108 Seel Street, was to be important in the Beatles' next phase. Larry Parnes, a famous name from London, had a reputation for creating top British pop stars and giving them names that evoked a positive image in a pop scene that was mostly spineless. After discovering Tommy Steele in the 2 I's coffee bar in Soho, Parnes had gone on to launch such luminaries as Marty Wilde, Vince Eager, Duffy Power, Johnny Gentle, and Dickie Pride. It was a pop stable with Elvis Presley stereotypes, painfully British in its imitative stance, and people laughed. But in the late 1950s Parnes was a name to be noted by anyone with an eye on making headway in the pop music world.

Through Allan Williams John's group, then known as the Silver Beetles, secured an audition with Larry Parnes in Liverpool. The winning group would accompany another Liverpool singer from the Larry Parnes stable, Billy Fury, on a nationwide concert tour. The Silver Beetles failed that audition, but were offered something equally attractive—the grand sum of £18 a week to accompany one of his lesser-known singers, Johnny Gentle, on a tour of the far north of Scotland. John and Stuart were ecstatic. They would find it simple to skip college for one week. Paul was equally determined to make the break from his studies for school exams. He had an uphill job persuading his father that the break would rest his brain and be beneficial, but with the aid of his brother Michael he clinched it. With Tommy Moore, George and Stuart, the Silver Beetles set off from Liverpool's Lime Street Station, and for a week enjoyed for the first time the life of hotels, autograph hunters, and importantly, non-Liverpool audiences. The money proved barely adequate but the freedom from home and school was wonderful, particularly for the wanderlust in John, who did not have parental security as a backdrop to his life.

Two people were to be the butt of John's cruel streak on that Scottish tour. Curiously, neither was prepared to join in his verbal jousting or retaliate, and since John preferred fighters to pacifists, they were easy targets. He got a special delight out of taunting Stuart, whose attempts to keep up with the music were simply beyond his capabilities. It didn't seem to occur to John that it was he who had dragged a reluctant Stuart into playing bass in the first place. Now, Stuart was verbally pummelled by his best mate for not coming up to scratch. More cold-bloodedly, Lennon had no patience whatsoever for Tommy Moore. When the group van, which singer Johnny Gentle was driving, had a bump with a car, and Moore was taken to hospital, it was Lennon who went to his bedside and insisted that he got up in time for that night's show.

Scotland had a more profound effect on John than on the other four. Tommy Moore left the Silver Beetles immediately on their return, feeling the age gap too much and the prospects not too rosy. Paul and George went back to the Liverpool Institute, while John's art college days were sliding into disarray. While he was away in Scotland, Cynthia had heard of his failure in lettering. Nothing could redeem his all-round lack of art college application. It was at this time that he hit his worst patch with Mimi, too. 'What was I going to do with someone who had no certificates from school and who appeared to be going the same way at college? I didn't stop worrying,' says Mimi. 'I'd say: "You must think about getting a job instead of messing about with the guitar, John. Concentrate on your studies. You know you're good at drawing."

'And he always replied along the same lines: "I'll be OK, I don't need the bits of paper to tell me where I'm going." '

Rock 'n' roll as a livelihood was clearly established in his mind by now, though he was less sure about how he would manage it. He increased the pressure on Allan Williams to get them work. Weekly sessions at Mona Best's Casbah Club, and the support work at the Jac, as well as the occasional accompaniment of a stripper in the New Cabaret Artistes Club, were not enough. Fresh from the taste of a proper concert tour in Scotland, John was fired with a hunger for engagements almost nightly. Allan Williams was now more convinced of their potential. They were even rivalling Derry and the Seniors and Gerry and the Pacemakers as local favourites. Before long, Allan Williams was getting the Silver Beetles engagements at the Grosvenor Ballroom in Seacombe and at the Neston Institute. The teddy boy movement plummeted to its nadir at some of these halls. Boozed-up teds were infuriated by the fact that the band on stage was highly fancied by the 'birds' they had brought along, and they took it out on the musicians. The aggression usually stopped short of fist fights, but not always. John, faster with his reflexes than anyone in the group, had come to the rescue of the physically slighter Stuart one night. A group of teds set on Stu and kicked him in the head after a dance. Lennon set about Sutcliffe's assailant with a ferocity rarely seen. It was as if John needed a good excuse, like the battering of his best friend, to show even himself the strength he now had at twenty. Though there was a lot of blood, and Stuart went home with a gashed forehead, it could have been much worse without John's retaliation.

Most of John's energy was not used for punch-ups, however: it was going into his passionate love affair with Cynthia; his songwriting sessions with Paul; the night-time shows whenever they came up; perfecting his mean, Elvis-like looks; and into trying to get more work for the group, which he now feared was probably going to be his only real hope of making money. Not surprisingly, he pestered Allan Williams more than anyone. 'Al, get us some work.' 'Al, what's next for us?' John would say when they played the Jacaranda. 'What have you got lined up for us next?' Williams was as enthusiastic as they were, but he had a roster of other bands to protect. Williams was to relinquish his link with the group and Brian Epstein eventually became manager of the Beatles. Fourteen years later Allan Williams wrote a book about his experiences with the Beatles, entitled *The Man Who Gave the Beatles Away*. After reading it Lennon, in a classic example of his rapier-like wit, referred to Allan as 'The Man Who Couldn't Give the Beatles Away'.

A strange quirk of fate led John, Paul, George, and Stuart from struggling through £10-a-night dances in Liverpool to kicking their act into blistering, world-breaking energy in Hamburg. Allan Williams was again the man who caused that trip to happen.

The Royal Caribbean Steel Band, his regular act at the Jacaranda, went to Hamburg and wrote to him saying there were great opportunities for British pop groups there. About the same time, the Silver Beetles had dropped the 'Silver' because John felt it was too twee and reminded him of the absurd suggestion that he should call himself Long John Silver. From a show in June 1960 they were styled as the Beatles. Other groups in Liverpool, who traded under more thrusting imagery (the Seniors, the Pacemakers, the Hurricanes, the Searchers), laughed at the corniness of merging the still-new word 'beat' with something else. It had no precedent but then neither had John Lennon. He was as perverse about the decision to change the name permanently to Beatles as he was in many other directions.

It was the Beatles, then, that Allan Williams sold, during a visit to Hamburg to follow up the attractive-sounding letter he had received from his beloved steel band. His first call was to a club on the Reeperbahn, then as now a neon-flashing street teeming with sex shows, clubs, bars and prostitutes. The manager of the Kaiserkeller club, one Bruno Koschmider, hired the Beatles and they were booked for their first shows there in September 1960.

It was just as well for John: college was a write-off. He was never formally expelled like his best mate Geoff Mohammed, because Arthur Ballard, his faithful mentor, was lobbying for him to be moved on to a new section called the Faculty of Design. But Ballard's pleas were falling on obstinate, more conservative ears. Other tutors now regarded Lennon as definitely more trouble than he was worth. During this period of debate about whether John was to remain an art student the Hamburg offer came in and clinched it: he was off, and told everyone so. Even Mimi had no argument against John's proud claim that they would be earning £100 a week each. 'I feared the worst,' says Mimi. 'But of course, he was getting older by then, not a child, so it was not so much a question of telling him what I thought as advising him. I couldn't see any future in going to Germany but he told me the money would be good.'

Before they went, they needed a drummer. At the Casbah Mona Best's son, a handsome, mean, moody-looking boy named Peter, had often sat in with John, Paul, George, and Stuart. He was rather more introverted than John and Paul, and they had little in common beyond the music, but that was enough: he was a good, lusty drummer. Other forces were causing ripples in the group. Paul and Stuart were starting to clash. The perfectionist inside McCartney had no patience with Stuart's thinly veiled attempts to play bass guitar properly, and Paul was constantly criticizing his playing. With George improving all the time and functioning strongly as the lead guitarist, individual roles needed defining more clearly. John was a competent rhythm guitarist, but there was no need for two. McCartney fancied the bass playing role himself, instead of Stuart. There was also jealousy for Lennon's attention. McCartney could not understand why John, as hard a man as one could wish to meet, could be so stupidly loyal as to have his incompetent best friend in the group against his better judgement. Stuart was also competition for the attention of girls, a fact the vain Paul did not like. On several fronts, then, Stuart Sutcliffe was bad news to Paul McCartney.

But for the Hamburg trip, expediency was essential. Peter Best lacked a sense of humour but had been hugely popular with the girls at his mother's coffee bar. He was in.

There was a problem finding John's birth certificate, which was essential to get a passport for the German trip. The problem in getting documentation for Paul, George, Stuart, and Pete was worrying enough for Allan Williams. In the case of Lennon, with no parents to sign the papers, and the vital birth certificate only found at the last moment, it was touch and go.

He also won the difficult battle of persuading the parents of every member of the group that they would be safe and that a profitable trip lay ahead in Germany for the band, which was, he assured everyone, full of potential.

And so on 16 August 1960 the Beatles' first journey to Hamburg began. This was the trip that was to convert John Lennon, aged nineteen, Paul McCartney, aged eighteen, and George Harrison, aged seventeen into world beaters. The Hamburg Experience, as they later called it, was to teach them not only to hurl themselves full-bloodedly into making a great show; it was to teach them survival, and introduce them to stimulants in the form of pep pills.

Parting from Cynthia was painful. For two years John and Cyn had hardly been out of each other's company—and even then only a twenty-minute train journey away—and the thought of separation for an unknown time in a foreign country was worrying for Cynthia. As four months elapsed, Cynthia's feelings for John increased. He kept a simple promise, and hardly a day went by without a letter from Hamburg arriving at Hoylake. Envelopes were emblazoned with all the messages of teenage love: kisses and hearts, codes like SWALK (sealed with a loving kiss), 'Postman, postman, don't be slow, I'm in love with Cyn so go, man, go.' John's loving verse would almost obliterate the address. Inside, John would tell her of how much he wanted her—particularly sexually—needed her and missed her, but also how well the Beatles were doing in Hamburg, despite the fact that Bruno Koschmider was exploiting them, working them hard and giving them living quarters consisting of three filthy rooms containing only camp beds and blankets. He also said the washing and toilet facilities were appalling and that their rooms were situated behind a cinema screen, the cinema having been converted from an old theatre. Cynthia still worried about the girls available to John in promiscuous, dangerous Hamburg—'the love and warmth of his letters made me feel wonderful and miserable at the same time,' she says candidly.

Immediately John went abroad, Cynthia realized that she and John did not have photographs of each other. So she took to going to a Woolworth's photo booth every week. Carefully combing her hair, she dressed in her finest and turned on her most seductive pout for John to receive a picture of her. That, she hoped, would dissuade him from the German blondes who were worrying her.

With one of these photographs, Cynthia asked John to send in return pictures of himself from a coin-in-the-slot machine. The result was an unmistakable stroke of Lennon. He mailed Cynthia pictures of himself in grotesque poses: his face would contort, he would pretend to be a hunchback, his eyes would leer maniacally, and he would try to make each picture more sick than the last. Despite this, from the scores of letters she received from Germany Cynthia decided that John's aggression was waning. He was more ambitious for the Beatles, more enthusiastic about their success, than anything else, she says. 'I could sense his feeling that it was all starting to happen for him. It was just as well, as there was nothing much for him to come back to in England, as far as work was concerned.'

The Indra club, which they played almost immediately on their arrival, was a small and seedy basement. The audience was only about half a dozen strong, but the opportunistic promoter who had booked them, Bruno Koschmider, was scarcely a man with whom Liverpool teenagers would argue. He had a limp, a crooked nose, and all the authority that came with having fought in the war with the German Panzer Divisions. His idea in booking the Beatles was to inject some life into the place, and to try to get them to do for the Indra what their Liverpool rivals, Derry and the Seniors, had done for the Kaiserkeller: swell audiences and thereby raise the bar takings.

The Indra had previously been used as a strip club, and had a tiny, cramped stage. The Beatles' performance was stifled, and when a woman in the flat above the club complained to the police about the noise, Koschmider decided that the energy of the group would be better used in his much larger Kaiserkeller club. Derry and the Seniors had played there to packed houses; in Germany there was no admission charge but patrons had to buy drink, and plenty of it, which had a boisterous effect on many of them, resulting in fights. Here was born the full-blooded, almost animal-like rock 'n' roll in John Lennon.

Koschmider had heard Allan Williams trying to instil a touch of show business razzmatazz into the Beatles' act. Allan had often told them 'to make a show', to attract customers.

Soon, the forceful Koschmider was using the phrase 'Mak show, mak show' to the boys all the time. Lennon, more than the other four, realized the *carte blanche* he was being given to perfect a wild stage personality. Besides, the demands Koschmider was making on them were physically punishing, so something more than music was essential. The contract called for the Beatles to perform from eight in the evening until two in the morning, with the occasional fifteen-minute break. What this amounted to was about six sets of forty-five minutes each. The schedule taxed the group's repertoire to its limit, and the chance of varying from set to set was minimal. It was little wonder that they tired of 'Roll Over Beethoven', 'Be-Bop-A-Lula' and 'Long Tall Sally'.

Survival was everything to John and the others. From the tough audiences, beer would arrive on stage together with an occasional request for a song. Hamburg John, often drunk but never incapable of delivering a power-crazed blast of rock 'n' roll to 'the bloody Krauts' as he called them, revelled in the challenge of it all. For a group of teenagers fresh from Liverpool, the violence as the waiters jostled with drunken customers, gangsters and prostitutes in the audience, and the hilarious language barrier made it all larger than life. Customers who got out of hand were often threatened by the bouncers with coshes and flick knives. John said later: 'I grew up in Hamburg, not Liverpool.' But the key to the Beatles' endurance lay in their first serious use of stimulants, in the form of pep pills.

Preludin was a mild stimulant which John and the others acquired mostly from the waiters, and in John's case, not surprisingly, from a barmaid girlfriend. Basically they were slimming pills which had to be taken with beer to have the right effect: they stirred the brain and the body into such activity that, until the effects of the pills wore off after twelve hours, the pill-taker could not bear to be still. Adrenalin poured from the system. Conveniently, the pills killed the appetite for food.

One effect of Prellys, as John and the Beatles christened them, was to give them a false confidence. After a few weeks John had grown to dislike the innate aggressiveness of the Germans. His waspish wit, born on Merseyside, was to be sharpened to perfection in Hamburg as the easy targets of nationalism and inhumanity during the war dawned on the super-sensitive John that hid beneath the loudmouth. 'What did you do during the fucking war? Bloody Krauts, Heil Hitler, back to your tank,' he would shout from the stand to nobody in particular, when he knew that amid the din nothing could be heard. John totally refused to learn German, though Paul and George and Stuart managed a few words and Pete Best had an O-level in the language. For John the Hamburg Experience, like hundreds of other very important periods in his life, was to be absorbed, used, then disposed of.

Hamburg was a hard baptism but there were side benefits. The young teenage girls who went to the clubs and the Reeper-bahn cafés looking for men were attracted by the five good-looking, comparatively innocent young British lads. The girls warmed to John, Paul, George, Stuart, and Pete as a refreshing change from the tired businessmen and sex-starved sailors. There was not a lot of time for much besides working, sleeping, and playing cards—usually 'brag', a variation on poker. John, like the others, had the occasional relationship with girls during his first four-month visit to Hamburg. But to paint a picture of five teenagers wallowing in scenes of orgies and depravity—which has regrettably become part of the Beatles mythology during those years—is to fall victim to rumour and exagger-ation. They dabbled with girls from time to time, but work, music, Prellys, and sheer exhaustion were by far the most important factors in their lives.

One girl, particularly, was to make an indelible impression on the Beatles, especially on Stuart and John. Astrid Kirchherr, born in 1938, the daughter of a sales director of Ford Motors in West Germany, was at first sight the least likely fan to visit the tacky Kaiserkeller club in which the Beatles played seven nights a week. Her visit there, and her subsequent closeness, particularly to Stuart and John, came through her boyfriend, Klaus Voormann. From childhood, and particularly during her teenage years, Astrid had taken a keen interest in art and had designed and made all her own clothes. Her friendship with the Berlin-born doctor's son had blossomed at a private art academy, Hamburg's Meisterschule. Klaus was crazy on rock 'n' roll and, as an illustrator, kept saying how much he wanted to design pop album covers. Astrid's emergent talent lay in photography, and she switched to studying that after first entering the college for dress design.

Klaus lived in a room in the house occupied by Astrid and her mother in the middle-class Hamburg suburb of Altona. Astrid's father had died when she was seventeen. When the Beatles arrived in Hamburg she was twenty-two, with an air of cool, independent assertiveness that perfectly matched her riveting good looks. Her cropped blonde hair, pure white skin, and big expressive eyes put John once again in mind of his goddess, Brigitte Bardot.

It was a row with Klaus that took Astrid to the Reeperbahn one summer evening in 1960. A few days earlier Klaus had walked out after their argument, gone to the cinema, and then drifted into the seedy St Pauli district of Hamburg. Nice people never went there, still less inside the Reeperbahn clubs. But Klaus, hungry for the sounds of rock 'n' roll, was drawn to a noise coming from a street called the Grosse Freiheit. He went downstairs in search of the sound and, once inside, unknowingly sat next to the Beatles who were watching the group on stage. They happened to be another Liverpool group, Rory Storm and the Hurricanes, featuring Ringo Starr on drums.

Klaus's first memory of that night is vivid, 'I couldn't believe the look of the boys whom I sat next to, and there wasn't much conversation as they couldn't speak German. But the sound when the Beatles eventually went on stage was amazing.' When John tore into rockers like 'Sweet Little Sixteen' and 'Roll Over Beethoven', the combination of teddy boy hairstyles and their music bowled over the enthusiastic Klaus. He wanted to talk to the group, judged Lennon to be the leader, and, when the session ended, asked John about designing album covers, which was his ambition. Lennon beckoned Klaus in the direction of Stuart, saying: 'Show it to him, he's the artist in the group.'

The next evening Klaus Voormann returned to the club to see the Beatles' full session. As an artist, as much as a rock 'n' roll fan, he was particularly fascinated by Stuart's appearance, for despite his lack of musical prominence he looked like the artist he was: scrawny, fragile, James Dean-like, with moody dark glasses, winklepicker shoes, and an air of shyness.

Klaus did not consider for a moment that in persuading Astrid to visit the club, three nights after his discovery of it, he would be marking the end of his own love affair. But immediately the leather-jacketed Astrid entered the Kaiserkeller with the Beatles on stage, her eyes fell on Stuart. The magnetism she radiated, all elfin-chic with a detached beauty that lifted her a million miles from the Reeperbahn scrubbers they had been used to, attracted Stuart.

Astrid's effect on the Beatles was enormous. On their four further visits to Hamburg in the two years that followed she was to offer them much more than the warmth, eggs and steaks and chips which they desperately missed, and total commitment as their closest German friend. She was to invest them with style and point them in a direction that would stir the world.

Her own firm leanings were towards the 'exis', who formed most of her friends at the Meisterschule. Derived from the existentialists, they were in the forefront of the avant garde. They believed firmly in rejecting universal values, and stamped their own imprimatur on everything from appearance to opinions: in art, fashion, music, and in personal behaviour the 'exis' were fiercely independent. Most of all, they wanted to define youthful freedom.

Stuart and Astrid were together, surprisingly without any resentment from Klaus, within a few nights, and both Astrid and Klaus and another friend, photographer Jürgen Vollmer, were to become part of the Beatles' coterie, inseparable from them when they played the club, and during the day too. Astrid persuaded her to let them take their photographs, and within a few weeks Stuart had moved into the Kirchherr home. Astrid's mother worried about his thin frame and decided he needed food and care.

Astrid and Klaus were the first intellectual Beatles fans. Before they arrived John and Stuart had enjoyed a long-standing special relationship, and Paul and John both felt passionately about music, but as a unit they came together only for blazing rock 'n' roll. Now Astrid and Klaus introduced them all to her home, to her friendly mother who spoke not a word of English but loved cooking them egg and chips. And Astrid gave them a glimpse of her style, mirrored in her all-black bedroom with its floor-to-ceiling silk sheets and huge mirrors which screamed individualism.

Today Astrid remains in the Hamburg she loves, her memories of Stuart and John indelibly etched in her mind. She carries her attachments to them both, for both John and Stuart gave her their guitar plectrums which she wears in her pierced right ear, as earrings. Her reflections on John and Stuart as twenty-year-olds, and the interaction of the Beatles before their meteoric rise to fame, are tempered with her visible love for the two.

'When I first met him,' she says, 'John had this knowledge of everything that surrounded him, because he had particularly high intelligence. But he didn't have much experience, and he was so *nosey*. He wanted to keep finding out everything. He had an innocence and didn't stop investigating, asking questions—about art, about clothes, about the German people, who fascinated him. Of course, he would take the mickey out of us: "Bloody Krauts", and all that. But I thought of him as a gentle, sentimental boy who was in such a hurry to find out about everything. Stuart was the same, but really he had a deeper natural intelligence than John. When they were together, it was very powerful for them both.'

No serious photographer had been near the Beatles. When Astrid took them to pose for her in the parks and fairgrounds they were 'incredibly excited', she says, at the results. 'I did big prints showing their expressions naturally, not asking them to pose, and they went crazy. They'd never seen anything like these in their lives. Jürgen Vollmer came down to take pictures of them too. He was fascinated by their appearance.' Indeed, one picture of Lennon standing in a Hamburg doorway was chosen by John fourteen years later as the cover for his 1975 album, *Rock 'n' Roll*.

Astrid says her clique dressed mostly in suede or velvet clothes, always black with white collars, and she often wore a short leather skirt. 'They'd never seen anything like the way we looked.' Still less had they witnessed a hairstyle like Klaus's. Tired of the fast-scissored traditional formula of Hamburg hairdressers, and looking for something that would emulate her own sense of the eccentric, Astrid had cut Klaus's hair herself for years. She *never* combed his hair backwards, always out

from the side, and it was always longer than the accepted length.
'The Beatles were dressed like teddy boys, with these very,
very pointed shoes which we in Hamburg had never seen before. We were fascinated with those, just like they were with
our things,' says Astrid. 'And their very tight trousers and little
tiny grey jackets. They didn't have many clothes, of course.
And their hair was combed back with sideboards, like teddy
boys.'

Stuart, the first to have his hair cut and styled by Astrid,
faced John's scorn when, one night, he arrived at the club for
work with what later became known as the Beatle haircut. 'John
collapsed laughing,' Astrid says. 'He didn't have the guts to
say, ''Hey, that looks great'', which is what he really thought.
John was a complicated person when it came to showing his
feelings like that: he hid his emotions. Because he could not
bring himself to say what he really thought, he would cover it
up and in doing that he would hurt people.' Shy Stuart was an
easy target. The situation was not helped by the obviously
strong love affair that had bloomed between him and Astrid.

'Stu at that time was really mad on her,' remembers Paul
McCartney. 'We all fancied her a bit but it was, kind of, you
know—''Hands off, I'm serious.'' I know you lot, you just
like her, OK, but I mean this one, for me. . . . And anyway,
she liked Stu. They hit it off very well and we used to chat
with her friends. There was Klaus and Jürgen and Astrid, who
were like the gang, and they used to have a couple of other
mates of theirs who were from art school. They used to hang
around the club, and got to like our band particularly because
we were sort of different, too, from all the other groups. We
were a bit more into the black leather and black polo sweaters.
It was a different look at that time, like new wave or punk
later. Astrid and her friends were great. They were like a
different race of people because they dressed very differently.
They dressed in all the black leather and black polo necks, and
she had blonde, short-cut hair. She looked really great. I think
all of us thought she looked great. But Stu. . . .'

Paul, always more conscious than the others about his appearance, was the next to ask Astrid to style his hair. 'He asked
me what started me in cutting Klaus's hair. I told him I couldn't
stand my boyfriend having greasy hair swept back, and the

same with all my friends at art school. The boys did the girls'
hair, and the girls did the boys'.'

John was the last Beatle to succumb to the Beatle cut. Only
Pete Best declined, retaining his quiff and teddy boy aura that
attracted the girls. 'John was the same with the collarless jackets
which I designed and Stuart was the first to wear,' recalls
Astrid. 'They all laughed when Stuart went in wearing one,
and John always said he fancied my leather pants and jacket.
But it took all of them to adopt the jacket before John could
be bothered. He was defiant about clothes and appearances.
He didn't like to be led, you know—for someone else to have
thought of something before him.'

Astrid and Klaus had been together for two years, but she
and Stuart became serious after two weeks. 'It was very hard
for all of us. Klaus liked Stuart a lot, and Stuart had a conscious
hurt about falling in love with me and hurting Klaus. John and
Stuart had no problem about our love—we were in a sense all
together, laughing at the same jokes, and John and Stuart had
the same sense of humour, very black, very sick.'

It was Astrid, then, who injected a sense of style, in hair
and clothes, into the Beatles. It wasn't just a question of how
they looked, and what they wore, she would tell them at the
club and at her home: it was their general presence, the way
they moved, off stage as well as on it. The message got home
years later when, as international stars, they acknowledged their
debt to their Hamburg days and to Astrid.

If John and Paul got together as opposites, then Stuart was
John's foil in an utterly different way. 'They had similar out-
looks on life, and attitudes,' says Astrid. 'John really loved
Stuart, in the best sense, but Stuart was never made aware of
that love and worried about it. John always had to be the hard
man, teasing Stuart about his looks, his bass playing, his singing, anything. Stuart took it all, and, being highly intelligent
and sensitive, never replied much. John would know how far
he could go. But something deep inside John stopped him from
putting his hand on Stuart's shoulder and saying: "Hey, I love
you." Which he did. I think John regarded Stuart as a mental
rival.'

Stuart was less reticent about his friendship with John. Most
of the time, when they were not working, John and Stuart were

together. 'At first Stuart was very tight about talking because he was together with four boys who acted very rough. But when Stuart became loose, he talked to me about his love for John, how John was the only one in the group he could relate to. Stuart knew he was not a musician and only came into the group for John. Stuart was a genius and would have been a very, very great writer and painter.'

While John was heavy on Stuart from a paternal standpoint, Paul waded in with the impatience of a long-suffering perfectionist who was exerting his ambition and ability. Paul was playing the piano frequently between belting out 'Long Tall Sally' and other Little Richard rockers. When Stuart stepped forward with his tiny physique to take a singing solo with the Elvis Presley ballad 'Love Me Tender', McCartney would berate him. Paul didn't like the slowness of the song after the rockers, says Astrid. It is more likely that the ballad-loving Paul was just looking for a good excuse to dig at Stu.

But while Stuart would take John's knocks for his weak singing, Paul's digs cut more deeply. Stuart felt very inferior, with reason. 'He knew he couldn't play, and criticism coming from Paul was more than he could take,' says Astrid. 'John had persuaded Stuart to play bass guitar but he knew in his heart it was ridiculous. He was simply not a good player. Paul played bass better than Stuart, Paul played piano better than Stuart and John, and Paul played guitar as good as John, and Paul played drums. His heart and soul were in music. Paul used to have a lot of arguments with Stuart. He didn't like his singing much. But Paul was in a difficult situation. John was the leader, up there on stage. However good a musician Paul was, John just gave off this feeling of being the leader. And John wanted Stuart in the group. It was bound to lead to tension.'

Paul remembers Stuart as 'a great fellow, a very good painter who used to get picked on by us generally'. On the clashes, Paul says: 'One of the main problems was: he wasn't that good on bass. So what you had to do, if you were having a photo taken, was tell Stu to turn away, do a mean moody thing looking over his shoulder, 'cos you didn't want anyone to see what he was actually playing. 'Cos anyone who knew would realize he couldn't play it. He just used to turn his amp down and sort of make a bass noise. It was quite good. But he didn't know what key we were in half the time. He just put a lot of bass on it and sort of bluffed and stamped a lot, you know.'

An insight into the twenty-year-old Lennon comes from Astrid's memories of her drug experiences with him. 'I was always close to John,' she says, 'but he never allowed anyone to get inside him. Only when we took the pills did he open up about himself.' And to set the record straight about the pills, she says: 'Drugs? It was just a big laugh. The stories that the Beatles were all doped up during their visits to Hamburg is so much rubbish. We were young kids. George, particularly, was a baby of seventeen. We could only afford to drink beer, which was the cheapest, and then one of us discovered these little pills called Preludin. They were pep pills so that when you took them you felt no hunger. We called them slimming pills. We discovered that when you took them and drank beer, you felt great. You didn't get drunk but you got all speedy and talked away like mad. They were fifty pfennigs each and my Mummy used to get them for us from the chemist—you had to have a prescription for them, but my Mummy knew somebody at the chemist.

'We had maybe one and a half for the whole night. They'd last for seven or eight hours. And it was from those pep pills that I had my best talks with John. He and I would take them and then go out of the club for a long talk. The pills would make a person feel more relaxed. When John took one, he lost all his inhibitions.

'He would talk about his feelings and the things he liked. He'd say: "Oh, I want to tell you so much how I feel. I love you and I love Stu." Without the pills, he would never have given me this honesty. He would have choked up at telling the truth. And so most nights John would say: "Come on, Astrid, let's take some beans and talk." But to say he was kept going by pills in Hamburg is really rubbish. He was kept going by something deep within himself,' says Astrid forcefully.

Beatles mythology says that the five young men on their Hamburg trip wallowed in a sea of orgies and carried on as depraved sex maniacs, drug addicts, and alcoholics. John, Paul, George, Stuart, and Pete have been painted as five Liverpool louts rampaging through the Reeperbahn red light district, high on pep pills, using prostitutes all the time. Astrid, who was closer to the group than anyone, says adamantly that the stories are inaccurate, and have grown over the years into sheer fantasy. 'Prostitutes!' she laughs. 'First, they were too frightened to go anywhere near them, and secondly, they didn't have the money. Thirdly, and most importantly, they didn't need them. There were girls in the club sitting around waiting for John or Paul or George to go and sleep with them. But there were no sexual orgies. They all had their little affairs in Hamburg, but in 1960 even teenagers had a totally different sexual attitude towards one another. The girls were not prostitutes, they were seventeen or eighteen years old, and officially couldn't get into the club until they were eighteen. They were salesgirls or workers or students like me.

'The Beatles were five sweet, innocent young men, and they couldn't believe girls were falling in love with them. Yes, they had the occasional affairs, but definitely there was nothing wild about their behaviour.' In the popularity stakes, Paul was the most popular with the girls in the audience. 'He was always so neat and clean and the girls loved that,' says Astrid. But among the student friends whom she brought along John and Stuart carried the honours. 'We all thought they had more style,' says Astrid. It was John who christened Astrid and her friends the 'exis'.

On their relationship, the subject of much speculation by Beatles watchers, she says, 'He was attracted to me, and me to him, but it was more mental than sexual. We would hold hands occasionally but he would find it hard even to do that, because he would never, never have done anything to hurt his best friend Stuart. John always called me the German Brigitte Bardot and he admired my long blonde hair and small waist. I used to dress in the style he found fantastic—he went on and on about my black leather gear.

'I loved his mentality, not because I thought he was a sexy boy. That was reserved by me for Stuart, whom I adored and fancied right from the start. John was pleased for Stuart. Also, John told me he had left his girlfriend at home in Liverpool, so that was that.'

Alone among the Beatles, John would trudge to the Hamburg post office every week to send back to Cynthia the £35 he eventually earned at the Star-Club. 'I couldn't believe what he was doing,' says Henry Henroid, one of the club's booking agents who often walked with John to the post office. 'I said, "If you do this every week, what do you live on?"

'He said, "Oh I can earn a few marks by playing for this stripper round the back street in the afternoons." It was incredible—very responsible behaviour for a boy of that age. All the musicians seemed to booze their money away. John had to get it back to Liverpool quickly.'

John's obsessive 'noseyness', as Astrid describes it, was especially evident at her home. He raided her book collection, taking a particular interest in works by the Marquis de Sade, and looking for any connection with sadism. 'You read books like *that*?' he said to Astrid once. 'It's dirty!' She reminded him of his own tendency to learn the rudest words in the German language, to augment what she described as 'John's most basic version of Hitler Deutsch'. 'He loved poking fun at the Krauts, shouting "Where's your tank?" at audiences. I told him about Jean Cocteau and books I'd read, whenever I met him, and he wanted to know everything. I'd end up buying them for him, in English, which was not easy to find.' Classical records formed most of Astrid's collection, with the odd Nat King Cole thrown in. Paul often went straight for her Stravinsky records, but John would shout: 'Take that off.'

Routine for the Beatles during their first Hamburg visit was totally bound up with work. They would collapse into bed around dawn after all-night sessions, sleep until midday, and often be collected by Astrid in the early afternoon for the ten-minute drive to her home. Nostalgic for British breakfasts, which Astrid or her mother cooked, they tucked into bacon, eggs, beans and toast at their whim. John struck up a particular affection for Astrid's mother: 'George and Paul just shook her hand and said hello, that was all. But never John. He always kissed her and put his arms around her. My Mummy admired John most after Stuart.'

Astrid smiles at aspects of the John Lennon she knew so closely. He choked up at the mention of the death of his mother two years before he went to Hamburg. 'John was rough and sweet and gentle all together, I often used to wonder if this was a mixture of his emotions at losing his mother and the fact that his father wasn't there during his childhood. If you asked him a question he would answer, but without being asked he wouldn't tell you anything about himself, unless he had taken a pill. You had to work very, very hard to get deep thoughts from inside him. But if you asked and you were sincere, as I was, he'd pour them out. "Yeah, most of my friends grew up with a Dad and a Mum," he'd say. "I missed all that." '

Because music and success meant much more to him than to Stuart, John adopted a fiercer, more penetrating character in Hamburg. Realizing that it was a heaven-sent make-or-break city for them to knock their act into shape, his humour was even blacker than during his Liverpool Art College years. 'Stuart shared the sick sense of humour,' says Astrid, 'but his was much happier than John's, which was always mean and cruel. I never knew why.' Postcards and letters to Mimi would be conventional, and tell nothing of the exhausting test that was Hamburg. He told her nothing of the money problems, either; the £100 a week they expected fizzled into more like £15 a week each, says Paul McCartney. 'They were always broke, always,' says Astrid.

'John used to have his dreams about being as famous as Elvis Presley. George would say it would be OK to be as popular as Cliff Richard, that would be a start! Stuart said: "When I'm a famous painter, I'll buy you a Rolls-Royce." I said, "When I sell my first picture of you all to *Life* magazine I'll buy you a new leather jacket." '

John did indeed grow up in Hamburg, but the experience was to be more valuable to him than profitable. Word about the lively British teenagers' energetic appearances at the Kaiser-keller, and their indefatigable improvement in the face of the demon promoter Koschmider, soon spread around the tough city. Peter Eckhorn, a reputable promoter who ran the rival, bigger Top Ten club, invited the band over to watch another British act, Tony Sheridan, who worked as a solo singer. Un-known to John and the other Beatles, Koschmider had a friend who told him the fateful truth: the Beatles had appeared on stage with Tony Sheridan in a jam session, which was strictly forbidden under the terms of Koschmider's iron-fisted contract.

He also feared that, like Tony Sheridan before them, the Beatles intended to leave the Kaiserkeller for the more sophisticated surroundings of the Top Ten club. In Hamburg, inter-club warfare was almost as intense as the fights that broke out inside them.

Koschmider struck back at the Beatles for their truancy in a devastating way. He called the police. George Harrison, aged seventeen, was arrested and jailed for a day for being under age while working in a foreign country, and deported home. Paul and Pete Best were ordered by Koschmider to leave, after allegedly causing a small fire to some sacks by using candles in their tacky digs behind the cinema screen in the club. John Lennon, unscathed but broken by the anti-climax of it all, wended his way home alone, leaving Stuart to the comfort of Astrid's home. They had become engaged, and Stu wanted to pursue painting in Hamburg.

John was penniless. The dreams of riches had been illusory. They had not made nearly so much money as expected, and what Deutschmarks they had earned had gone on clothes, beer, cigarettes, and food. Dejectedly, he had drifted across on the ferry from the Hook of Holland to Harwich and by train to Lime Street Station and taxi home to Menlove Avenue.

Cynthia was at once pleased and sad at his return. Mimi, once more vindicated by the unlucky turn of events, had the additional irritation of having to pay his cab fare. 'What happened to the £100 a week you mentioned?' she asked John.

John's reply was to typify his sharp retorts as the Beatles story got into its stride later. 'Spent it all, Mimi.'

He was contrite, recalls Mimi, but with all her spirit she respected the streak in him that was to strike terror into the hearts of those who asked him 'damned stupid questions'.

'Once his mind was set on something,' says Mimi, 'nobody and nothing could shake him. He was down but not out.'

9
LIVERPOOL

'Right then, Brian, manage us'

Returning to Liverpool ignominiously from Hamburg, penniless and with an uncertain future, was bad enough. Going back to Aunt Mimi after experiencing the liberation of Gambier Terrace, the illicit nights with Cynthia, and Hamburg's wildness, was stultifying for John. With his best friend left behind, in love with Astrid, Lennon was at one of his lowest psychological ebbs during December 1960.

There were two consolations to add to the physical improvements of being back in a comfortable house, with Mimi's cooking and Cynthia's faithful knock on the front door, which came within a day of his return.

Both were musical. First, he was now equipped with a Rickenbacker guitar, a much sought-after Club 40 model which was his pride and joy. Secondly, less tangibly, the reputation of the Beatles' huge impact on Hamburg audiences had spread back to Liverpool's burgeoning beat scene. Derry and the Seniors had put the word about that the Beatles had taken the Kaiserkeller by storm and had only been ejected from Germany by an act of spite.

They had improved their act beyond all recognition in Hamburg, developing an almost manic energy and a repertoire twice as big as when they left Liverpool. Yet John knew that while he was a dominant leader on stage, he was not pushy or organized enough to give the group its thrust. His own ambition,

125

to be bigger than Elvis, was unshaken. He had a new aggression after Hamburg. What he needed now, for his band so curiously called the Beatles, was a stroke of luck.

The twist of events throughout early 1961 and the rest of that year was to put the Beatles on the fastest-moving escalator to fame and fortune in the history of entertainment. Throughout his school and college years, and in the fights at the ballrooms and clubs of Liverpool and Hamburg, John had relied intuitively on fate smiling on him. It was as if someone was watching over him, bailing him out of disasters in every step of his twenty years. Now, having flounced out of college, blown it in Hamburg where their name was being sullied by Koschmider as unreliable, and having to persuade Mimi that all would come right, John was irritable.

The biggest problem was, as ever, getting work for the Beatles in an increasingly competitive Liverpool beat scene. They sought refuge back at the Casbah in West Derby, where Mona Best welcomed her son's group with a triumphant poster on the door of the cellar in which they played: 'The Fabulous Beatles Are Back!' The coffee, snacks and Cokes were a far cry from the beer and Prellys of the Kaiserkeller, but in Liverpool, in December 1960, the Casbah was a haven for four young men facing the spectre of failure. Nor was there much joy at the Jacaranda, where Allan Williams was licking his own Hamburg wounds. But it was then, in that coffee bar, that the Beatles met the man who was to mark their career so forcefully.

Bob Wooler was a twenty-eight-year-old ex-railway clerk turned disc jockey whose knowledge of the mushrooming Liverpool beat group scene was encyclopaedic. John and Paul found a receptive ear in the man who was to be a vital link in the chain that ensured they got work. Wooler, with his un-equalled grapevine knowledge of which group was coming up, sensed that the Beatles' Hamburg experience had made them special. He got them a date for £6, first at Litherland Town Hall where promoter Brian Kelly was amazed by their fiery energy. 'On their first appearance I was completely knocked out by them. They had a pounding, pulsating beat which I knew would be big box office. When they had finished playing I posted some bouncers on the door of their dressing-room to prevent some other promoters, who were in the hall, entering. I went inside and booked them solidly for months ahead.'

The Litherland dates became important for the Beatles, but Wooler was yet to deal his ace to them. He urged Ray McFall, owner of the Cavern club, a dingy, dank cellar and stronghold of traditional jazz at 10 Mathew Street in Liverpool's city centre, to give them a try. Lennon was ecstatic at the chain of events that was slowly but surely unfolding through Wooler.

Cynthia was still at art college. As far as Mimi was concerned, so was John. But in his mind he had quit college the day he set out for Hamburg, and had returned hell bent on music as a career. Until he was successful, he decided, it was best not to rock any boats with Mimi.

Wooler's memory of John in that desperate year of 1961 is of a hungry, difficult young man. He knew, says Wooler, that the Beatles were on the precipice of something, but worried that, instead of becoming successful, the scales might tip against them for want of both work and luck.

The Cavern, however, was to be the turning point for John and the Beatles. From their first appearance there the Beatles attracted not only their regular fans from West Derby, the area of the Casbah, but from Aintree and Litherland. Girls with beehive hairstyles from the typing pools nearby, in North John Street and Whitechapel, formed a new, quickly growing army of Beatles fans.

The Cavern, with little ventilation, appalling acoustics, walls dripping with dampness, stale air and cramped stage conditions, would tax even the most enthusiastic of young musicians. Its history was similar to dozens of cellar clubs in Britain in the late 1950s. It was a hotbed of traditional jazz featuring Liverpool's favourites, the Merseysippi Jazz Band and Manchester's Saints, with regular attacks from top London names such as Acker Bilk and Kenny Ball. The audiences were, in John Lennon's opinion, snobs against rock 'n' roll. He hated them for their superior attitude as trained musicians, their anti-pop attitude, and most of all because they always seemed to be well educated.

Over the next two and a half years the Beatles played the Cavern 292 times. They would play lunchtime and evening sessions, for a payment of around twenty-five shillings a session. The Cavern was to represent, to John, something much more than success for the Beatles. He saw it as a crusade against jazz and all it stood for, 'with all those bloody musicians and their G.C.E.s' (a British school education certificate).

John told jazz singer George Melly, who had played the club with the Mick Mulligan Band: 'You lot kept us from getting into the Cavern and other places much earlier. All that jazz crap held us back.' Melly conceded this point to Lennon; once the steamroller of rock 'n' roll had gathered speed, the death knell of traditional jazz's boom years was sounded. Through Acker Bilk, Chris Barber, and Kenny Ball 'trad' had enjoyed a brief flirtation with pop success. But with rock 'n' roll groups, led by the Beatles, pulling in students, previously the jazz fans' natural audience, 'the game was up' as Melly succinctly puts it. Lennon relished the kill. The tiny Cavern stage bulged with Pete Best's drum kit and cheap amplification, part of which had been 'permanently borrowed' from Liverpool Art College music room. Lennon's demeanour on that stage could be likened to that of a caged tiger: this was his domain. Here, he honed his short-sighted, head-tilted, legs-astride stance into a statement of defiance, much more than mere music. By the time that Lennon reached the Cavern, the Hamburg experience had galvanized his lithe, tallish frame into demonic energy.

Even now, the creative tension between John and Paul was rearing itself as they vied for the choice of songs. John made most of the announcements, taking the mickey out of the 'men in suits' who came. 'Shurrup, you with the suits on' became a regular Lennon message, especially to young teenagers who came during their lunch breaks from the insurance offices nearby. He mocked them for taking 'regular jobs'.

Among the regulars at the Cavern lunchtime sessions (admission one shilling) was Liz Hughes. She was a fourteen-year-old schoolgirl from Rock Ferry, across the Mersey, who saved the five shillings dinner money her parents gave her every week to spend on ferries and buses across to the city centre. Cavern sessions began at noon. At 11:45 precisely, dozens of Liverpool schoolgirls like Liz would eye the clock and get their belongings together to make a dash for it when the bell sounded. 'It was twelve-forty or even one o'clock before we reached the Cavern if we missed the first ferry,' says Liz. 'But it was worth it. Going to the Cavern and seeing the Beatles, the Big Three and later the Clayton Squares was almost like religion to certain kids of my age in those years.'

Today Liz Hughes and her husband Jim—another Cavern regular—are leading defenders of Liverpool's Beatles faith. They opened the Magical Mystery Store in 1978, and the Cavern Mecca in Mathew Street in 1981: this featured a Beatles museum and the re-creation of the old Cavern, complete with arches. As if in a time warp, Beatles music played non-stop. Liz and Jim were the proud curators of what for millions was pop music's most important period. Their mecca closed in 1984 and a heavily financed successor, Beatle City, opened as a museum in Liverpool.

Few women in Liverpool, outside the Beatles' family, can feel the warm nostalgia of that period with Liz Hughes' passion and intensity. She studied the style of John Lennon during the year that was, for him, the turning point of his life, the switch from potential bum to success beyond his wildest dreams.

'John always had this air about him,' says Liz. 'It gave all us kids the impression that if the audience had dropped dead, it would have gone right over his head. His attitude was as if he was saying: "I can take yer or leave yer. I'm here because this is something I wanna do, and I'm doing you lot a favour, not for the money."

'He looked as if he'd just stepped off the back of a motor bike. He usually wore dark clothes, crumpled trousers or jeans and a polo neck, but it was always unironed. They weren't in uniforms. It seemed that whatever caught their eye, or was on the back of the bedroom chair when he got out of bed, went on their backs. Except for Paul. He was the gentleman, the neat and tidy one who all the girls thought would be lovely to take home to their Mum. Paul played the part of the nice guy. But that John—he was the *animal*. The girls stood a bit back from him, a bit frightened. You never really knew which way he'd jump.

'I think John fed off Paul, but it was John who made most of the announcements. Paul would add to what John had said, but John made most of the first moves. They were obviously having a lot of fun. George was very quiet. A lot of the girls said he shouldn't be up there, he looked so embarrassed.' In the tiny dressing-room from which Bob Wooler would make his introductions of the Beatles, so much more majestically than for any other group, a few lucky teenage girls would huddle with the sweating Beatles after the session. They giggled at George's admission that he stuffed cardboard in the toes of his precious winklepicker shoes to ensure they remained pointed.

'Paul was safe and pretty, neat and tidy. George was so vulnerable. John looked like the sort of lad who would whip you up an entry, say thank you very much after he'd pleased himself, and ta-ra. All the girls were wary of him. He gave the impression of being so hard.'

What separated John, particularly, from all the other musicians who got on that three-feet-high Cavern stage, was his complete lack of professionalism. He would just stop singing or playing a song—dead—in the middle and start talking to Paul, for no apparent reason. He would light a cigarette, announce a new song, and carry on, with no explanation to the audience. 'It was like a permanent rehearsal. But he was someone you couldn't take your eyes from,' says Liz Hughes. 'My friend Deidre was absolutely crazy about him, but if he'd spoken to her, she'd have run a mile. That was a typical reaction. Her admiration was mixed with a fear of John. He was dangerous to all the girls, and that's what made him so attractive.

'The men in the audience took to him. He was a real man's man.' Jim Hughes agrees. 'Some of the lads modelled themselves on him. They'd lounge around the walls of the Cavern trying to imitate his stance, the way he held a cigarette, the legs astride, the lot.'

The music was like nothing else heard in Britain at that time. John's favourite songs, giving full rein to his leathery vocal work which had been hardened by the Kaiserkeller, were included in a set which usually featured this repertoire, refined in Hamburg: 'What'd I Say', 'Boys', 'Will You Love Me Tomorrow', 'Wooden Heart', 'C'mon Everybody', 'Twenty Flight Rock', 'Hallelujah I Love Her So', 'Mailman', 'Red Sails In The Sunset', 'Crying, Waiting, Hoping', 'Over The Rainbow', 'Mean Woman Blues', 'Lucille', 'Hey Good Looking', 'Blue Moon of Kentucky', 'Love Me Tender', 'Corinne Corinna'.

But it was John's magnetism, and his merciless mickey-taking of anyone in the audience who proved an easy target, that gave them that edge. There was no alcohol in the Cavern, and the Coca-Cola the Beatles always had by their side was in bottles, for these were the days before cans. It was just as well, for one day, early in their residency at the lunchtime sessions, Aunt Mimi decided to visit the Cavern. John had still not told her that he had left college. His days were spent hanging round the record shops, playing at the Cavern, or meeting Paul wherever they could manage it, to develop their songwriting. Mimi, uncharacteristically lost for words at the sight of Lennon in full flight amid the sweat in such unsalubrious surroundings, could manage just eight sardonic words when he came off stage to take a break. She awaited him in the dressing-room.

'This is nice, John. This is *very* nice.'

John put his arm around her, but she stomped off.

The longer the Beatles dug in as the resident band at the Cavern, the more confident and more aggressively ambitious he became. Soon they were so popular that they played on Monday, Wednesday and Friday lunchtimes as well as on Wednesday and Sunday nights. It was a claustrophobic hell-hole but a massive breakthrough to Lennon; apart from Cynthia, this was the greatest anchor of his life so far. Even Mimi, who now knew by mid-1961 that he was channelling everything into a life in music, had to concede that at least he had a goal, however errant. He was also earning a little money.

The fans, who hung on their every song, soon developed unswerving loyalties. The roles were cast. John, the tough, abrasive, fiercely masculine leader whose quick mouth could wound in a flash, carried the male vote. Paul wooed the girls with his flashing big eyes, comparatively immaculate dress, and romanticism set to music. George, enigmatic, shy, getting the music right, the apprentice electrician at Blackler's department store opposite Lime Street Station, was by far the best guitarist. And Pete Best at the back, on drums, had those sharply defined features but slightly sulky detached air that made him very popular with the girls. The contrasts, together with the electricity within the group, meshed perfectly.

Even in 1971, when the Beatles had split amid acrimony, Paul was admitting that his 'best playing days were at the Cavern lunchtime sessions'.

'We'd go on stage with a cheese roll and a cigarette and we felt we had really something going in that place. The amps used to fuse and we'd stop and sing a Sunblest bread commercial while they were being repaired. We used to do skits. . . . I'd do a Jet Harris impersonation because he'd played there. He fell off the stage once and I'd fall off it, too. You couldn't beat it.'

There was no contest between Lennon and McCartney for attention. They knew they attracted different people. Paul developed a warm friendship with the fans, while John tended to keep at a distance, retaining his slightly sinister mystique compounded by his increasing short-sightedness and refusal to wear glasses.

Before long, Lennon had nicknamed the crowd of schoolgirls who surrounded the stage most lunchtimes 'the Beatlettes'. Aged between fourteen and seventeen, the eight members of this elite clan shouted song requests, fetched the boys Cokes, and were the group's earliest known entourage. After evening sessions, the Beatles' blue Commer van, driven by Pete Best's friend Neil Aspinall, would even drop the girls at their homes to demonstrate to their parents that everything was 'above board' and that nothing was happening to their daughters, whatever the hour.

Hilary Williams, then a confirmed Beatlette of sixteen and now a Liverpool nurse, says that for all John's toughness he showed her and her schoolgirl friends a different side to his character at lunchtime or evening sessions. 'It was he who realized we were too young to have much money. The Beatles were each allowed one guest free in the club and John said we should be given that free ticket because we had been with them from the start. And one day he bought me a cup of tea for threepence. I couldn't believe it. Neither could my friends. ''*What*?'' they said. ''Lennon, the big he-man, bought you a cup of tea? Why?'' It was because he asked me how I could afford to keep coming, and I said I couldn't and I was broke that lunchtime. He just came up and put the cup by my side.'

John was palpably sexual, even to sixteen-year-old girls in 1961. But Hilary Williams remembers that he had a code of honour with her and her innocent friends. 'John would swear more than anyone else from that stage. If a string broke on his guitar, or if he was angry with the way a show was going, he'd curse all right! But in the 1960s, there were either decent, well-brought up girls, or there were tarts. He knew the Beatlettes were not tarts and treated us kindly and carefully.' Hilary Williams still has a rare memento of those years, a leather jacket she dared to wear on her Cavern outings. It still reeks of the unmistakable Cavern dampness, which the author experienced.

When the Beatles adjourned for beer to the Grapes, the pub just along Mathew Street from the Cavern, the Beatlettes and other supporters who were under drinking age would mournfully leave them and go into the Kardomah coffee bar in nearby Whitechapel. John and Paul would follow them later and buy them tea. Lennon's staple lunch would be a cheese sandwich followed by his own special weakness, red jelly. Hilary Williams said to her two brothers, who admonished her for bothering with the ruffians at the Cavern: 'They'll be famous one day, just you wait and see.'

For the schoolgirls who went to the Cavern and lived and breathed Beatles as a hobby, there was one major problem: Cynthia Powell. She was known to be John's art student girlfriend, and the very sight of her entering the Cavern made the possessive Beatlettes go schoolgirl crimson with a combination of jealousy and embarrassment. Outwardly, they were friendly to the twenty-two-year-old, but as they huddled together beneath the stage and in the Kardomah they could not contain their resentment. 'We called her Cindy to try to appear friendly, but it was no use,' says Hilary Williams. 'We couldn't compete. She had long blonde hair, and black leather, a real arty look, whereas we were dressed in denim. Looking back now, it's obvious she was a lovely girl, but at the time feelings were very strong against her. She'd got our John!'

When Cynthia went to the Cavern, John's behaviour changed. 'He swore less from the stage and was more gentle. There was even a rumour that Cindy was not his steady girlfriend but that he'd been out with another girl named Iris. Well, a few of us decided that was a cover-up to put us off knowing that he was serious with Cindy.' Hilary and other Beatlettes saw their defeat at the hands of Cynthia avenged one night. After a Cavern session, Paul McCartney conscientiously drove the girls to their homes in the Allerton area. First to be dropped off, in Menlove Avenue, was John. 'It was two o'clock in the morning, very late. We'd all just been talking after a session,' recalls Hilary Williams. 'Cynthia came out of his Auntie's house and hit him over the head with a bread board. We all collapsed with laughter in the van.'

The Beatles' popularity in Liverpool spread like an epidemic throughout 1961. 'It was horrible when that happened,' says Hilary Williams. 'They weren't ours any more. Girls used to come in at lunchtime and in the evenings from Widnes, St Helens, and Aintree. They were the ones who started the screaming for John or Paul. The earliest fans never screamed. But the new ones took sides with whichever Beatle they fancied.'

Competition was intense among the groups. Although they had different sets of fans, there was a special rivalry between the Beatles and Gerry and the Pacemakers. 'There was this contest for who was the best band in Liverpool,' says Gerry Marsden. 'But the nice thing was, we never nicked songs from each other. For a start, the Beatles didn't have a pianist as we did, so that gave us more room for Jerry Lee Lewis-type songs. We watched the Beats, as I called them, and they watched us, but there was this unbreakable rule that we never nicked songs. It was all done very politely, as a swap: John would say: "'Ere, can we have 'Jambalaya' if we give you 'Some Other Guy' or something like that?" '

Gerry remembers Lennon as more outgoing than the other Beatles. 'He was always more involved in more things than the others were. It wasn't just the group to him during the Cavern and ballroom dates. He was interested in seeing whatever else was happening around him. I spent more time with John because he was always up and ready.'

The Beatles and Gerry and the Pacemakers shared the bill on scores of Merseyside dates, even combining forces, at one memorable, crazy night at Litherland Town Hall, to become the Beatmakers. 'After a show, it would always be John who'd be the first one to say, "Yeah", if I said, "Coming for a pint, then?" Paul or the others would more often say: "No, I'm just going to run through this song." '

Marsden, the former British Railways van driver, and Lennon, whose caustic wit was more than a match for Gerry's sharpness, became firm friends. That closeness developed in Hamburg, where Gerry's group played the Top Ten club while the Beatles played the Kaiserkeller. 'So we never had a chance to see them on stage in Hamburg. We played the sets and met for drinks or meals afterwards.' Gerry went to the Cavern to see them immediately they returned from Germany. 'And I said to my brother Fred, who played drums with my band: "John and Paul are going to be big, big, big. Never mind what happens to the Beatles, there's nothing can stop those two." I couldn't believe how good they were. The energy, the way they shaped up to the microphone together, you know—Paul, the left-handed bass player, John standing there, couldn't give a shit, the *attitude* of the man. I thought: "They'll be the first band out of Liverpool to make it." '

Lennon was not even a great guitarist, says Gerry. 'John never claimed to be a great player: "I'm a cinema-verité player," he once said. Nor was he a good pianist, although he dabbled on it when there was no one around. But I could always tell a Lennon guitar touch, even when he was just strumming. It came at you from an angle. It wasn't like anyone else. And that voice! In the Cavern, on the stage at Litherland, he'd belt out "Memphis Tennessee" or any Chuck Berry songs and I'd say to myself immediately: "*That*'s John Lennon!" Much more important than anything is to have a distinctive voice. It's more important than any other quality. It doesn't have to be fantastic in any way, or never sound flat, or never raunchy. It's got to be a voice on its own for rock 'n' roll, and John had that like nobody else I know. His vibration on stage was special, because he simply stood there, with this attitude: "I'm going to have a bloody good time, hope you'll join me." '

Gerry shared John's sick humour. 'He'd sit in a pub doing a drawing, which appeared quite straight, a doodle. Then suddenly at the back would be a pair of crutches. I'd fall about laughing, because he had this black macabre sense of sick humour. He was always taking the mickey out of cripples, or walking down the street around Liverpool he'd pretend to be one. I went along with it because I found it funny, too.' Once, in a Paris jazz club, a drunken John and Gerry did a crushingly accurate imitation of cripples. As the two men lurched uproariously around the club, the mostly sober audience sat back, flabbergasted at the sight.

Another who was at the Cavern one lunchtime was a girl named Priscilla Maria Veronica White. She was never the official hat check girl at the cellar but occasionally, when she was broke, Priscilla asked the doorman if she could be allowed in free if she volunteered to help with the cloaks.

It was John Lennon who remarked, 'Pretty girl, Brian,' to Epstein one lunchtime, when Epstein had become their manager. And the girl went on to become, under the name Cilla Black, a singing star and comedienne in the Gracie Fields tradition.

Cilla recalls: 'I played truant from Anfield Commercial College to see the Beatles at lunchtime sessions. At that time I was singing with some of the local bands, billed as "Swingin' Cilla", on a semi-professional basis. But this was the first time I had my chance to sing with the Beatles.

' "What's your name, girl?" asked John.

'When I told him he yelled: "Do you hear that, lads? She's got a boy's name. This is Cyril who is going to have a bash at singing something with us."

'John went on: "What key do you sing in, Cyril?"

'When I said I had no idea—because I'd never had a lesson in my life!—he shouted: "Let's try a Yale!"

'The group had just come back from Germany and wore gear they'd bought in Hamburg. John's hair was much longer then than Brian Epstein ever let him wear it later on. It was brushed forward instead of back and he had an enormous pink leather hat over it. He had black leather pants on, lined with red satin, black T-shirt, black leather jacket, and high black boots with Cuban heels. I took one look and thought: "Oh, my God!"

'At the end of 1961 I was appearing with Kingsize Taylor and the Dominoes at the Tower Ballroom in New Brighton. The Beatles were on the same bill. I noticed a very smart man deep in conversation with John. John told me it was their new manager, but I just laughed because I thought this was another of John's jokes. Then he took me over and introduced me. It was Brian Epstein and he'd just signed the Beatles. Even then

John was still doing his "Cyril" thing with me: "Come over here, Cyril, I want you to meet Brian Epstein."

'It was John who persuaded Brian to listen to me. He told Brian that he should sign me up. I did an audition at a club in Birkenhead with the Beatles backing me. I must have been dreadful because I was very nervous. Brian didn't say anything at all and I didn't like to ask him what he thought. Eight months later he signed me. I remember I used to be dead scared of John, although he was the one who had helped me most. He had this aura of super-intelligence. I hated being left alone to speak to him. Once he said: "What's wrong with you, girl? Don't you like me?"'

'I confessed, "I'm frightened of you, John."'

'He roared with laughter: "And I thought you were a snob!"'

'After that we often talked. John loved coloured singers—many of my own American favourites. He talked about his songs, but the memory which stands out is the way he admitted he longed to become a famous actor one day.'

John loathed crowds. He told me, in the midst of the Beatles fans' wildest scenes, when he was waving at thousands of them from a hotel balcony in Munich: 'I'd hate to be in the middle of that. I couldn't stand being hemmed in.' The seething Cavern crowds made him feel claustrophobic, too.

If Liverpool rock 'n' roll was a religion in the early 1960s, then the parish priest was Bob Wooler. Until the old Cavern was closed on 27 May 1973 to make way for an excavation shaft for an underground railway link, Wooler was able to take people down there and affectionately recreate those halcyon days. Today, the great Cavern compère is an institution among Beatles fans who marvel at his place in history, having survived the stifling, sweaty cubby hole they called a dressing-room which he shared with the Beatles. His memories of Lennon tempered by an historic punch-up with him, are warm and respectful. When the Beatles returned to Liverpool for the northern première of their film *A Hard Day's Night* in 1964, Wooler went to Speke airport and was greeted by a typical Lennon remark: 'Hi, Bob. Has anyone given you a black eye lately?'

McCartney was his perfect foil, says Wooler; both John

and Paul realized that the group needed John's edge, but Paul was there to apologize when John offended people. 'I have rarely seen any one person embody youth so much as Lennon did in those years,' says Bob Wooler. 'He had aggressiveness, but not aggression. He would stand straddling the far left of the stage and look, unseeingly, into the audience because he was *so* short-sighted. It was obvious the applause was washing over him, but he loved it. He managed to give off this attitude of not caring two hoots, but deep down I know he did. He loved every minute. I told him he reminded me of the actor Kirk Douglas and he said that was rather high-sounding. He did have a cleft chin like Kirk Douglas and that was part of his appeal to the girls. But he was adored by both sexes.'

Wooler remembers John as a 'very black and white character who couldn't be bothered with people'. The identification of Lennon in black and white is significant: the Cavern was totally black and white in appearance and in atmosphere, and John often told his friends that he preferred the earthy simplicity of mono films and art to colour: it was partly because the film *Help!* was in unreal colour that he felt it ended up looking tawdry. 'In the Cavern,' says Bob Wooler, 'the shadows and the starkness helped the Beatles create a great drama from their music. It was love us or loathe us, but that's how we are, straight ahead, black and white.'

From his close encounters with Lennon, Bob Wooler's overall view is that there was so much loneliness in his life that the thing he most feared was showing his tears. As an example of John's vulnerability, Wooler recalls the day Aunt Mimi went to the Cavern lunchtime session. 'It was the custom, if a father like Jim McCartney or any close relative came to see the group, to dedicate a record to him or her,' says Wooler. 'But John insisted that no record should ever be played for Mimi or any of his mates. I think she would have loved it, but it might have given people in the crowd the feeling that John was a softie, and that image was never allowed to register.'

The problem for John, when the Beatles became famous, was that, never having believed in himself, he could not fully absorb what was happening. 'Paul's horizon had already been in focus, so he was ready. But John was really thrown by it all,' says Bob Wooler. Lennon, he says, had a love/hate relationship with the Cavern but often admitted that, because it was so difficult to play on account of its acoustics, it had played a big part in forcing the Beatles to 'play hard'.

Coincidentally, Liverpool Art College canteen, where they first played, was also a basement with arches. But, in a totally different sense, the ambition to climb out of that damp, sweaty, unlicensed catacomb that had no acoustics became John's greatest incentive for the Beatles. 'We couldn't get out of the place fast enough,' he said. He wasn't ungrateful for what the Cavern had done for them, but to John any form of regularity very quickly became monotony. This was the restlessness that was to mark his life, and make him so utterly different from his partner, Paul McCartney. Once a thing was rolling along, Lennon wanted to move on: a new kick, a fresh challenge, something a little dangerous. Thus the Cavern had to be escaped from.

Many people who were in Liverpool during 1961 could claim to have played a big role in giving the Beatles the thrust that enabled them to break out of the confines of the city into a London recording studio, with all that led to. Bill Harry, who saw most of their Cavern shows and had been at art college with John, encouraged John in his early writings, diverted Brian Epstein to the Cavern, which was to lead to a great partnership, and can claim to have been the first to publish John's words.

Harry saw the rumblings of a big beat group scene on Merseyside in 1960. With Stuart Sutcliffe, he was on the students' union committee, so it was inevitable that Sutcliffe would lobby for his best friend's band to get work. As a friend of Stuart's, Bill had been to the Gambier Terrace flat which Lennon shared with him. There he first became aware of John's weird sense of humour, his special way with words, and his ability to draw. 'We'd drink at Ye Cracke and then spend entire evenings at the flat in Gambier Terrace or at another student's flat in Huskisson Street,' says Bill. They played games, many of them invented by John. They sat in a circle, including Rod Murray and his girlfriend Dizzy who occupied the flat next to Stuart's. 'John suggested we create stories by saying whatever came into our heads. One person would reel off a few sentences, and the following person would continue unfolding the story. We laughed till the tears ran down our cheeks at some of the tales, particularly John's, which were often cruelly suggestive with references to spastics, cripples, and crutches.

'When Margaret Duxbury fell asleep on the bed, John suggested we get potatoes and use matchstick legs to make them look like spiders. We suspended them from the ceiling so that she'd get a shock when she woke up. All this made me realize that John had a macabre sense of humour and a creative turn of mind.'

It was that electricity from Lennon that connected with Bill Harry when he was about to launch, with great foresight, a newspaper called *Mersey Beat*. Bill had talked about poetry with John in Ye Cracke. Lennon said he wrote it occasionally and grudgingly showed some of his rough work to Bill. 'I liked it, particularly since it wasn't a pastiche of Beat Generation poetry which was all the rage with other students,' says Bill. 'It once again indicated his individuality. In fact, the group actually backed a beat poet named Royston Ellis. He'd been booked by Liverpool University to read his poetry there, and he later talked the Beatles into providing backing for his readings at the Jacaranda.

'In 1961, when I was preparing *Mersey Beat*, I remembered John's poetry and decided to ask him to write for the paper, beginning with a biography of the Beatles.' Bill was a fan of the group and saw them perform several hundred times.

'I met him at the Jacaranda for the copy and he shoved two pieces of paper torn from an exercise book into my hands. He seemed embarrassed by the piece. It was like no other biography of a band and I told him I'd be pleased to print it, which cheered him up no end.' In the piece, John spelled Paul's surname wrongly, calling him McArtrey, as he had done in letters to Cynthia from Hamburg. The humour and light touch of John's first printed work was a talking point among the local beat population; it read like this:

Being a Short Diversion on the Dubious Origins of Beatles
Translated from the John Lennon.

Once upon a time there were three little boys called John, George and Paul, by name christened. They de-

cided to get together because they were the getting together type. When they were together they wondered
what for after all, what for? So all of a sudden they all
grew guitars and fashioned a noise. Funnily enough, no
one was interested, least of all the three little men.
So-o-o on discovering a fourth little even littler man
called Stuart Sutcliffe running about them they said,
quote 'Sonny get a bass guitar and you will be alright'
and he did—but he wasn't alright because he couldn't
play it. So they sat on him with comfort 'til he could
play. Still, there was no beat, and a kindly old man
said, quote 'Thou hast not drums!' We had no drums!
they coffed. So a series of drums came and went and
came.

Suddenly, in Scotland, touring with Johnny Gentle,
the group (called the Beatles called) discovered they
had not a very nice sound,—because they had no amplifiers. They got some. Many people ask what are the
Beatles? Why Beatles? Ugh, Beatles how did the name
arrive? So we will tell you. It came in a vision—a man
appeared on a flaming pie and said unto them 'From
this day on you are Beatles with an A'. Thank you,
Mister Man, they said, thanking him.

But before we could go we had to grow a drummer,
so we grew one in West Derby in a club called Some
Casbah and his trouble was Pete Best. We called 'Hello
Pete, come off to Germany!' 'Yes!' Zooooom. After a
few months, Peter and Paul (who is called McArtrey,
son of Jim McArtrey, his father) lit a Kino (cinema)
and the German police said, 'Bad Beatles, you must go
home and light your English cinemas.' Zooooom, half
a group. But even before this, the Gestapo had taken
my friend little George Harrison (of Speke) away because he was only twelve and too young to vote in
Germany: but after two months in England he grew
eighteen, and the Gestapoes said 'you can come.' So
suddenly back in Liverpool Village were many groups
playing in grey suits and Jim said 'Why have you no
grey suits?' 'We don't like them, Jim' we said speaking
to Jim. After playing in the clubs a bit, everyone said

'Go to Germany!' So we are. Zooooom. Stuart gone.
Zoom zoom, John (of Woolton) George (of Speke) Peter
and Paul zoom zoom. All of them gone.

Thank you club members, from John and George
(what are friends).

Readers told Bill Harry they liked the piece, so he asked John
to contribute a regular column. 'He turned up at the office with
an untidy bundle of papers and I leafed through them, completely enchanted by the strange stories, drawings, short tales,
and political satires.' As a fan of the *Daily Express* column
Beachcomber, Bill Harry decided to call John's column Beatcomber because John's work seemed to have 'inspired lunacy'.

His first piece under the name Beatcomber was headlined
SMALL SAM, and read:

Once upon a Tom there was a small little Stan, who
was very small. 'You are very small, Stan,' they said.
'I am only little,' replied Stan answering, feeling very
small. Who could blame him, for Stan was only small.
'You must be small, Stan,' people were oft heard to
cry, noticing how extremely small Stan was in fact. But
being small (Stan was small) had its condensations.
Who else but Stan (the small) could wear all those small
clothes?

Stan was highly regarded by everyone (for Stan was
small and little). However, one day Stan saw an adverse
in the Mersey Bean for 'Club you quickly grow your
boots.' So on that very day Small Stan (by name called)
purchased a pair of the very same. So now when Stan
passes by, folks say, 'Is that not small Stan wearing a
pair of those clubs you quickly grow you boots?' And
it is.

In a satire on the hit record 'The Lion Sleeps Tonight', by
the Tokens, John's Beatcomber column one week had a safari
theme:

On Safairy With Whide Hunter

In the jumble . . . the mighty jumble . . . Whide Hunter
sleeps tonight. At the foot of the bed, Otumba kept

wogs for poisonous snacks such as the deadly Cobbler and Apple Python.

Otumba awoke him with a cup of teeth, and they lit up towards the jumble.

'Ain't dat Elepoon Pill?' said Wipe Hudnose, 'wearing his new Basuti?'

'Could be the flying Docker on a case.'

'No he's walking,' said Otumba in swahily which is not arf from here as the crowbarks. All too soon they reached a cleaner in the jumble and set up cramp.' Jumble Jim, whom shall remain nameless, was slowly, but slowly asking his way through the underpants (underware he was being washed by Whide Hunter).

'Beat the bus Otumbath!' commanded Whide Hunter.

'No, but mayble next week it will be my turn to beat the bus now standing at platofrbe nine.'

Jumping Gym, who shall remain Norman, spotted Whit Monday and the Barking Doctrine shooting some rhinostrills and hipposthumous and Otumbark.

'Stop shouting those animoles!' But it hab no influence upod them. They carried on shotting, alligarters, wild boats, garriffes, lepers and Uncle Tom Cobra and all . . . Old Buncle Ron Gabble and all . . . Bold Rumple Bom Dobby and all . . . Bad Runcorn Sad Toddy and all.

Walking into the *Mersey Beat* office at 81A Renshaw Street one day, John forked out with his own cash to place these five classified advertisements in the paper, asking that they should definitely not be printed in sequence, but should be scattered among other adverts:

HOT LIPS, missed you Friday, RED NOSE
RED NOSE, missed you Friday, HOT LIPS
ACCRINGTON welcomes HOT LIPS and RED NOSE.
Whistling Jock Lennon wishes to contact HOT NOSE.
RED SCUNTHORPE wishes to jock HOT ACCRINGTON

Clearly, John's early poems, together with his famous exercise book of lampooning called the *Daily Howl* which he had invented at Quarry Bank, was an indication of the literary style for which he was to be lavishly praised only a few years later. *In His Own Write*, and *A Spaniard In The Works*, were more sophisticated continuations of these early stabs at poetry and satire. There was an Englishness to his work that ran in sharp contrast to the stream-of-consciousness poetry of the American beat poets of the day, like Allen Ginsberg. John's work was to presage the rise of Liverpool beat poets and can now be seen as an indicator of the assertiveness of Liverpool people in various arts, away from the American influence of the time.

Mersey Beat acquired another occasional contributor: Brian Epstein. Aged twenty-seven, he ran the record department of the local NEMS store in Whitechapel. Fascinated by the activity of local beat groups, he had read the newspaper from cover to cover after first stocking it at Bill Harry's request. The first issue sold out a dozen copies in Epstein's department; the second sold two hundred and forty copies. 'It was a musical wonderland on his own doorstep which he hadn't been aware of, and he asked if he could contribute a regular record review column,' says Bill Harry. 'He'd call me each week and I'd visit him in his office for chats about the local scene.' About this time, the expanding *Mersey Beat* needed new offices, and during the paper's move many of John's poems were lost. When he was told, Lennon wept on the shoulder of Bill Harry's wife, Virginia.

Theoretically, Brian Epstein was the least likely mentor of the Beatles, particularly after the rumbustious Allan Williams. He spoke articulately, or, as the Beatles would describe it, 'posh'. He dressed immaculately, in suit and tie, and carried a briefcase. He was painfully shy and would wilt at the slightest dig against his personality. And he was from a middle-class, respectable, Jewish family.

Pride and punctiliousness, rather than a love for pop music, led Brian Epstein to the Beatles. He was more interested in Sibelius than any other sounds. As a businessman, though, he wanted all his teenage customers to be satisfied. One of his biggest boasts was that if he did not have a record in stock when it was asked for, he would get it.

So when Raymond Jones, a regular NEMS record buyer,

walked into the shop on 28 October 1961, and asked for 'My Bonnie', by the Beatles, Brian Epstein was flummoxed. He had heard of neither the group, whose weird name he could not spell, nor the record. Jones explained that it was a Liverpool group and the record had been made in Hamburg. Epstein promised to investigate, and wrote down on his familiar pad: 'My Bonnie, The Beatles. Check on Monday'.

A few phone calls on Monday elicited some facts. The Beatles had made the record in Hamburg as a backing group and copies of it were available on the Polydor label. And not only did the group still exist—they played regularly, unknown to Brian, a little more than two hundred yards away in a cellar club he had never heard of, called the Cavern. He suddenly clicked with the familiarity of the names from the pages of *Mersey Beat*, and he asked Bill Harry to arrange for him to go to the club.

The man who was to become the Beatles manager was a complex character. His background, although more genteel and conservative, shared one striking characteristic with the Beatles. He had been expelled from Liverpool College at the age of ten 'for inattention and for being below standard'. The crunch that caused his expulsion came when, during a maths lesson, he designed beneath his desk a programme featuring dancing girls. 'My parents despaired many times over the years, and I don't blame them, for throughout my schooldays I was one of those out-of-sorts boys who never quite fit,' Epstein wrote later. 'I was ragged, nagged and bullied and beloved of neither boys nor masters.' By ten, he had been to three schools and settled in none of them. He was top of his class at art, poor at mathematics and the sciences, and, after failing many entrance examinations for public schools, was accepted at Wrekin College in Shropshire. He went to RADA before deciding that actors were too narcissistic, and subsequently returned to Liverpool and the family business after an apprenticeship in salesmanship at Times Furnishing in Lord Street, Liverpool.

By the time he reached the Cavern, Epstein had seen the Beatles without realizing it. They had visited his record department in the afternoons, and he had dismissed them in his mind as scruffy layabouts whom he hoped would go away. 'I had been bothered a little with the frequent visits of a group of scruffy lads in leather and jeans . . . chatting to the girls and lounging on the counters listening to records. They were pleasant enough boys, untidy and a little wild, and they needed haircuts,' said Brian.

'I mentioned to the girls in the shop that I thought the youth of Liverpool might while their afternoons away somewhere else but they assured me that the boys were well behaved and they occasionally bought records. Also, said the girls, they seemed to know good discs from bad. Though I didn't know it, the four lads were the Beatles, filling in part of the long afternoons between the lunchtime and evening shows in the beat cellars.'

Brian Epstein's visit to the Cavern embarrassed him for two reasons. First, he felt conspicuous as the well-dressed adult amid a surging crowd of schoolgirls with beehive hairstyles who spoke a language all their own between Cokes and ham rolls. Secondly, Bob Wooler, the Cavern disc jockey, marked Brian's arrival with a magisterial announcement that 'Mr Epstein of NEMS' was in the audience and would the crowd please give him a big hand. Brian blushed.

'I had never seen anything like the Beatles on any stage,' Epstein recalled later. 'They smoked as they played and they ate and talked and pretended to hit each other. They turned their backs on the audience and shouted at them and laughed at private jokes.' Epstein was both irritated and mesmerized at the unruly group that radiated raw talent. Whatever it was coming from that stage in a dungeon, he could not take his eyes from it.

Although he had several girlfriends, Brian Epstein was a homosexual. It has been said that he had a fixation for John Lennon in particular, from that first sight of him on the Cavern stage. Since both men are dead, and neither spoke on the subject during his life, it is a matter of pure conjecture. Brian had a deep fascination for John, but Lennon was an extremely active heterosexual with the traditional contempt of those years for the people who, in 1961, were called 'queers' and who kept their preferences secret. Homosexuality was a taboo then and to Brian it was not something he allowed to be known, even among his family. To say, as some commentators have, that Brian Epstein's ambition for the Beatles was based mostly on his initial love of Lennon, is speculative nonsense. The memories of two good men should not be contaminated by rumours that can never be corroborated.

I knew Brian Epstein well enough to know that he was in love with the Beatles as an entity. He was fiercely protective of them all, ambitious for all four of them individually, and totally committed to making them the world's best-known pop act. It was something that went way beyond any sexual preferences.

'Sitting right here today,' Epstein told me in a Liverpool restaurant one night in 1962, 'I can't think why I didn't walk out of the Cavern within a few minutes. I can still remember these four ill-presented youths and their untidy hair.' Brian had invited me, as a writer with the weekly music paper *Melody Maker*, to Liverpool; I was the first London music journalist to go to the city to hear about the Beatles. He told me of his great hopes for the group, how they would be world-beaters, and how lucky I was to be in at the birth of such an explosion. I was interested, but cynically apprehensive. The British pop scene, dominated for so long by America, was slowly developing its own identity. With it came a new breed of swaggering managers who phoned me and many other writers every day to tout the new sensation. Elvis Presley and Cliff Richard had been joined by Acker Bilk's 'Stranger on the Shore', Frank Ifield's yodelling 'I Remember You', and the Tornados' number one hit 'Telstar', to mark America's first communications satellite, launched that year. John Lennon was getting heavily influenced by a raunchy American single, 'Hey Baby', by Bruce Channel which was to inspire John's harmonica playing. Against the general background of gimmicks and ballads and the trickle of good records, and the ubiquitous Elvis Presley, a group of Liverpool boys with the unlikely name of the Beatles sounded doubtful starters. Epstein, who exuded charm, impeccable manners, and persistence, was insistent. 'Stay and meet them in my office tomorrow,' he said to me.

Brian told me how, a few months previously, he had invited the Beatles to his shop one afternoon. Although he had no firm plan of what they should do together, 'the idea of management occurred on both sides'. They had arrived at the NEMS store in Whitechapel, taking along Bob Wooler as if to mark the seriousness of the occasion. It was Lennon who broke the ice, saying 'This is me Dad,' when introducing Wooler to Epstein.

Wooler, who had seen the group's popularity soar, had confided in Epstein earlier that the Beatles were enormously popular but lacking regular work. Brian confirmed this with the group, had a general vague talk about contracts and their future, and invited them to return a week later. This time he got to the point briskly. 'Quite simply, you need a manager. Would you like me to do it?'

No one spoke for a moment or two and then John, in a low, husky voice, blurted: 'Yes.'

The others nodded. Paul, ever wary, asked: 'Will it make much difference to us? I mean, it won't make any difference to the way we play.'

Assured that it would not and assured of Epstein's enthusiasm, the five men sat looking at each other for a few minutes, not knowing what to say next.

Lennon again broke the silence. 'Right, then, Brian, manage us, now. Where's the contract? I'll sign it.'

I did meet the Beatles the day after that dinner with Brian Epstein. It was a brief encounter in Brian's office above a magic shop. John and George bounded in and asked for cigarettes. 'Love Me Do' had just been released. They were cheerful, optimistic, and not at all unkempt. John got in a quick dig that the *Melody Maker* 'only ever writes about jazz', but he said it with the cynical smile that was to become endearing even when he was at his most cutting. I remember thinking it was difficult, though, to reconcile the tidy men with the uncouth image which Brian had described from the Cavern.

Even in those early days, Brian Epstein's impact was considerable. Before he began the long, frustrating search for a record contract, he informally laid down certain rules for them. First, he was a stickler for punctuality. Bob Wooler had trouble getting them on stage on time, and also in getting them off it. That needed tightening up, Epstein told John. Next, Brian suggested they stop drinking Cokes and eating sandwiches on stage, and they were not to shout abuse to people in the audience. He insisted on a tighter act of a maximum of an hour, and that they built a fairly rigid repertoire. The Hamburg experience of playing everything by ear and lambasting the audience was to be dropped. Their music on stage was, under Epstein, never to be as free and easy, but it was the sure route to directing their talent into mass popularity.

With slight reluctance, John accepted Epstein's theory. In a coffee bar Lennon bumped into the art college model June Furlong, who asked him how the group was progressing. He said they had met a posh man named Brian Epstein who had definite ideas for them but it would mean a radical change. 'He seemed unsure of whether it was a good thing,' says June Furlong. 'I said: "Go with it, John. What have you got to lose?" And he roared with laughter.

' "Yeah, June, how true. What have we got to *lose*?" '

He went also to the Renshaw Street offices of *Mersey Beat* and demanded back some of his ruder poems from Bill Harry, lest they should be published. They would, he thought, clash with the new, cleaner image that Brian Epstein intended to project. On two visits to Mendips, Epstein secured Aunt Mimi's seal of approval. 'A charming gentle man, a restless soul just like John,' she says. 'Always so polite.'

But the next part of Epstein's master plan was to shock John to the bone. As a successful salesman, Brian believed that the great British public would never go for an act that looked scruffy, however primitive their music was to remain. He insisted that the Beatles should wear suits, shirts and ties. Brian pointed to the Shadows as an example of success. Cliff Richard's backing group were the epitome of that antiseptic pop which John loathed. But secretly, however much Lennon resented Epstein's grooming, he was prepared to give it a whirl. Brian's salesmanship law said that, once a brand name had set a pattern, if it was successful then it should be followed. The Beatles would retain control over their music, of which he knew nothing but that it was spine-tingling with earthy excitement. But when it came to packaging, he told John, he knew what he was talking about: the Shadows were successful, and they wore suits.

It was a major decision, and a successful one. But John was going against his instincts in letting Brian mould the group in this direction. It might have been the first moment the group polarized, with John and George rebelling against the 'super packaging' idea which was propounded by Epstein and strongly supported by Paul McCartney.

Clive Epstein, Brian's brother, says John was a frequent visitor to the Epstein family home long before the first single was made. 'Brian and John had long, serious discussions about how to project the group,' says Clive. Lennon was keen on learning about Brian's marketing techniques, something utterly foreign to him. 'He had a lot to say and they became very animated. Brian told me privately he believed John was a genius, and of course he assured my parents and me that they would be bigger than Elvis Presley, even before the first single was a small hit. Brian was definitely closer to John than the others; there was a mental contact between them that was perfect and really vital for the group's future.'

Long after the euphoria of Beatlemania John said in the *Melody Maker*, 'In the beginning it was a constant fight between Brian and Paul on one side, and me and George on the other. Brian put us in neat suits and shirts and Paul was right behind him. I didn't dig that and I tried to get George to rebel with me. I'd say to George: "Look, we don't need these suits. Let's chuck them out of the window." My little rebellion was to have my tie loose with the top button of my shirt undone, but Paul'd always come up to me and put it straight.

'On the first television film we ever did, the Granada people came down to film us, and there we were in suits and everything. It just wasn't us, and watching that film I knew that that was where we started to sell out.' In most pictures of John he is seen with his tie at least a little askew and, often, with his top shirt button undone.

He said all that with the benefit of hindsight. But in 1962, even for John, the end justified the means. Epstein's logic was unarguable: the devoted fans who thronged the Cavern and the ballrooms for the Beatles would have to be augmented by much wider appeal if they were to be a successful concert, television, and recording group. And the route to real pop success in Britain in 1962 was through the hit parade charts. While Brian tidied them up and slowly improved their fees and number of engagements, he set about the major task of getting them a record contract. It was to prove a heartbreaking hurdle.

Meanwhile, the virtual emigration of his best friend to Germany had left Lennon feeling isolated. John missed Stuart. 'The only real friend John ever had', is how Aunt Mimi describes him. 'The bond was beautiful, whenever they met. You could see it immediately,' says Cynthia. Astrid, Stuart's fiancée, would work away in her photographic studio in Hamburg while Stuart worked in an attic in her Hamburg home, alternately painting or writing long letters to John in Liverpool.

Equally, Lennon wrote letters to Stuart with an open-hearted intensity he usually reserved for Cynthia. His twenty-page letters to Stuart were different. Each bemoaned the state of the world, and little was said of the Beatles' progress. What came through, from John to Stuart, and then from Stuart to John, was a restlessness about life, and from John the freedom at last to feel he could unleash his innermost emotions, perhaps about his own venomous tongue which had hurt so many people. Once he wrote to Stuart:

I can't remember anything without a sadness
So deep that it hardly becomes known to me
So deep that its tears leave me a spectator of my own
   stupidity.

As the Epstein plan gathered momentum, the Beatles were to fulfil, on 13 April 1962, an engagement to open Hamburg's Star-Club, their most prestigious appearance so far in a city which they had grown to adopt as their second home. With a new manager behind them, a fresh confidence surged within the group as they travelled. This time, Epstein's style insisted on the Beatles flying to Germany rather than going by train and boat. He wanted to impress them with his largesse and give them confidence that he was serious about making them gigantically successful.

John had been aware of Stuart's very bad headaches through his letters, but only Astrid and her mother knew how really serious they were becoming. 'There were days when poor Stu was convulsed with pain,' says Astrid. 'When I went back to Liverpool with him at Christmas in 1961, everybody said how ill he looked. He fainted at art college once and we all decided that as he was in such agony, and it was impossible to know when a severe headache was caused, he had better stay at my home in bed or in the attic, and at least my mother and I could be near him when he needed help.' It also gave Stuart the attention of the Kirchherr family doctor. He sent him for X-rays but nothing untoward showed itself.

On 10 April, as the plane carrying the Beatles took off from Manchester to Hamburg, Astrid received a phone call from her mother saying that Stuart was in such pain from headaches that she could not even contemplate calling the family doctor. 'He has to go to the hospital right now,' said Frau Kirchherr. Astrid sped home and insisted on accompanying her fiancé in the ambulance. 'He died in my arms on that journey,' says Astrid. 'I cannot say it was unexpected but the suddenness was. . . .' Her voice trails off. Cause of death was given as cerebral paralysis.

Astrid went from the hospital to Hamburg airport to meet John, Paul, and Pete Best. (George did not arrive until next day.) They knew nothing of the drama of the day, still less of twenty-one-year-old Stuart's death. 'I don't know how I got through that moment, after what happened,' says Astrid. 'I can see John walking into the airport hall and he got sight of me and came over, waving his arms, "Hello, I'm *here*, how are you . . . oh, what's the matter?" ' He could see darkness in Astrid's doleful, expressive eyes.

'Stuart died, John. He's gone.'

Lennon's reaction was to burst into laughter. He said nothing at all to anyone. 'He never cried,' says Astrid. 'Not once. He went into this hysterical laughter, and couldn't stop. It was his way of not wanting to face the truth. John went deep into himself for just a little while after the news. But he and I didn't speak much about Stuart. I knew that he and Stuart genuinely loved each other. They told me so, when they got loose. I know Stu would have preferred to have died rather than go on in the pain he was suffering. But the loss to me was great, and to anyone who knew him, because he was a genius, with a great mind and an original talent as an artist. He would have been outstanding, if he'd lived. How John got over that period I'll never know.'

Lennon's method of recovery was the same that he had adopted when first he had that awful choice between his mother and father, then the death of Uncle George, then the death of his mother. His period of mourning was quiet, totally personal and not shared with anyone else. He believed in getting on with living immediately.

Astrid suffered a deep depression for months afterwards, and it was mostly John who pulled her out of it. 'He saved me,' she said. Paul and George particularly were sweet to her, she says, but John knew the onus was on him to look after her because of his relationship with Stu. 'In his rough way, he was so beautiful, and he imposed his own method of recovery on me without me knowing it,' says Astrid. 'Come on, make up your mind, live or die,' he would say. 'You're coming to the Star-Club with us tonight. Stop sitting at home—it won't bring Stu back.' John showed many times his demonstrativeness towards Astrid's mother, who had borne the brunt of Stuart's illness when Astrid was away in her photographic studio so often during the days. 'My mother would say: "John, you are supposed to be rough rocker." He would put his arms around her and carry on as if he lived in the house, which she loved.' Astrid says John kept her from becoming morose and she did, indeed, go to the Star-Club when the Beatles opened there on 13 April for seven weeks.

They were in a mood of despondency at Stuart's death, and optimism at their career prospects: the Star-Club was a step up and they had, after all, been chosen to open it. One of the men who helped run the club, Horst Fascher, recalls John as being the one with the most bizarre behaviour during the seven weeks they were at the Star-Club. 'On that opening night, we had the Beatles and other groups and Brian Epstein also came. There was lots to drink. The next morning we all went to a club and Brian was a bit drunk and John Lennon poured beer all over him. There was a slight argument.'

Fascher knew the Beatles from 1960 when he had worked in the Kaiserkeller, the second Hamburg club they had played. He was also the manager of Tony Sheridan, with whom the Beatles had made their first record in Hamburg, called 'My Bonnie', which had been the subject of that first request to Brian Epstein. Fascher recalls: 'They were different from the start. There was something I liked about them, and their clothes and special sound impressed me.' He was also amused by their eccentricity: 'One day,' he says, 'they all went to the fish market in Hamburg and bought a pig. They walked it, on a lead, up and down the Reeperbahn. Some people who saw it were annoyed and called the police, who took it away to be slaughtered. It was typical of their outlandish behaviour.'

As the kings of the Cavern back home, and now knowing Hamburg where their reputation was soaring, John, Paul, George, and Pete Best were in a lively mood. They stayed in a flat above the Star-Club. John's often outrageous behaviour, during that month, may have been traceable to his submerging of Stuart's death. The Star-Club owner, Manfred Weissleder, sometimes travelled to Africa and bought animal skins which he suggested the Beatles wore on stage. So on one occasion John appeared on the Star-Club stage as a monkey. When the show ended, he walked outside, up and down the Grosse Freiheit and the Reeperbahn, in the same outfit. Then he and the others went into a club and Horst Fascher had a call from the police, saying the Beatles had gone into a club and 'scared people to death'. People had run away and not paid their bills, so the owner insisted the Beatles should pay the bills. 'They had no money, so I had to pay.'

One Saturday night, after the Beatles had been playing at the Star-Club until nearly dawn, thirty people attended a party at their flat in the Grosse Freiheit. The toilet facilities were inadequate, with just one lavatory shared among the flats, up five flights of stairs; John urinated over the edge of the balcony. 'We were all just normal human beings,' says Paul McCartney, confirming the event. 'I seem to remember John had a pee over the edge. But what happens is that all these stories grow into great legends.' McCartney says that the story that John urinated on nuns who were going to the St Joseph's Catholic Church, next door to the flats, was untrue. 'On a separate occasion, there were some nuns and we shouted at them, not crazily, but like "Oy oy, sister" and generally like young people do. The two stories got together, so we get this really outrageous story where John's peeing on nuns. It never really was like that. It all just grew into really crazy stories out of what most people would agree is boyish craziness.'

A drunken John did take the stage of the club with a toilet seat around his neck, but it was at the end of a show when most of the audience wanted a bit of a cabaret, and he went along with it. But during that trip in Hamburg John was certainly often wild. Says Gerry Marsden, who was playing at the Top Ten club and who saw the Beatles socially: 'Remember we were all kids who had basically never been anywhere apart from Liverpool. You're suddenly free of parents, friends, anybody who knows you, and getting paid decent money. So John did his own thing more freely because his Auntie wasn't there to say: "Stop it." Like all of us, John went a little bit mad.

'As for booze, yes, we all drank too much, including John. He started work around seven in the evening and played half a dozen sets or so, ending at around two in the morning. Rum and Coke was sixpence a big glass, and we couldn't afford that stuff in England. So by the early hours of the next morning, we'd all had quite a lot of bevvies. And you'll still be high because the adrenalin was pumping away from performing your heart out. So then you'd go out to eat, until four or five in the morning, maybe with the Horst Fascher family, and of course sleep in till about three o'clock next afternoon. Then it was down to the Seamen's Mission on the dockside for a fry-up breakfast. That was the pattern for all the groups in Hamburg. It was like a rehearsal every night, and John told me many times afterwards that it was an experience he could never have got anywhere else. If you can survive Hamburg, with all its audiences giving you hell, and the demands of the nights, you can survive even Beatlemania! It trained John to have the really hard voice that became famous as part of the Beatles. It wrecked everybody's vocal cords singing for such long periods, but when you keep on singing every night like that, and shouting back the first thing that comes into your head at the crowds, your voice's power increases. John used to enjoy the hurly burly of it all.'

Gerry saw Lennon in many punch-ups in Liverpool and Hamburg. 'But I'd not describe him as a hard lad. He'd lose his temper and hit people, but more often than not he'd get a smack right back in the mouth. In Liverpool, John was lucky that he had a strong reputation and the name of the Beatles behind him, otherwise he'd have got beaten up even more than he did. He behaved like a typical Scouse teddy boy, a ruffian, but he was no harder than lots of other people of those days. But when he hit, he got smashed back. You don't walk away often, on Merseyside, when you give a mouthful of abuse to someone. I saw him get many a pasting.'

The worst scene Gerry Marsden saw involving John happened in Hamburg. Playing cards in the flat above the Star-Club, John was drunk. There was an argument. 'John got up and hit the fellow over the head with a bottle. I thought: "That's really out of order." Within seconds the fellow had got up and knocked hell out of John, pasting him all over the flat. And all of us just stood there and let him do it, because we agreed that you just don't go round hitting people over the head with bottles and expect to get away with it. I saw John bashed about many times, but never so hard. He really took it that night. But he asked for it, and he said later it was fair because he shouldn't have done what he did. Put it like this: I'd never have employed John as a bodyguard. He wasn't that hard.'

Twenty years after the Beatles were in Hamburg, there were still people closely connected with that period who warmed to the memories. Rosa, for example: two decades later, at eighty-six years old, she was still the toilet attendant in the Top Ten club in the Reeperbahn, extolling, through a translator, her love of the boys whom she cooked, laundered, and made beds for, and provided with her husband's houseboat for accommodation. 'John's reputation as the wild one was true,' says Rosa. 'He was like the devil on that stage. I remember John as the ambitious one. He said that one day they would be very famous. "Mama," he would say, "*Mutti*! We go to America, be very big, very famous, make LOTS of money." '

She says that he often drank too much and would lie on the dance floor and cry. 'He was really angry sometimes, but the public thought it was a show. What he was angry about was the group sound, when it was not as he liked. Then he would drink as a kind of consolation. I heard them quarrelling a lot. I would worry about the amount John was going to drink when they argued.'

Hamburg, with its punishing physical demands on stage, the absurd time-keeping and irregular sleep and food, and the combativeness of the audience, was John's gruelling training ground. With the sadness evoked by the city's constant reminder of his best friend's death, it provided him with a steely exterior. As the years went on, that characteristic became confused with toughness. The curious fact is that the older he became, the less tough and abrasive and the more human John Lennon emerged.

He was given to odd streaks of sentimentality. In Hamburg that bleak spring, trying to console Astrid and Stuart's heartbroken mother, Millie Sutcliffe, John Lennon asked particularly for Stuart's long, woollen college scarf, striped in navy and pale blue and yellow and cream. It was to remain his most prized souvenir of their bond. It reminded John of their days together, huddled in Gambier Terrace and the alleyways of Liverpool 8.

10
MARRIAGE

'Don't worry, Cyn. We'll get married'

John's obsession with deformities and afflictions has been mentioned before. On one of his private drawings, which he gave to a student as a gift, John captioned a particularly gruesome-looking figure 'The Wife', almost as a commentary about what he feared the role of a woman in his life could be: overbearing and domineering, hideously ugly.

But the first serious woman in his life, who was inseparable from him when they met at college in 1957 and became his wife during Beatlemania as well as the mother of his first child, was the opposite of that fearsome drawing. Cynthia scarcely realized how John's macabre sense of the absurd would manifest itself into a tender moment in their lives, a year after their marriage. On 8 April 1963 their only son, John Charles Julian Lennon, was born at Sefton General Hospital, Liverpool.

It was not an easy birth. Cynthia says, 'I was something like three days in hospital before Julian arrived and then he had jaundice, the umbilical cord was around his neck, and he had a very large mole on his head. He had to be left alone for twenty-four hours; I couldn't touch him. I was petrified about all these things. But I was scared more than anything about the birth mark, the mole. Knowing John's horror of deformities, I was absolutely panic-stricken about what John's reaction would be.' When Julian was born, John and the Beatles were busy

158

criss-crossing Britain on a hectic schedule of ballroom appearances to consolidate their new fame. John phoned the hospital, excitedly enquiring about his wife and baby, and was triumphant at the news that it was a boy.

After three days Cynthia welcomed John to the hospital—and made sure that the baby's head was resting against a pillow so that the prominent mole could not be seen by the sensitive, eagle-eyed father. 'When John came in, I decided not to hide it. I said: "Oh he's beautiful, wonderful, John, but he has this birth mark on his head."

'John replied: "Oh, it doesn't matter. His hair will grow over that."

'I was still bothered because I wanted the perfect child for John, but he couldn't have cared less. He was just thrilled, the typical father.'

In the weeks that followed, Cynthia carefully covered the baby's head with a hat at every possible moment—so that John would not have his attention drawn to the mole. The prospect of a baby Lennon that was anything less than physically perfect haunted her.

Julian Lennon was conceived at Cynthia's £3-a-week bedsitter at 93 Garmoyle Road, off Smithdown Road, a stone's throw from Penny Lane. It was also very close to Sefton General Hospital, where Julian was born. They had never taken birth control precautions, from their first experience together in Stuart's flat.

'There was no planning. There was no pill in those days. We considered nothing except ourselves and didn't consider the consequences. As far as I was concerned, ignorance was bliss. Neither John nor I gave pregnancy a thought. My parents didn't advise me and I didn't ask them, and I'm sure John wouldn't dream of asking Mimi. We weren't thinking about anything like prevention, just enjoying each other naturally as two kids.

'But when the reality dawned first on me, I was full of absolute shock. "My God, what am I going to tell my Mum?"

'And he had the same reaction: "What am I going to tell Mimi?"

'It was guilt. Even though we didn't have the pill, we did

have respect for our elders. Aged twenty in 1962 was rather like being aged sixteen by today's standards,' Cynthia observes. 'We were both kids basically.'

But John's reaction, on being told, was that if a girl became pregnant, the man must 'do the right thing' and marry her.

'I don't think we'd have been married if I hadn't become pregnant,' she says. 'He wasn't the sort at the age of twenty-one to say: "Will you marry me?" It was all so immediate we hardly realized the seriousness of it all: making love, getting pregnant, getting married.

'If we had carried on seeing each other without a child arriving, I had it in mind to obtain my qualification as an art teacher. That would have enabled me to support John whatever happened, because his life at that time was music and I couldn't see his future in it. He was messing around at college and within music and I thought: "Well, I love him. Whatever happens, if he can't make money, I'll be there and I'll have my art teacher's diploma and I'll be able to teach." That was at the back of my mind.'

But her attention to her studies suffered when she got involved with John. Cynthia failed her art teacher's diploma exam. And John went on to do rather well with his music.

'One thing's for sure,' says Cynthia. 'I didn't marry John for his money. He didn't have any, I didn't appreciate it, and it's never done me any good. I had more money than he did in the early days of our love affair and I was funding him every day at college. So if money was important to me I'd have chosen a rich boyfriend.'

John's attitude to being a father was similar to his approach to everything else, from the launching of the Beatles to pursuing art, to getting married and divorced, and buying houses. The same principle applied throughout his life: first decide, then do it, then move on to the next situation—a new challenge. Although whatever he became involved in was done wholeheartedly, the restless spirit inside him was always powerful. Lennon had many varied and brilliant assets within his character, but stability was never among them.

'I don't think he was ready for a child any more than I was,' says Cynthia. 'He wasn't ready to settle down.' When they married he was twenty-one and she was twenty-two.

'Whatever happened with John was always a compromise. He had to get everything over with quickly. He was committed to it while it had to be done, but he'd want to be moving on to the next thing fast.'

Cynthia's cramped flat in Garmoyle Road was not far from Woolworth's in Penny Lane where she worked as a counter assistant during summer vacations from college. When Cynthia's father died—uncannily about the same time that John was hit by the death of his mother—her mother went to Canada to act as nanny to Cynthia's cousin. The family house at Hoylake was rented out, and Cynthia fancied a flat of her own.

In August 1962 John was visiting Cynthia at her flat when he found her particularly quiet.

'Is everything OK?' he asked.

Cynthia was in the kitchen, washing up. 'No, it's not OK.'

'What's the matter?'

'I'm pregnant, that's what's the matter.'

'Oh Christ, what are we going to do?' said John, moving over to put his arm around her. Panic seized him, then a quick flash of practicality: 'Look, I'll go and tell Mimi. Don't worry, Cyn. We'll get married.'

John's instinctive decision to 'do the right thing' and marry a girl who was pregnant in 1962 was very much a reflection of the times. They had been having an affair, but nobody knew and the first time John's Aunt Mimi knew that they had slept together was when he went home that night and said, 'Cyn's pregnant.'

Mimi erupted. 'John told me there had been the most tremendous scene, one of the worst things he'd ever had to go through,' Cynthia says. 'Mimi threw everything at him—"You stupid children, getting yourselves into this situation! The whole family will have nothing to do with you. You've got yourself into this mess, now get yourselves out of it." '

Lennon certainly did not *want* marriage at this stage. He told several people close to him that he had to get married to protect Cynthia and the child, and Cynthia will always doubt that he would ever have married her if she had not become pregnant. But Cynthia's closest friend throughout and after college years, Phyllis McKenzie, disagrees. 'They were totally opposite but right for each other and, although they came from different backgrounds, they were a perfect match,' she says. 'I think they would obviously have taken longer to get married, but it *would* have happened. They loved each other very much. There was no separating them.'

Once the decision was made, John panicked about the ceremony. 'Christ,' he said to Brian Epstein. 'What am I going to do? How can I fix it all up and get on with it quickly?'

If ever John needed evidence that he had the right manager, this was that moment. The smooth, organized skill of Epstein rose to the occasion. 'Don't worry, John. I'll fix it.'

An early sign of her acceptance of the situation came when Aunt Mimi gave John the money to buy the wedding ring. He went with Cynthia to a jeweller just a few doors from Epstein's NEMS store in Whitechapel. She chose a simple £10 gold wedding ring and there was no sentimentality attached to buying it.

For all his bravery when he was with Cynthia, John broke down with his Aunt Mimi the night before his wedding. 'I don't want to get married,' he said, wandering restlessly around Mendips. He was choking back the tears at the seriousness of the situation.

'I told you before, John. You're too young. But what's done's done.' She regarded Cynthia as not bright enough for her brilliant nephew. 'Now, John, I've said it. Once the ring's on the finger, I shall hold my peace.' She pointedly refused to attend the wedding.

Brian Epstein arranged a special licence for the marriage at Mount Pleasant Register Office. He arranged for a car to collect Cynthia from her flat, where, shaking with nerves, she had dressed in a well-worn purple and black check two-piece suit. John was dressed formally, almost funereally, in black suit and tie, with a white shirt, and his friends Paul McCartney and George Harrison were dressed exactly the same. The other guests were Cynthia's brother Tony and his wife, Margery, who shared the honour of signing their names as witnesses on the marriage certificate with 'James Paul McCartney'.

The mood at the wedding was one of controlled panic. In the register office waiting-room John fidgeted nervously with his tie and his hair. During the three-minute ceremony a pneumatic drill outside started up bang on cue, just as the Registrar began his short speech. The noise virtually drowned the event: that broke the ice.

Giggling nervously, they walked out into torrential rain, down the hill past Liverpool's grand old Adelphi Hotel. At Brian's suggestion, the wedding celebration was a lunch in the unlicensed Reece's restaurant. John did not realize that the same register office and Reece's had been his parents' wedding day rendezvous. It was just noon, and the Beatles party had to queue for a table before sitting down to the set lunch of soup, chicken and trifle. They toasted the bride and groom with glasses of water. The bill came to fifteen shillings a head and Epstein paid.

'It was hysterical. We were like nervous children going to the dentist, from start to finish. We were laughing uncontrollably at anything in sight,' says Cynthia. 'People's hats, the women who go into Reece's—we were laughing all the time at anything to make sure we didn't take it seriously. I was the only one thinking about the future, I think, because I knew what I was in for.'

At Reece's Epstein told John and Cynthia of his special gift to them—free, unlimited use of his flat at 36 Falkner Street, a street almost opposite the art college. Cynthia believes that the shrewd Epstein did not relish the thought of the leader of the Beatles living in her spartan bed-sitter in Garmoyle Road —'it might have been bad for the image.' Brian's flat was, anyway, comparatively luxurious and in what was at that time a fashionable area of the city. They even had use of a small, walled garden.

On the wedding night, John and the Beatles had a show at Chester. The new Mrs Lennon, relieved that one of the most testing days of her life was over, moved her meagre possessions from Garmoyle Road to Brian's flat, and relaxed. For John, though, the speed of events in his musical career was a perfect diversion from what had just happened. Brian Epstein's industrious efforts to obtain a recording contract had achieved success three months before John's wedding. Twelve days after his marriage to Cynthia, John was excitedly in London recording the McCartney song that was to start the most astonishing, influential event in entertainment, and rocket John and the Beatles into a prominence previously known only to film stars and statesmen.

On the van journey to London for that recording session they would all wait for the signal from John to recite the short poem which he had concocted. It was a little rhyme that in a year became even truer than he ever dared hope:

> *John:*   Where are we going fellas?
> *Chorus:*   To the top, Johnny to the TOP!
> *John:*   And where *is* the top, fellas?
> *Chorus:*   To the toppermost of the poppermost!

With the Beatles' career moving ahead decisively, Epstein was adding to John Lennon's arrogance a remarkable new factor: confidence that he had a spectacular future. Repeatedly, Eppy told anyone who would listen that 'the boys' would one day be bigger than Elvis Presley. Events proved Epstein absolutely accurate, but at that time most people were convulsed with laughter at Brian's promise that Liverpool lads could achieve anything like Presley status. Elvis was an untouchable god. Moreover he was American, and America always led in pop. British artists were consigned to plagiarism at best, weedy pap like Cliff Richard or Frankie Vaughan at worst. Four Liverpool scruffs to dominate the world? Forget it, Brian!

But the Beatles thrust happened so quickly under Brian's devotion and the prescience of George Martin that it needed John's total attention. Their roots at St Peter's church fete, Woolton, may have been a dim, distant memory, but John and Paul were able to draw on a formidable reserve of experience—particularly of live shows, and tough audiences in ballrooms and clubs—by the time they were pitchforked by Epstein into the big time. Lennon, more than the other three, loved the hoop which Brian was putting them through. When George Martin told Epstein that Pete Best needed replacing as Beatles' drummer before he would offer a record contract, John's reaction to an anguished Brian at Mendips one night was immediate: 'OK, but you tell Pete he's out and I'll get Ringo in.' John and Paul had always admired Ringo Starr's work with another local band, Rory Storm and the Hurricanes.

Next night, John phoned Ringo, who was playing at Butlin's holiday camp in Skegness. 'You're in, Ringo—the sidies will have to go, though.' John's remark recognized that Ringo's cheek-length sideburns would clash with Epstein's master plan to tidy the Beatles up.

Mentally high on the Hamburg experiences, and having a faster instinct than any of the other Beatles, John knew that once they had recorded a song and marshalled their image and their fans properly, they would be unstoppable. From childhood he had never lacked confidence in his ability; the only difference was that now it was not a wayward, artistic talent. It had direction. It was blazing enthusiasm for music to the exclusion of everything else. When John got hold of something— anything—he became blinkered to the world beyond it.

The qualities John admired in Paul McCartney were exactly those that John lacked: Paul was artistic, creative, and a wonderful foil to offset John. But he had a valuable extra ingredient: determination to see a job through. He insisted on every detail being completed. His appearance reflected the inner man; he looked casual, but he was always pin-clean, like his tidy mind.

When John talked to Cynthia about Paul, it was in terms of incredulity at Paul's self-discipline. John, who had stalked his way through grammar school and college, and lurched into a rock band, was thrilled at the prospect of moving ahead in music with McCartney's methodical touches at his elbow. He would not have said so at the time.

There was another quality in the immensely heterosexual Lennon that he admired in Paul: an ability to attract a woman, and have a fling with her, and then move on very quickly. John did not master that art until later, in his mid-twenties. Adventurousness, and the appetite for moving on, applied to John in everything except his associations with women. It could not have been related to the death of his mother, for long before she died he was having an affair with a girl in Woolton named Barbara whom he had dated for two years before her parents warned her to drop him. The length of that affair, and his intense relationship with Cynthia, demonstrated that he never did things by halves.

Now, as a married twenty-two-year-old, John was pulled in two directions. His wife and baby were in Epstein's flat just as the Beatles caravan began to look as if it would roll. After the row with Aunt Mimi about Cynthia's pregnancy, and her boycott of the wedding, John now felt he had to crack on with music to the exclusion of everything else.

In what must rank as one of the world's most bizarre honeymoons, John—after going to Chester on their wedding night —continued to travel, first to London, then to Manchester and other cities as the Beatles' success gained momentum in the north-west. After the Beatles' first entry into the hit parade, preparations for their first proper concert tour around Britain, with Helen Shapiro, took John away from Cynthia at the very time that they should have been consolidating their relationship.

'We were both sort of bowled over by the fact that we were married,' says Cynthia. 'It wasn't a question of "What's happened to us, have we done the right thing?" It was all perfectly natural that we should be together. But John didn't get a chance to be first a real husband or later a real father. He was too busy, and put himself under a lot of pressure to make sure that, once the Beatles ball was rolling, he kept pushing it.'

After three months of pregnancy, Cynthia had a threatened miscarriage. 'I was alone, John was away, and I started panicking.' Her brother, Tony, rushed over to be with her, but the doctor's orders were straightforward: stay in bed for three days. John phoned her at the flat, but she didn't tell him, in case he should be diverted from what she knew was vital to him at this time: success with the Beatles.

'When John came home I told him about it, and said I was particularly frightened while I was pregnant, because if I had lost Julian there was nobody there to help me at all. I suddenly said, "Why don't we go and see Mimi, ask her advice." ' He had often said to her, 'I wonder how Mimi and Mendips is.' He was nervous about seeing her after the terrible scenes that took place before the wedding. He hadn't seen her for three months—the first time in his life they had been separated since childhood.

Cynthia said, 'Come on John, she's your Auntie, I'm sure she'll be OK now.'

He said, 'Are you sure?'

Cynthia reflects now: 'I knew in my heart of hearts that she was missing John like mad, that she was upset about the whole business, and wanted peace. Knowing Mimi and John, I also knew it was always a quickfire temper, soon over with. She was obviously going to be missing her "son" and John was, I think, missing her.' He felt isolated from his family.

On a sunny day they got the bus, and with some trepidation walked down the drive at Mendips. John knocked at the door, Mimi opened it with outstretched arms, and the three of them went in for a warmer welcome than John and Cynthia had dared hope for. Mimi made eggs and chips and tea and asked the now visibly pregnant Cynthia how she was feeling. Cynthia told her of the threatened miscarriage.

'I'm very worried about you,' said Mimi. 'You can't stay in that flat on your own. Come and live with me. I'll move upstairs and you and John can live downstairs. It will be cheaper, and better for you because you need someone with you while you're pregnant.' The garden outside would soon be essential for the pram, Mimi added.

The move to Mimi's house was speedy and practical, but disastrous for Cynthia. Cynthia felt that Mimi resented the intrusion on her home, despite her earlier invitation. There was another torment for Cynthia: at a meeting before she became pregnant, at Cynthia's home in Hoylake, Mimi and Cynthia's mother had clashed. Their temperaments were totally opposite: Mimi was artistic, bookish, and utterly possessive of John whom she regarded as very special; Lilian Powell was the archetypal protector of her daughter's virtues. At the frosty encounter, which had been suggested by John and Cynthia, the two women sought refuge in picking faults in John and Cynthia. John and Cynthia left the room in red-faced embarrassment as the two women carried on grumbling about them and poured scorn on their relationship. Eventually John took Mimi home, silently, on the bus; but he was never to forgive his future mother-in-law for hosting such a destructive meeting.

'John and I were very upset. We were both in love with each other,' says Cynthia, 'and for the two dearest people in our lives to stand in front of us saying what terrible people we were, and how they hated us for getting together, was awful. I think they did it because they didn't get on and they didn't want us to get on either. But the experience was horrible.'

As soon as Cynthia moved into Mendips John was off on

the road again. Cynthia now felt terribly exposed: she felt uneasy because Mimi was ill with bronchitis and Cynthia's arrival had meant she had to move upstairs; and to increase her tension, John had told her that Brian Epstein insisted she keep her pregnancy secret because a married Beatle would be bad for the group's image.

In those years, pop stars were expected to be 'available' in the eyes of girl fans. A chief Beatle with a wife, heaven forbid a pregnant one, might have turned away the teenage girls who were now rallying round the Beatles as they travelled the country. At stage doors, in dressing-rooms, and as their van drove them away to their digs or cheap hotel for the night, sixties girls with beehive hairstyles, hopelessly high heels, and heavy mascara would queue in wait for a glimpse of their favourite Beatle. A chatting-up would be even better, and if it led to a night together—great. Paul McCartney's handsome, brown-eyed stare made him the early favourite among the girls, but John's tough guy stance and leer, plus his raw aggression on stage, made him a very close second. Cynthia was to be kept firmly and privately at home.

Epstein's rule suited Lennon perfectly. It tied in with his maxim that, whatever the job in hand, it must be concentrated upon one hundred per cent. The job was the Beatles, and the pace of events was speeding up.

During Cynthia's pregnancy John travelled all over England as the Beatles set about consolidating their record success with 'Love Me Do'. On tour with Helen Shapiro, he phoned Cynthia at Mendips regularly. He sounded tremendously excited that things were taking off for them, and relieved that she had had no recurrences of the threatened miscarriage. 'His music was coming together well, the crowds were gathering for them, and it was a terribly exciting time,' says Cynthia.

The pressure on her was considerable. Mimi took in students who knew that John Lennon of the Beatles was her nephew; the same students, or their friends, had lodged with her year after year. Mimi took pride now in the fact that the Beatles were having a little success, but Cynthia had to play out a charade. 'I said to these students, and people nearby, that I was John's girlfriend, but I was also a student and that's the reason I gave them for wearing smocks. "I'm an artist and I do some work here at home," I'd say. What they didn't realize, I hope, was that the smocks were getting bigger and bigger to hide the baby.'

John, on the phone, was sounding excited at the prospect of being a father. He never minded whether it was a boy or a girl as long as it was healthy. Mimi, however, repeatedly told Cynthia: 'It's got to be a boy, just like John.'

The choice of names came quickly and easily: John after the father, Julian because it was close to John's mother's name, and Charles in memory of Cynthia's father. One thing worried John in the maternity ward when he and Cynthia discussed it: 'Hey,' he said, 'someone said Julian sounds a bit poofy.' But they laughed it away and decided that the closeness to his mother was what really mattered.

Three factors had always made Cynthia's relationship with Mimi difficult and tense. Mimi was constantly worried that John's poor school results would mean that he would end up unemployed; she felt incredibly possessive about her surrogate son; and her dislike of Cynthia's mother was reflected in her attitude towards Cynthia.

'When John first took me home,' says Cynthia, 'I suppose Mimi looked on it as a childhood romance, nothing serious. We were about eighteen and no aunt would expect her nephew to be seriously involved at that age. The more it drifted on for months, the greater I could see Mimi worrying and looking concerned. It wasn't anything she said, just her general attitude towards me at that stage, after a few months of John and me together and me visiting Mendips. I don't think she went overboard.'

Mimi's full wrath had come one afternoon. For the very first time John had earned some money from some of their Cavern dates, and other work, in 1961. He proudly asked Cynthia what she would like as a celebration present. She asked for a brown suede coat. John went with her to C & A's store and spent £17 on the three-quarter-length coat. 'It wasn't very high quality, it was rough suede, but for me at the time it was the most wonderful gift,' says Cynthia.

They went straight from Liverpool city centre to show it

off to Mimi. Cynthia said they shouldn't go empty-handed, so they took her a cooked chicken for their tea. Neither John nor Cynthia could believe the fury that greeted them.

'Do you like Cyn's new coat?' John said as they entered the hall.

Mimi flew into an immediate rage. How could John go buying things like that when he didn't have a proper job? 'But we've brought you a cooked chicken, Mimi.'

'Take your chicken and your gangster's moll and get out,' Mimi roared. 'You get a bit of money in your pocket and go and blow it on *her*.' Finally Mimi sat down in tears and Cynthia tried to calm her down.

'I'm sorry if you're upset, but we'll be all right,' said Cynthia. 'Take it easy, Mimi.'

'Go away. Don't talk to me,' sobbed Mimi, inconsolable.

And that's just what John and Cynthia did. When John returned later, after taking Cynthia home to Garmoyle Road, Mimi was silent. John crept up to bed and the next morning the row had been forgotten.

But it had been a sharp example to John and Cynthia of Mimi's touchiness. John knew she was not a woman to cross lightly. Now he had proof. 'All over a bloody coat,' he mused to Cyn.

Mimi's fury at John's display of largesse was, of course, justified by the facts. With no O-levels at school, and now apparently having left art college, on to which she had pinned all her hopes, John was drifting into full-time pop music. That future was not secure enough for Mimi. The Beatles' success was a mere pipe dream to her.

One day she called his bluff and put the fear of God inside him. 'I said: "All right, so you don't want college and you don't want any more education. But what are you earning? Five shillings, which you're spending on your way out of that Cavern. You're just not earning enough at this music game, John, so I've found a proper job for you." '

'What are you talking about?' John said, shaken.

'It's no good, John,' Mimi went on. 'I can't go on like this. The worry's too much. I've got a job for you on the buses—as a conductor. They can't get staff anywhere. I've signed you on.'

'Me, me!!! I'm not a *working man*. If you think I'm going to go out at nine o'clock in the morning and come home at five, well I won't.'

Mimi retorted: 'What do you think you've been studying for if it isn't to be a working man? Think about it, John. It's either that or brushing the snow. I've had it with you.'

John's face went scarlet and he ran up to his room. Here was his privacy. Mimi was never allowed there. A picture of Brigitte Bardot was stuck to the ceiling above his bed.

Half an hour elapsed before John slowly walked downstairs. He said nothing but sidled up behind Mimi who was sitting in his favourite armchair. 'Make up your mind, John,' she said. But she could not keep it up any longer and her face cracked into a smile. 'I wasn't serious, but I was just trying to stir him up and worry him into work,' says Mimi now.

The scene ended when John said, 'I knew you were joking, Mimi.'

'Oh, no, I'm not, John.'

'Yes you are. I can't add two and two together—how can I be a bus conductor?'

11
FAME

'I battered his bloody ribs in'

Satire and comedy that leaned towards innuendo, rather than knockabout humour of the custard pie variety, had always attracted John. He grew up listening carefully, and tittering under his breath, to two radio programmes, *Up the Pole*, starring Jimmy Jewel and Ben Warris, a double act who lampooned each other, and, more significantly, *The Goon Show*. Spike Milligan and Harry Secombe's voices were clever, but John particularly loved the droll Peter Sellers, whose dry satire was captured on one of Lennon's favourite records of the period, *The Best of Sellers*. Another favourite was Stanley Unwin, who specialized in converting the English language into gibberish. He was a major influence on John's word-play in his own two books.

John's saltiness gave the Beatles their edge, on and off stage, in the recording studio and when they were travelling. It was a characteristic felt early on in the desperate attempt by Brian Epstein to secure them a recording contract.

Returning one night from London to Lime Street Station, Epstein had grim news for the Beatles: he was not getting any interest from the record companies. Their future was in jeopardy, although his hopes and determination were undimmed. He called Paul McCartney and asked the Beatles to meet him in Joe's Café in Duke Street, a haunt of night workers, lorry drivers and anyone else needing a cup of tea until 4 a.m.

'I'm afraid it's no use, I've had a flat "No",' Epstein began. Decca had turned them down, in what was to become one of the legendary rejections in the history of music. Pye had also said no.

John broke the spell and the gloom. As they all sat drinking tea and smoking, he flicked a teaspoon high into the air and said, 'Right. Try Embassy.' Embassy was then something of a joke record label, run by Woolworth's and featuring pale copies of the hits of the day.

John's remark was worthy of *The Goon Show*. He did not realize then that the Beatles' eventual recording contract was to be secured by Brian with the man who had been the Goons' recording manager, and who had been with them in the studios during the recording of phrases immortal to John's ears, such as 'Ying Tong'. It was a neat irony.

George Martin, trained as a classical pianist at the Guildhall School of Music, also played the oboe, and was artists and recording manager in charge of the Parlophone label at E.M.I. Although he got on immediately with Brian Epstein, whose refined accent he shared, the odds were that four young rock 'n' rollers from Liverpool would be at odds with his attitudes and his musical preferences. He was steeped in light orchestral music, but had a penchant for comedy. Lennon relished the prospect of making records with a man who had rubbed shoulders with such wonderful mimics.

It was during that fateful visit to Hamburg, with news of the death of Stuart so fresh in their minds, that Epstein's telegram arrived: 'E.M.I. CONTRACT SIGNED, SEALED. TREMENDOUS IMPORTANCE TO US ALL. WONDERFUL.' They returned their delight in crisp messages on postcards. Paul wrote: 'Please wire £10,000 advance royalties.' George wrote: 'Please order four new guitars.' John wrote: 'When are we going to be millionaires?'

Their recording career took off like lightning, with 'Love Me Do' as their début hit, helped by John's catchy harmonica playing. When they moved to London, and met the Rolling Stones, John was teased about that solo by the late Brian Jones, who played the harmonica on the Stones' first records.

On a visit to the Crawdaddy Club in Richmond, John was

asked by Brian during the Stones' set: 'Are you playing harmonica or a blues harp on "Love Me Do"?'

Lennon replied: 'A harmonica, y'know, with a button.'

John recalled later that Brian wondered how he got such a deep bottom note during the record. John told Brian that it was 'impossible to get "Hey Baby" licks from a blues harp'. A top favourite of the Beatles at the time was Bruce Channel's harmonica-based hit, 'Hey Baby'. John did his utmost to copy that style when he played the harmonica.

One of John's most adamant statements, during the years I knew him, was that there was nothing original in rock 'n' roll, or in what he and the Beatles were doing. 'It's all rip-off,' he would say repeatedly. Reading the music papers, particularly the outlandish and pompous claims of some musicians, John would blurt out: 'This is a load of crap' when singers or musicians claimed originality. Rock 'n' roll to him was totally derivative. Elvis Presley, Buddy Holly, and the newer sounds of the Miracles and Tamla Motown were the *real* music, he kept saying. 'We're the receivers, we're just interpreting it as English kids. Don't let anybody ever kid you it's original. It's all a RIP OFF!' Depending on the quantity of alcohol he'd consumed, the five words would be either emphasized or screamed.

The momentum of the Beatles that began in that autumn of 1962 with 'Love Me Do' gathered with a speed that is often forgotten. Brian Epstein summed up the astounding pace of events after George Martin's offer of a recording session. 'Two years later', wrote Epstein, 'the Beatles were the greatest entertainers in the world; they had met the Queen Mother and the Duke of Edinburgh and their pictures were on the walls of the noble bedrooms of the young aristocracy. Prince Charles had all their records and San Francisco had the ticker-tape ready. They played the Hollywood Bowl, had the freedom of Liverpool. Ringo Starr was asked to be President of London University and John Lennon was the world's bestselling writer.'

In a single turbulent year for John, the Beatles had acquired an active and ambitious manager; they had an audition in the big city, London, resulting in a record contract with E.M.I.;

his best friend had died in Hamburg; Pete Best had been fired
as drummer, to be replaced by Ringo Starr; his girlfriend had
broken the news that she was pregnant and they had hurriedly
married; and the Beatles had made their television début before
going to Hamburg for their fifth and final club trip.

Against that year's background, the Beatles began 1963 in a
remarkable frenzy. They were booked for their first major British concert tour by package tour promoter Arthur Howes, who
specialized in putting artists of the calibre of Cliff Richard and
the Shadows around the cinema halls of Britain. John was
particularly elated, particularly as the tour coincided with the
release of 'Please Please Me', their second single which shot
to number one in the bestselling record charts. Top-of-the-bill
singer on their tour was the most popular girl singer in Britain
that year—Helen Shapiro, aged sixteen. A teenage prodigy,
Helen had burst on the pop scene two years earlier as a schoolgirl, with her E.M.I. records 'Don't Treat Me Like A Child',
'You Don't Know' and 'Walkin' Back To Happiness'. Because
of her youth, she became a national phenomenon.

   Helen Shapiro was beside herself with excitement that the
Beatles would be touring with her and that she would top the
bill, because she had a colossal crush on John Lennon. On the
coach that carried her with the Beatles across a Britain gripped
by arctic weather conditions, on that one-night stand tour, she
contrived to sit next to him and hoped he would not guess that
her blushing hid a teenage fancy for the Beatle who was six
years older than she was.

   'I had a special feeling for John,' says Helen. 'He probably
realized I had a crush on him. He called me "Helly" and was
incredibly protective. I was mad on him, really mad. I had the
biggest crush on him any sixteen-year-old could have on a guy.

   'On the coach once between cities, I picked up a copy of
the *Melody Maker* and opened it up to a headline: "Is Helen
a has-been at sixteen?" John was sitting right behind me then,
reading over my shoulder. I was really upset, but it was he
who comforted me. "Don't let the swines get you down," he
said to me.'

   Helen had met the Beatles on stage where they were setting

up their equipment. John told her that he and Paul had written a song for her, called 'Misery', but it had been rejected by her management.

In a Sheffield hotel room, Helen sat with John watching the Beatles on television. 'He was fascinated but rather put off by the way he looked, because he used to have this stance with the guitar across his chest and the legs rather bowed, going up and down. He was quite horrified. But he was excited at seeing himself on the screen. Then Gerry and the Pacemakers came on and John said: "Hey, this is our mate." We were leaning out of hotel windows, throwing photographs of ourselves at fans, and it was an incredible period, looking back.'

The protectiveness of John towards 'Helly' contrasted sharply with the 'hard man' image which built up even in the early days of the Beatles. She saw, so early in his successful career, the tender, caring side of the man. 'He would always look after me. I looked up to him not in a fatherlike way, but as a teenage girl with a wild crush. He never took advantage of me. He was always such a soft, warm, attentive fellow.

'He'd make sure I ate properly when we were travelling. He'd put his arm round me and make sure I crossed the road properly. Of all the Beatles he was by far the most polite.' At the Abbey Road recording studios the Beatles were occupying studio two, which Helen normally used, and she had to make do with studio three. 'It was John who came in with a cup of tea and kind of apologized because he'd heard I had been moved to make way for them,' says Helen. 'He came in with a cup of tea for me and a big hug.'

At Great Yarmouth in 1963, however, Helen was doing a summer season and the Beatles came in to do a Sunday concert. 'Then I realized how big they were. Everybody was all over them and I could hardly reach John. There were girls everywhere. I was incredibly jealous, for no reason, in my sweet innocence. I remember thinking: "Oh, they go with *girls*! And they drink *Scotch* and Coke." '

On the band coach, Lennon would both embarrass and amuse Helen and the rest of the cast: singers Kenny Lynch, Danny Williams, the Kestrels (featuring Roger Greenaway, later to become a major British songwriter and chairman of the Performing Right Society), and compère Dave Allen. There were jam sessions, John with guitar breaking into Beach Boys' and Shirelles' songs, and Helen joining in. A strong favourite of John's was Little Eva's hit, 'Keep Your Hands Off My Baby'. Then, suddenly, Lennon would take on the role of the court jester. He would launch into his manic impersonation of cripples and spastics. He'd pull faces out of the window. Passers-by in busy High Streets would look on aghast at the absurd facial contortions of the leather-jacketed man with uncommonly long hair. 'He was very sick,' says Helen Shapiro. 'Especially if he saw a couple of nuns walking by. He'd pull the crudest faces at them.' One night in Sunderland, the practical joker in John petrified Helen when she awoke in her bedroom in the middle of the night, in virtual darkness, to see him standing there with a hat and a raincoat on.

For a cynic Lennon was acutely aware of his responsibility to fans. Autograph signing was a chore he undertook, if not enthusiastically, then fairly conscientiously. (Tragically, John's openness with fans who cared and waited was to be one reason for his ultimate murder in New York in December 1980. His assassin had lain in wait for him after getting his autograph earlier in the day and waited for him to return home to the Dakota Building the same night.) In 1963, before demands for autographs and Beatles' photographs had become so big that their road managers would forge their signatures, John was as diligent a signatory as any Beatle. 'He was portrayed, partly by himself, as the hard man of the group. But I recall him as a softie,' says Helen Shapiro. 'He certainly did care about the fans, in hotel foyers and stage doors. More than the other three, I think he valued the fans.'

Her memories of the man she fell for crystallize into quick images. 'I loved his very raw, bluesy voice, and told him so. He was surprised. He said I obviously didn't realize that it was him singing the high falsetto voice on "From Me To You". He said: "I can do the high stuff better than Paul." I do remember that.'

He moaned to Helen about his rotten teeth after seeing a picture of himself smiling. He told her to sing more songs by his favourite, Mary Wells, then Tamla Motown's undiscovered star, whom the Beatles eventually brought to their British tour when she had a huge hit with 'My Guy'. He used to mock

Helen at the Ad Lib club in London's Soho, every time she went to the toilet. 'Ha, Helly, been for a secret ciggie, have we?' Helen used to smoke secretly at that time, as she was below the smoking age. 'Helly's a secret smoker,' he'd shout.

Although Beatlemania had not gripped Britain like the fever it became by autumn of that year, there were early signs as the Helen Shapiro package tour criss-crossed the country's cinemas. Despite Helen's popularity, John, Paul, George and Ringo were getting more cheers. The promoter, Arthur Howes, had to keep changing the concert running order around so the Beatles would get more than their allotted twenty minutes. Nobody wanted to go on just before the Beatles. It was a 'dead spot', with the girls in the audience getting too excited about the next act. Most of the bill resented the attention being focused on four relatively unknown lads from Liverpool. 'One day,' recalls singer Kenny Lynch, 'Arthur Howes came to me and said, "Look, you'd better go on just before the Beatles. You're the only one who doesn't care how badly you go down." ' Lynch became the man who introduced the Beatles every night. 'I'd only got to mention "the lads" and a cheer went up. I'd say: "I'm not bringing *them* on until you're quiet." There was bedlam. I knew it was a bloodless revolution the music business was experiencing. I'd say: "Ladies and gentlemen, *the lads*," and the kids would rush the stage. For a virtually unknown group, it was incredible. The game was up.'

Kenny, a warm-hearted, tough East End Londoner, struck up a strong friendship with Lennon. Both shared an abrasiveness, a dislike for humbug and convention. Lynch's first meeting with the Beatles had been at Liverpool Empire, before that tour, when Brian Epstein had presented them in concert. 'I'd been asked by Brian who I'd like backing me and I said: "Who's on the bill with me?"

'He said he had his own group, the Beatles.

'I said, "Oh, they'll do, then, but I've brought my own group."

'When I arrived, the Beatles said, "Do you want us to back you?"

'I said, "No thanks, I have my own musicians who always back me."

'They said, "Well, we'd like to back you."'

'I couldn't let my people down, but John never let me forget the moment later on. He reckoned that I was one of the first guys to turn the Beatles down.'

A clear view of John's ambition during that first tour comes from Kenny Lynch's memory of a conversation, across a grand piano on the stage of the A.B.C. cinema, Carlisle.

'I said to John: "Well, what do you expect to get out of this game then?"'

'He replied quickly: "All we want to do is earn a million quid each and then piss off." '

Lynch guffawed. 'Listen, you've got some chance! I've been at it for years and I haven't got two halfpennies to rub together.'

In those days, before the British motorway system expanded, the coach journeys took longer. The pop package tours forced creative people together for four or five hours at a stretch. Apart from sleeping and jam sessions, songwriting was often done on the coach, and stage acts were debated.

'I remember John and Paul saying they were thinking of running up to the microphone together and shaking their heads and singing, "Whoooooooooooo". It later became a very important, terrifically popular part of their act when they sang "She Loves You". But at the time they were planning it, even before the song was written, I remember everybody on the coach fell about laughing. I said, "You can't do that. They'll think you're a bunch of poofs." I remember John saying to me he thought it sounded great and they were having it in their act.'

But Lennon was less pleased when Kenny Lynch played him his version of the song 'Misery', which was mostly John's own composition. The song had been intended for Helen Shapiro, but Kenny remembers her saying she disliked it because it sounded dreary. 'I'll have it,' said the eager Lynch.

But when he played his record to John and Paul, in the offices of their music publisher Dick James off Charing Cross Road, Lennon said, 'Your singing's OK, but who's that playing the telephone?'

It was John's way of blasting the guitarist.

Lynch replied: 'Don't blame me, I don't pick the musicians. Anyway, he's OK. It's Bert Weedon.'

Weedon, a solidly established player from the old school, played with great technical efficiency but little individuality. He epitomized the stylistic barrier between the Beatles' new vibrancy and the Old Guard of British musicianship. 'I said I thought Bert was OK, and that made things worse,' says Kenny Lynch. 'Lennon didn't stop bollocking me for days and weeks about Bert Weedon being on the first recording by somebody else of his song. "Bert WEEDON—he's fookin' LAST!" John kept saying.' The word became popular among the Beatles in denigrating what they mocked or regarded as unhip.

As the Beatles' popularity increased, and they made their first album in one eleven-hour recording session, John and Paul emerged as incredibly prolific songwriters, and John's aspirations to improve his writing became more and more evident. On the road, he would always be writing down phrases that occurred on the coach, in conversation. 'There was no booze and certainly no drugs on the road,' says Kenny Lynch. 'It was transport cafés, eggs and chips, Cokes and milk. John always smoked a lot but, whatever they'd done in Hamburg, they were getting the kicks from just performing and making such a quick impact on audiences all over England. They didn't need any false effects from drugs.'

Slowly, the contrasting personalities of Lennon and McCartney were becoming obvious. Although the Beatles as a group attracted girl fans by the million, Britain's fans, and later the world's, were dividing and uniting behind their own favourite within the group. 'Paul was more of the spokesman, but John had the veto,' says Kenny Lynch. 'John stood there in the dressing-room, for example, listening to Paul saying: "We're going to do this and we're going to do that," and John would suddenly stop him by saying: "Fuck it, we're NOT." And that would be it. John's word was law. It was like an offer nobody in the Beatles could refuse. There was very often this sudden interjection by John after Paul had tried to lead everything his way.' At later press conferences, Paul did most of the talking. He seemed to be taking the role of the most articulate of them. But John was the 'heavy'.

John's creativity was evident as much during that first tour as during the prolific songwriting years that were to follow. In hotels and theatre dressing-rooms and on the band coach, three Beatles went through a passion for ciné cameras. John would film horses and cattle in the fields as they travelled around; but, significantly, he was the first to drop the hobby.

What separated John from the others in the eyes of Ron King, the highly efficient coach driver who took them everywhere on that first tour, was his interest in the written word. He remembers John burying himself in the newspapers more than anyone else on the coach. 'And I remember him telling me he could get ideas for his songs from reading. He'd be watching television in his hotel, or in a dressing-room, and suddenly he'd jump for his cigarette packet on which he'd write a phrase or something he'd heard. Later, I'd hear it crop up in a song, like "I Wanna Be Your Man". I thought how clever he was. He always had books or magazines or newspapers when he was on the coach for hours on end. We'd forget he was there, or somebody would doze off, and suddenly John's voice would come up from the back: "Anyone got a ciggy?" ' In the dressing-rooms, Lennon was addicted to tea.

If 1962 had been a turbulent year for John, with Stuart's death, his own marriage and the Beatles' breakthrough, 1963 was his year of tumult. As well as the birth of his son John experienced four long, major tours of Britain including the one with Helen Shapiro. The other three found the Beatles sharing the bill with both Tommy Roe and Chris Montez, and then topping the bill over their old friends Gerry and the Pacemakers and Roy Orbison, the American singer who had influenced their work, and over Peter Jay and the Jaywalkers. They had such a close physical resemblance to the Beatles that they were used as decoys to fool the crowd into believing John, Paul, George, and Ringo had arrived at the theatre. Then, half an hour later, the real Beatles could coast in quietly after the stage door siege had dispersed.

Although Beatlemania did not properly grip Britain until the autumn, they were still making news and causing more adulation than any other British group. It was a year of sociological, political, and musical ferment. A British government minister, John Profumo, figured in a sex scandal with names that have since passed into history: Christine Keeler and Mandy Rice-Davies. A telephone 'hot line' was established that year

between the White House and the Kremlin, Pope John XXIII
died, aged eighty-one. President Kennedy visited the Berlin
Wall. One thousand people died in an earthquake in Yugoslavia. Back in Britain, £2 million was stolen in the legendary
Great Train Robbery. The Rev. Martin Luther King made a
vital speech that united Black Americans. And on 22 November, the night the Beatles played the Globe Cinema, Stockton
to mounting scenes of fanmania, President Kennedy was assassinated in Dallas, Texas.

I saw a lot of the Beatles that year. The *Melody Maker*, on
which I was then assistant editor, had its roots in jazz. Started
in 1928, the paper had a tradition for upholding 'good musicianship'. Pop singers who 'sang in tune', like Frank Sinatra,
were often allowed to cross the line into the paper, but teenage
pop had been treated with contempt, as if it had nothing to do
with music. It was regarded as the preserve of teenagers who
were tone-deaf. The events of that year, and the infectious
change in emphasis of the bestselling record charts towards
new 'beat music', forced the paper to switch its policy and
report the new sounds. The Beatles were front-page news every
week and I went in and out of their tours, nagging Brian Epstein
for exclusive access and for news stories.

One major reason the Beatles were so acceptable to the Old
Guard, and even to jazz snobs, was the outspoken style of John
Lennon. Quite apart from their records that were pounding up
the charts ('She Loves You' was at the top for seven weeks,
and 'I Want To Hold Your Hand' for four weeks), Lennon's
acrid interviews became the group's unexpected strength. The
music could take care of itself, but the electricity generated by
John, more than any of the Fab Four, was so alive that he
quickly became the most sought-after Beatle.

Most pop stars before John had had a problem sustaining
a conversation beyond the bland talk of their latest record and
their narcissism. Lennon single-handedly stood that credo on
its head. In his speech alone, pop music grew up. The worlds
of jazz and adult music, which had grown too holy and insular,
found themselves threatened not merely by great, energetic,
self-made music led by the Beatles; in Lennon, above all, they
faced an articulacy unheard of in popular music. He would talk
about anything and everything, he would criticize himself and

claim nothing whatsoever for his group, unlike the established singers who placed themselves on a pedestal. And to clinch it all, he didn't care if the Beatles were denigrated.

The rapport I built up with John Lennon in 1963 was, curiously, based partly on the musical snobbery of the old *Melody Maker*. Because the paper had a slightly older readership than other pop papers, we tended to ask more adult questions of everyone we interviewed. Glossy fan magazines pestered the Beatles for the names of their dogs and their aunts, and asked whether they preferred marmalade or honey for breakfast, as well as their height and weight. The *Melody Maker* treated the beat group players as the new musicians, and they would be invited to weigh in on any interesting subject, even old taboos like politics and religion. Lennon loved this. He hated jazz, anyway, but enjoyed talking to a paper that at least gave him credit for being intelligent—and fallible.

What made John stand apart, to me, was the interest he took in everything. He was always inquisitive, rarely pleased with a stage show, and generated intelligence as well as almost belligerent energy. It was obvious to me that, while the Beatles caravan was gaining speed, he was not satisfied merely with being rich and famous. There was always 'but . . .' in his armoury. Millionaire status and all that went with it as success came so quickly was lovely, he would imply. 'But then what?' Clearly, this was no moronic idol.

It was not a matter of self-improvement: that was not in his plan. Paul McCartney, with his keen eye on being the Beatles' diplomat and self-appointed publicist, was the social climber. He desperately needed self-improvement, and worked towards it. John once said to me: 'I've got a built-in shit detector.' He was talking specifically about music, but he might as well have been referring to his entire outlook.

Our interviews would be in dressing-rooms and hotel rooms, in the back of the Beatles' Austin Princess, on the phone, on a plane or train, or at his home in Weybridge, Surrey. There, John and Cynthia spent £19,000 on a Tudor-style mansion, Kenwood, in St George's Hill in the stockbroker belt. He told me he never liked it: he felt hemmed in, he said, by its 'bourgeois' atmosphere. Possibly, because he spent so little time there it didn't have a chance. His moods at Kenwood ranged from restless, creative, and talkative to monosyllabic and depressed.

At the height of Beatlemania I caught up with John on the road: I was with them on 1 November 1963 for the opening of their big autumn tour at Cheltenham Gaumont. Before the show, in the dressing-room, he had just washed his hair. 'I get such terrible dandruff, I think it'd be better if we cut it all off, nice and short. Think what that would do for the Beatles!' He relished the thought of rocking the boat.

He signed autographs, as he often did, while watching television or having a conversation. He rarely looked at the paper or book or programme as he signed his name on it. That night, John was at his most acerbic. In conversation with someone else, Paul McCartney had joked: 'Two things I hate in life, y'know: racial discrimination and coloured people.'

John weighed in instantly and uncomfortably at Paul: 'People who talk like that really don't like coloured people, otherwise they wouldn't think that way at all. I've heard it all before.' Adopting a broad Lancashire accent, he went on: 'Aye, theer all reet but they're so dirty and they bring down the value of property.'

Even at the age of twenty-three, John was contemplating his future from a position of pop supremacy. The Beatles were *en route* to big things, and when the Rolling Stones became friends of the Beatles he had discussed with Mick Jagger how long they would all last at the top. 'I said during a conversation with Mick Jagger that I didn't want to be fiddling round the world singing "Please Please Me" when I'm thirty. If we move into films, and they work out OK, I'll like that. People say that's where the Beatles are heading and I suppose that makes sense. But I also like A & R-ing records. Haven't done much of it but I've enjoyed watching it being done, like by Uncle George Martin. I'd like to see more of it. Recording interests me more than anything.

'I'd like to continue writing for other people and I hope we still carry on making records for a long time. I still enjoy playing live. I get slightly less kick out of things now compared with a few years ago before we had any hits. But that's natural.'

As the tours continued, and John and the others became trapped by Beatlemania, John became furious at the enormous demands made on him as a celebrity. The standing joke between them was the requests for autographs and signed photographs from mayors and mayoresses and police chiefs throughout Britain. These would usually be accompanied by the civic leaders saying: 'It's not for me, it's for my daughter.'

Lennon exploded once to me: 'I don't mind the *fans*. They've paid for a good show and they can go potty. That's OK. But I'm sick of meeting people I don't want to meet. Boring lord mayors and all that. It spoils things for me because I suppose I'm a bit intolerant. But is it any wonder I get fed up? They keep sending in autograph books and we sign them only to find they belong to officials, promoters, police and all that lot. Real fans, who'd wait for hours and days, get treated by the same cops as half-wits because they want our signatures. But the cops make sure they get theirs. I bet every bloody policeman's daughter in Britain's got an autograph. Half of them aren't our fans. It's unfair on the kids who really want them.'

Paul McCartney, sitting opposite and listening to John's anger, shouted: 'Hey, I've had enough of you blasting off, John.'

Lennon retorted: 'You say what you want to say and I'll say what I want to say, OK?'

The sharp division between John and Paul was getting easier to define. John didn't care much for coating what he said with a veneer of acceptability: he spoke as he felt. Paul not only adopted the role of diplomat, but sometimes trespassed into John's independence. The banter between them, joking but with serious undertones, continued during that evening.

Paul said, 'You're bad for my image!'

John retorted, 'You're soft. Shurrup and watch the telly like a good boy.'

John's waspish wit was at its most crushing when the adrenalin of travelling on concert tours gave him a special, edgy thrust. In October 1964 I was travelling with him in the Beatles' limousine when word came that the Duke of Edinburgh was reported as having said that the Beatles were 'on the wane'. Lennon's trenchant retort was immediate: 'The bloke's getting no money for his playing fields from me.'

Later, the Duke said he had been misreported or misheard: he had actually said the Beatles were 'away', meaning out of the country. John's dig at his playing fields referred to the Duke's involvement with the National Playing Fields Association.

John dealt savagely with journalists who asked absurd questions. In 1964 you'd have had to have been a monk, at least, not to know where the Beatles had come from.

One reporter asked him: 'Where's your home town, John?'

Lennon answered: 'Huddersfield.' That ended the interview.

A Leicester policeman, thrusting his autograph book into the limousine and into John's hand, fancied himself as a comedian. 'I see you have the same limousine that you came in last year. Money getting tight then, boys?'

John weighed in: 'Yeah, and you've got the same bloody uniform on that you wore last year. I recognize it.'

The perennial questions about the Beatles' trend-setting long hair were met with some classic Lennon one-liners: 'Our popularity will never decline. It will *recede*. . . . No, we don't have our hair cut, we have it *diminished* every now and then.' He often wore a trilby hat when entering restaurants or hotels in a vain attempt to pass unnoticed. But the stealth and intuition of Beatles fans in seeking them out always impressed him. When a fan broke through the security net, John was always fascinated to ask how he or she had achieved it.

John rebelled against anything that he regarded as a compromise with the truth. In the early 1960s, pop stars were theoretically supposed to be unmarried. As the Beatles' fans were now being counted in millions, Brian Epstein regarded John's marriage and fatherhood as dangerous. When John and Cynthia moved to London and the news trickled out, Epstein was furious. John scarcely cared what was said about him by the Press and revelled in being quoted and photographed, as long as he was interestingly presented as someone other than a brainless 'moptop', as papers called the Beatles. John's wife and child became public knowledge early in 1964 when the couple moved into a flat found for them by their friend, photographer Robert Freeman, at 13 Emperor's Gate, West Kensington. Within weeks the flat became known as the Beatles residence and the fans began to lay siege outside. Cynthia became exhausted, too, with carrying the baby and her shopping up five flights of stairs, so they started househunting and headed for the suburbs.

Lennon fought with Epstein about maintaining secrecy. 'Brian had an obsession about not letting the marriage become public,' says Tony Barrow, who was the Beatles' press officer at that time. 'At a very early stage of my involvement, John mentioned the fact that he was married and Brian went berserk about it to me. He said: "I don't know why he's told you that. Yes, of course it's true, but he's told awfully few people and I want you to make quite sure you don't tell anybody else." '

Barrow believes that Epstein's determination to hold back the truth about John was directly linked to his own homosexuality. 'He feared that some of his own private life could be made public. He was particularly touchy about conceding any part of his artists' private lives, simply because he had so much of a scandalous nature to conceal in his own.' Lennon regarded Eppy's edict as wrong for two reasons: it was going to come out later, anyway, so why not get it over with; and it would make no difference to the Beatles' popularity. He was proved right, for when Cynthia 'went public' the Beatles' popularity continued to rise. She, meanwhile, knew nothing of John's battle with Epstein about their marriage. 'He kept so many things from me, bad and good,' says Cynthia. 'I only heard much later that Brian wanted me kept quiet.' John knew, however, when to draw the line. Shortly after they moved to London, I asked him if I could interview Cynthia to prepare an unusual profile of him. 'I'd like to ask her what it's like being married to you, and what it's like being the envy of millions of girls,' I said, when John asked me why.

He fixed me with a withering look. 'No bloody fear,' he said. 'I'm the bloody star around here.'

Fielding the Press, radio and television, became an art and a full-time job. Tony Barrow, Liverpool-born and the record reviewer of the *Liverpool Echo* under the pseudonym of Disker, had been pestered by Epstein from the early days to write about 'the boys'. When eventually he was lured to London to take on the job of press officer for Epstein's fast-growing NEMS organization, Barrow was invited by Brian to meet them for the first time in a pub, the Devonshire Arms, near E.M.I.'s Manchester Square headquarters.

'John was relatively quiet that night,' says Tony Barrow. 'Paul McCartney seemed to dominate the proceedings. He came round asking everybody what they wanted to drink and I was very impressed by this, until I realized that he relayed the whole order to Brian Epstein, who picked up the bill.'

Lennon did not speak for a while to the man who would handle his press work. When he eventually was introduced to him, John said: 'Well, Tony, if you're not queer and you're not Jewish, why are you joining NEMS?' Brian overheard the remark, but ignored it. It was among many taunts which John was to toss at Brian. When Eppy was writing his autobiography in 1964, he asked John if he had a suggestion for a title. 'Why don't you call it *Queer Jew*?' said John. The book was called *A Cellarful of Noise*. John parodied that as *A Cellarful of Boys*. The crushing remarks made by John simply increased Epstein's admiration and respect for him.

John's fascination for Brian was obvious, and Lennon interpreted it as a kind of weakness. It was John's clear masculinity, fearlessness, abrasiveness, and aggression, which Epstein could not match, that proved such a powerful attraction. Nor did Lennon shrink from cruelly putting Brian down in public. At Abbey Road recording studios one day, Epstein ventured an opinion about the sound they were making. Across the studio, with everyone listening, John said: 'You stick to your percentages, Brian. We'll make the music.' When he put the verbal knife in like that, his voice would have a toughness that invited no reply.

John's resentment of Brian Epstein's involvement with their music went back a long way. He maintained that they had been turned down by Decca mostly because Brian had insisted that at their audition they did mostly standards like 'September In The Rain' and not 'ravers which we went down well with at the Cavern'. John never forgot or forgave Brian for inflicting his own, wrong choice of material on the Beatles which resulted in that rejection, and he decided that never again would he let Brian near a decision about their music. Epstein kept his peace—reluctantly, because he considered he had a good ear for music.

Three weeks after the birth of Julian, and between the vital British tours with Chris Montez/Tommy Roe and Roy Orbison/ Gerry and the Pacemakers, the Beatles were officially on holiday. John went to Spain for twelve days with Brian Epstein. 'I didn't think anything about it,' said Cynthia. 'John said he'd been working very hard, with the concert tours and the album. He needed a break.' She was frantically busy, anyway, with a new baby and setting up temporary home in Mendips.

Lennon knew, of course, about Brian's fixation on him, but he could not have anticipated the campaign of whispering that holiday would give rise to. As one who was close to him during the Beatles' rise to fame, I saw a solidly heterosexual man. He did not boast about his exploits, but he made it abundantly clear that he enjoyed women. John would hardly have taunted Brian so mercilessly about his sexual preferences if he felt any empathy with him as a homosexual.

When John returned, he was livid at the rumours. The girls in the NEMS office, naïve about homosexuality, which was illegal, giggled nervously and were told by John, patiently, and for the first time in their lives, what homosexuality meant. He told them in general conversation and 'from a distance'.

But his Spanish trip with Epstein erupted into a scandal. John and Cynthia, along with many Liverpool musicians, like Gerry and the Pacemakers, Billy J. Kramer, and the Shadows from London, went to Paul McCartney's twenty-first birthday party on 18 June 1963, a party held mostly in the garden, and in a marquee, at the house of Paul's Auntie Jin, in Dinas Lane, Huyton.

John had little to eat and too much to drink at the party. Bob Wooler, the old friend who had introduced the Beatles on stage at the Cavern nearly three hundred times, said something to John about his visit to Spain with Epstein. John laid into Wooler with a ferocity that landed the disc jockey in hospital with a black eye, bruised ribs, and torn knuckles. Brian Epstein drove Bob Wooler to hospital.

The party broke up in disarray. Cynthia, who left with John, recalls: 'John said: "He called me a queer so I battered his bloody ribs in." '

Billy J. Kramer was at that party. (John had injected the

'J' into his name during a chat in Epstein's office. 'He thought it had more flow. I said: "What's the J. for, if anyone asks me?" John said it was for Julian.') Billy J., as John called him, was in the marquee at Paul's party with several show business personalities. 'I remember asking Bruce Welch of the Shadows what he thought of the Beatles, and his reply: "They've written a few catchy songs, nothing special. Once they dry up that'll be the end of them." ' Kramer recalls the conversation because John had said it was one of his greatest ambitions to 'blow the Shadows out—he couldn't stand their clean music'. Kramer recalls that after he had laid into Bob Wooler, John grabbed the body of a girl who was standing next to him. 'I said: "Lay off, John." But he lashed into her. He'd had too much booze. I was semi-professional at the time, and he was winding me up as I left before him, shouting: "You're nothing, Kramer, and we're the top." ' Lennon was at his most withering when the demon drink fuelled his insecurities.

Kramer was furious. Epstein apologized for John to him next day, but Billy said: 'I refuse to take a second-hand apology.' A few days later, Lennon met Kramer in a Liverpool street, and immediately put out his hand to shake: 'I'm really sorry about what happened that night,' said John.

News of John's fisticuffs with Bob Wooler filtered through to the northern newsdesks of Britain's national papers. Tony Barrow received several phone calls next day. 'What's your lad John Lennon been up to? Been a naughty boy, has he?' Barrow's first thoughts were that news of John's marriage to Cynthia had leaked and he would face trouble from Epstein. 'Although Julian was two months old by then,' says Barrow, 'the news that John was married, let alone a father, was still a secret. Some fans in Liverpool knew, but nationally it was still unknown.' When the Press confronted Barrow with the news of the Lennon–Wooler punch-up, Tony phoned John to find out what his reply should be. 'He was completely unrepentant. He said: "The bastard was saying I was bloody queer so I smacked him one, I punched him one, he deserved it, he went a bit too far, and I don't care what the Press make of that, sod it." '

But by the time the *Daily Mirror*, through its show business reporter Don Short, had got to Lennon, his story had become either more apologetic or more diplomatic, on Epstein's advice. In the first national newspaper recognition of the Beatles' importance, Don Short wrote in the *Mirror* under the headline: 'Beatle in Brawl—Sorry I Socked You':

> Guitarist John Lennon, twenty-two-year-old leader of the Beatles pop group, said last night: 'Why did I have to go and punch my best friend? I was so high I didn't realize what I was doing.' Then he sent off a telegram apologizing to twenty-nine-year-old [*sic*] Liverpool rock show compère and disc jockey Bob Wooler . . . who said: 'I don't know why he did it. I have been a friend of the Beatles for a long time. I have often compèred shows where they have appeared. I am terribly upset about this, physically as well as mentally.'
>
> John Lennon said: 'Bob is the last person in the world I would want to have a fight with. I can only hope he realizes that I was too far gone to know what I was doing.'

John badly damaged his forefinger. Back at Mendips, he walked around hiding his right hand from Mimi for several days in case she should see his injuries and ask him how it happened.

Years later, the homosexual leader of a rock band, Tom Robinson, maintained that the first gay rock song was written by Lennon in 1965. Millions heard the song, 'You've Got To Hide Your Love Away', as a sentimental ballad written in John's period of great influence by the songwriting style of Bob Dylan. But Robinson believes the words were a message to Brian Epstein.

A few years later, John wrote a message to an American publication called the *Gay Liberation Book*. The editors had solicited contributions from prominent people, and John's read as follows:

> Why make it sad to be gay?
> Doing your thing is okay.
> Our body's our own, so leave us alone
> And play with yourself today.

Anyone who knew John Lennon would dismiss the suggestion that he was a homosexual. On tour, he was an aggressive woman hunter, something he was to confess to Cynthia when their marriage foundered. He had a massive sexual appetite for women, and particularly for new conquests. Women who had been with him spoke of John as an enthusiastic lover but 'rough and ready, never kind and considerate'. All through his life, he was a woman chaser.

'I slept in a million hotel rooms, as we all did, with John and there was never any hint that he was gay,' says Paul McCartney. The rumour that caused Lennon to punch Bob Wooler for a suggestive remark was explained by Paul in an interview on London's Capital Radio with Roger Scott:

> When the group was formed John was a smart cookie. Brian Epstein was going on holiday to Spain and Brian was gay. He invited John along. John, not being stupid, saw his opportunity to impress upon Mr Epstein who was the boss of this group. And I think that's why John went on holiday. And good luck to him, too—he was that kind of guy, he wanted Brian to know who he should listen to in this group, and that was the relationship.
>
> John was very much the leader in that kind of sense, although it was never actually said, we were all sort of leaders. But in truth . . . John was probably the deciding vote. He was into that.
>
> So they say he went on holiday with someone who was known to be gay and therefore he is gay.

Paul recalls someone asking John once if he had ever tried homosexuality, and Lennon's crunching reply, 'No. I haven't met a fellow I fancy enough!'

And the girls at college with him echo Cynthia's statement on the subject: 'You'd have to look a long way to find a more heterosexual man. The suggestion that he was anything else is too ridiculous for words.'

For people inside the Beatles circle, John needed to be treated with kid gloves. Paul, ever charming, polite, informative, was never a media problem. Ringo assumed the air of a cuddly, amiable guy, lucky to be hoisted aboard the Beatles just before the group shot to fame. George, who hated invasions of his privacy, was not comfortable with the Press but he was tolerant and spoke intelligently. John was different. 'I was sometimes nervous of what impression he would make upon third parties, rather in the same way one sent home sensitive aunts and uncles if John Lennon was due to drop in,' recalls Tony Barrow. 'I wasn't wary of asking him to do interviews. He was co-operative, although he'd grumble and curse if it wasn't convenient. But I was selective about the journalists I sent to him. It had to be someone sufficiently worldly, or sophisticated, with a decent and preferably way-out sense of humour, to accept John as he was. The journalist didn't have to be offended by the guy. John always asked for someone who shared his outrageous sense of humour, who would come back at him with something as nasty and cynical as he gave them. Otherwise he might just turn a bit nasty on an ill-informed or inexperienced journalist. Or he'd particularly turn on one who thought he knew too much or knew all about the Beatles.'

Billy J. Kramer later had good reason to appreciate their healed relationship. The first song given to him by Brian Epstein was a tape of John Lennon playing acoustic guitar and singing the demonstration of a song he'd written called 'Do You Want To Know A Secret'. 'John later apologized for the tape quality but said he'd done the demo in the toilet, as it was the quietest place he could find.' The sound of the loo flushing at the end confirmed John's story. 'God,' says Billy J. Kramer, 'if I had that tape now it would be worth a fortune.' John and Paul went on to give him several hits that boosted his career: a number one with 'Bad To Me' plus 'From A Window' and 'I'll Keep You Satisfied'.

John's intake of alcohol rose a lot during the heady Beatles years. As undisputed kings of the Swinging London decade, the Beatles held court at the Ad Lib club, above the Prince Charles cinema in Leicester Street, Soho. It vied with two other clubs as the focal point for pop and cinema stars, photographers and fashion people. The other night spots were the Scotch of St James in Masons Yard near Piccadilly, and the Bag o' Nails in Cromwell Road, West Kensington. The night began around one o'clock after a concert. Often, Lennon, getting steadily more drunk on Scotch and Coke, and smoking incessantly his favourite brand, Peter Stuyvesant, would become more and more emotional as the drink took hold.

A favourite habit when he was lubricated was to seize one person for a verbal hammering and not let go until that person was utterly exhausted by the sheer persistence of John's argument. There was a streak in John that could not bear to lose a battle. With Mick Jagger or Alan Price, both intelligent men with plenty of opinions, John would rant all night about music or a city or who was winning the popularity race between the Beatles, the Rolling Stones, the Animals, and the Hollies. He particularly hated Manchester's Hollies. He regarded them as syrupy copyists of the Beatles' vocal style.

It could be argued that John Lennon was always worldly, even as a Quarry Bank pupil lampooning the teachers and as a perverse Liverpool Art College student. But those qualities grew within the fast-moving Beatles story. Music aside, and there were some catatonic moments in which he and Paul touched the heights, John was intuitive enough to understand that it was an unstoppable bandwagon. If it wasn't exactly out of control, it was moving too fast for him to have a lot of impact on it, so he might as well get stuck in and enjoy it, particularly the money, while Beatlemania gripped Britain, and quickly, the impossible dream happened: they conquered America.

Just before that happened, Britain had its first national glimpse of the subtle difference in personalities within the Beatles whom they had previously regarded as four lovable Liverpool lads with perhaps equal brightness. At the Royal Variety Show in London, it was John who entered the history books with the irreverent, hilarious line: 'Will the people in the cheaper seats clap your hands? All the rest of you, if you'll just rattle your jewellery. . . .' John was determined to have a dig of some kind at royalty. John learned, very early, the art of manipulating an event, a situation, and also a person. Cynical about the royal patronage, he told Epstein of the joke he planned backstage. Brian used every ounce of his persuasion in stopping John from saying: '. . . the rest of you just rattle your fucking jewellery'.

No group, before or since, could have 'closed ranks' more

forcefully than the Beatles. However close to the band anyone felt, when the hotel suite, or limousine, or dressing-room door was shut, the four men insisted on privacy and group unity when they needed it. The only man who could remotely be described as the fifth Beatle was Neil Aspinall, who went to Liverpool Institute with Paul and George. He was the man who drove their Commer van for them back in the Cavern days, and who gave up a solid career in accountancy to become their utterly trusted friend, confidant, and world-travelling tour manager. 'Nell', as he was to the Beatles, is still today the managing director in London of Apple, the bizarre company left by the Beatles since they split.

Brian Epstein liked to regard himself as the fifth Beatle, yet for all their affection for his loyalty and what he achieved for them, the Beatles did not consider him a true insider. Precision, style, presentation and urbanity were his strengths. The more the media screamed that the Rolling Stones were unkempt and a danger to daughters, the more Epstein concentrated on projecting his 'boys', as he insisted on calling them, as intelligent and clean. It worked perfectly. As hair everywhere got longer and skirts were shorter, Beatlemania became the acceptable face of Swinging Britain.

Brian Epstein's admiration of John directly affected what the Beatles did. Eppy clashed with Paul about many things, from the timing of tours to the lists of people in the Beatles' entourage who should accompany them. There was an unwritten rule that the Beatles and the Rolling Stones would never have a single record out at the same time because a 'same day' release might split and confuse the fans—and one of the two supergroups would be kept from the coveted number one spot. It was Paul who did the arranging of the timing, usually with Mick Jagger. Epstein did not like Paul's intrusion, but just how adept McCartney was at managing his career became obvious when the Beatles split and he became the world's most successful popular musician and songwriter.

'Paul can be temperamental and moody and difficult to deal with,' said Epstein. 'This means that we compromise on our clash of personalities. He is a great one for not wishing to hear about things and if he doesn't want to know he switches himself off, settles down in a chair, puts one booted foot across his knee and pretends to read a newspaper, having consciously made his face an impassive mask.'

Epstein's interpretation of John was, predictably, more convoluted. Writing in his autobiography, Epstein said:

> John Lennon, his [Paul's] friend from boyhood, his co-writer of so many songs, the dominant figure in a group which is virtually without a leader, is in my opinion a most exceptional man. Had there been no Beatles and no Epstein participation, John would have emerged from the mass of the population as a man to reckon with. He may not have been a singer or a guitarist, a writer or a painter, but he would most certainly have been a Something. You cannot contain a talent like this. There is in the set of his head a controlled aggression which demands respect.

Brian went on to say how John had sometimes been abominably rude to him.

But because he loved him so much, Brian would take it. As the speed of Beatlemania demanded decisions faster than subtlety, McCartney realized that Lennon was able to influence Epstein very strongly on any matter involving the group. So when he thought there might be a clash with Epstein, Paul would feed his demands through John, who could get his own way every time. Because he was such a smoothie, Epstein was intrigued by John's cruel tongue. Though it hurt him, he would take it.

Yet for all his foibles, and for all the warts, business and personal, attached to his discovery and management of the Beatles, Brian Epstein was a superb manager for them. His devotion was unyielding, his belief in their originality infectious, his sense of fairness a byword. When he died in 1967, the Beatles began to fall apart as a group. Brian Epstein was a man of strong principles, right for his time as the mentor of the world's greatest pop group. He succeeded in helping them become 'bigger than Elvis'. Those of us who knew him well remember his warmth, his passion, and his precision which was more important to the success story than we knew at the time. 'Paul has the glamour, John the command,' said Epstein. It was an astute observation in 1964, which will always hold true.

Listening to John on stage, it was difficult to believe he was the master of the sharp jibe. On the British and European tours, the screams were so loud that the Beatles' performance became more of a ritual than a show. The music was unimportant. 'It's like we're four freaks being wheeled out to be seen, shake our hair about, and get back in our cage afterwards,' he said to me. He became irritable about it but grew reconciled to Beatle-mania. He expected the Beatles to last about five years, and in terms of live performances he was not far wrong. His stage personality was electrifying in 1963 and 1964. Legs arrogantly apart, head tilted back slightly to emphasize his prominent nose, guitar across his chest, John exuded an air of detached uninterest. By then he wore contact lenses, recommended to John by Bobby Goldsboro during the British tour by Roy Orbison and the Beatles. (Goldsboro, then Orbison's guitarist, later emerged as a successful solo singer, with records like 'Honey' and 'Summer (The First Time)'.) John told me that Goldsboro's recommendation was a great idea and a drag as well. 'I mean, I couldn't be seen in horn-rimmed specs on stage, that would never do for a Beatle, folks! But the contacts are not easy to control.' They were regularly falling out either on stage, causing him visual chaos, or in dressing-rooms or hotels where I, like many others who were with him, spent many an hour fumbling in thick pile carpet looking for a missing lens. 'Can you imagine what it's like,' he once said, 'hearing all that noise and playing, and not seeing a *thing*? It's frightening.'

John's reputation for repartee was certainly not born from his communications on stage. 'We'd like to sing a number from our new L.P.,' was typical of the inanity that he managed above the roar. But the difference between John and Paul was as easy to define in a concert as millions have found on records.

John would be at his blistering best on his cherished favourites, rockers like 'Twist and Shout' and 'Money', while Paul would woo the girls in the crowd with his romantic specialities, 'All My Loving' and 'Till There Was You', the unlikely song from the show *The Music Man* which the Beatles used on stage to break up their rock 'n' roll diet. John would roar into his own song 'I Feel Fine', which he claimed was the first-ever record to feature the feedback technique, and would lead on the autobiographical 'Help!' Paul dominated on 'Can't Buy Me Love' and, as if to reclaim his rock 'n' roll roots, often hammered out a powerful 'Long Tall Sally'.

Lennon's lack of interest in live performing struck me forcefully one night in Exeter. He had forgotten the words to 'I Want To Hold Your Hand', and asked me to write down what I could remember of them on the back of his hand. They were ingrained into my consciousness at the time, so I did it, in biro.

'It wouldn't matter if I never sang,' he said cynically. 'Often I don't anyway. I just stand there and make mouth movements. Nobody knows. I reckon we could send out four waxwork dummies of ourselves and that would satisfy the crowds. Beatles concerts are nothing to do with music any more. They're just bloody tribal rites.'

Just as he got no thrill from performing, John took no interest whatsoever, in the sixties, in seeing other artists on stage. 'I'm a record man,' he said. 'I just like records. It always spoils it for me when I see someone whose records I like— they're never as good live.'

The squeals of Beatlemania seemed insane to John. The debasement of the music, the pandemonium, the hurling on stage of dolls and teddy bears, and jelly babies once they had said they liked to eat them, was all too juvenile for his speedy mind. He went along for the ride, but, as always in his life, there was a 'get-out' clause. He devised his own method of coping with the lunacy. 'Nice endings to songs don't work in that situation,' said John. 'The kids are all getting worked up about something that's not music.' He let out that pent-up shriek of resentment at what he had to do to get to the top and stay there. At the end of a song, as a wave of screaming cascaded around the hall, John would screech out an obscenity to complete the song. It was his own release.

'The others didn't have John's resentment of having to do what he was doing to be a Beatle,' says Mike McCartney. 'They thought they were just bloody lucky they were getting away with it for so long. But John always had that drive, something ticking over, the need to do something else. It was:

"Ah, so *this* is what we have to do to be bigger than Elvis? OK, let's go, but I'm not going to give it one hundred per cent of me." ' That individuality stayed and marked him out as the most original of the four.

'On the road, in dressing-rooms and hotels, John usually had an aggressive attitude,' says British tour promoter Arthur Howes, who presented most of their concerts right from the start of their nationwide popularity. 'But I could see it was defensive, a cover-up for the real John who was a nice, soft-hearted man. At dinner after concerts he would launch into Stanley Unwin-type double-talk. I'd never met anyone with such a fast style in one-liners. At Dublin airport once, a reporter asked the Beatles where Brian Epstein was, and, quick as a flash, John replied: "Oh, he's in America signing up a new rhythm-and-Jews group." On aggression alone, John was the leader of the Beatles.'

'When he wasn't bullying or bellowing, he could be very kind and considerate,' says Tony Barrow. 'He was very friendly and very popular with the NEMS office staff in Liverpool. And once, when Brian Epstein fired a girl typist in a fit of temper, merely for messing up a Dictaphone tape, John was there and turned the whole episode into a joke. He laughed a lot about it. And if Lennon laughed, Epstein laughed. So the girl got her job back.'

His sense of the absurd and obsession with deformity in people gave him both laughter and tears on the road. This was another escape route. He once autographed a programme: 'Sodoffy from John Leper'. And when he spoke of things he did not like, he would sometimes say: 'It was horrible—really spastic.' I challenged him about it one night over one of Cynthia's chicken dinners at Weybridge. He had made a strong little speech about success. It was in 1965.

'I want no more from being a record star. I'm not uninterested but there is more, now, than making good records and selling them. I'd like to see us making better and better films. That's very difficult. Unlike pop music, it allows you to grow up as a person. I'm not craving for any more gold discs even though they're a nice boost. That's all over. I just want to be an all-round spastic—think how awful it would be to be an old Beatle, or a grey-haired Beatle, or a spastic Beatle.'

Cynthia gave him a crushing look.

'Enjoying your dinner?' said John. 'Look, I mean nothing *nasty* about these spastics. I don't think I'd know a real spastic from a Polaroid lens. I'm not hung up about them. When I use the word "spastic" in general conversation, I don't mean it literally. I feel terrible sympathy for these people. It seems to be like the end of the world when you see deformed spastics, and we've had quite a lot of them on our travels.

'In the States, they were bringing hundreds of 'em along backstage and it was fantastic. I can't stand looking at 'em. I have to turn away. I have to laugh or I'd collapse from hate *of the situation*. Listen, in the States, they lined 'em up and you got the impression the Beatles were being treated as bloody faith healers. It was sickening.'

Tough, cantankerous, and iconoclastic John was, but there were also signs of enormous wit and compassion. That night, after dinner, we all went out to a private showing of the Michael Caine film *The Ipcress File*. On the twenty-mile journey from Surrey back into London, John's Rolls-Royce was smeared with lipstick and dented by fans as they waited at traffic lights and they spotted a Beatle in the back. Girls banged on the doors and wings and blocked the road. 'John, John,' they screamed. He carried on reading and locked himself in. The chauffeur became irritable and was about to get out and push them away. 'Leave them,' snapped John. 'They bought the car. They've got the right to smash it up.'

12
DRUGS

'But Cyn, it's fantastic, it's wonderful'

It was not a normal marriage and he could never be a normal father. When Cynthia was heavily pregnant in February and March 1963, John was touring Britain; he was also appearing with the Beatles when Julian was born on 8 April in Liverpool; and by 18 May he was off again for another three-week tour, this time with Gerry and the Pacemakers and Roy Orbison.

The Beatles did four major tours that year, and went on to become one of the busiest travelling groups in pop before they finally ended live work in 1966. John was the only Beatle who had embarked on that long and winding road with a wife and son.

The first clash in John and Cynthia's marriage occurred when Julian was nine months old. John was appearing in the Beatles' Christmas Show in London and had not been in touch for several days. Cynthia decided the time was right for the baby to be christened, and went ahead with organizing it in Hoylake Parish Church, opposite her home in Trinity Road. She had gone to Sunday School there as a child.

The christening passed off quietly one Sunday morning, except for Julian's show-stopping habit of knocking the vicar's glasses off his face. But when Cynthia carried him outside the church, there were photographers. Next day, newspapers featured pictures of a Beatle's baby being carried away from his christening.

John phoned Cynthia when he read about it in the newspaper during his tour. He was livid. 'What's all *this*? He didn't need baptizing or christening.'

Cynthia argued that he did, to give him a seal of religious belief in his life. 'It's simple, it doesn't harm anybody, and it's over and done with.'

John's anger continued: 'Well I didn't want it done, and you should have told me.'

Cynthia said she was sorry, but with John away on tour she had to get things done and she did not expect him to react so strongly.

There were, says Cynthia, four major changes in John's personality during their marriage: the student, the father, the meeting with Brian Epstein that shaped his future, and the rich, famous Beatle. But the one over which John agonized the most was his fatherhood.

'As far as our marriage was concerned,' says Cynthia, 'we got on great. It wasn't the greatest whizzo-active relationship and once he became a Beatle we didn't go out much and see the sights, as husband and wife. But we had holidays with the other Beatles and we were strong as a unit in that home.'

Apart from the christening eruption, Cynthia recalls one other major blow-up by John. Returning from another tour to family life at Weybridge, John was having breakfast with Cynthia and Julian one morning. While eating, Julian made a typical three-year-old's mess of the food and everything else on the table. 'John stood up and blew his top, screaming at this little boy who couldn't understand this man who he very rarely saw!' says Cynthia. 'Julian wasn't the tidiest of eaters as a child and needed coaxing and he was a crying baby too.

'When John screamed at Julian, I flew off the handle. I disappeared upstairs in a fit of tears. I said: "If you were here more often, you'd understand your child. You can't just come home, blow your top and take it out on a little boy who doesn't understand." John was sweet then, very apologetic and understanding. It was the only real row we ever had. He'd just come home from a tour, all hyped up and nervous and, somebody was going to get it. It was unfair that Julian and I were the people he chose.'

The stress of life with this agitated, extraordinary pop star who darted in and out of their home took a heavy toll on their marriage. 'It was very hard for him to adjust to home after two or three weeks of all the adrenalin of screams and being hyped up after concerts here or in America or Europe,' she says. 'We were on different wavelengths. The patterns of our thoughts were obviously different. I decided to offer him security. I tried to stay the same person for him. It was probably the worst thing I could have done. I should have gone out and got on with other things, developed my own activities. But I didn't. I thought: "Well, at least if I'm here and Julian's fine and he has me, he has these roots." But there were too many people pulling on these roots in those Beatle days. I couldn't get them into the ground quickly enough.'

The magic moments for Cynthia were when they took off on holidays, at the height of Beatlemania. There was Tahiti with George and Pattie Boyd, St Vincent in the Caribbean with Ringo and Maureen Starr, St Moritz with George and Judy Martin, swimming in the sea, playing Monopoly and drinking Scotch and Coke and eating well. 'John became quite hefty and was really enjoying the pleasure of being rich. I could see he felt under pressure, but I didn't know how much. But he enjoyed the holidays, there were no drugs, and he reverted to being a Liverpool lad.' They managed to stay anonymously in hotels: the machinery of Brian Epstein's organization ensured that manager and staff did not blurt out the news of their presence to anyone.

Indulgence, in fact, was John's pleasure for a time. On buying Kenwood in Weybridge, the value of the house was quickly doubled by the building of a swimming pool. John wanted the pool bottom to be a full-sized mirror, but ended up accepting a gigantic eye painted on the bottom. The pool and its adaptations cost £20,000. John didn't blink an eye at the cost.

Despite his absence from home, Lennon enjoyed the fact that he was a father. The tears of joy that welled up in him when he first visited Cynthia in hospital and held his son for the first time stayed true during the boy's years as a toddler. 'He often said it was a shame his family had to be pushed into the background,' says Cynthia. 'He regretted it, but once the Beatles wagon was rolling, he could not get off it if he wanted to. He became exhausted and irritable when he was at home, and angry at his own absence when he wasn't there.' In 1966, by which time he was heavily into smoking marijuana and sleeping until two or three in the afternoon when he was at Weybridge, John let out his thoughts in his song 'I'm Only Sleeping':

> When I wake up early in the morning
> Lift my head, I'm still yawning
> When I'm in the middle of a dream
> Stay in bed, float upstream
> Please don't wake me, no, don't shake me
> Leave me where I am, I'm only sleeping.
> Everybody seems to think I'm lazy
> I don't mind, I think they're crazy
> Running everywhere at such a speed
> Till they find there's no such need
> Please don't spoil my day, I'm miles away
> And after all, I'm only sleeping.

'One big change I noticed in his habits, once the Beatles got going, was in his sleeping,' says Cynthia. 'He would collapse into a dead sleep and be immovable until afternoons unless there was an appointment to be kept earlier. We were both book fanatics and read until the early hours. I'd usually fall asleep before he did.' An avid collector as well as reader, John would stop his chauffeur and make weekly swoops on bookshops throughout London and Surrey. Tennyson, Swift, Tolstoy, Oscar Wilde, Aldous Huxley, and all the *Just William* books from his childhood ranged across the huge bookcase in the lounge. When Cynthia's mother lived at the house, John asked her, 'Lil, go and fill the bookshelves.' He could not stand the sight of empty bookshelves. He chauvinistically told Cynthia she could not have a full-time nanny for Julian; he wanted his son to have the mother he had been deprived of when he was a child.

John was keen on spending money. He would make unscheduled stops with his chauffeur and return with expensive clocks, a huge leather-bound Bible, or a compendium of toys, and one day a suit of armour which he had ordered was deliv-

ered. 'This is Sidney,' John announced: the armour occupied
pride of place in the hall. Nearby reposed a more quixotic,
priceless gift from George Harrison: a pair of crutches.

When they closed Harrods for the Beatles to do their Christmas shopping, John arrived home and presented Cynthia with
several fur coats and 'naughty nighties'. But he always forgot
birthdays. 'It wasn't important to me,' says Cynthia. 'John was
soft, generous, and gave when it was least expected. He never
was tight, going right back to college. If he had a cigarette he
would always offer you one, and light it.' But she always gazed
jealously at something Ringo did when he and Maureen joined
John and Cynthia at either one of their houses. 'Ringo had this
habit of lighting up two cigarettes, one for Maureen at the same
time that he lit his own. I remember thinking it was a loving
thing to do, and wishing John did it for me. But that would
have been too obviously demonstrative, maybe, for John. . . .'

Her pocket money was £50 in cash a week, and a similar
amount was arranged by John to go to Aunt Mimi. 'It was
quite a lot, considering I didn't have any bills to pay,' says
Cynthia. 'All the food and nearly everything else was on accounts, so there was nothing to spend it on.' Like royalty,
John rarely carried any cash or a cheque book. 'Send the bill in,'
he would say, whenever he was in a club or restaurant or
bookshop.

John, as always, was in a hurry. Once Beatlemania arrived it
was great, but it left him feeling strangely unfulfilled, for all
the tangible benefits it brought. What Beatlemania brought
John, above all, was freedom. Or so he thought.

Drugs entered their marriage, and contributed to its eventual
collapse, quite innocently. 'John was always seeking interesting
ways to get rid of the mundane and close a chapter. The Beatles
were so big, the pressure on him and Paul so much, that he
kept looking for new things to occupy his mind. We all went
to a party at Brian Epstein's flat in Williams Mews, Knights-
bridge, and that was the first time John and I smoked marijuana.' Paul McCartney was the only Beatle not there.

After several puffs, John said: 'The only thing this is doing
to me is giving me the giggles.' Cynthia's reaction after smoking the joint was to be violently sick. She rejected offers of

more marijuana at the round of dinners to which she and John were invited; but John got steadily more engrossed in smoking during 1965.

When a dentist spiked their coffee with L.S.D. the first effects were again horrific and John thought it was potentially enlightening and worth investigation.

'I warned him against it,' says Cynthia. 'At times I felt like a mother, shouting at him for being a naughty boy but he'd say: "But Cyn, it's FANTASTIC, it's WONDERFUL. Why don't you do it?"

'I said, "No, because I know what it does, it makes me ill, sick."

' "But it's great, Cyn," John continued, "you've got to be with me, you've *got* to do it." '

Says Cynthia, 'He was so enthusiastic and so happy about the whole thing, and I just couldn't be. We couldn't meet on that level, and although I did try I didn't see what he saw. He obviously saw his escape from whatever he was running away from. I wasn't running away from it. So I didn't really need it.

'What I think John wanted was a kind of mental freedom. He was trying to shed responsibility. I don't think John was a very responsible person. He didn't want to account all the time to anybody but himself. He didn't want to account to Mimi all the time when he was living with her, and now he didn't want to account to me. He's a man who should have been unencumbered until he was about thirty. He wasn't prepared for the two big things running side by side: one or the other, marriage or the pop scene, and certainly not marriage with a growing son. It was a bit too hard to take, and he was wide open when all the pushers kept offering him more and more of what he thought were interesting drugs. He was a sitting target.'

Although she does not feel drugs themselves ended their marriage, Cynthia says, 'They had an important effect in that they separated us. We were on different mental planes. John's thoughts would always be much more expansive than mine. I'd seen the effects of drugs and I didn't want to be there. He did. He kept saying that on his trips he was seeing beautiful things.'

One heavy drug-taking weekend occurred when John went,

alone, to the Ascot house of Derek Taylor, the former *Daily Express* writer who had been lured into the Beatles' coterie by Brian Epstein, to whom he became personal assistant. Taylor, an early convert to marijuana and L.S.D., had a particularly strong intellectual rapport with John.

Derek and Joan Taylor also had five children. Returning from their home, John was aglow at the L.S.D.-tripping he had enjoyed during the weekend. Derek had done wonders for John's ego, 'telling me what a good person I am', he explained to Cynthia. Normally, during drug experiences John was the more experienced one, guiding less frequent users; this time Derek had assumed the dominant role.

Derek had just returned from a lengthy stay in California, where the blossoming of flower power had made drug-taking almost mandatory. Taylor strongly advocated its use at the time, and to John he was virtually a guru. Mentally, John was going through a period of uncertainty about his marriage, his fatherhood, the Beatles, and himself. During several L.S.D. trips that weekend away from Cynthia, John had his ego massaged by Taylor: it was just the kind of pampering John needed. 'You're OK, you're clever, and you have no real problems,' Derek Taylor told John Lennon in many different ways. John returned to Kenwood smiling through the haze.

'Oh, Cyn,' he said when they reunited at Weybridge. 'It was wonderful. Why don't we have lots of children, a big, big family, and everything will be wonderful? That's what we should do. . . .'

Cynthia nodded. She knew he was tripping but felt her hands tied behind her back. She remembered the last time John was so clearly high on dope. He had talked gibberish then, about 'buying an island in the sun, switching the sun on and off and totally controlling the weather'.

'I couldn't switch John's brain off, could I?' asks Cynthia. 'One normal person couldn't compete against that barrage of experiences. Unless they were extraordinary, dominant, and in a position of power. Which I wasn't. I was just Mum.'

Reading about the new drug culture, and the Beatles' endorsement of it, Aunt Mimi was on the phone immediately to John in Weybridge.

'By jove, I had a lot to say very quickly,' she recalls. 'John said: "Mimi, I'm *old enough* now. You don't understand the kind of lives we lead. The tension. I've had lots of tensions. And anyway, I used to see you taking aspirins."

'I said: "Yes, John, but only when I had a very bad head-ache. Look, the worry of it is nearly killing me. I don't approve of it any more than your Scouse accent. I still can't understand a word you're saying in all these interviews, and now there's this worry over drugs. What do you need drugs for and a Scouse accent?"

'And he answered: "Don't worry, Mimi. The accent's put on for money. They love it in Brooklyn. And I can handle the drugs." '

Mimi was equally strong with her final words: 'Well, don't have me to come over to your house while all this is happening.'

Julian Lennon has two prized possessions: one is a big brown floppy hat on which is embroidered 'Dr Winston O'Boogie', John's nickname for himself; the other is an electric guitar, a Les Paul copy, which Julian received as a Christmas present in 1974. Featuring a plaque with the inscription 'To Julian, Happy Christmas', the guitar is adorned with mirrors. Both were unique gifts from John to his son.

What John could not give Julian during his growing years was time. From his birth at the onslaught of Beatlemania through the turbulent years at Weybridge, Julian was a toddler and a growing boy with an absent Dad.

When John was at his most frenetic as a Beatle, from 1964 to 1966, Julian registered very little of his father's fame. 'All I knew was that he was away a lot. When he came home, and we were together, I recall most of all the fun like flying a kite in the garden, or the riding on the back of Dad's motorbike down to Ringo's home. The rest of my childhood with Dad is a fog.' He says he has picked up the full story of his father's old group from news clips and films. 'More than anything, I can remember Dad's way with words, his humour and sense of fun. I know he used to say something about enjoying a good laugh.'

Julian has grown into a great admirer of his father's work —more his non-Beatle songwriting and efforts for peace than his straight Beatles hits. But he finds life today, as Lennon's first son, hazardous. He has regrets about the lack of father–son relationship which he says he desperately needed. 'But if Dad was going to be a musician, then he obviously had to be away from home a lot. Nobody's blaming him. I just missed him and wished he was around more.'

Educated at private schools, Julian went first to Heath House, Weybridge, then to Kingsmead in Hoylake, Cheshire, going to a variety of preparatory schools and finally settling at Ruthin School in North Wales. There, he followed the family tradition of John and his mother, leaning heavily towards art and hoping for an A-level in the subject. He lacked interest in most other subjects and planned a career in engineering. But he failed all his O-levels, just like his father, and set his sights firmly on music. At school in Hoylake he had a year's tuition on guitar, and with his close friend Justin Clayton played rock 'n' roll classics like 'Roll Over Beethoven', 'Rock Around The Clock' and 'Kansas City'.

As he grew up and listened to his father's work, particularly his lyrics, Julian decided to carry on his tradition. 'But in my own way, and playing mostly piano,' says Julian. 'I prefer ballads to hard driving rock 'n' roll. I don't want to face any comparison with my father for the songs I'm writing, although I'd have to agree that his work has been a big influence.' His favourite song is 'Isolation', with tracks like 'Dear Prudence', 'Sexy Sadie' and 'A Day In The Life' among the ones he particularly loves.

Growing up as John Lennon's son brought its hurdles for Julian as a schoolboy. 'The other kids thought I was a rich brat, and made jokes like: "He's got ten pound notes as wall-paper", but there were only a couple of times the kids in North Wales tried to beat me up just because of jealousy over who I am. The kids at Ruthin School really thought I had a fortune, and it was never like that.'

While he had attended Ruthin School, Julian was taunted by other boys. 'They took the mickey out of me for having a millionaire father, and that wasn't easy,' he recalls. But it was at that school that a crucial friendship developed for Julian, with an equally quiet boy named Justin Clayton. By the time he was seventeen, Julian had jammed around with Justin and other musicians and toyed with calling his group the Lennon

Drops. But the progress of that activity, as well as the entire fabric of Julian's life during that period, changed when his father was murdered and Julian went to New York to stay with Yoko and Sean.

Returning to London, Julian pondered his future from an apartment in London's Notting Hill district. Contrary to popular notion, he had little cash. After a few months of quiet mourning and reflection in Britain, and regular visits to his mother who then lived in Wiltshire, Julian hit the 'young socialite' scene, visiting the London clubs, being exploited and exposed, and generally living it up. It was not the happiest of periods for him; the British newspapers revelled in the sight of the 'playboy millionaire', the son of a murdered legend, the 'poor little rich boy' who drank too much, talked too much, and had a pretty girl on his arm as he came out of the London clubs in the early hours.

This 'backlash' was the natural behaviour of a teenager whose life would, from then, forever be under the spotlight. At his flat, Julian gradually gathered around him a commune of friends who were also musicians.

During much of 1981 and 1982, Julian veered towards the piano, but he was not enamoured with the synthesizer bands dominating the rock scene. There was, he told me, something cold and clinical about their sound. For about eighteen months he contemplated the route his music should take, as well as the flak he could expect if he launched himself into music as a career.

But there was little alternative. The extraordinary parallel with his father's life was now obvious: he had not been an academic success, excelled only in art, and now could only think of popular music.

Slowly, and with the streak of independence that so marked his father, Julian became determined to become a musician. But he also decided firmly that his work would not necessarily be as trendy as the best-selling records, but would have powerful lyrics as well as an individual sound. That way, he thought, he might just avoid being compared with anyone contemporary. And he was reconciled to inevitable comparisons with his father.

In the fall of 1983, during my work on this biography of

his father, I visited Julian and drove him around London. The cassette in my car was one which I could not stop playing repeatedly: an early demonstration of *The Nylon Curtain*, an album by a favourite artist, Billy Joel. Julian had scarcely heard of Joel's work and was mesmerized, particularly by the track 'Scandinavian Skies' in which Billy did a virtual parody of the Beatles sound. The whole album, though, impressed Julian for a totally different reason. He thought the production ideas and techniques were sensational. I told him the name of the producer: Phil Ramone, a man with an impeccable pedigree, having produced records by such giant names as Frank Sinatra, Bob Dylan, and Paul Simon. That day, Julian left my car clutching the demonstration tape of Billy Joel's new album. Julian seemed both elated and defeated: it was a stunning record which made a great impact on him as we drove around town; yet he reflected sadly that he might never achieve such standards himself.

His first goal, though, was to get a record contract. After some frustrating months for Julian and his musician friends and his manager and friend Dean Gordon, Julian signed in London with Charisma Records, who licensed him to Atlantic in the United States. The head of Charisma, a vastly experienced and intuitive record man, Tony Stratton Smith, loved Julian's demonstration cassette but was acutely aware of the explosion that would be caused by the launch of a son of John Lennon as a singer-songwriter. His first, wise decision was not to rush anything but to finance and generally support Julian in his writing and general planning of his debut album.

Tony Stratton Smith sent Julian and his musicians (Justin Clayton, guitar, and Jamaican-born bassist Carlos Morales) to France. There, in the isolation of a beautiful castle, the Manoir de Valotte, remotely tucked away near the town of Nevers, Julian worked for nearly three months on songwriting. He had to: there was nothing else to do except write, make demonstration tapes, and live the life of the solitary artist. Motorcycling, a favourite hobby of Julian's, was the only other pursuit.

News from New York that Phil Ramone had agreed to produce his first album galvanized Julian into great energy. I visited him in France and found a man both apprehensive and thrilled that the jigsaw of his life heading towards music was taking shape. 'I only hope I don't let anyone down,' he kept saying, an obvious reference to his family name.

The nurturing of Julian's debut album, called Valotte as a mark of attachment and memory of the unique retreat that inspired the music, went into a crucial final stage. He flew with his band to New York for the recording sessions, and the result was a triumphant entry into the professional music arena like few others in recent years. Julian's songs, 'Well I Don't Know', which related to his father, 'OK For You', and 'Too Late For Goodbyes', showed a fertile imagination that had both abrasive touches and melodicism; in Britain, he scored an immediate hit single with 'Too Late For Goodbyes', and appeared on many television and radio programmes, answering the obvious observations that he sounded very much like his father.

Once Julian had achieved instant success in Britain, the next target was America. After the album release, Julian's first major concert tour of the U.S. proved a resounding success. For a newcomer to the stage, he displayed great confidence and verve; and at the end of his shows, he demonstrated that he was not going to be afraid of confronting his identity. He sang three songs associated with his father: 'Day Tripper', 'Slippin' And Slidin' ', and—the biggest crowd-pleaser—'Stand By Me'.

When Julian felt sufficient confidence in his stage work, he invited Cynthia to see his three Los Angeles performances. She glowed as she realized that Julian was indeed going to be capable of continuing his father's great name in the world of music. 'There are similarities, obviously in the voices for genetic reasons,' observes Cynthia, 'but Julian is very much an individual. He was fully aware of what he was in for, and that he would be accused of cashing in on his father. But that's rubbish. I know he's had music inside him all his life. He was determined to do it his way, and his talent proves he was right.'

She was not always so calm and relaxed about Julian's physical similarities to John. Cynthia says that since his teenage years, Julian has thought, walked, stood, and spoken just like John, a true son. 'Once, in our house in North Wales, I came downstairs and Julian was standing with his back to me, astride a piano stool. Suddenly I saw the vision of John. It freaked me out, and the memory still does.

'Julian told me he has memories and sadnesses which he wants to hold on to privately. He feels, as I do, that all the talk of his father and the comparisons with his singing will never bring to life someone who was special and who is dead. We all love John and miss him. It's like a weeping sore. It seems to get worse the more attention we have to give it.

'Julian was so like his dad when John was alive. But now the likeness is just staggering. He thinks the same, moves the same, reacts the same, does not suffer fools gladly, and even talks to people in the same style as John. It's both unnerving and beautiful to see.'

While Julian moved onwards and upwards in his career, and as America, particularly, adopted him as a gifted artist, Cynthia too felt the need to actively assert her individuality. She returned to her first love, art, as a career, working for a top British company in textile and fabric design. She helped design the exterior of the newly-established Cavern Walks mall in Liverpool. And she became a television interviewer near her new home in the picturesque north of England. Ironically, her first assignment from the television station was to interview her son for a heart-to-heart chat about his life, his career, his hopes, and his recollections of his early years. She approached the task with trepidation, but Julian was utterly relaxed. 'It could have been traumatic. Instead it was a fantastic therapy for us both,' says Cynthia. When she saw the programme she wept with joy, realizing that mother and son had talked honestly to each other for the first time.

'We had never spoken about our emotions,' she says. 'For the television programme, we *had* to. We had our first proper conversation in public! It was nerve-wracking and for me a frightening baptism into my new job.'

Cynthia's memory flashes back to 8 April 1963, in Sefton Park hospital so close to Penny Lane in Liverpool. Shortly after she had given birth to Julian, John arrived. It was a mere five weeks after the Beatles had scored their first number one British hit with 'Please Please Me', and there were signs that the group would be a success.

'Who's a clever little Miss Powell then?' John said to Cynthia. And then, proudly lifting the six-pound, eleven-ounce baby into the air, John said: 'Who's going to be a famous little rocker like his Dad?'

Julian recalls very few conversations with his father about his life as a musician, songwriter, or pop star. 'He didn't like to talk to me about it much when I was growing up,' says Julian. 'He'd had enough of talking about the Beatles by the time he got home. He just talked about normal things—like my school work, my games, my clothes. I remember asking him once if he regretted anything about the Beatles and he answered: "No, it was great fun, but I'd hate to have to go through it again." '

In 1984, as Julian prepared for his own entry into a musical career, as a songwriter, pianist and bandleader, his father's words echoed in his mind. Julian wants to keep the Lennon tradition of songwriting aflame. 'My father's name and reputation has made me even more keen to follow on. I see my work as a continuation, though I'm aware of the dangers of comparison. I'll do it my way, and don't want to be compared with him. I'm just glad I had a father with so much talent.' And what would John say to him if he saw his son launching himself into a career in music? Julian thought for a long time. 'I think my father would say: "Do it—but don't blame me." '

Living life as the son of John Lennon, despite its problems, fills him with pride. 'I know everything my Dad did, good and bad,' says Julian. 'He said I was born out of a whisky bottle on a Saturday night. Makes no difference. I love him and respect him and I'm really proud of him.'

13
MONEY

'A room and a car and a car and a room'

Fame was hemming him in, but there was one massive compensation—money. By mid-1964, with American success assured, and record sales and songwriting royalties pouring in, John was a millionaire. Only four years after leaving art college, and only two years after signing with E.M.I., the material world was at his feet. In America, merchandising of Beatle-related paraphernalia (wigs, pillows, scarves) swelled their income beyond John's wildest dreams. Only George, who nursed a grievance even bigger than John's at the craziness of Beatlemania, shared John's understanding of the mayhem that was surrounding them.

Yet for all the status and all his money, which he enjoyed, John kept his feet firmly on the ground. He told me on tour once that he still had Mimi buy his combs from Woolworth's in Penny Lane because they were the best and he'd grown up with them. He was a great experimenter with fads: he tried vegetarianism but quickly rejected it. 'Nut cutlets! Ugh! I chucked them away and asked Cyn for a fry up of bacon and eggs.' Mentally he was on a fame planet, but deep down his roots were unshaken.

George was absorbed by the money. He prodded Brian Epstein as much as he dared about how much this record had made, how much their royalties were, what concerts would yield. Quickly, Harrison was dubbed the 'money Beatle'. He fought a vain battle for recognition by John and Paul of his own songs, but was mostly held off by the sheer weight of Lennon and McCartney's output. In their sense of humour, the more time the Beatles spent together the closer John and George became. The friendship was strengthened when, cost being of little consideration, John bought his Surrey house, Kenwood, in St George's Hill, Weybridge, while George bought Kinfauns, Claremont Estate, Esher, four miles away. His girlfriend and wife-to-be Pattie Boyd soon moved in with him. She got on well with Cynthia. Ringo was a neighbour of John's at Sunny Heights, on the same estate. Paul stayed in London, initially at Jane Asher's flat in the West End, but he eventually bought his own home at 7 Cavendish Avenue, St John's Wood.

George was a regular visitor to John's home, which was a pop star mansion, a symbol of success. It was bought hurriedly by John and Cynthia as a refuge from the fan-besieged flat in West Kensington. Within a month of buying it, John was off to America on tour. When John returned, the home and possessions began to interest him more. There was his art nouveau Rolls-Royce eventually painted in a rainbow of swirling floral patterns on a bright yellow background, with smoked one-way glass in the side and rear windows to keep the curious at bay. It had a television and drinks-packed refrigerator inside. He bought a Ferrari and a black Mini Cooper, and took driving lessons, successfully passing his test in February 1965. 'He was a terrible driver,' says Neil Aspinall. He had no sense of direction, often getting lost on the way home. The décor of the house was both spectacular and bizarre, a distinct contrast to the conformity of the sedate estate on which the house stood: purple velvet lined the dining-room walls—'It sets off the old scrubbed table we eat off,' said John. Most rooms had a television set, which John liked to have permanently switched on with the sound off. He was a self-confessed T.V. addict: 'I get lots of ideas from it,' he explained to me. 'I think with it on.'

'Then there's the funny room upstairs. I painted that pink and green, changing from one can to another as I emptied each can of paint.' A conducted tour of the house by John gave me an insight into the Beatle insisting on his individuality when he felt it was threatened by Beatlemania. Shortly after he moved

in and took me on a tour of Kenwood, I asked him for a list
of prized possessions, and he came up with this list:

My first Rickenbacker guitar: it's a bit hammered now,
I just keep it for kicks. I bought it in Germany on the
hire purchase—whatever it cost, it was a hell of a lot
of money to me at the time.

Three cars: a Rolls, Mini Cooper and Ferrari. The
Mini for pottering about in, the Rolls for relaxing in
and the Ferrari for zoom. I do very little driving. I'm
not a good driver.

Swimming pool: I enjoy a swim at home. It's a
luxury. All rich people have to have a pool.

Two pictures drawn by Stuart Sutcliffe, our old bass
player. I'll always keep those, for sentimental reasons.

A lump of stone: we found it on the doorstep and
somebody said it was prehistoric. I've since been en-
lightened and I believe it's a load of crap.

A stone frog: I like to see this in the fireplace, near
the T.V. set, looking at us all.

About twenty suits; but I only wear about two, both
black. I've got an evening dress but I only wear it when
I have to because it's so uncomfortable. I get my clothes
from Dougie Millings.

The Singing Postman's record: just part of my huge
record collection, but I particularly like this 'cos it's
stupid. I've got everything, electronic, Indian, classical
and modern jazz.

Pin table: football game machine and fruit machine:
in my 'den' here at home, just for a laugh.

Juke box: it's got forty-eight records on it, but I
keep it mainly for rock 'n' roll standards like Gene
Vincent's 'Be Bop A Lula', and the Big Three's 'Some
Other Guy'.

A studio which has two very good tape recorders
from which I can make my own records. And twelve
guitars, some of which are wrecked.

Aldous Huxley books. I've just started reading him,
because he's the new guvnor, it seems to me.

There were several tape recorders on which John would write his songs. He claimed to be the first British owner of the Mellotron, which occupied pride of place in the middle of the lounge. And on the mantelpiece was the winking 'nothing box' which begged the question: 'What's it do?' John enjoyed replying: 'It does nothing. It's a nothing box. It just winks all day and all night, but you can't tell where it's going to wink next.' The red flashing lights on his cherished nothing box had a hypnotic effect on all visitors. Its useless absurdity made John smile every time he looked at it.

John was always determined to move forward creatively, particularly in the Beatles' use of instruments. When he adopted the harmonica on 'Love Me Do', their début single, he hoped it would mark a breakthrough for the instrument, but he was just beaten to the bestsellers by Frank Ifield with his harmonica-accompanied number one, 'I Remember You'. In 1963, John became interested in the first 'organ-guitar' being developed in Britain by the entrepreneurial instrument manufacturer Jim Burns. John became deeply involved in all stages of the instrument's development. 'I played a Hammond organ on our second L.P.,' said John, 'and I fancy a guitar that plays like an organ as well as a guitar. It'd be gear (a favorite word to show enthusiasm).'

By the time the Beatles went on tour and into the recording studios as a successful group, John's pride and joy was the guitar he had hankered after during his lean, struggling years. It was a Rickenbacker model number 1996, slimline. It cost an astronomical 159 guineas at the beginning of 1964. John cherished it like a child with a new toy and asked the Beatles' road manager 'Big Mal' Evans to take great care of it. It can be heard making the particularly pretty guitar figures during one of John's most under-rated solos, 'You Can't Do That'.

John enjoyed indulging himself. 'I do get fits worrying about money,' he told me about this time. 'I worry about being one of those idiots who spend, spend, spend and do it all by the time I'm thirty. I thought I'd been a bit extravagant and bought too many cars, so I put the Mini and the Ferrari up for sale. Then one of the accountants said I was all right, so I got the cars back from the showroom.'

The problem was that he did not know how much money

he had. 'I've tried to find out, but with income tax to be deducted and royalties coming in from all over the place, the sums get too complicated for me. I can't even do my times table. Every now and again the accountant clears some money of tax and puts it in my account and says: "That's yours but don't spend it all at once." But I have learned this much: to spend £10,000 I have to earn £30,000 before tax to get it.' His generosity often overtook him: on the rare occasions when he carried money he would give £5 or £10 tips to astonished waiters in restaurants.

He would leave messages on the answering machine of Wendy Hanson, Brian Epstein's personal assistant. One said: 'Wendy, send Aunt Mimi one of those maps of the world that has bottles in it.' She had several similarly enigmatic instructions from him. 'I knew he'd have seen it in Asprey's,' says Wendy Hanson. 'He was always rushing through there making mental notes. It was a globe. He was very impetuous, rather than acquisitive. Asprey's was a favourite. I once had John Asprey keep the place open late just for the Beatles to tour the shop, like they did at Harrods one Christmas. John thought it was a joke. He simply bought some jam.'

Wendy, who as Epstein's chief lieutenant was on the receiving end of John during what she feels was 'one of the most extraordinary phenomena of modern times', describes him as 'like a crab, a tough shell outside, a softie inside. . . . He wasn't tough at all. In France a fourteen-year-old girl fan hid in Lennon's bedroom to await his arrival at the Negresco Hotel, Nice. Her mother phoned Wendy to say: "A Beatle has raped my daughter."

'John was distraught for this girl,' Wendy continues. 'He said: "Wendy, call this woman up and tell her that her child hasn't been touched. She's hiding under my bed and won't come out. She's absolutely fine but worried because she says her mother's going to beat her up when she gets home." It was extraordinary. We got the girl out, but I remember how much John cared and was very gentle about it. He made sure long after the chaos of the event that we checked to make sure the girl got home safely. I remember saying to someone: "So much for the tough guy." '

The change in status, from a college student who had had to scrounge cigarettes and cinema money only four years previously, to being one of the most sought-after personalities in the world, amused John. His telephone answering machine at Weybridge reflected his frivolity. A favourite game would be to play the messages over and over again, laughing maniacally at people's accents, mimicking them, and rarely returning phone calls. It was John's Goon-like sense of humour surfacing. Guests at the house, like singer P.J. Proby, whose audacity Lennon admired, Liverpool schoolfriends like Ivan and Jean Vaughan and Pete Shotton, were bemused by the new Lennon.

As Beatlemania mounted, John became irritable at the lack of privacy. Kenwood was invaded on Saturdays and Sundays by fans who regarded the sighting of a Beatle at home as a pilgrimage to the Promised Land. 'I'm fed up with it,' he told me during one particularly exasperated night. 'Some weekends it gets so bad we go away, anywhere, to get away from the fans who come to gawp. No, stop that word, they're not *fans*! They treat my house like a bloody holiday camp, sitting in the grounds with flasks of tea and sandwiches. What do they think this is, a Beatle National Park? They're adults too, not all kids. I went out and told them all to sod off once, and they said they wouldn't buy any more of my records! I said they should find something better to do with their spare time.'

The fans collected anything as mementoes of their visits. They took photographs of the strange brass doorknocker in the shape of a naked woman. They took blades of grass from the lawn as souvenirs of a Beatle mansion. John wanted it to be a haven for himself, Cynthia and Julian, their two tabby cats, called Mimi and Babaghi, and their brown labrador dog, Nigel. But it was an uphill fight. He never knew what was going to await him when he returned home.

John's own spare time, when he had not been writing songs or travelling or in the recording studio, had been spent writing and doodling. On the backs of envelopes, in cars and trains and planes and hotel rooms, John scribbled away and drew caricatures of the characters he invented. It was his private diversion from the mayhem of Beatlemania. The stories were continuations of the theme he had begun, seven years earlier, at Quarry Bank school, in the *Daily Howl* exercise book. Brian Epstein, seeing John's verse and doodles one day, offered to get them published. It had not occurred to Lennon, but the result was the début, in 1964, of John as an author.

In His Own Write, published by Jonathan Cape in 1964, was lionized by the literary establishment. 'Worth the attention of anyone who fears for the impoverishment of the English language and the British imagination,' said *The Times Literary Supplement*.

The obvious influences at work in the book were Lewis Carroll, Spike Milligan and *The Goon Show*, and the gobbledegook linguistic comedian Stanley Unwin. The 'Alice' books had exerted a strong influence on John since childhood and were later to percolate into his writing, notably 'I Am The Walrus' which derived from Carroll's 'The Walrus and the Carpenter'. The first verse of 'Lucy In The Sky With Diamonds' recalls Alice's gentle voyage with the sheep in *Alice Through the Looking Glass*. Lennon was familiar with Carroll's lengthier, surrealistic poems like 'Jabberwocky' and 'The Hunting of the Snark', and loved his verbal word-play and jumbling of images. The titles of John's hilarious essays told their own story of the satirical slants. 'On Safairy With Whide Hunter' (written, as John put it, 'in conjugal with Paul') and 'No Flies On Frank', 'The Fat Growth On Eric Hearble', and 'At The Denis', demonstrated a grasp of humour that had the critics showering praise. One Conservative M.P., Charles Curran, seemed to miss the point. He stated in Parliament that John's book highlighted the poor education in Liverpool, and claimed Lennon was illiterate.

John's first book topped the British bestseller list. It sold more than 100,000 copies in its first printing, and he was feted at a prestigious Foyle's literary luncheon at London's Dorchester Hotel. Immediately, John was recognized as the intelligent Beatle. Demand for tickets at the lunch exceeded the requests when George Bernard Shaw was the guest. The lunch itself was animated enough, with a high attendance of the literary establishment, but John was not to be drawn into making the customary speech for a guest of honour. He rose and said: 'Thank you very much, God bless you.' Many were disappointed, but he explained later that he did not feel up to it.

'Give me another fifteen years, and I may make a speech. Anyway I daren't today. I was scared stiff.'

John's speechlessness did nothing to dent his mystique among the expensively dressed debutantes, bejewelled dowagers, waiters and aristocrats who jostled outside the Dorchester Hotel like teenage fans, demanding John's autograph. 'For my daughter,' of course.

One woman clutched ten copies of his book and thrust them into his hand, saying: 'Put your name clearly here.'

John looked at her, astonished, as she said to her friend: 'I never thought I would stoop to asking for such an autograph.'

John cut her with: 'And I never thought I would be forced to sign my name for someone like *you*.'

John's second book, *A Spaniard In The Works*, was more disciplined than the first. 'It was starting from scratch,' explained John. 'The publisher said you've got so many months to write a book in. With the first book, I'd written a lot of it at odd times during my life.'

John had nearly a year to produce *A Spaniard In The Works*, during which he observed, as always, the passing scene and was able to develop his thoughts into prose and satire. There was a tilt at the *Daily Mirror* columnist Cassandra (whom John called Cassandle), which John said was because the writer had been knocking the Beatles. There was a send-up of newspaper letter columns called Readers Lettuce. There was John's glorious irreverence captured in Last Will and Testicle:

I, Barrold Reginald Bunker-Harquart being of sound mind you, limp and bodie, do on this day the 18 of September 1924th, leave all my belongings estate and brown suits to my nice neice Elsie. The above afformentioned hereafter to be kept in a large box until she is 21 of age. . . .

'The National Health Cow', 'Snore Wife and some Several Dwarts', and 'The Singularge Experience of Miss Anne Duffield'—in which John had some help in writing from George while they were on holiday in Tahiti—were more examples of John's acute sense of the ridiculous.

A keen insight into the literary Lennon came with his broadcast in July 1965 on B.B.C. radio's *World of Books* programme. Interviewed by Wilfred De'Ath, John said his books were mostly spontaneous and undisciplined productions.

'I'm selfish about what I write, or big-headed about it. Once I've written it I like it and the publishers sometimes say, "Should we leave this out or change that?" And I fight like mad because once I've done it, I like to keep it. But I always write it straight off. I might add things when I go over it, before it's published, but I seldom take anything out, so it's spontaneous.'

That desire reflected John's recording preferences. He hated songs to linger for long, to be refined in the studio. He liked to work, in records as apparently in books and all his art, rather like a daily newspaperman: write it, see it released very quickly, then move on. He wanted his records out overnight, and when his life as a Beatle was replaced by the Plastic Ono Band John did have records out within days of completion. It mirrored, also, his philosophy of life as a fast run.

On that radio interview John admitted only two influences in his literary work: Conan Doyle, who had marked his work in the Sherlock Holmes-inspired tale, 'The Singularge Experience of Miss Anne Duffield', and Lewis Carroll. 'I always admit to that because I love *Alice in Wonderland* and *Through the Looking Glass*, but I didn't even know he'd written anything else, I was that ignorant. I just had it as a birthday present as a child and liked them.'

'A lot of people say your pieces are sick. What do you say to that?' asked the interviewer.

'If it makes people sick. But I can read it and it doesn't appear sick to me,' replied John.

Denying other influences tossed around by literary reviewers, who quoted Edward Lear, James Thurber and others as his evident inspirations, John said: 'I deny it because I'm ignorant of it. Lear I'd never heard of. Well, I'd heard the name obviously somewhere but we didn't do him at school. The only classic or very highbrow anything I read at school or knew of is Chaucer. I might have read a bit of Chaucer at school because I think they do that. And so I bought all the books they said it was like. I bought one book on Edward Lear, I bought *Finnegan's Wake*, Chaucer, and I couldn't see any resemblance to any of them.'

He only read what he stumbled across, he said, not what it was 'right' or accepted to read. He had never read anything by Jonathan Swift. 'Charles Dickens I don't like too much. I've got to be in a certain mood. It's too *school*. I'm too near school to read Dickens or Shakespeare. I hate Shakespeare. I don't care whether you should like him or not. It doesn't mean anything to me.' He had just discovered Winnie the Pooh, 'which I'd never read as a child. I just discovered him about a year ago.'

By far the longest essay in *Spaniard In The Works*, 'The Singular Experience', spread over nine pages. When Wilfred De'Ath described his written works as 'mini pieces', John said: 'To you they're mini pieces, to me they're *marathons*. With Sherlock Holmes, I was seeing how far I could go. I forget which characters have come in and I just get lost and fed up and bored. That's why I usually either kill them off—well, I killed the lot off in the first book.'

On his Cassandra lampoon, he said, 'I did it mainly because he knocked us. We get a lot of knocking which we don't mind. We don't want everybody to love us, if somebody doesn't like us they're entitled to but we have no defence against people like that writing about us in newspapers, because we can't say anything back. And this is just my way of having a go back. It was just a sort of personal joke amongst ourselves. I'm definitely planning on Bernard Levin for the next one.'

Singer George Melly met John at a party to launch John's first book. Melly had written a glowing review of the book in the *Observer*. 'I approached him,' says George, 'in what I thought was a friendly manner, with perhaps an element of patronization. He was quite drunk and so was I.

'He started on me about the fact that I came from trad jazz which he hated because it blocked him and his friends from the Cavern. So he called me one of the blockers. He was quite aggressive.

'I said, "Did you like the review?"

'He said he hadn't read it.

'I said how much I enjoyed it, and referred to his James Joyce influence.

'He said: "I don't know who you're talking about. I've never heard of him. Who the hell's Joyce?" '

This was not true, because he *had* heard of James Joyce.

Finally Lennon and Melly nearly came to blows when Melly brought up the subject of black singers. George said: 'Of course, you must feel as I feel in my sphere, that one's real debt is to black singers like Muddy Waters and Chuck Berry, who invented the idiom in which we both sing.'

John became furious. He said he accepted nothing of the sort. He refuted all influences. 'I could eat 'em for breakfast . . . they don't make anything like I make,' he roared, the drink talking. The shout-up continued, with Melly insisting that Lennon's music was as derivative as his own. 'It nearly came to a fight,' says Melly. 'I'm glad it didn't because he would certainly have won.'

Yet once he had achieved success, John felt ambivalent about singing on the same concert bill as black acts. With the other Beatles, notably George Harrison, he had invited cult Tamla Motown singer Mary Wells ('My Guy') to tour with them in Britain in 1964; but when she came, superb though she was, John felt uncomfortable. 'I hate singing "Twist and Shout" when there's a coloured artist on the bill,' he told me. 'It doesn't seem right, you know. It seems to be their music and I feel sort of embarrassed. Makes me curl up . . . they can do these songs much better than us.'

He had no patience with other beat groups, who, he declared, 'are pinching our musical arrangements down to the last note'. He said to me: 'Look, we copied nobody. I am not a Negro so I can't copy a Negro singer. We've got our own style based on the music we grew up with, and it annoys me a lot to find groups getting on the wagon by copying sounds we were playing two years ago. Why can't these copyists make their own styles like we did? It happens in hairstyles as well. I see players in some groups have even the same length of hair as us. It's no good them saying they're students and they just happen to have long hair. *We* were students, as well, before we came to London, and we didn't have these hairstyles then. The difference between the Beatles and some of these others is that we didn't sit around in the 'Pool saying: "We're going to be big stars." Music was part of our lives. We played it because we loved doing it, not just for the loot. Unlike some groups, we don't go around even now saying: "Look, we're stars." I just consider myself a lucky layabout from Liverpool who has had some success. My auntie used to say (and here he would brilliantly mimic Mimi's authoritarian voice): "You're not seriously thinking of making a career in *that* line! The guitar's all right as a hobby, John, but you'll never make a living from it."

'And I'd say: "No, it's just a passing thing." '

When he was speaking fast and furiously and wanting it reported, John would urge a journalist: 'Get it *down*, get it down in that book.'

Asked by a radio interviewer whether he would prefer to be remembered as a writer or as a Beatle, John replied: "I don't care whether I'm remembered or not. After I'm gone, I don't care what happens.'

John adapted to the lifestyle of a millionaire star with ease. He drank too much, but some kind of release from the pressures of being in what he later called a 'goldfish bowl' was essential. He had a few formal dinner guests at his Weybridge home, and those who did stay, like the pianist-singer Alan Price, would find themselves driven there nearer breakfast-time after all-night drinking at the Ad Lib club, exchanging hilarious tales of fights in their mad youth—John regaling people with stories of Hamburg, Price with ones of his Geordie childhood.

Spectators who did not participate in debates, like American singers Dionne Warwick and Mary Wells, would look on in disbelief at Lennon's Scotch-and-Coke-soaked antics. This was not the cosy Beatle whose moptop image had been pumped across the Atlantic as something clean and pure. Here was a drunk!

John's realization of just how enormous his group had become occurred when the Beatles returned home for a civic reception at Liverpool Town Hall. More than one hundred thousand people turned out for the day, and John, on a secret visit to Mendips, found his old home had become a shrine. Fans and journalists from all over the world were besieging his house, and Aunt Mimi was too exposed for comfort. She lived there alone, since John's move to London, save for Tim, the fat ginger cat.

'I kept changing the phone number,' says Mimi, 'but the

fans would keep discovering the new one within a few days.'
Rich and successful with the world at his feet, John's welcome
was tempered by Mimi with her traditional reserve. 'He knew
better than to tell me how well they were doing,' says Mimi.

'I simply said: "I'm glad it's working out well, John."

'He said: "I told you it would."

'And that was that.'

A year later, John persuaded Mimi to stay with him at
Weybridge. 'I'm going to buy you a new house, Mimi,' he
said to her over his usual breakfast of two or three bowls of
cornflakes topped with bananas. 'Where's it to be?'

Mimi, stumped for a reply, said the first seaside place that
came into her head: 'Bournemouth.' That morning, John and
Mimi set off in his Rolls-Royce, chauffeured by the faithful
Les Anthony, armed with maps of Hampshire. John never just
sat in his Rolls. He lay down in it. He operated the electrically
controlled windows with his feet, playing ups and downs with
them all the time. He smoked a lot, often passing a cigarette
to his chauffeur. At traffic lights, people glanced inside in
disbelief at sighting a Beatle. He gave them the world's most
freezing stare.

The estate agents in Bournemouth provided them with some
suitable houses for sale, and Mimi took a fancy to a white-
painted bungalow overlooking Poole Harbour. She particularly
loved the view, with its lounge window facing the terrace which
led down to the water. Mimi pictured herself here, watching
the pleasure launches and seeing the seagulls. 'Like it, Mimi?'
said John. Within hours of starting the search, he was on the
phone to his accountant and had bought the house in Panorama
Road, Sandbanks.

Mimi sold Mendips, finally persuading John, who wanted
the backdrop to his childhood years preserved, that there could
be no turning back the clock. For the next eight years, John
rang her phone several times a week on his world travels as
he developed increasing love and respect for the daunting woman
who had brought him up. He visited her regularly too, slumping
in the armchair with its sea view and over cups of tea confiding
his innermost thoughts about the Beatles, his marriage, and his
restlessness. 'The older he got, the better we got to know each
other,' reflects his aunt.

When the time came for Mimi to leave Liverpool, John asked her to take special care of his childhood books and the huge grandfather clock on which Uncle George had taught him to tell the time. 'I'll need it some day,' said John.

During an interview I had in 1964 with Bob Dylan, he referred to a song whose title he could not remember: the Beatles' 'I Want To Hold Your Hand'. It held the number one position for seven weeks in America. 'You know,' he said, 'that song about dope?' I must have looked even more baffled than I felt.

It transpired that Bob believed the real words, 'I can hide, I can hide', at the end of one chorus, were 'I get high, I get high'. Dylan was astonished that it was not a drugs song, and by his discovery, on meeting them in America, that they were not into marijuana. British pop stars were several years behind their American counterparts in adopting drugs as part of their lifestyle.

Dylan is popularly regarded as having switched the Beatles on to marijuana during their visit to America. But his significance to John, during the mid-1960s, was his spectacular command of words and ability to combine intelligent imagery with electric folk music. Lennon was quickly hypnotized by Dylan's album *Bringing It All Back Home*, a brave adventure by a former folk singer–guitarist into the world of rock. John played the album a lot at home, but would not be drawn much on it. It was as if he felt the presence of a genuine literary rival.

His inquisitiveness, though, triumphed over his apprehension. There followed a distinct 'Dylan period' as John called it, when he wrote songs in Bob's style and even invited the singer to his home. But there was an edginess, a nervousness of each other, in the air, and the Weybridge meeting did not form the basis of a long and lasting friendship. Spiritually, as totally original artists, Lennon and Dylan were too alike to become close. Recognition of each other was enough, and John, who before Dylan turned him on to marijuana had only got high on booze or 'Prellys' in Hamburg, acknowledged the maestro with songs like 'I'm A Loser' and 'Norwegian Wood', both introspective. One of his favourite 1965 singles was Dylan's 'Subterranean Homesick Blues', which John described as 'very Chuck Berry-ish'. He and I spent a lot of time at his Weybridge home trying to work out the words.

Dylan, and Lennon's fresh songwriting phase of looking inwards, had arrived at an important juncture in John's life. It was natural, thought Brian Epstein, for the boys' personalities to be captured in films. Their first tentative move was in *A Hard Day's Night*, followed the next year by *Help!* and subsequently by John's solo role in *How I Won The War*, alongside Michael Crawford. The director of all three films was Richard Lester. John struck up an immediate rapport with the laconic American, partly because, like George Martin, Lester had been involved with John's cherished Goons, having filmed Spike Milligan and Peter Sellers, in *The Running, Jumping and Standing Still Film*. Zany comedy was still John's favourite brand and he envisaged a desperately needed switch from the rigours of Beatlemania. The scriptwriter was Alun Owen, a Liverpudlian who went with Lester to meet the Beatles during their Paris trip in January 1964.

A Hard Day's Night was devised, simply, as a black and white fictionalized documentary of the Beatles' crazy life as pop stars, covering their experiences as musicians, in the recording studios, their television appearances, their pressures in concerts. 'The film was based on their life living in small boxes, as prisoners of their own success,' says Richard Lester. 'The concept came from John's reply to a question I asked him about a trip they'd made to Sweden.

' "How did you like it?" I said.

'John said: "Oh, it was a room and a car and a car and a room and a room and a car."

'That became our signal of how to do *A Hard Day's Night*.' The film was shot on location at Marylebone Station in London and on trains.

'We tried very hard to make sure that nobody had more than one sentence to learn at any given time,' says Richard Lester, 'and John fell into line with the rest of them. It was eight o'clock every morning make-up and eight-thirty on the set, no arguments. I think that came as a great shock to them, but their road managers, Neil Aspinall and Mal Evans, made sure that they were all there on time.'

Wherever the Beatles went in the public eye in the mid-sixties, fans gathered in their hundreds or thousands very quickly. 'The biggest problem in making *A Hard Day's Night* on location was that we could, at best, get two takes on anything when we were on a street,' says Richard Lester. 'The streets would get so blocked with fans we'd have to change locations and start again. We had to get the Beatles on and off the set very quickly!' This meant the Beatles tearing quickly into a shop, doing their scene, and making a rapid exit at the other side of the shop to fool the crowds. All this had to be done in minutes, and led to one of the most expensive days in John Lennon's life.

Darting in and out of Asprey's, the exclusive and ultra-expensive store in Bond Street, John managed to spend about £80,000 within minutes. 'God knows how he managed it. I think even John was amazed at how much he ordered from the place,' says Richard Lester. He ordered furniture, jewellery, and bric-à-brac.

The song title became the title for the film after Ringo had come up with the phrase to recall a heavy night. John's composition, and his searing vocal, make it one of the most enduring Beatles songs.

Help! was a more adventurous enterprise. Filmed over a nine-week period, it had a weak story similar to the James Bond themes. A crazy scientist joined a search for a valuable ring that ended up on Ringo's hand. The movie began life as *Eight Arms To Hold You*, but when John wrote the title track it was such a powerful song that it was adopted as the film's title.

Shooting began over two weeks in the Bahamas, where John quickly showed that, even as a multi-millionaire pop and film star, he was not likely to be conned into high society. 'One didn't want to have a tongue lashing from John, but it did come out in Nassau,' recalls Richard Lester. 'We were all guests at dinner of the Governor, and we had been filming in a mental hospital where conditions were outrageous.'

Actor Victor Spinetti, who was there and who developed a strong friendship with John, says, 'We all went looking around what appeared to be an army barracks. We thought it was deserted. In fact there were a lot of spastics and cripples and old people in there and John was shocked that they had been shoved away under this terrible corrugated-iron army hut.'

'It was a black tie affair,' says Richard Lester, 'with the equivalent of all the hoorays of the Bahamas. John let loose. It was a perfectly justifiable sense of outrage for anyone with a sense of social conscience.'

Victor Spinetti says Lennon was especially appalled by the contrast between the champagne and caviare they were offered at dinner, and the living conditions of the afflicted. John said to the Minister of Finance: 'I saw this place today which was meant to be a hospital. People were in there under the most terrible conditions.'

'The Minister replied: "I do my best, you know. I'm not being paid for being the Minister of Finance."

'To which John answered: "Oh, in that case you're doing better than I thought you were doing." '

The press turned on the Beatles because of John's sharpness, but he was unrepentant and told everyone he loathed the Bahamas.

'He made the very strong point,' says Richard Lester, 'that these people were hypocrites and condescending to the Beatles because they *were* the Beatles, and that he couldn't stand. He was very, very tough on the authorities after that. The power of John's attack on that government figure makes me remember him very strongly from the weeks in the Bahamas, much more than the others at that time.'

After the Bahamas, the location work moved to the ski slopes of Austria, in a small town called Obertauren, two hours' drive from Salzburg. By now John and the others were smoking marijuana heavily, but not so much that they could not work. They would hardly have been able to work so vigorously, or write the songs, or drink until the early hours in the hotel, if they had been heavily stoned. But John's euphoria after going to his room for a smoke, and his enlarged pupils, made it obvious when he was high.

Perhaps it was a release from the Bahamas, but John was in a particularly buoyant mood when I visited Austria for a week during location work. He was agile at skiing, which he enjoyed. He thought the film story was ludicrous but was able to laugh at the fact that it was unstoppable, expensive, and a waste of such a lot of time and money; he struck up a warm friendship with actress Eleanor Bron and was often to be heard in conversation with her, talking politics and philosophy, over drinks in the hotel bar. In political beliefs John thought like a socialist but said he would have to vote Conservative because they knew how to manage the country. Money came into it quite strongly, he used to tell me. 'Deep down,' he said, 'I'm Labour. Politics is a state of mind but you've got to protect your money, haven't you?'

It was in Austria that John and Paul and I concocted an amusing, childish, but absorbing word-game one night in the hotel bar. The game was called Winners and Losers, and appealed immensely to John. One person called out the name of a person, country, drink or anything tangible, and the others would pronounce it a winner or a loser. There were no hard rules for this daft, arbitrary game. It relied purely on intuition rather than definition. Thus, John pronounced E.M.I. a winner, Decca a loser; France (where the Beatles had just appeared, with only moderate success) a loser country, America a winner; Coca-Cola was a winner, Pepsi-Cola a loser; New York was a winner, Los Angeles a loser; tea a winner, coffee a loser; the whole of Fleet Street a loser because the journalists were so very late realizing the Beatles were a force. And so it went on, becoming highly personalized, argumentative, often cruel and great fun.

In a chance remark to a British musician he greatly admired, Tony Sheridan, John said, as the Beatles' success grew: 'I've sold my soul to the devil.' Sheridan, who had recorded with the Beatles in Hamburg, had been particularly friendly with John and knew immediately what John meant, for fame of this kind was never what Lennon expected.

The *Help!* film coincided with what John later called his 'fat Elvis' period. It was difficult to realize it until later, but John was slightly overweight, eating and drinking too much, materialistically collecting possessions, but too much of an artist to be swept along by show business. He was more dissatisfied even than he realized: he thought he had lost his art. Cynthia, however, maintains that 1965 was his finest songwriting year.

When he wrote 'Help!' something from deep within him gave vent to his insecurity, his feeling that all was not well, despite the millions of record sales, the adoration, the frustrating mansion in Weybridge which he described as 'like a bus stop, you wait until something comes along . . .'.

John's *cri de coeur* emerged with painful honesty, although nobody was listening carefully to his title song as the autobiography it was . . .

When I was younger, so much younger than today,
I never needed anybody's help in any way.
But now these days are gone, I'm not so self-assured
Now I find I've changed my mind, I've opened up
    the doors.

Help me if you can, I'm feeling down
And I do appreciate you being 'round
Help me get my feet back on the ground, won't you
    please, please help me?

And now my life has changed in oh so many ways
My independence seems to vanish in the haze,
But every now and then I feel so insecure
I know that I just need you like I've never done
    before . . .
Help, I need somebody, help, not just anybody,
    help . . . help!

Characteristically, John was the first Beatle to debunk the Beatles. He could not stand the inflated descriptions of what the Beatles were, or being constantly paraded, or the dukes and lords who regarded it as a social cachet to be photographed with a Beatle. To John what had begun as rock 'n' roll had become an industry. He did not see himself as a profound performer, and while he admired Paul McCartney's musical strengths, the two men were not reacting in the same way to fame. Paul loved it.

One rainy afternoon in 1965, in an interview with me at Weybridge, John was in a morose mood. His restlessness was evident as he took me up to the music room where, amid countless tapes, recorders, and amplifiers, and a mess of paper, he was strumming his guitar and writing a song which turned out later as 'Nowhere Man'. With hindsight, it was a prophetic title: a moment, a day, when the change in John Winston Lennon was more evident than at any time since they first scored a hit record.

He was both defensive and confused about fame as he ate his afternoon breakfast of cornflakes, a dish he was likely to eat at any time of the day. He smoked incessantly and started talking about how he felt old at the age of twenty-five. 'According to the rules of the pop world, we're old,' he said. 'But we don't look any older than the Stones, do we? We certainly don't act any older. I've seen Jagger looking a hundred and The Who looking at least thirty some nights. Christ, we felt old when we started, when Brian Epstein found us. We thought we'd left it too late to make it. Years don't affect your mind. They can give your face wrinkles, but it's your attitude and outlook that counts. I've met people of thirty who aren't thirty in their mentality. The calendar alone says they've lived thirty years, and although age can give you experience, some people aren't capable of using that experience. I'm twenty-six next year. The rules say that I'm a fully grown man, settled down and all that. I'm not—I've still got a young outlook!'

What nagged away at him was the fear that the Beatles were no longer a rock 'n' roll group but were generally appealing to mothers and fathers and adults. 'There was a time back there when we seemed to be doing everything at once—getting older people interested in what we're doing as well as the young. But I don't like that.' He said he had not enjoyed their Christmas concerts in London for that reason. 'It doesn't seem natural to see old people out there looking at us. They should be at home doing the knitting.'

Asked if he regretted the size of the Beatles' popularity, John said, 'No, I'm glad things got as big as they did. Because when we got *nearly* big, people started saying to us: "You're the biggest thing since. . . ." And I hated that. I wanted the Beatles to be just *the* biggest thing. It's like gold. The more you get the more you want.'

John said British fan mail for the Beatles was declining from the peak it had reached a year or so earlier. 'I'm talking about the stuff I get myself now. Paul gets a lot every day.

Mine fluctuates—goes up when we've got a new record out. Since our European tour we've been getting plenty of mail from Yugoslavia, Italy, and for some reason, Japan.'

The attitude of the fans still bothered him, he told me. 'It's annoying when people turn round and say: "But we MADE you, you ungrateful swines." They did, in a way, but there's a limit to what we're bound to do, as if it's a duty. When I had black windows put in my Rolls-Royce, a fan wrote to me: "You're hiding, turning your back and running away from the people who made you."

'Rubbish! If I go to a shop down the road and buy a bunch of roses I don't expect the bloke to be so grateful that he spends his life bowing and scraping. I like the roses, so I buy them, and that's that.

'I don't want to sound as if we don't like being liked. We appreciate it,' said John, his Aunt Mimi's training conspicuously keeping him balanced. 'But we can't spend our lives being dictated to.

'Think about these Kellogg's cornflakes. If you buy cornflakes, do you expect Mr Kellogg to spend his life being told how to do everything, how to behave? No. And if you buy a loaf of bread and it's lousy, you just don't buy it again.

'It's not all that different with us. We make a record and if you like it you buy it. If you don't, don't buy it. It's up to the public to decide.

'The Beatles can't win at the moment. If we try to please everybody, right across the age groups, it's impossible. We'd end up in the middle with nobody liking us. People think of us as a machine. They pay six shillings and eight pence for a record and we have to do what they say, like Jack-in-the-box. I don't like that side of being a pop star.'

Cynthia came into the room, with Julian and John's cup of tea. Julian stayed a while, and I casually asked John how old the boy was. 'He's two, I think,' said John. And then, in a rare flash of correction. 'That's awful. I'm away so much I've forgotten how old he is. Yeah, two it must be.'

When Cynthia left the room, John said how glad he was that his, and Ringo's, marriage had been accepted by fans. 'I don't think the two of us being married has had any bad effects on our popularity. Remember, when it got out that both Ringo

and I were married, there hadn't been anybody in such a position as we were in, who had got married. It was Silver Disc,
as opposed to Gold Disc, people, who'd got married before
us! People who relied on the fact that they wiggled, sexily, in
their stage acts. We didn't rely on wiggling, we still don't, and
we won't. We were never dependent on fans being in love with
us so much as others are. Not like Jagger. He's the Charlie
Chaplin of rock 'n' roll. Now *he* can't afford to get married!
The Stones would be all over.'

Although John and Mick got on well superficially, there
was a distinct impression that Lennon thought Jagger was trying,
through the Stones, to overtake the Beatles, and John regarded
that as pathetic. Later, John slammed the Stones' *Satanic Maj-
esties Request* album as an imitation of *Sgt Pepper*, and loathed
the Stones' record 'We Love You' which John said was 'She
Loves You' backwards. Coincidentally, both John and Paul
had sung on the record which Lennon blasted so forcefully.
John had very little artistic respect for the Rolling Stones. When
he was drinking, he tore into them for merely copying black
music.

The trappings and status of fame seemed strangely, suddenly shallow. The fine wines in the cellar at Weybridge were
ordered by John or Cynthia or the housekeeper, Dorothy Jarlett,
at random. Expensive restaurant dinners were nice but were
making him mentally, as well as physically, bloated. He and
Cynthia dined with good friends, like Victor Spinetti, who
introduced him to light escapism in the theatre and shows like
The Student Prince and *The Desert Song*. Afterwards, they
would adjourn to La Cappannina, an Italian restaurant in Rom-
illy Street, Soho, and talk the night away. John enjoyed visiting
the home of Peter Cook, whose sense of humour was endearing,
and he was a regular, often alone, at the trendy discotheque
called the Scotch of St James, where he traded stories with
visiting American musicians. 'Before going out for a night on
the booze,' he said, 'I drink a pint of milk and take two Aspro.
Stops you getting a hangover.' John was funny when inebriated,
but could be aggressive if he didn't win an argument. And in
that period, he was subconsciously seeking new routes. He
would vent his tension in odd ways.

In Paris, at the posh Hôtel Georges V, John stubbed a cigarette out in the middle of a giant, extravagant cake which reposed in the Beatles' suite. It was John's way of commenting on the sickliness of the cake and the stupidity of its appearance and extravagance. Next to the Queen, nothing in Britain was a better-known institution than the Beatles, and privately that was precisely what bothered John. At Kenwood, he had spent nearly £50,000 on decorating and furnishing a house which had cost only £19,000 to buy. Now, nourished by his success as the author of two books, he started looking around outside the Beatles for activities.

Touring was a drag. The film *Help!* had been a disaster to John, whatever anyone else said. 'I was only an extra in my own film,' he told Richard Lester. He was encouraged to make another film, away from the Beatles, the following year, but by then John had a built-in distrust of acting. 'Of the four, he would have been the best actor, an unexpected actor,' says Lester.

'I told him: "You're obviously a good actor if you want to be."

'He replied: "Acting's silly and daft." '

Concert tours were a wider issue. Live work was what the Beatles had been born from, yet now, mounting a tour was more like a military operation than ever. The 'car and a room and a room and a car' syndrome had gone beyond anyone's comprehension and was no longer a joke. On the road, particularly in America, the compensations were the women and the speedy American way of life. But to the Beatles on stage the shows were charades. They could hear only deafening screams, and the music counted for nothing. They were like a circus act. 'Just dummies,' John said. 'They can't even see us from that distance. We're specks on the horizon. Why they pay money to come and see us, like fifty-five thousand at Shea Stadium in New York, I'll never know.'

And then there was flying. John had always hated it. Next to George, who had a pathological fear of getting on a plane, John was the worst flier. He joked his way nervously through most flights, and shored himself up with alcohol. Yet the jokes flowed when he was aboard. Flying Lufthansa from London to

Munich, he said to me in a voice that thankfully none of the German crew heard as we climbed the steps: 'It's good to fly Lufthansa to London—all the pilots know the way.'

John's tongue was at once his most endearing characteristic and his worst enemy. On stage in Hamburg during the Beatles' emotional return there in 1966 for a triumphant German concert tour, John told the crowd, 'Don't listen to our music. We're terrible these days.' He meant that their stage work had lost its bite. It was the truth, but he hurt a lot of people with the remark. And he could not understand why all those millions of screams came from people who simply wanted to attend an *event*.

Lennon had a macabre sense of humour about dying in a plane crash. 'We'll either go in a plane crash or we'll be popped off by some loony,' he said to me on a plane in America. The remark was to echo with devastating, appalling irony in New York fourteen years later.

Once, as the Beatles' plane was coming in to land at Portland, Oregon, the group were joking with the *Daily Mirror*'s Don Short that they were so famous, there could be no more big stories. They had cracked America wide open, and they would soon no longer be newsworthy. John and Don sat together drawing up a list of what could be concocted to spin out the Beatles' news value.

John said, 'I know. I'll run off with Ringo's wife on Howard Hughes' plane.' Just then, one of the plane's engines caught fire and the plane started billowing black smoke.

Short said: 'Well, John, this is one story we haven't accounted for yet.'

And John answered: 'Oh Christ, how are we going to tell this?'

John then wrote his own obituary, got a film spool from a travelling photographer, wound the paper round the spool and sealed it down, so that when the plane crashed his own 'black box' would be there to tell the story of his death in his own words.

The plane landed safely, amid ambulances and fire engines and general pandemonium. John roared above the madness: 'Beatles and children off first!' In Paris, before that tour, John had studied a list of American cities they might visit. They had escaped from the Hôtel Georges V at four in the morning for a stroll and wandered into one of the cafés on the Champs-Elysées, just like they used to on the Reeperbahn in Hamburg after their club work. Someone reflected on that forthcoming American tour, and pondered how Beatlemania, which was so enormous, could possibly end. 'It will all end in an air crash,' John said, throatily through his Gauloise. 'It's got to be Cincinnati. Just as the plane is landing. Cincinnati sounds a great place to die.'

Meeting Elvis Presley was something that John Lennon could never have comprehended when he was a devoted fan as an art student five years earlier. But in the summer of 1965 he was to come face to face with the idol who had changed his life. It happened during the Beatles' stay in Los Angeles when they rented a house on Mulholland Drive, and the meeting was arranged by journalist Chris Hutchins of London's *New Musical Express*. He persuaded Colonel Tom Parker, Presley's manager, and Brian Epstein, to get them all together. Hutchins had no trouble persuading the Beatles, but for days there was tension over who should be the host: the Beatles were undoubtedly hotter than Elvis, but Presley was the more senior act and it was his town. 'In the end,' says Hutchins, 'the Colonel's wisdom and experience won over Brian Epstein's lack of determination and basic politeness.' An evening was set for the Beatles to glide in their limousines to Elvis's gigantic mansion in Bel Air.

John was full of genuine anticipation as Elvis entered the room dressed casually in red shirt and grey trousers. But the first few minutes seemed like hours: both Elvis and the four Beatles were struck dumb at the size of the occasion. Finally, John and Paul wandered off to corner Elvis and talk about songwriting.

Presley asked how many hits they had written and it was Lennon who confronted the King with the question all self-respecting rock 'n' roll fans throughout the world were asking: 'Why don't you go back to making rock 'n' roll records?' Presley had been pummelled by all his old fans, like John, for slumping into a tiring routine of making trashy Hollywood movies and his records were soundtracks.

'It's my movie schedule,' Elvis said. 'It's so tight! I might just do one soon, though.'

John retorted: 'Then we'll buy that!'

They jammed a while on Elvis's guitars, only riffs and no complete song tunes, and adjourned to the games room to play the pinball machines. But the atmosphere was stilted and, although he enjoyed the occasion, John was disillusioned by his idol. 'It was like meeting Engelbert Humperdinck,' he later said scathingly. The Beatles' mementoes of the uneventful meeting, handed to them by Colonel Parker, were a complete set of Presley albums each, a table lamp shaped like a wagon, and holsters with gold leather belts. 'It was obvious Elvis was high and the Beatles knew very little about dope then,' says Chris Hutchins. 'Neither side desired the meeting that much and the politics of it made it so heavy.'

(Bob Gruen/Star File)

October 1950. Ten-year-old John outside Mendips, Menlove Avenue, Woolton, the middle-class home where his Aunt Mimi brought him up

(Tom Hanley)

John's familiar hunched frame was captured by fellow student Ann Mason when he sat for more than two hours for this painting in March 1958   *(Ann Mason)*

One of the earliest photographs of John and his future wife Cynthia together, before she dyed her hair blonde at his request. This was taken in October 1958 in the alleyway alongside John's regular college pub, Ye Cracke in Rice Street. Seated in the front, from left to right, are students June Harry, Pat Jordon, Jim Reynolds and Hazel Dorothy *(Thelma Pickles)*

(Thelma Pickles)

In this college photograph taken in September 1958 by Thelma Pickles, one of his girlfriends, John's greased-back hairstyle shows his affinity with Elvis Presley. The students in the picture, taken near Liverpool College of Art, are (from the left on the back row), John Lennon, Carol Balfour, John Wild, Jeff Cane, Gill Taylor, Peter Williams; (seated, from left) Marcia Coleman, Ann Preece, Violet Upton, Helen Anderson, Diane Molyneux; (front from left) Ann Curtis, Sheila Jones

Aunt Mimi, whom John grew to love and respect. This picture, taken in March 1971, shows her with a cat John brought home as a stray

(Tom Hanley)

September 1947, Aged six, a
pupil of Dovedale Primary
School, Allerton
(Dezo Hoffmann/Rex Features)

A childhood Christmas
sketch by John and a note
on a telegraph form to
Mimi's husband, George.
The postcard is from his
Aunt Elizabeth in Scotland
(Tom Hanley)

May 1948. John, aged
seven outside the front
porch of Mendips. Aunt
Mimi would banish him
there when his guitar
playing became too much
for her
(Tom Hanley)

John with his mother,
Julia, in the garden of
her sister's house
(John's Aunt Anne) in
Rock Ferry on the
Wirral, July 1949
(Tom Hanley)

June 1964. Aunt Mimi,
smiling in Sydney,
Australia, has her first
experience of Beatlemania
(Tom Hanley)

John's vision of a church
wedding. This is one of many
cartoons he gave to a fellow
art student

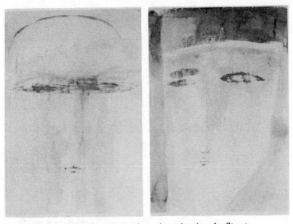

John's sharp facial features dominate these drawings by Stuart
Sutcliffe of his best friend. 'Stuart drew these at my mother's house
three months before he died,' says Astrid. 'He never drew likenesses,
always impressions.'   *(Astrid Kirchherr)*

'John and Stuart loved our days at the seaside and had lots of pleasure
drawing pictures on the sand,' says Astrid, who took this picture on
the beach at Ostsee, near Hamburg, in July 1961

(Astrid Kirchherr)

The early days of romance, as
seen by John. He drew this
Christmas card for Cynthia in 1958

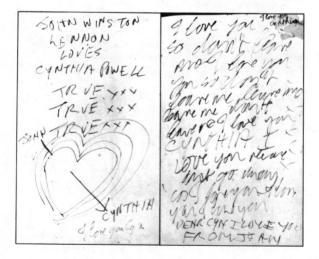

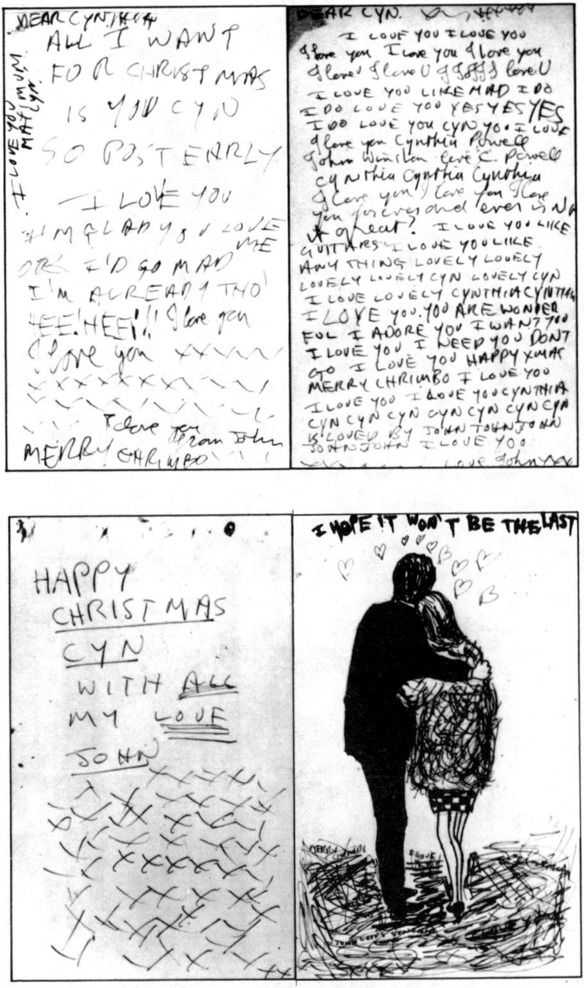

DEAR CYN, 1964
ALL I WANT
FOR CHRISTMAS
IS YOU CYN
SO POSTERRLY
I LOVE YOU
I'M GLAD YE I LOVE ME
OR I'D GO MAD
I'M ALREADY THO'
HEE! HEE!!! I love you
I love you xxx
xxxxxxxx
I love you
from John
MERRY CHRIMBO

I LOVE YOU MUM MAT CYN

DEAR CYN. 1964
I LOVE YOU I LOVE YOU
I love you I love you I love you
I love I love U q qqqqq loveU
I LOVE YOU LIKE MAD I DO
I DO LOVE YOU YES YES YES
I DO LOVE YOU CYN YES I LOVE
you Cynthia Powell
John Winilon love C Powell
Cynthia Cynthia Cynthia
I love you I love you I love
you forever and ever is NA
a great? I LOVE YOU LIKE
GUITARS I LOVE YOU LIKE
ANYTHING LOVELY LOVELY
LOVELY LOVELY CYN LOVELY CYN
I LOVE LOVELY CYNTHIA CYNTHA
I LOVE YOU. YOU ARE WONDER
FUL I ADORE YOU I WANT YOU
I LOVE YOU I NEED YOU DON'T
GO I LOVE YOU HAPPY XMAS
MERRY CHRIMBO I LOVE YOU
I LOVE YOU I LOVE YOU CYNTHIA
CYN CYN CYN CYN CYN CYN CYN
I LOVED BY JOHN JOHN JOHN
JOHN JOHN I LOVE YOU
Love John xx

HAPPY
CHRISTMAS
CYN
WITH ALL
MY LOVE
JOHN

I HOPE IT WON'T BE THE LAST

(Cynthia Lennon)

Thelma Pickles photographed during her intense relationship with John which began at Liverpool College of Art in 1958
(Thelma Pickles Collection)

The elegant love match: Stuart Sutcliffe and Astrid Kirchherr at her Hamburg home in November 1961, just five months before Stuart died. Stuart's clothes uncannily anticipate the uniform Brian Epstein was to devise for the Beatles much later
(Reinhard Wolf/Astrid Kirchherr)

At the time of John's twentieth birthday, in October 1960, George, Stuart and John are pictured at a funfair at a Hamburg park where they often played to boost their income

(Reinhard Wolf/Astrid Kirchherr)

October 1962. Behind closed doors at Liverpool's Cavern Club John plays harmonica and Paul piano at rehearsal. McCartney's chair had been 'borrowed' from the Star-Club, Hamburg. Mike McCartney is standing by the piano
(Mike McCartney)

October 1962. John launches into one of his imitations of deformity in a jokey backstage session at the Cavern. Paul gives a helping hand, Cavern owner Ray McFall joins in, and Cynthia watches the camera
(Mike McCartney)

A scruffily dressed John with Paul and drummer Pete Best prepare for a 'Riverboat Shuffle' down the Mersey on the ship *Royal Iris* in July 1962. Top of the bill was Acker Bilk's jazz band
(Mike McCartney)

John wrote this letter, parts of which have been cut out by Cynthia, from Hamburg a few days after Stuart Sutcliffe's death in April 1962. 'Dot' was Dot Rhone, Paul McCartney's first serious girlfriend

STAR CLUB
39 GROSE FRIEHES
ALTONA HAMBURG

Dear Cyn

I love love love you and I'm missing you like mad whereas you my little _____
I wonder why all the newspapers wrote about Stu' especially the 'People'- and how the hell did they find out who could have told them as I wrote that I suddenly remembered there a fellow at Ki' 'Susannah' who's a free lance journalist it ... ed have been him 'cause Allan Williams has be.... telling poor Mrs Sutcliffe or something. I haven't seen Astrid since the day we arrived I've thought of going to see her but I would be so awkward – and probably the others would come as well and it would be even more, I won't write any more about it 'cause its not much fun. I love you – I don't like the idea of Dot moving in permanently with you 'cause we could never be alone really – however when I come home – can't she have the other room or find another flat – imagine having her there all the time when we were in bed – and imagine Paul coming all the time – and especially when I want to sleep. I'd hate the idea. I love you Cyn x

The club is massive and we only play 3 hrs are eight and the next ... and we play an hour – then an hours break so it loesn't seem long at all really. The boss

Continued overleaf

(continued overleaf)

of this place is a good skin – we're off tomorrow 'cause its Good Friday and they can't have music so the boss – (Manfred) is taking us and the other group out for the day in his car and all the rest of them like them that are coming so it will all tag inds in two 5 cars. We're going somewhere healthy like the Oor Sea (Stu's again).

God I'm knackered its 6 o'clock in the morning and I want you (I've just found out that theres no post tomorrow so I will pack in good night. I love you boo! hoo! I hate this place). That was Friday night now its Sunday afternoon, I've just wakened up and theres no post today or tomorrow (Easter Monday I think) anyway happy Easter Cyn. I love you. We went out but all we did was eat and eat and eat (Good Friday) it was all free so it was ok, we drove somewhere about 30 mls away and ate.

My voice has been gone since I got here (it was gone before I came if I remember rightly). I can't seem to find it John well I love you Cyn. Powell and I with Imos on the way to post but with the Sunday papers and choices and ideotions! Oh yes! I forgot to tell you the art gift life – wide overcoat with a belt so I'll look quite life news! Pauls leaping about in my head he's a bank as proud and he's saving! I can hardly get in a position to write to you anyway stairs captain, Shurrup Mcartney! ....

I can't wait to see your new room it will be great
seeing it for the first time, and having chips and
all and a ciggie (don't tell me some noise for the
noises please Miss Powell) Hmm I can just see you
and Dot puffing away, I suppose thats the
heart of my worries. I love you Cyn I miss miss
miss you miss powell — I keep remembering
all the parts of Hamburg that we went to
together. The fact I can't get away from you.
— especially in the ways and inside the
Seamans. Miss you powell I love love love you. X
       Did I tell you that we have a
good bathroom with a shower too! didn't
tell you? well I've had ONE while I've been
here! I'm a clean little cocker! Heelheel Have you
I haven't written to them yet but I know how
to send them money so it gets there in time. XXX

       I can't think what to write now
so I will pack in and write some tomorrow
seeing as how like I can't POST IT anyway
so good afternoon Cyn I love you. Yum Yum.
Will you send me the words to "A SHOT OF
RYTHEM + BLUES" Peax? there's not many.
       Its Monday night and we finished
playing about ¾ hr ago (its 2 o'clock) I'm dead
beat my sweet so I hope you won't mind if I

Continued overleaf

(4)
finish now and have lovely sleep (without you but
still I'll be lonely — double the hurt that this so
so so tired). I love you Cyn I hope you realize
why this letter took so long, but there has been no
post Fri Sat Sun Mon and this one will go
by the early morning Tuesday post cause I will
nip downstairs and post it any minute (hardly
Cyn it?). I love you I love you please write for
me and don't be mad and work hard and
be a clever little Cyn Powell. I love you
I love you I love you I love you I love you
I love you, write soon ooh its a naughty
old Hamburg we're living in, XX

       All my Love for Ever and ever
                from
                John
                XXXXY
                YXXYY

P.S.
Their's leather not pants!
PANTIES not pants).
(just in case you)

♡ I love you ♡
Goodnight
X Y Y Y Y

(Cynthia Lennon)

Togetherness on the beach. A youthful-looking John and Cynthia at the resort of Ostsee just outside Hamburg in July 1961. The snapshot unfortunately shows the effects of having been carried around for years in Cynthia's handbag *(Astrid Kirchherr/Cynthia Lennon)*

Before Beatlemania. John at the Abbey Road studios in London during the recording of their first E.M.I. single, 'Love Me Do', in September 1962 *(Dezo Hoffmann/Rex Features)*

Top: John's arrogant stance—head slightly back, guitar across his chest, legs firmly astride—seen in close-up at a special reception thrown by E.M.I. Records at their offices in Manchester Square, London, to celebrate the success of 'Please Please Me' and launch the album of the same name in April 1963

(Dezo Hoffmann/Rex Features)

Above: At the Abbey Road studios—John casts an eye towards George Martin's control room during the recording of *With The Beatles* in September 1963 *(Times Newspapers)*

November 1963. High jinks during a British tour as John, towel around his head, and Paul play around with McCartney's two Hofner violin bass guitars
(Pictorial Press)

John and Brian Epstein relaxing in Miami, Florida, where the Beatles did two television shows during their triumphant first American tour in February 1964

(Dezo Hoffmann/Rex Features)

Top: Author Ray Coleman is at John's right shoulder during a walk down the Champs-Elysées during the Beatles' three-week season at the Paris Olympia in January 1964 *(Melody Maker)*

Above: February 1964. Stepping out in New York with Paul and Ringo, John is pictured in Central Park against a background of the home where he was to settle eight years later

(Syndication International)

Top: A straw sunhat for John as he relaxes in Miami in February
1964   *(Syndication International)*

Above: November 1963. John chatting to the secretaries at the offices
of NEMS Enterprises and the Beatles fan club headquarters in
Monmouth Street, London   *(David Magnus/Rex Features)*

June 1965. John and Cynthia pose in the garden at Weybridge

(Cynthia Lennon)

On a skiing holiday in St Moritz, Switzerland, in 1965

(Cynthia Lennon)

Part of a letter from John to Cynthia, written in August 1965 when he was in California during a Beatles tour of America. 'Dot' was Dorothy Jarlett, the housekeeper at Weybridge, and 'Lil' was Lilian Powell, Cynthia's mother. The other names are those of occasional staff and friends

(9) what we said about it. It's not much bother really, is it? When you think about it — I'm sure I'm sure Dot and Lil' and Bernie, Tommy, Dorley etc can understand something as simple as us wanting to be alone for a day. — I don't mean Julian tho' — I mean don't pack him off to Dot's or anywhere — I really miss him as a person now — do you know what I mean, — he's not so much 'The Baby' or 'my baby!' anymore he's a real living part of me now — you know he's Julian and everything and I can't wait to see him, I miss him more than I've ever done before — I think it's been a slow process my feeling like a real father! I hope all this is clean and understandable, I spend hours in dressing rooms and things thinking about the times I've wasted not being with him — and playing with him — you know I keep thinking of those stupid bastard times when I keep reading bloody newspapers and other shit whether he's in the room with me and I've decided it's ALL WRONG! He doesn't see enough of me as it is and I really want him to

I know and loves me, and miss me like I seem to be missing both of you so much still so now 'cause I'm bringing myself down thinking what a thoughtless bastard I seem to be — and it's only sort of three o'clock in the afternoon and its seems the wrong time of day to feel so emotional — I really feel like crying it's stupid — and I'm choking up now as I'm writing — I don't know what the matter with me — it's not the tour that's so different from other times — I mean I'm having lots of laughs (you know the type he he!) but in between the laughs there is such a drop — I mean there seems no in between feelings). Anyway I'm going now so that this letter doesn't get to draggy. I love you very much. to Cyn XXXX Nana John XXXXXX Julian XX XX XXX

P.S. Say hello to Charles etc. for us.
P.P.S. I think you can ring me if you have a phone there try — if not I'll see you in about a week.
271-6565 LOS ANGELES, CALIFORNIA.

P.P.P.S. It's Monday now 23rd today and I leave this house next Monday the 30th of August — so you can see how.

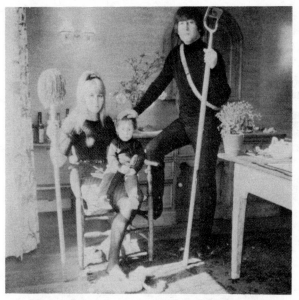

Top: June 1965. Domestic bliss at Weybridge with Cynthia and two-year-old Julian   *(Cynthia Lennon)*

Above: Cynthia and John happy on holiday in Miami in February 1964   *(Cynthia Lennon)*

April 1964. Red wine, lots of it, was required by John to endure the formality of the Foyle's Literary Luncheon at London's Dorchester Hotel to mark the publication of his first book, *In His Own Write*. He is sitting with songwriter Lionel Bart   *(Keystone Press)*

John bought Aunt Mimi this bungalow overlooking the harbour at Poole, Dorset, in August 1965. Pleasure launches soon included the spot on guided tours of the area   *(Tom Hanley)*

Waiting for the action during the filming of *A Hard Day's Night* on a platform covered with broken glass

(David Hurn/The John Hillelson Agency)

February 1965. A pensive
John pictured during the
filming of *Help!*
(Rex Features)

John, in Paris during the
Beatles' three-week season at
the Olympia in January 1964,
prepares to go for a stroll
down the Champs-Elysées
(Dezo Hoffmann/Rex Features)

February 1964. Tie askew and
a shirt button undone, John is
watched by 73 million viewers
on America's *Ed Sullivan
Show*
(Dezo Hoffmann/Rex Features)

At the height of the twist dance craze, in February 1964, John and Cynthia went to the club that was its birthplace, New York's Peppermint Lounge—fake 'Beetles' were already installed there

(Camera Press)

This 'postcard', made by tearing an autographed publicity photograph in half, was sent to the author from Genoa in Italy, during a European tour in June 1965. The message is typical of John's laconic sense of humour

John fingers his beloved Rickenbacker guitar during the recording, with producer George Martin, of *A Hard Day's Night* in June 1964

(Robert Freeman)

January 1966. John's father, Freddy Lennon, launched forth with his one and only single, 'That's My Life (My Love And My Home)', much to John's embarrassment

(Popperfoto)

March 1964. Seen here with Harold Wilson, John gives the V for victory sign made famous by the man who inspired his name, Winston Churchill. The occasion was the Variety Club of Great Britain lunch in London at which the Beatles were named Show Business Personalities of 1963. John used to call the Labour Party Leader 'Harassed Wilsod'

(Keystone Press)

October 1965. Tie loose and top shirt button undone, John looks suitably bored at a press conference ('All those damned stupid questions,' he used to say). This one was at Brian Epstein's Savile Theatre after the Beatles had been invested with the M.B.E. Four years later John sent back the medal he never really wanted, incurring the full fury of his Aunt Mimi

(Dezo Hoffmann/Rex Features)

Yoko as John saw her for the first time. This picture is taken from the inside cover of the catalogue which was handed to John when he walked into the Indica Gallery in London on 9 November 1966
(Adrian Morris)

September 1966. In Almeria, Spain, John had his locks shorn and adopted 'granny' glasses for the first time during the filming of *How I Won The War*
(Cynthia Lennon)

John in 1967, posing for a promotional picture to launch the *Sgt Pepper* album at his home in Weybridge *(Henry Grossman/Colorific!)*

John at the party at Brian Epstein's home in Belgravia to launch *Sgt Pepper's Lonely Hearts Club Band*. He was taking a lot of drugs at this time, and looked gaunt and under-nourished *(Dezo Hoffmann/Rex Features)*

En route to North Wales for a weekend of meditation in August 1967, John leans out of the carriage at Euston Station to see a forlorn Cynthia narrowly missing the train
(top-Syndication International
(bottom-Rex Features)

14
MUSIC

'DO something with my voice'

The combination of John Lennon and Paul McCartney, as friends as well as songwriters, must rank as one of the great examples of opposites being drawn to each other like magnets. McCartney's background, with a father as a jazz pianist and a mother determined that her academic son stayed on course to a 'proper job' in one of the professions, was traditional and musically conventional.

John carried the scars of a lost father and a mother killed in a road accident, at the time he and Paul set off on their musical collaboration. Lennon had been a teddy boy who had virtually roared through Liverpool, leaving broken hearts and many scars among the hundreds who knew that he would either end up a catastrophic loser, or that his streak of artistic genius and prescience might carry him through to the heights. McCartney was simply an orthodox teenager.

By the time they reached London and became immersed in recording, the general opinion was that it was easy, despite the songwriting credit line of Lennon–McCartney which appeared everywhere, to detect who wrote what.

Whoever sang the lead vocal had usually written the song. If it haunted you, it was a McCartney. If it baffled you, made you think, it was a Lennon. If it grabbed you by the heart ('Yesterday', 'All My Loving'), it was one of Paul's. If it was

241

autobiographical, and made a pungent personal statement ('In My Life', 'Norwegian Wood'), it was John's.

It was certainly music, rather than their contrasting personalities, that drew John and Paul together. Although John had established that he, as a Libran, was theoretically supposed to get on well with Paul, a Gemini, they were poles apart in personality and temperament. That difference extended deeply into their musical collaboration, with great mutual benefits.

Or so it seemed. In reality, both men were utter contradictions. Lennon's apparent toughness was always a complete cover-up. Inside that fierce exterior beat a softie's heart. He was a complex man who seemed afraid to let his inner self be seen. The hard front was without a shred of doubt a screen for the real, tender man of which there were hundreds of examples, particularly when the Beatles split.

McCartney, conversely, came across during the Beatles years as the Beatle who melted most girls' hearts, with his big brown eyes and his songs of unashamed love. On the surface, he was the suave, smooth, debonair romantic. This misconception paralleled the inaccurate theory that John was a tough nut. In fact, McCartney was always the tougher of the two. He totally outstripped John when it came to business acumen, planning his life with a fine eye for detail that later made him popular music's richest man.

From the moment the Beatles went to London and marshalled their raw talent as musicians and songwriters into tunes the world could whistle, one man stood beside them in what at first seemed an incongruous partnership. John, in particular, had always made blistering remarks about 'the men in suits'. Yet when it came to associating the Beatles with them, he would always say that the end would justify the means. John always said he wanted to be rich and famous—particularly rich. Brian Epstein was attractive because his respectability seemed a good bet to get them a record contract, John and Paul's most cherished ambition.

The man who eventually came to be linked with the Beatles as their record producer, and forge a unique bond with them at a critically formative peak in their lives, was George Martin. He wore a suit and a tie. He was a staff producer at the giant E.M.I. Records and recorded classical music, jazz, pop and particularly comedy by such artists as Peter Sellers, Bernard Cribbins, Spike Milligan, and Flanders and Swann.

Heard today, 'Love Me Do' is simple, catchy, earthy—a natural début sound from the Beatles as we grew to love and understand their music. But at the time George Martin was unimpressed. 'To begin with, they gave me very few songs,' says Martin. 'Love Me Do' had been written by Paul when he was sixteen, with John contributing to the middle. 'That was the best of the stuff they had, and I thought it pretty poor,' says Martin. 'I offered them "How Do You Do It" as their first song (later this became a number one hit for Gerry and the Pacemakers) although this was not written by them. They didn't fancy it and we pressed on with "Love Me Do". But they learned very quickly after that and when they got the success of "Please Please Me" under their belt they were fired by it, and from then on everything they brought me was pure gold.' 'Please Please Me' was written totally by John; he later told the author that he was imitating the falsetto sound of American singer Roy Orbison. The harmonica player on the disc whose style Lennon admired was Delbert McClinton.

Success came so rapidly to John and Paul, and their creativity flowered so speedily as a result, that George Martin's role as a catalyst became a joy to him. George believes that rivalry, rather than competitiveness, was the key to their mutual respect. A spark of tension, each songwriter wondering what the other would do or say next, gave them both a thrusting edge. 'It was like a tug of war,' says Martin.

'In the studio, their rivalry was based purely on friendship. They had a very close relationship because in many ways they were incredibly similar. Some people accentuated the differences between them—John being the acrid, bitter one and Paul the soft one. That was basically an image built up by the Press.

'The truth is that deep down they were very, very similar indeed. Each had a soft underbelly, each was very much hurt by certain things. John had a very soft side to him. But you see, each had a bitter turn of phrase and could be quite nasty to the other, which each one expected at certain times.

'They did love each other very much throughout the time I knew them in the studio. But the tension was there mostly because they never really collaborated. They were never Rodgers and Hart. They were always songwriters who helped each other out with little bits and pieces. One would have most of a song finished, play it to the other, and he'd say: "Well, why don't you do this?" That was just about the way their collaboration worked.' Gradually, as they were always individual songwriters, they became positively solo operators as success led them on.

'Imagine two people pulling on a rope, smiling at each other and pulling all the time with all their might. The tension between the two of them made for the bond.

'John was such a creative thinker, one notch higher than most,' says Dick James, the man whom Brian Epstein turned to on his arrival in London, and who became the publisher of the Beatles' songs. 'He had more sensitivity. John *had* to be cynical, because he was very vulnerable and could hurt very easily, and so he surrounded himself with this cynical crust. He was very difficult, particularly later in his career.'

Dick James had the unique position of hearing all the Beatles' early work before it went on record. 'To this day,' he says, 'my office receives tapes from groups who are trying to sound uncannily like Paul or John, as lead singer, with the same kind of appeal. But the original model was so special. I could hardly believe my ears when Brian Epstein would come into my office and play me the next song.

' "What do you think, Jamesy?" John would say.

'And right after "Please Please Me", I'd have to say: "Dare I say it, John and Paul? Another number one." '

In 1963 James borrowed £10,000 and handed it to Brian Epstein as an 'advance' on their royalties. 'It's usually six to eight months before the initial income comes in from world sales. The boys were in debt to Brian, who had given them eating money. They couldn't believe the figures we were talking about. They'd been in poverty street. I hadn't known them then, but I did know the song publishing world and knew they would be earning a lot of money. I had to borrow the money for them against that first number one, "Please Please Me". I had no trouble getting the cash. I knew it was a winning investment.'

As a veteran of the old school of songwriters, Dick James

looked on the new school of beat musicians led by the Beatles with a critical ear. 'If the songs came around today, brand new, they'd still be world-wide smashes. The quality was amazing. I could not believe what I was hearing. It was the perfect entertainment machine: John, Paul, marvellous songwriters, George a splendid musician, Ringo a wonderful drummer for them, and a foil.'

His outstanding memory of John was of 'a great stubbornness which was essential to them in their early days. His contribution to the Beatles' success was definitely equal to Paul's, not one iota less.' Lennon looked on James as an amiable benevolent uncle. It was a view that was to change in 1969 when a business clash divided John and Dick. 'But when we went public with Northern Songs in 1965, I said to John: "The songs will go on earning money well into the next century."

'He smiled. "Good on yer, Jamesy." '

Visitors to London's Abbey Road number two studio during Beatles recording sessions could not be aware that pop music history was being made. A Liverpool group, bucking the trends of the time (Cliff Richard, traditional jazz, and Chubby Checker's big Twist craze), did not represent an overnight phenomenon at the recording studios. Martin, tall, angular, punctilious, was an easy target for the Beatles' quicksilver, raw sense of humour. And so because of that they would rarely tease him. They respected him and enjoyed his straightforwardness and particularly his expertise.

As the lynchpins for the group, writing hit after hit, John and Paul had a special relationship with George Martin. It began as record producer and young pop stars and then developed into that of a wise uncle, and eventually to friendship. But when their popularity began moving swiftly upwards, a marked difference became apparent in John and Paul's make-up.

Typically John would want to move from song to song in a hurry. He would be involved in a song for only as long as it took to get it recorded satisfactorily. Then he was on to the next. McCartney took a different, more thorough attitude. Later, Paul's persistence in worrying a session to death, until one of his songs had been drained dry of every possibility and permutation, irritated John.

John nursed an inner grievance that McCartney's songs got more studio attention and finishing touches than his. 'That's probably true,' Martin reflects, 'but that's because Paul was more interested. John's irritation was a little unfair. John's songs got a great deal of attention, but possibly what he meant was that they never got the attention to detail that he thought they needed. So they didn't quite work out the way he wanted them. But they worked out the way I wanted them.

'Maybe I thought my communication was pretty good in getting inside his brain and finding out what he wanted. He would always say: "Yes great, lovely, OK, fine," at the play-backs. But only later did he tell people he'd never been really happy with anything he'd written.

'Some of John's works we recorded in the Beatles days were some of the best stuff I've ever heard, so it's a matter of opinion.' As he outgrew the early Beatles, John asserted that George was 'always more like a Paul McCartney producer than for my music'.

John's reputation as the most intelligent Beatle with literary aspirations was firmly established by 1964. Each one of the four was quick-witted, but none of the other three matched Lennon's perception and lucidity. Only in the recording studios, with Paul's melodic strengths and eagerness to discover every twitch of every switch, was there any contest. That was because John's restlessness to move on to the next song differed from Paul's need to get the current work meticulously right. That year, George Martin released his own orchestral album of Beatles hits. Despite Martin's natural affinity with McCartney, his album featured a commercially powerful sleeve note written by John which allowed Lennon to hark back in dry literary style to his satirical *Mersey Beat* newspaper ramblings. He wrote:

> George Martin is a tall man. He is also a musician with short hair. In spite of this he records rock groups such as (Beatles, Billy J. Kramer, Gerry and the Pacemakers) to name four, and has earned the respect of everyone in the business (what business you might well ask). We all owe a great deal of our success to George, especially for his patient guidance of our enthusiasm in the right

directions (it was a patient George Martin who, on one of our early sessions, explained to a puzzled Ringo that it was a bit much playing a full drum kit, tambourine and maracas at the same time).

Us Beatles are genuinely flattered that a 'real musician' as we call him should turn his talents to arranging an L.P. of our songs, considering that he has previously worked with such great artists as Peter Sellers, Shirley Bassey, Jimmy Shand and a machine that sings 'Daisy Daisy'. Some of the sounds on the album may be new to you (and me), that's 'cause George has a great habit of matching unlikely instruments together (like a Jew's harp and a twelve-stringed finger) but the results are great and I think he should get a raise. So plug yourselves in and listen.

P.S. Please tell all your friends to buy it too, so George can be rich and famous—after all why not?

> Good George Martin is our friend
> Buddy Pal and Mate
> Buy this record and he'll send
> A dog for your front gate
> *Chorus:* With an arf arf here
> And an arf arf there, etc.

Sung to the tune of Old Macdonald Had An Arm by the Beatles a band.

Martin felt the sharp end of Lennon's tongue when John went to New York and publicly attacked old friends like Derek Taylor and George Martin, for, as he implied, having too big an idea of their own importance. Lennon snapped his frequent jibe that nobody made the Beatles, the Beatles made themselves. It was always true . . . but this time he chose old pals like Martin and Taylor as his targets. They were deeply hurt.

When the Beatles split, John adopted a fiercely defensive stance on behalf of his old group. It seemed that only he, or the other three, were allowed to damn the achievements, particularly, of the Beatles. John's comment about George was: 'Who does he think he is, anyway? What songs has he ever written?' But Martin remembers going for dinner with John in Los Angeles in 1973 and, typically, John apologized for his outburst which had embarrassed Martin. 'I'm sorry George,' John said. 'I didn't really mean those things about you and all the others. I was smashed out of my mind when I was speaking.'

The difference inside the studios between John and Paul was obvious to George from the start. 'Paul would sit down and ask what I planned to do with his songs, every note virtually. "What do you think the cellos should be doing here, George?" and I'd have to describe to him on the piano what it would be. He'd say: "Yeah, OK, but what about changing that note?" Lots of the arrangements to his songs were very much his ideas which I would have to implement.

'John would be more vague in what he wanted. He would talk in metaphors about his ideas. I'd have to get inside his brain to find out what he wanted. It would be more of a psychological approach. He'd say—for example, on "Being For The Benefit Of Mr Kite!"—"This song's about a fairground. A little bit mystified. I want to get the feeling of the sawdust and the feel of the ring. Can you do something about it?" I'd then have to think how that imagery could be transformed into sound. The difference between John and Paul, fundamentally, was that Paul would want to know *how* I was going to go about achieving what he wanted. John couldn't care less. He just wanted the result.

'On "Strawberry Fields Forever", we did one track and he said: "Well, I like it but it's worked out much harder than I thought it would be. I'd like you to do a score and maybe use a few cellos and a bit of brass." That was it.'

Another odd clash of opinion between Lennon and Martin occurred from the start of the Beatles' success. John's singing voice—leathery, raw, lung-bursting on their anthems like 'Twist And Shout' and 'Money'—was a stark contrast with Paul's melodic qualities. But John had that distinctive, lived-in, untrained hardness in his voice. It made him stand out; it was the voice of a new breed of rock 'n' roll guitarist who couldn't give a damn. There was nothing crude about it, but it was the voice of someone who had lived, for all his youth. John was genuinely bashful about his voice. I remember telling him how much I liked it on one particular track, 'You Can't Do That', and he was astonished that anyone should single out his vocal work for any praise. 'You really mean it?' he asked incredulously. 'I can't say I ever liked hearing myself.'

The nagging self-doubts about his vocal abilities were to manifest themselves into a considerable issue with George Martin. 'John was a great admirer of Elvis Presley's early records, particularly the "Heartbreak Hotel" kind of sound. He also had an inborn dislike of his own voice which I could never understand, as it was one of the best voices I've heard,' recalls Martin.

'He was always saying to me: "*Do* something with my voice! You know, put something on it. Smother it with tomato ketchup or something. Make it *different*." And he was obsessed with tape delay. In technical terms, it's only a delay of about thirty milliseconds which gives you that kind of effect John sought, a sort of very near-echo which he used a lot when he made his own records. I used to do other things to him, and as long as it wasn't his natural voice coming through, he was reasonably happy. But he'd always want his vocals to get special treatment.

'On "Tomorrow Never Knows", he wanted to sound like a Dalai Lama singing on a hilltop. He actually said to me: "That's the kind of sound I need." So I put his voice through a loudspeaker and rotated it. It actually did come out as that strangled sort of cry from the hillside.

'He simply always wanted to distort his voice. But I wanted to hear it in its own natural quality. So after he left me, he did all his own distortion to his heart's content. And I didn't like that—after all, the raw material was so good.'

Martin looks on John's work since the Beatles split with mixed feelings: 'There were lots of things I didn't like about them and that I would have done differently. My favourite song of all was "Imagine" and that was a great album—I loved that. Some of the stuff he did on that was pure magic. I'd like to have produced that.'

Conversely, Martin was disappointed with John's final album, *Double Fantasy*. 'He hadn't been in the studios for a long time, and it shows. It's not vintage Lennon, not the greatest stuff he ever did.'

And to the question that concerns Beatles students throughout the world: who was the more important to the group, Lennon or McCartney, Martin reflects: 'I'm a melody man rather than a lyric man, being a musician and not a lyric writer. My brain accommodates music much more easily than it does words. Paul's melodies and his harmonic structures appealed to me more than John's because John's melodies and his music were tailor-made to fit his words rather than the other way round. The lyrics would lead and develop John's songs. He would write one verse and the music was already there once the words told him the way the line would go.

'As for comparing their value to the Beatles, it's impossible. It's like asking what's the most important constituent in a sauce vinaigrette, the oil or the vinegar. Both were fundamentally important: one without the other would have been unthinkable in terms of the Beatles' success.

'It's quite likely that, in terms of success, Paul's songs will last longer than John's because they get more to the average man, to the heart strings, than John's did. That's being really commercial about it. But I couldn't put a cigarette paper between them.'

On a British concert tour in 1964, I interviewed John specifically about his attitude to his guitar. Asked if he ever practised, he laughed and took another drag on his cigarette, 'I never *did* practise! I only ever wanted to learn to play to back myself. In the early days, we all used to sing. Originally, I'd do one, then Paul'd do one, then George and so on. So you didn't need to be a genius of a guitarist to back yourself.'

Did he find it a handicap, not being able to read music? 'It's not essential for what I'm doing. No, I've never found it a handicap. These dance bands that play pop on the B.B.C. radio programmes—they sound all right at *that* because they can read it off music sheets. But have you heard some of them trying to play rock? It's rotten!

'If I wanted to read music I'd have to pack all this in and start from scratch. Sometimes I think I'd like to, but I'm a cheat. I can't play finger style. I just manage to do something that makes it sound like I can. I started with a banjo when I was fifteen, when my mother taught me some banjo chords. She could play it pretty good. When I was young, I played the guitar like a banjo, with the sixth string hanging loose! I always thought Lonnie and Elvis were the greatest and all I ever wanted to do was vamp. I got some banjo things off OK, then George and Paul came along and taught me other things.'

Asked why he took to the guitar, he told me: 'Oh, the usual kid's desire to get up on stage, I suppose. And my mother was a big encouragement. She said she could play any stringed instrument and was able to give me the first ideas.'

Of his musical role within the Beatles, John, who was officially described as rhythm guitarist, said: 'The job of the normal group rhythm guitarist is to back the solo guitarist like the left hand does on a piano. Unless the lead guitarist is very good and can back himself like the finger-style guitarists can, he needs someone else to help fill out. Most of our stuff in the early days was twelve-bar stuff. I'd play boogie and George would play lead. I'd vamp like Bruce Welch [of the Shadows] does, in that style of rhythm.

'We always have someone playing rhythm in the set style all the time, although it's too thin for records so we just both go full-out.

'I'd find it a drag to play rhythm all the time so I always work myself out something interesting to play. The best example I can think of is like I did on "You Can't Do That". There wasn't really a lead guitarist and a rhythm guitarist on that because I feel that the rhythm guitarist role sounds too thin for records. Anyway, it'd drive me potty to play chunk-chunk rhythm all the time. I never play anything as lead guitarist that George couldn't do better. But I like playing lead sometimes, so I do it.'

Of his songwriting tactics, he said: 'When Paul and I started writing stuff, we did it in the key of A because we thought that was the key Buddy Holly did all his songs in. Holly was a big thing then, an inspiration, sort of. Anyway, later on I found out he played in C and other keys but it was too late and it didn't worry us anyway. It all sounded OK in A so that's the way we played our stuff. Oh yeah, we keep up with all the keys—C, D, G, F (joking) but we keep out of B flat and that. It doesn't give you an artistic sound. Heh Heh!'

John Lennon was an addicted rock 'n' roll *fan*, just like the teenage Paul Simon or Bruce Springsteen and thousands of other musicians for whom it was a force as tribal as it was musical. All were mesmerized by Elvis Presley, who brought colour and meaning into their lives. Rock 'n' roll was the foundation for John Lennon. The ensuing years may have seen him stray into strange unconnected territories; may have seen him put his head on the chopping block of public scorn and ridicule, but right to the end Lennon stayed true to the *idea* of rock 'n' roll. On record and in print, Lennon was moved to the core, and that music still had ability and power throughout his life, even when it was obvious that the music he was making far transcended in impact and quality the music which inspired him. 'There is nothing conceptually better than rock 'n' roll,' he said. 'No group, Beatles, Dylan, or Stones, have ever improved on "Whole Lotta Shakin' " for my money, or maybe I'm like our parents: that's my period and I dig it, and I'll never leave it.'

When 'Heartbreak Hotel' floated across the Radio Luxembourg airwaves into Mendips, John Lennon succumbed and was forever lost. 'When I heard it, I dropped everything!' Elvis across the ether was followed by dozens more, each as glamorous, raucous and liberating—Buddy Holly, Jerry Lee Lewis, Gene Vincent, Little Richard, Lloyd Price, Chuck Berry, Eddie Cochran, Larry Williams. That music, those performances, made real the world which had been glimpsed in the movies. Part of the appeal of rock 'n' roll was its remoteness, which helped create a code amongst the young English audience. The terms used were alien, but the emotions were direct. In a whole generation of English teenagers, those raw emotions touched a chord.

Lennon's first group, the Quarry Men, was formed with school mates and everybody mucking in for fun. The gigs were standard for the time—working men's clubs, club dates, ballrooms, and fortuitously, village fetes. Rock 'n' roll was for (and by) the young. Rock 'n' roll was for NOW! Lennon remembered the time: 'As kids we were all opposed to folk songs, because they were so middle-class. It was all college students with big scarves and a pint of beer in their hands, singing folk songs in what we called la-di-da voices. When I started, rock 'n' roll was the basic revolution to people of my age and situation.' That revolutionary aspect obviously ap-

pealed to the rebellious Lennon. Before—so the cliché ran—
the only way out was through crime or boxing. Now there was
a third, more glamorous, alternative—music. It meant you
could get girls, get drunk, and get somewhere. That early,
classic rock 'n' roll was raw and primitive, it could be learned,
if you practised, which was boring, or if someone taught you.
That was the sound that John Lennon wanted George Martin
to record.

Years later, Lennon could remember with great accuracy
and affection the music which so moved him as a restless
teenager: ' "Long Tall Sally"—when I first heard it, it was
so great, I couldn't speak! "Bony Moronie"—I remember
singing it the only time my mother saw me perform before she
died. "Ain't That A Shame"—the first rock 'n' roll song I
ever learned. My mother taught it to me on the banjo before I
learned the guitar. "Whole Lotta Shakin' "—I like the take
he did in 1956, on the record. I'm not interested in the variation
of a theme . . . I'm a record fan . . . Those are the records I
dug then, I dig them now, and I'm still trying to reproduce
"Some Other Guy" or "Be-Bop-A-Lula".'

Thrown together in Liverpool and Hamburg, Lennon and
McCartney collaborated, bolstering each other, goading each
other to reach new heights. Such was their diversity, they could
assimilate virtually any style into their songwriting; the lyrical
dexterity of Leiber and Stoller, the touching teen pains of Goffin
and King, the hiccuping sensitivity of Buddy Holly. The evidence of the earliest Beatles recordings demonstrates Lennon
tearing into such rock classics as 'Ain't She Sweet', 'Memphis',
'Money', and 'Sweet Little Sixteen'. Even early on in their
career, the Beatles were typecast—Paul was cute and John was
hard. Like all clichés, there was an element of truth in it, but
Paul was also capable of whipping up a storm on rock standards,
and John proved he could be a sensitive performer handling
ballads.

For fans tired of the saccharine sweetness of British and
American pop, tired of the manufactured idols, they found
something raw and refreshing in the Beatles' performances.
There was a healthy irreverence in Lennon's crashing about
the stage, cajoling and insulting the audiences. They poured
their hearts into the music, sweating it out night after night,

playing from dawn to dusk, with an astonishing turnover of music. The music came from diverse sources—show tunes like 'Besame Mucho', 'Falling In Love Again', 'Till There Was You', the first tentative performances of their own songs, 'I Saw Her Standing There', and 'Ask Me Why', classic rockers like 'Twist and Shout', 'Honey, Don't', and contemporary hits like Joe Brown's 'A Picture Of You'. These marathon sessions proved invaluable in shaping the Beatles' music. It gave them an edge and a variety their contemporaries never matched. While the pop world sank in the quicksand of mediocrity, and Elvis went missing in trashy Hollywood films like *Blue Hawaii*, the Beatles kept a flame burning for the music which had so moved them as teenagers.

The earliest known live recordings of the Beatles available on disc were recorded by Ted 'Kingsize' Taylor, at the Star-Club in Hamburg at the end of 1962. Despite the dreadful sound quality they make great listening and provide a fascinating insight into the roots of the Beatles' music. Recorded during one of those marathon sessions, the group are ragged and committed, tearing into their songs, young and full of fervour, determined to rattle the walls. It was that musical baptism, forged in Hamburg and honed in Liverpool, that gave the Beatles their musical edge. But, tellingly, one of the reasons the Beatles came out ahead of Faron's Flamingoes, Rory Storm, and Gerry and the Pacemakers—all of whom paid their musical dues in Hamburg—was that they had their own two songwriters, and didn't have to go on endlessly pillaging the familiar pool of material which all the Mersey beat groups dipped into.

The evidence contained on the album of the Beatles' Decca audition displays just how Brian Epstein had cleaned the group up (and how he was thinking of 'the end of the pier show' as the ultimate ambition). The Beatles sound stilted and uncomfortable as they meander through 'The Sheik of Araby' and 'To Know Her Is To Love Her'. Their collective studio knowledge was minimal. Aside from some late fifties' Quarry Men demonstration recordings, the Beatles' inauguration in recording took place in Hamburg. John, Paul and George cut 'Fever', 'September Song', and 'Summertime', in a Record-Your-Voice booth at the back of Hamburg Railway Station in 1960. They were backing a singer called Wally—Lou Walters—from Rory

Storm's group, the Hurricanes. Rory's drummer Ringo Starr also sat in on the impromptu session, two years before he joined the Beatles.

The best-known pre-Parlophone recordings were with the Hamburg-based singer Tony Sheridan in May 1961. The subsequent album (issued long after their initial success) is of historic interest, featuring a raucous Lennon vocal on 'Ain't She Sweet', and the only known Harrison–Lennon collaboration on the instrumental 'Cry For A Shadow'. But it took those sessions to bring the Beatles to Brian Epstein's attention. The Sheridan/Beatles version of 'My Bonnie' was a moderate chart success in Germany.

By the time the Beatles arrived at Parlophone in 1962, they were pretty near the bottom of the pile. Decca turned them down in favour of Brian Poole and the Tremeloes, because they were more accessibly based in Dagenham. It took the intuitive sympathy and knowledge of house producer George Martin to realize the Beatles' sound fully and coalesce it on record.

Those early Parlophone sessions harnessed the Beatles' enthusiasm and Martin's studio mastery—a combination which was to prove unbeatable over the next seven years. Parlophone was always regarded as a joke by E.M.I., its parent company. But by working closely together, Martin and the Beatles came together. They respected his innate musical pedigree, and he saw their strengths as lying in their harmonies, and the fact that they wrote their own material—with strong views on how it should be recorded—rather than accepting their manager's hand-me-downs. The fruits of that collaboration were first seen on 5 October 1962, when the Beatles' first single, 'Love Me Do', was released.

It eventually reached a healthy number seventeen on the British charts (in competition with the perennial Cliff Richard and 'Bachelor Boy' and Little Eva's 'The Loco-Motion').

It was the release of the second single, 'Please Please Me' in early 1963, that really established the group. It's hard to imagine the effect it had on the record-buying public. Initially Lennon's harmonica was the novelty that drew the casual listener in. The prominent guitars and driving rhythm were emphasized by the rudimentary harmonies. Hearing it again now, what still strikes the listener is the Englishness of the vocals. Until then, English pop stars adopted mid-Atlantic accents, or went for stage Cockney like Anthony Newley. The Beatles made no effort to disguise their Liverpudlian origins, even if the vocal mannerisms were American. 'Please Please Me' was a Lennon original: 'I remember the pink eyelet down over the bed, sitting in one of the bedrooms in my aunt's house on Menlove Avenue. I heard Roy Orbison doing "Only The Lonely" on the radio. I was intrigued by the double use of the word "please" in a Bing Crosby song. So it was a combination of Bing Crosby and Roy Orbison.'

As a writer, Lennon was a great one for plucking individual lines or phrases from other songs, and expanding them into his own material. 'Run For Your Life' came from Elvis's 'Baby Let's Play House'; 'Do You Want To Know A Secret?' was a line from 'Snow White And The Seven Dwarfs'; 'I'll Be Back' was based on a chord variation from a Del Shannon song.

The infectious 'From Me To You' repeated the Beatles' hit formula, and went to number one in May 1963. But by then the Beatles had proved their merit on album. *Please Please Me* was released in March, and proved remarkable in a number of ways—there were eight Lennon–McCartney originals, a remarkable achievement in those days of manufactured product. Hit songs either came from established shows, or writers were chosen by a manager or, more likely, British pop songs were innocuous covers of American hits. To write and perform your own material was revolutionary, and threatened the Tin Pan Alley stranglehold.

The bulk of material on the Beatles' début album encapsulated their influences to date. Much of the original material was jointly written while touring Britain, on the long coach journeys up and down the newly opened motorways. 'I Saw Her Standing There', though, was a composition John and Paul knocked off in Paul's front room, playing truant from school. Of equal interest, though, were the cover versions. Instead of going for the obvious versions of Elvis or Pat Boone hits, the Beatles chose obscure songs which they admired—the Shirelles and the Cookies were not names English audiences were too familiar with. 'Twist And Shout' had been a hit in America for the Isley Brothers and was written by Bert Russell and Phil Medley.

It is to George Martin's credit that, in an eleven-hour spurt, he managed to capture the verve and enthusiasm of the Beatles on record. But the vigour sprang from *them*. As writers and performers, the Beatles obviously had something fresh to offer a jaded public. Lennon is seen and heard as a sensitive interpreter on that first album, notably on 'Ask Me Why' and 'Anna' (written by Arthur Alexander, who also wrote the Stones' 'You Better Move On' and Ry Cooder's 'Go Home Girl'). Lennon also sounds plaintive on 'There's A Place', a place where he can go, when he feels low. Conversely, his manic version of 'Twist And Shout', which closes the album, recalls the ardent rocker from the Cavern. Nothing that demented had been heard on record since 'Hound Dog'.

It was that hard side which the world saw in Lennon—the hard rocker, embittered by his mother's early death and his father's desertion, his own belief in himself, his inability to display a softer side. Lennon was painted the hard man of the Beatles.

Despite the typecasting—the 'hard' Lennon and the 'soft' McCartney—it helped give their partnership a balance which was crucial. Their individual writing efforts were born out of a desire to prove themselves, out of individual insecurity. Once they gained confidence in themselves, they grew apart, but there was still that question of balance. They sparked each other off, and even if it was only altering a word, suggesting a title, Lennon and McCartney could, and did, inspire each other. That balance saw them through the hysteria. They couldn't go out, so they stayed in, and—among other things—wrote songs. That partnership lasted a long time and only grew irrevocably apart when they found other partners.

With their second album, Lennon and McCartney were already being called 'the outstanding English composers of 1963' and William Mann of *The Times* singled out 'the Aeolian cadence at the end of "Not A Second Time" ' (the chord progression which ends Mahler's *Song Of The Earth*). Lennon said he thought 'Aeolian cadences were some sort of exotic birds!' William Mann's eulogy, which finally set the seal on

the Beatles as being more than 'just another pop group', is of
interest for his comments on the group's early impact. Leaving
aside the 'pandiatonic clusters' and 'melismas with altered vow-
els', he does make a number of interesting points: 'For several
decades in fact, since the decline of the music hall, England
has taken her popular songs from the United States, either
directly, or by mimicry. But the songs of Lennon and Mc-
Cartney are distinctly indigenous in character. . . .' Mann went
on to cite 'the exhilarating and often quasi-instrumental duet-
ting' and the 'discreet, and sometimes subtle, varieties of instrumentation', which led him to conclude: 'These are some
of the qualities that make one wonder with interest what the
Beatles and particularly Lennon and McCartney, will do next,
and if America will spoil them or hold on to them, and if their
next record will wear as well as the others.' If only he had
known; if only *they* had known.

With The Beatles had been preceded by the fourth Beatles
single, 'She Loves You', which established them as *the* British
showbiz phenomenon. The song became an anthem, which
helped a nation Yeah, yeah, yeah its way into 'the swinging
sixties'. Lennon remembered that crucial song thus: ' "She
Loves You" was written by the two of us together. I remember
it was Paul's idea. Instead of singing I love you, again, Paul
decided we would have a third party passing by and latch on
to something else . . . the woo-woo was taken from the Isley
Brothers' "Twist And Shout". We stuck it in everything—
thinking when Elvis did "All Shook Up", that was the first
time I heard "uh huh", "oh yeah" and "yeah yeah" all in
the same song.'

By the end of 1963 it was apparent to everyone in Britain
that the Beatles were more than just a pop group about to be
usurped by the Dave Clark Five. There were invitations to
perform before royalty, eulogies in the press, and hysteria at
their every appearance. But they were still judged by their
music. *With The Beatles* (released on the day of President
Kennedy's assassination) again dipped back to the Hamburg
days ('Roll Over Beethoven'; 'Till There Was You') and, despite the prolific Lennon–McCartney partnership, the album
contained six cover versions. But this time, drawing heavily
on the contemporary music sound of black America—'Please

Mister Postman', 'Money', and 'You Really Got A Hold On Me', all emanated from the burgeoning Tamla Motown. Here was the 'hard side' of Lennon, screaming 'Money', and 'It Won't Be Long', while Paul opted for the softer 'All My Loving' and 'Till There Was You'. With George Martin drafted in as ancillary pianist, the Beatles made their first tentative steps to expanding their group sound in the studio.

From *With The Beatles* on, things started getting crazy: 'I Want To Hold Your Hand' sold 12 million copies. There was the first American tour, their first film, endless concerts. Brian Epstein still saw touring as the logical step to ensure that the cash came in, and that the Beatles' name was kept in the public eye. Who could blame him? There had never been any precedent on how to handle a phenomenon such as the Beatles. Touring kept John and Paul together, and in the interminable gaps between shows and venues they stared out of their cocooned existence and wrote. Fragments, images and catchphrases cropped up in their songs. Hermetically sealed, they poured their energies into their songs. Creatively, those rigorous years of touring paid off.

A Hard Day's Night was the first album consisting solely of Lennon–McCartney originals. Composed during their visits to France and America, and when filming in England, the finished album reflected a remarkable variety and assurance. Remarkable too was the prolificacy of the partnership. Consider the pressure they were under from the moment Beatlemania broke at the end of 1963, and indeed the pressures which lasted until the end of touring in 1966—the Beatles were expected to undertake at least two major tours every year, and come up with three original singles, two albums of original material, plus T.V. and film work. It is an itinerary which would make many of today's pampered groups blink with disbelief. What makes the Beatles' achievements so astounding is not only the quantity, but more importantly the *quality*, of their music those years inside the bubble.

Once the hysteria began, the Beatles' performances became little more than a charade. They *were* a fine live band, as evidenced by *The Beatles Live At The Hollywood Bowl*. The album of those 1964–5 concerts was only released, finally, in 1977, at the height of the punk explosion. What comes across from those recordings is how good they still sounded. Given that there were no feedback monitors, so they couldn't hear themselves play, nothing could beat the persistent, cacophonous screaming. The Beatles still sounded hungry, angry! It is a testament to their musical inventiveness and ability. The studio recordings are the ultimate proof, but contained on *The Beatles Live At The Hollywood Bowl* is the proof that there was a certain chemistry, or *magic*, which sustained them.

Concerts by then offered fans little more than an opportunity to see the gods made mortal. There were the constant problems of security, isolation, and safety. Then there was the music. Within a year, the Beatles had found themselves elevated from a 'beat group phenomenon' to an international showbiz institution. It was a double-edged sword, and one which Lennon particularly resented. He told *Rolling Stone* magazine editor Jann Wenner, in 1970: 'Brian put us in suits and all that, and we made it very, very big. But we sold out, you know, the music was dead before we even went to the first theatre tour of Britain. We were feeling shit already, because we had to reduce an hour or two hours' playing, which we were glad about in oné way, to twenty minutes, and we would go on and repeat the same twenty minutes every night. The Beatles died then as musicians . . . because in spite of all the things, the Beatles could really play music together.' The Beatles had, after all, only set out to make it 'bigger than Elvis'. Within months, they had already achieved that. And after that, where else was there to go?

Lennon found the whole thing developing into a macabre charade, which was, inevitably, reflected in his music, the only place where he could relax, create, and be himself. Listening to the album of *A Hard Day's Night*, one is struck by the aching cries for help and the feelings of isolation. Here he was, the idol of millions, one of the world's most eligible men, an acclaimed author and composer; but in his songs you find introverted sentiments, and feelings of great sadness and lost innocence. That innate sadness was, of course, buried beneath the ebullient high quality of the Beatles' music. By the time of *A Hard Day's Night*, Beatle fans, like Lennon himself, only listened to the *sound* of the record. The lyrics, if they made any impact at all, were simply the choruses the fans could memorize and sing along with.

'Tell Me Why' is full of tears, lies, moans, apologies, pleas; 'I'll Cry Instead' has tears and loss, 'a chip on my shoulder that's bigger than my feet'; 'Any Time At All' cries for a response, begs a friendly response. 'I've got no time for trivialities,' sang Lennon on 'When I Get Home'. The public and the private Lennon merged on *A Hard Day's Night*.

Lennon's musical experiments were encouraged by George Martin and the other three Beatles, notably the first recorded use of feedback on 1964's 'I Feel Fine'. Lennon had a small studio at Kenwood, where he tinkered with tape recorders and fragments of songs, the results of which would manifest themselves the following year. But the greatest impact on Lennon's music during those crazy 'Beatlemania' years was made from the only man who could be said to have rivalled the group in terms of influence—Bob Dylan.

During the early and mid-1960s, Bob Dylan gave pop music a voice. His songs had lyrics of personal and political relevance—even his early love songs were bitter and aching, hardly the fodder for unthinking pop fans. But Dylan swiftly found an audience and articulated their dissatisfaction and compassion in striking, vivid images. Dylan was now tiring of his typecasting as 'spokesman for a generation'. From adolescence he'd been a fervent rock 'n' roller. His high school ambition, he said, had been 'to join Little Richard'. When Dylan heard the Animals' electric re-working of the traditional 'House Of The Rising Sun', and the Beatles' 'I Want To Hold Your Hand' in 1964, it helped him decide which direction his music was to take. The British invasion was a prime force in making Dylan switch to 'folk-rock', with his devastating *Bringing It All Back Home* and *Highway 61 Revisited* albums of 1965.

Dylan first met the Beatles on their first American tour in 1964 and turned them on to marijuana, but made a more permanent impact in shaping their musical direction. Latterly, Lennon denied Dylan's influence on the group, saying he never listened to anything after the seminal 1965 albums, and was quoted as saying: 'I remember the early meetings with Dylan, he was always saying "Listen to the words, man" and I said

"I can't be bothered. I listen to the sound of it, the overall sound." ' Lennon did admit, though, that, like so many others, Dylan's music helped him think for himself and inject more honesty into his own lyrics. The two did enjoy a sporadic friendship. Lennon appears in the rarely seen *Eat the Document*, a surreal account of Dylan's controversial 1966 British tour.

Dylan's achievements then became Lennon's goal, an attempt to marry the power of rock 'n' roll to lyrics of some substantiality. The Dylan influence first manifested itself on the Beatles' fourth album, *Beatles For Sale*. Derek Taylor's sleeve notes announced that the album was 'straightforward 1964 disc-making . . . there is little or nothing on the album which cannot be reproduced on stage!' Such jolliness disguised the intensity with which Lennon approached the album. *Beatles For Sale* displayed the bleaker side of the Lennon persona. 'No Reply', 'I'm A Loser', and 'Baby's In Black' formed a pretty bleak trilogy to open an album by the Fabs at the height of their power.

'No Reply' opens with the jaundiced 'This happened once before', a song which bitterly sifts through the embers of a dying relationship, symbolized by the failure to communicate. The song is conveyed by a particularly lugubrious Lennon vocal, a dispirited opening to an album which was meant to celebrate *triumph*. On 'I'm A Loser', the title says it all, and Lennon's singing is suitably atmospheric as the song traces the disintegration of a love affair. It may not match Dylan's searing sense of loneliness or loss evoked by his contemporary 'Boots Of Spanish Leather' or 'Ballad in Plain D', but it was an attempt to inject some honesty and genuine emotion into the fairytale world of the Beatles.

Similarly, while never reaching Dylan's heights of absurdity or depths of despair, Lennon's couplet 'Although I laugh and act like a clown/Beneath this mask I am wearing a frown' seemed an ironic comment coming from a man with the world at his feet. 'Baby's In Black' continues in the Dylan vein, another splint to help bolster up a shattered soul: 'Baby's in black and I'm feeling blue.' He was juggling with dark colours, but questioning, probing, pleading rather than celebrating.

Hindsight reveals the internal friction in the group by then, which subsequently led to open antipathy. Lennon's character was always the rebel, the cynic, and he was the one to express his dissatisfaction most forcefully. As he admitted in a *Playboy* magazine interview: 'I was always like that, you know. I was like that before the Beatles. I always asked why people did things and why society was like it was. I didn't just accept it for what it was apparently doing. I always looked below the surface.' The overt politicizing didn't come till much later, but Lennon was keen to avoid the showbiz stereotypes: 'We don't want to learn to tap dance or take elocution lessons,' he told Michael Braun in his 1964 book, *Love Me Do*.

Critics have pointed out that *Beatles For Sale* was cut at the height of Beatlemania, which accounted for the number of cover versions. In many ways, though, the Beatles' fourth album is perhaps their most revealing in terms of musical influences. The six covers take them right back to those manic all-night rave-ups in Hamburg—Carl Perkins' 'Everybody's Trying To Be My Baby' and 'Honey, Don't'; Buddy Holly's 'Words Of Love'; Leiber and Stoller's classic 'Kansas City', sung by Little Richard; and Chuck Berry's anthemic 'Rock and Roll Music'. Such was the Beatles' enthusiasm that they disinterred 'Mr Moonlight' from the B-side of a single by the original Dr Feelgood, Willie Perryman (Piano Red). It took the Beatles' championing for these (by now) forgotten rockers to re-acquaint American audiences with their own rock 'n' roll history. It was only by studying the songwriting credits that thousands of American fans realized that 'Words Of Love' wasn't a Lennon–McCartney original, and the dedicated pursued it back to its source, thereby discovering the joys of Buddy Holly. The Beatles' pioneering work in helping Americans trace their rock heritage did not go unrecognized by musicians. Bob Dylan's 'Bringing It All Back Home', his first wholesale rock 'n' roll work, was a title which acknowledged the group's efforts.

The Beatles' fifth album, *Help!*, was also the soundtrack of their second film. Although removed from the documentary pressures of *A Hard Day's Night*, the Beatles were, by their own admission, constantly high on marijuana during filming. Lennon was also obsessed about his obesity, concerned about the state of his marriage, and worried that his role as 'pop singer' was too insubstantial for someone of his abilities. ('If there is such a thing as genius, I am one! If there isn't, I don't care.') On the surface 'Help!' was another catchy Beatles single which went automatically to number one. It contained all their hallmarks—an unforgettable chorus, infectious harmonies, and quaintly memorable lyrics. But, as Lennon admitted, it really *was* a cry for help.

The finished album is riddled with insecurities, lack of assurance, and self-doubt. Lennon gratefully accepted the instant obliteration offered by drugs, barely disguising his distaste for the parody he felt the Beatles had become. That distaste is nowhere more evident than in 'You've Got To Hide Your Love Away'. The Dylan influence is particularly strong, vocally, musically and lyrically. ('That's me in my Dylan period. I am like a chameleon, influenced by whatever is going on. If Elvis can do it, I can do it. If the Everly Brothers can do it, me and Paul can. Same with Dylan.') The song finds Lennon as the poet alone, head buried deep in hands, surrounded by clowns. The paranoia is obvious; twitchy at what people will think, he is told to hide his love away, fearful that any open display of emotion will be ridiculed.

The growing distance between Lennon and McCartney musically was demonstrated by the sequence of two of their tracks on the finished album—Paul's rather smug 'Another Girl' ('She's sweeter than all the girls, and I've met quite a few'), and John's jaundiced 'You're Going To Lose That Girl'.

Help! is probably remembered for the haunting McCartney ballad, 'Yesterday'. Lennon was predictably scathing about McCartney's best-known song, and, as if emphasizing his rocker credibility, finished the album with a blistering version of Larry Williams' 'Dizzy Miss Lizzy'. Williams was one of Lennon's early musical heroes. The Beatles recorded his 'Bad Boy' in 1965; 'Slow Down' appeared on their 1964 'Long Tall Sally' E.P. and Lennon included Williams' classic 'Bony Moronie' on his 1975 *Rock 'n' Roll* album. 'It's Only Love' displayed Lennon's softer side on *Help!* but even that is tainted by druggy imagery and a reliance on Dylanesque word-play.

The use of a string quartet on 'Yesterday' and the flutes on 'You've Got To Hide Your Love Away' marked the first inclusion of musicians outside the Beatles' immediate orbit on their material. With such an intuitive and astute interpreter as

George Martin, the group could experiment in the studio and feel genuinely creative. Live, it was impossible—the screams obliterated everything. Even with the intolerable pressure of touring and filming, the Beatles could relax in the studio and were receptive to Martin's ideas and suggestions on how to expand their sound. Lennon and McCartney's compelling musical codes found swift acceptance with George Martin's classically trained musical mind. By the middle of 1965 they were setting themselves dauntingly high standards. Creatively, George Martin was certainly 'the fifth Beatle', but he could only work with what was presented to him *by* them. In a 1983 interview, Martin said: 'I've always held that the role of the producer is the person who can look back on the picture, and not just at the detail. When you have your picture taken in a school form, the first thing you look for is "Where am I?" You don't look at the picture, you look at yourself. And this is true of most instrumentalists, of most people who make records, they tend to listen to the bit they were doing.

'I also believe that the producer's role is a minor one compared to the performer's. There's been a tendency in recent years for that to be a reversal. I think that the fellow who creates it is the important thing, and the producer is the guy who helps him shape it. I don't see the producer as a Svengali mastermind. The role of the producer has become slightly inflated, and it's strange for me to say that, because maybe I've had something to do with that. But it's something I haven't been comfortable with.'

The high standards the Beatles had attained can be seen simply by looking at their two film soundtracks. The normal thing for soundtracks (particularly 'pop' film soundtracks) was to stretch one theme song over an album, patched up with 'mood' instrumentals. The Beatles changed all that—*A Hard Day's Night* and *Help!* were crammed full of potential hit singles, and there wasn't an ounce of surplus flesh on either. By *Help!*, the sound of the Beatles on record was a lot deeper, deferring to Martin's orthodox musical knowledge; the group were keen to enrich the standard two guitars, bass and drums sound. The percussive effects on 'Tell Me What You See', John's harmonium on 'We Can Work It Out', and the pianos and organs, strings and woodwinds dotted around their records of the period all point towards a flexing of the Beatles' musical muscles, which would culminate with the majestic *Sgt Pepper* only two years later.

Running parallel to the album, of course, were the astonishingly assured and varied singles. Again, the Beatles set new standards, even down to the packaging of their material. Prior to them, L.P.s were simply regarded as vehicles for collected singles, B-sides and cover versions, which the record company duly issued to extract the final penny from diehard fans of these short-lived phenomena—pop groups! The Beatles changed all that.

By the middle of 1965, Beatles' songs like 'She Loves You', 'I Want To Hold Your Hand' and 'Can't Buy Me Love', had entered the public consciousness. The experimentation started with 'I Feel Fine' (with its use of feedback and jagged rhythms); the Motown feel of 'Day Tripper' and the fairground atmosphere of 'We Can Work It Out'; the fluid 'Ticket To Ride'. The quality of those singles is reflected by the variety of artists who covered them, an astonishing cross-section—Ella Fitzgerald, Otis Redding, The Carpenters, Dollar, and Stevie Wonder.

From early on, the Beatles were determined that their albums should be regarded as separate entities. It helped, of course, having what press agent Tony Barrow called 'their own built-in tunesmith team of Lennon and McCartney'. Even at the time it was apparent that the compositions were no way split fifty–fifty. If John sang a 'Lennon and McCartney' song, you could bet that the majority of the work had been his, and vice versa. There were arguments in the studio about whose songs should get priority as A-sides.

Even as they grew apart as writers, there was still that balance to the Lennon and McCartney partnership. The individual contributions to joint compositions may have been minimal, but they mattered, and helped shape the songs. Such was their intuitive reading of each other that they played off against each other, goading each other into making the song perfect. It may only have been a change of tense, a switch in direction, but this joint honing strengthened the song.

Lennon defined the partnership around this time when he told *Playboy*: 'In ''We Can Work It Out'', Paul did the first half, I did the middle eight. But you've got Paul writing "We can work it out", real optimistic, y'know, and me, impatient: "Life is very short and there's no time for fussing and fighting, my friend. . . ." ' The full flowering of that creativity was to come with the Beatles' sixth album, the punningly titled *Rubber Soul*. Newly honoured by Queen and Country, despite the unremitting pressures (the album was recorded in under a fortnight) the Beatles, M.B.E., showed they were well ahead of the field. In these days of high-technology recording, where months and sometimes years are spent preparing an album, it is remarkable to look back on the pressure under which the Beatles recorded, and see how confident and progressive, in the best possible sense, their music sounded. By the end of 1965, rock 'n' roll had grown up. Dylan's electric experiments had spawned a clutch of imitators who gradually grew into their own style (Simon and Garfunkel, The Byrds) and the Beatles were under pressure from their contemporaries (Who, Stones, Animals, Yardbirds) to stay one step ahead. They were no longer the cocky rockers of only three years earlier but they hadn't forgotten their roots. And they proved they could still whip up a storm on a song like 'Dizzy Miss Lizzy'. But with their growing confidence as writers, and their growing understanding of the studio, the Beatles' material grew in stature.

Lyrically, at the end of 1965, they found themselves commenting on the craziness of their situation, occasionally distorted by drugs. 'Norwegian Wood' was John's veiled admission of an affair; 'Nowhere Man', his observations on the unreality of it all; there was also the wistful nostalgia of 'In My Life'. Paul's 'You Won't See Me', and 'I'm Looking Through You', were remarkably bitter comments on the price of fame and the superficiality of the Beatles' status.

Musically, too, *Rubber Soul* was a progression. The public noticed the introduction to pop of the sitar on 'Norwegian Wood'. But there was also a greater reliance on keyboards than before. *Rubber Soul* catches them between the hysteria of Beatlemania and the acid excesses of *Sgt Pepper*. They finally sound comfortable in the studio, willing to experiment, but never straying too far away from the three-minute pop song, a form they had perfected. *Rubber Soul* will always stand superbly on its own merits.

For Lennon, particularly, the album marked a personal progression in his craft. Personal honesty and confession, which were to characterize his later work, were inherent. His songs are marked by a more poetic approach, and he was beginning to find his own voice, rather than copy Dylan's. 'Girl' opens with the plaintive 'Is there anybody going to listen to my story . . .? ' before moving on to what would become a familiar Lennon preoccupation. Was she told when she was young that pain would lead to pleasure? He later remarked that the song was a personal favourite, a move away from the Tin Pan Alley style of songwriting.

'Nowhere Man' is a curiously nihilistic 'pop' song, casting Lennon as a monarch of nothingness, without opinion, power or desire. The Nowhere Man is an impotent, hollow symbol of the swinging sixties—'Nowhere Man, don't worry/Take your time, don't hurry/Leave it all till somebody else/Lends you a hand.' It was his view of life from the emptiness of the mansion he called a 'bus stop, awaiting action'. 'Norwegian Wood' is the vacuous swinging sixties again. Druggy, floating, random ('She told me she worked in the morning, and started to laugh'). Lennon's vocal is weary, dispassionate, that of an outsider viewing something intensely personal. The song is a thinly veiled message to his wife, Cynthia, that he has had an affair outside their marriage.

'In My Life' is the curtain-raiser for a trip down to Strawberry Fields. Although nothing is mentioned by name, there is that overriding impression of nostalgia and yearning for home. Lennon said: 'It was the first song I wrote that was consciously about my life. . . . "In My Life" started out as a bus journey from my house at 251 Menlove Avenue to town, mentioning all the places I could recall. I wrote it all down, and it was so *boring*. So I forgot about it and laid back, and these lyrics started coming to me about friends and lovers of the past. . . .' It was an extraordinary position to be in. Only five years before he had been 'Lennon', a scruffy Liverpudlian rocker, with prospects as bleak as the view across the Mersey. Half a decade later, he was J.W. Lennon M.B.E., millionaire, surveying his world from the stockbroker security of Weybridge. 'In My Life' echoes the theory that 'you can never go home again', 'Though I know I'll never lose affection/For people and things that went before/I know I'll often stop and think about them. . . .' The song marked a rare moment of retrospection and sentimentality for Lennon; the lyrics are tinged with a resignation that all is gone, that the only security lies ahead.

As 1965 drew to a close the Beatles stood untouched, at the height of their influence and powers. The extent of the Beatles' popularity at that time is hard to imagine today, when every group that manages two consecutive number ones, is cited as 'the new Beatles'. No cracks had appeared in their façade; they could still be *seen*, screamed at, touched. But the drive to the 'toppermost of the poppermost' had ended. They had reached their summit. Like kings, they viewed the world at their feet.

By the Beatles' gruelling standards, 1966 was a relatively quiet year which saw them pour their creative energies into recording, rather than squeezing in sessions between tours. The earliest fruit of those labours came with the 'Paperback Writer' single in June: a bubbly, clever Beatles single, just like the old days. But the B-side, 'Rain', was of particular interest. 'Rain' was written at John's home studio, where he was experimenting with tape loops, which explains the weird, distorted atmosphere on the song. The dreamy feel was accentuated by the druggy lyrics ('I can show you, when it starts to rain/Everything's the same'). There are echoes in the song of future Lennon classics: 'Can you hear me that when it rains and shines/It's just a state of mind.' It precedes 'Strawberry Fields Forever' and 'Lucy In The Sky With Diamonds' with its remote and ethereal feel. Spiked on acid, Lennon was seeing the world through hazy shades. The drugs added a translucent element to his music, and aided and abetted the desire to drift into the dream world of Lewis Carroll, where nothing was real, and 'the slithy toves/ Did gyre and gimble in the wabe'. To be a Beatle meant that reality was distorted anyway. Their cocooned existence saw them grow more and more remote. By mid-1966 touring had become a physical and mental strain, particularly after the American reaction to Lennon's 'We're bigger than Jesus' quote and their hostile reception in Manila.

The spring of that year was spent in the studio, recording what turned out to be the *Revolver* album. The first track they recorded was the last to appear on the album—Lennon's mysterious 'Tomorrow Never Knows'. It marked the zenith of the Beatles and George Martin's studio ingenuity at the time— backward tapes, loops, chanting choirs, oddball lyrics, all underpinned by some relentless Ringo drumming.

Still ahead of its time, 'Tomorrow Never Knows' has John hurling himself into the psychedelic maelstrom, with lyrics drawn from the Tibetan Book of the Dead, although the actual title was a Ringoism Lennon used to diffuse the lyrical obtuseness. It was one of the earliest attempts by Lennon actually to make music that, until then, had been confined to his mind. For the first time, it let us 'see the meaning of within'. It had been a long, crazy journey from 'Be-Bop-A-Lula'!

All sorts of other wondrous potions can be found inside the jar which is the *Revolver* album—'I'm Only Sleeping' carried on the theme of floating, of dreaming of being at the centre of something, and letting others glimpse in through layers of sound and mystery, of being a reluctant idol, at the centre of attention, but needing to look inward, and find out exactly what makes him/them tick ('Please don't spoil my day, I'm only sleeping').

'She Said, She Said' evoked images of his druggy dreams in Laurel Canyon, California, where the song was written. It played out John's private agony in public: 'I know what it's like to be dead! Who also knows what it's like to never have been born/sad/mad.' It was a trippy odyssey from birth to death, with Lennon returning to the precious world of his childhood, to the home he never had: 'I said no, no, you're wrong, when I was a boy/Everything was right.' It never had been, but by then, he could convince himself that it was.

In 'And Your Bird Can Sing' John issued his early message of independence from the Beatles' cocoon: 'Tell them that you've got everything you want . . . But you won't get me!' For they had seen the Seven Wonders, they had heard 'every sound there is', and it still wasn't enough.

Isolated and immunized, John called, more and more, on 'Dr Robert', a euphemism for drugs, and took 'a drink from his special cup'. He had all the answers. The more the Beatles dipped into that special cup, the more reliant they became. With distorted perspective and lost time, they knew that there was always one constant: 'Day or night, he'll be there, anytime at all'. Any time at all grew into the void of 'Tomorrow Never

Knows', and they were gone! They disappeared on 29 August 1966. It was actually in Candlestick Park, San Francisco. It could have been anywhere. To all intents and purposes, outside of the comfortable insularity of the recording studio, the Beatles ceased to exist.

After leaving the stage at Candlestick Park, the Beatles became their own bosses. For the first time in three years, Parlophone didn't have the obligatory Beatles album for Christmas. Without that, for many people Christmas was not complete. *A Collection of Beatles' Oldies* did appear, with its cover that epitomized the Swinging London which the Beatles had helped so much to shape. There they were, all their best songs. Created in the fiery furnace of a three-year burst, here was the vinyl proof of rock's maturing. With touring definitely vetoed, with no film projects to occupy them seriously, for the first time in a decade, the Beatles were suddenly no longer a group. From now on there would be no more 'songs', no more product manufactured to meet a particular schedule. The balloon had come down to earth. They tasted freedom. It was the end of 1966. Ahead lay the unknown.

15
PRESSURES

'We're more popular than Jesus now'

A fantastic scene awaited John one day in 1965 on his return to Weybridge from London in his chauffeured Rolls. Sitting in his lounge, drinking a cup of tea, was his father, whom he had not seen since he was five years old in Blackpool.

Dishevelled, with long greasy grey hair and a shabby suit, totally unkempt, fifty-two-year-old Fred Lennon was working as a kitchen hand, washing up dishes in the Greyhound Hotel, Hampton Court, a few miles from John's home. Drinking in a pub one day, he had got chatting to a man who drove the Beatles occasionally for a car hire firm.

'If you're Fred Lennon,' said the man, 'I drive your son.'

Fred said: 'Oh, well give me a lift to his house. I haven't seen him for years and I'd like to see him.'

When Fred arrived, Cynthia answered the knock on the door. 'Hello, Cyn, I'm John's Dad and you haven't seen me before.' He had his foot in the hall before she could react.

'He was a charmer in his own way,' says Cynthia. 'There was no way I could have shut the door on him. He looked like a tramp but he was John's Dad. I had no alternative but to ask him to wait for John to return.'

John was staggered. After the initial shock of seeing his father sitting there, and Cynthia's obvious discomfort, John said, in the scathing voice that people feared: 'Where have *you* been for the last twenty years?' John was dumbfounded not only at his father's appearance, but at his demeanour. As a child, he had built up a totally different image of his Dad as a swashbuckling, seafaring Errol Flynn-type character romantically sailing around the world.

'Discovering him to be a pretty foul-mouthed washer-up of dishes, with a real Scouse accent which John, with his upbringing, never had, was not a pretty sight,' says Cynthia.

Freddy Lennon, an inveterate beer drinker, made good money as a ship's steward, and when he worked as a hotel porter. But he was always broke, and scrounging cash from friends and relatives.

The atmosphere grew steadily worse. 'He kept on about what a hard life he'd had, how he was having to work as a skivvy to earn a few bob, and John and I never had it so good,' recalls Cynthia. 'Within an hour or so of coming in the door, he was saying how he didn't want to take anything from his son. But it was obvious he was coming for a handout.'

John felt uncomfortable for his father almost as much as he felt irritable with himself. He remembered how his relatives, his aunts and cousins, older than him, felt suddenly different in *his* company now that he was a famous Beatle. But try though he did, he could not take the arrival of his lost father with a hard luck story.

'He was so embarrassed,' says Cynthia. 'He was in and out of the room like a cat on a hot tin roof. He was nervous and said he suddenly felt ill at ease in his own home.' John's feelings were not helped by the obvious fact that his father had come primarily for money. 'I suppose Fred was proud of what John had achieved,' says Cynthia, 'but his main object was to rip off some cash from John.'

Out of sympathy and to relieve the tension, Cynthia asked Fred if he would like to stay at Kenwood for the night, hoping that it would help the atmosphere. John fixed Cynthia with a stare that asked: 'Do you realize what you're doing?' Fred stayed for three nights and the pressures on John mounted so much that he was out more often than he was at home, leaving Cynthia with the unpleasant job of talking to his father.

When he was with his father, John's insatiable quest for

the truth about his childhood and his father's reported desertion of his mother forced several confrontations. 'Why did you leave Julia—she would have had you back, y'know,' said John.

'How could I, John? Julia left *me*. I didn't leave Julia, she decided she would leave me.'

And so the conversation went on, with John insisting that his mother would have welcomed Fred back to rebuild their marriage, and giving him a happy parental background, while Fred argued that Julia had found another man while he was at sea, and didn't want him back.

It was a fruitless discussion which only confused John even more about his childhood and reminded him of his mother's death.

To Mimi, who had a low opinion of Fred, John said on the phone: 'Oh Mimi, how could my mother marry a man like that? Why didn't you tell me what kind of father I had?'

Mimi answered: 'Dear boy, how would I know what kind of father you had? I didn't know him well myself. Did you want me to bring you up telling you he was a bad man who left you? Would that have made you any happier? You've been happy, haven't you?'

Mimi says John replied: 'Yes, I'm the happiest person in the whole family.'

Three years later Fred presented John and Cynthia with a further problem. He had met a girl and wanted to marry her, but she was only nineteen and had been made a ward of court.

John groaned to his father: 'Oh, no, isn't one failed marriage enough?'

'Fred said he was madly in love with her but didn't have enough money to set himself and her up in a home,' says Cynthia.

The girl was Pauline Jones, a former Exeter University student. Fred persuaded John and Cynthia that his life with her would be easier if she had some work to do, and as she would make a great secretary, she could help John and Cynthia typing their letters.

'John and I talked about it for a while and although he didn't like the idea much, he said he'd like to help his Dad if he could,' says Cynthia.

'I said: "Let's give it a try." '

John dealt brusquely with his father, saying, 'I think it's time for you to leave,' when it became obvious that he would have stayed there for ever, given half a chance. Pauline worked as a live-in secretary for about five months, but her sobbing and wailing kept John and Cynthia up at nights. She was tearful about her difficult relationship with Fred.

And there was not enough work for her. 'She was at as much of a loss about knowing what to do as we were,' says Cynthia. 'We'd never had a permanent secretary and she was going through a bad emotional patch in her life.' Eventually Pauline was asked to leave, but John eased the way for Fred by paying for his court cases and eventually for Fred and Pauline's wedding in Scotland.

'I want you to be happy,' he told his father, finally. He bought him a £15,000 house near Kew Gardens, Surrey, and gave him *carte blanche* to order furniture. He arranged for him to receive £30 a week from the Beatles' company, and established a reasonable, if distant, relationship with him.

Fred and Pauline had two children—John, then, had two half-brothers, David Henry Lennon, born in Brighton in 1969, and Robin Francis Lennon, born in Brighton in 1973. So when John was murdered in 1980, at the age of forty, he had a seven-year-old half-brother living in England whom he had never met.

Fred Lennon became an embarrassment to John. When Fred arrived one day after that first meeting John was under particular Beatles' pressure. He could not face another conversation with the father who had ingratiated himself into his life. John simply slammed the door in his face. Later Fred delivered his ultimate insult to his brilliant son by condemning the decorations at his Weybridge house, criticizing Beatles music as unlike the ballads he sang, 'not as good as the old stuff, say "Begin the Beguine" ', and by hawking himself to national newspapers and magazines as the father of a Beatle. He arrived at the *Melody Maker* office to promote his unspeakable record, 'That's My Life (My Love And My Home)', and told me his record company wanted him to make more. They were even paying for him to get his teeth capped, he said. John Lennon kept up a remarkably dignified silence throughout all this. But not for nothing did he christen his father 'The Ignoble Alf'.

John had proved his generosity, and in spite of provocation had done the right thing for his father. There were other examples of his big heart. He did a special drawing for charity Christmas cards to help famine relief. He was an easy touch for many worthwhile causes like orphans. And to divert his own interest a little from the Beatles and songwriting he became, with George Harrison, a founding director of Hayling Supermarkets Ltd on the Hampshire coast. The other director, and active in running the supermarket towards which John gave £20,000, was his old Quarry Bank school mate and Quarry Men washboard player, Pete Shotton. John and George resigned their directorships in September 1969, leaving Pete in control of the supermarket.

It was impossible to compute John's fortune by 1965. Albums and singles were selling by the million all around the world. Concerts, films, and assorted tie-ins with Beatles merchandise made all four of them millionaires as well as Brian Epstein, who received a percentage of their income on a sliding scale of up to twenty-five per cent. The key to John and Paul's equal money lay in that handshake at the McCartney home at Forthlin Road, Allerton, only eight years earlier; they would write as Lennon–McCartney, whether one wrote a song alone or not. The link resulted in Lenmac, their own company within Northern Songs, the company that raised eyebrows when it went public in February 1965. There was astonishment in the city at pop stars, even the Beatles, considering themselves mighty enough to go public on the London Stock Exchange, but shares were snapped up quickly. John and Paul's income from songwriting alone made them millionaires, and the royalties soared as hundreds of artists around the world clamoured to 'cover' their work, notably Paul's romantic ballads like 'Yesterday' and 'And I Love Her'.

It was said during that year that, at any single moment in any twenty-four hours around the world, a Beatles song was being played on the radio somewhere, just as their records were selling as fast as E.M.I. in London and Capitol in America could press them. America's *Time* magazine said the 'most conservative estimate' put the net worth of George Harrison and Ringo Starr at 3 million dollars each, with John and Paul at 4 million dollars each because of their extra earnings as songwriters. 'The figures could easily be twice as high,' said *Time*. They were out of date before the magazine was published.

The Beatles were not merely bigger than Elvis, as Brian Epstein had vowed they would be. In three bewildering years they had become kings of pop, virtually a royal family of youth. The world hung on their every word, particularly John's, and he retained the title of the Most Outspoken Beatle.

Ever since the Beatles had triumphed at the Royal Variety Show in 1963, they had been courted by the Establishment. It was this very fact that got under John's skin. Rock 'n' roll, he said, was the antithesis of comfortable upper-class values. He had parodied Sir Alec Douglas-Home, the British Prime Minister, as Sir Alec Doubtless Whom, and had a generally healthy disregard for the aristocracy.

One day at Weybridge, among his usual batch of letters from Brian Epstein's office and American fans who simply addressed their envelopes: 'John Lennon, England', there was an official letter saying that he had been selected as a potential recipient of the M.B.E. He was asked if he would accept it publicly. Offering the Beatles the medal of Member of the British Empire, an award bestowed by the Queen, was staggering for pop musicians. It had been building up, surely, but the reality of it was front-page news in all Britain's newspapers that June in 1965.

John's first reaction was to say no. He had already had quite enough of the canonization of the Beatles. The knowledge that lords and ladies and debutantes were fawning over them, and the colossal distance they had travelled from enjoying the beer and sweat of Hamburg and the Cavern, was all too much. 'The money's nice,' he said to me, 'but *this*', pointing to the sweeping lawns of his Weybridge mansion, 'is not necessary. It's all too much. What I'd have liked would have been the money and the hit records without the fame.'

John threw the letter from Buckingham Palace into a pile of fan mail. 'I thought when I saw a brown envelope saying "On Her Majesty's Service" that I was being called up,' said John. A few days later, Brian Epstein asked him on the phone

if he had received it. John said yes, but his instinct was to turn
it down. What were the others doing? Epstein pointed out that
they would all have to accept the honour, and that was that.
John reluctantly agreed that to refuse an award from the Queen
would do colossal damage to the Beatles. Paul, George, and
Ringo felt honoured. So John grunted and agreed. He was
always a terrible compromiser. 'Taking the M.B.E. was a sell-
out for me,' John said later. 'We did manage to refuse all sorts
of things that people don't know about. For instance, we did
the Royal Variety Show [in 1963] and we were asked discreetly
to do it every year after that, but we always said: "Stuff it."
So every year there was always a story in the newspapers
saying, "Why no Beatles for the Queen?" Which was pretty
funny, because they didn't know we refused it. That show's a
bad gig anyway. Everybody's very nervous and uptight and
nobody performs well. The time we did do it, I cracked a joke
on stage. I was fantastically nervous but I wanted to say something, just to rebel a bit, and that was the best I could do.'

   John's witticisms, usually laced with a slice of irony or
invective, were aroused when the Beatles' M.B.E. award became known. He said: 'I thought people got these things for
driving tanks, winning wars.' Retired colonels erupted in fury
at a pop group like the long-haired Beatles receiving such an
award. And some people returned their awards to Buckingham
Palace in protest. John rounded on them with blistering attacks.
Army officers received their medals for killing people, he said.
'We got ours for entertaining. On balance, I'd say we deserve
ours more.' In any case, he pointed out, the Beatles had received their medals for exports, bringing into Britain millions
of pounds' worth of trade.

   'Beatles M.B.E.' stayed as national news in Britain for
weeks, confirming John's private theory that they should never
have accepted it.

   Lord Wilson, then Harold Wilson, British Prime Minister,
had recommended the award of the M.B.E. by the Queen. He
was criticized by many for jumping on the bandwagon of youth,
but Lord Wilson defends his decision: 'Some of the heavy-
weights in the Press had probably never heard of the Beatles,
and if they had, they wouldn't have understood the role the

Beatles had come to play in young people's lives. I saw the
Beatles as having a transforming effect on the minds of youth,
mostly for the good. It kept a lot of kids off the streets. They
introduced many, many young people to music, which in itself
was a good thing. A lot of old stagers might have regarded it
as idiosyncratic music, but the Mersey sound was a new, important thing. That's why they deserved such recognition,' Lord
Wilson told me in 1982.

Lord Wilson recalls a chat with John Lennon at the Variety
Club luncheon in 1964, when the Beatles were named Show
Business Personalities of the Year. As a Merseyside Member
of Parliament, Lord Wilson talked to him about his background.
'John recalled they had started their learning as a group in the
Labour clubs and trade union clubs near his home in Woolton.
I recall that Penny Lane is a mile or so outside my constituency,
so a lot of young people from my constituency would do their
courting there. I thought John Lennon had an irrepressible sense
of humour.'

John's wit struck Lord Wilson at the Variety Club lunch.
The Beatle had risen to accept the award for the group. He
was sitting between the then Leader of the Opposition and
Prince Philip. Addressing the Variety Club chief, John said:
'Mr Chief Barker . . . and [turning to the Opposition
Leader] . . . Mr Dobson.' The confectionery firm of Barker
and Dobson was known mostly to Merseysiders: it was a beautifully timed line. Says Lord Wilson: 'It got very few laughs
because they were all ignorant southerners on our table. But
we enjoyed it.'

There was a typically Lennonesque twist to the M.B.E.
affair. On the day of the investiture at Buckingham Palace,
with thousands of fans crowding the gates outside, the Beatles'
limousine drew up and the immaculately suited moptops stepped
out. John's secret was that inside one of his black boots were
several marijuana joints. Just as the investiture was about to
start the Beatles adjourned together to a small toilet inside
Buckingham Palace where they passed around one joint between them.

The M.B.E. presentation passed uneventfully through their
good cheer. That Christmas, John took his medal down to Aunt

Mimi's new seaside bungalow. 'Keep it, Mimi,' he said. It occupied pride of place on the sideboard, underneath Mimi's favourite picture of John, a huge print taken by Astrid.

John very rarely, if ever, apologized. He believed it to be a sign of weakness, and that to refuse to capitulate was an example of strength. Only Aunt Mimi could elicit a 'sorry' from him, and that was when he knew that, if he didn't say it, the after-effects would last for months.

Still less had John been known to cry. The 'tough guy' bravado approach, a complete veneer for the soft, humanitarian inside, meant that he could never be seen to shed a tear. 'I never once saw John cry,' says Cynthia, 'in the ten years we were together.'

The spring of 1966 became a débâcle for John Lennon. In London's *Evening Standard* he had been profiled, as always, as an iconoclastic, deep-thinking, restless man, way ahead of Beatledom and the perimeters of pop stardom. The writer, Maureen Cleave, was a friend and confidante of John's. He admired her intellect, trusted her, and was always at his frankest when journalists of her calibre treated him as a person with thoughts, outside the confines of pop music. Most sixties' stars projected themselves as vacuous. John set out to impress informed writers like Maureen Cleave that he had a sharp mind and wanted to learn. Talking to her was, for John, cathartic. As always, Maureen Cleave portrayed Lennon as a thinker; she coolly reported him as saying: 'Christianity will go. It will vanish and shrink. I needn't argue with that; I'm right and I will be proved right. We're more popular than Jesus now; I don't know which will go first—rock 'n' roll or Christianity. Jesus was all right but his disciples were thick and ordinary. It's them twisting it that ruins it for me.' He was, she reported, reading extensively about religion. And that was the end of the sermon.

Britain, numbed by four years of some pretty outrageous Lennonisms, did not react to the remarks. The comments had appeared, unsensationally, midway through an erudite article. The Beatles family applauded their leader for again projecting himself intelligently.

Four whole months after Maureen Cleave's article appeared, and had been forgotten, it reappeared under a syndication arrangement with an American magazine, *Datebook*. This time it was not submerged within the context of a general article, but was front-paged: Lennon was claiming that the Beatles were bigger than Jesus Christ!

American reaction, two weeks before the Beatles were due to begin a long concert tour, was instantaneous and devastating. The Beatles, and particularly John, were denounced as sacrilegious, and a wave of anti-Beatle demonstrations fanned out across the American South, the Bible Belt. The Ku Klux Klan marched, there were bonfires of Beatles records, and an estimated thirty-five radio stations across America banned Beatles records. The country that had adopted the Beatles as the 1960s' biggest single social phenomenon was rejecting them. Love and hate, those two closely related emotions, had met. The Beatles were bad news, and Lennon's tongue had caused it.

Promoters who had planned the Beatles' concerts of America were worried about guaranteeing the safety of the group on stage. The Vatican commented that 'some subjects must not be dealt with profanely, even in the world of beatniks'. One minister threatened to excommunicate any member of his congregation who attended a Beatles concert.

Responding to alarming phone calls from America, Brian Epstein immediately flew to New York. His first instinct was to cancel the tour, to protect the Beatles' safety. But he was told that if John made an apology at a press conference in the United States, then things might cool down sufficiently for the tour to proceed. Brian telephoned John at his home in Weybridge. John's immediate reaction was: 'Tell them to get stuffed. I've got nothing to apologize for.' He asked Brian to cancel the tour. 'I'd rather that than have to get up and lie. What I said stands.'

The seriousness of the anti-Beatles campaign was more evident to Brian, in America, than to John in the seclusion of his home in Surrey. There were hundreds of letters arriving daily, addressed simply: 'John Lennon, England', or, searingly, 'Jesus Lennon'. John took a dispassionate interest in reading some. 'How many for and against today?' he would ask Cynthia. Epstein cajoled and pleaded with John, insisting that, unless he made an exception of his golden rule never to apologize, the Beatles' future in America looked bleak, not just for the forthcoming tour but for ever. Next day, South African radio banned all records composed or played by the Beatles. Faced with mounting pressure, John had little choice; he called Epstein and said he would deal with the matter at the Beatles' press conference in Chicago three days later.

Brian, meanwhile, had tried his best to damp down the flames. He said at his own press conference in New York: 'The quote which John Lennon made to a London columnist nearly three months ago [*sic*] has been quoted and misrepresented entirely out of the context of the article, which was in fact highly complimentary to Lennon as a person and was understood by him to be exclusive to the *Evening Standard*. It was not anticipated that it would be displayed out of context and in such a manner as it was in an American teenage magazine.'

In London, Maureen Cleave did her utmost to place John's remarks in their true perspective. 'John was certainly not comparing the Beatles with Christ,' she said. 'He was simply observing that so weak was the state of Christianity that the Beatles were, to many people, better known. He was deploring, rather than approving, this.' The irony of the American uproar was, to many British clergymen, the uncomfortable truth that John was right—witness the number of people who attended the Beatles' concerts and bought their records, compared with church attendance figures.

When John arrived, distraught, in Chicago, he was met by Brian Epstein and Tony Barrow. They took him to a hotel room to brief him on what to expect from the hostile journalists and disc jockeys who were waiting to eat him at the press conference.

'We discussed very, very seriously what should be said by John,' says Tony Barrow. 'It was most unusual for John because for the first and only time in his life that I knew him, he was very willing and ready to apologize.' But under pressure, John broke down and cried: Epstein was explaining what was involved in cancelling the whole Beatle American tour, and Barrow was telling John what the line of questioning would be from the baying journalists. 'I said to John he should try to *explain*.' Brian feared the Beatles might be assassinated during the tour.

John was immediately worried for the safety of the others. He threw his head down into his lap and sobbed loudly, holding his head in his hands. 'I'll do anything,' he said. 'Anything, whatever you say I should do, I'll have to say. How on earth am I going to face the others if this whole tour is called off? Just because of me, just because of something I've said. I didn't mean to cause all of this.'

Epstein's mention of death threats made no impact on John personally. This was odd, because to be 'level' with a Beatle on such major problems and fears when there was an element of potential trouble was most unusual. All four of them were always protected from grim truths and left alone with the job of being Beatles. For Epstein to tell Lennon of his real worries was a big break with tradition. For John not to react puzzled Brian. He asked John if he realized the seriousness of what he'd said. But it was more what Paul, George and Ringo would think of him, if a remark by him had caused the danger of cancellation, that bothered John. Here was John's conscience, exposed for perhaps the first time in his life. He was definitely ready to do whatever was necessary to quell the pandemonium that was gripping America on the subject of the Beatles.

When John took the microphone at the press conference in Chicago that night he looked shaken and apprehensive as he faced a crowd of newsmen on the scent of a cowering Beatle. 'If I had said television is more popular than Jesus, I might have got away with it,' he began, 'but I just happened to be talking to a friend and I used the words "Beatles" as a remote thing, not as what I think—as Beatles, as those other Beatles like other people see us. I just said "they" are having more influence on kids and things than anything else, including Jesus. But I said it in that way which is the wrong way.'

Some journalists were dissatisfied. They thought John had made a stumbling apology, and was virtually restating his original folly.

Said one reporter to him: 'Some teenagers have repeated your statements—"I like the Beatles more than Jesus Christ." What do you think about that?'

John replied: 'Well, originally I pointed out that fact in reference to England. That we meant more to kids than Jesus did, or religion at that time. I wasn't knocking it or putting it

down. I was just saying it as a fact and it is true more for
England than here. I'm not saying that we're better or greater,
or comparing us with Jesus Christ as a person or God as a thing
or whatever it is. I just said what I said and it was wrong. Or
it was taken wrong. And now it's all this.'

The apology that John had conceded would be forthcoming
when he had spoken earlier to Brian Epstein and Tony Barrow
was not coming out clearly. A radio interviewer brought the
matter to a head: 'But are you prepared to apologize?'

John thought he had done so. His face reddened with anguish and his voice became firmer. 'I'm not anti-God, anti-
Christ, or anti-religion. I was not saying we're greater or better.
I believe in God but not as an old man in the sky. I believe
what people call God is something in all of us. I wasn't saying
the Beatles are better than God or Jesus. I used "Beatles"
because it was easy for me to talk about the Beatles.'

But would he apologize?

'I wasn't saying whatever they're saying I was saying. I'm
sorry I said it really. I never meant it to be a lousy anti-religious
thing. I apologize if that will make you happy. I still don't
know quite what I've done. I've tried to tell you what I did do
but if you want me to apologize, if that will make you happy,
then OK, I'm sorry.'

The press conference broke up amid the usual clatter of
microphones and newspapermen fighting for the telephones. In
the more traditional line of questioning that followed, few people took much notice of the resurfacing of the old Lennon
venom. He condemned American involvement in the Vietnam
war. Two months before that day, American planes had bombed
Hanoi. John said he thought American action was unnecessarily
warlike. It was his way of reasserting the real John Lennon.
Public opinion on the Beatles being what it was in America at
that time, he was lucky that his remark on the Vietnam controversy was not picked up and exploited. Fortunately, the
general news line was that Lennon had apologized. Behind all
that furore America wanted its Beatles back, cuddly, tuneful,
joyful. The apology did not reach Alabama, deep in the Bible
Belt, in time to prevent two thousand screaming teenagers
tossing records and pictures of the Unfab Four on to a bonfire
in a ceremony organized by a radio station, WAAX. But across

the street, a smaller group of fans chanted: 'Yeah Beatles, Boo WAAX.' And a disc jockey, announcing the cancellation of another bonfire arranged for later that week, said he accepted the Lennon apology in the same spirit in which it had been made. The Beatles, he suggested, were now aware that they must use 'some degree of judgement and wisdom'.

Against that uncomfortable backdrop, the Beatles' 1966 tour of America could hardly lack tension. They were off the hook, but psychologically weakened and defensive. The 'Jesus' eruption had followed some riotous scenes in the Philippines. After a concert in Manila, the Beatles were alleged to have snubbed the President's wife by not attending a party. Paul said they were never invited, but the word got out that they had been rude, and they were jeered by many and jostled at the airport by thirty thugs, some with guns.

As always, the party invitation was simply a matter of confusion. But on their way out to the airport, thousands cheered while a few booed. 'All along the route there were people waving,' said John back at Heathrow, 'but I could see a few old men booing us. When they started on us at the airport, I was petrified.

'I thought I was going to get hurt so I headed for three nuns and two monks, thinking that if I was close to these people that might stop them. I was just pushed around. But that's the Philippines finished for me. No plane's going through the Philippines with me on it. I wouldn't even fly over it.'

America, in the aftermath of the 'Jesus' affair, threatened worse. With the real danger of assassination by the 'loony' John had so often joked about, it had little chance of being a coast-to-coast celebration. Fifteen concerts, two in the 55,000-capacity Shea Stadium in New York, one before a similar crowd at the Los Angeles Dodger Stadium, testified to the power of America's love of the Beatles. But something had happened deep inside; as far as John was concerned, a chapter had closed. It was turning sour and a drag. The Beatles road show was over. It had been a bore for long enough. Now it was also dangerous.

That tour was the finale of the Beatles' live work. Their last appearance, at Candlestick Park, San Francisco, on 29

August 1966, was a firm decision they made early on during that tour. When they told Brian Epstein, he was dejected. He realized his paternal role with the Beatles whom he loved would be virtually over, except for business relationships. For in the recording studio, as he had found to his cost, he was only welcome if he played no artistic role.

George Harrison had been instrumental in forcing an end to touring. Fed up with the poor sound and never enthralled by Beatlemania, he wanted to spend more time in the studios perfecting their finished recordings. There, there could be no duff notes going unchecked, unlike at the concerts where nobody cared. Now they'd proved they were enormous they didn't need the hassle, he argued. He was able to win over John because Lennon disliked the discomfort of touring. He was shouting more obscenities at the screaming crowds who knew nothing of this curious 'release' when he was on stage. He was second only to George in his nervousness of flying. The restrictions and lack of freedom, and scarcely knowing which town they were in, had finally become too much. The nail in the coffin was the bitter taste in the mouth from the Philippines and America from things that had happened *off* stage.

Paul McCartney enjoyed touring. He strongly resisted the Harrison–Lennon partnership and argued that that was what a rock 'n' roll band was all about. A showman in the grand tradition, Paul needed an audience's approval and applause. He said that was a vital part of the act. But while George laid out the unarguable facts about the quality of their music in the huge stadiums, John weighed in with: 'It's got too far from the Cavern.' Even though Ringo enjoyed touring, there could be no road show with John and George so reluctant. The only bright aspects of tours were the women and drugs and parties which customarily marked the end of the American tours: the camaraderie between the Beatles and other musicians which became a ritual in the rented house high in the Hollywood Hills. But now, that too had lost its appeal.

Britain was hopeless, anyway. The halls were too small to contain their millions of fans. A tour would disappoint more people than it would please. So on the road, at least, it was all over. On the plane back from San Francisco, George breathed a sigh of relief: 'Now I don't have to pretend to be a Beatle any more.' Brian Epstein, who had not been able to bring himself to attend the final concert, just got drunk on champagne. In London, weeks later, when Brian told John of the concern of promoter Arthur Howes that they would never tour Britain again, Lennon snorted down the phone: 'Tell him to send out four wax dummies of the Beatles that shake their heads at the right time. The kids won't know the difference.'

Returning from the tumult of touring to Weybridge proved very hard for John. Cynthia was there to welcome him, with Julian and a big batch of post from religious zealots, particularly from America, seeking to educate John about Jesus. For a few days John enjoyed domesticity, putting Julian to bed, reading him a story, making his tea occasionally. There was, though, a fear inside him: though the Beatles had not disbanded, 'What the hell am I going to do?' All his working life the Beatles had been a travelling band. Now they were not. Of all the Beatles he was the most individualistic, and the least reliant on the group. But he felt suddenly alone. The rungs on the ladder from the Cavern had been quickly climbed until he had reached the very pinnacle: hit songs, no money worries, films, wife, child, fame, power of a frightening nature, and two bestselling books.

The restlessness that had driven him since childhood now gnawed away at him. 'Doing more of the same was never my solution to a problem,' he said. The Beatles, although they still had years of good music to make, was no longer a challenge. John was now an insatiable newspaper reader, particularly of the *Daily Mirror* and *Daily Mail*.

Cynthia noticed a softening in John in the aftermath of the American débâcle. The tongue was not so quick. The battle for the Beatles had been won and an era closed, and John seemed more like his old self than the cocky Beatle-on-the-road. He told her that he was pleased touring was all over.

His ego remained strong. Offers for him to build up his literary and artistic career poured in. Would he design another charity Christmas card? Would he open this, give his blessing to that, donate some money here, there, and everywhere? John sought refuge by accepting his first solo acting role in the film *How I Won The War*. John would take the role of Private

Gripweed in a story that tilted against war, a favourite theme
for John, and, importantly, the producer and director was Richard Lester. 'I was flattered at being asked,' said John. 'The
ego needed feeding, with the Beatles at a kind of crossroads.'

It was the first move by a Beatle outside the Beatles. And
for John it involved not merely an acting role, but a significant
change in his looks. First he was symbolically shorn of all his
long Beatles hair, and next he needed to look like a soldier,
so he adopted wire-framed National Health spectacles—'granny
glasses' as they became known. The specs, a bizarre flashback
to the ones he had rejected when Aunt Mimi took him to an
optician in Liverpool as a schoolboy, started a craze as surely
as the Beatles' haircuts had seen to it that any self-respecting
man of 1966 in the Western world had a hairstyle resembling
that of the moptops.

Shooting for *How I Won The War* was in Germany, where
John's locks were cut, and Almeria, Spain. Ringo and Maureen
went out to socialize with John, who broke with his own tradition and invited Cynthia to visit him in Spain. Conditions
were primitive in the rented house, but there was glorious
solitude. After four years of relying to some degree on Paul,
George, and Ringo, John was now alone in a creative situation.
He played cricket with Richard Lester, enjoyed the company
of actor Michael Crawford, and practised music making for
much of the time. 'The harmonica was with him throughout
the filming,' says Richard Lester.

Lennon identified completely with what the film projected:
'It represented a genuine, heartfelt emotional attitude in response to its time,' says Richard Lester. 'It will live on because
it doesn't lead, it doesn't change society, but it does reflect a
desperately sincere attitude towards the glorification of war by
show business that was prevalent in the mid-sixties.'

In the wake of the Vietnam conflict John was vocal about
war, even though he felt like a novice as the actor. 'I was an
apprentice in the middle of professionals,' he said of his colleagues in the picture. When the film was completed, he took
to wearing a badge with the initials C.N.D., supporting the
Campaign for Nuclear Disarmament.

What had attracted Lennon to the film was Richard Lester's

theory at the time: 'One of the gross obscenities about war is the war film itself. War on the screen is treated like a great big adventure with extras being killed in the way of a Western.'

John said: 'I hate war. The Vietnam war and all that is being done there made me feel like that. If there is another war I won't fight—and although the youngsters may be asked to fight I'll stand up there and try to tell them not to. I hate all the sham about war.'

John liked the experience of that solo film, but it was not enough to propel him into a serious acting career. He loathed the endless waiting in the desert, or on film sets in Germany and Spain, and learning lines, however short, drained his patience. No matter how often Richard Lester told him sincerely that he had the ability to develop a role as a fine actor, John would have none of it. He reverted to his lifelong theory about the stage and the cinema: '. . . people up there trying to pretend they're somewhere else.'

On his return home, it was obvious to Lennon that he had already lived at a pace, and absorbed enough, that matched three times his age. Doors had opened and closed during his twenty-six years with fantastic speed: art, music, books, dramatic acting, recording, concerts, success on a scale undreamed of. Yet they all left him feeling empty, and without much sense of achievement. His scepticism about politics remained: in a British General Election year, he said to me during an interview on his political beliefs: 'The motto seems to be: "Keep the people happy with a few fags and beer and they won't ask any questions." I'm not an anarchist, but it would be good if people started realizing the difference between political propaganda and truth.'

His own search for the truth manifested itself that autumn in two diversions that were dramatically and tangibly to affect the next two years of his life, and his years beyond them. Those diversions were drugs and his desire to get back in some way to the world of art from which he sprang. Combined, drugs and artistic visions would produce the psychedelic sounds, the next year, of *Sgt Pepper's Lonely Hearts Club Band*. But in 1966, desperate for a new route that nourished his own psyche,

John Lennon believed he had found spiritual and physical uplift in the drug L.S.D. (lysergic acid) and a constant round of London art galleries.

Lysergic acid was slipped quietly into John and Cynthia's drinks one night when they were out with George and his wife Pattie, the model whom he had met on the set of *A Hard Day's Night*. For John, the mind expansion, the discovery of oneself within, the check on one's ego, the release, the heightening of his perceptions, were not just the perfect backdrop for the new vibrancy of Swinging London. The drug's ability to detach him from the mundane and transport his mind into a kind of nirvana was, he told me, an answer to his prayer. Attending a round of parties in London connected with the art world, John found out how to get what he described to me as 'the best stuff it's possible to get in the world'. He took large amounts of L.S.D. in the autumn of 1966, mixing up potions at home. He became a vegetarian, ate infrequently, and looked dangerously wasted within a few short months.

John tried unsuccessfully to lure Cynthia into his never-ending use of marijuana or L.S.D. 'It seemed to be all right for him, although I was totally against it,' she recalls. 'It opened the floodgates of his mind and he seemed to escape from the imprisonment of fame. Tensions, and bad tempers, were replaced by understanding and love as his message.' Pressured by John's constant pleading, Cynthia did relent and tried an L.S.D. trip, during which John carefully guided her. But she was not mentally receptive.

When she 'came back' from her horrifying experience of a bad trip, she decided categorically that she would never dabble again. 'This upset John, but I could not handle it,' she says. 'Suddenly there was this new mental barrier between us.' Her rejection erected an even bigger wall between them than already existed. For weeks she had become increasingly worried about the retinue of drug pushers and the undesirable caravan of hangers-on who were arriving back home with John, pouring out of his Rolls-Royce at dawn, after a night of clubbing and hard drinking in London. A drunken John was something Cynthia had learned to cope with for years, but a combination of drink and drugs and a coterie of odd unknown people who dossed down in the sumptuous lounge of their home drove her to despair. She told John she was worried about the environment in which Julian was having to grow up and go to school from, each morning. But John was deep within himself, and when he did not want to reply he would pretend not to have heard. 'I knew then that our marriage was in trouble,' says Cynthia. 'We had lost communication. John was on another planet.'

John was looking for something way beyond the Beatles, and even he did not know what it was. Slowly, his songwriting as well as his life was infiltrated by the hallucinatory effects of soft and hard drugs, though the world did not know it. He hid his marijuana and L.S.D. in the garden at Kenwood, fearing a police raid. The evidence was there in two songs in particular: 'Day Tripper' alluded to anyone who was not properly into drugs, but was what John called a weekend hippie; and in 'We Can Work It Out', written mostly by Paul, John composed the middle part. McCartney was still optimistically looking at life with the sunny outlook that inspired the title, while the suspicious John interjected the words in the middle: 'Life is very short and there's no time . . . for fussing and fighting, my friend.' Love and peace, man, was now his chief passion. The man who had told me at Weybridge at the height of Beatlemania that he was 'waiting for something to happen' set about *making* it happen.

As the seeds of flower power and psychedelia were planted in Swinging London, two of the most thriving industries were boutiques and art galleries, which opened by the score. The Chelsea set, and the tourists, gravitated to the King's Road. Art people headed for Mayfair, Piccadilly, or South Kensington.

Through Mick Jagger and singer Marianne Faithfull, one of the least durable partnerships of the Swinging Scene, Lennon was introduced to John Dunbar, Marianne's former husband and owner of a small art gallery, the Indica, in Mason's Yard, off St James's, Piccadilly. One of its investors was Peter Asher, whose sister Jane was Paul McCartney's girlfriend at the time. Peter had also, as half of the vocal duo Peter and Gordon, recorded a McCartney song, 'A World Without Love', whose lyrical corniness sent Lennon into fits of derisive laughter. 'Please lock me away' was, to John, hilarious.

Dunbar told John that an interesting and unusual exhibition would be opening on 10 November 1966 and that, to ensure that he wasn't harassed as part of a crowd, John might consider popping in to a private preview.

John and Cynthia often did different things in the evenings; she would draw or paint, or do needlework, happy to play the role of contented mother and wife in Weybridge. Besides, drugs had started to rock their partnership. John often went out alone.

On 9 November John's chauffeur-driven Mini Cooper with its tinted windows drew up outside the Indica and he stepped inside for what Dunbar had told him by telephone would be 'a happening'. John was intrigued. Anything that was off-beat, that fed his druggy inspirations, was going to attract him. This sounded an extraordinary exhibition. He thought 'a happening' might mean an orgy, he said. He was mentally geared up for an *event*.

The exhibition was called *Unfinished Paintings and Objects*. As he leafed through the catalogue John thought it was very freaky but fascinating, off-beat and weird enough for him to take his time walking round. The catalogue featured pictures of objects like wall cabinets, glassware, a big black bag captioned 'with a member of the audience inside', an apple, apparently meaningless to John: 'a mirror to see your behind', a 'sky T.V.' described more fully as closed-circuit T.V. set up in the gallery for looking at the sky; an 'eternal time clock'. Accompanying the pictures were words describing the exhibits: 'I would like to see the sky machine on every corner of the street instead of the Coke machine. We need more skies than Coke.' And: 'The mind is omnipresent. Events in life never happen alone and the history is forever increasing its volume. The natural state of life and mind is complexity. At this point, what art can offer is an absence of complexity, a vacuum through which you are led to a state of complete relaxation of mind. After that, you may return to the complexity of life again. It may not be the same, or it may be, or you may never return, but that is your problem.' And: 'Man is born, educates himself, builds a house and a life and then all that vanishes when he dies. What is real? Is anything real? A thing becomes real to us when it is functional and necessary to us. As long as we strive for truth we live in self-induced misery, expecting in life something that is not an illusion. If we recognize that nothing is true nor illusory . . . then we can proceed from there on to be optimistic and swallow life as it comes.'

The catalogue offered John the most bizarre introduction to 'the happening'. There was a 'Painting To Shake Hands— a painting for cowards: drill a hole in a canvas and put your hand out from behind. Receive your guests in that position. Shake hands and converse with hands.'

The carefully designed, handsomely printed catalogue had pictures on stickers for tearing out and placing over captions to feed the imagination: 'Painting to hammer a nail': 'Painting to let the evening light go through'; 'bag wear'.

A commercial sales list in the catalogue increased the smile on John's face. On offer, through mail order, were items like this: 'Soundtape of the snow falling at dawn, twenty-five cents per inch (types: snow of India, snow of Kyo, snow of Aos).

'Crying machine: machine drops tears and cries for you when coin is deposited. 3,000 dollars.

'Word machine: machine produces a word when coin is deposited: 1,500 dollars.

'Disappearing machine: machine that allows an object to disappear when button is pressed: 1,600 dollars.

'Danger box: machine that you will never come back the same from (we cannot guarantee your safety in its use), 1,100 dollars.

'Sky machine: machine produces nothing when coin is deposited, 1,500 dollars.'

The list went on: a transparent house, intended so that the people inside cannot see out and the people outside can see in; special defects underwear for men; underwear to make you high, for women, description upon request; imaginary music; books called *Grapefruit*.

'What's all this *about*?' an incredulous Lennon asked John Dunbar.

'Bringing you here,' replied Dunbar, 'is my conceptual work of art.'

As John finished reading and moved round the gallery to look at the startling exhibits the artist herself, a slight woman, under five feet tall, dressed all in black, her head framed by thick, long black hair, handed him a card on which was printed one word: BREATHE.

Her name was Yoko Ono.

16
DIVORCE

'When I met Yoko, I had to drop everything!'

'I think,' says Yoko Ono, 'that I was probably the successor to Aunt Mimi in John's life.' Her comparison of herself with the formidable but intensely caring woman who raised John Lennon through his entire childhood is both brave and astute. The qualities in his stern Aunt Mimi, which John grew to admire and respect, were to be re-created in a much more bizarre fashion by Yoko Ono. And she too had a profound, devastating effect on him.

Their first meeting set the pattern of their loving, creative and often tempestuous relationship. At London's Indica art gallery in late 1966 one of the exhibits in Yoko's show as an avant-garde artist was an apple which she had on sale for £200. John was taken aback by the absurdity of it. 'Look, I don't have to pay all that money for an apple,' he said, smiling cynically with that familiar curled bottom lip. He appreciated the dry humour in her work immediately. Yoko Ono had won her point: she had elicited a firm response. For the artist in her, contact had been made.

Next she asked John to climb a stepladder and hammer an imaginary nail into the wall. This, she said, would cost him five shillings. John's retort was as swift as one might have expected from a no-nonsense Liverpudlian: 'I'll give you an imaginary five shillings,' he said, 'if you'll let me hammer the imaginary nail.' The joke was that there were no nails left.

Yoko permitted herself a rare smile. John said later that he regarded the event as 'nutty'. But Yoko remembers that they both felt a certain electricity in the air as they 'connected'. Lennon was a sucker for experimentation. Yoko says she recognized in him that evening an artistic sense of humour that placed him apart from his professional role as Millionaire Beatle. She was anyway totally unimpressed by the fact that he was rich and famous: 'I was a conceptual artist and had no interest in pop music. The Beatles' thing, rock 'n' roll, had passed me by.' Lennon, conversely, was drawn to the art world like a magnet. The restlessness that simmered underneath the pop star at the end of 1966 had resulted from his deep involvement with drugs.

The evening he first met Yoko he had been up for three nights, stoned on marijuana and L.S.D. His demeanour virtually reflected his inner self: confused and dissatisfied with the mad whirl of Beatlemania. Crucially, at the time of his meeting with Yoko he was looking for a new force in his life. With the uncanny sixth sense of communication that was to manifest itself between them as the years unfolded, Yoko realized after that odd encounter at the Indica Gallery that something had happened to her too. 'He played exactly the same mind game as me,' she says.

John's account of that first meeting is somewhat longer but just as immediate. 'Imagine two cars of the same make heading towards each other and they're gonna crash, head-on. Well, it's like one of those scenes from a film—they're doing a hundred miles an hour, they both slam their brakes on and there's smoke everywhere on the floor and they stop just in the nick of time with their bumpers almost touching but not quite. That's what it was like from the first time I got to know her.' The analogy was perfect.

There was a problem, however. Both John Winston Lennon and Yoko Ono were married . . .

Back at home in Weybridge, Surrey, John's wife Cynthia firmly believed her role was to continue as before Beatlemania: as the rock-solid, unquestioning, loving, home-building wife and devoted mother to their three-year-old son Julian. John's absence as a travelling Beatle had forced her to shoulder all the domestic chores. Passive, maternal, at all times understanding, except on the subject of drugs, Cynthia was still the contented, tasteful, resilient Hoylake girl who had first won John's heart at art college. Being the wife of a millionaire star whose face was in the newspapers and on television every week had not changed her one scrap. The problem was that John *had* changed. And he regretted that Cyn had not changed with him. He was looking for new action. And he wanted it quickly, like everything else.

'There was nothing basically wrong with my marriage to Cyn,' John told me. 'It was just like an amber light. It wasn't on go and it wasn't on stop. I suppose that me being away so much during the early years of our marriage, I never did feel like the average married man.'

His artistic flirtation with Yoko took months, and a determined pursuit by her, before it developed; in the beginning he was sceptical of her strange world but intrigued too. Soon after their meeting Yoko sent John a copy of her small book, *Grapefruit*. Its simplicity infuriated him but it played on his imagination just as Yoko had intended. Effectively it was a continuation of the odd images conjured up in the catalogue which he had smiled over at the Indica Gallery. *Grapefruit* featured Yoko's instructions to: 'Cut a hole in a bag filled with seeds and place the bag where there is wind.' One entry read: 'Hide until everybody goes home. Hide until everybody forgets about you. Hide until everybody dies.'

John read *Grapefruit* in bed at night. Beside him lay Cynthia, who once asked what he was reading. 'Oh, something that weird artist woman sent me,' he replied. Neither husband nor wife realized that within two years that same 'weird artist woman' would radically re-shape both their lives and that John would write as his introduction to the reprinted version of *Grapefruit*: 'Hi, my name is John Lennon. I'd like you to meet Yoko Ono.' Alongside the terse message would be his drawing of the woman who by then had won his heart as well as his head.

John was no saint and Cynthia knew it. The temptations for a Beatle, who was one of the most famous people in the world in 1966, adored, mentally and physically, by thousands of women, would have been almost impossible for a full-blooded male to resist.

'But I had blind faith,' says Cynthia. 'I couldn't imagine John being involved with another woman. And even if he had, I would have ignored it because he always came back. Whatever John did outside our marriage, he didn't flaunt anything. So when I learned later about the temptations he had succumbed to, I had the satisfaction of knowing he had protected me at the time, just like he had since we first met.'

Cynthia says she had more fears about his desirability when he was a student than when he was a Beatle. 'Once he became famous, he was like a national institution, not easy to be picked off for flings—well, easy maybe, but he had to be careful about it, be careful who knew.'

Honesty, one of John's most endearing characteristics, forced him to confess to Cynthia one day early in 1967. Cynthia was washing the dishes when John came behind her, put his arms around her waist and said: 'I want to get it off my chest, Cyn. There have been hundreds of other women.'

It could have been an explosive moment. But such was Cynthia's love and devotion to John that his honesty and his tender way of breaking the news of his affairs developed into one of the frankest moments in their marriage since the turbulence of Beatlemania and drugs had pulled them apart. 'Strangely,' says Cynthia, 'it was a very loving moment. I was in tears, not of anger or shock, but tears of happiness that he could tell me, that we'd once again got close enough for him to get rid of it, talk it through and put it on a different level. Perhaps it would have been better if I'd been able to be a bit more aggressive. But I was so happy that at last he felt he could open his heart and tell me what was on his mind.'

Their marriage had been 'rolling along nicely with no fireworks,' she recalls. Although she had suspected that John had been involved with other women, she had shut herself away from the possibility, preoccupied with running a house, bringing up Julian and cosseting John when he returned from work. His extra-marital affairs did not concern her.

Mentally the rift between them had begun more than a year before with John's increased interest in drugs and Cynthia's steadfast refusal to join him on his trips. Now, in 1967, the full flowering of John's personality was to take shape; his own confrontation with his marriage was a central part of this.

'When John told me he'd had all these affairs, I felt as though we were being brought together again,' says Cynthia. 'He'd been leading his life as a musician and pop star and I'd led mine as a wife and mother. Conversation had become very thin on the ground. He was doing so many things I wasn't involved in.'

John's confession had a strange irony. A few weeks earlier he and Cynthia had been watching television when a programme mentioned the number of times a week an average married couple would make love. They fell far short of it, says Cynthia, because John was away so much. He said to her: 'God, we're just like brother and sister, aren't we?' But their marriage had ticked over until that crucial session of owning up. And that was the major problem. John's mind was expanding so fast by then that he did not want anything in his life to 'tick over'.

'Our relationship was one of friendship—we were always mates and we'd gone through a lot together,' says Cynthia. 'But I did know we couldn't pretend it was like the student days once he'd made it to the top. Once Julian was born, we were parents, responsible people and John was a big star. If any of John's agony, self-torment or torture was worrying him, then he kept it hidden from me. I wasn't aware of it.'

John's admission of other women in his life might have been therapeutic for both him and Cynthia but the physical flings were only a surface indication of something which ran much deeper. What he would not say to her, because he did not want to hurt her, was that he was desperately looking for some new milestone in his life. He did not feel comfortable in his Weybridge mansion in the stockbroker belt. The house was merely a status symbol, bought hurriedly to hide from fans thronging their central London flat. The roller-coaster of Beatlemania had lost its attraction for him. Drugs were increasing their hold over him and the continuing clash with Cynthia over his use of L.S.D. rocked their marriage still further. He became increasingly irritable when, as he took L.S.D. at home, Cynthia said: 'Please, John, it would be wise for you not to do it. You will go mental if you're not careful. Think about Julian, think about everything.'

Cynthia comments: 'But his reasoning power over what was important had gone. Whatever anyone said when he was taking L.S.D. was not to be treated seriously. Me, I didn't get involved because I saw my role as his wife, and Julian's Mum, as running the house and being the mainstay of his life when he was there.' She regrets not having been more positive, perhaps even slightly more aggressive, to counter John's excesses. 'I couldn't change my character, though, could I?' But Cynthia had miscalculated the degree of intellectual stimulus John was now seeking.

In midsummer 1967 the Beatles' manager Brian Epstein threw a small party at his house at 24 Chapel Street, Belgravia, to mark a very special event in the career of the four men to whom he still paternally referred as 'the boys'. Few of the guests, including me, expected the new album from the Beatles to be so revolutionary. The record that blared out from behind tables groaning with exquisitely chosen gourmet food was *Sgt Pepper's Lonely Hearts Club Band*. The music perfectly captured the mood of that psychedelic, flowerpower summer when swinging London, mini skirts, Carnaby Street's fashion liberation and love and peace were precursors of a generation's change. It became a soundtrack for psychedelia.

There had been little indication to the public that the Beatles had gone so far down the road with drugs. A few months earlier John's song 'Strawberry Fields Forever'—one of his finest— evoked nothing more spiky than his childhood memories of ice-creams in a Salvation Army children's fete, while Paul's 'Penny Lane', on the reverse side, completed the Liverpool connection with flashbacks to the bus shelter where John and Paul, as fiendish schoolboys, would meet and eye the girls. But *Sgt Pepper* was different, a triumphant leap forward in songwriting ideas by John and Paul. Two Lennon songs in particular—'A Day In The Life' and 'Lucy In The Sky With Diamonds'—were revolutionary even for the ever-questing John, the first being banned by the B.B.C. for its implied condoning of drugs, the second being a haunting stream-of-consciousness song which John had written after Julian had come home from school (Heath House, Weybridge) one afternoon and shown him a picture he had drawn, inspired by his friend Lucy.

At Epstein's party John looked haggard, old, ill, and hopelessly addicted to drugs. His eyes were glazed, his speech slow and slurred. I had a brief chat with him about music and he said he was worried that they had gone too far for public taste with the new album. 'Will they buy it? I like it, we all feel it's another step up, but will it sell?' I was astonished at his coherence while he was clearly under the influence of drugs. We spoke a little about the state of the music scene and he said there was one 'dope' record which he couldn't get off his mind. He couldn't remember the title. All other pop music of the period was 'crap', one of his favourite words at the time. John said he wasn't eating much and was on a vegetarian diet.

He smoked and drank wine incessantly. Talking later to Brian Epstein I said how horrifying and worrying John's physical state seemed. 'Don't worry. He's a survivor,' said Brian.

Next day John phoned me. 'I remembered after I'd gone what the record is that I can't stop playing,' he said. 'It's that dope song, Procol Harum's "Whiter Shade Of Pale". It's the best song I've heard for a while. You play it when you take some acid and . . . whooooooooooooo.' What was most surprising about the phone call was that he'd actually remembered our conversation the previous evening. As he was later to prove, his eye and ear for detail and his memory, even when on drugs, would surprise anyone who thought him inattentive.

Talking of the making of *Sgt Pepper*, producer George Martin says: 'That was an incredible thing because it took on its own character, it grew despite us. It was a complete change of life, a very long and arduous series of recordings and I suppose that looking back on it, *Pepper* would never have been formed in exactly that way if the boys hadn't got into the drug scene, and if I hadn't been a normal person. I don't think it would have been as coherent. . . . I just had to be patient. You can't do much with a guy when he's giggling all the time. If they hadn't been on drugs, it's possible something like *Pepper* would have happened but not quite so flowery, maybe.'

Drugs, *Sgt Pepper*, his psychedelically painted Rolls-Royce, the gipsy caravan in his garden at Weybridge, and his total embrace of a more freewheeling way of life hardened John's attitude to his home environment. Yoko both fascinated and annoyed him. A steady stream of letters arrived at Weybridge from her and for a period, postcards arrived daily, saying:

'Dance' or 'Breathe' or 'Watch all the lights until dawn.' John alternately found them intriguing or simply dismissed them.

At this point in his life John was at his most vulnerable. The Beatles had stopped touring and had just produced an album which was critically acclaimed as setting new standards for popular music, lifting Lennon and McCartney into a new echelon of composers. This crossroads in the Beatles' position, coupled with his foundering marriage and his enthusiasm for drugs, made him easy prey to anything that offered new kicks.

As for the other Beatles, George Harrison had succumbed to Eastern mysticism, entranced by the sitar-playing of his tutor and new friend, Ravi Shankar. Paul McCartney, with actress Jane Asher at his side, moved ever upwards in the social whirl of London hip society, which held no appeal for John. Ringo, living a few minutes away on the same estate at Weybridge, enjoyed dispensing drinks from his private bar, the Flying Cow, and was useful to John when he wanted to lock into light-heartedly playing the Beatle role. But when Pattie Harrison, George's wife, said she had heard from a friend about transcendental meditation, which encouraged a deeper, cooler form of consciousness and awareness, John was hooked. Together with Cynthia, George and Pattie, and Paul and Jane he attended a lecture on meditation by the Maharishi Mahesh Yogi at London's Hilton Hotel.

By now the phone calls from Yoko had increased; she sought his support for her artistic ventures and even visited his home when neither he nor Cynthia was there. The housekeeper, Dorothy Jarlett, allowed her in one day to make a phone call and next day Yoko phoned John to say she must return because she had left her 'very precious' ring by the phone. John was getting used to her unpredictable behaviour and her spacey conversation attracted him, especially when he was high on drugs. Cynthia was blissfully ignorant that their relationship had any potential until that night after their baptism into transcendental meditation. Yoko was also at the meeting—alone.

As John and Cynthia climbed into their chauffeur-driven Rolls-Royce afterwards Yoko followed them into the car. 'John and I both looked at each other as though we'd gone crazy,' says Cynthia. 'I said to him: "What's going on?" He said: "I dunno." Neither of us had the courage to say: "Excuse me,

madam, but where are you going?'' She got in the car and
asked to be dropped off down the road, which we duly did.
For all I knew, there could have been something going on
between John and Yoko even then but I don't think so judging
from the look on his face. It was pure shock. It couldn't have
been put on.' Yoko was dressed all in black. With her long
hair and tiny figure even Cynthia admits she was fascinating.
'We thought it was quite amusing afterwards,' she recalls. 'We
joked about it.' When John introduced Yoko to Cynthia, Yoko
almost immediately propelled herself into talking about *Grapefruit*. Cynthia drew long and hard on her ever-present cigarette
and pondered the weird woman in black who, according to
John's reports, 'kept popping up all over the place' in his life.

At home later that evening Cynthia confronted John about
Yoko and her strange behaviour.

'What is it with Yoko then?'

John replied: 'Oh nothing, she's crackers, she's just a weirdo
artist. Don't worry about it.'

Cynthia persisted: 'Well what's all the phoning about, all
these letters and leaving rings behind and knocking at the door?'

'Oh don't worry about it,' John insisted, 'it's not important.
Crazy crazy crazy, Cyn! She's another nutter wanting money
for all that avant-garde bullshit.'

Cynthia recalls: 'There was, though, something coming
across constantly. It was worrying me but I had no tangible
evidence . . . Although he and I didn't properly argue about
it, the fact that he was smoking and taking L.S.D. made it hard
to communicate. He kept pleading with me to join him and
take it, but I wanted to keep my sanity. . . . During one of
these scenes, I said to him: "Perhaps Yoko's the one for you,
John." I remember he said: "Don't be stupid. That weird
artist!" '

The day after that bizarre encounter John went with the
other Beatles to Bangor, North Wales to be properly taught
transcendental meditation during a Bank Holiday weekend seminar. After a frantic dash to London's Euston Station Cynthia
arrived to see the train leaving and John, hanging from the
window, a face in the distance. The moment flashed before
both John and Cynthia's eyes as strangely underlining the split
in their marriage. When she eventually arrived alone John sar-

castically berated her for 'always being late' and brought Cynthia to the brink of tears during what was supposed to be a weekend of tranquillity. The weekend, as well as widening the rift in John's marriage, proved to be a turning point for the Beatles.

On 27 August 1967, a day before he was due to travel north to join the Beatles for the meditation course, Brian Epstein died, a victim of an accidental drug overdose at his London home. Amid his beads and robes and peace in the North Wales countryside John reacted to the news with the same pent-up emotion which he had felt at the deaths of his mother, his Uncle George, and his best friend Stuart Sutcliffe. Lennon did not believe in prolonged grief. The Beatles returned to London to face the Press and try to marshal their thoughts about the millionaire, thirty-two-year-old manager who had steered them to the dizziest heights of world fame.

His death, so unexpected in the context of his success, was a puzzle. Brian was a complex, narcissistic man, very much a loner, and yet in a mere six years he had converted four scruffy rock 'n' rollers from Liverpool to legendary status and international social phenomena. It was a stupendous achievement. John had a love-hate feeling about Brian's triumph. He wanted the riches and fame which Brian's zeal had made possible, but he resented the fact that Epstein had cleaned them up and robbed them of their raw roots. Even so, John often demonstrated his big heart, sending Brian flowers or little gifts when Eppy was low.

That Bank Holiday Monday afternoon John invited me over to Weybridge to talk about the impact of Brian's death. Robed in white and lazing with Ringo by the pool, he seemed dazed as the words came together slowly.

'We all feel very sad but it's controlled grief, controlled emotion. As soon as I find myself feeling depressed, I think of something nice about him. But you can't hide the hurt— you know, I went to the phone book and saw his name and it hit me a few minutes ago. The memory must be kept nice but of course there's something inside us that tells us that Brian's death is sad.

'It hurts when someone close dies and Brian was very close.

You know, we've all been through that feeling of wanting a good cry. But that wouldn't get us anywhere, would it?

'We all feel it but these talks on transcendental meditation have helped us to stand up to it so much better. You don't get upset, do you, when a young kid becomes a teenager or a teenager becomes an adult or when an adult gets old? Well, Brian is just passing into the next phase.

'His spirit is still around and always will be. It's a physical memory we have of him and as men we will build on that memory. It's a loss of genius, but other genius's bodies have died as well, and the world gains from their spirits.

'It's up to us now to sort out the way we, and Brian, wanted things to go. He might be dead physically but that's a negative way of thinking. He helped to give us the strength to do what we did and the same urge is still alive. It's a drag he didn't come up to the meditation course with the Maharishi.'

I asked John for his evaluation of Epstein's role in the Beatles' success and whether they would still have broken through without him. 'Not the same as we know it, no. But if he hadn't come along, we would all—the four of us and Brian—have been working towards the same thing, even though it might have been with different aims. We all knew what we wanted to get over; he helped us and we helped him.

'We're all going to India soon for a couple of months to study transcendental meditation properly. The only plans we had, before Brian died, were to make a record, do a T.V. show, and make a film. But meeting the Maharishi changed our thoughts a bit and Brian's death has changed it a lot. It makes it more worthwhile, now, somehow, to go to India.

'We want to learn the meditation thing properly so we can propagate it and sell the whole idea to everyone. This is how we plan to use our power now—they've always called us leaders of youth and we believe this is a good way to give a lead. We want to set up an academy in London and use all the power we've got to get it moving. And all the people who are worried about youth and drugs and that scene—all these people with the short back and sides, they can come along and dig it, too.

'It's no gospel, Bible-thumping, singalong thing and it needn't be religion if people don't want to connect it with religion. It's all in the mind.

'It strengthens understanding, makes people relaxed. The whole world wants to relax more and the people who get to know a bit about meditation will see it's not just a fad or a gimmick but the way to calm down tensions. You learn about thoughts, the meaning of thoughts, how to trace your thoughts—and it's much better than acid.

'We have no idea of whether we'll get a new manager. We have always been in control of what we're doing and we'll have to do what we have to, now. We know what we should do and what we shouldn't do. Brian was a natural guide and we'll certainly miss him.

'If Brian had been in on the lectures on meditation he would have understood. This is the biggest thing in my life now and it's come at the time when I need it most. It's nothing to do with mysticism. It's about *understanding*.

'Brian has died only in body and his spirit will always be working with us. His power and force were everything, and that will linger on. When we were on the right track he knew it, and when we were on the wrong track he told us so and he was usually right. But anyway, he isn't really dead.'

Just before he died Epstein had tried, unsuccessfully, to persuade the Beatles to re-consider their decision to stop touring. But John and George were resolute in their determination that the 1966 American trail had been the last. Brian died a dispirited man, empty at the realization that 'the boys' no longer needed him and that they did not respond to his requests. If they were to be a group that existed mostly for recording, John's whiplash tongue would see to it that, like any other visitor to their sessions, Brian kept silent when the music was being rehearsed or completed. Epstein had simply been left with an untenable role—a manager with no power and little control. His 'boys' had become men: rich, independent individuals with positive plans, widening horizons, and the talent to move on.

Or so it seemed that heady midsummer in 1967. That year, as the message of love and peace wafted from California to London on a tidal wave of good vibrations, as Scott McKenzie sang 'If you go to San Francisco be sure to wear some flowers in your hair' and John Lennon chewed gum before 400 million people on world television singing 'All You Need Is Love',

John stayed cool. But later he would be forced to admit, 'The Beatles were finished when Eppy died. I knew, deep inside me, that that was it. Without him, we'd had it.'

As John and Cynthia left Heathrow Airport for the concrete chalets of Rishikesh, India, early in 1968 to accompany George and Pattie Harrison at the Maharishi's meditation academy, he looked, felt and spoke like a man with problems gnawing away inside him. He was no longer the lovable moptop Beatle whose steely wit had won the admiration of millions.

In Rishikesh the meditation was a healing influence and the changed environment was good for John but Cynthia noticed his jittery behaviour. 'Every morning he would be up and out of our room before me, at seven o'clock, saying he was off to meditate alone,' she says. 'He cut me dead in the mornings. The first week we were in India he was fine, but after that, he cut me off from himself. We'd always done things together . . . "Hang on wait for me John," I said.

' "No, no, I'm off," was his answer. I couldn't understand why at the time; I put it down to being away and his changed attitudes to meditation and the beauty that there were now no drugs. Meditation had killed the pushers stone dead, which I was thrilled about because it was getting to a very dangerous state. I thought heroin had to be the next stage. But now he was on edge. I realized later that he was going to collect the morning mail with letters from Yoko, but at the time I had no idea.

'It got to the stage when we were in the same room together that we would get on each others' nerves. Meditation has different patterns and I would sometimes go into deep meditation when John wasn't in the mood, and when we shared the same room, it was bad for both of us. . . . He seemed very isolated and would spend days on end with the Maharishi, emerging bleary-eyed and not wanting to communicate with me or anyone. So I believe he underwent a big change in Rishikesh. He went so deeply within himself through meditation that he separated himself from everything.'

John took meditation very seriously. He and George believed in its calming powers far more than the others in the party. For eight hours a day John would meditate and for the rest of the time during the eight weeks spent at the academy he wrote fifteen songs.

Yoko's flow of letters, some handwritten, others which she had typed immaculately, struck just the right mood for John's relaxed frame of mind. 'I'm a cloud. Watch for me in the sky', she wrote. John, who quickly moved to a separate bedroom from Cynthia, reflected on her hypnotic words back in Weybridge: 'Perhaps Yoko's the one for you.' Perhaps, he decided, she was dead right. He could hardly wait to see her again.

Coupled with this was a growing disaffection with the Maharishi's behaviour and personality (although not with his methods). John and Cynthia announced they were leaving two weeks ahead of their original plan. Paul and Jane Asher, and Ringo and his wife Maureen had already returned home. There were too many Indian flies in the air for Maureen and Ringo commented with his dry humour that the academy resembled a Butlin's holiday camp. Lennon, asked by the Maharishi, whom he had grown to distrust, why he was leaving early, replied tersely: 'If you're so bloody cosmic, you'll know why.'

With his interest in Yoko growing rapidly John was eager to get back to England. On his return, however, he was bedevilled by problems which even he found hard to face.

With no manager, he and the other three Beatles decided to launch their own company, Apple, and a new album was also in the offing. By far the biggest issue in his mind, however, was his relationship with Cynthia. It wasn't that they were quarrelling much. It was more of a communication barrier. The mental rift caused by drugs was now increased by the meditation scene. 'We went through some bad times,' Cynthia says. 'It was very confusing, coming back to reality after meditating in India.'

John said to her that as he had an album to prepare and business to attend to he would be in the studios a lot. 'Cyn, why don't you get away for a couple of weeks on that holiday in Greece that Jenny and Alex are going on?' he said. Jenny Boyd was the sister of Pattie Harrison; Alex was 'Magic Alex' (his real name was John Alexis Mardas), a Greek-born electronics wizard who had inveigled himself into John's life and was a constant visitor to the Lennon home.

Cynthia agreed. 'We both needed space to breathe,' she says. 'I don't think he was intentionally getting rid of me. He just wanted to sort himself out, after India, just as I did. He was unsure of himself and the way his life was going. He felt he'd been let down by the Maharishi, the Beatles were obviously going to have to re-consider everything now Brian Epstein was dead, and then there were the uncertainties between us. It seemed a good thing for me to get away and let him concentrate on work.'

John's first major sign to Cynthia that he was going through agonizing decisions came the day she was packing for her Greek holiday. 'He was upstairs lying, fully clothed, on our bed, staring into space, not saying a word. It was as though he had so much on his mind he couldn't speak. Normally he'd have come down and waved me off in the taxi, but he was on a different planet that day I left. There was no getting through to him. He'd obviously got to the brink of planning what he wanted from his life and what was going to happen a week later with me on holiday. And what John wanted, he usually got.'

Cynthia left Weybridge under a cloud. John had decided that it was now or never with Yoko Ono. It was time to resolve their clandestine relationship and follow up the stream of curious, intriguing letters.

The only other person living at Weybridge during Cynthia's absence was his old schoolfriend from Quarry Bank, Liverpool. Pete Shotton was a little surprised when John said he thought he would invite Yoko Ono over for an evening the night before Cynthia's return. Shotton said he was going to bed anyway. John phoned Yoko in her London flat and his chauffeur-driven Rolls-Royce was sent to bring her, clad in her customary black, up the gravel drive into Kenwood by mid-evening.

John was apprehensive; he realized this might not be another of his fast affairs. He and Yoko sat talking nervously downstairs in the lounge for several hours: he about the pressures of being a famous millionaire Beatle and how he now no longer felt the same sense of challenge as before; she about the frustrations of being an artist. 'Yoko and I were on the same wavelength right from the start, from that first night,' John told me years later. 'That first night convinced me I'd have to end my marriage to Cyn.'

John took Yoko to his upstairs den with its two tape recorders on which he had first practised some of his songwriting
gems like 'Nowhere Man', 'I'm A Loser' and the classic 'Norwegian Wood' which told of his affair with a prominent woman
journalist. John and Yoko introduced each other to their different worlds. Lennon had always experimented with sounds
and was interested in electronic effects and comedy; Yoko's
interest was the human voice and extending its potential beyond
the realms of orthodox singing. 'We improvised for many hours,'
she recalls. 'He used the two tape recorders and put through
them any sounds that came into his hands, you know: old
recorded sounds. I sat down and did the voice. We were both
involved and enjoying the uncertainty of how it would all turn
out. And that was it. We called it *Unfinished Music*. The idea
is that the listener can take from it, or add to it in his mind,
or her mind.' Challenging her public was a central theme in
Yoko's work. John was mesmerized by her sense of artistic
adventure. From his guitar and pen, everything had been channelled into straightforward commercial songs. Yoko's world,
he suddenly decided, was not 'avant-garde crap' as he had
earlier feared. It opened up real possibilities. They went to bed
together at dawn as the birds were waking. 'It was very beautiful', John recalled. 'I had no doubt I'd met The One.'

Next morning Pete Shotton became the first person to know.
John told him that he was going to look for a new house in
which he and Yoko could live. A flabbergasted Shotton asked
him what he was talking about. John replied that he had met
the person he'd been looking for and was prepared to cash in
everything, whatever the cost, to be with her. Beatles, houses,
money, fame—nothing counted except his future with Yoko
Ono. The chemistry between them was unbelievable; her physical attraction was strengthened by her intuitive knowledge of
what fired John's thoughts. If there was one moment when John
Lennon ceased to be a committed Beatle and chose, instead,
to become an artist, it was that spring night and dawn in May
1968. And, as always when John decided on something, it was
irrevocable.

By mid-afternoon, a joyful, refreshed Cynthia arrived home.
After her holiday she was bubbling and optimistic that the short

separation might now improve her life with John. Mysteriously the outside porch light was on and all the curtains were drawn. 'It was eerily silent,' she recalls. 'Normally there would be a gardener around, or Dot the housekeeper, or Julian playing, but it was deserted, as if there had been an all-night party. I had no idea what would confront me when I got in. I knocked on the door like mad at first but there was no reply. The whole of the front of the house was in darkness but looking through to the big lounge there was a light coming through, rather eerily.' A back door was opened.

Once inside Cynthia, followed by Jenny Boyd and Magic Alex, walked slowly around shouting: 'Is anybody there? John? Julian? Dot?' Still there was no sound. Cynthia ran round all the rooms on the ground floor, until finally reaching the dining-room and kitchen. Off this, in the sun-room, the sight that faced her left her 'dumbstruck'. John, in his green-and-white-striped towelling robe, hair dishevelled, mug of tea in his hand, sat on the small settee, facing Cynthia as she walked in. Yoko, her mass of black hair cascading down the back of a chair, making her instantly recognizable, sat on a chair facing John. She was motionless, her back to Cynthia who had stopped dead at the doorway. 'It was like walking into a brick wall, as if I didn't belong any more. I felt absolutely shut out from communication,' says Cynthia. Within seconds Jenny and Alex were standing behind her, open-mouthed.

John broke the silence of what seemed hours and was probably a minute. 'Oh hi,' he said coolly, taking a drag from his cigarette. He might have been addressing the gardener or a waiter.

Cynthia, feeling the unreality of the situation, was shattered and lost for words. She attempted to pacify the ugliness of the experience. 'Oh hi,' she said to John. 'I had this great idea,' she went on quietly. 'We had breakfast in Greece, lunch in Rome and Jenny and Alex and I thought it would be great if we all went out to dinner in London to carry on the whole holiday.'

With no expression in his voice, John answered bluntly: 'No thanks.'

At this point Yoko turned round and gave Cynthia 'a very positive, confident look'. She was dressed in a black silk kimono. 'I suppose I should have been prepared for it but I wasn't,' says Cynthia. 'It took my breath away. I wasn't angry. I was just absolutely shattered at the vision. John wasn't talking to anybody—not just me, but to nobody. He was just staring, expressionless. So instead of starting a battle and asking questions about what was going on, I felt I had to get out of that house immediately.' She went upstairs and, in the panic, repacked the kind of things she had just returned with from her holiday in the sun: toothbrush, shoes, make-up, coat, toilet bag. Passing the guest bedroom, Cynthia saw a pair of Japanese slippers outside the door: the final, crushing evidence, if she needed it, that Yoko had spent a night there.

Seized by a need to get out of the house as soon as she could, Cynthia was ready to leave within fifteen minutes of her arrival and confrontation. 'I decided John had been almost willing me to go. I took his silence as saying, "Don't interrupt this fantastic situation. Get lost. You're spoiling things." I got the message immediately without any more words.' She says she travelled faster than the speed of sound.

Cynthia went to stay with Jenny Boyd and Alex Mardas at their mews house in central London. 'I knew Julian would be safe with Dot, the housekeeper. He often went there,' she says. Three days later, having collected her thoughts, Cynthia warily phoned Kenwood. Dorothy Jarlett, the loyal housekeeper, now in an impossible situation, answered. No, she said, John was not in. Cynthia enquired if Julian was all right and said she was returning home that day.

To her amazement John greeted her as if nothing had happened. 'I can't understand why you went off,' he said. 'What have you been up to?' Cynthia apologized and said she couldn't cope with seeing him and Yoko looking so together. John insisted that their liaison was purely intellectual, Yoko and he had 'messed around with tapes all night' and it was quite wrong for Cynthia to misconstrue the situation. He would not talk about his association with Yoko. Cynthia says: 'It was strange that he would talk about the other women he'd been involved with, but with Yoko he stopped the conversation flat.'

Superficially, a warm, welcoming John gave Cynthia the impression all was well with their marriage. 'But I noticed his unease when I said, several times: "I see a great similarity between you and Yoko. John, there's something about her that's just like you. Look, you may say these things about Yoko, that she's crazy, just a weird artist, but there's an aura about her that's going to click with you." ' Cynthia succeeded only in irritating John when she said: 'I can see more into your situation with her than you can.' As she says: 'I knew immediately I saw them together that they were right for each other. I knew I'd lost him.'

Despite John's assurances, Cynthia knew in her heart that their relationship was now threatened. Superficially, however, life seemed to return to normal and she had no reason to fear an immediate marriage crisis. For several weeks during their reunion she asked if she should cancel the family holiday in Italy she had planned for herself, Julian, and her mother. 'No, no, you go ahead and have a lovely time,' said John. But he became increasingly distant as the time neared for them to go to Pesaro. There was no chance of his going with them: he had work to do, and besides, the prospect of John going on holiday with his mother-in-law was unthinkable. They had always kept their distance and he told several people how much he resented the intrusion of Lilian Powell into his domain.

Cynthia felt that she should press on with the holiday 'for Julian's sake'. If she had feared that her absence would crucially affect their marriage, she would never have gone. 'But I didn't. We were back together again and everything seemed fine.' Until, that was, her day of packing and flying. John was in a panic-stricken mood. 'He obviously knew something was going to happen while I was away and he was upset and frightened because he didn't know how it would turn out. Also he was probably worried about losing his son and he was already concerned that he'd spent a lot of time away from Julian when he was growing up.' But John was very distant as Les Anthony, their chauffeur, packed the Rolls-Royce that took them to Heathrow. 'We left with a cloud over the holiday,' says Cynthia. 'John was in a trance. He didn't even come to the door to say goodbye.'

John had decided to end his marriage to Cynthia but he didn't want to be the one to pass her the painful news. She thought it odd that, just before she left, he asked her if she had any affairs outside their marriage. 'No way. I've been totally faithful to you,' she answered. 'There have been mild flirtations but nothing serious that would jeopardize our marriage.' John seemed pleased, she says. His feeling for Yoko was now an obsession. As soon as Cynthia left, John saw as much of her as he could, despite a very busy work period.

An Italian newspaper brought home to Cynthia for the first time the fact that John and Yoko were now inseparable and her marriage irretrievable. Resting in bed with a sore throat, Cynthia was brought a newspaper by the hotel owner, Roberto Bassanini. It contained pictures of 'John Lennon, the Beatle, hand in hand with Japanese artist Yoko Ono', attending the opening night of a play, *In His Own Write*.

'I knew when I saw the picture that that was *it*,' says Cynthia. 'He'd obviously waited for me to go away to appear in the open with Yoko. He probably thought it would be easier for both of us. I knew it was the end because he would never flaunt something like an involvement with another woman if it were not very serious. It had been building up, I suppose, and was obvious to outsiders but not to me because John had kept up his same attitude, not hurting me.'

Next day John sent an unlikely emissary to give Cynthia a message—Magic Alex Mardas. Alex was to pass on his message to Cynthia and also to hire a private detective to monitor every move she made in Italy. After a tense breakfast with Cynthia, Roberto Bassanini, Julian, and Cynthia's mother he insisted on speaking to Cynthia alone. His message could not have been blunter: 'Well, John says he's going to divorce you. He's going to take Julian away from you and he's going to send you back to Hoylake.' His job done, he left immediately for London.

Cynthia's immediate reaction had been that John could not possibly do as he threatened and ignore her rights in this way. Her mother, vowing she would 'get to the bottom of this', also left immediately and headed for 34 Montagu Square, in London's West End, a flat which had been used alternately by rock star Jimi Hendrix and Ringo Starr, and to which she had moved after Cynthia's first encounter with John and Yoko. On her arrival she found a bouquet of flowers from John at the door with the cryptic message: 'Beat you to it, Lil.' It was his caustic way of telling Cynthia's mother he knew she had got home quickly to try to play the role of amateur detective and to try to rock the boat between him and Yoko.

Back in London with Julian, Cynthia also went to Montagu Square. She had been shadowed by John's private detective, for within five minutes of her arrival there was a knock at the door and a solicitor handed her a writ for divorce on the grounds of her alleged adultery.

In the five months that followed before John and Cynthia's eventual divorce, rancour and mistrust ran alongside John's frenzied involvement with Yoko which he never sought to hide. His image with the Beatles' public changed dramatically as he openly courted the woman who was to change his life. The last six months of 1968 were electrifying for him: Yoko became pregnant; they began their artistic activities together; Apple was launched; he met Brigitte Bardot, his teenage idol, in a formally set-up meeting in London's Mayfair Hotel; he was arrested for possessing drugs; and he was divorced. John always loved fast action but this rapid turn of events, combined with the tensions surfacing within the Beatles, pushed him to the limits of his endurance. He leaned increasingly on L.S.D. and drink, usually Scotch.

The run-up to the divorce was complex and often ugly. Cynthia was angry at the speed with which her contact with John was severed. 'One minute I was with him at Weybridge, the next the whole fabric of my life and Julian's was destroyed.' After appointing her own solicitor, she phoned the Beatles' office and said she needed to talk to John.

She arrived at Weybridge with Julian and her mother in tow, probably a psychological blunder considering John's dislike of Mrs Powell. Yoko and John met her looking as one: both all in black, John extremely tense. Cynthia's mother waded in instantly by saying to Yoko: 'I think you should go in the other room and leave these two together.'

John interjected: 'No, Yoko, you stay here.'

Eventually Yoko left of her own volition: she could not stand the tension any longer as John and Cynthia lumbered into a battle neither could win. For fifteen minutes they argued about who had committed adultery. John insisted that Cynthia had done so; Cynthia denied this: 'You're totally unjust in putting me on the spot when you're the one breaking up the marriage.'

John said: 'We'd better get it in the hands of solicitors and get it all sorted out.' Cynthia said *she* was suing for divorce. Cynthia's mother fussed in and out saying her daughter should not be left on her own.

Finally John could stand her no longer: 'This is my house—you get out,' he roared.

In the end John and Cynthia agreed to disagree and to hand the divorce arrangements to their solicitors. Practicality was then re-established amid the thick cigarette smoke that filled the library. John said that as Cynthia was caring for Julian, it would be best if he and Yoko moved out to Montagu Square, and Cynthia, her mother, and Julian moved back into Kenwood. The house swap happened next day.

The lawyers began their work and there followed some attempts by Cynthia, by telephone, to arrange the terms of the separation. Her personal savings amounted to a mere £2,500 and she clearly needed provision for her immediate future if she was to maintain Julian. She told John on the phone that it might be better if they fixed all the details privately because lawyers wanted her to 'screw him for hundreds of thousands of pounds'. An irate John roared: 'Look, my last offer to you is seventy-five thousand. What have you done to deserve it? Christ, it's like winning the bloody pools!'

A disastrous attempt at harmonious separation took place next on neutral territory: Paul McCartney's house at 7 Cavendish Avenue, St John's Wood, London. Against her solicitor's advice Cynthia went along to try to arrange things with John. But Yoko was there, apologizing for not being able to make English tea, and John's demeanour was still aggressive. Cynthia left in tears, frustrated at her failure to break any ground in talking things over with him.

The lawyers set to work. In August Cynthia filed a counter petition against John, alleging his adultery with Yoko, which their solicitors said they denied. But by 25 October John and Yoko announced that they were expecting a baby the next February. That decided the legalities of the case: Cynthia was granted a decree nisi on 8 November 1968 and a settlement payment to her of £100,000 was agreed. She was granted custody of Julian and John was said in court to have made 'generous and proper provision for Julian'. Additionally she received £2,400 a year for Julian's school fees from a separate trust.

This trust was set up by John for Julian, providing him with £100,000 at the age of twenty-five. He would be the sole beneficiary unless any further children were born to John. When Yoko gave birth to Sean, Julian's entitlement from the trust became £50,000 plus the accrued interest, and Sean's the same.

Emotionally battered, Cynthia withdrew from John's life. Inevitably their paths would cross many times in the future, for John had said he wanted proper access to Julian who was five at the time of the divorce. Cynthia went on to marry Roberto Bassanini, the Italian hotelier from Pesaro. That marriage, and another to Liverpool electrical engineer John Twist, ended in divorce. 'I'll always be in love with John Lennon,' says Cynthia. 'We went through some great times and bad times together, but whatever happened he made such an impression on everyone he touched.' The relationship between Cynthia and Yoko was tense. Cynthia was heart-broken in the early days of their break-up. Eventually, however, she accepted that John had met his match. 'It was a meeting of two minds and nobody could fight that,' Cynthia says candidly.

John had changed. Yoko, he said, took him back partly to how he was as a Liverpool rebel: fiercely independent, opinionated, an activist, a champion of causes. 'The Beatles had got rid of all that in me. The Beatles had turned me into a puppet. It was OK, but once we'd made it so big, the fun had gone and so had my own strength. The Beatles, if you must know, sapped me.'

In Yoko Ono he faced a formidable counterpart. 'But when I met her,' he told me later, 'I had to drop everything.' It was 'Goodbye to the boys in the band!' Jealous of her previous lovers, John questioned her closely and repeatedly about the men she had been with in addition to her husbands. And he wanted to know everything, quickly, about the art world from which she sprang into his life.

Her world was populated with dilettantes, artists with great inspiration but little notion of how to communicate. In the parlance of the art world, so few of them 'got it together'. Yoko was not among them. A shrewd communicator whose outlandish conceptual art exhibitions had gained her under-ground notoriety for originality, she believed firmly that if an artist produced a piece of work and then failed to get it through to the public, 'Then what's the point?' One of her greatest strengths lay in that simple truth: she was, and is, a gifted and thrusting communicator. She never believed that being de-scribed as avant-garde or underground meant she should lie fallow and hope the people would discover her. She believed implicitly in packaging an original product and marketing it with a degree of humour. By 1968 the stage was set for the launch of a partnership that was a perfect foil for her sometimes fanciful ideas and a magic carpet ride for John's submerged personality. Amid the dying embers of the Beatles, the public had to understand just what Lennon meant when he repeatedly wrote of his new world as *JohnandYoko*.

17
BEATLES

'I'm breaking the group up'

Yoko Ono—her first name means Ocean Child—was born on 18 February 1933 in Tokyo. Her father Eisuke left Tokyo University with degrees in mathematics and economics. He was a pianist before taking up a banking career and quickly rising to head a Japanese bank in San Francisco. Because of his move from the East in pursuit of his career, he did not meet Yoko until she was two; she had stayed in Japan with her mother.

Yoko's aristocratic mother Isoko came from one of Japan's richest business families, specializing in property investment, insurance, and banking. Yoko grew up in an environment with maids and tutors and a strikingly attractive, slightly aloof, though caring, mother who enjoyed the material things of life like jewellery and good clothes. That may, Yoko believes, account partly for her own eventual adoption of art as her way of life: 'Inside me I could feel a certain rejection of my mother's show of her possessions but I got over that as I grew older,' she says. She coolly points out, however, that she was never the pauper seeking the millionaire pop star: in her life money had never been a problem. Yoko has a brother, Keisuke, three years younger, and a sister, Setsuko, eight years younger.

By the time Yoko was eighteen her father had been appointed president of the Bank of Tokyo in New York and the

Ono family had moved from Japan to the high-class suburb of Scarsdale. Yoko attended the prestigious Sarah Lawrence College in New York but dropped out to elope with her first husband, Japanese-born Toshi Ichiyanagi. He proved to be her early partner in the discovery of the world of avant-garde artists. In her loft apartment at 112 Chambers Street, Greenwich Village, Yoko began her lifelong association with art, staging informal events, writing poetry and developing the conceptual theories which marked her out as an artistic radical. For years her work met either derision or a dull local response. 'I *do* know what it is like to be a frustrated artist,' she says with irony. One of her early liaisons was with American jazz musician–film producer Anthony Cox; he linked up with her to encourage her to stage exhibitions of art objects which demanded a response and some input from the observer rather than answering all the questions. Cox became Yoko's second husband and their only child, a daughter, Kyoko, was born on 8 August 1963, four months after John and Cynthia Lennon's son Julian.

As an ambitious and highly organized partnership, Yoko and Tony Cox had a reputation in Europe in the underground art world for staging uncanny exhibitions. There was, as London art people recall, some kudos to be gained from staging a show planned by a talked-about Japanese woman who lived in New York; thus they arrived for their first trip to London in 1962 if not to rapturous acclaim, then certainly amid considerable curiosity. They came back frequently during the next four years.

London artist Adrian Morris, in whose flat Yoko stayed in 1967 soon after going to London from New York, recalls his first meeting with her at a party off the King's Road. He asked her what kind of artist she was, and she answered: 'I deal with music of the mind.' She had been heavily influenced by the 'extended and repeated image' work of Andy Warhol in New York. As their conversation flowed and Adrian Morris warmed to her, she said she was waiting to move into a flat but there was a complication. Adrian Morris said she and Tony Cox could stay the weekend with him and his wife Audrey at their home at 57 Tedworth Square, Chelsea. Yoko accepted with enthusiasm:

the weekend lasted three months. The couples became friends and Adrian Morris attended several of her artistic events.

Yoko had arrived in London with a reputation for having made a film in New York about famous people's bottoms. She decided to repeat and extend the movie, called *Four Square*, in London, this time using 365 people's bottoms.

'I enjoyed their company and I was broadly sympathetic to what they were doing,' says Morris. He saw Yoko at London's Roundhouse, then a base for embryonic artists. She was performing a 'Word Piece', throwing a word into the audience and asking them to respond. Morris was intrigued by her determination and surrealist humour.

A day at London Zoo with the two couples joined by four-year-old Kyoko, who was staying elsewhere with friends, turned into humour when Yoko asked someone to take her photograph alongside the bottoms of the baboons. 'Yoko,' Morris says tellingly, 'was always aware of what she was doing, observing and always profound. Once I came home to my house and, walking towards the kitchen from the back garden, I saw her listening to a clock with a stethoscope. She was running an exhibition at the time called *Time Piece*. Photographers were taking pictures of her and I then realized she was unique.' The kitchen was the scene of a favourite Yoko activity: cooking steamed mackerel on a bed of beanshoots, a dish that impressed everyone.

Yoko's marriage to Tony Cox was fraught with tension. Adrian and Audrey Morris were not surprised when Yoko told them privately that she was 'hung up on this guy' who later turned out to be John Lennon. Soon after Yoko had told her friends she was 'miserable out of this guy's company', the newspapers were full of their liaison and her split from Tony was inevitable.

Although the Morrises recognized her talent as an artist working in a difficult field, they were equally impressed by her business acumen. 'She was clearly an entrepreneur and absolutely brilliant at working things out,' says Adrian. 'One day in the kitchen, I playfully patted her on the head during a conversation and called her Little Yoko. I vividly remember her response: "You say *little* Yoko," she said. "But I have a *universe* in my head." '

While John's relationship with Yoko deepened, leading eventually to the break-up of his marriage, the Beatles loomed as a parallel crisis. With Brian Epstein dead and the meditation honeymoon over, the Beatles decided to grasp the business nettle. They launched the Apple organization, first as a boutique and then as a record label and management company. John was never quite as confident as Paul or George in the utopian hope that Apple would be a freewheeling 'umbrella for new talent'. But he accepted that there was an urgent and immediate need to do something about the management of their affairs. With Epstein gone, John felt that not even a tenuous link remained with NEMS Enterprises, now run by Brian's affable brother Clive. Apple, set up in London at 95 Wigmore Street, with a boutique at 94 Baker Street and later with offices at 3 Savile Row, was intended to be both philanthropic and efficient in handling the Beatles' business affairs. It was originally conceived to invest in new talent in music, electronics, films, publishing, retailing, and records. 'Those were the days, my friend, I thought they'd never end,' sang sweet-voiced Mary Hopkin on her number one hit for Apple Records, produced by Paul McCartney. But they *did* end and quickly. Apple was doomed. And with John feverishly re-shaping his life and his attitude around Yoko and art, so were the Beatles.

Lifestyles and aspirations were at the root of the quarrel that erupted between John and Paul, eventually causing John, who had never been content with his achievements with the group, to inform the Beatles he was leaving. Despite the fact that he was high on drugs in 1967 and 1968, he characteristically remained, throughout his life, exceptionally clear-headed whenever business was called for and hard decisions were needed.

The rift with Paul dated back to McCartney's assumption of the leadership of the Beatles when Epstein died. It was Paul who concocted the ill-fated *Magical Mystery Tour* T.V. film. The Beatles' first real failure, it was never screened in America. It had a threadbare plot which consisted of a busload of Beatles and others travelling around the West Country as a kind of circus act. The songs were weak and decidedly McCartney-ish. John loathed the whole affair. He was angry at the cost—£75,000 for what he derisively called 'the most expensive home movie ever'. It came, also, right at the time when John was becoming intrigued with Yoko. The *Magical Mystery Tour* was McCartney's attempt to have the Beatles continue just as before, only under his aegis. With Epstein—who had considered Paul the most truculent Beatle—now dead, and with John's attention diverted, the stage was set for Paul to assert himself as king pin.

John, however, was not prepared to sit back and be ordered about. McCartney also underestimated John's dedication to Yoko and his boredom with the Beatles. The two of them had launched Apple in America, at a press conference at New York's Americana Hotel and on nationwide television on the *Tonight* show. John had fainted on the plane *en route* to New York, a victim of too many late nights, too much dope and not enough food. He arrived in New York with a plaster on his cut chin but he was in fine form, taking the chance to scorn the Maharishi publicly as well as to boost the Apple idea and prop up the Beatles' declining popularity in America.

It had taken a beating when they went to India and *Sgt Pepper*, released the previous summer, had made little impact with the millions of screaming fans in America: it was too far from 'She Loves You' and the Beatles most Americans loved. It was, however, a giant hit with the more discerning listeners, staying at number one for fifteen consecutive weeks and half a year in the top three.

When the job of publicizing Apple had to be done, John was semi-serious. 'We've decided to sell India and buy the Garden of Eden,' he said. As for the Maharishi, 'We thought he was God,' said John. 'I told him not to go on tour with the Beach Boys,' he jibed at the Maharishi's pretence to showmanship.

The entire American trip was an anathema to John. He was a lousy hypocrite. Privately he knew the Beatles were doomed. His polarization from Paul was accelerated by McCartney's acceptance of the show business embrace. However talented he was as a songwriter, Paul was, in John's view, content to continue churning out more of the same. The massive acclaim for 'Yesterday', the all-McCartney classic, had gone to Paul's head, John decided. The Beatles, Paul's bossiness, Apple—the whole package was stultifying to John, more than even he would admit. For the sake of unity he kept the peace for a few months to give himself time to develop his relationship with Yoko.

But soon that too became a vital issue. The other Beatles treated her shabbily and provocatively. In the Abbey Road studios during the summer of 1968, the Beatles were recording the 'White Album'. (The album was officially titled *The Beatles* but because of its all-white cover, and for easier identification, it became known colloquially around the world as the 'White Album'.) It consisted mainly of songs they had written in India including 'Yer Blues', 'Sexy Sadie' and 'The Continuing Story Of Bungalow Bill'. John broke a rigid, unwritten rule of the group: that their women would never be allowed in the studios. Getting inside a Beatles recording session was hard even for the accredited inner circle—Brian Epstein and song publisher Dick James were often invited to stay away and judge the *results* rather than see the group fiddling for hours with an embryonic song. John perversely attended every session for the 'White Album' with Yoko at his side. His message, unspoken, was obvious to all: they were inseparable. She sat on the speakers, offering suggestions and, incredibly, criticisms.

Their chauvinist pique apart, George, Paul, and Ringo were in a sticky situation in their resentment of Yoko's arrival. John, the leader and genius, was obviously changing even more tangibly than they had realized if he brought this peculiar Japanese artist so deeply into his life that she was even allowed to sing on one of his compositions ('Bungalow Bill') and help on another song, 'Revolution 9'. What flabbergasted them was John allowing Yoko to comment on the Beatles' work. Only the four of them, plus George Martin, had ever been allowed that privilege. But they might have guessed his seriousness when he sang on 'Julia', the song about his mother: 'Ocean child calls me', his first recorded reference to Yoko's letters to him in India.

George Martin was unconvinced of the merits of enough of the songs to justify putting it out as a double album but John loved the record's individualism and persuaded him. The album remained John's favourite Beatles work because it demonstrated the development of personalities rather than the Beatles as an entity, of which by 1968 he had become tired.

With her thick, cascading black hair and unsmiling demeanour, Yoko was also destined for a difficult time at the Apple offices, where she and John held court in their own ground-floor office overlooking Savile Row. At Apple, where she usually dressed in white and exchanged ideas with a beleaguered staff coping with a daily invasion of artists, wayfarers, and good causes wanting money and the Beatle seal of approval, Yoko was treated with disdain. George, Paul, and Ringo, particularly, did not give her the warmth and fair reception she deserved, both as their leader's new woman and as an artist. 'I'll never forgive them,' John said later. 'They were bastards to Yoko and they knew it mattered to me.'

John naturally regarded the coolness towards Yoko as an insult to himself. How, he reasoned, could people applaud him as a force for good and as a fine artist while condemning his choice of woman? He could not be great and dumb at the same time. When Yoko's increased melodicism on *Double Fantasy* was noted by reviewers in 1980, John was thrilled that at last she appeared to be getting recognition. She had always been ahead of her time. 'I've had two partners in my life, Paul McCartney and Yoko. That's not a bad record, is it?' he once said to me.

In 1968 and 1969, the most important years of his life, John had few friends, inside or outside the Beatles family. 'Yes, it was hard,' recalls Yoko, 'but he and I had no doubt we would get through. John's excitement at doing things together with me as an artist was so obvious that he didn't have that much time to get upset about what people were thinking, you know.'

The relationship was too important for both of them for any opposition to dissuade them: 'We both think alike,' said John. 'We've both been alone. And we seem to have had the same kind of dreams when we *were* alone. I can see now that I always dreamed of a woman like this one coming into my life. You can't go out *looking* for this kind of relationship. It's like somebody was planning it from above.'

While relationships with George, Paul, and Ringo simmered, with George as always the one with the best rapport with John in his new life, John and Yoko boldly stepped out in public to emphasize their togetherness, artistically and as man and woman. By now he was parting his hair in the centre to match Yoko's style and they both invariably dressed in all-white suits.

Their first 'event' in June 1968 fuelled the cynics' view that John had gone crazy. As part of the National Sculpture Exhibition John and Yoko decided to plant two acorns, one facing east, the other facing west, in the grounds of Coventry Cathedral. The idea, which was John's, was to symbolize the meeting of John and Yoko as the combination of two different cultures, and the phrase 'Plant an acorn for peace', coined by John, was to accompany the event.

The couple were driven from London in John's Rolls-Royce for the 100-mile trip to Coventry, where the event attracted only minor interest, considering it was an activity by a Beatle. The acorns were duly planted, the media scoffed and Beatles fans everywhere knew that whatever John Lennon was now up to, he meant it. The planting of acorns in the cathedral precincts—disallowed on consecrated ground lest the Church should be seen to condone the couple's liaison—was of great significance to John, more so than to Yoko. It marked his concentration on art and his first conscious proclamation of peace.

In contrast, John and Yoko's second public outing in the same month faced the full glare of national publicity. Word spread to a gleeful newspaper world that John's marriage was on the rocks and he was living with Yoko at 34 Montagu Square, London W.1. The couple were pursued by photographers twenty-four hours a day: a married Beatle escorting an unknown Japanese artist/actress had strong news value. But the couple faced the music, going hand in hand to the opening of the play *In His Own Write*. Photographers shouted: 'Where's your wife then, John?'

Angrily but firmly he retorted: 'I don't know.'

The play was directed by John's old friend from the films *A Hard Day's Night* and *Help!*, actor Victor Spinetti. When Victor phoned John with an idea from American writer Adrienne Kennedy, that Lennon books be converted into a play, John burst into laughter. 'They must be fucking mad!' he screamed into the phone. But then he quickly added that he always thought that *he* was mad until he came across a word called surrealism and had thought: 'Oh, that's what I am, I'm a *surrealist*.' When Spinetti brought the conversation back to earth John readily agreed to grant him the theatrical rights.

They began working on the adaptation and John and Yoko attended a meeting with Sir Laurence Olivier, who ran the Old Vic, then the home of the National Theatre where the play was to be staged. During the meeting Sir Laurence told John that when the play went ahead, they might be faced with other business decisions, such as film and record rights. Lennon, sitting next to the white-hatted Yoko and looking like a bored hippie, suddenly stunned the assembled company. In a mildly peremptory manner he said slowly to Sir Laurence: 'Don't you have people that you pay to talk about these kind of things who can talk to the people that I pay to talk about these kind of things?'

Spinetti had immediate proof of the speed of Lennon's thought. He had asked John for a Queen's speech for one sequence in his adaptation. 'Without thinking,' says Victor, 'and instantly, he took hold of a piece of cardboard used to keep a new shirt firmly in place, and started writing:

> One second's pause. . . .
> 'My housebound and eyeball take pressure in denounc-
> ing his ship. . . .'

Spinetti points out that although John often said he had no knowledge of Chaucer, his instinct was distinctly Chaucerian, and the word 'housebound' was a variant of 'husband' in Middle English. John, however, was adamant that the expression was his own.

John and Yoko's child was expected in February 1969, but in November 1968 Yoko was rushed to Queen Charlotte's Hospital, Hammersmith, where she suffered a painful miscarriage. She was thirty-five, and the nursing staff said she might have expected problems. John insisted on staying in a spare bed alongside her and when that was no longer acceptable to the hospital he slept on the floor.

Although he had officially given up smoking during that period, Lennon persuaded Victor Spinetti to pop in at eight-thirty each morning 'before the crowds arrive' and sneak him a packet of twenty Players Gold Leaf. 'He looked truly awful,' recalls Spinetti. 'I said to him: "Which one of you had the miscarriage?" ' The loss of the child had a traumatic effect on John and, coming on top of all the other dilemmas that clouded his love of Yoko, he became nervous, edgy and less happy than ever with his role as a public Beatle.

That autumn developed into a harrowing period for John. The one problem he did not expect to face was a drugs charge. For some five years various pop stars had been closely associated with the use of cannabis but so far the 'Holy Beatles' had escaped the law. Anyone talking to them was aware that they smoked pot and in the pop world it was commonplace. But now the public view of the Beatles, and particularly John Lennon, was not so cosy. To be ensconced with a crazy Japanese actress who made a film about bottoms was bad enough. To be *en route* to the divorce court, having planted acorns for peace and having embraced and subsequently rejected the Maharishi and meditation, condemned John to public scorn.

John and Yoko were in bed at the Montagu Square flat when police with Alsatian sniffer dogs hammered on the door. John, shocked and confused by this rough awakening, did not open the door immediately. He phoned solicitor Nicholas Cowan, the partner of David Jacobs, who was representing Brian Epstein's estate and doing other work for the Beatles. 'John said there were a number of people outside the flat who said they had a search warrant and were threatening to break the door down,' says Cowan. By the time Cowan arrived half a dozen police and a dog were inside the flat. The police made a quick and thorough search of the premises. 'The basement was full of recording equipment,' says Cowan, 'all of which appeared to have been on for some time and the temperature was extremely high. In one room there was a large trunk full of clothes in which the dog was showing interest. A search of the trunk revealed a small piece of hash. John and Yoko were asked to go to Marylebone police station where they were formally charged and fingerprinted in my presence.'

A cuddly Beatle no more. Lennon's anguish showed on his face in the days that followed. A Beatle being busted for dope was big news; journalists besieged the police station and John and Yoko were given permission to leave by the police head-quarters back door. They lay low for the night at Nicholas Cowan's home in Redcliffe Road, Fulham. Next day their case was adjourned for six weeks.

When the court case finally came up, John pleaded guilty to a charge of unauthorized possession of 219 grains of cannabis. He was fined £150 with 20 guineas costs. John and Yoko were found not guilty of obstructing the police in execution of a search warrant. It was a terrifying episode, John confessed later. He was always convinced that the bust was a 'set-up'. Don Short of the *Daily Mirror* had warned him three weeks previously that the police were on their way, so John said he had 'cleaned the place up, especially as I knew Jimi Hendrix had this flat before Ringo and me'. He maintained that the dope had been planted in the trunk, a spot in which he would never have tried to hide it. 'It was a frame-up. I guess they didn't like the way the image was looking. The Beatles thing was over. No reason to protect us for being soft and cuddly any more—so bust us! That's what happened.'

The drugs conviction in itself did not concern him but he was well aware of the problems it might cause if he wanted to visit America. Musicians lived in dread of being busted because American immigration authorities were so hot about it. But even John did not realize, during that heady period, that the straight conviction for possession of pot would so painfully affect his future. At the time, however, there were enough pressures to divert him. He could handle his own change of identity perfectly well: his metamorphosis from hit-making pop star to thinking artist, and his publicly declared love for a ridiculed avant-garde artist, were things he revelled in. He loved taking on the public at the game of 'Who is Lennon?' What he found exhausting was the continuing problem of Apple and the Beatles.

By the summer of 1968 Apple Music, the Apple boutique, Apple Films, and Apple Electronics had not made a film, sold a single invention or opened shops outside London. When the Baker Street boutique closed, thousands of pounds' worth of clothes were given away to the public in an astonishing—and unbusinesslike—gesture of largesse. What Apple *had* done was spend £1 million of Beatles money, which had been frittered away on overstaffing, extravagant salaries, and an endless supply of alcohol for visitors.

Apple, beautifully described as 'the longest cocktail party' by one of its employees, Richard DiLello, in a hilarious book on the episode, was great fun. It was also cripplingly expensive and not functioning well. In its earliest days, with visitors like Peter Sellers, Harry Nilsson, Twiggy, and Kenny Everett, John enjoyed the fantasy of playing host to the world's artists. He also grew to believe more in Apple's philanthropy. But it surprised some who believed him to be the dopey Beatle, the druggy one, the one hopelessly diverted by Yokoism, that he became the first to say, effectively, 'enough is enough'. At the time John decided to sound the warning shots Apple was costing the Beatles £50,000 a week.

During an interview with me in January 1969 for the pop weekly *Disc and Music Echo* I asked John if he was happy with the way Apple was shaping. He answered: 'No, not really. I think it's a bit messy and it wants tightening up. We haven't got half the money people think we have. We have enough to live on but we can't let Apple go on like it is. We started off with loads of ideas of what we wanted to do—an umbrella for different activities. But like one or two Beatle things, it didn't work because we aren't practical and we weren't quick enough to realize that we need a businessman's brain to run the whole thing.

'You can't offer facilities to poets and charities and film makers unless you have money definitely coming in. It's been pie-in-the-sky from the start. . . . We did it all wrong—you know, Paul and me running to New York saying we'll do this and encourage this and that. It's got to be a business first; we realize that now.

'It needs a new broom and a lot of people there will have to go. . . . It doesn't need to make vast profits but if it carries on like this all of us will be broke in the next six months.' (Typically Lennon did show the accounts to someone right at the top—Lord Beeching. After studying the books he gave Lennon terse but sound advice: 'Go back to music!')

I asked whether he and the Beatles missed Brian Epstein's guidance. 'Sure we miss him,' John replied. 'His death was a loss. That's probably what's the matter with Apple or the Beatles at the moment—Brian's death left us on our own. He handled the business and we find it hard to.'

Lennon's outburst rocked Savile Row and reverberated around the world as international newspapers, television, and radio picked up on the confession by a Beatle that they had made a colossal mistake and might go broke. The Beatles had no more desire to be shopkeepers, John told me, than to become rock 'n' roll museum pieces and part of the showbiz Establishment. It was time for them to own up. The interview confirmed the unpleasant truth that nobody had wanted to face since the disastrous *Magical Mystery Tour* and optimistic founding of Apple: the Beatles, as an operating company, was in an appalling mess. While the fans were shocked, the media had a field day. It also brought the uneasy relationship between John and Paul to breaking-point.

A week after my interview with John I visited Apple to see him again. Coming out of John's office I met the heavily bearded McCartney. He was furious with my decision to publish John's comments. 'What did you want to go and use all that for?' he snapped. 'You know this is a small and young company, just trying to get along. And you know John always shoots his mouth off. It's not that bad. We've got a few problems but they'll be sorted out. I'm surprised it was you—we thought we had a few friends in the Press we could trust.'

Paul was suggesting that John's remarks should have been considered as 'off the record'. Like many writers who had been close to the Beatles from the start, I had used discretion when secrets were either unimportant to the public or impolitic to reveal for the sake of the Beatles or their families. But on this occasion Lennon talking about Apple's looming disaster for the first time was manifestly an on-the-record interview. John knew it would be used and that it would be big news: he was an avid media freak, he knew the value of a quote and always said what he wanted, on reflection, to be left out of any interview. The day he spoke he was as clear-minded as he had ever been. Thus began the long, bitter battle between John and Paul. A few weeks later I saw John again and he did not mention his explosive comments on Apple. Had he regretted them or their ramifications he would certainly have told me. For Apple, and the Beatles, the end was in sight.

The musical rapport between them had long gone as well as the accord. But before the end they had a commitment to fulfil: to complete their third film, *Let It Be*, which was to show their album being made. The four, with Yoko, shuffled desultorily into Twickenham Film Studios in early January 1969 to undertake the multi-media project. The internal bickering and antipathy can be seen in the finished film. Ironically it also shows them performing much of their early Hamburg/Liverpool repertoire, joyously together, and revelling in the therapeutic qualities of the music. It was a painful, if evocative affair, in particular the twenty-minute session on the roof at Apple. John's words to the crowd spoke the Beatles' epitaph as poetically as we had come to expect from him: 'I'd like to say thank you on behalf of the group and ourselves . . . and I hope we passed the audition.' It had been a long journey from Liverpool Cavern but for John, life was just beginning.

By now the Beatles were virtually dead as far as he was concerned. Paul, who had steadfastly been arriving at Apple each morning at ten o'clock (often travelling in from his home in St John's Wood by bus), did not realize how serious John was about quitting the Beatles. It wasn't simply a question of his utter absorption with Yoko. It was the growing mental distance between him and Paul. Apple Records' first number one hit, and one of the Beatles' greatest single successes, had been 'Hey Jude', a song which Paul wrote during John's separation from Cynthia and composed partly on his way to Weybridge to comfort Cynthia on the breakdown of the marriage. Paul later admitted that John had helped him decide on some lyrics for the song, particularly Paul's line which John loved best, 'The movement you need is on your shoulder.' John had reluctantly agreed to it being the major side of the record, rather than his own song, 'Revolution', which became the B-side.

Commercially there was no choice. But it emphasized finally to him the different directions he and Paul were taking. While Paul was still composing beautiful melodies and writing of love, John's words tilted at the student revolutions in Europe during 1968.

But if you want money for people with minds that hate
All I can tell you is brother, you have to wait. . . .

But if you go carrying pictures of Chairman Mao
You ain't gonna make it with anyone, anyhow.

John simply believed that his new rock 'n' roll should have his mind and his message in the music. The old Chuck Berry and Little Richard rave-ups would always be his roots but mentally he was moving quickly and his profound new music had to accommodate the change in him. Paul, intimidated by Yoko's presence, felt that every time he was in John's company and making music, he ought to be producing something avant-garde. It was not in his nature. The split was inevitable and acrimonious.

John broke the news of the break-up of the Beatles in his usual rapier-like style. Paul remembers a meeting at Savile Row in which all the Beatles sat stonily discussing business. 'The group was getting very tense,' says Paul. 'It was looking like we were breaking up.

'One day we came in, had a meeting, all Apple business, and it was getting very hairy and nobody was really enjoying themselves. We had forgotten the music bit; it was just business. I said: "I think we should get back on the road, small band, go and do the clubs, sod it. Let's get back to square one and remember what we're all about." ' McCartney suggested several other projects which he thought would be the only thing to occupy the group's creativity to the full and hold them together: a concert—no ordinary show but the Beatles playing a Roman amphitheatre in North Africa; or the Beatles as a house band on a round-the-world cruise. John would have none of it.

'John's actual words were: "I think you're daft. I wasn't going to tell you but I'm breaking the group up. It feels good. It feels like a divorce." And he just sat there. And our jaws dropped. And that was it. No one quite knew what to say. Then after that we thought we should give it a couple of months. It was a big act to break up just like that. We talked for a couple of months but it was never going to be on. Looking back, it was largely that John needed a new direction that he went into headlong, helter skelter. He went right in there and did all sorts of stuff he had never done before—with Yoko. And you can't blame him because he was that kind of guy. He wanted to live life, do stuff and there was no holding back with John. And it was what we all admired him for. So we couldn't really say: "Oh we don't want you to do that, John. Stay with us." You'd feel so wimpy. It *had* to happen.'

What was remarkable about John and Yoko's frenzied activities together is that they managed to do so much despite the business problems of 1968, 1969, and 1970. Between John's divorce, Yoko's miscarriage, the drugs bust and the bickering between the Beatles and worry over Apple, John and Yoko released their first album and continued their assault on a now punch-drunk public by appearing in a large white bag on stage at the Royal Albert Hall, London. This was an event called the Alchemical Wedding, the underground art movement's Christmas party.

The move that was to shake the foundations of John's most ardent supporters was the release of their début album. *Unfinished Music No.1: Two Virgins*, a collection of bizarre sounds and effects, the result of their first collaboration that night in Weybridge when Cynthia was away, was neither surprising nor important musically. It was their decision to have themselves photographed nude on the front and back of the album sleeve, however, that convinced Lennon's detractors—and many of his supporters—that he had now indeed gone insane.

The pictures were taken by John with an automatic camera. The *Two Virgins* concept was his: Yoko was 'terribly embarrassed' by it. Any theory that it was a continuation of her film theme of people's bottoms was absurd, she says. 'We were both very shy about it, really,' she recalls. 'But John had the original idea. He thought it suited what we were doing at the time.' In those days nudity on the London theatre stage in the show *Hair* was making front-page news. John, who told me eventually that he was 'testing people's reactions, and it was mostly bad', enjoyed extending his and Yoko's audacity as far as he dared.

The nude pictures caused an immediate censorship problem. Apple Records were distributed through the Beatles' original record company, E.M.I., whose chairman at the time was Sir Joseph Lockwood. He remembers the Beatles arriving for lunch at his official dining-room in Manchester Square, a few weeks before the problem with the nude pictures arose. 'When the four boys came they had with them this person all in white, surrounded by hair, and I couldn't see anything. I wasn't sure if it was a human being or an animal. John Lennon introduced her to me: "This is my secretary," he said. After the lunch, he told me she had tape-recorded everything we had said. It was a business meeting. John was pretty clued up on everything that was going on.'

Sir Joseph's meeting with John and Yoko a few weeks later was more pointed. They arrived at his office with the nude pictures which they wanted released by E.M.I./Apple for their *Two Virgins* sleeve. Paul McCartney went with them to act as diplomat. 'He didn't want any row,' says Sir Joseph. 'At that time he was very anxious to prevent a falling-out with E.M.I.'

As he looked at the picture Sir Joseph was asked by John: 'Well, aren't you shocked?'

The E.M.I. chief said: 'No, I've seen worse than this.'

John weighed in quickly: 'So it's all right then, is it?'

'No, it's not all right,' said Sir Joseph. 'I'm not worried about the rich people, the duchesses and those people who follow you. But your mums and dads and girl fans will object strongly. You will be damaged and what will you gain? What's the purpose of it?'

Yoko said: 'It's art.'

Sir Joseph answered sharply: 'Well, I should find some better bodies to put on the cover than your two. They're not very attractive. Paul McCartney would look better naked than you.'

Sir Joseph recalls: 'It didn't go down too badly, except that poor old Paul McCartney blushed. We went on and on for a long time. They wouldn't give way. They were pressing and pressing.

'Paul McCartney was not in favour of it, I'm sure. He just wanted to prevent me from blowing up with them, which I had no intention of doing.'

Finally Sir Joseph established a perfect British compromise. E.M.I. would press the album but Apple would have to distribute it themselves. E.M.I. would have nothing to do with the actual sale of *Two Virgins*. John reluctantly agreed and Paul, whose great commercial future was bound up with E.M.I., breathed a sigh of relief. Sir Joseph, who regarded John as the most talented Beatle, even if Paul was the most commercial, felt vindicated when thousands of exported copies of *Two Virgins* were impounded by customs men and eventually confiscated. The record was a critical and commercial failure both in Britain and America but John felt it was 'a statement'.

On 12 March 1969 Paul McCartney married New York photographer Linda Eastman in London. No other Beatle was invited to the wedding.

Paul's choice of bride had a marked effect on the cauldron that was by then the Beatles' business empire. John and Yoko, on the advice of Mick Jagger, had decided that a fast-talking American show business lawyer, Allen Klein, should be hired to weed out the chaos at Apple. George and Ringo went along with the Lennon line, eventually signing a business management contract with Klein, who convinced John that he could streamline Apple and negotiate better record deals for the Beatles. Paul flatly refused to become involved, but was outvoted at a board meeting by three to one. Klein was in. Paul had wanted his new father-in-law, widely respected American entertainment lawyer Lee Eastman, to handle his affairs, and he went ahead and appointed him to manage his personal business concerns. The stage was set for the rift to become even wider.

Klein, whose openly stated ambition was to manage the Beatles, had flown to London immediately he heard of John's interview with me in which he laid bare the Apple financial quandary. All his life, Klein, the New Jersey orphan who had clawed his way through the pop jungle, wanted the 'fabulous Beedles'. Once in Britain, through Jagger, he quickly met John Lennon who told him that he did not 'want to end up broke like Mickey Rooney'.

The American went about his work with savage determination, alienating Sir Joseph Lockwood at E.M.I. with his foulmouthed demands—on one occasion Sir Joseph ordered him out of the building—and encountering stubborn resistance from McCartney. Paul's tactic was simply to stay away from the Apple he had so conscientiously nurtured. Len Wood, managing director of E.M.I., noticed that John had confidence in Klein during their meetings together; even when letters with

major proposals for an Apple takeover came in and Klein wanted
John's views, Lennon waved him away saying it was his job
to deal with them. Allen was visibly thrilled at such a vote of
confidence.

By mid-1969 the only question unanswered about the Beatles' future was how the group could split formally. John simply
didn't care. He was off and running with Yoko. As far as he
was concerned he'd served notice on Paul, George, and Ringo
and Klein could hammer out the details with Lee Eastman.

The Plastic Ono Band had utterly eclipsed the Beatles in
John's affections. Its appeal lay in its spontaneity: in September
1969 John and Yoko had been asked to appear at a rock concert
in Toronto and Lennon actually did what McCartney had urged
the Beatles to do—get back on the road as a small band. Instead
of talking about it, John got a band together, literally overnight.
Eric Clapton recalls a phone call from John twenty-four hours
before the show: 'He said: "We're doing this concert in Toronto. Why don't you come over with us?" ' Eric, thinking it
would be fun, agreed and bass player Klaus Voormann, John's
old friend from Hamburg, joined in. They rehearsed old rock
'n' roll songs on the plane on the way over. The music on
stage, though scrappy, had a raw quality John liked. On the
plane he had told Clapton and Voormann that the Beatles were
finished.

On his return I asked John about the Plastic Ono Band, the
Beatles and his current attitude to Paul. Was the Plastic Ono
Band more crucial to him than the Beatles? 'Neither more
important nor less,' he said. 'Sometimes the Plastic Ono Band
sessions are a drag, sometimes great. Sessions with the Beatles
likewise. Just meself and a tape recorder can be good, sometimes it's boring. I like *change*.' Were the Beatles split? I asked.
'We're going through changes, sure. The thing is—we change
in public. It's a menopause or something like that.'

When had he last seen Paul? 'About two months ago. I
keep meaning to go and see him. We write a lot—postcards
to each other. I see Ringo and George every other day because
they're here at Apple but Paul hasn't been here for ages. I want
to ask him why.' It was an astonishing turnaround in the pair's
behaviour: Paul had until this period been the determined executive, always keen on discovering and nurturing new talent

Top: Garlands of flowers from the Maharishi Mahesh Yogi greet Paul and John as they arrive at Bangor railway station in August 1967 for a weekend of transcendental meditation *(Times Newspapers)*

Above: John and Julian, aged four, with the Lennon Rolls-Royce that became a major talking-point in Britain during the psychedelic era. The picture was taken at Weybridge in June 1967

(Keystone Press)

An early public
appearance with
Yoko Ono. They
were launching
John's first art
exhibition, 'You
Are Here', at
London's Robert
Fraser Gallery in
July 1968
(Rex Features)

John as seen by Don
McCullin in July 1968
(John Hillelson Agency)

Top: In December 1968, a month after his divorce from Cynthia, John took Julian and Yoko to Wembley Television Studios for the filming of the Rolling Stones TV documentary *Rock And Roll Circus.* The show also featured Eric Clapton, the Rolling Stones and The Who, but it became entangled in legal and artistic problems and was never shown
(Rex Features)

Above: John shields Yoko, a week after her miscarriage, as they both leave Marylebone Magistrates Court in November 1968, surrounded by police. John's conviction for possession of cannabis was to cause him some big problems four years later in the U.S.
(Kenneth Mason/Daily Telegraph)

John and Yoko outside their new home, Tittenhurst Park, Ascot, Berkshire, in September 1969, a month after moving in
(Tom Blau/Camera Press)

John was a compulsive filler-in of forms and sent this Yoko-laden handwritten voting coupon to *Disc and Music Echo* for its Valentine Day Awards in 1969: in the Top Radio Show section he votes for one of his favourite childhood programmes, *Life With The Lyons*; and in the '1969 Hope' category he names Berenice Kinn, wife of the founder of the *New Musical Express*

A signing session in Selfridge's in July 1971 to promote Yoko's book, *Grapefruit*. John had written the foreword
(Keystone Press)

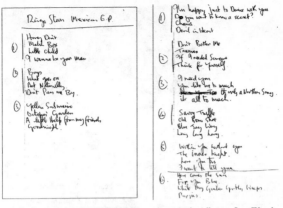

Ringo Starr Mexican E.P.

1) Honey Don't
   Match Box
   Little Child
   I wanna be your man

2) Boys
   What goes on
   Act Naturally
   Don't Pass me By.

3) Yellow Submarine
   Octopus' Garden
   A little help from my friends
   Goodnight.

1) I'm happy just to Dance with you
   Do you want to know a secret?
   Chains
   Devil in Heart

2) Don't Bother Me
   Taxman
   If I needed Someone
   Think for Yourself

3) I need you
   You like me to much
   it's all to much
   the inner a Northern Song.

4) Savoy Truffle
   Old Brown Shoe
   Blue Jay Way
   Long long long.

5) Within you without you
   The Inner light.
   Love you to
   I want to tell you.

6) Here Comes the Sun
   For you Blue.
   While my Guitar Gently Weeps
   Piggies.

In the summer of 1974 E.M.I. Records managing director Len Wood asked John to 'pair off' some Beatles songs for release as E.P.s in Mexico. John took the time to write these suggested lists of Ringo Starr and George Harrison tracks *(Len Wood)*

On the roof of the Apple building in April 1969, John formally changes his name by deed poll from John Winston Lennon to John Ono Lennon *(David Nutter/*
Camera Press)

The famous Bed-in for Peace at Amsterdam's Hilton Hotel in March 1969: John and Yoko, in their favourite colour, white, with their drawings and slogans pinned to the wall of their suite, gave seven days of interviews to propound their peace message

(Popperfoto)

With Yoko at his feet covered in a white sheet, John is clearly having a ball onstage at London's Lyceum during the concert by the Plastic Ono Supergroup in December 1969

(Barry Plummer)

The launch of the 'War Is Over! (If You Want It)' campaign by John and Yoko in their Apple office, December 1969. He is holding the poster that was displayed on billboards in eleven cities
(Times Newspapers)

John's drawing for the readers of *Disc and Music Echo*, after they had named him Britain's Most Popular Beatle in 1969

John telephones journalists around the world from his Apple office in November 1969 to explain why he has returned his M.B.E. medal to the Queen. A copy of his laconic letter lies on the desk in front of him
(Popperfoto)

John's first meeting with Kyoko, daughter of Yoko by her second marriage to film producer Tony Cox, in May 1969. Kyoko, aged five, had just flown in to London's Heathrow Airport from New York
(The Times)

Yoko's second husband Tony Cox, his second wife Melinda, Yoko and John, the four of them together in apparent harmony. The picture was taken in Majorca in April 1971
(Rex Features)

Yoko, almost unrecognizable in her wig, and John waiting to fly home from Majorca after failing to retrieve Yoko's daughter, Kyoko, from her father, Tony Cox, during the battle for custody
(Rex Features)

John, naturally horrified by the lingerie advertisements in a Spanish magazine bought in Majorca
(Rex Features)

Happiness exudes from John and Yoko in this picture taken at
the Cannes Film Festival in May 1971. They went to attend the world
premiere of their films *Fly* and *Apotheosis*

(Claude Breuer/John Hillelson Agency)

Informal shots taken in July 1971 at Tittenhurst
Park, the £150,000 house John described as 'functional': the cluttered
spare room, the bathroom, and the bedroom

(Tom Hanley)

(top and bottom—Tom Hanley)

John with a blindfolded Yoko behind him appears on BBC television's *Top Of The Pops* in February 1970 to sing 'Instant Karma!' It was the first appearance by a Beatle on *Top Of The Pops* for four years; they recorded two shows, and the next week showed Yoko knitting behind John *(Rex Features)*

An unkempt-looking John photographed during October 1969, the month of Yoko's second miscarriage *(Tom Hanley)*

Top: A masterpiece of music in the making: Paul and John in Number 2 studio at Abbey Road in May 1967, writing and recording *Sgt Pepper's Lonely Hearts Club Band*

(Henry Grossman/Colorific!)

Above: John in his small recording studio at Tittenhurst Park immediately after recording 'Imagine' in 1971

(Tom Hanley)

An invitation to the launch of
the Unique Plastic Ono Band;
the party took place in the
absence of John and Yoko,
who were in the hospital after
a car crash in Scotland

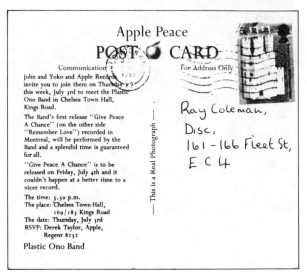

Apple Peace

POST CARD

Communication

John and Yoko and Apple Records
invite you to join them on Thursday
this week, July 3rd to meet the Plastic
Ono Band in Chelsea Town Hall,
Kings Road.

The Band's first release "Give Peace
A Chance" (on the other side
"Remember Love") recorded in
Montreal, will be performed by the
Band and a splendid time is guaranteed
for all.

"Give Peace A Chance" is to be
released on Friday, July 4th and it
couldn't happen at a better time to a
nicer record.

The time: 5.30 p.m.
The place: Chelsea Town Hall,
          169/183 Kings Road
The date: Thursday, July 3rd
RSVP: Derek Taylor, Apple,
      Regent 8232

Plastic Ono Band

For Address Only

Ray Coleman,
Disc,
161-166 Fleet St,
E.C.4

— This is a Real Photograph —

Bob Dylan was one of John's inspirations as a songwriter, and he took Yoko to see his giant open-air Isle of Wight concert in September 1969; folk singer Tom Paxton is on John's right

John and Yoko during rehearsals for the 'One To One' concert at Madison Square Garden in August 1972

At the piano
on which Jóhn wrote
his best loved song,
'Imagine', at
Tittenhurst Park in
July 1971; the piano is
now in Yoko's lounge
at the Dakota
apartment in New
York
(Tom Hanley)

May 1972. John and
Yoko became
enthusiasically
involved in the street
life of Greenwich
Village shortly after
arriving in New York.
They bought bicycles,
did their own
shopping, and rented
an apartment in Bank
Street where they met
some of the city's
controversial
personalities
*(Ben Ross/Camera
Press)*

The apartment in
Bank Street

T: Simonandgill   and M.M. Readers   December 13 '71

From JohnandYoko   *The People*

Dear Simonandgill   and M.M. Readers

Apple was/is a capitalist concern. We brought in a capitalist to prevent it sinking.
(with the Beatles on board). The whole problem the ex-Beatles have is concerned with
their commitment to Apple. I referred to tax in answer to Paul's article in M.M.
and other British Weeklies, i.e. 'let's just sign a bit of paper'. You may not worry
about our tax-scene, but if we don't, your fab four will end up like Mickey Rooney,
Joe Louis, etc. - performing for the rest of their lives to pay back the tax man.

We, John and Yoko, have asked them, Apple, to reduce the cost of Yoko's album FLY,
they told us they had.

I personally have had enough of Apple/Ascot and all other properties which tie me
down, mentally and physically. - I intend to cash in my chips as soon as I can - and
be FREE.

John/Yoko intend to do all performances around the world FREE and/or whatever
we've earned will go e.g. to prisons to release people who can't afford bail, etc.
- and many other ways of getting money back to the people.

This is one way of paying the people back.

Until we find an alternative, the Pete Bennettes and the Apples, EMIs, etc., are
the only way of getting our product to the people. (Not to mention the contractual
angle) - if you know of any other way - don't keep it a secret!

                                Power to the People

                              John Lennon&Yoko
                              JohnandYoko

P.S. The number of tracks per album is irrelevant - it''s the amount of time per
side that counts. Anything over - say 25 minutes at most results in less power-volume,
bass/drums, etc. But 'Live Jam' Plastic Ono Band - out soon - has about at least 30
minutes a side!

P.P.S. Dear ■■■■■ - who wants to sound like the Beatles?
P.P.P.S. We like Reggae, too! Paul likes Rock!
P.P.P.P.S. I personally have had enough of Apple/Ascot long before John has and
I'm very happy that John's coming around - and not only "Imagine no possessions"
but wanting to get rid of it - the things that interfere with our work and our life. (y.o.)
P.P.P.P.P.S. If you'd like to know where my earnings go - every cent of it goes
to various 'causes'. (y.o.)
P.P.P.P.P.P.S. Please stop attacking John for "How Do You Sleep", It happens to be
a good song (very powerful and full of pathos) and also, it happens to be an answer
to Paul's "Ram". Listen to "Ram" carefully and you'll see. (y.o.)
          this i'r t'e last word on that subject! x.
P.P.P.P.P.P.S. Rally on Friday for John Sinclair. Released on Monday
after 2 years of a 10 year sentence for possession of 2 joints.

From New York,
John's erratic typing
carries his usual
pungent words in
reply to a reader's
letter in *Melody
Maker*

Within months of settling in America, John and Yoko were heavily involved in radical politics. In February 1972, in temperatures well below freezing, they were out demonstrating their support for an airline union leaders's boycott of British exports as a protest against British policy in Northern Ireland

(Associated Press)

July 1973: John followed the Watergate hearings in New York, which indicted the government of President Richard Nixon, with keen interest, and attended them regularly with Yoko

(Associated Press)

In July 1976, after a four-year battle, John wins his vital Green Card from the U.S. Immigration Department. It gave him freedom to leave and re-enter the country
(Bob Gruen/Star File)

John in California: his life fell apart without Yoko. A note to jog his memory reads 'Jeans for Julian'
(Scope Features)

John filling in time in California

(Michael Brennan/Scope Features)

May Pang looks on as John attends to the styling of eleven-
year-old Julian's hair in December 1975

(Scope Features)

John at the opening of
the *Sgt Pepper's
Lonely Hearts Club
Band* musical in New
York in November
1974
*(Ann Phillips/John
Hillelson Agency)*

AN OPENED LETTUCE TO SODD HUMTLESTUMTLE. (from dr. winston o'boogie)

   Couldn't resist adding a few "islands of truth" of my
own, in answer to Turd Rundgreen's howl of hate (pain.)

Dear Todd,

   I like you, and some of your work, including "I Saw The
Light", which is not unlike "There's A Place" (Beatles), melody
wise.)

   1) I have never claimed to be a revolutionary. But I
       am allowed to sing about anything I want! Right?

   2) I never hit a waitress in the Troubador, I did act
       like an ass, I was too drunk. So shoot me!

   3) I guess we're all looking for attention Rodd, do
       you really think I don't know how to get it, without
       "revolution"? I could dye my hair green and pink for
       a start!

   4) I don't represent anyone but my SELF. It sounds like
       I represented something to you, or you wouldn't be so
       violent towards me. (Your dad perhaps?)

   5) Yes Dodd, violence comes in mysterious ways it's wonders
       to perform, including verbal. But you'd know that kind
       of mind game, wouldn't you? Of course you would.

   6) So the Nazz use to do "like heavy rock" then
       SUDDENLY a "light pretty ballad". How original!

   7) Which gets me to the Beatles, "who had no other style
       than being the Beatles"!! That covers a lot of style
       man, including your own, TO DATE.....

   Yes Godd, the one thing these Beatles did was to affect
PEOPLES' MINDS. Maybe you need another fix?

   Somebody played me your rock and roll pussy song, but I
never noticed anything. I think that the real reason you're mad
at me is cause I didn't know who you were at the Rainbow (L.A.)
Remember that time you came in with Wolfman Jack? When I found
out later, I was cursing, cause I wanted to tell you how good you were.
(I'd heard you on the radio.)

                                     Anyway,
                                       However much you hurt me darling;
                                     I'll always love you,

                              J. L.   *Johnlennun*

                                       30th Sept. 1974

John's reply to an interview
conducted by *Melody Maker*
with American singer-
writer Todd Rundgren in
which he criticized John and
the Beatles

A Japanese-style family, pictured in the Dakota apartment when Sean was just one month old. This was the beginning of John's time as a househusband and doting father *(Bob Gruen/Star File)*

(Allan Tannenbaum/John Hillelson Agency)

John and Yoko in front of the Dakota

MAMPEI HOTEL
KARUIZAWA JAPAN

PRONOUNCED "KA-RI-ZA."

Karuizawa, Japan.

Dear Julian,

we are just near
here in the mountains;
if you wish to 'phone
it would be great!
but if you are too busy
its o.k. too!
lots of love to you
+ God Bless!
Daddy / John / Sean

NO: KARUIZA: 2: 5327

JULIAN LENNON
BROW-Y-GOF
LLANFIRWROG
RUTHIN
NORTH WALES
BRITAIN
U.K.

Have a cool summer! Y.

A postcard sent to Julian from Japan

John, Yoko and their friend Elliot Mintz during their
five-month holiday in Japan in the summer of 1977.
Outside the *sushi* bar in Karuizawa where they
usually had lunch. *Below:* In a restaurant in the
ancient town of Kyoto.

(both—*Nishi F. Saimaru*)

Above: After a long walk to the top of a mountain John points dramatically to the mist (the city below was invisible).

Below: In the public gardens near their hotel, the Mampei in Karuizawa. 'John was at the healthiest point in his life during that period,' recalls Mintz   *(both—Nishi F. Saimaru)*

John and Yoko in New York, 6 December, 1980

(Bob Gruen/Star File)

'Farmer J. wrestling with an agricultural problem'—a postcard sent to Julian from New York. The picture had originally been included with John's *Imagine* L.P., as Lennon's jibe at McCartney's *Ram* album cover

'Every day, in every way, I'm getting better and better,' writes John in April 1979 on this postcard to Julian; it was a phrase that came into one of his final songs, 'Beautiful Boy', on his penultimate album, *Double Fantasy*

John looks every inch the teenage rock 'n' roller beside the giant guitar model in New York's Record Plant where some of the mixing for the *Double Fantasy* album was done
(Bob Gruen/Star File)

(Bob Gruen/Star File)

John the working musician and composer: taking a guitar break and at the piano

(David Spindel)

John makes a point to Yoko at the recording console, autumn 1980 *(David Spindel)*

John and Yoko perched on their favourite bench in Central Park. They used to spend hours walking and talking there *(Allan Tannenbaum/ John Hillelson Agency)*

Yoko and John in
New York,
6 December 1980
(Bob Gruen/Star File)

'I love New York
because I can walk
around feeling so
free,' said John. In
T-shirt and jeans, he
and Yoko stroll the
sidewalks in
September 1980
*(David McGough/
London Features
International)*

For years, Sean had been asking his parents to take him to Liverpool. In January 1984, Yoko took him on a tour of the city to all his father's old haunts . . . the Art College, the Cavern Mecca where they pinned a Cavern badge on Sean, and finally to John's childhood home in Woolton. This picture, taken outside the house, shows Yoko and Sean flanked by their ever-present bodyguards *(Pictorial Press)*

Julian Lennon clasps the shoulders of Sean Lennon at the dedication ceremony for 'Strawberry Fields', a garden in New York's Central Park, in March 1984; on the far left is long-time John Lennon supporter Mayor Ed Koch *(Bob Gruen/Star File)*

Julian Lennon on stage during his American concert tour debut in
Washington in 1985   *(Phyllis Rosney/Star File)*

like Mary Hopkin. John was not so keen on talent-hunting: he was too busy discovering himself.

Drastic change was affecting John, privately and professionally. With Allen Klein at the helm in Apple he was back in a buoyant mood, despite the rift with Paul. 'It's going to be great here at Apple,' he said as their record successes increased. He was trying to boost his confidence in Klein. But yet another business crisis hit him badly.

Dick James, the friendly, enthusiastic song publisher who was managing director of Northern Songs, which owned the copyright to nearly all the Lennon–McCartney songs, had been wooed for several months by Sir Lew Grade, then chairman of A.T.V., who wanted to take over the valuable Beatles song catalogue. With a vision that the songs would earn money for the copyright holders well into the twenty-first century and probably until the end of time, Grade repeatedly offered James a great deal of money but one man alone could not decide to sell about 200 songs that dated back to their earliest hits such as 'From Me To You', 'She Loves You' and 'I Want To Hold Your Hand' and went through to their now huge-selling album titles. 'When Brian Epstein died and the Beatles were visibly torn asunder, Grade began romancing me,' recalls Dick James. 'In old money the shares for Northern were marketing at seven shillings and ninepence at the start and fourteen shillings and sixpence when Brian died. Lew's final offer was thirty-five shillings a share, so the financial gain to everyone, including John and Paul, was very considerable.' James put Grade's offer to the board of Northern Songs, who represented more than 3,000 outside shareholders. The decision was unanimous: accept the offer, which would bring in £10 million in cash.

Dick James' theory was that he was doing the Beatles, and John and Paul as the major songwriters, a favour. Northern Songs was, he believed, very vulnerable to all kinds of City takeovers and with the Beatles at loggerheads they would suffer badly if different factions in the City pulled it to pieces. Better, he thought, to sell to A.T.V. where at least it would be under the roof of a serious, stable music publishing house. 'The protection the Beatles' songs could have within the framework of a much larger company like A.T.V., as has been proven, was much safer. When A.T.V. took it over the wolves stopped

baying. It would have been wrong to sell Northern Songs to
John or Paul individually and with Allen Klein and Lee Eastman
representing them each, they could hardly buy it jointly at that
stage.'

John was furious at what he considered a betrayal of his
interests without giving him any options. At a meeting at
Paul's house, Lennon tore into James. 'I tried to point out to
John that his capital gain was at the lowest rate of tax paid
anywhere in the world, as opposed to his tax from record
sales which were subject to ordinary income tax,' says James.
But John was inconsolable. Paul was annoyed but John, says
Dick James, was 'hurt and I was very sorry, and Yoko was
annoyed'.

Finally, after a tense meeting, James tried to win John over.
He told Lennon about the huge lump sum coming his way from
the sale: 'Well, John, at least this means you can put some
money by for your children.'

John's cynical retort ended any cosiness: 'I have no desire
to create another fucking aristocracy,' he said bitterly.

Relations between John and Paul began to decline swiftly
after John left the group. And although it had been John who
made the break, it was a public relations tactic by Paul that
broke the news to the world. With his first solo album, called
McCartney, he issued a press release with forty-one questions
and answers which left the world's media in no doubt that Paul
was out of the group. It contained barbed references to his non-
association with the Beatles. Issued in question-and-answer
form, part of the text ran:

Did you enjoy working as a solo?

Very much. I only had me to ask for a decision and I
agreed with me.

*Is this album a rest away from the Beatles or the start
of a solo career?*

Time will tell. . . .

*Is your break with the Beatles, temporary or permanent,
due to personal differences or musical ones?*

Personal differences. Business differences. Musical differences. But most of all because I have a better time with my family. Temporary or permanent? I don't know.

Is it true that neither Allen Klein nor ABCKO (his company) have been or will be in any way involved in the production, manufacturing, distribution or promotion of this new album?

Not if I can help it.

Lennon was furious at what appeared a pre-emptive strike by McCartney to gain the momentum and wrest the decision-making role from him. Paul's dislike of Yoko was one thing: to upstage him by causing the world to surmise that Paul was the one taking the initiative was another. John reacted with a beautifully laconic piece of venom: by telephone he told me for an article I wrote: 'I received a phone call from Paul last Thursday afternoon. He said: "I'm going to leave the Beatles as well." I was happy to hear from Paul. It was nice to find that he was still alive.

'Anyway, Paul hasn't left. I sacked him.'

The sour relationship with Paul continued right up until John and Yoko left to settle in America in 1971. John and Yoko and their newly named Plastic Ono Band had taken flight in a surge of activity that camouflaged the McCartney situation, from the public at least. But when Paul usurped him by releasing the press statement, John was livid. The two men had little contact but newspaper conjecture carried on. McCartney again ended the world's speculation with a letter to the *Melody Maker* on 29 August 1970:

In order to put out of its misery the limping dog of a news story which has been dragging itself across your pages for the past year, my answer to the question: 'Will the Beatles get together again?' is no.

Paul McCartney

By the end of 1970 Paul McCartney began proceedings in the High Court to wind up the Beatles partnership. Even against the background of bickering it was a difficult decision:

he made it during a sojourn with Linda at his farm in Camp-
beltown, Argyllshire. 'It's not easy being in a top job one
second and the next someone says: "Well, we're breaking
the group up." And you haven't got a job. It screwed my
head for years,' he says. As for the questions that persisted
about a reunion: 'It's like asking a divorced couple: Are you
getting back together? . . . when you can't stand to look at
each other.' It was agony, 'suing my best mates and being
seen to sue my best mates. That was the worst.' The Beatles
were formally ended as a performing group in the High Court
on 12 March 1971 and a receiver appointed to look after their
business interests. The Beatles continued only as a business
name.

On a personal level the wrangles continued and began to
manifest themselves in Paul and John's music. Four months
before John left for America in September 1971 Paul released
a solo album made with Linda McCartney, *Ram*. Two songs
in particular, 'Too Many People (Going Underground)' and
'Back Seat Of My Car' (ending with the chant, 'We believe
we can't be wrong') were unsubtle jibes at John and Yoko.
Quite why Paul, well known for his anodyne tendencies, chose
to pick a fight on record, and in public, with such a master of
invective as John, will always be a mystery. Lennon's reply
was the vitriolic 'How Do You Sleep?', on his classic *Imagine*
album. Unlike Paul's songs, John's tactics were not cloak-and-
dagger but a full frontal assault:

So Sgt Pepper took you by surprise
You better see right through that mother's eyes
Those freaks was right when they said you was dead
The one mistake you made was in your head . . .
You live with straights who tell you you was king
Jump when your mama tell you anything
The only thing you done was Yesterday
And since you've gone you're just Another Day
How do you sleep? . . .
A pretty face may last a year or two
But pretty soon they'll see what you can do
The sound you make is Muzak to my ears
You must have learned something in all those years

The rancour over Yoko, over Klein and Eastman and how best to end the Beatles had now turned bitterly personal. At the root of it lay the fundamental truth which millions of Beatles fans still find unpalatable: John and Paul never had much in common. They had different aspirations: Paul, with his gift for melody and musicianship, and love of popularity, headed securely for the world of entertainment where he will always be a giant figure. John was on a perpetual adventure, picking up and adopting, then quickly rejecting ideas and causes, writing poetry, and writing from within himself. He was an artist with a distinct anti-Establishment backbone. McCartney greatly admired John's mercurial, often whimsical, style, his originality, his arrogance, his wit. To a lesser extent Lennon acknowledged Paul's strengths as a songwriter. But John had little time for craftsmen, dismissing them as 'people who could write little ditties to order'. He sweated over his own work. His post-Beatles writing was inspired by personal relationships, observations and events. John could recognize Paul's commercial power but it was all too often vapid, mawkish, and sentimental in contrast with his hard edge. They were right for each other at a certain period of their lives. But put simply, where McCartney had great talent, Lennon was a genius. By 1971 they had irrevocably parted company, both personally and artistically, and John's feelings were further inflamed by Paul's digs at Yoko, whom John regarded as part of him.

The fight continued in public. Paul gave an interview to *Melody Maker* in November 1971, emphasizing that although the music had ended, business problems still faced them: 'I just want the four of us to get somewhere and sign a piece of paper saying it's all over and we want to divide the money four ways.

'No one else would be there, not even Linda or Yoko or Allen Klein. We'd just sign the paper and hand it to the business people and let them sort it all out. That's all I want now. But John won't do it. Everybody thinks I am the aggressor. But I'm not, you know. I just want out.

'John and Yoko are not cool in what they are doing. I saw them on television the other night and thought that what they are saying about what they wanted to do together was basically the same as what Linda and I want to do.

'John's whole image now is very honest and open. He's all right, is John. I like his *Imagine* album but I didn't like the others. *Imagine* is what John is really like but there was too much political stuff on the other albums. You know, I only really listen to them to see if there is something I can pinch.' (He laughed.)

What did Paul think of 'How Do You Sleep?'? 'I think it's silly. So what if I live with straights? I like straights. I have straight babies. It doesn't affect *him*. He says the only thing I did was "Yesterday". He knows that's wrong. He knows and I know it's not true.'

Referring to the Beatles' album, *Let It Be*, Paul said: 'There was a little bit of hype on the back of the sleeve for the first time ever on a Beatles album. At the time the Beatles were very strained with each other and it wasn't a happy time. It said it was a new-phase Beatles album and there was nothing further from the truth. That was the last Beatles album and everybody knew it. . . . Klein had it re-produced because he said it didn't sound commercial enough.'

Talking of John's Toronto concert with Eric Clapton, Yoko, and Klaus Voormann, Paul said: 'John wanted to do a big thing in Toronto but I didn't dig that at all. I hear that before he went on stage he was sick and that's just what I didn't want. Like anybody else I have been nervous because of the Beatles thing.

'I wanted to get in a van and do an unadvertised concert at a Saturday night hop at Slough Town Hall or somewhere like that. We'd call ourselves Rikki and the Red Streaks or something and just get up and play. There'd be no Press and we'd tell nobody about it. John thought it was a daft idea.

'Before John said he was leaving the Beatles I was lying in bed at home one night and I thought I would like to get a band together like his Plastic Ono Band. I felt the urge because we had never played live for four years. We all wanted to appear on a stage but not with the Beatles. We couldn't do it as the Beatles because it would be so big. We'd have to find a million-seater hall or something.' And in a remark which made John smile, Paul said what he thought of New York: 'I went for a walk in Central Park and there was a layer of dirt on the grass everywhere.' The grass on his farm in Scotland, where he had 100 sheep on sixty acres of land, was so much better than American grass.

John's letter of reply which was published in the *Melody Maker* two weeks later, was accompanied by a request that it be published in full to give 'equal time' to his side of the story. Part of the letter referred to McCartney's claim that if he (Paul) had appeared at George Harrison's summer 1971 Bangladesh concert in New York, Allen Klein would have taken the credit for pulling the Beatles back together again. John's classic letter, positively dripping with invective, ran as follows:

Dear Paul, Linda *et all* the wee McCartneys,

Thanks for your letter.

1. We give *you money* for your bits of Apple.

2. We give *you more money* in the form of royalties which legally belong to Apple (I know we're Apple, but on the other hand we're *not*).

Maybe there's an answer there somewhere . . . but for the millionth time in these past few years I repeat, *What about the TAX*? It's all very well, playing 'simple, honest ole Paul' in the *Melody Maker* but you know damn well we can't just sign a bit of paper.

You say, 'John won't do it.' I will if you'll *indemnify* us against the tax man! Anyway, you know that after we have *our* meeting, the fucking lawyers will have to implement whatever we agree on—right?

If they have some form of agreement between *them* before *we* met, it might make it even easier. It's up to you; as we've said many times, we'll meet you whenever you like. Just make up your mind! E.g. two weeks ago I asked you on the phone, 'Please let's meet without advisers, etc. and decide what we want', and I emphasized especially Maclen [John and Paul's songwriting partnership company within Northern Songs] which is mainly our concern, but you refused—right?

You said under *no condition* would you sell to us and if we didn't do what you wanted, you'd sue us again and that Ringo and George are going to break you John, etc. etc.

Now I was quite straight with you that day, and you tried to shoot me down with your emotional 'logic'. If *you're not* the aggressor (as you claim) who the hell took us to court and shat all over us in public?

As I've said before—have you ever thought that you might *possibly* be wrong about something? Your conceit about us and Klein is incredible—you say you 'made the mistake of trying to advise them against him [Klein] and that pissed them off' and we secretly feel that you're right! Good God! You must *know we're right about East-man. . . .*

One other little lie in your 'It's only Paulie' *MM* bit: *Let It Be* was not the 'first bit of hype' on a Beatle album. Remember Tony Barrow? And his wonderful writing on 'Please Please Me' etc. etc. the early Beatle Xmas records!

And you gotta admit it was a 'new-phase Beatle album', incidentally written in the style of the great Barrow himself! By the way what happened to my idea of putting the parody of our first album cover on the *Let It Be* cover?

Also, we were intending to parody Barrow originally, so it was hype. But what was your *Life* article? Tony Barrow couldn't have done it better. (And your writing inside of the *Wings* album isn't exactly the realist is it?) Anyway, enough of this petty bourgeois fun.

You were right about New York! I do love it; it's the ONLY PLACE TO BE. (Apart from anything else, they leave you alone too!) I see you prefer Scotland. . . . I'll bet you YOUR piece of Apple you'll be living in New York by 1974 (two years is the usual time it takes you—right?).

Another thing, whadya mean *big thing* in Toronto? It was completely spontaneous, they rang on the *Friday*—we flew there and we played on the *Saturday*. I was sick because I was stone pissed. Listen to the album, with no rehearsal too. Come on Macka! Own up! (We'd never played together before!) Half a dozen live shows—with no big fuss—in fact we've been *doing* what you've said the Beatles should do, Yoko and I have been doing it for three years! (I said it was daft for the Beatles to do it. I still think it's daft.) So go on and do it! Do it! Do it! E.g. *Cambridge*, 1969, completely unadvertised! (A *very* small hall.) *Lyceum*

Ballroom, (1969, no fuss, great show—thirty-piece rock band! 'Live Jam' out soon!) *Fillmore East* (1971) unannounced. Another good time had by all—out soon!!) We even played in the streets here in the Village (our spiritual home!?) with the great David Peel!! We were moved on by the cops even!! It's best just to DO IT.

I know you'll dig it, and they don't even expect the Beatles now anyway!

So *you* think *Imagine* ain't political, it's 'Working Class Hero' with sugar on it for conservatives like yourself!! You obviously didn't *dig the words*. Imagine! You took 'How Do You Sleep?' so literally (read my own review of the album in *Crawdaddy*). *Your* politics are very similar to Mary Whitehouse's—saying *nothing* is as loud as saying *something*.

Listen, my obsessive old pal, it was George's press conference not dat old debbil Klein! *He* said what *you* said—'I'd love to come but. . . .' Anyway, we did it for basically the same reasons—the Beatles bit. They still called it a Beatle show—with just two of them! [Ringo played drums in the superstar band George Harrison formed for the spectacular Bangladesh concert in New York.]

Join the Rock Liberation Front before it gets *you*.

Wanna put your photo on the label like uncool John and Yoko do ya? (Ain't ya got no shame!) If we're *not* cool, WHAT DOES THAT MAKE YOU?

No hard feelings to you either. I know basically we want the same, and as I said on the phone and in this letter, whenever you want to meet, all you have to do is call.

All you need is love
Power to the people
Free all prisoners
Jail the judges
Love and peace
Get it on and rip 'em off

John Lennon

P.S. The bit that really puzzled us was asking to meet WITHOUT LINDA AND YOKO. I thought you'd have understood BY NOW that I'm JOHNANDYOKO.

P.P.S. Even *your own* lawyers know you can't 'just sign
a bit of paper' (or don't they tell you?).

The wounds were deep and lasting. Relations between John
and Paul never fully recovered from the encounter. When John
wrote that letter, two months after arriving in New York, he
scarcely realized that he would never visit Britain again. And
it would be four years before Paul finally visited him in New
York, the Beatles dead and the business hatchet still not properly buried. At the time of their friction, George Martin said:
'I don't think Linda is a substitute for John Lennon any more
than Yoko is a substitute for Paul McCartney.' The producer
of the Beatles' records was judging each artist's new direction
in music. He was also, unknowingly, echoing their desires.
John had shed the Beatles, Paul, and Britain. And he was
opening his mind.

The Beatles phenomenon, he said, was so enormous that
he had had to be a Beatle and nothing else. 'It was not a monster
at the beginning. We communicated with people, in clubs and
ballrooms; we spoke to people and it was really great. But then
it became a kind of machine. It's like a guy who makes millions,
say Rockefeller or Getty. They become totally obsessed by
money, how to make more. That's how the Beatles became,
and that's what I could not accept. There wasn't a moment to
think about anything else, so the Beatles was just a period in
my life.' Before the Beatles, he had known nothing about world
politics, but he had been aware of his position within Liverpool
society—'trying to get into university and all the silly things
that go with that'.

But he accepted that the Beatles had a vital social influence.
He always seized on anyone who denied the importance of the
Beatles to the world. *He* was allowed to denigrate the group,
but woe betide anyone else who did, particularly musicians.
'The Beatles had a social impact then became sterile like a
government that has stayed in power too long. When that situation arises, you abdicate. So we abdicated.'

18
PEACE

*'We are willing to be clowns if it helps
spread the word'*

Just before going to America in 1971, John told me: 'We'd
like to be remembered as the Romeo and Juliet of the 1970s.'

Yoko continued: 'When people get cynical about love, they
should look at us and see that it *is* possible.' They were holding
hands, smiling and obviously meant every word. I had asked
them what their real aims were, in the heat of the great controversy surrounding their union and demonstrations for peace.

'I'd like everyone to remember us with a smile,' said John.
'But, if possible, just as John and Yoko who created world
peace for ever. The whole of life is a preparation for death.
I'm not worried about dying. When we go, we'd like to leave
behind a better place.'

In the wake of the limping Beatles and the *Two Virgins*
album furor, three other major landmarks had just re-shaped
John's life. The speed of events was breathtaking.

In February 1969 Yoko was divorced from her second husband, Anthony Cox. Seven weeks after that, John and Yoko
had married. Five days after that they staged the renowned bed-
in demonstration for peace in Amsterdam. And a month after
their wedding John formally changed his middle name by deed
poll from Winston to Ono. He was following his maxim to
Paul, 'Do it!' with a speed that was not to let up for the next
six years.

John's formal change of name from Winston to Ono was

a mark of togetherness but it had a diplomatic motive too. Yoko had said to John, light-heartedly but with meaning: 'I don't like being known as Mrs Lennon. How would *you* like it if you had to change your name upon marriage to Mr John Ono? Why should that not be?' (Ono is Yoko's given surname which she does not drop upon marriage.) She was intent on asserting her independence and even wrote a song, 'Mrs Lennon', which, she says now, summed up her cynicism at the irony of the situation.

'My God, it really is unfair,' admitted John as they joked about it.

Then, Yoko recalls, John 'showed what an incredible politician he was'. He had repeatedly told Yoko that he disliked his middle name, Winston, with its wartime connotation and implication that he was somehow a subscriber to the spirit of the upper-class 'British empire and all that'. It made him feel hypocritical. 'I don't want that name. It's always following me around,' John told Yoko.

'He hated being compared in any way with Winston Churchill,' she says. 'His incredible idea of having his middle name changed to Ono, to accommodate my request, made me feel good and amazed me at the same time. He said I could carry on being known as Yoko Ono, and why not, and he had made a step towards me without dropping Lennon, which nobody wanted him to do, anyway.'

John decided to have the ceremony performed by the Commissioner of Oaths on the roof at Apple. But there was a technical problem: he was told that day that, while he could adopt the name Ono, he could not renounce the given name of Winston. What he decided to call himself was totally up to him and he was re-registered as John Winston Ono Lennon that day. John grumbled: 'Why am I paying all these lawyers if I'm not getting rid of Winston?'

The legalities of whether John still owned the name Winston dragged on for months. 'I don't feel patriotic enough to keep the name,' he said. 'I am John Ono Lennon.' In all the oaths which he swore during his statements on the winding-up of the Beatles in 1970 John was written down as John Ono Lennon and all his personal documents were named accordingly. He often signed himself with just his new initials: J.O.L. But when it came to his American immigration battle between 1972 and 1976, he diplomatically added back the name Winston and the Green Card was eventually made out to him in the name of John Winston Ono Lennon. 'Although he may never have technically lost the Winston, he disliked it and never used it,' says Yoko. Her own situation is exactly the same: the world knows her as Yoko Ono, the name she prefers, but technically she is Yoko Ono Lennon. John particularly liked to add extra 'o's to his name because he and Yoko said the letter was a sign of intuitiveness and was good on psychic grounds, too. 'Between us,' Yoko says, 'we were very psychic. We knew all the time what the other was thinking, what was going to be said by the other, our responses, everything. It was sometimes unnerving.'

Their wedding was unconventional but romantic. Based in Paris for a couple of weeks in March 1969, they decided to charter a plane and marry in Gibraltar. The bride and groom wore white tennis shoes and their clothes were also white. Yoko wore a white linen mini dress and coat, a huge-brimmed white hat that contrasted vividly with her flowing black hair and white socks. John had a white jacket and off-white corduroy trousers. The man who had been cast as the waspish Beatle, hard and cynical, was old-fashioned about his marriage. 'We are two love birds,' he said. 'Intellectually we didn't believe in getting married. But one doesn't love someone just intellectually. For two people, marriage still has the edge over just living together.' At the ceremony he stood before the registrar in the British Consulate office with one hand in his pocket and the other holding a cigarette. 'Oh, that wasn't important at all,' he answered when asked if it was irreverent. 'The event was *ours*. If I can't stand and do what I like at my own wedding. . . .'

They had their honeymoon, he explained, before the wedding. 'Just eating, shopping and looking round Paris. In love in Paris in the spring was beautiful. We're both tremendous romantics!' They would have liked to have been married in church by the Archbishop of Canterbury but that was impossible because divorced people could not be married in church.

The scorn that had been directed at Yoko vanished immediately. People suddenly realized that she was human after all. 'I got so emotional at the wedding I broke down and John nearly did, too,' she said. 'This man, rabbiting on about "Do you take this woman for your wife?''—it was a tremendous experience.' Back in Paris after only a seventy-minute stay in Gibraltar, John and Yoko went to the Plaza Athénée Hotel. Yes, Yoko reflected, marriage was old-fashioned but both of them definitely respected it as an institution. John said that from then on they would do everything together, as artists and as husband and wife. Yoko said she would certainly not be the traditional wife, if that meant bringing him his slippers. She added that their marriage was one of their happenings, very important and indicative of the future. 'We're planning another one in the next seven days. You'll know soon enough when it is.'

The next stop, Amsterdam, a few days later, was to be the pivotal event of their peace campaign. Since they had already appeared on stage at London's Royal Albert Hall in a large white bag in December 1968 and as Yoko had fast gained a reputation for leading John into the realms of fantasy, it should not have been so surprising. But John and Yoko were in a hurry to ram home some principles. The mid-1960s had educated the world into accepting that rock stars could have brains; some saw their role as messianic. John, encouraged by Yoko, sensed the power that being a Beatle had given him and believed it could be used intelligently to advocate peace. He had first been encouraged to launch a peace campaign in a letter from Peter Watkins, producer of the film *The War Game*. Watkins spoke of the obscenity of war and the power of artists like John; reflecting on his appearance in the anti-war film *How I Won The War*, John became totally committed to the idea.

For seven days in the presidential suite of the Amsterdam Hilton John and Yoko lay in bed together in white pyjamas. They were surrounded by flowers and two notices adorned their bedhead: 'Bed Peace' and 'Hair Peace'. They invited the Press, and during that week nearly 100 reporters from all around the world came to watch the event that became known as the Amsterdam bed-in for peace. What was *this*? Mad John and crazy Yoko having a public honeymoon? In the eyes of the conventional world they had now cooked up the most outrageous happening of all.

'Ha! They all thought John and Yoko were going to fuck

in front of the world's Press for peace,' John laughed. 'That was never on, and anyway we're far too shy to do anything, *anything*, like that.' The idea was to stage a genuine demonstration when they knew that publicity would be guaranteed: 'The Press would have found us whatever we'd done for a honeymoon, so we decided to invite the Press along and get some publicity for something we both believe in,' John said later. Sporting a beard and with his hair at its longest, John urged others to grow their hair as a symbol of their peace campaign; strangely, John also seemed calmer during the week in Amsterdam. Fans besieged the hotel, listening patiently to the messages of peace that John and Yoko propounded. They kept the windows of their room open so they could hear the fans in the street outside. And the Press, at once bemused and amused by the whole episode, was cynically grateful. Good old John and Yoko had given them a decent story, at least. John saw it more profoundly: he believed the peace message had got across. Hundreds of newspapers and radio and television programmes had sent out their message. It was better propaganda than any prime minister had yet achieved. As for the fans: well, he was old now (twenty-eight at the time) and Yoko was thirty-six; he felt that his days as a pop idol had run out and that it was time to concentrate on more serious work.

At the time the Amsterdam bed-in was regarded by many as a stunt or a joke. A cynical British police chief described it as disgusting, adding: 'If wealth does this to people then I do not want it. Power corrupts.' But John and Yoko had optimism firmly on their side: if there was a wave of cynicism in 1969, then in the years since John and Yoko's palpable sincerity and the importance and urgency of their message and motive has rung true throughout the world.

There was never any let-up, either, in their proclamation of love for each other: signs proclaiming 'John loves Yoko' and 'Yoko loves John' hung next to them in bed for seven days. And when Yoko told John her £3 10s. wedding ring was too large and was slipping off her finger, John drew a temporary one in ink on Yoko's finger while the real one went for shrinking. A solid streak of conformity, convention, tradition, and romanticism bound them together while the world had exactly the opposite impression of them. They were much more demonstrative in their affection for each other than many 'normal' husbands and wives; and with John and Yoko, every facet of their partnership was played out in public. They quickly damped down any speculation that Yoko, because of her far-out stand in art, was an aggressive fighter for women's liberation who had hammered her views into a chauvinistic Beatle. 'John is a very aggressive, masculine man and I enjoy being submissive,' said Yoko. But three years of observing Yoko had changed John's outlook. By the time they married he was re-thinking his whole attitude to women. Yoko's strength convinced him that to go on looking for merely physical attributes would never satisfy him. As he commented: 'I guess I was looking for a woman who would give me everything I got from a man, intellectually, as well as the fact that she was female.' He took a keen interest in women's emancipation partly because Yoko had demonstrated her equality and often superiority. John resented very strongly the middle-class snubs that Yoko had suffered: after she had appeared nude with him on the *Two Virgins* album cover she was called an 'ugly old cow', and he felt she should fight back. 'How dare they? I think she's beautiful,' he said. More importantly he knew something that was going to be much harder to get across: mentally, intellectually, and conceptually Yoko not only suffered racial prejudice and opposition from all women and, naturally, Lennon's girl fans from the Beatles days, but as an artist she was years ahead of her time and her work was constantly misunderstood. What Amsterdam convinced him of was that she should strike out even more, together with him, for feminism, and articulate it, while he should also shed the mental restrictions of being labelled a Beatle.

The fecundity of their partnership was nourished more in Amsterdam than anywhere. 'We are willing,' said John, 'to become the world's clowns if it helps spread the word for peace. Too many people talk about it but not enough do anything.' With his famous name and Yoko's ideas they would continue doing things for years that would force people to react, he said. After the previous year's acorns in Coventry Cathedral and the 'bagism' on a London stage, Bag Productions, John and Yoko's film and production company was formed, based at the Apple headquarters. John Lennon, man of peace, had been launched.

As with everything he ever did, he was serious, intense, simple, hurried, and infectious. As he admitted in song, it wasn't easy, 'the way things are going, they're gonna crucify me'. The world had become used to the abrasive, opinionated Beatle. It had slowly realized he meant Yoko to be more than a passerby in his life when they married. For the next eleven years John Lennon was gradually to jump the biggest hurdle of all, the foundations of which had been set up in Amsterdam: the pop star idolized by millions was to become known as a spokesman and campaigner for goodwill and humanitarianism.

There was a double edge to John's adoption of the peace cause. It came at a perfect time in his life, with the Beatles at a crossroads. And he had reflected that, for six years as a pop star, he had reluctantly been conscious of his image, not getting too involved in politics or philosophy. It had always been against his nature: after he had tripped up over his remarks on Jesus Christ in 1966, Brian Epstein's rule that the Beatles should be non-controversial seemed to make sense. Lennon wanted to condemn publicly American aggression in Vietnam at the height of the Beatles' fame. Epstein warned him against it and John, who for a time did not want the roller-coaster of Beatlemania to wane, went along with the 'party line'. It was a bitter pill to swallow.

Now, with fame and wealth, he would pretend no more. He told the Amsterdam press conference: 'All I'm saying is peace. We're not pointing a finger at anybody. There are good guys and bad guys. The struggle is in the mind. We must bury our own monsters and stop condemning people. We're all Christ and we are all Hitler. We are trying to make Christ's message contemporary. We want Christ to win. What would He have done if He had advertisements, records, films, T.V. and newspapers? Well, the miracle today is communications. So let's use it!'

John and Yoko's method was expensive. Hotel suites and travelling expenses ran into thousands of pounds a week as they continued their European trip that spring. The critics tried another pin-prick: wouldn't it be better if John gave some money to the starving rather than indulging himself and his ego? He was ahead of them on that one: he regularly sent money to needy refugees, particularly in Biafra, that era's crisis point.

All his life John was to give away thousands of pounds to charities and good causes. He did it quietly, not wanting the publicity of the rich, demonstrative pop star displaying his wealth.

Amsterdam was only the start. As a continuation of the Coventry Cathedral acorn plantation, John and Yoko sent a pair of acorns to prime ministers throughout the world, urging them to plant them symbolically for peace, as they had done.

Films had always intrigued John and he and Yoko decided they would make them another aspect of their work together. Their first two, shot at Weybridge, were *Smile* and *Two Virgins*. *Smile* was Yoko's idea and was typically spare in its conception: simply a shot of John's face, smiling, in different expressions which were multiplied by the camera to complete a film lasting nearly an hour. *Two Virgins* was similar in theme, using John's face superimposed on Yoko's. Made early in their relationship, they were not so important as films as in sealing the chemistry between John and Yoko. Yoko was John's launching pad and it was she who showed him the true dimensions of his talent as a communicator.

He loved, too, the sense of humour in her work. Their third film, *Rape*, virtually parodied the story of the Beatles' escalator to success. A girl's reaction during her pursuit by journalists reaches a desperate finale in which she struggles violently and attacks a television camera. The film's première on Austrian T.V. followed the Amsterdam bed-in in March 1969. John and Yoko flew to Vienna and petrified the staid community by announcing that their press conference would be held where they were staying—the dignified and historic Hotel Sacher. The press conference rocked the august foundations of the grand old hotel. John and Yoko, by now christened 'Joko' by some cynics, appeared sitting on a trestle table covered totally by a white sheet. 'Bagism', they explained, was part of their peace drive.

John desperately wanted his propaganda machine for peace to have a big launch in America, then heavily involved in the Vietnam war. Asked why he had not had a bed-in there he had answered: 'Because I don't want to get shot.' His honesty usually got him through. The real reason, however, why they could not stage a bed-in in New York, as they wanted, was because John was refused a visa in May 1969: the London drugs conviction had blocked his freedom of movement. Montreal proved a happy alternative and John, by now an enthusiast of the telephone that he used to hate, used the proximity with North America to do literally hundreds of phone interviews with radio, television, and newspaper people anxious to learn what lay behind the Amsterdam idea.

'One problem with what we're doing,' he said, 'is that we'll never know how successful we are. With the Beatles, you put out a record and either it's a hit or it's a miss. I don't expect the prime ministers or kings and queens of the world to suddenly change their policies just because John and Yoko have said "Peace, brother". It would be nice! But it's *youth* we're addressing. Youth is the future. If we can get inside their minds and tell them to think in favour of non-violence, we'll be satisfied. What's the point of getting fame as a Beatle and not using it?!' John's urgency, his enthusiasm, and the still-glowing embers of Beatlemania in Canada and North America made for enormous press coverage. Since John never made any bones about his hunger for publicity for the peace cause, he viewed the seven-day Montreal bed-in as a winner.

He clinched it by making one of his strongest pieces of music. For months he had been using the phrase 'Give it a *chance*', when pleading with reporters to listen to the peace campaign fairly. Amid the huge spread of carnations in his hotel room, he was inspired to write the snappy little chant, 'Give Peace A Chance'. It quickly became popular with the entourage and John decided to order a portable eight-track tape recorder so that it could be recorded. Among the people singing along on the chorus were Timothy Leary, high priest of the drug culture, Montreal rabbi Abraham Feinberg, and comedian Tommy Smothers. The spontaneity of the song and John's unmistakable conviction gave it a sharp edge. The peace campaign now had an international anthem.

Just as with 'Give Peace A Chance', so many of John's phrases, inextricably linked with his humour and masterful word-play, serve as soundtracks for his life. Once his world was rolling with Yoko, John's one-liners and his song lyrics became even more memorable. 'The sixties were all about learning to swim,' he said once. 'So when you've learned to swim—swim!' Another classic summing up of the Beatles was: 'The dream is over . . . nothing's changed. Just a few of us are walking around with longer hair.' And, with his 1975 album of rock 'n' roll songs, John coined the phrase: 'You shoulda been there (signed) Dr Winston O'Boogie.' 'Imagine', his best-loved song, has a wealth of allegorical lines destined to enchant people for ever.

One of John's proudest word collaborations with Yoko came as the finale of their peace campaign in 1969. It had been a spine-tingling year. The simplicity of the slogan they invented gave it its power: 'WAR IS OVER! If you want it. Happy Christmas from John and Yoko.' Huge billboards went up in eleven cities around the world to display the poster and thousands of posters were distributed internationally. A full two years later, at Christmas 1971, John and Yoko joined together with the black children of the Harlem Community Choir in New York to make their classic Christmas song, 'Happy Xmas (War Is Over)'. The chorus, 'War Is Over, if you want it', lived on, which pleased John. 'And so this is Christmas,' he sang. 'And what have you done?/Another year over, a new one just begun.' By the end of 1969, though, John realized that the energy he had poured into the peace campaign needed one final boost. The answer, of course, lay in music.

To aid the United Nations Children's Emergency Fund he got together the Plastic Ono Band for a show at London's Lyceum ballroom. With the backdrop of the 'War Is Over!' billboard John assembled George Harrison, Eric Clapton, Klaus Voormann, the Who's Keith Moon, singer-pianist Billy Preston, and the Delaney and Bonnie Band. Yoko sat at John's feet on the stage, covered for much of the time by a white bag. Nobody was in any doubt, after a full year of propaganda, that they meant what they preached. On Christmas Eve they went to Rochester Cathedral, Kent, to join a sit-in and fast to spotlight world poverty. The cynics could not resist the temptation to take a negative view: Lennon was talking about poverty, they sneered, while arriving at the steps of the cathedral in a Rolls-Royce. John's retort was: 'Would they want me to walk here? The people who criticize us have cars. If they give up theirs, first, for peace, I'll give up my Rolls.'

It took Britain time to get used to John's antics. He was prepared for total rejection by Beatles fans because in his mind he had ceased to be a pop star. 'I've left all that to the Monkees,' he told me. But that summer, a heart-warming example of teenagers' support gave John and Yoko the feeling that the peace campaign, and their partnership, had succeeded.

In an opinion poll among readers of *Disc and Music Echo* John was voted the most popular Beatle and, the paper reported, his extrovert behaviour had 'made him a figure of respect rather than ridicule'. The paper asked: 'Some people think John Lennon's behaviour since he met his wife Yoko has been eccentric. What do you think?' The majority of young readers felt he was 'eccentric, but harmless and sincere'. A fifteen-year-old girl said: 'I thought he was very eccentric when he married Yoko but my opinions towards him are now changing because I can see some sense in what he's aiming at.' A nineteen-year-old Scotsman said: 'That John Lennon's behaviour pattern is tending towards the unorthodox cannot be denied, but Lennon is no orthodox character. He is an honest, sincere, Christ figure of a man in whom the passions of peace flow strongly and there are too many out to crucify him.' A Midlands teenager replied: 'I never used to take very much notice of the Beatles as individuals before but I do now. John isn't just a guitar stomper any more. He is . . . well, I suppose you could call him a saint.' And another said: 'He's doing more good than most politicians. At least he's taking action to try to get peace, which is better than sitting discussing it.' It was not all honey, however. One critical fan said: 'The Beatles would be better off without John Lennon. He's going downhill and unfortunately he has enough influence over the rest of the group that, unless he leaves, the Beatles could go down with him.'

John also emerged as the Beatle people would most like to meet. 'I'd like to talk to him about peace,' wrote a sixteen-year-old girl. 'I also admire the way he stands up in front of the public even though they treat him disgustingly.' And: 'I'd like to try to assess whether his endeavours on behalf of world peace are sincere or just the self-indulgent whims of a very rich, egotistical young man.' Among pop fans the news that

John had overtaken Paul as Britain's favourite Beatle was big news. And the fact that John achieved it for his ideas, rather than his music or his good looks, made an even greater impact. Crucially, too, John and Yoko's peace efforts, while scoring a direct hit for them, had not, in the main, affected public love of the Beatles, even though traditional British bluntness put a sting in the tail of a poll that boosted John's morale: 'Going off with the Maharishi to do this meditating lark ruined them,' said one boy. 'They should have retired after *Sgt Pepper*,' said another. But John was ecstatic at the results. He sent me, as the paper's editor, an enigmatic drawing 'as my way of saying thanks to all your readers who are with us'. He threw in a typical aside before the end of our phone conversation: 'Hey, why don't you ask the readers what they make of the drawing? We could have another poll on that!'

So we did. The response was enormous, the interpretations deep, patient, and understanding. 'The drawing is about peace, present and past,' said one reader. 'The two faces are reflected images of themselves, with John as a modern-day saviour. The scene is tranquillity—a pleasant day, sunshine, an animal in the foreground. . . . Peace. It could also represent the Nativity, with a stable on the horizon and an animal waiting for the birth.' And another went further: 'The Lennon cartoon is a visionary work showing John and Yoko after deification. The playing card symbolism in the representation of John and Yoko suggests that in the process they have lost their personal identity (as in the case of Henry VIII in a pack of cards) to be known only as "God" or "The Gods". This interpretation is supported by the fact that Lennon has no eyes. The title ("ART") suggests John and Yoko have attained divine status on artistic merit rather than through their efforts for peace.'

At last John felt vindicated. So many readers of *Disc and Music Echo*, a large proportion of them teenagers, felt a rapport with his cause for peace that he plunged headlong into a long and exhausting schedule of press interviews. The paper had also canvassed opinion on John and Yoko's new music, asking for reactions to their *Life With The Lions* album. (The title was a wry piece of word-play by John, invoking the radio series of his childhood, *Life with the Lyons*). Many young people sympathized with the new, avant-garde direction in which the chief

Beatle was going with this far-out Japanese artist. 'They are sending out feelers to explore new areas of experimental music,' wrote one enthusiast. 'Instead of taking tentative steps, like many groups, John and Yoko have gone in head first and are courageous to have done this. Although we cannot yet understand much of their music, I am sure it will be accepted in ten years' time.' Others wrote of how much they enjoyed its sound, simplicity, and emotion. Long-time Lennon observer David Stark wrote: '*Life With The Lions* is a haunting, intriguing experience. Its pure concept is so refreshing and the sadness of the music—it *is* music—just makes me happy.' As always one fan put the knife in but with humour: 'This new music by John and Yoko certainly has something to offer. It makes me appreciate my other albums much more than I did before!' John loved that. 'Tell him avant-garde is French for bullshit,' he said, laughing.

Despite his involvement in the cause for peace, John decided he had to find time, in mid-1969, to find a new home for him and Yoko and also to take her on a short holiday. Weybridge held too many memories of his old life as a trapped Beatle. So Kenwood was sold and he settled on Tittenhurst Park. The vast, thirty-roomed Georgian mansion just outside Sunningdale, Berkshire, cost John £150,000. When he went for a look at the 300-year-old house John floored the estate agent by describing its sprawling grandeur as 'functional'. Included in the estate were seventy-two acres of parkland, featuring formal gardens, a farm, cottages, outhouses, and a lodge at the entrance gates. The two-storey house had seven main bedrooms, three reception rooms, three bathrooms, a large kitchen area, and extensive staff quarters. The striking feature of Tittenhurst, which attracted John and Yoko, was its tranquillity. Only twenty-six miles from London, it offered an oasis of peace and space in which John could plan his recording studio so that no neighbours would be affected.

Just before moving in John and Yoko set off on a trip north. John had spent a year consistently telling Yoko about Aunt Mimi, his roots in Liverpool and his childhood holidays in Scotland with 'Mater', his Aunt Elizabeth.

The perfect holiday for them both would be by car. 'I took

Yoko round the streets of my youth in Liverpool and to meet all my relatives,' John said later. He also mentioned to me a vague plan to return one day to Liverpool and stage an event with Yoko at his old art college.

John kept up occasional contact with Cynthia because he felt guilt at the loss of his son, Julian, from his regular company. When he moved into Ascot John asked for Julian to be a regular weekend visitor. One weekend Yoko's daughter Kyoko was visiting her too, and the four of them set off for Liverpool and Aunt Mimi, and Durness, where Aunt Mater and Uncle Bert ran the croft where John had holidayed as a lad.

Mater gave him a cool reception. She had loved her nephew as a child, was proud of him as a Beatle with his wife and son, but the new-look John, complete with bushy, unkempt beard, biblical-length hair, a strange reputation for displaying himself in bed, and the new wife he introduced, was not so acceptable. John told her that he wanted to secure custody of Julian, then six years old. 'You've ruined all chances of that,' said Mater curtly. 'You've made your bed, now lie on it.' An angry John left, with Yoko, Julian, and Kyoko, with John driving a hired Austin Maxi saloon for the Highlands.

He was an erratic driver and his attention tended to wander. On a narrow country road not far from Mater's house at Golspie, Sutherland, he missed a bend and the car rolled over, ending up in a ditch. John was the most badly hurt and blood poured from his face. Yoko, too, had facial injuries. A passer-by called an ambulance and they were taken, with Kyoko and Julian, to hospital. John's face had seventeen stitches and Yoko fourteen. Kyoko needed four stitches, while Julian, the least affected, suffered shock.

Cynthia was astonished to hear the news of the car accident on the television news. She had no idea that John and Yoko were taking Julian on a long car journey. She phoned Peter Brown, the Beatles' assistant, and asked to be taken to the hospital so that she could bring Julian home. Unfortunately they got on a plane going to Belfast, not Scotland. Eventually, another flight from Belfast and a four-hour taxi ride later, Cynthia arrived at the cottage hospital to be told that Julian had just been sent to stay with Aunt Mater. John and Yoko did not want to see her. She set off immediately to collect Julian from Mater's and they returned to London next day.

The whole strategy behind the 'peace offensive' called for constant action. Headline hunting was, by John's admission, a key part of his philosophy. He had always felt uneasy about the Beatles' acceptance of the M.B.E. in 1965, which he thought symbolized the Beatles selling-out to the Establishment. Four years later, with the Beatles in ruins, John felt it was a good time to have the courage of his earlier convictions. He would send his medal back to the Queen and do it as a gesture for peace.

John's chauffeur, Les Anthony, was despatched from Tittenhurst to Poole, Dorset, and Aunt Mimi. She proudly kept the medal on top of her television set. 'Mr Lennon said would you lend him the M.B.E. medal for a while,' said Les Anthony when he arrived.

Says Mimi: 'I said, "Yes, but tell him, don't forget it's mine and I want it back." ' The next day she was as aghast as the rest of Britain to read that John had returned it to the Queen at Buckingham Palace, accompanied by the following letter:

Your Majesty,

    I am returning this M.B.E. in protest against Britain's involvement in the Nigeria–Biafra thing, against our support of America in Vietnam, and against 'Cold Turkey' slipping down the charts.

With love,
John Lennon of Bag

A copy was also sent to Prime Minister Harold Wilson. Reaction was immediate: it was a rare event for anyone, particularly a Beatle, to return an honour bestowed by the Queen. Cranky old Lennon hit the headlines again and achieved his purpose. He explained that he had always felt uncomfortable at receiving it; he believed the Beatles were part of the Establishment and he had accepted it because he was a Beatle. Now he was rejecting it as his right. The reason behind its return was to draw attention to his peace campaign. The mention of 'Cold Turkey', his latest record, was 'humour to stop it from sounding like it was another stupid letter to the Queen from some boring colonel'.

Aunt Mimi, furious, was on the phone immediately. 'Over my dead body would I have given you the medal back to insult the Queen with. She's just a figurehead. Why did you go and embarrass her?' John told her he meant to keep up his long protest for peace and that this was a good way. 'John, you can't worry about the whole world,' she sighed. 'It's good that you do contribute and give money but this way was so ridiculous.' John was used to Mimi's condemnations, but this time she left him in no doubt: 'He broke my heart over that. And also, he didn't tell me first why that medal was being taken away.'

Predictably irate lords and ladies, not to mention retired colonels, bellowed that what they feared all along had now been amply demonstrated by that young lout Lennon. He was a bad egg, a disgrace to the country, a mere pop idol, totally unworthy of receiving the honour in the first instance. (Although John had rejected the medal, the honour itself remained; he was still technically an M.B.E. Recipients can send back their medals but they cannot renounce an honour once it has been bestowed.)

Lord Wilson, who as prime minister had originally recommended the award to the Queen, remembers John fondly and now believes he was 'naïve' in sending his medal back. 'John Lennon lived his life from day to day,' Lord Wilson told me. 'He didn't have to look two, three, five years ahead and people in showbiz don't have to have a relationship with fifty to a hundred countries, all of whom have different ideas. The Prime Minister has got to think in terms of long-term relationships.'

Lord Wilson had no regrets over having recommended the award. 'John's rejection of it was his personal right. The award at the time shocked a great many people because the Press was mainly hostile to me. They'd spent all their time trying to keep Labour out of government. Many of them had not come to realize what the role of the Beatles in young people's lives had come to be. The award was well earned. . . . ' Many of John's critics at this time felt that he was setting a bad example to youth by his drug-taking. Lord Wilson takes a more understanding view: 'It's easy to condemn. He was living a very, very strange existence when on the platform, broadcasting, or doing music for a bit of fun. As a superb performer, he was under great strain and he would not at any cost want to fall below the performance standard he had set himself.

'It was tragic that he had to take something. I don't suppose it was necessary but a lot of people his age had a shot of it. But if he was going to do it it was a pity he didn't keep it to himself. People who worshipped the ground on which he walked would say that if he does it, it's all right, never mind what Dad and Mum say.' Resentment of John by the media, says Lord Wilson, stemmed partly from the fact that most journalists were of an older generation and 'resented the kids making all that money'. He adds: 'John Lennon used to put his hands very deep into his pockets if he heard of a good cause, and despite the lack of publicity, on which his trade sort of depends, most gifts were anonymous.'

Another aspect of John's past which reappeared in his life in that summer of 1969 was his father. Much as he often tried, John found it impossible to shake off his roots. He had never properly forgiven his father for deserting him in childhood. But his conscience and sentimentality won the day occasionally: he had for example invited Freddy Lennon to the party to launch the *Magical Mystery Tour* back in December 1967. The event, at London's Royal Lancaster Hotel, had ended with John and his father getting very drunk and dancing happily together. (John spent a lot of time chatting up women other than his wife. Singer Lulu was furious and remonstrated angrily with John for his bad behaviour.)

Relations with his father had always been strained, ever since he had reappeared in John's life during Beatlemania. In 1968 Fred had married student Pauline Jones and in the summer of 1969, John's first half-brother, David Henry Lennon, was born in Brighton. When Freddy phoned John at Tittenhurst Park to tell him his good news, John was delighted. He invited Freddy to his new home, with the child, so that he could meet

Yoko too. But when Freddy arrived, John was in a black mood and he happened to be in the firing line. 'How dare you come back into my life whenever you think you can?' roared John to his baffled father. 'You weren't around when I needed you most. Get out.' John added the final, crushing blow when he said he didn't want to see him again. Freddy, who had after all been invited, left, hurt.

That proved to be their last meeting. Freddy Lennon died, aged sixty-three, from cancer of the stomach at Brighton General Hospital on 1 April 1976. From his New York home John phoned the hospital during Freddy's illness and spoke to him, thinking back to their last ugly encounter. Over several hours of conversation he tried to instil in him the will to live. He told him of his new-born son Sean—'You can't die,' said John.

John told friends that he would have preferred to have totally resolved his relationship with his father but that obviously it was not possible. He always looked two ways at their division and his father's abdication of his responsibilities by going to sea when John was a toddler. 'Some parents,' said John, 'just can't take the responsibility of kids. I realize that now. I would like to have had a better relationship with him, but we didn't and that was OK, too. It's the way it was meant to be.' The loss of his ebullient mother, killed in a road accident, was different. He rarely spoke of her but when he thought of her tears were never far away.

The early 1970s found John and Yoko in complicated situations over Julian and Kyoko. Both their former partners were looking after their respective children but John and Yoko wanted regular contact. It proved harder to achieve than either expected.

Cynthia, with her second husband-to-be Roberto Bassanini, was so anxious to keep good relations with John and Yoko that she invited them to her housewarming party in Kensington, London. John and Yoko, Paul, George, Ringo and his wife Maureen, and Neil Aspinall all went. John had a good chat with Roberto, and Cynthia hoped she had staged a successful event. But suddenly tension developed as the Beatles recalled the factors that separated them, both professionally and as husband-and-wife teams. 'It wasn't successful,' agrees Cynthia. 'It taught me that you can't step back into the past. Too many dramatic things had happened to all of them and the break-up of the very first Beatle marriage came home to them. They were all shell-shocked after they'd been there a while. Tight, nervous, everybody watching everyone else.'

Shortly afterwards, John phoned Cynthia: 'I want to come round and see Julian.' Their son had started at a new school and John wanted to check on his progress. He spent two hours alone with Julian in his bedroom, talking and drawing with him on the six-year-old boy's blackboard. 'He was really bright, cheerful, and friendly,' says Cynthia. He gave her a book to read by an American psychologist, Dr Arthur Janov, saying it was proving a great eye-opener to him. 'Oh no,' said Cynthia to herself. 'Not another! Either it's Janov or the Maharishi or drugs and vegetarianism!' But John said he had been feeling guilty about his absence from Julian and that Janov had convinced him that he should see his son more often, alone.

Yoko's contact with Kyoko was much more complex. In December 1969 John and Yoko holidayed in Denmark with Anthony Cox, Yoko's second husband, together with his new wife, Melinda, and Kyoko. Anthony Cox pronounced John 'a great guy'. Everything looked set fair for harmonious access. But it was not to be so easy.

The issue of custody of Kyoko was never properly resolved when Yoko and Tony Cox were divorced, and Yoko expected free access to her daughter. But after an ugly experience in Majorca in 1971, when John and Yoko were detained by police for a day on suspicion of kidnapping her, Anthony Cox vanished with Kyoko. The search in Majorca had appalled John and Yoko. 'How can you kidnap your own daughter?' said Yoko. Anthony Cox's evasiveness with the eight-year-old girl was what decided John and Yoko to move to New York. They first visited there in June 1971, believing that Cox had taken the girl into the city. Courtroom appearances and visits to the Virgin Islands, plus private detectives and international publicity, never properly resolved Yoko's and John's desire for a peaceful relationship with Kyoko and Anthony Cox. But in September 1971, while they were living temporarily in Manhattan's St Regis Hotel in the hope of finding Kyoko, they decided to live permanently in America. Yoko, who knew every corner of the city in which she had grown up in the 1950s, took John walking round it, and he needed little urging to convince him that it was the right environment for an artist. John applied the same logic, and description, as he had when first seeing Tittenhurst Park. 'Yoko and I seemed to be forever coming to New York,' he explained later. 'It seemed more *functional* to come and live here.'

Two critical events preceded the emigration. In early 1970, while workmen were still re-structuring Tittenhurst to John and Yoko's specifications, Mr and Mrs Lennon began bickering. It was not surprising. For three intense years since their first meeting they had not been out of each other's sight. There was no danger of a split but every conversation was edgy. Yoko was very weary of the Apple battle and the resentful atmosphere towards her. She missed her daughter. John was tense too but he could see no way out of the forest. He was desperate to solve the Beatles' business wrangle. He buried himself in endless television, concentrating on very little except the commercials, which had always fascinated him and given him occasional lines for songs. John in a foul mood was bad news for anyone near him: he would bark or scream at the slightest intrusion into his self-imposed silence. But both he and Yoko realized the reason for their tension: 'We were close friends, twenty-four hours a day, as well as artists,' recalls Yoko. 'No relationship survives without highs and lows. It's realization of the situation that's vital.'

Luck had been a main ingredient in John's life. His childhood was marred but once he was in his teens his music and lucky breaks had been his salvation. The greatest break in helping him through this particular psychological barrier came from the book by Janov that he had tried to persuade Cynthia to read. It was called *The Primal Scream (Primal Therapy: The Cure for Neurosis)*. John was hooked as quickly as he had been on drugs and meditation. Janov's cool logic regarding the treatment of neurosis made total sense to John. Like everything he touched, he had to plunge into it at full tilt—and he could never go into something like this alone. Yoko was a quick believer too. They phoned Janov in California and invited him to Ascot. Primal therapy might well have been designed exactly for John in his state of mind at that time.

Its theory was simple. It worked on the assumption that the

patient had layers of defences which needed stripping down to reveal the real person. By owning up to fallibilities and frailties and confessing to oneself the struggle of childhood, particularly one's relationship with parents, the person who underwent therapy willingly would come face to face with his real self again, literally screaming away the pain. It was simple but in John's case, effective. Janov had his first sessions with John and Yoko over three weeks at Tittenhurst Park. Then he told them they would have to go to the Primal Institute in California to continue the course. There was no choice for John: he was deriving an enormous amount of personal strength from talking himself through the agony of his childhood and his inhibitions about his lost parents. He and Yoko stayed in California for four months, renting a house in Bel Air and plunging into what he later described to me as something 'much more important to my life than the Beatles'. He went on: 'Janov showed me how to feel my own fear and pain, therefore I can handle it better than I could before, that's all. I'm the same, only there's a channel. It doesn't just remain in me, it goes round and out.'

One of John's most endearing characteristics, honesty, was to pour out of him as a result of primal therapy. The new John sang of his childhood in heart-rending songs: in 'Mother', 'Mother you had me/But I never had you . . . Father, you left me/But I never left you.' In 'Working Class Hero' he sang of the pressures of his school years, which partly explained his outlandish behaviour; in 'Isolation', he pinpointed the dilemma of being John and Yoko: 'Just a boy and a little girl/Trying to change the whole wide world.' And in 'God' he therapeutically listed all the points of reference which his mind wanted to offload: 'I don't believe in magic . . . I don't believe in Jesus . . . I don't believe in Kennedy . . . I don't believe in kings . . . I don't believe in Elvis . . . I don't believe in Zimmerman [Bob Dylan] . . . I don't believe in Beatles/I just believe in me/Yoko and me/And that's reality.' The starkness of his confessional was searing, simple, and it made a staggering impact on those who had written off the post-Beatle Lennon as a freaky sideshow. A straight song, 'Love', demonstrated that he could easily outshine McCartney in this chosen route of romance; the poetic beauty of the song attracted Barbra Streisand who recorded her own version as did many other artists. *John Lennon/Plastic Ono Band*, with John often accompanying himself on the piano, featured Yoko, with Klaus Voormann on bass and Ringo on drums. It stands as an album many of John's contemporaries feel is one of rock's greatest works. Only Bob Dylan, with less introspective genius, can have his work compared with *Plastic Ono Band* and its successor, *Imagine,* for soul-baring intensity and such a forceful projection of intense emotions. And even Dylan never wrote so personally. The two albums, appearing in 1970 and 1971 in the wake of Dr Janov's primal therapy, were vital signposts for John's future psyche. He often described himself as a chameleon. With these two albums, he stepped outside the traditional rock 'n' roll formula to show his inner self and to prove that at least two of his old images were inadequate. Hard old Lennon, the Liverpool rocker, would no longer do. Nor would the image of the lunatic peacenik. John came of age in 1970 and 1971. A change of country, to accommodate his philosophy, seemed the natural next step.

On the eve of their final departure from British soil, John and Yoko appeared on B.B.C. television's Michael Parkinson chat show. Yoko read some excerpts from *Grapefruit*, which John praised; Parkinson described the book as incomprehensible. John retorted: 'It's so simple, it eludes you. A lot of people over here don't understand it but a lot of people in America understand it because there's a lot of avant-garde there, especially in New York, which is where she lived for ten years. A lot of people who read the book when it was published ten years ago in limited form are now professors in American universities and *Grapefruit* is part of the curriculum in film schools.'

Parkinson persisted: 'I think the creative phase that you're going through at present . . . you've got to accept, that it's alienated you, particularly John, from the people that originally loved you in this country.'

John replied, 'When I left Liverpool with the group, a lot of Liverpool people dropped us and said: "Now you've let us down." When we left England with the group to go to America, we lost a lot of fans who had begun to feel as if they owned us. Well, the Liverpool people did and they did until we decided to leave. The same in England, a lot of people dropped us because we went to America. But of course we got a whole pile more, a different audience. And it's the same now. I'm not going to sort of gear my life just to attract an audience. I started off playing music because that's what I wanted to do. And in front of an audience is how you do it. And now it's not very different. I mean, then I sang "All You Need Is Love", and now I might sing "Power To The People". And the message is basically the same. It's just sort of slogans. The alienation started when I met Yoko; people do not seem to like people getting a divorce, you know. It's all right to do it quietly but we can't do it quietly. So we fell in love and it's unfortunate! We fell in love and we married. A lot of people think that to be odd, but it happens all the time. Yoko just happened to be Japanese which didn't help much. And so everybody had this impression that John's gone crazy. All I did was fall in love like a lot of people do who are already married, who married somebody very young, and that's all we did. I know we did *Two Virgins* which didn't help much!'

Yoko added, 'I'd be a masochist if I loved this country, where I'm constantly abused. It's a bit tough on me, you know.'

Parkinson responded: 'Another reason for people taking a dislike of you is because you've become known, again through the newspapers in this country, as the woman who broke up the Beatles. But that's not true?'

'That's not true,' John answered. 'Listen, I'll tell you. People on the street and kids do not dislike us. It's the media. We go on the street and lorry drivers wave and say, "Hello, Yoko, hello, John," and all that jazz. I judge it by that. . . . Nobody could break the Beatles up. We broke ourselves up. When Brian [Epstein] died we got a bit lost because we needed a manager, all of us are artists and we're nothing else. We can't manage ourselves or look after ourselves in that way. But it's a lot for four big heads like the Beatles to stay together for such a long time. In the early days there was the thing of "making it" big, or breaking into America and we had that goal together . . . but when we reached twenty-eight or twenty-nine . . . our personalities developed and they were a bit stifled with the Beatles. And between us now we sell ten times more records than the Beatles did.' This was not true and, typically, John said it to demonstrate a point rather than accept the facts.

By the end of 1970 sales of Beatles records totalled approximately 500 million units worldwide. The *Guinness Book of Records* states that between February 1963 and January 1972 the Beatles sold 545 million records. In the period January 1963 to August 1966 when they ceased to tour, the estimated international attendance at Beatles concerts was 2,676,000. The four Beatles as soloists (taken either separately or together) did not fill anything like that number of seats, nor sell anything like that number of records.

Michael Parkinson asked John how deep the hurt was between him and Paul McCartney. 'It's fairly deep,' John replied. 'We're playing Monopoly now with real money and so it's pretty serious. But I can't see it lasting and I think it'll probably cool off. It'll take a year after the whole thing is settled, moneywise, probably for us to relax a bit.'

Getting immersed in the spirit of things, Parkinson got inside a bag in the studio while he questioned John and Yoko. 'Hey,' said John, 'imagine if a black guy went for a job at the B.B.C. and he had to wear a bag. They wouldn't know what coloured people were and there'd be no prejudice, for a kick-off!'

Staying on the theme of the bag and relating it to the Beatles, John continued: 'There's no conceivable reason why the Beatles should come back together again because we're all individuals and in the Beatles we grew out of it. The bag was too small. I can't impose far-out music and far-out films on George and Paul if they don't want to do it. We have to live our lives separately. We've grown up now. We've left school. We never *left* school. We went straight into showbiz.'

Yoko interjected: 'Michael, this is a typical example. We are so nostalgic and we're talking about the past. But we have to live in the present. You can burn the past. That's why even in this book, *Grapefruit*, I'd like people to burn it after they've read it.'

John said finally: 'There's a beautiful story Yoko told me about a Japanese monk, which happened within the last ten years. He loved this fantastic golden temple so much that he didn't want to see it disintegrate. So he burned it . . . that is what I did with the Beatles. I never wanted them to slide down, making comebacks. I said when I was twenty in the Beatles:

"I'm not going to be singing 'She Loves You' when I'm thirty." '
John had a fine memory for generalization but a terrible rec-
ollection of details. The interview he was referring to was with
me for the *Melody Maker* on 24 October 1964. He had actually
said: 'I don't want to be fiddling round the world singing "It's
Been A Hard Day's Night" when I'm thirty, do I? I said during
a conversation with Mick Jagger that I'd be out of it in a few
years. I enjoy playing really but in America it was spoiled for
me because of the crap there . . . meeting people we don't
want to meet. I suppose I'm a bit intolerant'. 'Well, I was
thirty this year *[sic]*. I didn't force it to happen this year. It
just happened naturally.

'I guessed that by the time I was thirty I would have grown
out of it. And I have, you know. And the guy burned the
temple. And most people still like the Beatles and have a
pleasant memory of them . . . let's remember them like that
and remember their music like we remember people from the
past. That's fine.'

British singer George Melly, whose clash with John over
his musical roots is discussed in Chapter 13 of this biography,
met a very different ex-Beatle in the television show. (Melly
was on the same Parkinson programme.) 'We had a very nice
talk this time,' says Melly. 'Not very productive because it
was difficult to understand what they were getting at, exactly,
except for peace and love. But their gentleness and affection
for each other was very, very powerful. I really felt warm to
them because I didn't expect to. They irritated me with their
bagism and the fact that they were very rich and constantly
making humble gestures. If only the acorns had done some
good or the bagism had persuaded people to be peaceful. But
it just irritated most people and I felt it wasn't very useful.
Together, though, she with her dreamy beads and long hair,
he with long hair and granny glasses, and both holding hands
constantly, they were charming, childlike.' Contrasting vividly
with the drunken John who had seven years earlier berated
Melly at a publisher's party, he was warm and polite.

'There you are, you see, Yoko,' John said, when they came
to leave Melly. 'There *are* nice people in England.'

19
CHANGE

'My function in society is to be an artist'

John firmly believed in the adage that the best method of defence is attack. In the late 1960s, when he had married Yoko and taken a battering from both the Press and public opinion about their liaison and 'stunts for peace', John countered with some of his most forceful interviews. He still loved talking, particularly about himself: One of his strongest lines of defence of his publicly declared love for Yoko was that they were doing the Establishment a favour by making marriage fashionable against all the odds.

Talking to the new, post-Beatle Lennon, one encountered the man as he had originally been in Liverpool: in a hurry, warm and generous, full of invective, incurably idealistic. Between his marriage to Yoko in 1969 and their move to New York in 1971 I had many interviews with him, covering a wide range of topics. He said to me in 1969: 'Go on—ask me some questions that will get on the front page of the dailies. I'm not a moptop any more. I can say what I like!'

His ego was always big, but he said that he would rather have a following that did not seek his autograph. 'If kids want my signature and I'm in the right mood and it's the right person, they can have it. But it depends on the person who asks.' Living with Yoko had changed his outlook: there was nothing he had, materially, that he could not do without, now that he had found inner peace. 'I'm glad to have got the pop star thing out of the way. It was good and it gave me this freedom. But we grew up, grew apart.' He always firmly declared that the Beatles did not set any trends. 'We never did start anything. We were just part of the whole sixties thing, the movement, the fashion, the change in attitude among a load of people. The Beatles were just in the middle of it.'

Because of his nudity on the *Two Virgins* album cover, John said people thought of him as 'a perverted crank. They think Yoko and I are ravers, only interested in sex and causing a stir. But really, we're the quietest pair of spinsters around.' He was a vegetarian, and Yoko usually baked their bread. He wanted a farm so that they could grow their own macrobiotic food. 'It works like Zen Buddhism or meditation—you eat what you think's best for you and it's commonsense to me that you shouldn't eat most of the chemically treated rubbish most people seem to stuff themselves with. The trouble is most vegetarians don't get enough protein. My diet's based on meal, bread which Yoko makes, rice and no sugar. We have honey if anything needs sweetening.' But he wore leather shoes, I pointed out. 'I still wear the shoes I had before I changed my views. I don't see the point of not using them. I won't buy any more leather ones, though. I'm always wearing sneakers. I don't think animals were meant to be eaten and worn. We have enough resources to do without them. But it's big business again, you see.' Did he feel better, I asked him, since giving up meat? 'Yeah, but a car can last a long time on the wrong petrol. One day it packs up. I feel better mentally but maybe my diet's not right for everyone.'

He told me the best thing to come out of the Beatles was the power it gave him to do other things from a platform people would notice. 'I'm using my power all the time by doing things like releasing an album called *Two Virgins*. There are generation gaps and other gaps, plenty of them, in this world and they all need closing. I'm trying to open people's minds. There's nothing horrible about nudity. People said the Rolling Stones, and Elvis, and long hair were all obscene but they accepted them in the end. I hope it's the same with my scene. A lot of narrow minds need expanding. People say I offend "normal" people. . . . Society's full of people who think of themselves as normal, who aren't. It's as wrong as judging me as a hippy because I happen to have long hair. It's more what a man's scene is in his mind than how he looks or what he wears. You can be a pretty cool bin man.'

He believed in religion and had not regarded the Maharishi as a substitute for it. 'The Maharishi was good for me, like anybody who has something to tell you that you don't know enough about. He was no substitute for anything, though. There's a lot of good in Christianity but you've got to learn the basics of it, and the basics from the Eastern beliefs, and work them together for yourself. . . . Yoko and I are fighting a bit of a fight to spread understanding and a kind of freedom. I don't expect everybody to understand us but I just wish they'd try to be a bit more open-minded, that's all. Beatles wives always had a hard time, probably because the fans resented us marrying. I got more stick because I was the loud-mouth—and then I went and got meself a new wife without asking permission. And a Japanese one at that! It's "How dare Lennon go off with this woman who's not a housewife?" ' They were hurt by a lot of anti-Japanese mail.

He pointed out that he wanted to use power constructively. 'When we say, "War is over, if you want it", we mean that if everybody demanded peace instead of another television set, there'd be peace. If you like, we're the Tolpuddle Martyrs of our day. People said the first trade union leaders were fighting a losing battle, but when people realized what they could achieve by banding together and demanding their rights, they got it. It's a communal thing. Everybody has power, not just John and Yoko. We want to spread awareness.' In himself he was striving for perfection but doubted if he would achieve it. 'I'd like to be like Christ.' He described himself as a Christian communist, 'in a pure sense, not in the way Russia or Italy think of Christianity or communism.'

He consistently denied that he wanted to be seen as a leader. 'I'm not falling for that one. Like Pete Seeger said, we don't have a leader, but we have a song, "Give Peace A Chance". I refuse to be a leader. . . . Our whole mistake is having leaders and people we can rely on or point a finger at.'

Yoko often took up a point during the interviews. 'For instance,' she said, 'many people say . . . don't do anything that is misleading, like showing your genitals. Always keep a clean image so that people can believe in your peace movement.

'But that's exactly what the Establishment is doing ['And that's what the Beatles did, too,' said John], taking their children to church on Sundays. This is showing that "I'm the President of the United States and I'm all right and I'm healthy and very moral et cetera." You don't get anywhere that way. You just become another hypocrite and you're playing the Establishment game. We don't want to do that. We try to be honest and the point is, if we are really honest, just to make it between us is really a lifetime thing. And if we can't make it together and endure each other the world is nowhere.

'If ordinary couples can make it together and make it with their children and so forth, love-wise ['She doesn't mean "make it" as in "lay",' interjected John], then you can look after the world.'

John said: 'One thing we've found out is that love is a great gift, like a precious flower or something.' He often harkened back to romantic analogies. 'You have to feed it and look after it and it has storms to go through, and snow, but you have to protect it. . . . It's like a pet cat. You know, people get a cat and they don't want to feed it, or they get a dog and they won't want to walk it. But love has to be nurtured like a very sensitive animal because that's what it is. And you have to work at love. You don't just sit round with it and it doesn't just do it for you. You've got to be very careful with it. It's the most delicate thing you can be given.'

'People hide from each other all the time,' he continued. 'Everybody's frightened of saying something nice about somebody in case they don't say something nice back or in case they get hurt. . . . Everybody's uptight and they're always building these walls around themselves. All you can do is try and break down the walls and show that there's nothing there but *people*. It's just like looking in the mirror. . . . Of course we mustn't take ourselves too seriously. What we try and do is be non-serious about things but we are very serious about being not serious!'

Yoko said: 'We may be too serious, even. We try to have a sense of humour and to smile at everyone, a really genuine smile from the bottom of our hearts.'

John's laconic humour always permeated his work, even at a peak of his peace campaign with Yoko. To a circle of friends at Christmas in 1969, he sent a dry, hilarious item called 'The John Lennon London Diary 1969'. He had handwritten an entry for each day. Most were a very slight variation on the same words: 'Got up, went to work, came home, watched telly, went to bed.' It was a beautiful parody of the routine of life. But, like John, it was unpredictable: forgetfulness and boredom set in as he continued and one or two entries read: 'Got up, went to work, came home, watched telly, went to bed, fucked the wife,' for example. It was reassuring for some to know that Lennon's wit was still intact, come drugs, bagism or peace.

Demonstrative humour was more difficult for Yoko. Critics constantly jibed at her expressionless demeanour. In truth she has a cool, subterranean sense of humour. Her smiles are few because, as a child, her mother warned her against too much smiling lest it be construed by people as a sign of weakness.

The theory that Yoko's inscrutability had vanquished John's sense of fun was knocked firmly aside when they released a 1970 calendar which, month-by-month, captured in photographs their lives together. The calendar featured excerpts from his songs, his writings in *A Spaniard In The Works* and *In His Own Write*, plus quotations from *Grapefruit*. John set off the calendar with this original piece, demonstrating that his gobble-degook type of wit was still intact:

> wonsaapoatime therewas two Balloons called Jock and Yono. They were strictly in love-bound to happen in a million years. They werer together man. Unfortunatime-table they both seemed to have previous experience—which kept calling them one way oranother. (you know howitis). But they battled on against overwhelming odd-ities, includo some of there beast friends. . . . Being in love they cloong even the more together man—but some of the poisonessmonster of outrated busloded-shithrowers did stick slightly and they occasionally had to resort to the drycleaners. Luckily this did not kill them and they werent banned from the olympic games. They lived hopefully ever after, and who could blame them.

Paradoxically, it was John, rather than Yoko, who wholeheartedly publicly championed the cause of women's liberation once he had met her in the early seventies. Len Wood of E.M.I. Records recalls a visit to the Apple office at Broadway, New York, which had to be cut short. 'Yoko was going to a rally for women's rights, but she was most insistent that John should be the only male there,' says Wood. She was on the phone for ages impressing on these women that if they banned her husband from attending the rally, that would be a kind of reverse bigotry; she won her case and John attended. And on her striking double album, called *Approximately Infinite Universe*, she satirized the women's liberation movement with a song called 'What A Bastard The World Is'. 'So they would scream and kick out all the men? *Then* what are they going to do?' asked Yoko. 'I told John, and he agreed, that feminism involves men too. John helped the movement towards equality more by *doing* something, like house-husbandry, than a million people demonstrating for it. . . . Initially, feminists thought that the fact that I was married was a betrayal of the whole idea. As for the idea of really *loving* John, and saying so— *loving a man*, what was *this*? I wrote a song called "I Want My Man To Rest Tonight", which was addressed to my feminist sisters and said: let's not blame our men too much. They are doing their best. That was sniggered at. But I think in a male chauvinist society it was just as difficult for men too. They had to adjust. The reason I did not become an extreme feminist was a lot to do with living with John. He was a good influence.'

Reflecting on her early years in London, Yoko says: 'I was getting sick and tired of the pseudo-intellectual, elitist atmosphere of the circle I was in in London. I was thinking: Am I going to end up as the Queen Mother of the avant-garde world, always meeting these snobs talking about elitist kicks? I was starting to feel frightened.

'When I started to make the bottoms film I became very known in England in a strange sort of way—like to taxi drivers, that sort of thing—and my elite friends were so very upset about that. They were saying: "Well, she copped out, she went commercial."

'I said: "It's great to communicate your art with the working class. What *is* this?'' But all the same they stopped inviting me to their tea party; just sort of inverted snobbery.

'Around this time I met John. The first song we recorded on *Approximately Infinite Universe* was ''Song for John''. It was a song I made actually before I met him. I was hoping to find somebody who'd fly with me, or whatever, and I made a demo record. It's the first demo of mine that John listened to when he visited me and that's why, for sentimental reasons, I called it ''Song for John''. It's the same tune, same lyrics.'

The Lennons at home were much more traditional as husband and wife than their public face indicated. 'There's nothing I like more,' John told the *Melody Maker*, 'than to get home at the end of the day and sit next to Yoko and say, ''Well, we're together at last.'' Although we may have been holding hands all day, it's not the same when we're working or talking to the Press. We feel a hundred miles apart by comparison.'

Yoko confessed that she was lonely before she met John. 'Most people in the world are very lonely. That's the biggest problem,' she said. 'Because of their loneliness, they become suspicious. When I met John I started to open up a little, through love, you know, and that's the greatest thing that happened to me yet. . . . I never met anybody else who could understand me. We understand each other so well and I'm not lonely any more. Through loneliness, I was starting to become a very firm and strong ego. That's melting away and that's nice.'

John described his pre-Yoko loneliness this way: 'I didn't have full communication with anybody and it took a bit of adjusting. She re-discovered or cultivated the thing that existed in me before I left Liverpool, maybe, and re-cultivated the natural John Lennon that had been lost in the Beatles thing and the world-wide thing. She encouraged me to be myself because it was me she fell in love with, not the Beatles or whatever I was.

'When you get sidetracked you believe it, and when you're in the dark you believe it. She came and reminded me that there was light and when you remember there's light you don't want to get back in the dark again.'

Yoko continued: 'It's the falling in love bit. You start to see all sorts of things that you don't see if you're not in love. I found that he has all these qualities that he was hiding away.

Music-wise, he was doing all sorts of freaky things at home, just recording it on a cassette, but not really showing it publicly.

'Publicly he was doing the Beatles things. But he showed me all these cassettes and things and I said: "Why don't you produce these as records?" I performed the role of a mirror in a way. He was doing all those things anyway. I didn't suggest them. It was there and that goes for his drawing, paintings, and poetry too, especially his drawings. I think he's better than Picasso.'

John stopped her: 'She's biased!'

On another visit to Ascot, John particularly wanted to talk to me about his rationale behind the peace crusade. How exactly did they seek to make the world more peaceful? I wanted to know. What would John do, for instance, if he was elected prime minister?

'I'd stop selling arms to Nigeria and all that. I'd get rid of the army and the air force and become a Sweden. I'm not a practical guy, I only know peace can exist, and the first thing is for the world to disarm.

'But would I have enough power, as a prime minister, to do this? How much control does Wilson have? What chance would a peacenik prime minister have? I don't know. I just know things are not very good now and it must be worth a try.'

Life with the Lennons down at Ascot was a communal affair: members of the Krishna Consciousness Society hung around and John and Yoko would join them in their chanting. The Lennons liked this scene: it appealed to John's ideas of 'mixing with the people'. He was philosophical and decisive in his attitude to his wealth.

'You don't have to be poor to be a communist,' he said, laughing. 'My money that was earned as a Beatle, it's almost a by-product. I'm not just going to give it all away to some people, just so that I can starve like a lot of others. What's *that* going to achieve?

'But the money doesn't give me any hang-ups. . . . Both Yoko and I have this dream of living in a small cottage in the country, eventually. But we ended up with this big Georgian house. Now we're going through this big house scene before moving on.'

'But for the moment we enjoy it,' said Yoko passively.

John said that he got more pleasure from old 78 records than from revelling in the size and glory of his home. 'It means nothing to me,' he declared. 'A little bit of ivory I bought in Japan, that's my grossest material possession which I like as much as anything.'

'Material pleasures are all right as long as they don't clog your mind,' observed Yoko.

'I wouldn't worry,' John said, 'if I never had a thing. If it took too much to carry on living in this big house I wouldn't want to stay and live here . . . but I'm hoping to farm some of the land. The Krishna people are helping me do this. . . . We're hoping to grow non-chemical food—maybe we can sell it to Harrods.'

He reflected on the Beatles' touring days like this: 'Those old tours were OK at the time but once we had taken over from Helen Shapiro, there was nothing else to do, except for us to go around and other people to see us standing there, doing the same songs and not hearing a note.

'The Stones seemed to get a good thing in Hyde Park but it's different for us. We're not that type. Jagger is the Charlie Chaplin of rock and roll—it's OK for Mick because he's dancing around like a puppet and putting on a show. We don't. We couldn't stand the shell of unreality, standing there like four dolls in the middle of Shea Stadium. It killed our music.

'But when I see a group like The Band playing, I think we should have got going again before now.'

Did he, I asked, think the Plastic Ono Band would survive as long as or longer than the Beatles? He dodged the answer with some facts: 'I think it will survive—you know my records with Yoko and the Plastic Ono have sold well. We sold twenty-five thousand copies of *Two Virgins* in the States and sixty thousand of *Life With the Lions*. That's good going in the States.

'Our new album, *John and Yoko's Wedding Album* is going to sell as well. But in Britain we only sold about five thousand of each of those albums. I can understand that though.

'See, Americans like our albums because if you land in New York, it's like *Life With The Lions* anyway. If you play it in Britain, it doesn't have the same urgency, because of the environment. It'll be a few years before they turn on to that sort of thing properly here.'

'But we are patient,' said Yoko, 'because we are doing something worthwhile.'

John summarized the division between himself and the Beatles: 'I am an artist and my art is peace and I happen to be a musician. My music is done with the Beatles—that's where I get my wages from. The peace thing isn't a gimmick. Other people make it a gimmick. Yoko and I are serious.'

He clearly believed passionately in the peace campaign. 'It's the goodies and the baddies, the Blue Meanies, and the rest. I think I'll win because I believe in what Jesus said.'

Drawing on his Gitanes cigarettes in the Apple office, John devoured newspapers with an intensity that floored those who worked with him. He surprised the Apple team by his contradiction of his own image. The tough-talking Beatle was replaced, with Yoko at his side, by a man who was funny, gentle, and kind but nobody's fool. He strutted down the corridors, hands on hips. Gradually it was conceded that their partnership was impregnable, their message pure and sincere. It took time though and probably only sank in when Apple turned sour, the Beatles were officially pronounced dead, and John and Yoko had moved on to the next phase of their lives.

But for three years, for every success John counted there were people with trip wires, testing him. John enjoyed the challenge; some of his finest eloquence came during self-justification.

The 'Smile' box was a favourite way of getting the conversation going. It was a box which you had to open and inside it was a mirror which told the truth about your expression. The box, concocted by John and Yoko, kept many baffled and bemused because it had no message other than how the 'viewer' reacted. This, John would repeat to anyone, was Art with a capital A. Yoko described it as 'con art', which was short for conceptual art; meaning that the idea behind the piece was more important than the exhibit. John described Yoko as 'straight from Duchamp and Dada, but she's Now'. As a book he said, *Grapefruit* stood alongside the Bible.

As a film maker he was definitely interested in the avant-garde and art. Two films took up his time in 1970: *Apotheosis* followed on from *Self Portrait*, and *Erection* followed on from *Rape*. *Apotheosis* featured a balloon taking off from a snowy field in an English village and climbing into the clouds. The soundtrack is the fading noise of barking dogs, a hunting horn, and a gun being fired. When the balloon reaches the clouds, silence reigns for five minutes. The onus is on the viewer to interpret. The same is true of *Erection*: this film, made over nine months, depicts a hotel being erected in London's West Cromwell Road. The bizarre touch is the inactivity and slow progress made by the builders.

Art possessed John by the time he and Yoko made plans to go to live in America. He reflected on what they had achieved since 'going public'. The Amsterdam bed-in, he considered, was one of the greatest happenings of the century. Not because of what they had done but because of people's reactions: it was illogical, *marvellous*, that they hit the headlines just by getting married and going to bed to ask for peace. It was an Event. Communication, he intoned, was everything. 'The English are eccentrics. I'm just another one from a long line of eccentrics.'

He thought advertising their art was not reprehensible, rather a clear duty. People who believed they were stunts were naïve. 'Andy Warhol—the biggest publicity man in the world! Salvador Dali! Or Duchamp!' All artists struggled for publicity if they knew what they had to do, he said.

He was a revolutionary artist and he'd been consistent, right from 'All You Need Is Love' to 'Power To The People'. He was dedicated to change and to revolution in forcing people to think and react positively. Art for art's sake was decadent; he was writing songs for people to express themselves with. For example, at concerts in America, 30,000 people had sung 'Give Peace A Chance', and 20,000 were singing 'Power To The People' on the streets. Use of art for propaganda was totally right. To deny that was 'like saying, don't make knives in case you kill with them'.

He wrote songs for himself, primarily. 'You can't blame me or the song. I'm not here to provide power to the people: I'm *singin'* about it. I'm the songwriter who sang the song about it that the people sang at the meetings they held. That's all. That's my job. Like, if we're a community on an island, I'd be the singer. Somebody would be the carpenter, somebody else would be the cook. My function in society is to be an artist.

'You see,' he went on, 'society is under the delusion that art is something you have extra, like crème de menthe or something. But societies don't exist with no artist. Art is a functional part of society: if you don't have artists you don't have society. We're not some kind of decadent strip show that appears on the side. We're as important as prime ministers or policemen. So "Power To The People" isn't expected to make a revolution. It's for the people to sing, like the Christians sing hymns.'

He liked slogans, he continued. 'I like advertising. I love the telly.' He hated classical music; it was too slow. 'It's "then" music. It really is a load of crap. I think I write much more relevant music for today than the classical composers. . . . And where's today's classical music? There isn't any.'

His song 'Instant Karma!' was much more important than most of the classical music he had heard. 'It's about human beings, which is more than can be said for the classics. "Instant Karma!" is about action and reaction. Whenever you do something, whatever it is, there's a reaction to it. Even if you cough, you cough germs out all over the place. If you cough love out, out goes love. That's what "Instant Karma!" is—it's a great step forward. The greatest artists always come round to simplicity. It took Picasso sixty years to go through the whole bit and learn to paint like a child. I hope to record and write songs like an adult child.'

He was always at his most vociferous on the subject of peace. 'I'm not under any illusion. My contribution will be small in the light of the universe. Compared with the size of the earth, what John and Yoko achieve will be small, but it's the best we can manage. It takes time to be taken seriously. It took the Beatles time and then they were taken too seriously sometimes.' Yes, he agreed, the peace campaign was costing him a fortune, 'but you reap what you sow. Whatever you do, you get something back for it.'

I asked him why he equated himself with Christ so frequently during this period of self-revelation. 'I was brought up a Christian, Sunday School and all that. It's OK, I have nothing against it except that it organizes itself as a business, the Church. What I do like about it is that Christians talk about being perfect; so was Christ and I was taught that as a child. Christ is the one who most people in the West refer to when they speak of good people. . . . If I could do what Christ did, be as Christ was, that's what being a Christian is all about. I try to live as Christ lived. It's tough, I can tell you.'

Did he believe in God? 'I don't know that anyone like me, who questions everything down to the colour of his socks, can believe in an old man in the sky.' He was very thoughtful and silent for several minutes. 'I believe in something, definitely. I believe there is a force at work that you can't physically account for.'

During talks like these John would often stop himself from getting carried away or sounding portentous. 'Hey,' he would say. 'My Auntie Mimi says I sound too serious when I go on like this. She also reckons that having my hair cut short like this has turned me into a skinhead. Mimi—I'm happier now than I've ever been!'

John and Yoko's unique partnership derived partly from the great difference in their backgrounds. 'She had hardly heard of the music that turned me on, like Elvis and "Heartbreak Hotel". I had all that to get through to her,' he explained. She gave John new insights into art. What constantly surprised them both was how, almost five years after first meeting, on the eve of their departure from London to New York, they could not get enough of each other's company. 'Her and Elvis, they both turned me on most in my life. They're the greatest influences. It's a miracle. We're more in love than ever,' he said. By then Yoko had suffered three miscarriages. John worried that they were his fault, that his heavy use of drugs had made him either infertile or had a bad effect on Yoko's body. 'John needs to rest,' said Yoko just before they left for America. 'No drugs except tobacco, and I've been off that for a year too.'

Their togetherness was precisely what alienated many people who considered them 'over the top' in mawkish sentimentality. 'People say that if we're together twenty-four hours a day, we must get sick and tired of each other but it's the contrary,' said Yoko. 'We got so addicted to that situation that we miss each other more. It's a very strange scene.'

John weighed in: 'Somebody said: "Won't you get so reliant on each other that you can't manage without each other?" and we said yes! The only thing that could split us is death and we have to face that . . . and we don't even believe we'll be split then, if we work on it.

'Our only worry in the world is that we die together, otherwise even if it's three minutes later it's going to be hell. . . . Most marriages have a little pretence going on and we thought: are we going to have to pretend that we're happy together because we daren't say that we want to be apart? But that doesn't happen. When two of you are together, man and wife, there's nothing that can touch you. You have the power of two people, the power of two minds, which is a pretty powerful thing.'

20
THE MUSIC:
1966–1971

'Let me take you down 'cos I'm going to . . .'

From 'Strawberry Fields Forever' through to 'Imagine', John Lennon's work, in and out of the Beatles, was distinct and highly personalized. While Paul McCartney's gift lay in composing love songs, John was incapable of songwriting as a craftsman, 'for other people'. None the less, he admired some less syrupy McCartney compositions, particularly 'Here There And Everywhere' and 'For No One.' Conversely, the extrovert McCartney found it hard to write about himself. In that, John Lennon excelled. For although he loved the speed of rock 'n' roll, he thought the golden oldies of that genre were unbeatable; his own writing would have to act as a mirror of his personality, particularly as he grew older and more observant, and wanted more from life than teenagers screaming his name. At twenty-six, John wanted his music to express the important things in his life: his childhood memories; his assiduous reading of newspapers and magazines; his love of words and sharp observation of the unexpected phrase; his own frailties and rejection of the tough-guy Beatle image; and an increasing interest in humanitarianism.

During his life Lennon had demystified rock 'n' roll, which he believed was conceptually the best form of communication through music. As an artist he had been vulnerable, idealistic, and a worrier, lapsing into a frequent insecure dissection of who-wrote-what in the Lennon–McCartney songs. He was never totally able to stand back sufficiently from his own songs and accept their social impact. What he did, inside the Beatles, long after they split, and even when he was dead, was to inject his unique personal experiences into popular music.

Often described as the best-ever pop single, 'Strawberry Fields Forever' released in 1967, marked the start of the vital change in John's music. It was attributable to several factors: his meeting with Yoko at the end of 1966; his disillusionment with the Beatles myth; his use of drugs; and the important influence of Bob Dylan who led the way in putting *himself* into his songs.

Strawberry Field was a real place, a Salvation Army home just down the road from Aunt Mimi's in Woolton. It was a special place where she sometimes took him for ice-cream cornets and garden fetes. John enjoyed his childhood memories: 'Nothing is real/And nothing to get hungabout. . . .' It was Lennon in wonderland, re-creating the era of childhood simplicity when he knew he was happy.

Musically it invoked the very spirit of psychedelia raging that year. To get the required dreamy effect of trees, fields, and escapism, Lennon and producer George Martin spliced together two quite different versions of the song. It was a superb piece of technical editing by Martin and conjured up perfectly the ethereal feeling of the lyrics. From 'Strawberry Fields' onwards it was a one-way ticket for John: his music would be more incisive, more personal, more reflective, and more adventurous.

John's public persona became more intimidating from 1967. His droopy moustache gave him a sombre, almost sinister look, and sometimes, when he was under the influence of drugs, he wore a manic leer. With his hair cut short, his confidence was now apparent: so much so that he now wore his glasses in public.

The genius of John's writing was first captured on *Sgt Pepper's Lonely Hearts Club Band* with the songs 'A Day In The Life' and 'Lucy In The Sky With Diamonds'. *Sgt Pepper* marked rock music's coming of age, its scope and intention resulting in critical respectability. John's input on it showed that rock 'n' roll had come a long way since Elvis Presley's first recording sessions thirteen years before. It was prime 'pop art', seminal psychedelia. It also marked the apogee of studio technology at the time: four-track machines, Mellotrons, and forty-one-piece orchestras. Six months in the making, the cost was enormous—£25,000. Just to have the album was to be part of a special world, with the jokes on the run-out grooves, the note for the family dog, the badges and cut-outs, the coloured inner sleeve, the pretty pictures, and lyrics printed for the first time on a rock album.

The original idea behind the album was that it should be a concept L.P.: a memory of a day in the life of Liverpool children (which was to have included both 'Penny Lane' and 'Strawberry Fields'). A double album, evoking lost innocence, adolescence, and maturity. But *Sgt Pepper* grew and grew and the original plan disappeared (although vestiges were retained with 'A Day In The Life' and 'When I'm Sixty-Four'). In its place came an album that broke new ground with the segueing of tracks, the lyrical obtuseness, the rich production, and lavish instrumentation.

The material on the album was culled from various sources: 'When I'm Sixty-Four' even went back to Liverpool in the late fifties. Lennon collaborated with McCartney on this song, adding the memorable names 'Vera, Chuck and Dave'. He also threw in the caustic: 'What do you see when you turn out the light/I can't tell you but I know it's mine', to Paul's 'With A Little Help From My Friends'.

In 'Lucy In The Sky With Diamonds' Lennon immersed himself in the fantasy world of Lewis Carroll. It is a vivid, colourful world. Just 'Climb in the back with your head in the clouds/And you're gone!' The girl 'with kaleidoscope eyes' represents some sort of salvation but it is transitory and you're back, forever caught in that marshmallow world of dreams and fantasy.

'Getting Better' was John continuing to obviate his guilt about the women in his life, coming to terms with it directly, following on from the oblique inferences in 'Norwegian Wood'. Although 'Getting Better' is generally considered a McCartney song, and Paul certainly had the germ of the idea in the studio, John contributed some crucial, highly personal words. It was a classic example of how they helped each other in their writing.

I used to be cruel to my woman
I beat her and kept her apart from the things she loved
Man I was mean but I'm changing my scene
And I'm doing the best that I can

It was an indication of how he had mellowed; the guilt was apparent and made public. 'I was a hitter,' John explained later. 'I couldn't express myself and I hit. I fought men and I hit women. That is why I am always on about peace. It is the most violent people who go for love and peace. I am a violent man who has learned not to be violent and regret his violence. I will have to be a lot older before I can face in public how I treated women as a youngster,' he told David Sheff in *Playboy* magazine in 1980.

'Being For The Benefit Of Mr Kite!' was taken straight from an antique circus poster, which John transposed—in conjunction with George Martin's imaginative tape loops and cutups—into a beguiling cameo. 'Good Morning Good Morning' was a throwaway, inspired by a Kellogg's cornflakes television advert, which was on in the background while Lennon was in a vaguely 'writing' mood. John's songs for *Sgt Pepper*, while technically superior to anything he had yet attempted, were pillaged from the usual random sources: circus posters, advertisements, and newspaper cuttings.

The album's supreme achievement is still the massive 'A Day In The Life'. Again Lennon culled the song from disparate sources—newspaper headlines, his filming of *How I Won The War* in Spain in 1966, and snatches of conversation. Paul's middle eight slotted neatly into the scenario. After hearing the words 'went upstairs and had a smoke', the B.B.C. screamed 'drugs' and promptly banned the song. Lennon's jaundiced vocal is perfectly suited to the distanced picture of a man seated, 'read[ing] the news today', and from that preface the song unfolds. The seemingly random flow ends with the enigmatic line which was inspired by a friend: 'Now they know how many holes it takes to fill the Albert Hall.' 'A Day In The Life' marked the pinnacle of the Beatles' recorded output. It tested George Martin's abilities to breaking-point, in his having to encourage a classical orchestra to 'freak out', and to come up with an arrangement that sounded like 'the end of the world', sustaining the final note for forty-two seconds.

George Martin translated the impossible into sensational reality. The cumulative effect of the album was devastating. After playing it for the first time there was no choice but go right back to the beginning again, rather than—as had been the way with previous Beatle records—searching out individual tracks. The depth and variety of the album led to acts as diverse as Joe Brown and Joe Cocker covering songs from it.

At the time the scope and flair of *Sgt Pepper* ensured that it stood alone, the very zenith of rock 'n' roll. It ushered in the prime era of English psychedelia, which others were still trying to equal well into the eighties.

The scope and triumph of the album gave John even greater impetus. Barely had the dust settled than the Beatles were back within a month with a new single. John's composition 'All You Need Is Love' was premièred on the global *Our World* T.V. show. (It was a mark of the Beatles' position by then that they were chosen as Britain's representatives for this prestigious satellite link-up.) Four hundred million people saw the group première the anthem of the Love Generation; it took the Beatles to set the seal of acceptability on the hippy movement—although in truth it had already begun to burn itself out in Haight Ashbury, San Francisco by the time the single was released. Hearing it now is like activating a museum piece, but then, all those years ago, there were enough people who believed that all you needed *was* love and that entry into Shangri La was gained simply by wearing flowers in your hair.

On the finished single, just as it is fading, Lennon can be heard singing a cheerfully distorted 'She Loves You', as though publicly burying the Beatles legacy. The single's B-side was 'Baby, You're A Rich Man', a question-and-answer song, which Lennon originally viciously 'dedicated' to Brian Epstein as 'Baby, You're A Rich Fag Jew'. 'How does it feel to be one of the beautiful people?' asked Lennon, a question millions asked of him. Like many other songs of the period it was a combination of two quite different songs: McCartney had the title and some odd lines in his head while Lennon supplied the questions.

And there was still more to come. 'Hello, Goodbye' was

the final Beatles single of 1967. It was Paul's all the way through, another question-and-answer song, which perfectly captured the querulous atmosphere of the time. The B-side was 'I Am The Walrus', a Lennon *tour de force*, a psychedelic maelstrom. Here was John tripping into wonderland again, with the lyrics inspired by Lewis Carroll's poem 'The Walrus and the Carpenter' from *Alice in Wonderland*: 'To me, it was a beautiful poem. It never occurred to me that Lewis Carroll was commenting on the capitalist and social system. I never went into that bit about what it really meant, like people are doing with Beatles work. Later I went back and looked at it and realized that the walrus was the bad guy in the story and the carpenter was the good guy. I thought, Oh shit, I picked the wrong guy!'

The riff came about when John was going through one of his 'Nowhere Man' periods, and was actually 'Sitting in an English garden waiting for the sun'. He heard a police siren in the distance and the first three lines of the song flashed through his head. The lyrical obscurity left the song wide open to interpretation and to the end even Lennon admitted that *he* never really knew what the song was actually *about*. Much of it was obviously devious Lennon word-play. He was absorbing acid like milk, which must be where lines like 'Semolina pilchards climbing up the Eiffel Tower' come from. 'I am he as you are he as you are me and we are all together' was very much the feeling of the period. The song was also Lennon's sole contribution to the *Magical Mystery Tour* film, which the B.B.C. premièred on Boxing Day 1967 (he also had a co-writing credit on the throwaway instrumental 'Flying'). *Magical Mystery Tour* was a scrappy project, conceived in the wake of Brian Epstein's death. But there were occasional highlights, including the surreal walrus sequence, with eggmen and walruses floating dreamily past the camera.

The Beatles psychedelia persisted. At one time the group's extraordinary and still unreleased 'What's The News Maryjane' was scheduled by John as an official Plastic Ono Band single. 'Maryjane' is a euphemism for marijuana and the song features Lennon dreamily intoning such lyrics as: 'She like to be married to Yeti/Be grooving such cooky spaghetti!'

The Beatles first single of 1968, 'Lady Madonna', was

another solo McCartney effort, which saw the group return to their rock 'n' roll roots, a decisive move away from the lyrical and musical complexities of *Sgt Pepper*. In August they inaugurated the Apple label, which was launched with the marathon 'Hey Jude' single, another solo McCartney work. The B-side, though, was pure Lennon: 'Revolution' was his explicit comment on the student riots which had split Europe and America in the summer of 1968. In France radical students came close to overthrowing the government and in America there were massive protests at the country's growing involvement in South-East Asia.

With Bob Dylan in seclusion the demonstrators looked to the Beatles and the Rolling Stones for guidance and leadership. The Stones offered the swaggering *Beggar's Banquet* album which included the call-to-the-barricades rock of 'Street Fighting Man'. John was much more cautious and when the Beatles' 'message' came through him it was almost pessimistic. 'Revolution' acknowledged that 'we all want to change the world' but sagely counselled: 'But when you talk about destruction/ Don't you know that you can count me out?' For the first time the Beatles sounded like another generation advising their young: 'You say you got a real solution/Well, you know, we'd all love to see the plan.' John sat firmly on the fence. He recorded two versions of the song, one in which he asked to be included 'in', and another in which he asks to be left out. It was to be a further three years before he would advocate 'Power To The People'. The radical element in him would take some years to develop, but, typically, when it did Lennon opted for it wholeheartedly. In 1968 'Revolution' still showed the Beatles adhering to 'flowerpower' values, 'love is all you need'. There was never any justification for violence, said John in his music. The ends could not justify the means.

Yoko's growing influence on John began to manifest itself in his music. The first real evidence of this came in November 1968 with the release of the controversial *Two Virgins* album. It was the third album issued on Apple (George Harrison's *Wonderwall* can claim the distinction of being the first Beatle solo album). *Two Virgins* was recorded at Weybridge, utilizing tape loops and splices. Most Beatles fans found it completely unacceptable, consisting as it did of random electronic gurglings and burps.

The Beatles' first real musical punch of the year, in addition to the 'Hey Jude' single, came with *The Beatles* (or 'White Album'), their first double album, released exactly five years after *With The Beatles* on 22 November 1968. Here was the first real proof that the Fab Four weren't the happy beat quartet of fond memory and there was a clear distinction between Lennon and McCartney songs. It took them away from the production complexities of *Sgt Pepper*, and even allowed for the inclusion of outside musicians (Eric Clapton, Nicky Hopkins, Dave Mason, and, of course, Yoko Ono). It was, again, very much an album of its period. 'Jamming' was a recent development in rock; Jimi Hendrix's *Electric Ladyland* of the same year included star guests; and 'supergroups' were developing as musicians broke away from the strictures that they felt record companies imposed on them.

Even the more orthodox rock 'n' roll of the 'White Album' showed Yoko's influence. John's prolificness is reflected in his total of thirteen songs on the album. The only real concession to the avant-garde was 'Revolution 9'; Lennon's other songs reflect his love for good, old-fashioned rock 'n' roll. Even from a visual angle the album is a reflection of the Beatles' desire to shake off their past—the plain white cover is a deliberate reaction against the colourful layers of *Sgt Pepper*.

The variety of Lennon's styles on the finished album are encouraging, from the beguiling 'Dear Prudence' to the nursery-rhyme charms of 'Cry Baby Cry'. Lennon's writing focused almost exclusively on Yoko: even 'Julia', his heartfelt tribute to his mother, was as much about Yoko. He told *Playboy*: 'She inspired *all* this creation in me. It wasn't that she inspired the songs, she inspired *me*!' The fans were not alone in thinking that Yoko was the one person responsible for John's barely veiled hostility towards the group. Paul, George, and Ringo saw her influence on John and their music as pernicious. Yoko herself commented in 1980: 'I went to bed with this guy I liked and suddenly the next morning I see these three in-laws standing there!'

Of the songs on the 'White Album', 'Dear Prudence' was

conceived during meditation in India and was written to coax Mia Farrow's sister Prudence out into the sun. 'Glass Onion' was a song designed to bemuse Beatle freaks ('The Walrus was Paul' was Lennon's concession to McCartney in the light of his obsession with his new partner). Lennon later described the song as 'just a throwaway', but his reference to former glories—'Strawberry Fields', 'Lady Madonna', 'The Fool On The Hill'—gave fans a field day in exercising their own interpretations.

The most tragic case of misinterpretation of Beatle lyrics came when Charles Manson convinced himself that on the 'White Album' the Beatles were exhorting him and his 'family' to rise and destroy. It was, according to Manson's warped mind, the Beatles giving him the go-ahead for a bloody revolution. He tragically misinterpreted Paul's 'Helter Skelter' as a prelude to Armageddon, unaware that it was simply an English expression for a fairground slide. Manson also convinced himself that Harrison's 'Piggies' was a licence to kill pigs and that somewhere in the electronic mayhem of John's 'Revolution 9' there was a call to arms; this subsequently resulted in his bloody murder of Sharon Tate in California.

'The Continuing Story of Bungalow Bill' was 'a sort of teenage social comment song', which marked the first orthodox Lennon/Ono collaboration. She can be clearly heard singing the line 'Not when he looked so fierce. . . .' It is populated by characters from comic books. 'So Captain Marvel zapped in right between the eyes' is straight from the territory of Stan 'The Man' Lee. It is a fragmentary, haunting song with echoes of Lennon's 'On Safairy With Whide Hunter' from his first book.

'Happiness Is A Warm Gun' was inspired by a caption in an American magazine, which George Martin showed John in the studio. The cruel irony of the phrase inspired the song and provided its title. The acid fragments are still there in sections such as 'Like a lizard on a window pane . . . the man in the crowd with the multicoloured mirrors on his hobnail boots. . . .' But a line like 'A soap impression of his wife which he ate and donated to the National Trust' is pure Spike Milligan, whose Goonish word-play John loved so much.

'I'm So Tired' is both Lennon's greatest song on the album

and one of his finest ever. Recorded very late one night at Abbey Road, it perfectly captures that weary resignation, that three o'clock in the morning feeling, with the bizarre couplet: 'Although I'm so tired, I'll have another cigarette/And curse Sir Walter Raleigh, he was such a stupid get!' Still at the centre of the song is that plea for calm, 'a little peace of mind', which was John's cry for help—except that now there was someone to answer that cry.

'Julia' is a haunting, wistful fragment, for the mother Lennon never had enough time to know and for the companion he so desperately needed. The song managed to reconcile past and present and found Lennon recognizing his own frailty in the first line: 'Half of what I say is meaningless. . . .' The impression of all the songs on the album is that they are fragments which developed into finished songs at the last moment. One feels that Lennon is pouring his heart out, for the past, the present, and the future. The songs are scraps of paper, riddled with ambiguity and tragedy, dry and lacerating humour, sometimes touching and affecting, sometimes throwaway and disposable.

'Yer Blues' was a tongue-in-cheek dig at the late sixties British blues boom, which boasted groups like Fleetwood Mac, Ten Years After, and Chicken Shack. It is none the less still a bleak and bitter song, which took shape in India—'trying to reach God and feeling suicidal'. 'Yer Blues' conjures up an iconoclastic, nihilistic world: 'Blue mist around my soul/feel so suicidal/even hate my rock 'n' roll.'

'Everybody's Got Something To Hide Except Me And My Monkey' prefaces later songs like 'I Want You' and 'Come Together', repetitive lyrics written in gratitude to Yoko. 'Your inside is out when your outside is in,' Lennon sang. And who knew it better than he?

'Sexy Sadie' was directed at the Maharishi, who 'made a fool of everyone', promising the Beatles peace on earth and spiritual enlightenment but ending up as someone they distrusted. Lennon admitted that he 'copped out' by not naming the Maharishi in the song but everyone knew who the bitter put-down was aimed at. The whimsy of 'Cry Baby Cry' took Lennon back to Alice's magic garden: for the King and Queen of Hearts read 'The King of Marigold' and 'The Duchess of

Kirkcaldy'. The song is cruel and spiteful—'Make your mother cry, she's old enough to know better'—as only children can be.

Following the cacophony of 'Revolution 9' comes the syrupy 'Good Night'. It is hard to believe that Lennon was responsible for two such different songs. 'Good Night' was written for Julian Lennon and given to Ringo to croon. It was a George Martin *tour de force*, Busby Berkeley colliding head on with a radio favourite of John's childhood, Uncle Mac: 'Good night, children . . . everywhere.' As Lennon later laconically admitted: 'It was possibly overlush!'

The *Yellow Submarine* soundtrack surfaced in January 1969. The film was a contractual obligation for the group and United Artists. For the finished animated film only four new songs were required, which duly appeared on the album (an example of the Beatles giving less than full value for money). It bore all the hallmarks of having been hastily finished, with John's 'Hey Bulldog' and George Harrison's 'Only A Northern Song' knocked off as fillers. 'Hey Bulldog' was an unusually bitter Lennon song of the period—'What makes you think you're something special when you smile?. . ./You think you know me, but you haven't got a clue!'

At the beginning of 1969 the Beatles were beginning to crumble. The making of the film *Let It Be*, which began in January, was, in the main, not a happy affair and tensions soon re-surfaced. On 2 March John and Yoko appeared at an avantgarde jazz concert in Cambridge (part of their set would appear on the *Life With The Lions* album a few months later). Significantly it marked the first time a Beatle had ever appeared solo on stage. 'Get Back' was the first Beatles single of 1969, a McCartney rocker. The other side was Lennon pouring his heart out to Yoko in 'Don't Let Me Down', a strong and persuasive riff with a stirring Lennon vocal.

As the *Let It Be* project sprawled on into an indefinite future and moved further and further away from its intended naturalism, the Beatles began recording what ended up as the *Abbey Road* album. John, meanwhile, launched his Plastic Ono Band project. Plastic Ono was never intended as a full-time group. The nucleus was always to be John and Yoko, and it involved whoever happened to be around. In the case of Lennon's anthem

'Give Peace A Chance' it was a cast of hundreds! While the flippancy of the verses recalled Lennon's *In His Own Write* and his love of word-association, the message of the chorus was imperative and sincere.

The Lennons' paranoia about the public's scorn was apparent on the next 'Beatles' single, 'The Ballad of John and Yoko' (only Paul and John actually appear on it). It was markedly autobiographical, a narrative account of John and Yoko's recent activities: 'Christ you know it ain't easy, you know how hard it can be/The way things are going, they're gonna crucify me.' Set to an infectious, shuffling, old-time rock 'n' roll rhythm, it was naïvely effective.

Plastic Ono gave Lennon the opportunity to escape from the Beatles' mantle; the band's product could be recorded and released as quickly as possible and need not have the same care and attention lavished on it that the world had come to expect from the Beatles. It was a safety valve and one of which Lennon grew increasingly fond. Lennon talked about its inception to B.B.C. Radio's Andy Peebles: 'Plastic Ono Band was a concept of Yoko's, which is an imaginary band. The first advert was a photograph . . . of some pieces of plastic with a tape recorder and a T.V. in it. . . . And her idea was a completely robot pop group. . . . There was supposed to be a party for the release of the "Give Peace A Chance" record but we'd had a car crash or something so we couldn't come; so at the dance hall where they had the party for the Plastic Ono Band, all the Press came to meet the band, and the band was onstage, which was just a machine with a camera pointing at them, showing them onstage themselves. So the Plastic Ono Band is a conceptual band that never was. There never had been any members of it, and the advert said "You are the Plastic Ono Band". So I just want to clear that, it wasn't the re-forming of a new band like Wings or a Hollies, or whatever, where you have a name and you belong to it. There's never been anybody in that band. There are no members.'

The album *Live Peace in Toronto* 1969, which resulted from Plastic Ono's appearance at the rock 'n' roll festival in September is something of a potted history of John Lennon's life at the end of the 1960s. Songs drawn from the early Hamburg days ('Blue Suede Shoes' and 'Money') nestled next to current Beatles hits like 'Yer Blues', which was included as Lennon had enjoyed performing it on the never completed TV show, *Rolling Stones' Rock and Roll Circus*. Lennon's dependence on drugs ('Cold Turkey') jostled with his desire for peace ('Give Peace A Chance'). The other side of the album comprised potent songs by Yoko with 'Don't Worry Kyoko' and 'John John (Let's Hope for Peace)'.

Meanwhile the Beatles limped on. Chronologically the set that ended up as *Abbey Road* was recorded *after* their final album *Let It Be*, but because of the concomitant problems surrounding that album, *Abbey Road* was released first in September 1969. There was no need for a title or a name on the album cover, despite the fact that the four figures diligently trooping over the zebra crossing were virtually unrecognizable as the quartet the world knew as the Beatles. Side one of *Abbey Road* consisted of separate songs—almost like the old days. Lennon's syncopated 'Come Together', which opened the album, was based around a line from Chuck Berry's 'You Can't Catch Me'. Lennon cited it as one of his favourite Beatle tracks, describing it as 'funky . . . bluesy'. The competition was strong on that album. George Harrison's two best-remembered Beatle songs were there, ('Something' and 'Here Comes The Sun') as well as a clutch of McCartney classics. 'I Want You (She's So Heavy)' could well be John's definitive song of the period. Lennon pours out remorseless lyrics, pleading with Yoko: 'I want you so bad/It's driving me mad.' 'Because' came about from some Beethoven chords Yoko was playing on the piano, which were re-shaped by John, who then added some touchingly devoted lyrics: 'Love is old, love is new/Love is all, love is you.'

The second side of the album was made up of fragments from India and from Weybridge. Songs that were started, alone and together, but never finished. Somehow they produce a seamless suite. After 'Because', Lennon's contributions were characters who flickered across his imagination, 'Mean Mr Mustard', 'Polythene Pam', and 'Sun King' sung in cod Spanish. All were rooted in reality but distorted by drugs and his tendency to leave projects incomplete. Following on the heels of the 'White Album', *Abbey Road* displayed the Beatles as four individuals, who were none the less somehow bound together by some strange, tenacious loyalty.

Before the end of 1969 Lennon released the second Plastic Ono Band single, the harrowing 'Cold Turkey', which came out at the end of October just before the Beatles 'new' single, 'Something'. The single was pulled off *Abbey Road* at the insistence of Allen Klein to bring in some immediate cash. It was the first time a Beatles single had been released *solely* to make money and it reached only number four in the charts.

'Cold Turkey' seemed only to emphasize the disparate musical directions in which the Beatles were going. It was raw and powerful with the terse message 'Play Loud' printed on the label. It was strong rock 'n' roll, with thunderous drumming from Alan White, and the lyrics drew on Lennon's harrowing experiences with heroin, graphically depicting the pain and suffering of addiction and withdrawal symptoms. It only reached number fourteen in the British charts, possibly because the subject was too spine-chilling for public taste. 'When I wrote it, I went to the other three Beatles and said, "Hey kids I think I've just written a new single!" But they all said, "Umm . . . aeee . . . well", because it was going to be my project and so I thought, bugger it, I'll put it out myself!'

Let It Be had by this time, in contrast to the free-and-easy Plastic Ono releases, developed into a monster with three separate producers,—George Martin, Glyn Johns, and Phil Spector—all trying to salvage something from the sessions at Twickenham and Apple studios.

By the middle of November 1969 the Lennons issued *The Wedding Album*, a verbal collage of their lives together during the year. Along with *Two Virgins* and *Life With The Lions* it stands on the shelf of those collectors determined to possess everything of the Beatles.

At the beginning of a new decade the Beatles were still together as a group but the ties which bound them were thin and close to snapping. The last rites had to be administered and the *Let It Be* album and film effectively did just that. Before the album's release a profusion of Beatle solo projects helped to fuel rumours of the eventual split—Ringo's *Sentimental Journey* and Paul's *McCartney* albums were released. John chipped in with another Plastic Ono single, the breezy 'Instant Karma!'. It was produced by Phil Spector because Lennon was one of the few people involved with *Let It Be* who felt that Spector had earned his salary for his work on the finished album. 'Instant Karma!' was written and recorded in one day, emphasizing Lennon's belief that records (particularly singles) should have the immediacy of newspapers. Lyrically, it marked Lennon's 'We all shine on' mood and his belief that together-ness and love could still save the world. 'It just came to me. Everybody was going on about karma, especially in the sixties. But it occurred to me that karma is instant as well as it influences your past life or your future life. . . . Also, I'm fascinated by commercials and promotions as an art form. I enjoy them. So the idea of instant karma was like the idea of instant coffee, presenting something in a new form.'

Prior to the release of the *Let It Be* album, the eponymous single was released in March 1970. It was a Paul McCartney epic, although he publicly voiced his dissatisfaction with Spec-tor's doctoring of the finished tapes. The B-side was a rarity —'You Know My Name (Look Up The Number)'. A throw-away number, written and recorded by Lennon in 1967, it features McCartney, the Beatles' road manager Mal Evans and saxophonist Brian Jones (not the late Brian Jones of the Rolling Stones but a session musician of the same name). It is an enchanting, sleazy cabaret number, set in a mythical night club—'Slaggers'—with Lennon acting as M.C. and showman and McCartney crooning in his best put-on Vic Damone style.

The *Let It Be* album was finally released in May 1970. What had originally been intended as spontaneous proof of the Beatles' very existence and vitality comes across as a doctored valediction. 'It was hell,' recalled Lennon bitterly. 'Even the biggest Beatles fan couldn't have sat through those six weeks of misery.' The whole saga surrounding the 'finished' album was a sad reflection of how disillusioned the Beatles had be-come about their recording, their future, themselves and, trag-ically, their music. The original intention was to show the group 'warts and all', deliberately stripping away all the lavish pro-duction of their albums of the previous four years, to capture their spontaneity in the studio. The world was to eavesdrop on the Beatles in rehearsal and see them shape their songs for their next album. Over thirty hours of music are on tape somewhere; much has surfaced on sporadic bootlegs. You can listen to the undoctored versions of 'The Long And Winding Road', 'Let It Be', 'Across The Universe', the full version of 'Dig It', and great original material like the rockabilly 'Suzy Parker'. You can also hear the Beatles work out on songs of their youth, Hank Williams' 'You Win Again', Cliff Richard's 'Move It', Elvis' 'Good Rockin' Tonight', Chuck Berry's 'Memphis, Tennessee', Lennon's ripe parody of 'House Of The Rising Sun', and workouts on Dylan's 'Blowin' In The Wind', and 'All Along The Watchtower'. Ironically John Lennon began collecting Beatles bootleg albums in 1974 when he could begin to enjoy re-living his past.

By the end of the film and recording sessions of January 1969 neither the Beatles nor George Martin could face wading through the miles of tapes. Given the original 'natural' idea of the project, Phil Spector was called in to edit and polish up the material and give the world the Beatles album it expected. Spector was a legend. He had virtually invented the idea of the record producer with his mini teen epics of the mid-sixties: 'Then He Kissed Me', 'River Deep, Mountain High', and 'You've Lost That Lovin' Feeling'. All were conceived and executed on a Wagnerian scale with Spector inventing the 'wall of sound', utilizing multi-tracking, massed instrumentation, and laborious overdubbing. He was a genius, but like all geniuses, he could be difficult and unpredictable. Lennon recalled the *Let It Be* débâcle: 'It just was a dreadful, dreadful feeling. . . . We were going to let it out in really shitty condition. I didn't care. I had thought it would be good to let the shitty version out because it would break the Beatles myth. It would just be us, with no trousers on and no glossy paint over the cover, and no hype. "This is what we are like with our trousers off—would you please end the game now?" '

But the old magic did surface, even during those acrimonious final days. The album's opening track, 'Two Of Us', was a McCartney song for Linda but (in context) it becomes a moving requiem to two Liverpool kids, burning with ambition and talent: 'Two of us sending postcards, writing letters on my wall/You and me burning matches, lifting latches, on our way back home.' It is a memory of Liverpool as it was, when the world was open and bright for conquest, not shrouded in the acid connotations of 'Strawberry Fields'. At the dismal end, 'Two Of Us' serves as a moving reminder of that bright beginning.

'Dig A Pony' celebrated Lennon's omniscience—'You can celebrate anything you want . . . You can penetrate any place you go . . . You can radiate everything you are. . . .' But as the refrain runs, 'I told you so, all I want is you.' That was definitely meant for Yoko. 'Across The Universe' was a song which infuriated Lennon at the time. He woke up one morning with the line 'Pools of sorrow, waves of joy' running through his head and proceeded to construct the song from it. The version on the album was 'subconscious sabotage' on his part, in the name of experimentation. One version ended up on a World Wildlife Fund charity album with two Beatles fans singing the 'Nothing's gonna change my world' chorus. 'The original track was a real piece of shit,' he recalled with some bitterness, 'I was singing out of tune and instead of getting a decent choir, we got fans from outside . . . Apple Scruffs or whatever you call them. They came in and were singing all off-key. Nobody was interested in doing the tune originally. . . . Phil slowed the tape down, added the strings. . . . He did a really special job.' The 'Jai Guru Deva OM' refrain harkens back to the days of gurus and avatars who could save the world. The song caught Lennon at a time when all his creativity and sexuality were being devoted to Yoko but when: 'Words are flowing out like endless rain into a paper cup . . . Thoughts meander like a restless wind.' Restless, the artist in him was beset by relentless images and a burning desire to create, while he wilfully stripped everything down for Yoko. 'Nothing's gonna change my world,' he sang. But it had.

'Dig It' was an example of the 'new-phase Beatles album' which the *Let It Be* album sleeve boasted. Distilled from a five-minute stream of consciousness rap, the existing forty-eight-second track finds Lennon invoking Manchester United boss Matt Busby, Doris Day, and a series of acronyms, ending with the emphatic 'Whatever it is, whoever you are—just dig it!' Lennon's sardonic comments pepper the finished album— opening the album with 'I dig a pygmy by Charles Hawtrey . . .', prefacing the beautiful 'Let It Be' with the iconoclastic 'Now we'd like to do 'ark the Angels come . . .', digging up the traditional 'Maggie Mae', disembowelling 'Danny Boy', and pre-empting 'Get Back' with an improvised chorus of 'Sweet Loretta Fart/Thought she was a cleaner, but she was a frying pan'. It is only the tip of the iceberg, though, and unfortunately it is the poor-quality bootlegs which give a greater indication of the album's original concept.

'I've Got A Feeling' was a Lennon/McCartney collaboration of sorts. The first half of the song is all Paul, while the 'Everybody had a hard year' section onwards is John. 'One After 909' was a genuine collaboration, written in 1959 in those dim and distant Liverpool days and disinterred for their last album together. Here was a joyous slice of Eddie Çochran-style rock, written by two teenagers with no real idea of that so-distant America, culled instead from images of contemporary rock 'n' roll songs, with John and Paul singing enthusiastically together on the chorus. Sharply evocative of those earlier, sunnier and simpler days, it seems now a glorious finale to the partnership of Lennon and McCartney; as the years passed and the acrimony between the two men subsided, their preferred memory was, indeed, of 'sagging off school' as Liverpool boys and writing songs in the back of the Beatles' van.

All of John Lennon's subsequent musical activities would, inevitably, be measured alongside his achievement in creating the Beatles. They were the single most influential pop group ever. Their sounds and personalities had irrevocably altered not only the music but the social fabric of the western world. They were synonymous with youth culture and pop art. At the onset of a new decade, Lennon—perhaps more than anyone—was aware of his responsibilities and of the legacy he was condemned to carry.

The public had been warned of the 'new' Lennon by 'Cold Turkey'. Released in October 1969, it was John's harrowing confession of withdrawal from heroin. As the third single from the Plastic Ono Band, it went into the charts both in Britain and America, although not high enough to please John, who cited its poor performance in his letter to the Queen returning his M.B.E.

To Beatles fans, the record was astonishing, even from

John. Yet it was perhaps his most honest moment in making his music a catalogue of his life. He sang

> Temperature's rising, fever is high
> Can't see no future, can't see no sky
> My feet are so heavy, so is my head
> I wish I was a baby, I wish I was dead.

The urgency of his voice, the nature of the record as a clear reference to his drug habits, the strength of Eric Clapton's guitar work on it and the dramatic departure from anything previously heard from John and the Beatles, mark it as a milestone in his life. 'Cold Turkey', uncomfortable at the time, now defines precisely the open heart of Lennon.

The Plastic Ono Band helped John to expunge the Beatles myth and the catharsis engendered by Janov's primal therapy manifested itself on the *John Lennon/Plastic Ono Band* album, which reached the shops a fortnight before Christmas 1970. It still stands as one of the bleakest, most compellingly honest albums ever released by a major rock artist. On it Lennon exorcized his past and offered precious little hope for his future. Its bleakness took root in his childhood, particularly on 'Mother' and 'My Mummy's Dead', a plaintive cry from a spiritual orphan. 'Mother' was harrowing; Lennon's hair-raising vocal, the sparse instrumentation and chilling lyrics were a public mourning of his dead mother and castigation of his absent father. There was no cosiness, no imagery, nothing to hide behind here. 'Working Class Hero' was bitterly dismissive of the system which bred Lennon, which 'gave you no time instead of it all'. It is a twentieth-century folk song, for Everyman; a withering, scornful attack on a society which 'Keeps you doped with religion and sex and T.V./But you're still fucking peasants as far as I can see.'

For many the album's most despairing track is 'God', Lennon's litany of rejection of his past which concludes with the withering 'I don't believe in Beatles.' The dream was finally over. As he commented: ' "God" was put together from three songs. I had the idea that God is the concept by which we measure pain, so that when you have a word like that, you just sit down and sing the first tune that comes into your head. . . .

I don't know when I realized that I was putting down all these things I didn't believe in. So I could have gone on, it was like a Christmas card list: where do I end: Churchill? Hoover? I thought I had to stop. I was going to leave a gap and just fill in your own words; whoever you don't believe in. It had just got out of hand. And Beatles was the final thing because I no longer believe in myth and Beatles is another myth.'

Lennon's writing was as sparse as the instrumentation. The album, in fact, must be the sparsest Phil Spector has ever given his name to. Lennon admitted later: 'I started from ''Mother'' onwards, trying to shave off all imagery, pretensions of poetry, illusions of grandeur, what I call à la Dylan, Dylanesque. . . . As they say, Northern people are blunt, right, so I was trying to write like I am.'

That very bluntness shook many people on what amounted to Lennon's first solo album. There were no walruses or glass onions, no more masks to hide behind—here was the soul of John Ono Lennon. That 'Northern bluntness' was apparent on 'Working Class Hero', with its two 'fucks' that E.M.I. cut out on the inner sleeve. (The censorship was applied only in Britain; Capitol, who released the album in America, printed the words.) By then Lennon didn't care. He'd been performing to order for too long. If the public wanted John Lennon, they would have to take him on his own terms. He wasn't John Beatle any more.

There *were* moments of softness on the album: the beautiful ballad 'Love' which spoke of 'needing to be loved'; 'Hold On' was Yoko's plea: 'Hold on John, it's gonna be alright.' But the overwhelming feeling of the album is one of sadness, sadness for a past he never had, for the mother he missed, for the growing up in public. For all the fake gurus. For Yoko. For himself. It was from the heart.

Lennon's deliberate denunciation of his past was a brutal beginning to a new decade. With the Beatles gone, there seemed nothing to replace them musically or as a full-time occupation. Coupled with the long, confessional interview he did with *Rolling Stone* editor Jann Wenner in 1970, *Plastic Ono Band* renounced the past with all the accumulated bitterness and rancour of John's thirty years.

By early 1971 John and Yoko had thrown their hats firmly

into the political arena. 'Power To The People' was a slogan echoing round the world at the time. The civil disturbances in Northern Ireland were erupting into civil war. The Nixon administration had taken the gloves off when they murdered four students at Kent State University during a demonstration in 1970. The Lennons became more and more active in radical politics. They donated money to Michael X's Black House, recorded a single, 'Do The Oz', for the defendants in the infamous 'Schoolkids Oz' trial, and Lennon gave an interview to Tariq Ali's left-wing paper *Red Mole*: 'I think we must make the workers aware of the really unhappy position they are in, break the dream they are surrounded by. They think they are in a wonderful, free-speaking country, they've all got cars and tellies and they don't want to think there's anything more to life. They are prepared to let the bosses run them, to see their children fucked up in school. They're dreaming someone else's dream, it's not even their own.' Lennon was expanding the resentment which had fuelled 'Working Class Hero'. Many found Lennon's avowed socialism at odds with his personal wealth but John was quick to counter his critics and always managed to equate it with his rapidly changing beliefs.

'Power To The People' was the most obvious musical indication of the Lennons' growing political involvement, even if it was only a type of catchy sloganeering which was to manifest itself more fully on the album *Some Time In New York City*. It recalled an earlier Lennon statement—'Revolution' but this time he committed himself: 'Say we want a revolution/We better get it on right away/Well you get on your feet/And out on the street.' Now he was advocating direct involvement and action. His fence-sitting days were over.

He could not have produced a greater contrast with his next album and in no way did he see it as ironic that he was following his most politically motivated single with his lushest and most romantic album to date.

Imagine was released in October 1971 and is probably the album most associated with John Lennon, with the haunting title track, the poignant 'Oh My Love', the vitriolic 'How Do You Sleep?' and the resonant 'Jealous Guy'. *Imagine* revealed a mellower Lennon. Although the basic themes of pain and suffering were still there its lavish instrumentation was light

years away from the primal starkness of *Plastic Ono Band*.
Virtually all the songs speak of his devotion to Yoko. Only 'I
Don't Want To Be A Soldier' and the resounding 'Give Me
Some Truth' strayed from the theme . . . as of course did 'How
Do You Sleep?', his attack on Paul McCartney. In case any
listener missed the object of his scorn, a postcard was included
with *Imagine* that showed Lennon in a delicious parody of
McCartney's *Ram* album cover. 'Those freaks was right when
they said you was dead' sang Lennon in a vicious put-down.
He was referring to bizarre rumours, particularly in America,
that McCartney was, in fact, dead.

Imagine was classic Lennon. The album's title track was a
beautifully melodic song which he had written in a plane, on
a hotel bill. He always took trouble to tell people that Yoko
had helped him with it, particularly its original inspiration on
the theme of Utopia. Such was the intrinsic beauty of the song
and the sincerity with which Lennon sang it that it will stand
for ever as an international anthem. All Lennon was asking
was that we should *imagine* a world without possessions or
religion.

The world was by now so used to an abrasive, hard-faced
Lennon, that a song like 'Jealous Guy', which actually apologized for causing hurt and pain and recognized his emotional
vulnerability, seemed uncharacteristic. On 'Crippled Inside' he
sang once again of pain but without sounding self-pitying. 'One
thing you can't hide/Is when you're crippled inside'—that was
something John Lennon never did and he was respected for his
honesty in conveying that pain by a world he viewed with an
artist's eye.

Lennon recognized the difficulties of sustaining a relationship, of shedding his hard-man image and becoming a fully
rounded person. On *Imagine* he finally reconciled his efforts
with his craft. The album makes comfortable listening, thanks
in no small part to Spector's co-production and the lavish arrangements, although lyrically Lennon was still speaking as
directly as ever.

The reason, of course, was Yoko who had helped round
John off as a person and had given him a perspective on his
life. She had taken him into whole new areas, which initially
proved to be dead ends (the avant-garde of *Two Virgins* and

Side Two of *Live Peace In Toronto*). Latterly, however, she had steered him in the more fruitful directions signposted by *Imagine*. John's devotion to her manifested itself particularly on the beautiful 'Oh My Love' and the ebullient 'Oh Yoko!'. It was hard to reconcile the man who could write such sensitive love songs with the juvenile tough guy who could also sharpen his knife for the malice of 'How Do You Sleep?' But then, John Lennon always was paradoxical.

The cumbersome 'I Don't Want To Be A Soldier' was a clumsy intrusion, a laborious protest song, railing against the 'straights' who let themselves be hoodwinked into the army or other Establishment professions. 'Give Me Some Truth', though, was a blisteringly effective and sustained attack on the falsity of Nixon's America.

Musically *Imagine* packed real punch with legendary saxophonist King Curtis, Nicky Hopkins, Badfinger's Tom Evans and Joey Molland, George Harrison, and Phil Spector all contributing. Lennon spoke fondly of the finished album and pinpointed its strengths: ' "Imagine", both the song itself and the album, is the same thing as "Working Class Hero" and "Mother" and "God" on the first disc. But the first record was too real for people, so nobody bought it. . . . You see "Imagine" was exactly the same message but sugar-coated. Now "Imagine" is a big hit almost everywhere—anti-religious, anti-nationalistic, anti-conventional, anti-capitalistic but because it is sugar-coated it is accepted. Now I understand what you have to do. Put your political message across with a little honey.'

But the honey was to stay in the jar during 1972. By the time *Imagine* was in the shops, John and Yoko had left England and settled in New York.

21
AMERICA

'New York is the Rome of today'

With the Beatles written out of his mind and the thrust of the peace campaign over, John by 1971 was a curious amalgam of superstar, artist, and mercenary. He reiterated that he could no longer be a 'slave to gold records', but he was too much of a realist to be dragged too deeply into the esoteric world of art. He imposed his own limits on everything.

He had lived his thirty-one years on a cliff, consistently pushing himself and his abilities to the edge. He often remarked on the 'nearly' situations which punctuated his life: how he nearly got kicked out of school; how he nearly got expelled from art college but escaped to Hamburg just in time; how he was nearly lulled into a safe, rich, bourgeois existence at Weybridge when Yoko entered his life; how the Beatles broke up at exactly the right time for him. What had anchored him to the wide world, whatever was happening in his life, was his obsession with looking outside, rather than inside, himself.

Yoko's battle for custody of her daughter Kyoko took her and John to New York in the autumn of 1971. John's attraction for the country had already been whetted by a visit that summer. He and Yoko had staggered fans by playing at a jam session with Frank Zappa and his Mothers of Invention at Fillmore East; in a show that ended at dawn, John had surprised even himself by announcing: 'This is a song I used to sing when I was in the Cavern in Liverpool.' It was called 'Well (Baby

Please Don't Go)'. He had a neat line in self-deprecation: 'I did rhythm and booze, and Yoko sang on stage with what she calls voice modulation, which to the layman is screaming!'

In Britain John had explained why he felt so drawn to America, both on a personal and on an artistic level. 'It's Yoko's old stamping ground,' he explained, 'and she felt the country would be more receptive to what we're up to . . . in the States we're treated like artists. Which we are! Or anywhere else for that matter. But here [in Britain] I'm like the lad who knew Paul, got a lucky break, won the pools and married the actress.

'It's like 1940 here,' he said, warming to the theme. 'It's like coming back to Denmark or somewhere. It's really the sticks, you know. While in New York there's these fantastic twenty or thirty artists who all understand what I'm doing and have the same kind of mind as me. It's just like heaven after being here. Oh, it's terrible. You've seen how they treat me in the Press. There is an avant-garde here, but it's small.'

Political and other events had also depressed him in London: he was unhappy with the persecution of the editors of *Oz*, the Northern Ireland crisis infuriated him and when internment without trial began there, he declared that Britain should pull out and let Northern Ireland sort out its own problems; he didn't like the adoption by Britain of the decimal currency system that year. The only thing that made him smile was a record by Dave Edmunds, 'I Hear You Knocking', which Lennon rated as one of the finest sounds he'd heard in years. He played it endlessly, together with a single by B.B. King, 'The Thrill Is Gone'.

On 3 September 1971 John and Yoko left London to settle in New York. For nine years it was to prove an artistic and spiritual haven for him. 'It's the Rome of today, a bit like a together Liverpool,' he said to me shortly after the move. 'I'd always like to be where the action is. In olden times I'd like to have lived in Rome or Paris or the East. The seventies are gonna be America's.'

When they arrived John and Yoko made for Greenwich Village, which Yoko knew well from her days as a loft artist. They took a two-room apartment there at 105 Bank Street. A piano was quickly moved in, but mostly they shunned possessions. The apartment was spartan; the bed was a mattress covered with an American flag as a bedspread. They lived and dressed frugally, John in jeans, denim jacket and T-shirt and Yoko in jeans, black turtle-neck sweater and boots.

An early visitor was Bob Dylan, re-acquainting himself with his musical roots. He took John on a sightseeing tour of the Village, pointing out all the clubs and explaining the diversity of artistic activities that went on. John was immediately captivated by the freewheeling atmosphere.

As well as renting the Bank Street apartment they rented another nearby from ex-Lovin' Spoonful drummer, Joe Butler. They also bought push-bikes, 'the best way to get around the Village,' Dylan advised them. John's was a conservative, English, sit-up-and-beg handlebar model, Yoko's Japanese—pure coincidence, she said.

Yet even in those heady first few months John kept in touch with what was happening at home. He phoned Apple in New York and London regularly; he telephoned Aunt Mimi in Dorset to be warned against living in bad old America for too long; and he often went with Yoko to the Apple office at 1700 Broadway.

One day, amid the mountain of mail waiting him, was a copy of the *Melody Maker* containing a reader's letter. Headlined 'Dear JohnandYoko', it read:

> We love you very much and if all rock stars save one were to be lined up against a wall tomorrow and shot, you would be the one we'd save.
>
> But we're finding it more and more difficult to understand your simultaneous espousal of Rock Liberation and Mr Pete 'the President's friend' Bennett, promo man extraordinary (do you like being a 'product'?).
>
> Allen Klein may be a beautiful person but as far as we simple record buyers are concerned he's just another shrewd capitalist taking his cut wherever he can. Apple may be a wonderful company but all we notice is that its records get steadily more expensive and shorter (*vide* the new Mary Hopkin album with five short songs a side. Once upon a time *With the Beatles* had fourteen solid tracks on it.). If we want some Yoko music we have to fork out over four

quid. Can you remember the time when you were lucky to afford an album a month? That's our upper limit.

Power to the people, yeah—but which people? We were the Beatles' people all right but we still don't know if we're yours. We're T. Rex's, and Slade's—there they are on *Top of the Pops* (it might be rubbish but it's all we've got) and at St George's Hall, Bradford (at sixty pence a bit cheaper than a super album of your Fillmore gig). Are you one of us?

So please, dear JohnandYoko, give us a break from your public nasties on Paul (we're not very interested in your tax situation) and start explaining what rock liberation can mean when art and money are so mixed up. There aren't many people who can explain it. Peter Townshend has had a go; now it's your turn. Happy Christmas. Love,

Simon and Gill Frith,
Keighley, Yorkshire

Lennon's reply was instantaneous and revealing. On Apple headed notepaper he personally typed the reply which is reproduced as he typed it (see second insert of illustrations).

John's postscript about John Sinclair indicated his affinities during those early months in New York. As Lennon comments, Sinclair, a left-wing writer, had been jailed for possessing two joints of marijuana and John and Yoko attended a benefit rally at Ann Arbor, Michigan which resulted in Sinclair being freed within three days after serving two years of his sentence. The breakthrough thrilled John.

Left-wing personalities and political activists began to infiltrate his life. They, for their part, saw John as their Pied Piper. An early cohort in the Village was David Peel, an underground personality who amused John with his songs 'The Pope Smokes Dope' and 'Have A Marijuana'. Recalling that period, John said: 'I'd just arrived in New York and all these people, Jerry Rubin, Abbie Hoffman, David Peel, they were right on the corner when I was going out for a walk in the Village. It was that kind of community. I loved it. As usual, Lennon falls in the deep end, goes overboard, no half measures. At the time, though, it was a good scene and they meant no harm.'

Yoko felt safe in the Village; she was particularly keen on Jerry Rubin's philosophical book *Do It*, which had been in the Japanese bestseller list. John's first confrontation with the Village scene came when he dropped in, alone, to a clothes shop, the Limbo Shop, on St Mark's Place, only two weeks after arriving in New York. The best-known hippie in the Village ran up to him to shake hands and say: 'Hello, my name is David Peel, I work for Elektra Records.' They chatted for some time and a couple of nights later Peel was astonished when John and Yoko turned up at his concert in Washington Square Park. They enjoyed the irreverence of it all, and left the show chanting 'The Pope Smokes Dope.' It was the first of several encounters with Peel, who could scarcely believe that a Beatle was drawn to his scene, for whatever reason.

Shortly afterwards, Jerry Rubin told Lennon that Peel was going to do a 'walkabout', singing on the streets. John, with guitar, called on Peel and with Yoko went along Second Avenue singing 'The Pope Smokes Dope'. Fifty people joined the sidewalk minstrels. 'It was totally natural, spontaneous, and great.' Unfortunately the police thought a wandering Beatle was a security risk and broke it up.

Lennon loved street people as long as they were not phonies. What irritated him was when hangers-on bothered him, asking for money, drugs, or started to talk of the Beatles. He wanted to communicate with people on an ordinary level. New York, and particularly the crowd he was introduced to by Jerry Rubin, seemed to offer that; coupled with the radical politics preached by Rubin and his friends, it was John's automatic haven for the early months in the Village. Rubin effectively screened most of the people who wanted to get near John.

Peel's memory of those days with John is of a superstar who intuitively grasped the Village vibrations but could not become totally involved because he was a 'millionaire trendy'. Says Peel: 'John and Yoko were brilliant. They knew how to ad lib quicker than anybody I've ever met. What they liked doing best was getting things done quickly. They hated wasting time. John was open-minded, learned a lot, he had access to a lot of people, and he always *listened*. He wasn't as committed to the radical thing as a lot of us but because he was a Beatle he could make a call and get things done.'

Life for John and Yoko in the Village was a series of moments. John was so high on his freedom there that he even produced an album by David Peel and his band, the Lower East Side. 'John was an excellent producer,' says Peel. 'He had that Phil Spector Wall of Sound down pat, with everything exaggerated. He was heavily into *action* in the studio. . . . We had six guitars and ten congas and Yoko even played congas a little. "All right, let's go, *next*," he'd shout. . . . He was deadly serious but knew how to have fun. I never saw Lennon so happy as he was doing my album. John said: "Go in and play like you play on the street"—but how could I with that fantastic sound behind me?' The album, out on the Apple label, was instantly banned all over the world because it included 'The Pope Smokes Dope'.

Peel and his band played several times with John and Yoko. He was at the benefit rally for John Sinclair and on the David Frost T.V. show, and he jammed many times in their Bank Street apartment with John often playing washboard. Peel also played on their Dick Cavett T.V. appearance and at a Madison Square Garden charity concert for retarded children and adults. Peel was moved to write a song, 'Lennon for President'.

'I used to go over to Bank Street a lot to jam, especially to eat dinner,' he says. 'I knew a good free meal when I saw one. Yoko was a terrific cook of macrobiotic food.' Only one thing irritated Peel: that John maintained his bodyguards while he was in the Village. 'Nobody would bother him when he was with us. Allen Klein said to Lennon that the reason he liked hanging around me was because Peel does everything Lennon was afraid to do himself: That's what I did. I brought out the side of John that just wanted to go crazy, party all night. But the bodyguards . . . he was cynical and mistrustful. A lot of people wanted handouts. He was paranoid about it.

'When you are close to John Lennon, the guy's so powerful and aware of the world events that you start losing your own identity. Being so close to him for a year or so was good and bad, you know. Look . . . as soon as the carriage turned back to a pumpkin, Cinderella was a housemaid. When you're with John Lennon you're a prince. When his trendy thing is over, you go home a pumpkin. Twelve midnight, you're back in your rags doing what you did before. Like me.'

Life among the Greenwich Village hippies was a natural diversion of fun and freedom for John. But President Nixon's American government viewed it as something almost sinister. From the start of 1972, only a few months after setting foot on American soil, John was faced with an immigration battle that proved almost stranger than fiction.

John was in America on a temporary visa which expired on 29 February 1972. As early as January he and Yoko realized that staying in America permanently might not be easy and that the government could use John's 1968 drugs conviction to refuse them a visa, known as a Green Card. Lawyer Leon Wildes was among those interviewed by them that month in their Bank Street apartment before the real problems began. 'John was quieter than Yoko,' recalls the urbane Wildes. 'While she asked us questions, he was making us tea.' At that time there was no interest expressed in permanent residence in the U.S.A. 'The interest was only in staying a couple of months so they could continue their efforts to find Kyoko; they were in the middle of some complicated custody proceedings.'

Wildes told them that if all they wanted was an extension of another month or even three, 'You don't really need my help. The Apple solicitor can handle it as the custody problem is one of the strongest reasons you can give for the extension of a temporary stay.'

But Yoko answered: 'Yes, we really *do* need your help.' A puzzled Wildes was appointed as their immigration lawyer; he was, frankly, too much of a heavyweight lawyer to be dealing with a simple extension of John's visa. He had no idea, initially, that John was being harassed.

One of the Beatles' classic songs, 'We Can Work It Out', had been written by Paul. But John had injected the middle lines which made the song special: 'Life is very short and there's no time/For fussing and fighting my friend.' But as his initial foray into the relaxed New York lifestyle gave way to tension and worry, he began to realize that fussing and fighting was precisely what he would have to do to clear his sullied name and stay in the country he wanted to adopt.

The source of the government's hounding lay in the little-known Senate Internal Security Sub-Committee. Many politicians were surprised that the committee still existed; it had originated in the 1950s during the scares of communist infiltration. Even in 1972 it apparently operated on the same philosophy: anyone with a view different from the government's was subject to investigation.

The committee received a memorandum suggesting that Lennon might be bankrolling or otherwise supporting the group that had disturbed the 1968 Democratic Convention and, it was feared, might do the same at the Republican Convention due to be held in 1972. Says Leon Wildes: 'Lennon, of course, always denied that he had anything to do with, or had any knowledge of, this plan, if it existed. Nor was he really interested, he said. I always believed this, because he was a principled kind of guy and he wasn't interested in disturbing, rather in stating his piece, explaining his position.' (John's denials were underlined by David Peel's opinion that Lennon was never a believing radical and by John's statements throughout his life that his true role was to write songs and make music. His liaison with Jerry Rubin and others had, however, left him exposed to the charge. When he deviated from the role of writer-musician, he always ran into problems.)

The committee chairman sent the memorandum to John Mitchell, who was Attorney-General, with jurisdiction over the entire immigration process and also chairman of CREEP, the 'Committee to Re-elect the President'. A note at the foot of a covering letter said that a copy had been sent to the White House. 'There was obviously an interest by the Nixon administration, at the highest levels, in what John was doing,' says Wildes.

Evidence of a government campaign mounted. The *New York Times* summed it up:

> According to the government documents which Mr Lennon's lawyer Leon Wildes obtained from the government under court orders, Senator Strom Thurmond, Republican, of South Carolina, wrote a personal and confidential letter to the then Attorney General, John N. Mitchell, on 4 February 1972 suggesting that action against Mr Lennon could avoid 'many headaches'. Attached to the Thurmond letter was a memorandum from

the files of the Senate Internal Security Sub-Committee, asserting that a commune group was preparing to go to California to disrupt the 1972 Republican National Convention, and that a confidential source had learned 'that the activities of this group are being financed by John Lennon.' A second memo from the same files contended that 'radical New Left leaders plan to use Mr Lennon as a drawing card to promote the success of rock festivals, to obtain funds for a "dump Nixon" programme.'

The Thurmond letter discovered by Wildes had a handwritten footnote: 'Can we keep him [Lennon] out?' And the New York District Director of Immigration acknowledged that he had been specifically told from 'on high' what action to take on Lennon and exactly when to start deportation proceedings.

Initially, in March 1972, John was ordered to leave America within two months, which allowed some breathing space. John became extremely tense. Winning the right to stay in America was a matter of principle and other worries were adding to his jitters. There was the complex lawsuit with Northern Songs and Maclen Music in London dating back to the rights to his songs written since 1965, with Yoko. There was a simmering battle with Allen Klein. John was a confused, angry man during the early days in America. He drank too much and smoked too many Kool cigarettes.

He suspected that his immigration problem might have been part of a wider plan to split the unity of youth which, in the early seventies, was such a potent force. With Paul McCartney marooned in Britain because of his own drugs bust, John afraid to leave the U.S. because he wouldn't get back in, Jimi Hendrix and Jim Morrison, two catalysts of the youth culture, dead, and the Rolling Stones being carefully watched, Lennon thought that it was perhaps a plot. 'They're chopping off the "revolution" at its source,' he said. 'So there'll be no more mass gatherings like the Woodstock peace festival. These things inspire change. Politicians don't want change, so it's in their interests to split us all up.

'I'm not the only rock star who's harassed, but nobody else tried to stay here in America. And nobody else hung out with the baddies like I did. Maybe I'm dumb but I'm interested in people. I wanted to find out what they had to say about everything. I didn't want to read a book on them, so I met them all to find out where it's at, y'know. Now in 1968, the cops beat up some people at a Chicago convention. I'm discussing with Jerry Rubin, Allen Ginsberg and everybody what they're talking about—and they're saying, "Shall we go to San Francisco to have an anti-war rally?" Next thing it's in the papers that John and Yoko are going to lead a vast rally in San Diego with all these people!'

In April 1972, John and Yoko addressed a crowd in New York which was protesting against America's bombing of North Vietnam. Clearly John would not be hounded or compromised by any threat of deportation. At the same time he wanted the freedom to stay in New York. The pulse of the city was right for him.

Once the machine was rolling on checking Lennon out, it was unstoppable. Agents from the F.B.I. (Federal Bureau of Investigation) attended his concerts, studied his song lyrics—particularly those on the heavily political *Some Time In New York City* album—and C.I.A. (Central Intelligence Agency) men shadowed him in his private life. John's phone conversations were tapped so much that he rarely bothered to use it; instead Yoko did most of the talking. The F.B.I. strongly suggested at one point that John 'be arrested, if at all possible, on possession of narcotics charges' so that he might be 'immediately deportable'. Why this was not followed through is unknown; John was smoking marijuana in Bank Street quite often and it would have been easy for police to arrest him.

Leon Wildes now set to work with a counter plan of meticulous detail and careful strategy. 'The government wanted to be able to prove that Lennon was an undesirable because of his 1968 marijuana conviction,' he says. 'They planned to ease him out by bringing proceedings against him as an "overstay" on his temporary visa, telling him that unless he accepted this deal and got out voluntarily, they could always charge him with being deportable as a person with a drugs conviction. That way, he would be seen to be not leaving voluntarily but forcibly. They thought he would not want that and they believed that with a carrot-and-stick routine they could force him out within a month or two in mid-1972.'

While accumulating his proof of the government vendetta, Wildes managed to secure a 'waiver', a six-month extension for John and Yoko, which changed their status from Non-Immigrant Visa to that of Visitor of Distinguished Merit and Ability. John Lindsay, Mayor of New York and one of Lennon's main protagonists, had in former years helped to write and reform America's immigration laws: 'There's a thing called Suspension of Deportation by which, if a good character is proved, and there are sound and equitable reasons not to execute a technical deportation, the Attorney-General can suspend it. John Lennon was not the first by any means to be the beneficiary of a waiver of the technicality.'

This enabled John to appear on the influential Dick Cavett T.V. show. Typically he didn't shrink from confronting the situation head-on, telling millions of viewers that he was being followed by government detectives and that his phones and Wildes' were being tapped.

Although he was nervous about it, John's friend, the black comedian Dick Gregory, who had also been the victim of phone tapping, had convinced him he should tell the world about it.

John described his feelings at the time: 'I'm not saying they had plans other than just keeping tabs on me, to see what I was up to, who I was seeing. But I felt followed everywhere by government agents. Every time I picked up my phone there was a lot of noise. Somebody gave me a number that if you call it, you get this feedback sound that confirms your phone is being tapped. And I did it and it did. Suddenly I realized this was serious, they were coming for me, one way or another. They were harassing me. I'd open the door and there'd be guys standing on the other side of the street. I'd get in the car and they'd be following me and not hiding. That's what got me paranoid. They wanted me to see I was being followed. Anyway, after I said it out on the air, on T.V., the next day there was nobody there. Was I dreaming? No, I wasn't. Look, my lawyer, who's as square as the next one, started to agree. He found his phones were being tapped and he didn't know how to prove it either.'

What the Nixon government had not considered was the enormous groundswell of public opinion in John's favour. During several lawsuits, which included Leon Wildes suing the government at one stage over a technicality in the irregularity of a temporary visa, he pleaded humanitarianism under the Freedom of Information Act. 'There were people in the United States completely deportable, who nevertheless were allowed to remain here; I claimed that Lennon would probably fit within those standards, but since the standards had never been published we were entitled to the benefit of any doubt.' Further, Wildes claimed that Lennon was suffering Selective Prosecution for political rather than legal reasons.

The battle to get a Green Card took four agonizing, exhausting years. It was a long, dark tunnel, but during nerve-wracking days when Leon Wildes would call once or twice daily with news of an advance or a setback, John received heartening support from some of the most influential people in the U.S.A.

Mayor John Lindsay was one. 'This town,' he told me, 'always had a very important history of welcoming contributing talent. I could see no over-compelling reason to get rid of this kind of artist. John Lennon was a major force as we saw it, far more good than bad. Some people just didn't understand the nature of the beast. They didn't really know what Lennon stood for, didn't understand his world, his music, his behaviour, his whole theory of life. A lot of middle-aged politicians, and people who didn't want to stick their neck out, sometimes through fear, took the ''pull up the drawbridge'' attitude. I was interested in the cause and in this city, and anxious that this country demonstrated to John Lennon that he was welcome here. It seemed unthinkable that a major artist should be shown the door. This city has good Philharmonic, and good opera, and good Carnegie Hall, but it also has the John Lennons.

'Unless there's vigilance, civil liberties suffer. Governments start poking about and letting you know they're using police tactics. My colleagues in city government could sense that this was no hula-hoop thing, here today and gone tomorrow. We sensed that John Lennon's threatened deportation was affecting young people very deeply. It was in the tradition of New York that there remained a mixture of talent in the city.' He also stressed that his role in the Lennon battle, writing to the Commissioner of Immigration in Washington pleading for the deportation order to be dropped, was not to condone John's use of drugs. He did not consider that Lennon was damaging the community by his drug-taking.

John was particularly grateful also for the interest and campaign of Jack Anderson, the highly-rated writer with the *Washington Post*. Anderson, who has a reputation for tenacity and exposé reporting, had written about the 'Watergate tactics' being used to hound Lennon. 'When Jack Anderson started writing about what was happening,' Lennon told me, 'I knew I had to go on fighting until I won.' When John was murdered, Anderson recalled the immigration battle in a column in the *New York Daily News*:

> The immigration service reserves a special bureaucratic hell for aliens who have the slightest taint of narcotics in their past. Thieves, rapists, and even murderers have less trouble gaining admission to the United States than someone convicted of even the most minor drug charge. Six years ago, John Lennon . . . came close to being deported because of a 1968 marijuana charge in England. I took up his case in 1974. I reported that the deportation move was really a political vendetta against Lennon who had been outspoken in his opposition to the Vietnam war. Lennon was able to beat the trumped-up deportation order partly because of official embarrassment over my columns and partly because of the superb legal work of his attorney, Leon Wildes. Since that time the public attitude has changed towards both the Vietnam war and the drug habits it spawned. Most Americans now agree with Lennon that the war was a tragic mistake and his arrest for possessing a small amount of marijuana for personal use is no longer considered a horrendous crime.

Another ally was the Washington lawyer, Steve Martindale. Visiting New York, he met the Lennons at a party also attended by Mayor Lindsay and his wife Mary. 'John and Yoko were extremely shy,' says Martindale. 'Yoko took the lead in explaining the problems they were having with the U.S. government. I suggested they come and spend some time in Washington and we would get to the bottom of it.

'When they came I had a dinner for them. Henry Kissinger was there, so was Senator Alan Cranston. John and Yoko were awed by it all. . . . As I remember it, Henry [Kissinger] put in a call to John Mitchell [the Attorney-General] and we succeeded in softening the government up somewhat.'

The political and diplomatic ramifications of the case were lost on John. He reacted strongly, though, to one twist to Leon Wildes' reports to him. When Yoko was granted permission to remain a permanent resident he erupted. Wildes told him to cool it; the government was playing into their hands, he argued, by putting itself in a position of attempting to split up a married couple. 'That was why I applied separately for Yoko's permit,' says Wildes. 'I got her acknowledged to be an outstanding artist.'

Wildes' ace lay, ironically, in tracing with Yoko the circumstances of John's 1968 drugs bust. John had told Wildes that at the time he had been forced to plead guilty because of Yoko. That was the only action he could take: 'If I pleaded innocent, I would still have been convicted. Yoko at that time in England was an alien, and unless I took the rap they would have charged her and she would have been deported.' Wildes surmised that, since John had been advised by the best legal counsellors in London, what he said could be true. After all, the police pounced on him in a flat which he didn't own, where John had been tipped off by a *Daily Mirror* reporter in advance about their coming and had even cleaned up the flat. He *could* have been framed. And pleading guilty might well have been the best way out. Wildes decided to pursue this, and hoped to win the point in the U.S. Court of Appeals.

Chief Judge Kaufman, with two other judges, provided a positive answer. By a two-to-one vote, they ruled that John's conviction could not be recognized as a conviction for the '*illicit*' possession of marijuana. He had been convicted purely on the discovery of the marijuana on his premises—under British law at the time guilty *knowledge* was not something that needed proving before a conviction could be made. 'In the U.S.,' says Wildes, emphasizing the legal difference, 'there's no such thing as a crime where the government doesn't have the burden of proving that the man had a guilty intent.' The Court of Appeals remanded Lennon's case until the immigration service could re-consider the discretionary aspects of the case. They also admonished the government.

News of this triumph, a major hurdle in the case which virtually broke the government's back, came to Leon Wildes unofficially. A clerk at the Court of Appeals phoned: 'Mr Wildes, I shouldn't be doing this because it's still not in final form, but I'm a long-time Lennon fan . . . there is a decision here which will be in final form in an hour or two, and if you want to send someone down I'll give them a copy of it, in which you win the case two to one.'

Under the headline 'Deportation of Lennon barred by Court of Appeals', the *New York Times* reported the case on 8 October 1975:

> In the twenty-four-page decision Judge Irving R. Kaufman issued a strong warning that the courts will not condone selective deportation based upon secret political grounds. This alluded to government documents that were submitted to the court, indications that the Nixon administration started deportation proceedings against Lennon in 1972 for fear that the former Beatle would make appearances in the United States promoting opposition to the then President.
>
> In his summing-up and ruling in John's favour, Judge Kaufman said the court did not take lightly Lennon's claim that he was the victim of a move to oust him on political grounds. 'If in our two hundred years of independence we have in some measure realized our ideals, it is in large part because we have always found a place for those committed to the spirit of liberty, and willing to help implement it. Lennon's four-year battle to remain in our country is testimony to his faith in the American dream.'

Says Wildes: 'I can't describe how my feelings were after four years of courtroom appearances, with and without John.' He called Lennon immediately.

'What do you *mean*? We've won?' John asked.

The cautious Wildes said he must remember they agreed they would never claim victory. 'But John, what I thought

couldn't happen has happened. The court is remanding the case
back to the immigration service, saying they may not consider
your conviction. I think the government is now wiped out and
they're not going to get into all the other political things they've
been threatening, your writing and your songs and all the nonsense they were going to scrape together.'

The following morning John had double cause for jubila-
tion. His son Sean Ono Lennon had been born safely at 2 a.m.
and the precious Green Card was on the horizon.

It was nearly a year before John actually received the Green
Card (which is actually blue). On the appointed day John,
dressed in suit and black tie, went to court. Paradoxically, the
effect of the immigration battle had been to transform lawyer
Wildes' dress style from suits into jeans and long hair, while
John began veering towards the formal every time there was
immigration business to discuss. In court John ritualistically
answered the questions put to him by Wildes:

> *Have you ever been convicted of any crime anywhere
> in the U.S.?*
>
> No.
>
> *Have you ever been a member of the Communist Party
> or any other organization that may seek to overthrow
> the U.S. government by force?*
>
> No.
>
> *Do you intend to make the U.S. your home?*
>
> I do.
>
> *Will you continue your work here?*
>
> Yes. I wish to continue to live here with my family and
> continue making music.

The speeches in John's favour were eloquent and forceful.
Sam Trust, president of A.T.V. Music which owned the rights
to John's compositions, told the court: 'There are two very
positive reasons why Mr Lennon should be allowed to remain

in the U.S. The music scene in the U.S. is in the doldrums right now and the current resurgence of interest in the Beatles and their material proves that they are the most powerful source of music in the last thirty years. I believe we can look forward to many new innovations in music if Mr Lennon is allowed to remain in this country.'

Trust's second point was that Lennon was a tremendous revenue generator. 'The U.S. will be the scene for the reception of that revenue if he is allowed to remain here,' he said.

Writer Norman Mailer was next to take the stand. He described John as 'a great artist who has made an enormous contribution to popular culture. He is one of the great artists of the Western world. We lost T.S. Eliot to England and only got Auden back.'

Leon Wildes read out a letter from the Bishop of New York, the Rt Rev Paul Moore. Emphasizing John's contribution to the culture of New York, the bishop praised him as a 'gentleman of integrity'.

Gloria Swanson told the court that for years she had been actively interested in the physical fitness of New York's youth. 'My husband met John Lennon in a health food store in this city and we found we had feelings in common on this subject. Good food is essential to physical well-being and we are anti-junk-food. I hope very much that he will help us in this sphere. We must educate the country and the Lennons will help do something about it.'

Among the other witnesses who had given evidence to support John's claim to stay in the U.S. were the noted sculptor Noguchi and T.V. personality Geraldo Rivera. Also in the courtroom were composer John Cage and actor Peter Boyle, both close friends of John and Yoko.

As Judge Ira Fieldsteel announced his verdict John embraced Yoko, dressed radiantly in white, and the packed courtroom burst into spontaneous cheering.

Outside the courtroom John was buoyant but he spoke quietly. 'The Immigration Service has finally seen the light of day. It's been a long and slow road but I am not bitter. On the contrary, I can now go and see my relations in Japan and elsewhere. I can travel now! Until today my attorney wouldn't even let me go to Hawaii for a vacation in case I couldn't get back. Whenever I flew to Los Angeles I was paranoid in case the plane was diverted to Tokyo on the way!'

Leon Wildes' celebratory gift to John to mark the success was a leather passport case, bearing the bald eagle and the seal of the United States.

The emotional stress on John during the four-year campaign had been enormous. 'I didn't know him before it, but he'd obviously been a light, airy, *up* person,' says Leon Wildes. 'The psychological strain showed. It had a big effect on him, putting him down.'

John's dry humour did, however, surface on a television show discussion about the case. He went with Leon Wildes. John said to his announcer: 'I want you to interview *Leon*.' The announcer diplomatically said he wanted more time with John. Lennon pleaded for his lawyer: 'Look, let Leon go on. His mother's watching!'

John always remained both puzzled and angry at the immigration hassle. He summed up his feelings in a typically incisive sentence: 'I can't understand it. I always thought the Statue of Liberty said "*Come*". . . . Now I'm going home to crack open a tea-bag and start looking at some travel catalogues.'

John felt completely at home in New York where he had battled for so long to stay. 'My life here is not dissimilar to what it was in England, actually. One's life revolves around family or friends or the work you do. My life for the past ten years since I became "famous" has changed, but basically it's a bedroom, a studio, a T.V., a night out, back home! And they talk an American version of English on T.V. and it goes on a bit longer, all night. But beyond that there's not much difference.

'I imagine New York is like London must have been in the Victorian days when Britain was at the height of its power or on the decline. The American Empire is now what the British Empire used to be. The French had their empire—Paris was cooking. And America now has the empire of the world even though they're losing bits of it. It has that quality about it. And although Washington's the capital, a lot of the action is in New York because that's where the monied people are and it's an old place that's been built up, so that although it's not physically big it's big in the amount of power and the number of people here. I reckon it must have been like this in Queen Victoria's day in London, when everybody wanted to be there. Or even when that Bloomsbury group, Virginia Woolf and all those people were writing their books and poetry. This is like that: it's where a lot of people come to and I became enamoured of it.'

He also liked the fact that there was no language problem. 'Fortunately or unfortunately they speak English so I just fitted in. It's pretty hard to pinpoint what an American is: they're all Italian-Americans or Irish-Americans or African-Americans or Afro-Americans. It's *nice* here.'

During the period of worry over the Green Card his mind had travelled back to his English roots. He particularly enjoyed an invitation from the *New York Times* to review scripts of *The Goon Show* which he and his Uncle George had chortled over back in Liverpool when John was fourteen. The Goons, especially Spike Milligan, inspired the Beatles, he often said, as much as Elvis Presley and Chuck Berry had. They were to the Beatles' generation what the Beatles were to the next.

When Princess Anne married Captain Mark Phillips John stayed up all night in Los Angeles to watch the royal wedding on television. 'It was the right and proper thing for an Englishman abroad to do such a thing,' he explained, tongue in cheek. 'It was a good excuse to have a few drinks to toast the royal family.'

He took special pleasure in teasing the public about a Beatles reunion, rumours of which continued to simmer in the early seventies.

'Beatles to re-form?' screamed the writers excitedly in 1973 when John, George, and Ringo got together in Los Angeles for a Ringo Starr solo album session. In a parody of the Paul McCartney press release which still irritated him, John released this statement under the headline of 'Newswecanalldowithout':

Although John and Yoko and George, and George and Ringo, had played together often, it was the first time the three ex-Beauties had played together since—well, since they last played together. As usual, an awful lot of rumours, if not downright lies, were going on, including the possibility of impresario Allen De Klein of grABCKO playing bass for the other three in an as-yet-untitled album called *I Was A Teenage Fat Cat*. Producer Richard Perry, who planned to take the tapes along to sell them to Paul McCartney, told a friend: 'I'll take the tapes to Paul McCartney.'

The extreme humility that existed between John and Paul seems to have evaporated. 'They've spoken to each other on the telephone—and in English, that's a change,' said a McCartney associate. 'If only everything were as simple and unaffected as McCartney's new single "My Love", then maybe Dean Martin and Jerry Lewis would be reunited with the Marx Bros and *Newsweak* could get a job,' said an East African official.—Yours Up To The Teeth, John Lennon and Yoko Ono.

The two years preceding Sean's birth while the immigration battle continued were packed with dramatic events for John. As a musician, he encountered many peaks and troughs. His rock 'n' roll album produced by the legendary Phil Spector, one of his all-time heroes, was fraught with personal clashes. As a man, he descended into the worst period of his life, lurching in a drunken haze around California. The reason for that appalling episode was traceable to his marriage. In the autumn of 1973 he and Yoko split up.

'Yoko and I had a breakdown, one way or another,' John told me during their separation. 'We'd been together seven years, y'know, and it wasn't like a normal marriage where the man goes off to work all day, or even the accepted showbiz marriage where one of the partners gets involved in something that splits them up for months through work. We were together *just about twenty-four hours of every day*! So it was bound to happen that we'd snap.' Their private problem was exacerbated by the pressure of the immigration issue.

John and Yoko's split took everyone by surprise. They had been together as friends and artists, as well as man and wife, in one of the most publicly demonstrated love matches of the century. But John was a notoriously difficult, volatile, moody man to live with; during a creative lull, such as he experienced around this time, his insecurities manifested themselves in immature behaviour. He smoked too much, becoming edgy, and spent days on end in his bedroom in solitude. His hands went clammy with nervousness and worry at meeting even his closest friends. And, given the chance, he drank too much. Yoko knew only too well of the danger signs when booze was readily available, and kept a tight grip on its visibility in the Dakota.

She decided that a temporary split was essential. 'There was never any need for a divorce,' she says coolly. 'I knew we would be back together again, eventually.' But John needed time to straighten himself out and, perhaps, they should learn for a while to live without each other. If drinking and having a wild time was something he was missing, she reasoned, it was best that he got it out of his system and played out his fantasies while retaining contact with her by phone.

John was not happy about the decision. 'She kicked me out, pure and simple,' he said later. 'I was behaving stupidly and I'd lost whatever it was about me that she found good in the first place. It was grow-up time and I'm glad she made me do it.'

Yoko says: 'John and I were artists together and husband and wife together. We were competitive, also, to a point: he would write something and I'd say something like, ''Well, that's nice, I've got something now *I've* just written,'' and we would try to stretch each other as writers. It wasn't so surprising, really that we should separate for a while. It turned out to be the best thing that could happen.'

By then, they had moved into an apartment in the Dakota building at 1 West 72nd Street in Manhattan, from where they also ran their company, Lenono. Working as their secretary at the Dakota was a twenty-two-year-old girl born in New York of Chinese parents. May Pang was trusted. She was loyal, efficient, and hardworking for two very demanding people and she loved John's music. When John and Yoko agreed on the split, Yoko suggested John should head for California; to go outside America was impossible at the time because of the Green Card problem, and anyway, Yoko said, he should experience Los Angeles.

Elliot Mintz, John's closest male friend in America since 1971, says it was Yoko who said May should accompany John.

'Obviously,' says Mintz, 'for John Lennon to go alone to Los Angeles, where he'd never been before except with the Beatles, was out of the question. Here was a man who had not driven a car in America, could not walk into a supermarket and purchase food, who couldn't take his laundry to the corner, who didn't make phone calls, didn't know how to compute a tip on a bill, didn't know where to locate restaurants, and who knew hardly anyone in Los Angeles except me. He would have been totally helpless. It was practical to send his secretary, May Pang, with him to look after him. I suppose Yoko knew it was likely there would be intimacy between the two of them. She took a mature view, knowing John: "Better with May than galloping around with the golden groupies."

'And Yoko believed May could handle it. May did not smoke, drink or take drugs, she was not part of any weird Los Angeles orgy scene.' But it was never a love match, says Mintz, who saw them together often. 'To think that John ran off with May to leave Yoko Ono would require a remarkable suspension in logic. John could not sustain May's company for more than a matter of hours without incredible fatigue setting in. It was not a love affair. It was a relationship born out of the convenience of the moment. I do not wish to publicly embarrass the lady. She did a fairly effective job of doing just that in her own book. It is one thing to merchandise the memories but her contention that she was the other woman in John's life is nonsense. May contrived a quasi-fictional scenario in an attempt to give form to a relationship that was not there. From the moment John met Yoko to the last hour of his life, she was the only woman who shared his love.'

Elliot Mintz's closeness to John developed, curiously, from his first association with Yoko. In 1972 Mintz was working as a disc jockey and star television interviewer, well on the road to becoming a Dick Cavett-style commentator; in Los Angeles he reported for *Eye-Witness News* and had a growing reputation as a penetrating interviewer of statesmen, politicians and celebrities. When John and Yoko's controversial album *Some Time In New York City* was released in June of that year, Mintz conducted a one-hour interview/profile for the radio station KLOS with Yoko, tracing the background to her meeting with John. He asked her unusual questions: whether the people in her dreams spoke English or Japanese, what quotes from her book *Grapefruit* meant to her and how she wanted to be remembered when she died. Her answer was, 'Just say that John and I loved, lived, and died.' Next day she called to ask for a correction to be taped to that sentence: it was re-recorded to say: 'John and I lived, loved, and died.' Mintz had never really understood her music or avant-garde stance but he sensed a 'wonderful quality' in the lady over the telephone. Still, it was one of 2,000 radio interviews he had conducted over a decade, and he thought it would probably go no further. 'It was really quite a beautiful interview,' said Yoko, 'and we loved the tone of it.'

A few days later about 300 letters had arrived at Mintz's office enthusiastically enquiring about the Yoko interview. Hesitantly Mintz phoned Yoko to tell her about the letters. To his surprise she was fascinated to hear about every one. And that conversation began a unique telephone friendship between Yoko and Mintz that went on nightly for many months. Yoko believes it is sometimes possible to tell more of a person on the phone than in person, when appearances can sometimes distract or inhibit both parties. With Mintz in California and Yoko in New York, they spoke every night on 'everything—religion, films, politics, love, death, books, romance. And every time I spoke to Yoko her perceptions on anything we talked about, even something innocuous, brought a perspective on the subject that had never occurred to me,' says Mintz. 'I was beginning to understand why John, who had seen it all, done it all, knew it all, been around the block four million times, had to stop when he met Yoko. All her thoughts were original.'

Finally, after months of these nightly conversations, John could stand the curiosity no longer. Who was this disc jockey his wife was always talking to? Typically he decided to get in on the act and did a radio interview with Mintz.

Within months of striking up the telephone friendship, John and Yoko decided to take a car journey across America in their old station wagon, with a driver. John often remarked on how little he had seen of the country: 'We only went to America to buy records unavailable back home and give concerts in the old days. I needed to go in some of the coffee shops at four in the morning and get a chocolate milk shake, that kind of thing, just do it normally like the rest of the people do. Yoko and I wanted to experience the heartland of this country.'

A meeting with the mysterious Mintz was part of the programme. When they met him at the house they had rented in Santa Barbara, they presented him with the demonstration record of *Some Time In New York City*, the highly charged political album containing 'Woman Is The Nigger Of The World' and a song about Attica State Prison. After spending the day with John and Yoko, Mintz returned to Los Angeles and broadcast the entire album, freezing all commercials and inviting listeners' reaction. Next day John and Yoko phoned him to ask how it went.

'I have the good news and the bad news,' replied Mintz. 'The good news is that it went great, the bad news is that I was fired.' The lyrical content of the album had offended the sponsors. John and Yoko thought it was hilarious.

'My radio career had just collapsed,' says Mintz, 'and they just sat there laughing.'

John said: 'Oh well, now you don't have a job, you might as well come with us. We're going up to San Francisco.' Mintz did just that, spending a month with them at the Miyako Hotel in San Francisco, and from that first meeting he became John and Yoko's close friend and confidant. Lennon trusted him completely.

Born on 16 February 1945, Mintz is, crucially, an Aquarian like Yoko. A man who speaks and moves with total precision, he shared with Lennon a similarly dry sense of humour and an interest in literature. During the fifteen-month period Lennon was away from Yoko Mintz saw him and also spoke to Yoko on the phone nearly every day. 'Don't ever ask me to keep a secret from the other,' he told both of them. 'You are both my friends.'

When John and May Pang stepped from the plane at Los Angeles airport in October 1973 Mintz was there to meet them in his 1956 Jaguar. John wanted to cash some traveller's cheques but they reached the bank—Lloyds on Sunset Boulevard—just after it had closed. 'I knocked on the window and the teller shook his head,' says Mintz. 'I took John and moved him in front of the window and suddenly the doors swung open, security guards came out and the vault opened and the president of the bank appeared.

' "Would you care for some coffee, Mr Lennon?"

'John said: "I just want to turn this into some money." '

The amount turned out to be $10,000, so John sat down and signed his name on the back of 100 cheques, each valued at $100.

'John,' said Elliot Mintz, 'maybe I should take that cash and put it in my cheque account for you. It's a lot to carry around.'

The bank manager said: 'Maybe we can interest you in a long-term checking account?'

John said: 'No, no. I'll keep the money in me pocket.' He'd never handled so much cash in his life and wanted the 'feel' of it. He took ten thousand dollars and stuffed it in his jacket. It was the very first time in his life, he said, he had been inside a bank.

Mintz joked: 'If things go well next week, I'll take you to the supermarket.' John laughed. 'How did it feel, being in a bank, then, John?'

Lennon answered: 'It felt exactly the same as anywhere else. All I did was autograph bits of paper.'

The famous record producer, Lou Adler, had loaned John and May Pang a house on Stone Canyon Road, Bel Air. 'He was incredibly unhappy because of his estrangement from Yoko during the entire "lost weekend",' says Mintz. 'It was the low point of his life. Three days after arriving, at 10 o'clock in the morning, he arrived outside my house shouting: "Wake up, wake up. I've been trying to get you on the phone." I was astonished to see him up so early. I asked: "How long have you been up?" He said: "I haven't been to sleep yet. Can you get Yoko on the phone for me?" He was having trouble with the phones and with the time difference between California and New York. I later asked him why he appeared so low, during that period, and he said that he felt alienated, lost, and consistently unhappy, especially when he was drunk. It was a vicious circle: the more morose John became, the more he drank and the more depressed he became. And the worst thing I can say about my old friend John Lennon,' says Mintz, 'is that he was a lousy drinker. He just couldn't handle booze.

'The Los Angeles months marked the end of an era for John. The wild streak that showed itself in the Lennon of the Liverpool back streets and, later, of Hamburg ended on the Sunset Strip in Hollywood. Later he told me that he just wanted to show the boys that he could get as low as any of them. He could drink more, stay awake longer, play more rock 'n' roll music and be just as outrageous as the rest of them. It was a restless farewell to a persona he had already outgrown. That crazy recording session with Phil Spector, whom he loved and admired; the bar hopping with Keith Moon, Harry Nilsson and Ringo; the Hollywood parties and the nights that knew no end; all of it was an exercise in letting go. If most people did any of those things it would mean nothing. When John Lennon did it, the effect became larger than the reality of the actual events.'

Lennon's behaviour in Los Angeles filled him with remorse and regret; it was infinitely worse than his days in Hamburg. There at least he had the excuse that he was a young man on the prowl. Now, in California with the woman he loved back in New York, monitoring his every move and telling him he was in no state to return to her, John plunged down and down. His wild behaviour included a drunken audience with Jerry Lee Lewis and a ridiculous exhibition of foul-mouthed drunkenness, interrupting the Smothers Brothers show at the Troubadour Club on Sunset Boulevard. Worst of all was when he went on the rampage in the house at Bel Air. With musicians who had been drinking at Phil Spector's record session John had returned to the house drunk on vodka. He became violent and went round smashing the gold records hanging on the wall (one for Carole King's multi-million-selling *Tapestry* album), throwing vases against stained glass windows, wrecking furniture, tables, and chairs. For his own safety Spector and his bodyguard put Lennon—who had smashed his spectacles—into bed, tying his wrists and ankles to prevent him doing any more damage. A horrified Mintz got an alarm call from May Pang and was at the house within minutes. May was concerned for John's safety. A drunken Lennon screamed at May: 'Keep that bastard Jew away from me.' Mintz left.

By next morning John had forgotten nearly everything. He told May Pang to assure Lou Adler that he would meet the cost of all the repairs to his house and contents. His first call of apology was to Mintz. 'In all the time I've known you,' he said contritely, 'the very worst thing I could think of to say to you was that you were a bastard Jew. I guess I really must love you.' Then he phoned everybody else.

John's drunkenness in California probably extended to about a dozen times in the whole fifteen months; unfortunately on too many occasions he got drunk in public. And he drank anything that had the right effect. 'Give me a Remy Martin, a B&B, a Courvoisier, an Amaretto, a Tia Maria, anything of that sort,' he'd tell the waitress or bartender. He ate chocolate and candies and junk food.

When John was sober, Mintz would try to tell him he was making a fool of himself. Lennon's rejoinders were as caustic as they had been during his Hamburg and Beatle days: 'Don't get real on me. If you don't like being around me when I'm that way, why don't you just fuck off?' Next day, full of regret, he would apologize—in his fashion: 'Why did you stay with me last night? God, if you were that way, I'd not stay with *you*!'

Tough, cynical, angry, bitter, and confused, John leaned on drink for the same reason he always had: he was insecure. He desperately wanted to return to Yoko after only a week but the sober lady, busy pursuing her career in New York as an avant-garde artist and poet, was not listening to his pleas. They talked frequently by telephone, sometimes for minutes, sometimes for hours. John explained that one of the reasons why he was getting drunk so easily was because his body's resistance to alcohol had been reduced by the drugs he had taken at the height of his days as a Beatle. 'All of his thoughts, all of his longing, had to do with his desperation to get back to Yoko, and to his frustration with her telling him he didn't sound ready,' says Mintz. 'Although he said he was ready to return it was clear he was not.' While he fretted, however, Yoko told her friends that she was certain she and John would re-unite one day. It was only a matter of time.

Confirming Lennon's inability to handle liquor, Mintz says: 'If he had one glass of wine, I'd have to cancel all plans for the next three days. And he was so argumentative! He would start an argument and keep it going just for the sake of having a row and winning it. The basis of the argument was not so

important as the row itself. But he was never evil or terrible—
just drunk. I saw him that way twice in Las Vegas, once in
Japan, twice in New York, and perhaps a dozen times in Los
Angeles.'

But John crossed certain personal frontiers in California.
Elliot Mintz took him to see one of his favourite artists, Jerry
Lee Lewis, at the Roxy in Los Angeles. 'I had only three
childhood idols,' he told Mintz. 'Elvis, Carl Perkins, and Jerry
Lee, and I haven't seen any live. Let's go!' John was totally
immersed in the driving rock 'n' roll that had first inspired
him, classics like 'Whole Lotta Shakin' ' and 'Great Balls of
Fire'. Jerry Lee did his wildest show, playing the piano with
his toes. Lennon led the applause at the end of each song. After
the show Elliot took John backstage and introduced him to
Lewis. John just sank to the floor, and kissed Jerry Lee's
shoes. 'That's all right, son,' drawled Jerry Lee. 'You just get
up now.'

The encounter had a strange parallel with the occasion on
which he had met Elvis. There was, he decided, no future in
talking to artists. 'I'm a record man,' he told me. 'I don't like
live work or going to concerts. They usually let you down.'

Ten years earlier, living at Weybridge with Cynthia, John had
a sign hanging in his kitchen. It said simply: 'The drunk and
the glutton shall come to poverty.' It would be easy to view
the California débâcle as a worthless alcoholic escapade but in
many ways it was essential because John had never had a chance
to grow up. It had all been done in public as a musician. This
gave him the opportunity. One of his biggest dreams was to
experience Las Vegas. 'What's it like, what's it like, Elliot?'
he kept asking Mintz. 'Take me there. Fix me a drink and we'll
go.' One drizzly day Mintz agreed to take him. 'But John, take
it easy. If we're going to Las Vegas, let's at least get there
sober.'

Driving down La Cienega, not far from Mintz's home,
John's eye was caught by a flashing sign: 'The Losers' Topless
Club'. 'Feels right,' he said to Mintz. 'Let's pull in.' Mintz
was incredulous: it was two o'clock in the afternoon. Once in
the bar, with the topless barmaid filling up his glass as quickly
as he drank and Motown records accompanying the two topless

dancers, John became more and more uneasy. He quickly realized the futility and sleaziness of it all. Even in California he was able to diagnose bad taste through his alcoholic hazes. After a few minutes John had seen enough. 'As we left The Losers,' recalls Mintz, 'John started singing softly in my ear: "We make them paint their face and dance—Woman is the Nigger of the world." He could be the observer and the observed simultaneously.'

In Las Vegas John acted out all his fantasies. At Caesar's Palace John 'was enchanted by the casino atmosphere for a while, but it was the longest weekend of my life,' says Elliot Mintz. 'The house kept us supplied with drinks and we sat in the chairs by the roulette wheel for hours. He devised the John Lennon Las Vegas system; taking a ten-dollar chip and placing it on every number on the table. John became convinced he had a system that would guarantee him a 35–1 win with each turn of the wheel. The plan was less than successful. The gambling over, we went for a walk around the casino until the spotlight fell on him and four hundred people besieged him. Cocktail hostesses began fawning over him, saying things like: "Hey, I grew up listening to the Beatles." And John was off. The plastic, crazy, neon city of Las Vegas was even more empty to him than Los Angeles. And even L.A. he had christened as "the place you stop off to buy a hamburger".'

John consoled his sorrows over drinking sessions with friends Harry Nilsson, Keith Moon, Klaus Voormann, Ringo Starr, Jim Keltner, and Mal Evans, 'Big Mal', the faithful friend from Liverpool days who had been the Beatles' road manager. Evans, whose giant frame belied his soft, warm personality, was a former telephone engineer who drifted into the Beatles camp by doing part-time work as a bouncer at the Cavern. As road manager alongside Neil Aspinall on all the Beatles' world tours, he had a particularly strong relationship—gruff but intuitive—with the moody Lennon during Beatlemania. When the Beatles split, Mal felt lost. He moved to Los Angeles, fell victim to drink and drugs, and allegedly pulled a gun on a girl in his Hollywood flat on 5 January 1976. The police were called but Mal barricaded himself in. They smashed the door down to be confronted by Mal holding a gun; they shot him dead. The news of yet another fatality in the Beatles family saddened John but he coped with it as he had with all other tragedies: by not dwelling on it for long.

George Melly, whose meetings with John seemed to punctuate key events in Lennon's life—the Beatles, meeting Yoko, and estrangement from her—was in a bungalow at Hollywood's Chateau Marmont Hotel when an aggressive John arrived at dawn with Harry Nilsson and Derek Taylor. 'I wouldn't guarantee what substances were involved in creating his condition,' says Melly, 'but certainly drink was a contributory one. They were all high on an all-night raid. Suddenly one of us mentioned Jackie Pye, the Liverpool wrestler. He was famous in Liverpool as the baddie of the wrestling circuit. Although John was much younger than me, Jackie Pye, it turned out, had spanned our youth. We had both seen him. His favourite trick was blowing his nose between his thumb and forefinger and flicking the snot at the referee. He was known as Dirty Jackie Pye. Once we hit this area of shared knowledge we were in hysterics.' Amid the palm trees of Hollywood, two lapsed Liverpudlians recalled an eccentric slice of their youth.

Four months later a similarly wild John arrived in New York and headed for Derek Taylor's suite at the Algonquin Hotel. With Harry Nilsson again, John was drunk and began trying to smash the chandeliers in Derek's suite. The next thing that happened was a 2 a.m. phone call in the hotel to George Melly's female publicity agent. 'He demanded sex with her,' says Melly. 'She replied: "I'm asleep. Go away." I couldn't help reflecting, when I heard about it next morning, on the number of girls around the world who would have received that phone call from John Lennon with a certain enthusiasm.'

As John described his songs as 'personalized diaries', it was not surprising that the music he made during the separation period comprised messages to Yoko and elements of self-pity. *Walls And Bridges*, an album made during the California period, included such songs as 'Nobody Loves You (When You're Down And Out)'. I asked him what he meant by the enigmatic album title. He answered: 'Walls you walk into and bridges you cross over. Deep stuff!'

The biggest psychological bridge John had to cross during his absence from Yoko was a meeting with Julian, who was then ten and living with Cynthia. They had spoken on the phone, on Cynthia's insistence, regularly since John had gone to America. But for nearly three years they had not met. Cynthia believed that as John was isolated in California, he should see Julian. This caused John anguish and torment right up until Julian's visit. He believed that he had been a neglectful father and he could not summon up the inner strength to pick up the pieces.

When Cynthia and Julian flew into Los Angeles Airport just after Christmas 1974, John was nervous. He had no idea of how his reunion with his son would go and whether the boy would warm to him. And he dreaded seeing Cynthia again. Once a link had been broken, especially such a strong one, John felt that it should be severed for ever. Mentally he was a million miles away from life with Cynthia in Liverpool and Weybridge. There was the extra complication of her meeting May Pang.

At the airport and in the limousine which took Cynthia and Julian to their hotel, John was jittery. He was cool with Cynthia; a 'hello' and a peck on the cheek was all he could manage. But Julian's excited chatter about the flight on a jumbo jet and arrival in America broke the ice on the car ride. John realized how thrilled he felt to see Julian and kissed him affectionately.

Next day, the plan was for John to take Julian, alone, to Disneyland. Says Cynthia: 'John wanted to whip into the hotel, take Julian away and not communicate with me which was fine by me. Unfortunately, Julian flew into a tantrum in his bedroom, screaming on the floor, hysterical.' Julian dug his heels in, insisting he wanted his mother *and* father on the outing.

'Look, John,' said Cynthia, 'I'm sorry but he won't go anywhere with you without me. You can hear him in the other room.' Reluctantly John gave in.

A tense day for John, Cynthia, and May and Mal Evans followed. 'I felt miserable trailing round Disneyland with them, but Julian had a great time and that's what mattered.' Still John would not face Cynthia, who stayed several stages behind the party for most of the time. 'John could not look me in the eyes,' says Cynthia. 'He seemed in a total panic that we might start talking and he avoided looking near me as much as he could for the whole day.' They were forced together for a lunch of bacon and flapjacks and syrup, with John talking in a stilted fashion about the virtues of American junk food, but the atmosphere was awful.

As well as being 'deeply upset' by John's aloofness, the ever-practical Cynthia was worried about Julian. 'I wanted a proper conversation with John about Julian's education, his future and what he thought should be done for our son. I pushed once or twice but John looked the other way. After two or three rebuffs I gave up. I just hoped that the relationship between John and Julian would gain strength.'

And it did. The boy went off with a handful of balloons and many hugs and kisses from his Dad. Their friendship developed warmly in later years, as Julian confirms. One of the reasons for this was Julian's own musical talent, which showed itself even at this age.

By the late seventies Julian as a teenager was establishing a friendship with John. 'It was more of one man to another than the usual father and son relationship,' says Julian, 'because he had been away from me a lot, and he said he realized that. I was just getting through to him and growing up myself and growing out of the silly giggling I did as a young teenager that really annoyed him, when Dad was killed.' He sorely regrets being robbed of the time to develop the bond that was growing between them.

As Julian moved inexorably towards a life in music, he developed a particularly strong rapport with Sean. 'I feel a terrific blood closeness with Sean,' says Julian. 'We're going to get on well.' His relationship with his stepmother, on the other hand, will always require diplomacy. Yoko and Cynthia have kept a wary distance from each other since the divorce. 'I'll feel better with both my mother and Yoko when I'm older and more established on my own ground as a musician,' said Julian in 1984. 'I like to keep an open line with everyone and not hurt anybody's feelings.' Both personally and professionally as a singer-songwriter, being the son of John Lennon will never be easy.

By 1983, at the age of twenty, Julian had dropped his teenage plans to launch a group with the name of the Lennon Drops, and arrived in London, alone, to set up a flat and tackle, head-on, the job of becoming a singer–songwriter–bandleader.

Tony Stratton Smith, boss of Charisma Records, was highly impressed with Julian's songwriting and sent him for six weeks to an obscure château in France where Julian's confidence, as well as his musicianship, improved enormously. He has now been signed to Charisma and has secured the support of the outstanding American producer Phil Ramone, who has worked with major artists of the calibre of Paul Simon, Billy Joel, Frank Sinatra, and Bob Dylan.

Julian is totally aware of the pitfalls and expects to be accused of cashing in on his father's name. Clearly he is in a 'no win' situation. However, 'I just have to do it,' he told me. 'Partly, I feel that with my father dead someone should keep the tradition alive. He was a major, successful singer and writer and it's up to me to try to carry on to keep the name Lennon going in the field of music.

'I feel music in my blood. It would be asking for trouble to do it my father's way and style.' Vocal similarities with John are obvious: 'I can tell the sound is similar when I hear myself, but I don't do it consciously. I did love the way Dad sang, and there's nothing wrong with taking a bit of inspiration from him, surely? Others do, so I don't see why I shouldn't. His work has influenced me, but I'm very self-conscious about the criticism that is bound to come. It's both an advantage and a disadvantage being the son of John Lennon. I'm determined to live it down and live it up! I feel confident I can handle it and grow as a songwriter and singer. Dad told me the Beatles thing was something he enjoyed breaking away from and in a sense I'm trying to break away from him while remaining Julian Lennon all my life. He would understand. Dad's best work came when the Beatles finished. . . . He told me the Beatles were fun while they lasted but he would never do it again.'

Cynthia's last, bitter experience of John occurred on a flight from New York to Los Angeles. Again, John was with May Pang, and Julian, who had been with him in New York during the making of the *Walls And Bridges* album; Julian had even played the drums on one track called 'Ya Ya'. While Cynthia had stayed at the Pierre Hotel in New York, Julian had stayed with John and May. After a few days a cheery John had phoned his former wife and asked her to go with them to Los Angeles.

Cynthia thought that perhaps the breakthrough had come and they could have a decent relationship. She looked forward to the five-hour flight.

But when they boarded the plane, John's mental barricade went up again. He was with May and Julian in the first-class section, completely ignoring Cynthia, who was sitting behind them, for the entire journey. 'It was total and utter rejection,' she remembers. 'I couldn't get through. I'd fought hard to get John and Julian together, in ways John would never know about. But whenever we looked at each other, it was like utter panic by John. He couldn't cope with me. He must have felt threatened by me, that I was after him and wanted him and me to get back together. But I wasn't. All I wanted was mental communication for the sake of the one thing in life John and I still had in common: a son. I shall never understand why two people who had a child could not talk normally without threats or worries or fear.' Finally Cynthia broke down on the plane and wept. It was the last time she saw him.

Such was John's state during his separation from Yoko that it is amazing that he reached out to his son, establishing the basis for their future mental rapport, as well as making some superb music with lyrics sharply evocative of his mental condition. To cope with his former wife, in addition, and all memories she evoked, was impossible for him that year. At the time the estrangement from Yoko was enough of a problem.

In New York in mid-1974 I spent two days and nights with John while he was making *Walls And Bridges*. He talked openly about his depression, how he was missing Yoko, but that he expected they would re-unite. He was living with May Pang in a modest, one-roomed apartment at 434 East 52nd Street, overlooking the East River. He loved cities with rivers, he said; New York's affinity with Liverpool made him nostalgic. In the Record Plant studios John was at his mercurial best, changing lyrics and putting the gloss on some of his new songs. One evening over a Chinese meal he talked at length to me, both about his life as a New Yorker and how he was gradually coming to terms with realizing what went on in the Beatles years.

That year George Harrison played a solo tour of America

and John was rumoured to be planning to play at his New York concert. In the end he didn't because he had a row with George over what John called 'The Famous Beatles Agreement', the final dissolution of the group that required all four signatures. John was the last to sign. 'I was supposed to sign this on the day of the concert but I wouldn't. My astrologer told me it was the wrong day for business. [John finally signed the same day he visited Disneyland with Julian.] George was furious at the time because I hadn't signed it when I was supposed to and I was informed that I needn't bother to go to George's show. I was relieved because there wasn't any time for rehearsal and I didn't want it to be a case of John jumping up and playing a few chords. I went to see George at Nassau and it was a good, tight show. George's voice was shot but the atmosphere was good and George's performance was great. I saw George after the Madison Square Garden show and we were friends again.' Harrison had resolutely refused to sing major Beatles hits on the tour—'a basic mistake,' said John, 'easy to spot when you're not making one. But people definitely wanted to hear the old stuff.' The songs George did perform included John's 'In My Life', though with slightly altered lyrics; 'Something'; 'While My Guitar Gently Weeps'; and 'For You Blue'.

In the past two years, he said, he had changed his attitude towards the Beatles. 'The period when I rejected the Beatles years in my mind was when I was just out of the Janov therapy treatment,' he explained. 'I'd been mentally stripped bare and I wanted to shoot my mouth off to clear it all away. Now it's different.

'When I slagged off the Beatles thing, it was like divorce pangs and, me being me, it was blast this, fuck the past. Remember all those articles we did together in the old *Melody Maker*—"Lennon Blasts Hollies" all over the back page? And the *Daily Mirror* piece: "Lennon beats up local D.J. at Paul's 21st birthday party!" I've always had a bit of a mouth and when a thing begins that way, you have to live up to it. Then Paul and me had that fight in the pages of the *MM*. It was a period I had to go through. I sort of enjoy the fight at the time, that's the funny thing.

'Now we've all got it out and it's cool. I can see the Beatles from a new point of view. Can't remember much of what happened but I've started taking an interest in what went on while I was in that fish tank. It must have been incredible.'

Part of John's therapy in growing out of the Beatles was to recognize their importance to his life. On a long car journey across America he took a pile of Beatles cassettes to re-acquaint himself with the work which nobody would forget. And when, in 1974, America's devoted Beatles fans made it possible to stage a Beatlefest, John wanted to be counted in as a fan of his old group. Beatles films, guitars from John and Paul, Ringo's old drumsticks and other memorabilia were gathered by John when he met Mark Lapidos, who was then launching the Beatlefest at New York's Commodore Hotel, and who still runs the conventions several times a year all around America. 'John nearly even came to the first one to pick the winner of the charity raffle and see who won his old guitar,' says Lapidos. 'But he chickened out at the last minute.' John did, however, enthuse to Lapidos about the whole idea of Beatlefests, which have since become established throughout America.

Four years later a Beatlefest assistant, Roger Berkley, bumped into John in the street and told him that the 1978 convention was coming soon. Had John any message? 'Yeah, just tell them the music was the thing,' replied John. It had taken a long time, but John Lennon had come to terms with being an ex-Beatle. He even enjoyed it.

'I'm into collecting memorabilia as well,' he told me in our interviews. 'Elton John came in with these gifts for me, stills from the *Yellow Submarine* film. Great! He gave me these four dolls of John, Paul, George, and Ringo. I thought: Christ, what's *this*? A Beatle collecting Beatle dolls? But why not? It's history, man, history. I went through a phase of hating all those years and having to smile when I didn't want to, but now I'm out of it, it's great to look back on it, man. Great! Why haven't I ever considered the good times instead of moaning about what we had to go through?'

He had even gone some way towards mending his relationship with McCartney. 'He was here in New York recently. We spent two or three nights together talking about the old days. It was cool, seeing what each other remembered from Hamburg and Liverpool. So y'see, all that happened when I blew my mouth off was that it was like an abscess bursting, except that mine, as usual, burst in public.

'Look, when the Beatles did a tour, we hated it and loved it. There were great nights and lousy ones . . . It wasn't all pie and cookies being a Beatle but in 1970 people just wanted big-mouth Lennon to shout about the lows. So I made a quick trip [his therapy with Janov] to uncover the hidden stones of my mind and a lot of the bats flew and some of them are going to have to stay. I've got a perspective now, that's a fact.' He must have exorcized all the ghosts because he even went to the Broadway production of the successful theatrical production *Sgt Pepper*; watching it would have been like looking into the mirror of his own mind as well as his body.

John loved buttons. On the nights I saw him his badge was half an apple between bread slices. 'Work that one out,' he said. 'It doesn't mean I own half of Apple. Elton gave me the badge. It means I'm schizophrenic!'

John was alive, crackling with good humour and his old rapier-like observation. Leaving the recording studio, he walked with me for five minutes before hailing a cab. I mentioned that it was a strange contrast with the police-protected limousine rides he had been used to. Ah, he said, that was precisely what he loved about New York. 'I get 'em all the time. Not in California—they're looking for stars there and it's unsafe. But here in New York, I found all the paranoia was inside my own head. It's so safe here. I feel free, walking the streets. Nobody hassles you. I reckon most of the cab drivers in New York know me, I've taken so many, and I *love* seeing the city from the inside of a cab.'

At the end of the journey, John, always an enormously generous tipper, gave the cabbie $10 for a trip that cost less than half that amount.

'Excuse me, sir,' said the cab driver, 'but aren't you John Lennon?'

'Nah,' said John. 'I wish I was. I wish I had his money.'

Inside his apartment John regaled me and photographer Bob Gruen with the bizarre story that he had seen flying saucers from his window. He was serious. 'Look,' he said, 'it's true. I was standing, naked, by this window leading on to that roof when an oval-shaped object started flying from left to right. It had a red light on the top. After about twenty minutes it disappeared over the East River and behind the United Nations Building. I wonder if it might have been carrying out some research there.

'They all think I'm potty, but it's true. I shouted after it, "Wait for me, wait for me!" But I'm not kidding, May and I saw it. I didn't believe it either.' He had phoned the police, who said there had been other reports of the sighting of a flying saucer. 'But I didn't tell them who it was on the phone. I didn't want newspaper headlines saying: "Beatle Sees Flying Saucer". I've got enough trouble with the immigration people already.'

'And you'd not been smoking or drinking?' I said.

'No, God's honest truth. I only do that at weekends or when I see Harry Nilsson.'

We watched television for hours. John watched himself on a news bulletin coming out of court earlier that day where he had been to listen to yet another round in his immigration battle. Reporters, surprised to see John formally dressed in dark suit and tie, asked him if he was confident of winning his case.

'Yes, I'm confident,' said John.

'Why?' asked a reporter.

'Because I'm big-headed, as usual,' said John. 'I like it here. I want to stay. Amnesty! Amnesty!'

'It's absolutely alive, that's why I have got to live in New York and got sick of Los Angeles,' John told me. 'There's a buzz here. I like the way you can get or do anything you like at any time of the day or night. . . . If I couldn't live here, I'd live in Paris. I love the French. They're so bloody rude.

'Look here, New York gives you television all night. It's better than the B.B.C. Light Orchestra.'

John had been consumed by the Watergate scandal. 'Any country,' he said, 'that produces the Watergate affair has got to be number one with me. I sat watching every bit of it on T.V. and couldn't believe it. They kept asking the witnesses questions and the guy replied; "That is inoperative." Everything they were asked that was meant to make 'em tell the truth, they said: "That is inoperative." I'm gonna try it when they start asking me hard questions. ''Inoperative. All questions about the Beatles inoperative.'' '

Part of John's fascination for Watergate can be traced to his love of causes: he loved wearing buttons that championed people or attitudes and during 1975 wore one saying simply 'Elvis'. Other badges, or 'buttons' as he grew to call them when his language became peppered with Americanisms, included 'Indict Rockefeller for murder', 'Listen to this button' and 'Not Insane', a phrase coined by the parody group Firesign Theatre.

Throughout 1974 John made a determined, conscious effort to pull himself back from the precipice of emotional and intellectual disaster which threatened him during his Californian exile. He drank less. He made music. He immersed himself in serious subjects like Watergate during his own immigration battle. He even demonstrated to Britain that the appalling international publicity he had received in Los Angeles did not reflect a numbing of his sense or his memory. When singer–songwriter Todd Rundgren criticized his activities in the *Melody Maker*, John tore into him with the same ruthlessness he had used against Paul McCartney. In a style that combined his old satire with vitriol, John wrote Todd (whom he called Sodd Runtlestuntle) the 'Opened Lettuce' which is reproduced in second insert of illustrations.

One of the highlights of the year and a turning point in his life came when he went to Caribou recording studios in Colorado to record with Elton John. The two men were warm friends. Elton, a total fan of 1960s music, loved the mixture of hard man and soft romantic in John which all who knew him recognized under that sometimes manic exterior. Lennon, for his part, thought Elton's music and his industry was magnificent. He loved the nature of the man, his stage act, and his songs. Elton had worked in Dick James' music publishing office in London when the Beatles had sent in their demonstration tapes, so the link with John went back a long way. (Lennon was always attracted to extroverts; he sought only one autograph in his life, and that was Mae West's, secured for him by Elliot Mintz. 'Now, what's this fella's last name?' Mae West asked as she signed.)

John's song 'Whatever Gets You Thru The Night', on which Elton played keyboards, was his first chart-topper in America as a soloist. When they made the record Elton told John that it was a number one; John laughed at him. 'No, I'm out of favour here. It would be nice but it's not a number one.' Elton made John promise that if it did reach the top he would appear in concert with him. John was so certain it would not that he readily agreed. And so the stage was set for John to appear at Elton's Madison Square Garden concert on Thanksgiving Day, 28 November 1974.

Before he was committed to the New York show John went to see Elton's concert in Boston and he remembered thinking, Thank God it's not me, as he watched Elton dressing to go on. 'I got stage fright just looking at him!' said John. 'By the time I got on to the stage at Madison Square Garden with all the screaming and shouting [20,000 people gave Lennon a conquering hero's welcome], I thought what is *this*! I hadn't heard it since the Beatles. The place was really rocking.'

Elton wanted John to sing 'Imagine' but Lennon flatly refused. 'I didn't want to come on like Dean Martin, doing my classic hits. I wanted to have some fun and play some rock 'n' roll. And I didn't want to do more than three because it was Elton's show.' As well as the number one hit, John sang 'I Saw Her Standing There' and 'Lucy In The Sky With Diamonds'.

The significance of the show lay in much more than John's appearance. Elton had remained very friendly with Yoko during John's separation. Backstage before they went on, John received a gardenia with the message: 'Good luck, love, Yoko'. 'Hey,' John said to Elton. 'Look what Yoko sent me. I'm glad she's not here tonight. I'd never be able to go on.'

But Yoko was in the audience, shedding tears of joy at John's triumphant performance. Elton, in on the secret, had told her he wouldn't 'let on' to John, or neither Lennon nor he would have been able to perform. Backstage, John was floored when she walked into the dressing-room. Although they had spoken literally thousands of times on the phone, they had not seen each other for a year.

'You were great, John,' she said simply. She looked poised

and attractive; John was palpably emotional at seeing her. It was one of the best moments of his life.

Before the show John had talked about their separation to me: 'Yoko and I, well we had this little falling out. We're two artists and we found it hard living together. We'll see what happens. I still speak to her on the phone most days. She phoned me from London the other day and said: "Hey, it's nice here. Remember the autumn with all the leaves?" And I said: "What are you trying to say, Yoko? I know it's nice, but are you trying to unsettle me in New York? It's nice *here*—remember the noise?" '

January 1975 proved the watershed month. John had been for several talks with Yoko to maintain contact. Finally he phoned and told her he was fit and ready, in every way, to return. And he did, after a re-union cup of afternoon tea at the Plaza Hotel. Symbolically, that same month the Beatles as a business enterprise were finally dissolved in the High Court in London.

'I'm as happy as Larry to be back with her,' said John. 'It was a tough year for me. It's all right wondering whether the grass is greener on the other side but once you get there all you find is more grass. I don't know whether I'll ever learn that lesson about life. We had a mutual separation and a mutual getting back together. Look, she ain't no chick that you say: "OK, I'll see you Friday," or, "I'm coming back Monday." You're dealing with a fully aware human being. There's no treating her like your chick, you know . . .

'It fell in place again. It was like I never left. I realized this was where I belonged. I think we both knew we'd get back together again sooner or later, even if it was five years, and that's why we never bothered with divorce. I'm just glad she let me back in again. I was allowed back! It was like going out for a drink but it took me a year to get it.'

In talking about his love for Yoko John was able to look at their period of separation with a new perspective. 'I'm the one who's supposed to know everything, but she's my teacher. She's taught me everything I know. The lessons are hard and I can't take it sometimes and *that's* why I freaked out. When we were separate, it was *me* making an asshole of myself in the clubs and in the newspapers. It wasn't her. She missed me as a human being and she loved me but *her* life was ordered. *I* went back to *her* life. It wasn't the other way round.' Drily, he added: 'Yoko and I are proud to say that our separation was a failure.'

The period of estrangement and the terms of the reunion were an exceptional example of one woman's love of her man. Yoko's surveillance of John's activities, particularly with May Pang in Los Angeles when she monitored their every move from the Dakota—much to their chagrin and astonishment— reached epic proportions. Yoko's telephone calls to John were often less than five minutes apart; as soon as he put the phone down she would ring again, or *he* would ring back with something that was on his mind in connection with business, or to pass the time of day by recounting his activities. She knew every twist and turn of his drunken extravaganzas. And it said much for John's desire to rehabilitate himself that not once, given the freedom and 3,000-mile distance from New York to Los Angeles, did he move anywhere without Yoko knowing his phone number.

The fifteen-month 'lost weekend' ended after many pleas by John to be allowed back. 'I'm ready to come home,' he said, so often.

'No you're not, not yet,' she replied.

Yoko kept him totally informed about the business machinery which she was keeping well oiled, increasing their prosperity. Finally, when she eventually told him by telephone to come home, her conditions were, like her own personality, simple but serious and demanding: he would have to act with more maturity; not drink; travel alone frequently to keep their relationship fresh and assert his individuality; and not relapse into the self-pitying attitude that had caused their rift. In brief, she demanded that he return to the positive thinking and firm discipline that had marked the John Lennon she once knew. John reacted well to the unpalatable truth that he had been impossible to live with.

This reunion and John's house-husband period made Yoko seem to many people a manipulating, psychic, power-wielding egotist who would stop at nothing to get her way. This judgement hid the truth from people who didn't want to face it:

Yoko's appeal, to John and the people close to her, was that she was such a strong-minded, artistic individualist. She combined all this with a fearsome practicality. Above all, she would not tolerate weakness in people. Many people who were aware of their own frailties winced at Yoko's intuitive recognition of their failure to do anything about them. John did not; he wanted his woman forceful, intelligent, powerful, domineering, and one step ahead of the game.

He loved Yoko and knew he needed her to reassert himself both creatively and as a man. 'He was a simple, but complex man,' reflects Yoko. 'I mean, when we got back together after that separation, John said he had gone out for a walk for the morning paper and a cup of coffee and hadn't bothered to return. In a way, it *was* like that. At that time, we couldn't live together and we couldn't live apart properly either. But we did know it was just a matter of time straightening things out.'

Not for nothing did John call Yoko 'Mother'—to her face, and to their friends, and in little notes he left on the kitchen table. As well as being his lover, she was a distinctly maternal figure to him and, as Yoko herself says, a substitute for his Aunt Mimi, who raised him.

22
SECLUSION

*'Sean may not have come from my belly
but I'm gonna make his bones'*

By his early thirties John Ono Lennon had travelled mental and physical journeys that most people cannot hope for in a lifetime. Not all of his breadth of vision had stemmed from his millionaire status; if the money had given him freedom, it had also imprisoned him. Material possessions, anyway, had never been his first priority on becoming successful. As he had demonstrated when he embraced Yoko Ono in 1966, the star trip of being a Beatle was not enough to satisfy him. He always needed intellectual stimulation and New York provided it.

Back at the Dakota, he was a totally transformed man. He talked about the major change of direction in his life. 'The idea of being a rock 'n' roll musician and artist sort of suited my talents and mentality and the freedom was great,' said John. 'But then I felt boxed in. I found out I wasn't free, and it wasn't because of a contract. The contract was a physical manifestation of being in prison. I might as well have gone to a nine-to-five job, as carry on the way I was carrying on. And there's two ways to go. You either go to Las Vegas and sing your great hits, *if you're lucky*, or you go to hell, you know, actually literally *dying*,' he told David Sheff.

John was always a restless man, in constant need of new challenges. It took him a long time to throw off his rock 'n' roll restrictions but America was the melting pot in which he finally outgrew pop stardom and impressed himself on the world as a great man. The peace campaign had taken a long time to sink into the world's consciousness as something real and genuine. People had been slow to realize that even a young Beatle could have important qualities of leadership, however much he rejected the role. It took even longer for them to accept that the tough, loud-mouthed Lennon was, underneath, exactly the opposite. His ability to project that difference and articulate a warm humanitarianism, both in his music and by example, made him a model for generations of libertarians.

One of the popular myths about John Lennon has been that he was tough, hard-hearted, vicious, and unsentimental. One of the great myths about Yoko Ono is that she is a manipulative witch, power-hungry, and cold. The reverse is true in both cases. Lennon was incurably romantic all his life and that quality manifested itself with great intensity after his reunion with Yoko. Yoko too has always been emotional, tearful, and compassionate.

What gave her a reputation for toughness and what John loved was her industriousness, tenacity, and her enjoyment of business. Her concentration on detail and her memory are legendary. Her energy level floors everyone around her; she is not an orthodox sleeper by night but during the day takes five or six fifteen-minute 'catnaps'. Most mornings she is behind her office desk before nine.

'She's an original,' John told me. 'And she can come on as strong as any man. She's usually ahead of all of us. And at the same time, she's a woman. And when you meet someone like that, you drop everything. It's goodbye to the gang you used to drink with. Or, in my case, the guys in the band. You don't go and play football any more. Once I found *the* woman, the boys became of no interest whatsoever, other than that they were like old schoolfriends: "Hi, how are you, nice to see you. How's your wife?" That old gang of mine was over the moment I met Yoko—that was the end of the boys. It just so happened the boys were well known and weren't just the local guys at the bar. Coming face to face with anyone like her was something I never expected to do.' He was besotted with this woman who often gave him a hard time, rebuked him for his deficiencies and advised him to stop drinking and become a fanatical health enthusiast. Yoko, a non-drinker, eventually banned alcohol in the Dakota.

A few weeks after their reunion, John had good reason to heed her words. Yoko was pregnant. By spring 1975, a happy John was sending postcards to half a dozen of their closest friends: 'Here's a hard one for you to take: not only are John and Yoko back together. They're pregnant.'

Like so many major events surrounding the couple, the pregnancy was not an accident. And there had been problems leading up to it. In 1972, a year before their separation, they had visited San Francisco. There, through a journalist friend, they were introduced to a ninety-five-year-old Chinese herbalist and acupuncturist, Dr Hong. John was worried about his health. For about twelve years, since the Hamburg days and throughout Beatlemania and his early relationship with Yoko, he had abused his body. Pep pills in Hamburg had led to marijuana and L.S.D. in the Beatles years; he had tried heroin but, being in favour of living, had quickly rejected it.

He continued to smoke marijuana occasionally in his early days in New York. By 1972, however, John was found to have a low sperm count. It was thought it might be a result of the punishment he had meted out to his body. Dr Hong, he was advised, might be able to help. The doctor's advice was given to both: John had to renounce all drugs except cigarettes and go easy on alcohol. For Yoko, the doctor prescribed a 'magic potion' which would increase the chance of her fertility. Her age, thirty-nine then, was not a problem, said the doctor. They would eventually have a child, he said, if they lived cleanly and ate healthily. As it turned out John's 'lost weekend' got in the way of the doctor's advice, but by the time he returned to Yoko he was in good shape. The Lennon I saw frequently during the last six months of 1974 was sober, lean, fit, and clearly determined to stay that way.

So when Yoko announced her pregnancy John was thrilled but not completely surprised. The child was not merely a hope on the horizon. It had been desperately wanted and planned for—something of which they were both proud. It was, says Yoko, as if their getting back together was blessed.

John made one of the most crucial decisions of his life on

learning of Yoko's pregnancy. For twelve years he had been involved in music-making and being a public figure, and a break would be timely. He decided to retire from the business voluntarily. He would concentrate on being a father-to-be and then a Dad. Like a mother hen, he began fussing over Yoko in a way that amazed their friends. They perhaps did not realize that seven years earlier he had camped at Yoko's bedside during a miscarriage. True to his character John became totally immersed in every aspect of Yoko's pregnancy, reading baby books, going to health classes with her, cushioning her from stress, even to the point of being bossy. 'Stay right where you are. Don't move. If there's any rushing around to do, I'm gonna go.' He treated Yoko as if she were ill rather than pregnant. He was worried about her age—forty-two: she was very healthy but she was slight and had already suffered three miscarriages while with John. He was not taking any chances.

Many parents, according to John, conceived their children as 'Saturday night specials.' In America, the phrase he chose was unfortunate: it means handguns that have not sold well during the week and are offered as bargains on Saturdays. What John meant was that most parents conceived their babies 'after a couple of glasses of Scotch, when restraint was cast to the wind'. He was fascinated by the fact that about a hundred million people in America, half the population, were under the age of forty, and were born as a result of the 1945 post-war baby boom. John and Yoko were particularly proud that their child was sought after with love.

One of Yoko's favourite indulgences was chocolate cake. John insisted she stayed in bed every morning while he ordered it from the Silver Palate store for her, together with any other food or drink she fancied. One day Elliot Mintz arrived from Los Angeles. 'Let's go and buy Mother some clothes,' said John. John and Yoko felt strongly that the politics of pregnancy in America were bizarre: the country worshipped perfect bodies, youth and skinniness, and pregnancy seemed to be hidden. 'I think Yoko looks exquisite, beautiful,' John said as Yoko grew larger. He walked along Madison Avenue with Elliot until they saw a shop with beautiful silk and satin lingerie, and expensive dressing-gowns. Inside, he was characteristically generous, buying everything he thought Yoko might like. When it came to pay, John took out his gold American Express card, embossed with the name John Ono Lennon. Then the name of the store on the bill hit him straight between the eyes—it was called Lady Madonna. John burst out laughing.

The irony was that 'Lady Madonna' had been written by Paul. 'Another bloody McCartney song!' said John, laughing. In hotel lifts and restaurants everywhere he had been plagued for ten years by another McCartney gem, 'Yesterday'. In the Palm Court of New York's Plaza Hotel, where John liked to take afternoon tea, the violins would strike up 'Yesterday' in his honour, oblivious of the fact that he would have preferred 'Imagine'. Now 'Lady Madonna' was playing the same trick.

The usual crowd of about 300 gapers pressed against the windows of Lady Madonna. John Lennon shopping for maternity wear was special. As John sprinted away for a taxi, a chauffeur chased him and said: 'Hey, Elton's in a limousine over there. He just came in from London and wants to give you a ride.' John ran across and the two men embraced and went to Elton's hotel, the Pierre, where John told Elton of his 'retirement' plans.

Back at the Dakota Yoko looked appreciatively through the clothes which John had chosen. A woman who favoured simple and stark designs and colours, she was not particularly enamoured, particularly by the 'I love babies so much I'm having one' T-shirt which so amused John. She was touched though by his romantic shopping spree.

John and Yoko studied natural childbirth: 'It's not just Yoko giving birth to a child,' said John. 'It's both of us.' They attended classes for months and had very few visitors or doctors at the Dakota. The natural childbirth method, whereby the woman gives birth in a dark room and the father is present to see the baby placed immediately after birth against the mother's breast, excited both of them. 'Imagine, Elliot,' he said to Mintz, 'not having the baby touched by rubber gloves on its arrival in the world, but by skin straight away!'

John expected the child to be a boy and he and Yoko went through books of names to check their meanings. When John went shopping for toys, he was incredulous at the amount of junk on sale in various shops. At Macy's department store, he looked at beds and finally decided there would be no cribs, which he described as 'wooden cages for kids'. Their child would sleep between him and Yoko for as long as possible; and he did.

At the peak of Yoko's pregnancy she looked in superb health thanks to John's nursing. He, too, was sharp, aware and enjoying life. Just as Yoko went into hospital, John's long immigration battle was nearing its end. On 8 October 1975 a triumphant Leon Wildes phoned John to explain that he thought his Green Card application would be successful. 'Do me a favour, Leon,' John replied. 'I don't quite get this. I'm not following you. Look, Yoko's at the hospital, she's going to be induced in a couple of hours . . . stay right by your phone and I'll call you as soon as I'm there—you can explain it to Yoko.'

Yoko fully understood. Lying in bed in the New York Hospital private room in which Jacqueline Kennedy Onassis gave birth to Caroline Kennedy, she said on the phone: 'Come over with Ruth [Mrs Wildes] and let's all read the report together.' The four spent the night by Yoko's side. The Wildeses left the hospital at midnight. Two hours later, at 2 a.m., on John's thirty-fifth birthday, Yoko gave birth to a baby boy. It was a hazardous delivery. John was at the hospital throughout the period of the birth but when things became tense he was not allowed in. The baby was born by Caesarean section and Yoko, who had to be given a blood transfusion, nearly died.

John was well aware of the danger Yoko was in and the Lennon temper flared when Yoko was just coming round from sedation. John was jittery and wanted to get inside to see her immediately. A doctor walked up to John at a critical moment, saying: 'I love Beatle music. I just want to shake your hand.'

'Fuck off. Save my wife's life,' rasped an angry John. He was fuming with rage.

Nurses, too, had asked for his autograph. He was furious that the doctors and nurses were talking to him instead of attending to Yoko and the baby. It was an anger from which he would never recover. 'They were totally indifferent to Yoko's pain and to Sean—they wanted my *autograph* at a time like that!' Sean proved a healthy, happy baby, but both John and Yoko were sad that he had not been born by the active method, 'flesh touching flesh'.

Back home, John's first phone call was to his Aunt Mimi

in her seaside bungalow in Poole, Dorset. 'It's a boy, it's a boy, Mimi,' he said excitedly. 'And we've named him Sean.'

'Oh, John, you've *branded* him,' she said.

'It's Irish for John, Mimi,' John went on, 'but don't worry, Mimi, he'll be raised internationally and he'll be a citizen of the *world*.' At 6 a.m. a jubilant John phoned Leon Wildes. 'It's John. I'm a father!' There was no controlling him, says Wildes. 'He was ecstatic, bouncing around his room as he spoke.' A Polaroid snapshot of the baby was sent, triumphantly, to Dr Hong, who had been such a psychological boost to John and Yoko.

In the months following the birth John allowed very few visitors to the Dakota. He was afraid they might spread germs. Nobody except John or Yoko was allowed to touch Sean. It was the single most important thing in his life. Elliot Mintz, visiting the family a month after the birth, was asked to take the first picture of mother, father, and baby. Mintz's first view of Sean, sleeping with Yoko, was shadowed by John 'shushing' him to be quiet and not risk waking up the child. Telegrams of congratulation had poured in from all over the world, many remarking on the fact that Sean was born on John's birthday. 'It figures,' some joked, 'that the two of you would make this another one of your events!' But John took even that seriously: 'The baby decides the time and place and which family to have. Yoko did not give birth to Sean; Sean came through Yoko as a miracle and a gift to us. . . .'

'Well,' said Yoko shortly after the birth, with characteristic incisiveness, 'I've carried the baby for nine months and brought him into the world. Now it's your turn to look after him.' John was in full agreement. It was a good time for a total change in emphasis in his life. Yoko went into the office downstairs full-time to manage the family business, while he raised Sean in their seventh-floor apartment. John being John, it turned into a consuming passion of incredible intensity. Both he and Yoko fulfilled their new roles with distinction. Four months after Sean's birth John's recording contract with E.M.I./Capitol expired and he decided not to renew it, the first time in fifteen years that he had not been tied to a recording deal.

During the next five years John became, as he described

himself, a house-husband. His attention to Sean was total. The baby was fed, washed, bathed, dressed and taught to read by him. He hated changing his nappies but he did it all the same. No babysitters were needed. When Sean was about six months old John saw a pimple on him. Agitated, he went round to twenty members of office and domestic staff forbidding them to give Sean sugar of any kind in his diet: 'Sean may not have come out of my belly but I'm gonna make his bones.'

During the years of seclusion, Elliot Mintz visited John and Yoko dozens of times. 'We shared the special moments,' he recalls. 'Thanksgivings, Christmas Eves, Christmas Days, New Year's Eves, Sean's birthdays. They were the most glorious of times.

'I have never seen two people so much in love. They lived their lives with such conscious awareness. John would frequently walk over to Yoko, who might be sitting on the edge of the bed with Sean. He would hold her small hand in his and look deeply into her eyes and smile then whisper "Hello" very softly, as if he was making direct contact with her very essence. They would embrace and I would disappear. I remember reading that Brian Epstein once said he was happiest when the four Beatles and he were in a room together without anyone else, before a concert. For me, during those five years, John and Yoko and little Sean together as a family in the Dakota embodied everything that was special between lovers.'

Sean's full name is Sean Taro Ono Lennon. Says Yoko: 'John insisted that he should have one Japanese name. Taro is like Sean or John in Japanese, that kind of name. John loved it.

'In Japanese law a child belongs to the father's family. As a result of that mothers who have babies by accident sometimes have a terrible time . . . if they don't know who the father is and the mother cannot claim the child as hers. John and I wanted Sean to be as international as possible.' As well as having British and Japanese names and being born in New York, Sean Taro Ono Lennon has dual American and British nationality and his birth was registered in both New York and London.

There are already signs that Sean will emerge as formidable, strong-minded, and witty as his father. At the age of eight, he told me he was 'a real computer whizz'. At school, where the ever-present bodyguard accompanies him, standing within sight of him all day and every day, Sean says he is 'better at languages than adding up, but most of all I'm a real expert at using my free time'. He had a typical eight-year-old's contempt for the girls in his class, who outnumbered the boys: 'They're just not so nice as us so we beat them at dodge ball.' Although he agreed he was rather young to be considering his future, Sean said: 'I have been thinking about what to do but I haven't yet answered myself. I might be a singer or a crazy scientist or a geologist or an archaeologist.' As for his father's music: 'Sometimes it's good, sometimes not so good.' John would grudgingly have agreed with that one.

Elton John, whose concert was so instrumental in re-uniting John and Yoko, is Sean's godfather.

John scarcely needed the news of his father's death in April 1976 to persuade him to pour even more zeal into raising Sean. His own lack of parental stability as a child had nagged away at him over the years and he was determined that Sean would have a father he knew and grew up alongside. Although he could not claim to be a struggling 'mother figure', with the everyday physical pressures of millions of parents (he had a domestic staff to cushion him), John supervised everything that went into the boy's early years: food, drink, toys, books, sleep. After a year he helped Sean to toddle and walk. Television was banned. 'He's not gonna see people shooting each other,' said John. He even wheeled him in a pram around Central Park.

John was so immersed in baby-rearing that when Paul McCartney arrived, unscheduled, with a guitar at the Dakota one day and had the doorman announce him, John did not believe it could be him. Hoax phone calls were a regular problem. Paul had to be put on the phone by the doorman in the Dakota reception area to convince John that it was really him. When he went upstairs John gave him a frosty reception. 'Do you mind calling before you come round next time? This is not Liverpool, y'know. In New York, you don't just drop in on people like this without warning.' He went on to explain that he was tired from a hard day's work with Sean. Paul left in a huff. John's opinion of Paul's work at this time was very low. He described him to friends as 'like Engelbert Humperdinck'. Although he accepted that Paul was a competent songwriter, John was contemptuous of the fact that his old partner apparently wanted merely to continue as before; he referred to Mick Jagger and Paul jointly—and contemptuously—as the 'Rolling Wings'. There was more to life, implied John, than rock 'n' rolling into your forties. 'I've diarrhea'd on rock 'n' roll,' he said.

As he walked around New York's Central Park during his 'house-husband' years, one of the friendly faces John occasionally encountered was that of Sid Bernstein. The man who had promoted the Beatles' American tours from their first shows in 1964 had tried several times to re-unite them for massive charity concerts. Each time there had been no official response; John said he 'didn't go for all that Al Jolson, down-on-one-knee' pleading that became Bernstein's style in expensive appeals to the Beatles in the *New York Times*. But when John saw Bernstein walking around the park or on the Upper East Side, they embraced and did not mention the Beatles. 'It was always casual talk about my family and Sean, who was sometimes with him,' says Bernstein. 'I knew not to mention the Beatles. He only ever mentioned the past to me once, describing Shea Stadium as the top of the mountain.' John's forgetfulness made an impression on Bernstein: 'I saw him several times with Yoko and he introduced me to her every time as if we'd never met. Finally Yoko had to say to him: "John, I *know* Sid now." '

Their paths crossed twice. In 1974, John phoned Bernstein and asked him for the name of a really fine Italian restaurant in New York. After he had a good dinner at Palucci's, behaving perfectly with Harry Nilsson throughout the night, John sent a huge spray of flowers to Bernstein with a note of thanks for a good recommendation. And in 1975, John phoned to ask for tickets for a concert Bernstein was promoting at Carnegie Hall. The performer was Jimmy Cliff, a star of reggae, a music style which particularly captured John's affection in the cosmopolitan atmosphere of New York. Sid Bernstein had no tickets left, but his daughters gave up theirs when they heard John Lennon wanted to go.

Bernstein later presented the New York production of a play called *Lennon*, first shown at Liverpool's Everyman Theatre in 1981. It was artistically mediocre, concentrating heavily on John's 'tough guy' image and failing to capture his multi-faceted personality and sensitivity. Nevertheless, the play was notable for establishing the huge range in ages of John's appeal: children and teenagers who were not born when John formed the Beatles attended alongside their parents whose memories of Lennon were powerful. When shots rang out at the end of the play to simulate the murder, the audience sobbed. In New York, the play failed and came off at the Entermedia Theatre, off Broadway, after only nine weeks.

While John was busy nursing Sean, Yoko revelled in her role as businesswoman. By the evening, after a long programme of meetings in her office, she would say: 'It's been a hard day. I'm tired.'

John's house-husband wit was quick: 'Well, what do you think *I've* been doing? Bringing up a baby is work, as well! Don't give me that ''hard day at the office, dear'' bit.'

He pointed out that he had even begun reading cookery books to improve *his* performance.

Yoko set about demonstrating her business acumen with typical determination. 'It was a two-year plan,' she says, 'which quickly ran to five years when John told me how much money he wanted and I realized I couldn't achieve *that* amount within two years.'

Hitherto Yoko had been totally unmaterialistic. 'I survived throughout my earlier years,' she says, 'by not accumulating money, partly because my mother enjoyed luxury and was always showing me diamonds. Part of me rebelled against that and despised it. I felt I never wanted to lead a life like that, thinking so much about gold and diamonds and beautiful clothes.

'So until 1975 I was the opposite of a money person. But when John and I decided that I would be a businesswoman, I told myself that in order to attract money and do the new job well I'd have to reconstruct my psyche. My old attitude of not wanting to get into money just wasn't going to do.

'I meditated on it. I visualized all the materially good things in the world—diamonds, silk, velvets, art—and tried to see those things in my mind with love, which I never did before. I just opened my mind to all those things instead of rejecting them. And John immediately bought me this diamond, heart-shaped necklace, almost as a signal that I was changing. The usual me would have said, out of snobbery: "Oh, what do I want that for?" But instead I looked at its beauty and thanked him. I tried to see the beauty in the good properties we have. And we said: "If we are going to have it, we have to *act* as if we have it already, not as if we are just starting with money."

'So I went and bought great clothes most weeks and John would really enjoy seeing what I'd bought. It wasn't a question of getting these things in order to *own* them, more like reversing all my attitudes towards possessions. I really trained my mind to enjoy the things that were positive about money.'

With no head for statistics and without making any mathematical calculations Yoko began presiding over the Lenono business with a clear mind and intuitive powers that devastated all those who dealt with her. John and Yoko's first decision was that their cash would be invested in things that were ecologically inoffensive: 'We wanted nothing to do with energy or oil or big chemical corporations or any of the other things we could have invested in,' says Yoko. 'We wanted things that were peaceful to control and caused us, and the world, no problem.'

Yoko's first business venture was the gradual acquisition of five apartments in their beloved Dakota building on West 72nd Street. The setting for the film *Rosemary's Baby*, the intimidating Dakota was not easy to gain access to: major stars before John and Yoko had been refused permission by the committee which decides who may be granted residence there. John and Yoko had to attend a screening meeting to establish that they would be peaceful, respectable residents, particularly when Yoko set about buying each apartment that fell vacant. They so loved its decorous atmosphere that there was never any danger they would abuse it. John sat watching the sun set across Central Park. The all-white room (including the furniture and the white piano on which John wrote 'Imagine,' which now has Yoko's photographs of her family on it) was their *pièce de résistance*. The piano, John's gift to Yoko on her birthday in 1971, when they were living in Ascot, bears his inscription, 'This morning, a white piano for Yoko.' It remains in position. Asked why she needed all the apartments Yoko replied quixotically: 'It's just that John and I always wanted to live in a house.'

After the Dakota had been established as a major investment, Yoko turned to agriculture. Four farms were purchased, in the Catskill mountains, Virginia, Vermont, and upstate New York. Covering some 1,600 acres, the farms were reckoned to be worth nearly $1 million. Yoko's particular talent was her timing: her notoriety as a businesswoman went up several notches when one of her investments, a prize Holstein cow, one of 250 head of cattle they owned, fetched $265,000—a world record—at the New York State Fair at Syracuse. The exceptional Lenono cow was expected to produce over 6,000 gallons of milk a year. 'Only Yoko Ono,' said an amused John, reading about the sale in a newspaper while holidaying alone in Bermuda, 'could sell a cow for a quarter of a million dollars!'

A vital advantage of owning the farms was that their produce—eggs, milk, and vegetables, all produced without chemicals—was shipped down to New York at least once a week, ensuring that John, Yoko, and Sean had a healthy diet, which was as free of additives as possible.

Yoko's astute purchase of properties and the hiring of staff to run them became another time-consuming but profitable operation. For $450,000 the Lennons acquired a stunning weekend retreat, a house at Cold Spring Harbor, Long Island, overlooking the Atlantic. Yoko, particularly, loved this home, which was close to Manhattan but also in the fresh air of the countryside—important for Sean. They also bought a 63-foot ocean-going yacht called *Isis* and a sloop which John named *Strawberry Fields*.

Then there was West Palm Beach, Florida, where $700,000 bought the Lennons a beachfront mansion, El Salano, built in 1919 and once owned by the Vanderbilt family. With seven bedrooms, five servants' rooms, indoor and outdoor pools and its own fifty yards of sand by the ocean, the house proved the most expensive of all their properties: most of the year it stood empty, except for a small staff; John and Yoko managed only one month's visit a year. Art, a big collection of carpets, and Eastern artifacts were other assets.

Naturally their critics had an easy target. Here was the man who had sung 'Imagine no possessions' accumulating more, at the behest of his shrewd wife, than he would ever need. But a changed John had decided, as always, that if he was going to retire and be a non-musician for a few years and father Sean, then with the Beatles, Apple, and Allen Klein out of his system, he would have no better manager than Yoko. And, following the dictum of his life, 'Don't do things by halves', Yoko quickly enhanced their fortune. By the late seventies, John's estate was conservatively valued at $150 million with millions more coming in every year in royalties from record sales and songwriting.

Yoko talked to me about how she reconciled her business and her art. 'I think that most artists have this complex: they think they should suffer and struggle and always be miserable or else they can't be creative. John and I had that for a while. We were very aware of that side of being artists. But we tried to reverse the trap that artists fall into—because we didn't want to be miserable when we obviously had money and possessions. After all, being miserable is a pretty high price to pay for being an artist!' As to her business methods: 'Money, and making it, is fundamentally a state of mind. I often used to wonder why some people were rich and naturally talented at multiplying their money and others not. It sometimes comes down to attitude. A great many very intelligent people have no money and as a Greenwich Village artist wanting only recognition, I used to be one of them. But then I also had an inverted snobbery towards money. I thought it was silly to go looking for it. I've changed.' In business deals, however, men were chauvinistically distrustful of her judgement—'or, rather, they became upset by the fact that my judgement was right and it came from a woman. There *have* been some struggles with men in business because I am a woman.' Conversely, she had also benefited: 'Sometimes the men underestimate a woman so much that they reveal their tactics too soon. Then they find out how resilient I am.'

For John, walking away from music for a few years was much harder than carrying on: 'I know because I've done both. It was very hard because shouldn't I be going, like "to the office" or "producing something"? I don't exist if my name isn't in the charts or I'm not seen at the right club. It's like the guys aged sixty-five who've said: "Your life's over. Time for God." It's self-imposed, yes, but still the feeling was there, this whole big space that seems to be unfillable. And of course, it's nat-

urally got to be filled because that's the law of the universe. . . .
And it was filled by a fulfilling experience, to put it in a little
cute phrase.'

John and Yoko did not venture out much in 1976. John's
commitment to rearing Sean, supervising his every moment,
was total. He explained: 'People asked me: "What are you
doing now?"'

'And I'd say: "Looking after the baby and baking the bread."'

'And they'd say: "Ha ha. No, no, what else do you do?"'

'And I'd say: "Are you *kidding*? It's a full-time job, as
every housewife knows." There were no secret projects in the
basement.'

Making music was low on his agenda but a passion for
discovery was high. John's determination that Sean should be
healthy was stimulated by his own splendid health. As part of
a self-imposed diet he and Yoko had a forty-day fast when they
drank only fruit and vegetable juice. When they came off the
diet they were convinced of the importance of health foods and
vitamins.

Baking bread was a passion that lasted for a few months
and, while he enthused about it, everybody had to know.
'Elliot,' he told Mintz by phone one afternoon, 'an extraordinary thing has happened. I've just baked my first loaf of
bread. I saw it rise in the oven, I did it from start to finish.'
John took a Polaroid photo of the loaf and sent it by air courier
to his bemused pal 3,000 miles away. John was overjoyed and
proud of his achievement. 'I feel I've conquered something,'
he said to Yoko and he didn't mean merely by baking bread.
The thrill wore off somewhat when the entire staff of the Dakota
enjoyed his bread so much that 'drivers, and office boys, and
accountants, and everyone came for one and I'd make loaves
on Friday that'd be gone by Saturday afternoon.' He decided:
'Screw this for a lark. It was becoming routine. And I don't
get a gold record or a knighthood . . . nothing!'

John's cooking was enthusiastic but limited. He would chop
up a huge amount of vegetables, put them, occasionally with
fish, into a big crockpot, which simmered for days on the
cooker. Permanently beside it, loving the warmth, were the
three cats, Michu, Sasha and Charo. The longer the crockpot
simmered, he reasoned—quite fallaciously—the better the food

would taste. That, with perfectly cooked rice, and sometimes boiled eggs—rather watery and rarely cooked properly—was his culinary height, together with the bread.

He insisted that people follow the eating method which he had adopted from a macrobiotic guru: the practice of constant chewing. Drinking anything with meals was disallowed in the Dakota, as was alcohol. Every bite had to be chewed twenty times because John had been told that if he ate and washed it down with any liquid, he would be taking away the work of the digestive enzymes, particularly ptyalin, the enzyme in saliva that begins the digestion of food. Anybody eating a Lennon crockpot combination was ordered to chew until the ptyalin naturally dissolved it. Elliot Mintz recalls a visit by John and Yoko to Manhattan's East-West macrobiotic restaurant in which about 100 people sat facing each other, chewing, with no conversation. Mintz began: 'Well, it's great to see you two, how's it been going?' John rebuked him, placing fingers across his mouth to indicate that there should be no talking.

When Sean was two John decided to try to learn Japanese. For two hours a day, three days a week, he went to a language school in Manhattan. The technique was similar to that employed in many language classes: the complete immersion method with no English spoken. John also bought a series of cassettes. Much to Yoko's chagrin he would attempt to practise on her. But his combination of Liverpudlian and American made it hard for him: after two months of battling to absorb the intonation he could manage only about forty words. He gave up after a brave try, much to Yoko's relief.

The more successful his wife became 'downstairs', the more he trusted her vision. Yoko's business moves were supported by advice from a retinue of astrologers, numerologists, and tarot card readers. Every member of the Lenono staff, and most people who came into close proximity to them, was 'checked out' through their astrological sign in infinite detail. Thus Yoko arrived at the conclusion that there were good days for business and also days when she should sign nothing and just listen, days on which neither of them should travel, and days on which it would be bad to be in contact with someone who had the wrong 'sign rising'. Yoko had always been heavily into 'vibrations', good and bad. Her application of her hunches into a science began to shape their movements and those of their closest friends: 'If Yoko said it would be advisable for John or for me to fly 6,000 miles in an easterly direction and stay at that point for exactly four and a half days,' says Elliot Mintz, 'John would say: "Go with it. Trust her. She's always right." '

In June 1977 John, Yoko, and Sean went to Japan for an extended visit of several months. They had been there for nearly eight weeks when a phone call from Elliot Mintz in Los Angeles broke the news: Elvis Presley was dead. There was a pause on the line before John said of his teenage idol: 'Elvis died in the army.' Another pause. 'How? What happened?' The information was sketchy; Mintz had just heard the news on the radio. The impact on John was minimal, his reaction almost callous. He reserved his emotion for the living. Between pauses, John said to Mintz: 'Well, the difference between the Beatles and Elvis was that with Elvis the king died and the manager lived and with the Beatles the manager died and we lived. I never wanted to be a forty-year-old who virtually died singing his golden hits in a jump-suit in Las Vegas. Oh, please send two white gardenias to Elvis's grave, saying: "Rest In Peace, Love John and Yoko." '

Next day Mintz flew out to join the Lennons for a long Japanese holiday. Mintz, clearly affected by the death of a rock legend, was chastized by John. 'Don't talk to me about Elvis. He's dead. Don't try to sell me on the dreams and myths of these people. Elvis is dead. It's all over. It's unhealthy to live *through* anybody.'

Mintz flew to Tokyo and then took a train 200 miles north to the small town of Karuizawa. The Lennon he found there was a dramatically refreshed man. In two years, he had renounced rock 'n' roll for fatherhood and house-husbandry. It was now time to concentrate on the restoration of his own mind and body. For five months John enjoyed the cleanest, wisest, physically fittest period in his life, with no alcohol, no drugs, exercises of every kind from cycling and swimming to yoga every day, and none of the foods he had leaned on so much in New York: chocolate, honey, English muffins. He cut down drastically on his beloved French cigarettes. He had a constant diet of *sushi* and rice and joked that, 'Yoko likes to feed me dead fish.'

'In Karuizawa, we all did a lot of cycling and stayed at a very old, beautiful hotel, the Mampei,' says Mintz. 'Yoko's family has a home in this town; there were no Westerners or tourists and we did not have a car. John enjoyed having Sean sit on a seat across his crossbar in front of him.'

The Japanese experience proved idyllic for John. In their constant search for strong, black coffee, which both John and Yoko loved, they would drag Mintz on five-mile mountain road expeditions, Yoko's long hair flying behind her in the wind as she led the other two, John in T-shirt and shorts, with hair almost shoulder length, keeping up with her, and Mintz trailing 'and fully expecting a cardiac arrest' behind them. The coffee café, Mintz avers, was worth it. Yoko also took them to exclusive and exotic restaurants. Often the fish for their dinner would be pulled from a stream next to the restaurant. Their search for authenticity was not always felicitous. John was a little squeamish when he was asked to drink 'the best turtle soup in Japan' from the shell of the turtle he had seen alive only a few minutes earlier.

The fifteen-course traditional Japanese dinners, during which the three of them hardly spoke, were often preceded by the mineral baths which left John's skin glowing, his hair with a brilliant sheen, and Yoko's longer hair at its best. On one occasion when the two men were taken to a bathing area and Yoko went off to a women's area, two hostesses began to undress John and Elliot. John reacted incredulously: 'What's going on? Where's Mother?' As fast as the waitresses unbuttoned his shirt buttons, he would do them up again; finally, when he entered the water, he started swimming strongly.

'It's not for swimming,' Yoko rebuked him from the other side of the partition which separated men from women. 'It's for bathing, to refresh yourself before dinner.' But John was always a powerful, enthusiastic swimmer, and enjoyed teaching Sean.

In Karuizawa, John told Elliot how wonderful it was not to be recognized, not to have to be on guard or be attentive to strangers. A few Japanese smiled at him in recognition but he felt no pressure. At Yoko's mother's house, often wearing a suit and his old Quarry Bank school tie, he enjoyed many afternoons sitting on the porch, something similar to an old southern plantation verandah, drinking coffee, eating cakes and cycling back to the hotel later, singing songs and whistling.

In the ancient capital town of Kyoto John became immersed in the Buddhist temples. 'When we went into these and stood before the statues of Buddha, there were small areas where we wrote our prayers down,' says Mintz. 'John was genuinely into it. He clasped his hands, closed his eyes, bowed his head and prayed. . . . Yoko took us to a monastery in Kyoto where there was a religious order of very elderly women. It was irrelevant that John couldn't understand a word of the conversation. He was deeply moved. The religiosity of Japan definitely made an impression on him.'

En route home the family moved to the Okura Hotel in Tokyo, where they occupied the gigantic presidential suite. Here the throb of city life made John eager to get back to New York. 'He got out his acoustic guitar in the living-room of the suite and sang some old songs,' says Mintz. 'And he said he was getting a bit homesick.' The suite was so large that John even played football with Sean in it.

It was here that John quixotically played his last 'public' performance, which happened quite by accident. The gigantic hotel suite had lifts that arrived straight into the Lennon lounge. John was sitting quietly playing 'Jealous Guy' to himself and Elliot Mintz one evening when the lift doors opened and a Japanese couple—who had evidently arrived on the wrong floor—walked out to find a singer-guitarist whom they did not recognize. All the same they sat and listened as John continued the song. 'John was in a wonderful mood, playing gently and beautifully . . .' recalls Mintz. 'The people simply applauded and went back down the elevator.' They were the last two strangers who ever watched and listened as John performed.

When the time came to finish the Japanese holiday Yoko consulted her numerology. She decided that the 'signs' were all wrong for the two men to fly direct from Tokyo to New York. She would return straight home to the U.S. while John, Sean, and Elliot were to fly Tokyo–Hong Kong–Dubai–Frankfurt–New York. Their twenty-six-hour flight would mean changing planes at Dubai and Frankfurt. It sounded arduous but John believed implicitly in Yoko's prescience and totally trusted her ability to 'read the cards' which charted their movements.

On the long night flight from Dubai to Germany John became homesick, recalling the Beatles' early days in a conversation which Elliot Mintz will always remember as Lennon at his frankest. In the Lufthansa 747 jet Sean played with his car race track in the upper level of the plane with a nanny, while Mintz sat with Lennon with the seats on either side of them, as usual, empty. When flying he and Yoko always bought two seats on either side and in front of them to leave free. That way, John said, 'I make sure I don't sit next to somebody asking me when the Beatles will get back together again.'

Mintz had by that time known Lennon for six years but he had never seen him so sentimental, pensive, reflective, and talkative. Even his old Liverpool accent had partly returned. It was the side of John Lennon that the public had never seen. He spoke of his childhood, his sexual fantasies, how he felt when the Beatles first came to America and the feeling he had when the plane first touched down on the soil of the country that had first inspired his music. He talked of his relationship with his mother and the tears welled up as he recalled her premature death; he was in the reminiscent and confessional mood which often overcomes long-distance fliers; he repeatedly spoke of his love of Yoko, and his chattiness reassured Mintz, who was a nervous flier. John was particularly proud of the fact that he had his luggage down to a fine art: a large briefcase with one change of clothing and pyjamas.

The overnight stop in Frankfurt was John's one visit to Europe in nine years. It was marked by a bizarre encounter with a hotel receptionist, aghast at unexpectedly checking in a former Beatle. Rooms were not readily available, so John introduced Mintz as Paul McCartney. Rooms were suddenly found. 'I guess,' Mintz said to an unamused John, 'the clerk liked the fact that I wrote "Yesterday".'

Next day, John, Sean, and Elliot continued their journey to New York. At Kennedy Airport John got a special thrill from the passport controller's greeting. As John handed him his British passport and remembered the four-year immigration battle he had endured, the immigration man said to him: 'Welcome home, Mr Lennon.' John turned and smiled to Elliot, then caught sight of Yoko, standing alone to welcome him with an embrace. Back at the Dakota a revitalized John Lennon rediscovered with pleasure the forty hours of *Goon Show* tapes which Yoko had given him as a birthday gift.

John made other foreign trips. He went alone to Cape Town for a few days, staying at the Mount Nelson Hotel. He went to Hong Kong and Singapore and enjoyed walking incognito among the local population. His wit never deserted him. To Bob Gruen, his New York photographer friend, he sent a card from Hong Kong saying simply: 'Far East, man!' accompanied by the little doodle which told any recipient of a card that it was a genuine Lennon message. John and Yoko flew to spend one night in Cairo at the pyramids, where Yoko developed a fascination for Egyptian artifacts and bought the mummy that lies in her white room at the Dakota. John's solo journeys were a real education for a man who had been cushioned by company since his first travels out of Liverpool to Hamburg in 1960. Even dialling room service in a hotel was an adventure for him. Most of the time, he enjoyed simply sitting watching foreign television in blissful isolation in his room.

Few people recognized him on his foreign trips and in Hong Kong he enjoyed walking around the harbour among the local workers, 'just watching'. He had not enjoyed such freedom since his days in Hamburg before the lunacy of Beatlemania. The only occasions on which John was forced to admit his identity were when he handed his gold American Express card to the hotel desks. From each city he telephoned Yoko in the Dakota and Aunt Mimi in Dorset to give his hotel number, and to enthuse about the hum of a city, a skyline, a sunset, or even to crow over the fact that he was walking around shops and hotel lobbies without being hunted.

John was fortunate that he was not hounded, for in view of his name and his fame, he was astonishingly vulnerable. All public figures risk harassment by the public as soon as they step outside their front doors; for a lapsed Beatle and solo star of stature, who had a reputation as a recluse, to be travelling alone to the far-flung corners of the world, totally alone, was a brave adventure. In the case of John Lennon, it had an extra hazard: one of his most surprising flaws was an inability to detect hangers-on, phoneys, parasites or even dangerous people who sought his company, his approval, his warmth or his encouragement. There were two sides to his attitudes towards people and handling of them: the tough, abrasive, no-nonsense, street-wise Liverpudlian who believed everyone should battle their own way through life, as he had; and then there was John the sucker, the 'easy tap' for most causes that reached his ears, particularly if they were tinged with radicalism and sounded sincere. An incurable sentimentalist and fundamentally kind, John leaned this way, preferring to give any dubious characters the benefit of the doubt. It made him a poor judge of people who walked up to him. He did *not* possess a sound sixth sense of those who were around him to exploit him, because he tended to take people on face value. This became dangerous as he chose to confront his stardom and fly around the world alone, or walk the streets of New York and give his autograph to anybody who appeared, to him, to be innocuous. It was a trait that enabled him to break free of the strictures of stardom. It might also have cost him his life.

Nearly twelve years after their first meeting John and Yoko had achieved a serenity in their partnership that anyone might envy. 'We would argue, of course,' says Yoko. 'We were two very temperamental, very emotional, people. Friends and lovers, musicians and artists, man and woman, husband and wife.' Even when they fought, John had a unique method of breaking the deadlock. He would write a song or poem and either play the song to Yoko or strategically place the written poem where she would see it privately. 'That was part of our communication,' she says. 'We were both shy, we didn't go out often, certainly not to parties or anything like that. So we were literally together for fourteen years with very few breaks. John and I stood for peace and love but standing for peace doesn't make either of us holier than thou. John and I together were human beings, and by no means were both of us totally peaceful. Anger, hurt, vulnerability, were all a part of John. When we met, we were like two *driven* people and it was like a fantastic meeting of two crazy souls. John was more hurt than me by the public reaction to my early work. I was the "laugh". People said: "Oh, we can't listen to *her*." And John would be choked by that. But it's like John would say, everything takes its time and in a favourite phrase of his, *it will all work out in the end*.

'What people *did* take a long time realizing was that John might not have been a great, technically proficient guitarist, but listen now to "Why" on the *Plastic Ono Band* album and his playing is fantastic, far-out. Our fusion, with my singing and his playing, was something he realized was special much later. He said he could not have played like that with anybody, it was more than a duet of artists, but a coming together of the two of us.'

Yoko likens their partnership with that of Robert Browning and Elizabeth Barrett-Browning. John thought of them more like Scott and Zelda Fitzgerald. Whichever analogy one uses, their marriage and mutual love was a quite triumphant and justly celebrated public romance. It survived many hurdles: the ridicule of the public; the taunts of John's old 'friends', in and out of the Beatles' circle, and those of millions of Beatle fans in the early days; and a lengthy separation. As Yoko comments, 'We found that the love thing was bigger than both of us.'

During the first two years of his seclusion John was so immersed in being a father and taking an interest in Yoko's business transactions that the outside world virtually passed him by. He hardly ever went out shopping after that trip for Yoko's maternity wear. He rarely answered the flashing light of the telephone. He left the staff to order the food and on the occasions when he did phone a shop, he became irritated by shop assistants' refusal to believe that he really was John Lennon.

By the time of his Japanese visit, however, John had changed. Galvanized by Yoko's exceptional success in buying property, farms, and *objets d'art*, John began an excursion into acquisition. Like all his other enthusiasms, he went all the way while it lasted; this particular passion had its roots in planning Sean's life.

John decided to shower Sean with toys, games and books, practising a 'reverse materialism' on him. Lennon's theory was that he, and millions like him, were raised in the belief that he would grow up and be able to afford the first car, the first house, the first good suit, and the first guitar . . . and it was always 'tomorrow'. He wanted to try to wipe out that aspiration early in Sean's life: 'I don't want him hooked on being a consumer throughout his teenage years.' So Sean was given anything he fancied. A walk around the famous New York toy store, F.A.O. Schwarz, would cost John thousands of dollars. He spent vast sums on robot games at a store called Forbidden Planet in Greenwich Village; John also dabbled in computer games and bought Sean the most progressive ones. 'I'm giving him all the crap while he's young so that by the time he's ten, this kind of stuff won't mean anything to him. He'll have had his fix.'

It was a theory that only a rich man could apply. But it worked. By the time he was eight, Sean Lennon's proudest possession was a valueless collection of rocks. He had developed a great interest in the formation of stones, stalactites, minerals, and anything geological. His great hobby, besides computers, was hunting by the seashore for rare seashells. No expensive toys or brilliant pieces of engineering impressed him: beautiful electric train sets and gadgets by the crateload lay, forgotten, in a warehouse when I visited him in 1983.

When it came to spending and collecting for himself, however, John had immatured with age. In Japan a typical spending spree in Tokyo's 'electronic village' would find John walking down the aisles pointing out and ordering literally dozens of sophisticated amplifiers, turntables and speakers, which were shipped back to the Dakota and set up in each room. 'You know how Mother feels about wires,' he said to Elliot Mintz, who had accompanied him on the expedition, 'well, with this little lot, there'll be no need for any wires to trail around the house.'

Airline mail order catalogues fascinated him. He loved to be surprised by items he ordered on a plane, simply by filling in his American Express number: these arrived at the Dakota weeks or months afterwards, long after he had forgotten about them. A 'stereo pillow', a pillow with built-in speakers, amused him; there was a portable desk with foam-rubber backing; breakfast trays on which he would take Yoko her favourite extra strong, black coffee; and he developed a fetish for collecting attaché-cases. He had dozens in leather and other materials in all shapes and sizes, and carefully fixed the combination lock of each to include the figure nine which marked important events in his life. He was similarly attracted to manicure sets and collected dozens. If he walked into a store and found a pair of jeans that fitted him properly, he would ask for ten pairs in different colours to be sent to his home.

If that was the 'little child inside the man', there was plenty of seriousness in John to balance it out. An avid reader all his life, he spent the years of seclusion establishing a superb library of leatherbound, antiquarian books. He studied the history of the early slaves who were sent from Africa to his native Liverpool and were used, he said, to build the huge houses in the port alongside which he had grown up. He loved philosophy books, and sent Elliot Mintz *The Lazy Man's Guide to Enlightenment*.

When John and Yoko went out it was as if to re-live their early, simpler lives as student and artist. Away from the grandeur of the Dakota, light years away from rock 'n' roll, totally removed from Eastern influence, their choice was usually a small yet elegant coffee shop run by an Italian husband and wife. It was decidedly European in its atmosphere and sold only pastries and superb coffee and chocolate. For John and Yoko, for four years from the day it opened in 1976, Café La Fortuna at 69 West 71st Street, one block from their home, was a refuge.

Vincent Urwand, the owner, developed a bond with them. Only once did he have to chase away a gaggle of fans who gathered with cameras to disturb their peace. About four afternoons a week John would wander in, with or without Yoko, and sit down for his *cappuccino* and Gitanes and a read of any newspaper that had been lying around his home. In summer they sat in the garden at the back of the café.

When Sean was a toddler, John would bring him in with a rope around him. 'You got him like a dog, strapped up round his chest!' said Vincent.

'I've gotta have him tied up or else he runs wild. I can't keep up with him when he runs off,' explained John. Special ice-cream, without sugar and containing honey, was made for Sean at John's request.

John often struck up conversations with other people in La Fortuna. One, a German religious fanatic, tried unsuccessfully to stir John up about his ambivalent attitude to organized religion. For the most part, though, it was a haven, a grass roots contact with an unpretentious café. Vincent Urwand comments, 'John told me how they used to go round second-hand shops in this neighbourhood and buy old-fashioned hats and dresses. One day John phoned me and said that he and Yoko would provide me with the picture of themselves I'd asked for, for the wall. And when it came it was John wearing a derby hat with a paper moustache, Sean with the American flag draped around him, and Yoko in a big hat and an old-fashioned dress that you'd never see her in. They loved surprising people.'

Despite banning sugar for Sean, John's craving for chocolate remained undimmed: Vincent often sold him bars of imported dark, bittersweet Italian-made Luisa chocolate: with American Hershey bars they were his favourite. Years earlier John's sweet tooth had got the better of him in a phone conversation from New York to me in London: he asked me to bring him some of his childhood favourites, chocolate-covered Bath Oliver biscuits. He often asked British visitors to bring him foods which were unobtainable in New York. When he phoned his son Julian in North Wales in 1977, he also spoke to his former art college friend Helen Anderson. When she asked him if there was anything he was missing in America, he replied: 'Yes, I could do with a string of black puddings.' Helen realized that the man she remembered from nearly twenty years ago had fundamentally changed very little . . . particularly when he went on to ask her if she still had a Liverpool Art College scarf she could send him.

'When are you coming back here?' asked Helen.

'Oh, one of these days before long,' said John.

At the café, the Urwands had little interest in modern popular music. Coincidentally John was opening out in his music tastes at the time and Vincent successfully introduced him to his own favourites, jazz and the popular music of the veteran performers. 'I gave John some 78 r.p.m. records and he asked me to make up a tape for him. Next time he came in, he said how much he'd enjoyed it.' The music consisted of songs by Al Jolson, Benny Goodman, Mae West, Duke Ellington, and the jazz of Fats Waller and Louis Armstrong. 'I had a long discussion with John on opera and classical music but as it turned out he developed a real liking for stuff which I played and he really thought they were special: Bing Crosby, the jazz violinist Stephane Grappelli, and Gracie Fields singing "Now Is The Hour". John told me he loved her singing.' The visits, each week for four years when he was in New York, made John 'one of the family' inside that little café. Yoko even took her mother there, when she visited from Japan, to demonstrate a little how she and John lived.

John ignored rock music completely during the mid-seventies. It was as if the consolidation of his love for Yoko and the birth of Sean had brought out the true romantic in him. Although he hated overt, gushing, lovey-dovey sentimentality, John was a 'pushover' when it came to romantic music. John and Yoko's favourite song and movie at this time was Barbra Streisand's 'The Way We Were'. It was some distance from 'A Hard Day's Night' and Chuck Berry.

Yoko's gift to John for his thirty-eighth birthday was a very special antique; a 'bubble-top' Wurlitzer jukebox of the style popular in American soda fountain shops in the 1950s. It took only 78 r.p.m. records and its arrival coincided with John's increasing interest in nostalgic music. The first batch of records ordered for the Wurlitzer were mostly 1950s hits like 'Dream Lover' by Bobby Darin; Frankie Laine; Johnnie Ray's 'Little White Cloud That Cried'; and as many Bing Crosby records as he could get. Here was real irony: Bing Crosby's 'Please', which John had heard just as the Beatles were getting started eighteen years earlier in Liverpool, had inspired John to write their first big hit, 'Please Please Me'. Another favourite was 'As Time Goes By', by Dooley Wilson.

The Wurlitzer jukebox was the centrepoint of a creation by John on New Year's Eve 1979. He decided, with Elliot Mintz, to establish a private club called the Club Dakota, one small room which would be his equivalent of an Englishman's private club. With the Yamaha electric piano bought for his birthday by Elton John, he would give private recitals to a favoured few.

The Club Dakota's only members were John Lennon and Elliot Mintz. When Yoko attended, just once on that New Year's Eve, John was dressed in tails and his old Quarry Bank brown-and-yellow school tie. The appeal of the 'club' for John was its exclusivity. He even broke the hallowed 'no alcohol' rule there, agreed between himself and Yoko, allowing himself a bottle of old cognac.

Breakfasts in the Edwardian room of the Plaza Hotel were another regular pleasure. John had a special affinity with the hotel. The Beatles had stayed there when they first visited America in 1964. In the mornings the Lennons would have a late breakfast of black coffee (John ate eggs Benedict, Yoko split pea soup), before moving across to the tea-room where the violinist greeted them playing 'The Way We Were' and 'As Time Goes By' while they held hands. On Sean's seventh birthday the same violinist visited the Dakota to play 'Happy Birthday' for him. When they were out together, John and Yoko frequently held hands. 'When their kind of 1940s music struck up,' says Elliot Mintz, 'they behaved like high school sweethearts. They were *finished*, gazing at each other. . . .'

Memories of Liverpool permeated much of John's thinking from that day in 1976 when he secured his Green Card. Most nights he would telephone Aunt Mimi. Often he would reassure her that he had triumphed magnificently over the monster that was the Beatles. Several times he tried to persuade his aunt to go and live with him and take one of their Dakota apartments: 'No fear, John. You'll never catch me over there. I never have liked Americans. And *you* shouldn't be there, either. It's no good for you. Come back and live in England.' John told her he preferred New York but he now knew better than to argue with her.

Around the world Beatles fans had regarded John as a recluse since he had got his Green Card. His world travels to Japan, Hong Kong, Singapore, and South Africa had gone unnoticed. He and Yoko travelled incognito as the Revd Fred and Ada Ghurkin. Outside the Dakota the one person who knew precisely where he was on all his trips was Aunt Mimi. When he was travelling, he would phone her at 9.30 p.m. precisely British time, 4.30 p.m. New York time. 'I knew it was him; every night it rang almost on the dot,' she says. 'And it was, "Mimi, I'm in Bermuda, Cairo, Tokyo . . ." or wherever. Always gave me his phone number and said I could reverse the charges and call him back but I never wanted to do that. . . .'

For Sean's fourth birthday and John's thirty-ninth, on 9

October 1979, the Lennons threw a party at the Tavern on the Green, an elegant, glittering restaurant in Central Park. John was dressed soberly but wore his Quarry Bank tie to which he had grown attached. A Beatles fan sent a picture of John to a surprised Aunt Mimi, who challenged him about it. 'Who are your spies?' John said. 'Look, I've carried it around with me everywhere these past few years. I just like it.' It confirmed Mimi's lifelong suspicions about her nephew's sentimentality: 'He was a great big baby. He was no tough nut, never. I think he sometimes wanted people to think he was, but deep down, he was as soft as butter.'

Proof of this theory, which Mimi held all her life, sometimes against the odds, came at the start of 1980. In one of his daily phone conversations, John said: 'Right, Mimi, now I want you to put your affairs in order.'

'What affairs?'

'Now look, Mimi, everything belonging to you, I want it.'

'What do you mean, John? If it's that important to you, you can have anything you like now. But what have you on your mind?'

The next part of John's request shattered her. The degree of his memory of all her possessions, particularly the items he had grown up with back at 251 Menlove Avenue, was almost overpowering. 'Mimi, you remember that painting that Uncle George did when he was at Liverpool Institute in Form 4A? It was a watercolour of a kind of Chinese vase. I'd like that.' It was the picture at the far end of the hall that had faced John as he had walked in from school or college every day. Mimi found it in her loft.

'John wanted every single photograph of me that I could lay my hands on,' says Mimi. And he gave her a vivid description of the china that had been on a plate rack high on the wall of the entrance hall and dining-room at Mendips. 'It's gold, Mimi, and it's got blue in it and a sort of rusty red. Coalport, Spode and Crown Derby. And don't forget to send me the teapot.' Mimi always had a weakness for collecting china; it formed a central part of the decoration of the house in which John grew up. 'He asked for the really heavy cut-glass claret jugs, an enlargement of a photograph of my mother when she was a beautiful twenty-one-year-old. John wanted all my silver, all the cutlery I was not using that he'd seen at Mendips, any old cup and saucer, salt and pepperpots, anything. He said: "There's no need to do anything with it. Just leave it for collection." And John had a removal firm ship it all to him in crates.' John was developing an increasing fascination for his roots; he told friends he intended to write a *Forsyte Saga*-type story based on his family.

His final request was for Mimi to send him something that had been passed down in her late husband's family of Smiths for generations: an antique grandfather clock, inscribed 'George Toogood, Woolton Tavern'. Uncle George, whose full name was George Toogood Smith, had taught John the time on it. The Toogoods were John's ancestors, a fact he had discovered, says Mimi, in his teenage years when he walked his Woolton girlfriends around the graveyard of St Peter's Church. Mimi had the handsome wooden clock serviced and John arranged for it to be shipped over to New York. It ticks away loudly still in the Dakota kitchen, framed symbolically by pictures carefully chosen and positioned by John: one black-and-white picture of John and Yoko above it, and a Polaroid snapshot of John and Yoko on a boat, looking at each other, next to it.

John's emotional side came over loudly and clearly during 1980. 'Remember,' he would say to Mimi, 'those holidays you sent me on in Scotland with Mater [his Aunt Elizabeth]? And the postcard I sent you: "Dear Mimi and Uncle George, I caught my first trout today. . . ." Have you still got those cards, Mimi?' And the aunt who had lectured him so sternly about getting on with his studies would find it hard to keep the tears back.

Although Mimi had never seen Sean, whom she regarded as her grandson, she must have known everything there was to know about him. John regaled her most nights with a blow-by-blow account of what Sean was doing and how he was.

'John,' she said, 'don't make the same mistake that I did and wrap your life around a little boy. That's what *I* did, and what did I get?'

'Was I that bad? A worry to you?' And they would both laugh about the years when his conscientious aunt told him he was wasting his time playing the guitar at the Cavern Club instead of getting a proper career.

Throughout 1980 John sent out clear signs to his aunt that he loved and respected her for her strictness and her care of him. 'You were right,' he told her. 'But I knew I could paint and draw . . . and *write*. I'm forty this year. I'm going to make one more record, Mimi, then I'm going to do some writing.'

23
THE MUSIC:
1972–1980

'No longer riding on the merry-go-round,
I just had to let it go'

'Nobody told me there'd be days like *these*!' chanted John, alone and simply, in a record Yoko released four years after his death.

In 1984, four years after John's murder, it was a simple, stark reminder of the powerful, allegorical word-play with which he had mesmerized millions for twenty years. There had been diversions, of course: back to the roots rock 'n' roll; the tender, loving ballads on *Double Fantasy*. But here, now, in a song that was at once danceable to and which lyrically outclassed any contemporary rock 'n' roll, the words of 'Nobody Told Me' were as relevant to the eighties as the psychedelic anthems he created earlier were for the sixties. John Lennon's posthumously released album was a far more articulate, concerned, symbolic, and creative piece of work than that produced by any living artist in popular music. Together with the searing, chilling song he wrote for Yoko, 'Grow Old With Me', the album *Milk And Honey* demonstrated to all his friends—and those who had branded *Double Fantasy* as maudlin—that Lennon was a master who had not lost his muse.

Double Fantasy and *Milk And Honey* have provided the most moving love songs from John Lennon, because they feature lyrics written and sung around the time of his happiness as a husband and father in America. They were albums that accurately reflected his mood in 1980. But the man who had arrived in New York some nine years earlier, mentally high on his fixation for Yoko and the vibrancy of the country, with his eyes wide open seeking new mental horizons, provided some astonishingly provocative music and writing that demonstrated how he loved championing causes.

All the vitality Lennon felt he was getting from his new home poured into the *Some Time In New York City* album, which was released in 1972. Jerry Rubin, the political activist with whom John had become friendly, had put him in touch with a hard-rocking New York band, Elephants' Memory (three of whose songs were included on the soundtrack of the film *Midnight Cowboy*). Rejuvenated politically and musically, Lennon spontaneously plunged into the recording, finishing the album in nineteen days. It was a hasty decision and one which he later came to regret. *Some Time In New York City* does have moments of energy, particularly the driving 'New York City' which conveys Lennon's enthusiasm for his new home. You can even overlook such trite lines as 'His name is David Peel/ And we found that he was real', such is the vitality of the song. Yoko's songs on the record have a charm of their own. 'Sisters, O Sisters' and 'We're All Water' are lyrically invigorating. The haunting quality of her singing and the pile-driving Elephants Memory meant that the songs stood up on their own.

'Sunday Bloody Sunday' and 'The Luck Of The Irish' were drawn from Lennon's first-hand knowledge of the Irish community in Liverpool and they convey Lennon's rage at the British troops' occupation of Northern Ireland. 'The Luck Of The Irish' managed, however, to retain some of Lennon's charm.

Where the album falls down is in Lennon's trite and repetitious sloganeering. After being a leader for so long, Lennon was now being led. His direction was dominated by Rubin and Hoffman, who were hardly objective, and while the causes they championed were noble, 'John Sinclair', 'Attica State', 'Angela', and 'Woman Is The Nigger Of The World' for example, are almost offensively single-minded. The victimization of 'subversive elements' by the Nixon administration (which considered Lennon as one) was reprehensible and it was important that someone of Lennon's stature should speak out against such iniquities. Dylan's 1971 single 'George Jackson' was fired by that same sense of outrage but Dylan wisely confined his sentiments to a single. Lennon had proved throughout his career that he was one of rock's most articulate spokesmen, able to clarify and delineate problems with a perception and wry humour that few of his contemporaries could match. To hear him endlessly repeat other people's slogans was dispiriting.

Lennon resented the criticism that the album attracted— that he was writing simple lyrics—even though he had always claimed to dislike his songs 'being digested and analysed like the Mona Lisa'. 'I Want To Hold Your Hand' was simple, he said; if he constantly sought praise he could write more surrealistic material like 'I Am The Walrus'. What motivated him on his arrival in New York was the ease of writing political songs and rushing them out on a record, just as he had always wanted. 'Most other people express themselves by playing football at weekends or shouting. But here am I in New York and I hear about thirteen people shot dead in Ireland and I react immediately. And being what I am I react in four-to-the-bar with a guitar break in the middle,' he told Roy Carr in the *New Musical Express*. 'I don't say, "My God, what's happening, we should do something." I go: "It was Sunday Bloody Sunday/And they shot the people down . . ." It's not like the Bible. It's all over now. It's gone. It's finished.' Music, as a form of communication, was his main concern.

To its credit, the album did possess immediacy, as Lennon remembered: 'When we made that album, we weren't setting out to make the Brandenburg Concerto or the masterpiece everybody always tries to write, paint, draw, or film. . . . The point now is that I want to say whatever it is I've got to say, as simple as the music I like. And that's rock 'n' roll, and to match the lyrics to the music. So now it's . . . AWOPBOPALOOBOP Get Outta Ireland. I suppose it looks more preachy than it really is.'

Some Time In New York City was a realization of Lennon's ideal record at that time: it should have the immediacy of a newspaper and reflect current affairs (the album packaging was based on the *New York Times*). But *Some Time In New York City* did little to enhance Lennon's reputation. Side Three was recorded at the UNICEF Lyceum Benefit in 1969. It includes a workmanlike version of 'Cold Turkey' and continues with Yoko screeching that 'Britain killed Hanratty' (the A6 murderer who was hanged). Side Four included the Zappa jam, with a competent version of the old Olympics hit 'Well (Baby Please Don't Go)' dredged up from the Cavern days.

Lennon swiftly realized he had gone too far. He had lost objectivity and his craft had suffered. He told New York writer Peter Hamill in 1975: 'It almost *ruined* [my work]. It became journalism and not poetry. And I basically feel that I'm a poet. Then I began to take it seriously on another level, saying, "Well, I am reflecting what is going on, right?" '

Lennon had laid himself wide open for criticism and the reviews that the album received were a chastening experience for him. At the beginning of 1973 he and Yoko had moved into the Dakota Building and he kept a low profile. Just before Christmas 1972 John and Yoko's 'Happy Xmas (War Is Over)' single was belatedly released in the U.K. The Christmas novelty single is a great tradition in Britain. The Lennons' single took up their 'War Is Over, If You Want It' slogan and turned it into a memorable Christmas hit. The message is simply that we should work together and shed a little love, a suitably apposite message for Christmas, and one which echoes round the world every year when it is re-released. The choir on the record is the children's Harlem Community Choir.

Not until the end of 1973 did Lennon feel confident enough to release a new album. *Mind Games* marked a return to the melodicism of *Imagine* and was a distinct departure from the polemics of his previous album. As an indication of his commitment to the project, it was the first album he had produced by himself. He gathered the best session musicians New York could offer. Names like Jim Keltner, David Spinozza, Michael Brecker, and Sneaky Pete Kleinow, regularly featured on albums by Bob Dylan, Ry Cooder, the Rolling Stones, Bruce Springsteen, and the Flying Burrito Brothers. The inherent lushness and attempt to return to former glories could be found on the album's title track, which announced: 'Love is the answer, and you know that for sure.'

John was always one of the great rock 'n' roll vocalists, although he was reticent about his own vocal abilities. He had always allowed his voice to be buried on record, but on 'Tight A\$', the album's second track, there is a freewheeling return to rock 'n' roll with Lennon's voice well to the fore. It is not as hard as it could have been (the backing is far too polite) but Lennon is still in great voice and the song rolls along. 'Bring On The Lucie (Freda People)' is another of those cautious rockers—'OK boys, let's go over the hill,' he announces as the song plunges into its riff. But he doesn't go far enough and lapses back into vacuous sloganeering. The song is redeemed by some tasty dobro playing.

'Out The Blue' is a beautifully restrained love song, haunting and poignant. John's devotion to Yoko was aching: 'All my life's been a long slow knife/I was born just to get to you.' That feeling persisted on 'I Know (I Know)'. And there was the first indication of Lennon's efforts to bridge the gap between East and West with the schoolboy Japanese of 'Aisumasen (I'm Sorry)' and 'You Are Here', which overturned Kipling's maxim that 'East is East and West is West and never the twain shall meet.' Lennon maintains that the twain *shall* meet: 'From distant lands, one woman, one man. . . .'

Mind Games has several pleasant tracks—notably the title song—but it suffers from too many mid-paced rockers and lacks his usual lyrical inventiveness. The old radical Lennon had gone (as solace he offered a silent 'Nutopian International Anthem'). The love poet of *Imagine* had gone. The confessional troubador of *Plastic Ono Band* had gone. By the end of 1973 Lennon sounded listless and uninspired. After its release he went on his 'long weekend'.

Walls And Bridges, released in October 1974, was an open letter to the absent Yoko. Many of the songs were pleading, an uncharacteristic role for Lennon. The album was cockier than *Mind Games*, mainly because of Bobby Keys' raunchy sax playing and some generally fine instrumental back-up. The album was conceived and recorded while Lennon was just coming out of a bender of Dylan Thomas proportions. His old friend Harry Nilsson was closely involved. As far back as 1968 Lennon had congratulated him on his imaginative Beatle medley on his *Pandemonium Shadow Show* album and the two had collaborated on Nilsson's *Pussy Cats* L.P. in California earlier in the year.

Walls And Bridges was a beautifully packaged album, with drawings courtesy of the twelve-year-old John Winston Lennon, an imaginative cut-out sleeve, a lyric book and plenty of

Dr Winston O'Boogie's (a jokey pseudonym John sometimes used) aphorisms. Elton John, an ardent Lennon fan (and at the time himself the most successful British act since the Beatles) guested on the hit single 'Whatever Gets You Thru The Night', which turned out to be the album's best track. A cocky rocker, it had suitably irreverent lyrics: 'Whatever gets you thru the night, s'alright, s'alright.'

On the slower songs like 'Old Dirt Road' and 'Nobody Loves You (When You're Down And Out)'—which he always saw Sinatra as singing—Lennon sounded maudlin. On 'Bless You' he even comes over as sluggish. '#9 Dream' was a barely marked progression from 'Aisumasen'. It had the requisite dreamy atmosphere to match the lyrics, and was as much about the number nine, which Lennon always considered lucky, as it was about his state of mind.

'Scared' could lyrically have come from his first album, Lennon laying himself open to the world at large: 'I'm scared . . . No bell, book or candle/Can get you out of this . . . I'm tired of being so alone/No place to call my own/Like a rollin' stone.' 'Going Down On Love' was a plea to Yoko: 'Your love has gone . . . And you shoot out the light/Ain't coming home for the night.' The finished album was a definite improvement on the listless *Mind Games* but it was hardly vintage Lennon. He recalled the circumstances at the time: 'This last year has been an extraordinary one for me personally. And I'm almost amazed that I could get *anything* out. Musically, my mind was a clutter. It was apparent on *Walls And Bridges*, which was the work of a semi-sick craftsman. There was no inspiration and it gave an aura of misery.'

Significantly, two of the biggest stars of the seventies, Elton John and David Bowie, played a substantial role in getting Lennon back on the tracks: Elton because he coerced Lennon into appearing with him at his Madison Square Garden concert on Thanksgiving Night 1974 and Bowie because he asked Lennon along to help out on the sessions which made up his 1975 *Young Americans* album. In the studio Lennon backed vocals on what he said was always one of his favourite songs, Bowie's histrionic reading of 'Across The Universe'; John also co-wrote 'Fame' with Bowie and guitarist Carlos Alomar. The song gave

Bowie his first American number one hit while Elton also helped Lennon there with 'Whatever Gets You Thru The Night'.

Lennon's next album to be released was *Rock 'n' Roll* in February 1975. It was a project which had fascinated him for years and the story behind the album went back to when Chuck Berry's publisher, Morris Levy, had threatened to sue John for alleged plagiarism; Levy claimed that 'Come Together' from *Abbey Road* ripped off Berry's 1956 'You Can't Catch Me'. (Both songs do include the line: 'Here comes old flat top'.) In an out of court settlement, Lennon agreed to record a number of Chuck Berry songs for a forthcoming album, which laid the seeds for *Rock 'n' Roll*.

At an artistic and emotional crossroads in 1973, Lennon felt that he needed a producer to dictate how he sang, to help recreate the feel of those rock classics, to advise, and to inspire him. Having dropped Phil Spector after *Some Time In New York City*, and having produced *Mind Games* himself, Lennon now approached Spector again and asked him to work on the new album, originally called *Oldies but Mouldies*. (This was a neat parody on the sub-title of the first Beatles' hits collection released in 1966, *Oldies But Goldies*.) Although a virtual recluse, Spector agreed and they subsequently recorded many tracks together. But a growing estrangement developed between them, and the sessions grew more and more protracted. (Studio costs alone for the four tracks John considered to be rescuable were $90,000.) Finally Spector disappeared completely, taking the master tapes with him. There was talk of a car crash, rumour piled upon rumour, and not even John could get past the armed guards around the Spector mansion. Eventually Lennon retrieved the tapes but Spector (once again living the life of a recluse) was no longer interested in pursuing the project. In a burst of energy Lennon tore into the Record Plant in New York at the end of October 1974 and in a mere four days laid down ten new tracks to complete the album. Because of his enthusiasm for the project, and because of Levy's illegal *Roots* album suddenly being made available, *Rock 'n' Roll* was issued only four months after *Walls And Bridges*.

The cover picture alone, by Jurgen Vollmer, was worth the price of the album: John, sneering in a Hamburg doorway in

1961, fresh-faced, every inch a rocker. Blurred figures rush by hurrying to the future, while Lennon stands, as if waiting for the past to catch up with him. Lennon cherished the very *idea* of the album, and effortlessly pitched himself back in time: 'All the words to "Stand By Me" and "Be-Bop-A-Lula", I knew them all from being fifteen, they all just came back to me, just like that.'

In many ways *Rock 'n' Roll* is the definitive John Lennon album. Even when he had toyed with the avant-garde and radical politics John had remained a rocker at heart. He saw rock 'n' roll as 'the great motivator' and always paid homage to the greats who inspired him. He was genuinely modest about his own songwriting abilities and felt he had never written anything to equal 'Whole Lotta Shakin' Goin' On'. Now stripped of the peace and primals, he stands supreme as the cocky rocker who took on the world and almost beat it. *Rock 'n' Roll* is a human jukebox, with Lennon pouring his heart into his roots. It's far more than simply a rehash of twenty-year-old Chuck Berry and Little Richard songs. Each song on the album is stamped with his personality, infused with Lennon dynamism. The rockers are harder than anything Lennon had done in years, the ballads softer. While rock 'n' roll itself was looking for a direction in 1975, John Lennon was looking imaginatively back at its history.

The album spans the glory years of rock 'n' roll, from Little Richard's 1956 'Rip It Up' to Sam Cooke's 1962 'Bring It On Home To Me'. It covers John's adolescence, picking up the flickering signals of Radio Luxembourg, through art school and teenage groups, right up to the birth of the Beatles. Those songs were the soundtrack to his life, before the world went mad— the shuffle beat of Buddy Holly's 'Peggy Sue', the chilling 'Be-Bop-A-Lula', the raucous 'Ready Teddy' and 'Bony Moronie', the rolling 'Ain't That A Shame', the poignant 'Stand By Me'—Lennon hadn't sung better since *Plastic Ono Band*. His act of homage gave him the shot in the arm he needed.

The most touching aspect of the album comes right at the end of Side Two. He finishes a tender version of Lloyd Price's 'Just Because', treating it affectionately, delivering almost a parody of fifties' recording clichés. The spoken bridge and slow fade culminate with him saying: 'This is Dr Winston O'Boogie saying goodnight from the Record Plant East. We've had a swell time. Everybody here says Hi. Goodbye.' It was as if John knew the album was a watershed. He told Andy Peebles: 'Something flashed through my mind as I said it. Am I really saying farewell to the business? I looked at the cover I'd chosen, which was a picture of me in Hamburg the first time we got there *[sic]*. I thought, this is some sort of cosmic thing. Here I am with this old picture of me in Hamburg in sixty-one and I'm saying farewell from Record Plant, and I'm ending as I started, singing this straight rock 'n' roll stuff.'

With Yoko pregnant, Lennon channelled all his energies into caring for his wife. Nothing more was heard of him on record for five long years. A fortnight after Sean was born in October 1975 *Shaved Fish* was released. It was a timely, well-assembled collection, embracing the range of his work since 1969. Opening with a snatch of 'Give Peace A Chance', and finishing with 'Happy Xmas', the album ran through the facets of his career: Lennon as junkie ('Cold Turkey'), as political activist ('Power To The People'), as idealist ('Imagine', '#9 Dream'). It was an impressive roster. Perhaps more convincingly than any of the four Beatles, Lennon proved with this L.P. that he had achieved the impossible—he had forged his own identity. He had reconciled his art with his life and proved himself able to cope with his past.

During Lennon's years of silence the English music scene became convulsed with the iconoclasm of punk. 'No more Elvis, Beatles or Stones in 1977' screamed the Clash. The young punks were bored and angry with the remote rock élite. They wanted their own heroes and were not content with second-hand idols, whose lives and music bore no relation to their own.

It marked the first generation gap in music since the broad-side delivered by the Beatles and Bob Dylan all those years before. The anarchic approach of the Sex Pistols and the Clash to rock 'n' roll left many of the old guard marooned. Lennon remained one of the few rock establishment figures who was not ridiculed. Perhaps they remembered his struggles and the ridicule *he* had faced, which bore comparison with their own vendetta. For his own private reasons Lennon, wisely, did not opt for punk. He had other things on his mind during the punk upheaval—being a father and a husband, and becoming a human being instead of adopting roles and causes.

During those years of silence he listened to Hank Williams, Carl Perkins, Jerry Lee Lewis, the B52s, Lene Lovich, Bruce Springsteen, Madness, John Gielgud reading Shakespeare, and 'everything Bing Crosby had ever done'. He listened but did not comment. As the punks created their own idols, he breathed a sigh of relief as he watched the mantle pass on: 'God help Bruce Springsteen when they decide he's no longer God . . . when he gets down to facing his own success and growing older and having to produce it again and again, they'll turn on him and I hope he survives it.' John watched his idols and contemporaries fall, succumbing to the sort of pressures he had wisely managed to avoid.

During those five private years the anger seeped out of John Lennon. There is a school of rock theory that says the only *great* music comes out of anger and frustration, from the energy of youth. It has its point; that *is* where much of rock's motivation has come from. It follows that comfort and contentment see the original intentions vanish and disappear (McCartney's domesticity, Dylan's pulpit-bashing). And yet we have no right to expect our idols to suffer for the sake of their music. If they are enjoying security and happiness, then, inevitably, that is what will be reflected in their music. It is that feeling of contentment and domesticity which permeates *Double Fantasy*.

'(Just Like) Starting Over' was released on 24 October 1980, the first single from John Lennon in five years. Despite the convulsions in pop music during his silence, despite the contempt with which most icons of the sixties were held, a tremor ran through the music industry—Lennon was back! John now had something fresh to say musically. Sean was five, and he wanted to reflect the parental bliss he was experiencing. He also wanted to give his son a birthday present. And he chose the method he knew best.

The songs for the album were mostly written in a three-week burst in Bermuda. But then Lennon was never one to labour over a song. He once told David Bowie: 'Look, it's *very* simple: Say what you mean, make it rhyme and put a backbeat to it!' John and Yoko had a ball in the studio—Lennon was exultant at being back. 'We cut twenty-two tracks in two weeks!'

Double Fantasy was released at the end of November 1980 on the newly inaugurated Geffen label. With its release some ardent Lennon fans felt twinges of disappointment. They thought it simply showed John and Yoko washing their clean linen in public. Gone was the old *Angst*-ridden Lennon, the poet who carried the world's troubles on his shoulders. With the tracks evenly split between them, the Lennons now offered domestic bliss as the solution. It should have been obvious to everyone what public face the inscrutable Lennon would present. His wife and child were now his whole world. What else could he (or did he want to) write about? *Double Fantasy* was the most honest Lennon album since *Plastic Ono Band* in that it perfectly reflected his state of mind. The demons were vanquished. The past was firmly put in its place. With Yoko and Sean, and after forty years of trial and torment, John Lennon had found peace.

In all truth, and ridding ourselves of the poignancy which irrevocably surrounds *Double Fantasy*, it is not a great album. In retrospect it is, of course, John Lennon's final vinyl statement in which the tracks were produced, mixed, and sequenced exactly as he intended. A song like 'Beautiful Boy (Darling Boy)' takes on a terrible beauty in the aftermath of Lennon's murder, as he sings to his son: 'Close your eyes and have no fear/The monster's gone and your Daddy's here.' The morning he promised Sean at the end of the song never came.

'Starting Over' was the album opener, ushered in by the ringing of Yoko's personal 'wishing bell'—it was a deliberate ploy: 'I put it on *Double Fantasy* to show the likeness and difference from "Mother" to "Starting Over",' said John. Before, tolling bells had emphasized doom. Now there was a chirpy cheerful bell, indicating a willingness to start again. What was appealing was the diehard rock 'n' roll voice he chose (à la Elvis): 'It was the fifties-ish sound because I had never really written a song that sounded like that period, although that was my period, the music I identified with. So I just thought, why the hell not? In the Beatle days, that would have been taken as a joke. One avoided clichés. But now those clichés are not clichés any more,' he told *Playboy*.

'Woman' was a beautifully sustained Lennon ballad, written in fifteen minutes; it is already a classic. It recalls the fragility of 'Imagine' and touchingly recognizes that Yoko understands 'the little child inside the man'. 'Dear Yoko' finds Lennon again in fine fifties voice, pleading his love. It is a rockier version of 'Oh Yoko!' from 1971 and perfectly summarizes the intensity of their relationship: 'Without you I'm a one-track mind, dear Yoko/After all is really said and done/ The two of us are really one. . . .' (Yoko's seven songs on the album were her most accessible to date and proved she had an even more contemporary edge than her husband.)

'Watching The Wheels' is Lennon's answer to all those who speculated on his state of mind during his five-year silence: 'People have been saying I'm lazy, dreaming my life away, all my life,' John commented. 'Pop stars were getting indignant in the Press that I wasn't making records. I couldn't believe it, they were acting like mothers-in-law. . . .' To counter that speculation Lennon wrote of what he actually was doing: 'watching shadows on the wall . . . No longer riding on the merry-go-round/I just had to let it go.' Finally, after years of pressure, Lennon could slide off the helter skelter and leave the fairground. The song was powerfully autobiographical.

It could come as no surprise to him, though, that people were fascinated by his silence. Rock 'n' roll is a notoriously short-lived profession. The only comparable absences were when Elvis entered the army in 1958 and Dylan's enforced seclusion following his motorcycle crash of 1966. Rumours spread. The remote rock star becomes a mythical figure. People couldn't believe that John Lennon, probably the most talented rocker of his generation, could be *happy* simply making bread! He realized people still looked to him for answers but by 1980 the only answer he could offer was: 'Just sitting here watching the wheels go round/I really love to watch them roll. . . .' He told *Rolling Stone* in 1980: 'They're my own wheels, mainly. But you know, watching myself is like watching everybody else. The hardest thing is facing yourself. It's easier to shout "Revolution" and "Power To The People" than it is to look at yourself and try to find out what's real inside you and what isn't, when you're pulling the wool over your own eyes.' Lennon was well aware of the disappointment that his new-found peace would cause his fans but had no wish to compromise his own feelings to satisfy them: 'I cannot be a punk in Hamburg and Liverpool any more. I'm older now, I see the world through different eyes. . . . As Elvis Costello said—"What's so funny 'bout peace, love and understanding?" '

In the terrible aftermath of John's death in December 1980, 'Starting Over', 'Imagine', and 'Woman' all reached number one on the British charts. The three songs he performed with Elton John in 1974 appeared on a single and *The John Lennon Collection* was the number one album for Christmas 1982. Lennon's name was subsequently evoked by many of his disciples: on Elton John's 'Empty Garden', on Queen's 'Life Is Real', and on Paul Simon's 'The Late Great Johnny Ace'.

Paul McCartney movingly remembered Lennon on a song called 'Here Today', on his 1982 album *Tug of War*. McCartney admitted the gulf which had grown between the two men but, accompanied by a discreet string quartet, he unashamedly sang: 'I am holding back the tears no more/I love you.' In conversation with the late Alexis Korner he spoke of that song: 'It was being heralded as a kind of tribute album. Which I hadn't thought of, you know—"I will now make this a tribute album" . . . John would have been the first one to laugh at that kind of stuff. . . . He'd probably laugh and say that we're worlds apart anyway . . . but we weren't. I know if we had you back here right now you'd say, "Oh, load of bollocks." But it's not true, you know, that would be just bluff. We actually did know each other, we actually were very close. . . . There was always the competitive thing with John and I, which I know was very good for me and I think he appreciated it as it was very good for him too.'

When the shock of Lennon's murder eventually subsided, the *Milk and Honey* album was released in January 1984. Recorded at the *Double Fantasy* sessions in August 1980, the album follows the format of its predecessor, the tracks evenly divided between John and Yoko. The single, 'Nobody Told Me', was among John's best since 'Imagine', a jerky compelling rocker (with Lennon again favouring that fifties vocal style) which raced into the British charts. It stands as a tribute to his innate musical ability that 'Nobody Told Me' sounds as ebullient and infectious as anything Lennon had ever done.

Milk and Honey has a harder feel to it than *Double Fantasy* because of the obvious rawness of the Lennon tracks. As Yoko told Andy Peebles, the temptation for any outside producer would have been to over-produce the whole album (as Norman Petty did with Buddy Holly's posthumous recordings). So the resultant album retains its charm and spontaneity, notably on the lovely 'Grow Old With Me', with Lennon on piano, accompanied by a rhythm box. There is a grittiness on the album's rockier tracks, showing that, right to the end, Lennon was a rocker. Rock was both his heritage and his legacy.

There are moments of mawkishness as in '(Forgive Me) My Little Flower Princess', but on the whole it is the moments of touching greatness we remember. 'I Don't Wanna Face It' carries on the theme developed in 'Watching The Wheels' with Lennon advocating that people find another hero, he has had enough: 'Say you're looking for a place to go/Where nobody knows your name/You're looking for oblivion, with one eye on the Hall of Fame/I don't wanna face it . . . Well I can dish it out/But I just can't take it.' 'I'm Stepping Out' opens the album with Lennon taking on the character of Lonnie Donegan of 'Rock Island Line', vintage, before stepping into traditional blues territory, with John revelling in his role as house-husband.

The perfect marriage occurs at the end of Side One, as Lennon's 'Three, four . . .' ushers in 'Nobody Told Me', with his ruminating on Nazis in the bathroom and little yellow idols, punctuated by wistful cries of, 'Strange days indeed Momma'. Next to it, Yoko's poignant, brief ' "O" Sanity', probably her most incisive recorded song, ends with the terse: 'Let it go, cut it out!'

'Borrowed Time' has Lennon facing the uncertainties of middle age in a world no longer conveniently divided into black and white: 'The more I see, the less I know for sure,' he sings, although maintaining that 'It's good to be older.' For John, 'Grow Old With Me' had become a pleasant vision of his and Yoko's future. He wanted to include it on *Double Fantasy* but couldn't decide on the song's arrangement. As the album's deadline drew closer, it was held over for the follow-up and appears here in this charming, uncluttered version.

The album is peppered with Lennon's on-mike asides, his count-ins, and snatches of studio conversation, which add to the casual eavesdropping atmosphere for the listener. *Milk and Honey* is full of charm and tragedy. The tragedy lies in the fact that as a musician and poet John Lennon was back finding his musical feet. On the sleeve of his 1975 *Rock 'n' Roll* album, Dr Winston O'Boogie simply wrote: 'You should have been there.' Thanks to the music of John Lennon, we were and always will be.

24
THE COMEBACK

'Life begins at forty'

The word spread like a forest fire at the beginning of August 1980: John Lennon, the hermit, the Howard Hughes of rock, the man who had freaked out to become a house-husband and led a mysterious, reclusive life for five years, was back. At a New York recording studio he was recording a new album. With Yoko Ono. Amid U.S. election fever (Carter was to lose to Reagan in November), and as 54 Americans were held hostage in Iran, the news from the Lennon camp was like a beacon of light.

John's decision to return to recording had been made in Bermuda a month earlier. Bermuda proved yet another watershed for John. He had gone there because he felt that up until then he had done so few things alone in his life. He decided to go by sea with a five-man crew on his yacht *Isis*. The crossing from Newport, Rhode Island, is notoriously rough at certain times of the year and the yacht was tossed around in heavy seas. With the crew falling sick one by one, it fell to John to take the controls, which he did successfully. 'There was crockery falling all over the place and it was really rough with the waves coming up over the boat,' John recalled later. 'I thought I was supposed to be the passenger but I had a go.' He told Aunt Mimi of it by phone when he reached Bermuda; he had felt like an old sea captain, the sort that sailed into Liverpool. John said he had sung himself songs as he steered the yacht to keep up his morale: mostly Beatles oldies, 'Strawberry Fields Forever', 'Getting Better', 'Please Please Me'. Mentally he was slowly turning full circle.

In Bermuda, in a rented house, the idea was for John to relax totally and go swimming and sailing. But he could hardly stay off the phone each day, trying to reach Yoko. Incredibly he sometimes found his busy wife in business meetings, unable to be interrupted. It was then that he wrote the evocative song 'I'm Losing You', which he played to her over the telephone.

At the Forty Thieves discothèque and also on the radio John heard the music he was listening to being described as 'new wave'. It struck him that there was nothing new about it. Yoko had been writing and performing much more imaginative material, in the same genre, ten years earlier. At the time she was rejected as a freak. Perhaps, he mused, the world was ready for her now. It inspired him to write songs furiously. One of his first was 'Woman', that paean not only to Yoko but to women everywhere, which laid bare his deepest affections for them. Over the next week or two, on his daily phone conversations with Yoko, he sang and played her his latest compositions and she reciprocated with her new work. The stage was set. On his return to Manhattan he and Yoko had around twenty songs between them, some finished, some unfinished.

'(Just Like) Starting Over' epitomized precisely what John felt about his return to recording. His earliest influences in rock 'n' roll—Elvis Presley and Roy Orbison—were recalled on the sound and atmosphere of the song. The album's concept, a combination of songs by both husband and wife, was poetically captured by the title, *Double Fantasy*. John had been enraptured by a flower of this name while out walking in the summer in botanical gardens in Bermuda. It suited the tone of the album perfectly.

Back in New York, John was in superb mental and physical shape for the recording sessions. Seen outside the Hit Factory studios on West 54th Street, Manhattan, he looked sprightly and smiling. For the first time in eighteen years he was free of a contract: he had written the songs and was making the record purely for himself. No record deal was in the offing—the plan was to find a label when they had completed the work. The working pattern and atmosphere at the recording studios was both civilized and organized. There was no rock 'n' roll wildness or crazy behavior. Potted plants and flowers were ordered; there was a waiting room with comfortable chairs for everyone to relax; the musicians chosen to accompany John and Yoko were kindred spirits whom they admired as players: Andy Newmark (drums), Hugh McCracken (bass guitar), Earl Slick (guitar), Tony Levin (bass guitar). The competition among New York musicians to be on John Lennon's comeback album was enormous.

Yoko knew John was hungry for a successful return to work. He was particularly anxious for success in Britain. Phone calls to Aunt Mimi, imported tapes of British television shows like *Fawlty Towers* and *Monty Python*, and anything that gave him a sighting of the green British countryside, had made John almost misty-eyed when he thought of his native land. 'But England's not gonna go away,' he told anyone near him who asked when he was planning to return. 'It's still going to be there when I want to go and have a look at it. . . .'

He was in majestic form in the recording studios. His voice had achieved a resonance that was still the quintessential John Lennon but with a worldliness brilliantly mirrored in the lyrics of his songs.

Elliot Mintz had attended a number of *Double Fantasy* recording sessions. They were unlike any recording session for a John and Yoko album, he remembers. 'Yoko made it very clear to everyone that there was to be no alcohol or drugs of any kind during the making of that album. When it was time to break for dinner she had exquisite servings of fresh *sushi* delivered to the studio for the musicians and crew. A large colour photograph of Sean was taped over the television screen that faced the mixing console. There were dishes of raisins and sesame seeds placed around the control room. An assistant set up a small room with an interior look that resembled one of the rooms in the Dakota. Some pieces of furniture and art were placed in there so they would both feel comfortable and at home during the breaks.'

In November 1980 Elliot again flew in from Los Angeles to hear the final tape of *Double Fantasy*. John and Yoko had received the first complete master cassette on the night he arrived. 'John escorted me into the old bedroom and asked me to sit at the foot of the bed, while John and Yoko lay down with their heads propped up on the pillows—the stereo speakers were on the mantelpiece behind them. It was about ten at night and John dimmed the lights as he pushed the play button on the cassette. He played it loudly.'

As Mintz listened to the music he was reminded of another time. 'We had met for the first time almost ten years before. I thought about that first experience in California when we listened to the acetate of *Some Time In New York City*. John once told me he remembered points in his life by recalling the songs he was writing at the time. That night I was consciously reviewing the decade of adventure I had shared with John and Yoko; the birthdays, Christmases, trips around the world, months in Japan, John's Lost Weekend in California, the first time I saw Sean.'

The cassette ended and the three of them chatted excitedly into the night. When Elliot finally left John walked him to the front door of the apartment. He was wearing pyjamas under an antique Japanese robe. Elliot thought he had never looked better or seemed more optimistic. 'His enthusiasm was contagious—it was the best time of his life.'

'If you wake up before noon,' John said to his best male pal, 'we can meet for breakfast in the old hotel'. As he turned the brass doorknob Mintz recalls hearing the sound of bells.

'They used to have a string of chimes draped around the doorknob. Whenever anyone came or went, the bells would make a delicate sound as they rubbed against the door. We used to joke about it being a subtle, Zen-like alarm system.'

As the lift door closed, Mintz heard the bells chime again as John closed the door. They spoke by phone in the weeks ahead, but Elliot Mintz never saw John again.

With enough songs to make an album and plans for two more beyond that, John became apprehensive about signing a contract with the right record company. Free of both E.M.I./ Capitol and Apple, John was anxious not to sign with a major corporation. The album was sought by many companies but too many wanted to hear the music before talking about a deal. John regarded that as an insult to his integrity after eighteen years of making records. The album eventually went to David Geffen, whose empathy with major artists for more than a decade was matched by his acceptance of the record 'on trust', with not a note played to him before the deal was done. Geffen had been instrumental in discovering Joni Mitchell, Jackson Browne, and the Eagles. His Asylum label had also boasted Tom Waits and Linda Ronstadt. Before signing the Lennons his biggest coup had been to persuade Bob Dylan away from C.B.S. for two albums in the mid-seventies. *Double Fantasy* helped establish his label, which would later also attract Elton John, Asia and Peter Gabriel.

For the fans, the five-year wait had been a long one during pop music's darkest and least creative decade since its birth in 1955. John's return was a timely marker of rock's silver anniversary. He wanted to start a new decade and one which pointed up not down. As far as he was concerned the sixties were hip and the seventies appalling. Only the birth of Sean had redeemed the previous decade for him. Family relationships, love, and personal communication were now the foundation of his music and he applied all the passion and articulacy to his mature love songs that he had to his Beatles hits. John had too much sense to wade back with all the sounds of yesteryear and he avoided the trap of becoming an embarrassing forty-year-old rocker. For her part, Yoko responded to John telling her that her music of a decade before was now fashionable with the remark: 'I'm not going to do all that *old* stuff.' Fittingly sub-titled 'A Heart Play', *Double Fantasy* traced the path for family relationships which John had found so enriching and now wanted others to share.

It was a natural evolution for a man who had come full circle. When John had returned from seclusion and Bermuda he was heavily in favour of survival. He had seen too many of his rock 'n' roll contemporaries die prematurely, martyrs to their own myths: Elvis Presley, Jimi Hendrix, Brian Jones, Buddy Holly, Eddie Cochran, and also James Dean and Marilyn Monroe. John did not believe in any 'live fast die young' philosophy. He did not want to be a hero. He wanted to carry on making his marriage better, making music, raising his son. And in the year 1981 he would sail to Britain as part of a short concert tour, also taking in New York, Los Angeles, San Francisco, and Hamburg. 'Yes, we'll have real fun on this tour,' John said. To mark the new album Yoko gave John a gold watch inscribed on the back: 'To John. Just Like Starting Over. Love Yoko.'

At the age of thirty-nine, when he re-entered the recording studios, Lennon was at a mental peak. No other major rock star had achieved such intellectual and physical maturity yet maintained an aura of rugged warmth. As John put it succinctly but with his customary edge, when he spoke of people who wanted to carry on in rock bands into their forties: 'So the Stones have been going for a hundred and twelve years. Yippee!' That, he implied, was no achievement. *His* success could be measured by the fact that he had grown up, not grown old, in the same field. Many middle-aged pop stars from the sixties invited the question: 'What are you going to do when you grow up?' John was determined it would never be addressed to him. He confounded the cynics by returning with his own highly personal stance, that somehow reached out to old and new music fans. In defeating all the odds John had also beaten the system that chewed artists up before spitting them out as tired and worn.

John crystallized his outlook and his life as a family man on his new song 'Cleanup Time'.

'I'm not interested in being a sex symbol,' John said. He reiterated his pride and the unity with his wife and family: 'It was an enlightening experience for me, as the house-husband . . . because it was a complete reversal of my upbringing . . . I did it to experience what it was like being the women who've done it for me. And it's the way of the future. I'm glad to be in on the forefront of that.'

He felt that for a period he had lost the initial freedom of the artist by 'becoming enslaved to the image of the artist'. Many artists killed themselves because of that, John said. Yoko had been his mental liberation, salvation, inspiration.

'Life begins at forty, so they promised. I believe it, too. I feel fine. I'm . . . excited. It's like twenty-one, and saying: "Wow, what's gonna happen?" '

25
THE END

*'What does it mean that when you're such
a pacifist you get shot?'*

On the afternoon of Saturday 6 December 1980 John went alone
to Café La Fortuna for his customary *cappuccino* and read of
the newspapers. Vincent Urwand playfully teased him about
his comeback album.

'Look, you've had all those years of wildness and success
in the Beatles. You don't need the money. What are you doing
all this for? You're enjoying being a husband and father!'

John laughed. 'I swore I'd look after that boy until he was
five, and he's five and I feel like getting back to my music,'
he replied. 'The urge is there. It's been a long time since I
wrote a song, but they're coming thick and fast now.' John
sent Vincent a demonstration copy of *Double Fantasy*, autographed by him and Yoko.

That same evening John phoned Aunt Mimi. Enthusing
about his record he told her about its success, how pleased he
was with it, and how he was thinking about a world tour. Mimi,
used to his capriciousness and visions of Utopia, was unconvinced by his *bonhomie*. 'John,' she said, in the peremptory
voice he knew and secretly loved, 'John, you're an idealist
looking for a lost horizon. You would make a saint cry!' For
thirty-five years she had listened to him articulating his dreams.
They both enjoyed banter.

'Oh, Mimi don't be like that. . . . You see, I'll *see you
soon* and we'll bring Sean. Goodnight, God bless, Mimi.'

Two nights later John was dead.

At the Dakota John and Yoko were among the most popular residents. The exclusive apartment block's vetting committee, which had allowed them to buy up five apartments comprising thirty-four rooms in nine years, had been vindicated. The surest test of their acceptance came from the doormen and desk staff. While some celebrated Dakota residents treated the staff dismissively and bossily, John and Yoko always treated them as equals, with, in the words of several, perfect manners. John was so popular and such a generous tipper that the staff almost fought to deliver his packages to the seventh floor. Throughout his life John trusted everyone. A fatal flaw in him was a lack of perception in judging which people were 'on the level' with him. He was honest and expected the same of everyone.

Jay Hastings was a twenty-seven-year-old front desk clerk in the oak-panelled entrance hall of the Dakota. He checked every arrival and every package and phoned through to any apartment for permission to release the door lock and allow a visitor access. With the constant stream of artists, businessmen, and delivery people arriving at the Dakota's forbidding Gothic entrance, 'You get to be a pretty shrewd judge of character,' he says.

Growing a beard in midsummer 1980, John quizzed Jay Hastings about how he kept his facial hair looking so trim. Hastings told him he must buy a pair of plastic, snap-on guides for his razor. 'You mean as if I'm cutting grass?' said John. 'That's amazing. They make *that* kind of thing for people with beards?' But within a few weeks Lennon was in the lobby with neither beard nor spectacles, carrying a guitar case and *en route* for Bermuda. Jay asked him where the beard had gone. 'Oh, there was a picture of me with it in the paper and people recognized me everywhere after that,' replied John. 'I just wanna roam *free*! Nobody will expect me to look like this.'

On so many nights Jay Hastings had awaited John's cheery whistle as his five-foot-eleven frame strode distinctively the thirty-second walk from West 72nd Street up the steps into the hallway. '*Bonsoir*, Jay!' John would often say.

At the beginning of December 1980 John was particularly 'up', Hastings recalls. 'He had the album out, *Double Fantasy*. He was going back and forth two miles to the studio most days, leaving late afternoon and returning between ten-thirty and eleven-thirty, with Yoko. I'd listen out for the slam of their black limousine door. I could always tell his walk. And I waited for that whistle.'

The night of 8 December was particularly balmy. After spending five hours in the studio John and Yoko returned, their car pulling up at 10:49 p.m. José, the doorman, left his sentry box to open their car door. John walked ahead of Yoko into the archway. A man's voice called out: 'Mr Lennon?' As John turned round his murderer shot five bullets from a .38 revolver into his back. Contrary to popular belief, John was not shot in his chest. The bullets caught his arm and, mostly, his back as he turned his head to face his murderer.

Horrifying, chaotic scenes followed. Yoko, hysterical, screamed for an ambulance. John staggered up the six steps to Jay Hastings' office, eventually falling on his left side onto the floor, moaning, 'I'm shot, I'm shot.' Hastings ripped his own jacket off and covered John with it; then he immediately pressed an alarm button connected directly to the police precinct. Within two minutes a police car had arrived. They decided there was no time to wait for an ambulance. Jay Hastings helped the police carry John to their car which sped to Roosevelt Hospital. There doctors tried instant heart massage but to no avail. John died from a massive loss of blood.

At the Dakota the cassette recorder and tape which John was carrying when he fell were slowly picked up. Yoko later took possession of his spectacles. The music in his hand, destined for their next album, was Yoko's 'Walking On Thin Ice'. Back home from the hospital Yoko composed herself enough to issue a simple statement to a shattered world: 'John loved and prayed for the human race. Please do the same for him.'

As the news of his murder broke, the world's airwaves were filled with his music. Tragically, incredibly, the moment of his death was also the time he came alive in the minds of millions. He was guaranteed immortality on a scale that neither he, nor the world's ageing Beatles fans, would ever comprehend. Not since the murder of President John F. Kennedy in 1963 had the world been so enraged, stunned, and simply hurt by an assassination. Lennon's murder transcended that of even a major statesman because John was so much closer to his public.

For one awful moment, a world that didn't care was brought together, and in its grief remembered *how* to care. As shock turned to anger, as statesmen paid their tributes to his talent and human qualities, as the Dakota flag hung at half mast in his honour, the bitter irony sank in: the rebel who had finally found tranquillity in his life and who had preached peace and love, offered hope, inspired millions with his imagination, self-deprecating wit, compassion, and new example of family commitment, had died by the gun.

John was cremated at Hartsdale Crematorium, New York State. Millions mourned him, often with celebrations of his music which eclipsed the desire for revenge. Tributes poured in from around the world as people went on pilgrimages: to Menlove Avenue; to Liverpool College of Art; to Mathew Street, once the home of the Cavern; to New York's Central Park, where Yoko's request for a world-wide ten-minute silence was marked by 400,000 people assembling opposite John's home, heads bowed; and to Hamburg, where Astrid Kirchherr still remembers the terrible depression. 'The city seemed to close for days,' she says. Millions mourned the loss of their adolescence, for John had supplied the soundtrack to it. At a time when we could expect no more from rock 'n' roll, its voice as a form of youthful rebellion long gone and the battle for teenage assertiveness won, John had survived with a rare dignity. He had made the transition so few manage, from young rocker to artist and in forty years he had always refused to be bought. When he outgrew the Beatles he stayed true to himself. The world mourned the loss of his arrogance, his humour, his warmth, his frailties, and, above all, his humanity.

John was acutely aware of the fact that the number nine had dominated his life.

He was born on 9 October 1940. Sean was born on 9 October 1975. Brian Epstein first saw John and the Beatles at Liverpool's Cavern on 9 November 1961 and he secured their record contract with E.M.I. in London on 9 May 1962. The début record, 'Love Me Do', was on Parlophone R4949.

John met Yoko Ono on 9 November 1966. John and Yoko's apartment was located on West 72nd Street, New York City (seven plus two making nine) and their main Dakota apartment

Lennon

number was also, at first, 72. The bus he had travelled on as a student each morning from his home to Liverpool Art College had been the 72.

John's songs included 'Revolution 9', '#9 Dream', and 'One After 909', which he had written at his mother's home at 9 Newcastle Road, Wavertree, Liverpool. When he moved his Aunt Mimi from Liverpool to Sandbanks in Dorset her new address was 126 Panorama Road, the combination of figures striking John as his lucky number.

He even joked to me that one of his most important songs had nine key words: 'All we are saying is Give Peace A Chance'.

When John went gambling in Las Vegas, the number he repeatedly chose on the roulette wheel was nine . . . and he usually lost with it.

In Paris in 1964 during the Beatles' tour he received a death threat letter which made him nervous: 'I am going to shoot you at nine tonight.' John sold Tittenhurst Park to Ringo on 9 September 1973. He believed the sign of a marriage 'written in the stars' was that the names of John Ono Lennon and Yoko Ono Lennon together featured the letter 'o' nine times.

When John was killed, at 10:50 p.m. in New York on 8 December 1980, the five-hour time difference meant that it was 9 December in Britain. His body was taken to Roosevelt Hospital. It was situated on Ninth Avenue, Manhattan.

Within two hours of the shooting Elliot Mintz was on American Airlines Flight 10 from Los Angeles to New York. His mother had phoned from there to say she had heard a radio bulletin that John had been shot. Mintz's car radio was not working; as he drove to Los Angeles airport he hoped and believed that Lennon had survived. 'Just after take-off, I was sitting alone when the cockpit door opened. A stewardess appeared with tears streaming down her face. A lady asked her what was the matter. "John Lennon is dead," I overheard her say.' For the five-hour flight, Elliot remained in his seat in the darkened cabin in a state of shock. He went direct to the Dakota to be with Yoko.

'It was about six in the morning when I arrived. The police had not disturbed the spot where it happened. The image of the broken glass and the chalk marks and John's blood on the cement will haunt me for ever.

'I stood by the door to the old bedroom. For a long time I just listened to Yoko crying before I knocked.'

'It's me,' Mintz whispered. 'I'll be right here if you need me.' He stayed for the next two months, answering phones, sorting mail, meeting reporters, co-ordinating security, following up calls from psychics and psychotics and generally supporting Yoko and Sean. Later he was asked to inventory all John's precious possessions, noting the many photographs which Aunt Mimi had posted to her surrogate son months before.

'No one ever gets over a tragedy of this magnitude,' says Mintz. 'You just learn to readjust, to cope, to deal with a different reality. Yoko and Sean have been an inspiration to me. They are now the keepers of the wishing well. Her optimism and sense of dignity prevail. John and Yoko represent a prototype for couples of the future. Their love and honesty and conviction are now part of everyone whom they touched. He was very special.'

On 10 December 1980 Yoko, who had the appalling job of breaking the news to five-year-old Sean, issued the following statement from the Dakota:

> I told Sean what happened. I showed him the picture of his father on the cover of the paper and explained the situation. I took Sean to the spot where John lay after he was shot. Sean wanted to know why the person shot John if he liked John. I explained that he was probably a confused person. Sean said we should find out if he was confused or if he really had meant to kill John. I said that was up to the court. He asked what court—a tennis court or a basketball court? That's how Sean used to talk with his father. They were buddies. John would have been proud of Sean if he had heard this. Sean cried later. He also said, 'Now Daddy is part of God. I guess when you die you become much more bigger because you're part of everything.'
>
> I don't have much more to add to Sean's statement.

The silent vigil will take place December 14th at 2 p.m. for ten minutes.

Our thoughts will be with you.

Love, Yoko and Sean

None of the public responses were as simple and eloquent as those of the hundreds of fans who stood vigil for days outside the Dakota, with banners bearing quickly scrawled slogans like: 'Strawberry Fields Forever, John', 'We'll never forget him', and, movingly, 'Christmas In Heaven'.

Upstairs in her bedroom as the fans stayed there playing transistors with a non-stop, twenty-four-hour soundtrack of John's music, Yoko could scarcely stand the pressure. 'It began,' she recalls, 'on the night of the murder. As it wore on, throughout the week, it nearly drove me crazy. All day and all night, the music . . . after what had just happened, it was unbearable.' She valued the fans' touching letters, which still arrive every day.

Such spontaneous, heartfelt emotion came through a love of a man, his music and what he represented. For, although John shunned the role of leader, he was, despite his reluctance, the inspiration for a generation's ideals. He never wanted to be a god, certainly not a dead martyr. 'Make your own dreams and do things for yourself. I can't wake you up. You wake *you* up,' he said. All he had done, he implied, was leave a few signposts; but he positively rejected any theory that he was saying 'Follow me, this is how it is.' Gandhi and Martin Luther King were great examples, he pointed out, of non-violent people who had died violently. He never understood that, he said. Unnervingly, one of the last sentences he said to a friend, David Sheff, for *Playboy* magazine, was: 'What does it mean that when you're such a pacifist you get shot?'

In the weeks that followed, as the world's media were flooded with discussions of John's life and music, Yoko went into seclusion in the Dakota. She decided to cut off all her hair as a mark of respect for her husband. She closed off the bedroom they used to sleep in. Out of all the hundreds of gifts John had showered on her in the red velvet boxes he knew she loved, she took only two items to keep by her side—ironically they were *her* final gifts to *him*: the inscribed gold watch she had given him a month before he died, and a tiny American flag pin made up of red rubies, white diamonds, and blue sapphires. Yoko is rarely seen without the diamond necklace which John bought at Tiffany's and which she wears in the picture on the sleeve of *Double Fantasy*.

Inside the apartment Yoko instructed staff that every picture and painting on all the walls was to be left, for ever, precisely as John had wanted. There were, interestingly, no Beatles pictures or gold records hanging there. Significantly, the only one of John as a musician was the original picture of the twenty-year-old Lennon standing in a Hamburg doorway, every inch a rock 'n' roller.

'I think,' said Yoko when I met her a few months after the murder, 'that in many ways he was a simple Liverpool man right to the end. He was a chameleon, a bit of a chauvinist, but so human. In our fourteen years together he never stopped trying to improve himself *from within*. We were best friends but also competitive artists. To me, he is still alive. Death alone doesn't extinguish a flame and a spirit like John.'

John and Yoko probably saw more of each other in fourteen years than most married couples see of each other in a lifetime. It was hardly surprising that, in the wake of his assassination, Yoko became severely depressed alone in her bedroom. Staring out of the window, she ate only mushrooms and chocolate cake for nearly three months and smoked her Nat Sherman brown cigarettes until she felt that there was a clear choice facing her: she could either return to work, managing the family business as before, or she could go back to making a record. She finally decided on both: John would have liked that.

Her first decision astonished those who did not know her. She wanted to stay at the Dakota. John was part of the place. She felt him over her shoulder. And when she finally emerged, walking every day past the very spot where John was shot, she felt the inner strength of his invisible presence.

'I have strong emotions of sorrow, and hate, and resentment, but where do you put them?' she said to me. Gaunt, nervous of her first newspaper interview since the murder, she chainsmoked throughout and had carefully checked all the signs, astrologically, beforehand to ensure that we should talk. (The interviews, which took place at the Dakota, appeared in Lon-

don's *Daily Mirror* on 12 and 13 August and subsequently in
dozens of international publications.)

Scorned and vilified no more, Yoko Ono as a widow ironically gained a respect she would have preferred not to have
earned. The world which had once jeered suddenly applauded
her dignity. 'Do you know how that feels? For ten years I was
the devil,' she said to me. 'Now suddenly I'm an angel. Did
the world have to lose John for people to change their opinion
of me? It's unreal. If it brought John back, I'd rather remain
hated.'

To regain her sanity and to make some statements, Yoko
went back to the recording studio. When she went into the Hit
Factory to record *Season Of Glass* with many of the musicians
who had worked on *Double Fantasy*, she conquered a voice
choking with emotion and sang her compositions charged with
grief and anger. 'Making the record was definitely a therapy,
the only way I could survive,' she says. 'I felt John with me
all the time in the studio.' Her songs 'Goodbye Sadness' with
the sound of four gunshots and the ambulance siren on 'No,
No, No', are stunningly evocative of the murder. And at one
point she shouted on the record, 'You *bastards*. We had *everything*!' Yoko ran into a major controversy on her choice of
photograph for the sleeve which showed John's blood-covered
spectacles, which she had retrieved on the night of the murder.
'Tasteless,' said her critics.

Yoko disagreed: 'John would have approved and I will
explain why. I wanted the whole world to be reminded of what
happened. People are offended by the glasses and the blood?
The glasses are a tiny part of what happened. If people can't
stomach the glasses, I'm sorry. There was a dead body. There
was blood. His whole body was bloody. There was a load of
blood all over the floor. That's the reality. I want people to
face up to what happened. He did not commit suicide. He was
killed. People are offended by the glasses and the blood? John
had to stomach a lot more.'

John's assassin, Mark David Chapman, was twenty-five. He
came originally from Decatur, Georgia, but had been living in
Honolulu with his wife Gloria. He had worked as a hospital
security guard and a printer but had left, alone, for New York

several days before 8 December 1980. He stayed at the Olcott Hotel on West 72nd Street, just 200 yards from the scene of the murder. That day, clutching a copy of John and Yoko's *Double Fantasy* album, he loitered outside the Dakota building and succeeded in getting John's autograph. Nobody had any reason to regard the fans who often stood outside the Dakota as a threat.

In a fifteen-minute hearing on 9 December in a packed Manhattan Criminal Court, the district attorney said: 'This man came to New York with a specific purpose. He has done it. Chapman deliberately premeditated the execution of John Lennon in a cool, calm, rational and intelligent manner.' Chapman's lawyer said the murderer had told him he had always been a great fan of Lennon: 'He told me he had admired him very much ever since he was ten years old. My impression was of a very confused character.'

Chapman was subsequently sentenced to between twenty years and life imprisonment, first going to Rikers Jail and later to the top-security Attica State Prison, New York, as convict number 81A3860. There, he became arguably the most closely guarded man in the world, because of the distinct possibility of reprisals from other prisoners irate about having Lennon's murderer near them. Letters of hatred and requests from the world's media for interviews to discover his reasons for murdering John Lennon continued to arrive every day; not one, however, could equal the spine-chilling letter Chapman wrote to Yoko in 1982, seeking her approval in writing his story and giving the proceeds of any such book to charity. The letter, the content, and its signature which Yoko could scarcely absorb, still less reply to, brought back floods of tears. 'I was numbed by it,' she says. Chapman said he had written to her previously to apologize for what he had done. If Yoko objected to his book idea he would not do it, he added. This letter went unanswered but Yoko kept it 'for historical reasons, for future generations'.

A quarter of a million letters of sympathy arrived by the sack-load at the Dakota within two months of John's murder. The *Double Fantasy* album sold 7 million copies around the world within seven months. John's friend, the singer–songwriter Harry

Nilsson, involved himself in a campaign to ban handguns in America.

Yoko, warily opening John's drawers and books in the months after his death, found notes from him to her which she had never seen. 'Mother, don't forget the clocks are one hour fast . . . Daddy.' Others, more affectionate, brought her to tears. 'Don't forget the kettle's on.' 'Mother, I'll be back in an hour.' She cries often, and speaks of John in the present tense: 'His spirit is in the world for ever,' she declares.

It was three years before she could bear to listen to the songs he planned for their follow-up album to *Double Fantasy*. Finally, weeping openly when she re-discovered his aching love song to her, 'Grow Old With Me', she had a cassette recording of it encased in sweet-smelling, rare Bermudan cedarwood, a favourite aroma of John's. The music box, engraved 'Milk And Honey, Love Yoko and Sean, Xmas, '83, N.Y.C.', was sent to her friends one month before the final album, *Milk and Honey*, was released.

Back in England Aunt Mimi, suffering from a respiratory illness, went to live temporarily with her sister Anne near Liverpool. Heartbroken, she turned off the radio whenever John's voice came on. 'I shall never recover,' she says.

Liverpool was appallingly dilatory and mean in recognizing its four most famous sons. Not until 1982 was there any tangible civic recognition of the Beatles, when four roads were named after them (including John Lennon Drive). And when, in 1984, a statue was unveiled, and Beatle City and Cavern Walks established, it was through private enterprise and not civic pride.

In 1982, the twentieth anniversary year of the Beatles' first record release, the Performing Right Society in Britain launched its John Lennon Memorial Scholarship. This annual award supports postgraduate work incorporating recording techniques in the University of Surrey's department of music. John was a member of the Performing Right Society, an association of composers, authors, and music publishers, throughout his songwriting career. The scholarship was launched by two men instrumental in John's earliest work: George Martin and Dick James.

On a visit to Liverpool in 1984 with Sean, Yoko gave £10,000 for educational aid to students at Liverpool Polytechnic, once called the College of Art. She took Sean to the Pier Head, to all John's old haunts, to look at Menlove Avenue, and to meet an Aunt Mimi tearful with joy. 'Just like John,' said Mimi when she saw Sean.

John's will left half his wealth, calculated at the time of his death at more than $150 million and growing by more than $50,000 a day from songwriting and record royalties, to Yoko, with the other half held on trust for undisclosed beneficiaries. The will contained a provision that if any named beneficiary objected or took court action they were to receive nothing. Many of the beneficiaries would have been charities.

John and Yoko had launched the Spirit Foundation, a charitable organization which distributes money to all kinds of causes ranging from old people's homes to handicapped children. Their income was 'tithed'—10 per cent of it was automatically deducted and covenanted to the foundation. In what turned out to be an appalling irony, a year before he was shot dead John had donated $1,000 to a campaign to help provide New York policemen with bullet-proof vests.

Yoko continues to be heavily involved, anonymously, with a great deal of charity work. In 1983, she decided to simplify her life. After selling the house in West Palm Beach and their farms she planned to give approximately £3 million to charities and orphanages around the world. These included the Salvation Army hostel in Liverpool's Strawberry Field, John's childhood inspiration.

In New York's Central Park a triangular-shaped piece of land was designated Strawberry Fields in John's honour. At the opening ceremony, performed by long-time John Lennon admirer Mayor Ed Koch on 21 March 1984, Yoko broke down. It was a project she had begun shortly after John died. Sixteen years earlier John and Yoko had planted acorns in the precincts of Coventry Cathedral. That acorn was now symbolically a tree, she said. As a mark of world love and sharing, which John cared about, she had written to heads of state throughout the world asking for a plant, rock or stone of their nation to be sent for Strawberry Fields in Central Park. 'This is the nicest tribute we could give to John,' says Yoko. It was, fittingly, the place they had sat down and talked after their last walk together. Julian Lennon, in New York recording his début album, attended the ceremony. On 20 March, the date of John and Yoko's wedding anniversary, Yoko presented Sean with a full collection of his parents' recorded work.

In a bittersweet evening, Sean chose 'Instant Karma!' as his first favourite. Yoko broke down again when 'Imagine' came on. They played record after record through the night, totally absorbed in the music of the man they loved.

John Lennon was not only a genius. He was also a man of profound commitment, total integrity and intensive activity: a glance at the sheer volume and pattern of his life's work confirms that. His honesty and wit, his vulnerability, his lack of pomposity, his unique artistry, spirit and romanticism endeared him to millions. The grief that followed his murder, and the celebrations of his life and work, spanned the world.

As a twentieth-century philosopher, he set an example of imagination and humanitarianism. Although he would hate to be deified, a light went out on 8 December 1980. But his music and his spirit shine on.

CHRONOLOGY
1940–1980

1933
18 Feb.   Yoko Ono born in Tokyo

1938
3 Dec.   John's future mother, Julia Stanley, a cinema attendant, weds seaman Alfred (Fred) Lennon at Mount Pleasant Register Office, Liverpool.

1939
10 Sept.   Cynthia Powell born in Blackpool.

1940
9 Oct.   John Winston Lennon born at 6.30 p.m. at Oxford Street Maternity Hospital, Liverpool.

1941
Spring   John left in the care of his aunt, Mary Smith (Aunt Mimi) and Uncle George at 251 Menlove Avenue, Woolton.

1942
April   Fred Lennon, having been away at sea for long periods since his son's birth, leaves home for good while Julia Lennon moves in with her new man, John Dykins.

1945
Sept.   John starts at Dovedale Primary School, Liverpool.

1946
July   Fred Lennon suddenly returns and takes John to Blackpool, intending never to return. John's mother, Julia, tracks them down and gives her five-year-old son the choice of staying with his father or mother. He eventually chooses Julia, who returns him to Liverpool to stay with Aunt Mimi.

1952
July   John leaves Dovedale Primary School.
Sept.   John starts at Quarry Bank High School.

1955
5 June George Smith, John's uncle, dies, aged 52.

1957
May   John forms the Quarry Men skiffle group with some school friends.
24 May First ever Quarry Men public performance at a street carnival in Rosebery Street, Liverpool.
6 July Paul McCartney attends a Quarry Men performance at Woolton Parish Church Fete and meets John Lennon for the first time. He later joins the group.
July   John leaves Quarry Bank High School.
Sept.   John starts at Liverpool College of Art where he soon meets Cynthia Powell, his future wife, and Stuart Sutcliffe, to become his closest friend and a future Beatle.

1958
6 Feb. After seeing them perform at Wilson Hall, Garston, Liverpool, George Harrison joins the Quarry Men.
15 July Julia Lennon dies after a road accident outside Mimi's Menlove Avenue house.

1959

29 Aug.   The Quarry Men (John, Paul, George, and Ken Brown) play at the opening night of the Casbah coffee club, run by Mona Best, mother of the Beatles' future drummer, Peter.

15 Nov.   The group, now renamed Johnny and the Moondogs, fail an audition for 'star-maker' Carroll Levis at Manchester Hippodrome.

1960

5 May   The group, now renamed the Silver Beetles, fail an audition to back Billy Fury but are chosen to back another young singer, Johnny Gentle, on a Scottish tour.

20 May   That tour—the group's first—begins.

2 June   The group change their name to the Beatles for their first local 'professional' engagement at Neston Institute.

July   John leaves Liverpool College of Art.

16 Aug.   The Beatles travel to Hamburg and open at the Indra night club two days later.

5 Dec.   John arrives back in Liverpool penniless, after four months in Hamburg and a dispute with their employer there. George had been deported for being under age; Paul and Pete Best had been ordered to leave after allegedly causing a fire in their digs.

1961

21 Mar.   The Beatles make their début at the Cavern club, a jazz/beat cellar in Liverpool city centre.

June   A single, 'My Bonnie', by Tony Sheridan, with backing by the Beatles, is released in Germany.

6 July   The first edition of *Mersey Beat*, the Liverpool music paper, appears. John contributes a front-page article entitled 'Being a Short Diversion on the Dubious Origins of the Beatles' and, over the next two years, contributes many other poems and articles to the paper.

1 Oct.   John and Paul take a fourteen-day holiday in Paris.

28 Oct.	Brian Epstein, a local record shop owner, learns of the Beatles' existence.
9 Nov.	Epstein attends a lunchtime performance of the Beatles at the Cavern.
3 Dec.	Epstein invites the Beatles to his shop and offers to manage them.

1962

1 Jan.	The Beatles travel to London for an audition at Decca. They do not learn of their failure until March and are subsequently rejected by several other top record companies.
24 Jan.	Brian and the Beatles enter into an official management contract.
1 Feb.	The first Epstein-organized engagement, at a small café in West Kirby, Cheshire for £18.
2 Feb.	The Beatles' first official out-of-town date, in Manchester.
8 Mar.	The group appear on B.B.C. radio for the first time, on the Light Programme's *Teenager's Turn*.
10 April	Stuart Sutcliffe dies of a brain haemorrhage in Hamburg, aged twenty-one.
9 May	Brian Epstein secures a recording contract for the Beatles with Parlophone, a small label within E.M.I.
4 June	Epstein and the Beatles sign with E.M.I.
6 June	The Beatles' first recording session, at the Abbey Road studios, London N.W.8.
16 Aug.	Pete Best, the Beatles' drummer, is sacked.
18 Aug.	Ringo Starr leaves Rory Storm and the Hurricanes and fills the vacant drummer's seat with the Beatles.
22 Aug.	A Granada television film crew capture a few minutes of a lunchtime Beatles performance at the Cavern.
23 Aug.	John Lennon marries Cynthia Powell at Mount Pleasant Register Office, Liverpool. That same evening the Beatles, with John, fulfil an engagement in Chester.
4 Sept.	'Love Me Do', the group's first single, is recorded.
1 Oct.	Epstein and the Beatles sign a five-year management contract.

5 Oct.	'Love Me Do' is released.

5 Oct.   'Love Me Do' is released.

17 Oct.   The Beatles make their television début on Granada's north-west regional programme *People and Places*, singing 'Love Me Do'.

27 Oct.   'Love Me Do' enters the *Melody Maker* singles chart at number 48.

17 Dec.   The Beatles make their fifth and final club trip to Hamburg.

1963

19 Jan.   The Beatles make their nationwide television début, on *Thank Your Lucky Stars*.

2 Feb.   First U.K. tour, with Helen Shapiro, begins.

11 Feb.   In one eleven-hour session, the Beatles record their first L.P.

22 Feb.   Northern Songs, publishers of all future Lennon–McCartney compositions, is formed.

2 Mar.   'Please Please Me', the group's second single, hits number one on the *Melody Maker* chart.

8 April   A son, John Charles Julian, is born to Cynthia and John Lennon at 6.50 a.m. at Sefton General Hospital, Liverpool; he weighs 6 lb 11 oz.

28 April   John and Brian Epstein fly to Spain for a twelve-day holiday.

4 May   The Beatles' first L.P., *Please Please Me*, tops the *Melody Maker* chart.

18 June   John physically assaults Cavern compère Bob Wooler at Paul's twenty-first birthday party in Huyton, Liverpool.

21 June   The John/Bob Wooler incident is big news in the *Daily Mirror*.

29 June   John's first solo appearance on television, on B.B.C.'s *Juke Box Jury*. (The programme was recorded on 22 June.)

3 Aug.   The Beatles' 292nd, and last, appearance at the Cavern.

8 Aug.   A daughter, Kyoko, is born to Yoko Ono and her husband, Anthony Cox.

13 Oct.   First signs of Beatlemania as the Beatles appear on *Sunday Night at the London Palladium*.

31 Oct.	Hysteria at Heathrow Airport as the Beatles return from Sweden after a series of concerts.
4 Nov.	The Beatles appear in the Royal Variety Performance at the Prince of Wales Theatre, London. John utters his famous witticism.
27 Dec.	In *The Times*, John and Paul are described as 'the outstanding English composers of 1963'.

1964

1 Feb.	'I Want To Hold Your Hand' tops the singles chart in *Billboard*, the U.S.A.'s premier music trade magazine.
7 Feb.	Mass hysteria greets the Beatles' arrival at Kennedy Airport at the start of their American tour.
9 Feb.	An estimated 73 million people watch the Beatles perform on television on the *Ed Sullivan Show*.
11 Feb.	The Beatles' first American concert, at the Coliseum, Washington, D.C.
2 Mar.	Back in England, the Beatles begin shooting their first feature film, *A Hard Day's Night*.
23 Mar.	Jonathan Cape publish Lennon's first book, *In His Own Write*. It is an instant critical and commercial success.
4 April	The Beatles occupy the top five places on the *Billboard* American singles chart.
23 April	Foyle's holds a literary luncheon in John's honour at the Dorchester Hotel, London. John's speech, supposed to be the highlight of the occasion, lasts just five seconds.
19 June	Charles Curran, a Conservative M.P. states in Parliament that John's book highlights the poor education in Liverpool and that Lennon himself is illiterate.
6 July	The film *A Hard Day's Night* receives its world première in London.
10 July	Liverpool honours its four famous sons with a civic reception. Estimated crowds of 100,000 line the route of their procession from Speke Airport to the city centre.

15 July   John and Cynthia buy their first mansion, Kenwood, in the 'stockbroker belt' at Weybridge, Surrey.

19 Sept.   Oxfam print 500,000 Christmas cards using a specially donated Lennon drawing.

1965

9 Jan.   John appears on Peter Cook and Dudley Moore's *Not Only . . . But Also* B.B.C. television programme reading his poetry, accompanied by Moore and Norman Rossington.

15 Feb.   John passes his driving test.

18 Feb.   Northern Songs becomes a public company, quoted on the London Stock Exchange.

22 Feb.   Shooting of the Beatles' second feature film, *Help!* begins in the Bahamas (for tax reasons).

18 Mar.   John gives his former schoolfriend and one-time Quarry Man Pete Shotton £20,000, and together they form Hayling Supermarkets Ltd and open up for business on Hayling Island, off the Hampshire coast.

12 June   Buckingham Palace announces that the four Beatles are to be made Members of the Order of the British Empire (M.B.E.).

13 June   Several M.B.E. holders return their medals, furious over the Beatles' award.

24 June   *A Spaniard In The Works*, John's second book of poetry and nonsense prose, is published by Jonathan Cape.

29 July   *Help!* receives its world première in London.

3 Aug.   John buys Aunt Mimi a bungalow in Poole, Dorset, and she moves down from Liverpool in October.

15 Aug.   56,000 fans attend a Beatles concert at Shea Stadium in New York. The proceedings are filmed for a future television special.

26 Oct.   Hysteria at Buckingham Palace as the Beatles attend their M.B.E. investiture ceremony.

31 Dec.   Fred Lennon, John's father, releases his first and only single on Pye Records entitled 'That's My Life

(My Love And My Home)': it is an artistic and commercial disaster.

1966

1 Mar.   *The Beatles at Shea Stadium* receives its world première on B.B.C. television.

4 Mar.   London's *Evening Standard* publishes an interview with John by reporter Maureen Cleave. Tucked innocently in the middle of the article, John expresses an opinion that the Beatles are more popular than Jesus and that Christianity will vanish and shrink. There is no reaction from the British public.

1 May   The Beatles give what later turns out to be their last live performance in Britain, in the *New Musical Express* pollwinners' concert at the Empire Pool, Wembley.

26 June The Beatles' emotional return to Hamburg to play a concert.

5 July   Riots rage in Manila, capital of the Philippines, after the Beatles supposedly snub the President's wife.

29 July *Datebook* magazine re-publish in the U.S.A.—out of context—John's interview with Maureen Cleave.

31 July Radio stations in Birmingham, Alabama ban all Beatles music after learning of John's comments about Jesus. Other towns in the 'Bible Belt' soon follow and huge bonfires of Beatles records and memorabilia are organized.

6 Aug.   In the midst of the American uproar over John's comments, Brian Epstein hurriedly flies to New York to defend him publicly.

8 Aug.   After learning of John's Jesus comments the South African Broadcasting Corporation (S.A.B.C.) announce a ban on the playing of all records composed or played by the Beatles.

12 Aug. At the start of the Beatles' third official American tour in Chicago, John, under severe pressure, reluctantly apologizes to the world for his statement on Jesus.

29 Aug. Thoroughly fed-up after three years of constant

touring, the Beatles give their last live performance ever, at Candlestick Park in San Francisco.

6 Sept.   In a bar near Hanover, near the set of the film *How I Won The War*, John's Beatle locks are cut in preparation for his first solo acting role. He is given a pair of 'granny glasses' to wear.

19 Sept.   Shooting of *How I Won The War* switches to Almeria, Spain.

9 Nov.   John visits the Indica Gallery in Masons Yard, Duke Street, London S.W.1. for a preview of a nine-day exhibition by a Japanese artist, Yoko Ono, entitled *Unfinished Paintings and Objects*. He is introduced to Yoko by the gallery owner, John Dunbar.

26 Dec.   John appears in Peter Cook and Dudley Moore's *Not Only . . . But Also* T.V. programme in a comedy sketch, telerecorded on 27 November. The 'granny glasses' from the *How I Won The War* film are still there and they stay with John, forming part of his new image.

1967

17 Feb.   E.M.I. release a revolutionary new Beatles single —John's 'Strawberry Fields Forever' backed with Paul's 'Penny Lane'. Ironically it becomes their first record to fail to reach the coveted number one spot on some charts since 'Please Please Me', released four years earlier.

20 May   The B.B.C. ban John's 'A Day In The Life', from the forthcoming Beatles L.P., because its lyrics might encourage drug-taking.

1 June   *Sgt Pepper's Lonely Hearts Club Band*, the Beatles' most ambitious L.P. yet, is released.

25 June   The Beatles appear before an estimated audience of 400 million people from twenty-four countries, singing 'All You Need Is Love' on the world-wide T.V. link-up show *Our World*.

24 Aug.   Various Beatles with wives and relations, including John and Cynthia, attend a lecture on transcendental meditation by the Maharishi Mahesh Yogi at the Hilton Hotel, London.

25 Aug. The Beatles and their wives travel by train from London's Euston Station to Bangor, North Wales to attend a weekend seminar on meditation by the Maharishi. John's wife Cynthia, after a frantic dash, misses the train by seconds. John's disappearance down the platform without her seems symbolic of the future of their unsteady marriage.

27 Aug. While the Beatles are away in Bangor, Brian Epstein is found dead in his flat at 24 Chapel Street, Belgravia, London S.W.1. The Beatles hurriedly return to London.

11 Sept. Shooting of the ill-fated *Magical Mystery Tour* T.V. film starts in Cornwall.

30 Sept. John and George appear with the Maharishi on *The Frost Programme* on I.T.V. with presenter David Frost.

11 Oct. John anonymously sponsors an exhibition at the Lisson Art Gallery, London N.W.8. entitled *Yoko Plus Me*. It runs until 14 November.

17 Oct. John, Paul, George, and Ringo attend a memorial service for Brian Epstein at the New London Synagogue, Abbey Road, London N.W.8.

18 Oct. The world première of *How I Won The War* in London.

20 Nov. The B.B.C. ensure that John's composition 'I Am The Walrus' receives no radio or T.V. exposure although they officially deny actually banning it.

4 Dec. A new Beatles venture, the Apple Boutique, opens in Baker Street, London N.W.1.

16 Dec. John, George, and the Maharishi attend a UNICEF gala in Paris.

26 Dec. The world première of *Magical Mystery Tour* on B.B.C. television. A critical disaster, it is the Beatles' first public failure.

1968

5 Jan. John and his father Fred meet at John's Weybridge home. John gives his blessing to his father's impending marriage to nineteen-year-old former Exeter University student, Pauline Jones. The couple

announce that the wedding may have to wait until the bride is twenty-one years old as her mother refuses to give her consent. Instead they travel to Scotland, outside the English court jurisdiction, and marry there.

16 Feb. John and Cynthia, with George and his wife Pattie, fly to Rishikesh, India for an extensive course of meditation under the Maharishi. Paul, with fiancée Jane Asher, and Ringo and his wife Maureen, follow on four days later.

12 April John and George with their wives hurriedly leave Rishikesh two weeks earlier than expected. They feel that the Maharishi is not such a holy man after all. Paul, Jane, Ringo, and Maureen have already left.

15 May John and Paul appear on the *Tonight* show on American television to announce the formation of Apple Corps. John also takes the opportunity to denounce the Maharishi publicly.

15 June John and Yoko Ono plant two acorns outside Coventry Cathedral as part of the National Sculpture Exhibition. It is the couple's first 'event'.

18 June John and Yoko attend the opening night of *In His Own Write* at London's National Theatre, a play adapted from John's two books by his friend, actor Victor Spinetti.

21 June Apple Corps buys grandiose premises at 3 Savile Row, London W.1.

1 July The opening of John's first art exhibition, *You Are Here*, dedicated to Yoko, at the Robert Fraser Gallery in Duke Street, London W.1. Prior to the opening John and Yoko release 365 helium-filled balloons over London.

17 July World première of the Beatles' *Yellow Submarine* cartoon film in London.

31 July The Apple Boutique closes after two days of stock clearing free of charge to the general public.

22 Aug. Cynthia sues John for divorce on the grounds of adultery with Yoko Ono Cox.

18 Oct. Police raid the flat at 34 Montagu Square, London

	W.1., owned by Ringo but the temporary home of John and Yoko. They discover 219 grains of cannabis resin. The couple are also charged with obstructing police in the execution of a search warrant.
19 Oct.	At Marylebone Magistrates' Court John and Yoko are remanded on bail until 28 November.
25 Oct.	John and Yoko announce they are expecting a baby in February 1969.
8 Nov.	Cynthia is granted a decree nisi in the Divorce Court because of John's adultery with Yoko. The petition is uncontested but it is announced that John has made 'generous and proper provision' for his wife and child.
21 Nov.	Yoko has a miscarriage. John stays with her at Queen Charlotte's Maternity Hospital in Hammersmith, London W.6. in a spare bed. When that is no longer free he sleeps on the floor beside her.
28 Nov.	John pleads guilty to unauthorized possession of cannabis at Marylebone Magistrates' Court. He is fined £150 plus 20 guineas costs. Both John and Yoko are found not guilty of obstructing the police.
29 Nov.	*Unfinished Music No. 1: Two Virgins*, John and Yoko's first avant-garde album together is released. Its content is completely overshadowed by the furore over the album cover, which shows the couple stark naked in full-frontal pose on the front cover with a rear view on the back cover.
10 Dec.	Kenwood, John's Weybridge home, is put up for sale.
11 Dec.	John and Yoko participate in the never-completed Rolling Stones T.V. special *Rock and Roll Circus* at Wembley T.V. studios.
18 Dec.	John and Yoko appear onstage in a large white bag at the Royal Albert Hall during *Alchemical Wedding*, the underground art movement's Christmas party.
23 Dec.	John and Yoko dress up as Father and Mother Christmas, handing out presents, at the Apple Christmas party at Savile Row.

1969

2 Jan.   Shooting of the disastrous *Let It Be* film commences at the cold Twickenham Film Studios.

3 Jan.   30,000 copies of John and Yoko's *Two Virgins* are confiscated in New Jersey on the grounds that the sleeve is pornographic.

18 Jan.   John tells Ray Coleman in an interview for *Disc and Music Echo*: 'Apple's losing money every week . . . if it carries on like this, all of us will be broke in the next six months.'

30 Jan.   The Beatles perform live on the roof of the Apple building in Savile Row. The event is captured on film for the *Let It Be* project.

2 Feb.   Yoko Ono is divorced from Anthony Cox in the Virgin Islands.

3 Feb.   An American, Allen Klein, is appointed to look after the Beatles' financial affairs at the insistence of John, George, and Ringo. Paul opposes Klein's involvement.

2 Mar.   John and Yoko appear in an avant-garde jazz concert at the Lady Mitchell Hall in Cambridge.

20 Mar.   John and Yoko fly from Paris to Gibraltar where they stay for just seventy minutes. During that time they are married by registrar Cecil Wheeler in the British Consulate building. They then return to Paris. John comments: 'It was all very quick, quiet and British.'

24 Mar.   John and Yoko lunch with Salvador Dali in Paris.

25–31 Mar.   John and Yoko's first big 'event'—the Amsterdam bed-in for peace. For seven days the couple hold court in Room 902 of the Amsterdam Hilton and give literally hundreds of interviews and messages about peace.

31 Mar.   John and Yoko fly from Amsterdam straight to Vienna for the world T.V. première of their film *Rape*, shown later that evening. The couple also hold a quick press conference at the Hotel Sacher to launch the film and appear completely encased in a white bag, their voices being the only clue to their identity.

1 April Back in London, John and Yoko appear on Thames Television's *Today* programme, inviting host Eamonn Andrews to join them in bed before the cameras.

21 April Bag Productions, John and Yoko's film and production company, is formed.

22 April In a formal ceremony before Señor Bueno de Mesquita, the Commissioner of Oaths, John changes his middle name from Winston to Ono. The ceremony is on the roof of the Apple building at 3 Savile Row, London W.1.

4 May John and Yoko buy Tittenhurst Park, a mansion in Sunningdale, Ascot, Berkshire. They move in during August.

8 May John, George, and Ringo sign a business management contract with Allen Klein. Paul refuses.

9 May *Unfinished Music No. 2: Life With The Lions*, John and Yoko's second 'experimental' album, is released on the Zapple label, Apple's newly-formed avant-garde record label.

16 May John's application for a United States visa is rejected because of his drug conviction in November 1968. He planned to stage a New York bed-in.

24 May John and Yoko with Kyoko, Yoko's daughter from her marriage to Anthony Cox, fly to the Bahamas to stage their bed-in for peace at the Sheraton Oceanus Hotel. They leave the island within twenty-four hours because it is further from the United States than John had believed and because the humid 86° temperature is not conducive to seven days in bed.

25 May The Lennons arrive in Toronto but are detained at the airport for two and a half hours by the Canadian Immigration authorities. They are eventually released on their own recognizance. It is nearly midnight before they are able to check into a downtown motel.

26 May The Lennons and their entourage fly to Montreal and announce their intention to hold a bed-in at the Queen Elizabeth Hotel. John invites Canadian Prime

Minister, Pierre Trudeau, to join him and also to plant acorns for peace. Says Trudeau: 'I don't know about his acorns, but I'd like to see him if he's around. He's a good poet.'

26 May– John and Yoko hold another seven-day bed-in in
2 June   Room 1742 of the Queen Elizabeth Hotel.

30 May   The Australian Broadcasting Commission (A.B.C.) ban the new Beatles single, 'The Ballad of John And Yoko' on the grounds that it is blasphemous.

1 June   From their bed John and Yoko record 'Give Peace A Chance'. They are assisted by a roomful of people including the Smothers Brothers, Timmy Leary, the Canadian Radha Krishna Temple, Derek Taylor, Murray The K, and the local rabbi.

2 June   John and Yoko leave the hotel early in the afternoon and quickly move on to Ottawa for a university conference on peace. Later that evening they fly back to London.

1 July   After visiting John's aunt in Durness, Sutherland, Scotland, John, Yoko, Kyoko, and Julian, John's first child, have a car accident in Golspie. No other vehicle is involved. They are taken to the Lawson Memorial Hospital where John receives seventeen stitches in a facial wound, Yoko fourteen stitches and Kyoko four. Julian suffers shock.

2 July   Cynthia travels to Scotland to see and retrieve Julian.

3 July   Still hospitalized after their car crash, John and Yoko are unable to attend the press launch of the Plastic Ono Band at Chelsea Town Hall, London S.W.1. In their place stand perspex tubes with fitted microphones, tape recorders and amplifiers.

4 July   'Give Peace A Chance', John's first solo single, credited to the Plastic Ono Band, is released.

6 July   John, Yoko and Kyoko fly back to London from the Golspie Hospital in a specially chartered helicopter. John tells the delighted Golspie local newspaper: 'If you're going to have a car crash try to arrange for it to happen in the Highlands. The hospital there was just great.'

10 Sept. An evening of John and Yoko films at the New

Cinema Club in the Institute of Contemporary Arts (I.C.A.) in London's Pall Mall. Those shown are *Self Portrait*, *Smile*, *Honeymoon*, *Two Virgins*, and *Rape*. An unidentified couple sit on stage throughout encased in a white sack though nobody is quite sure whether it is John and Yoko themselves. The audience reaction to the evening is filmed by an infra-red camera hidden out of view.

12 Sept.   At very short notice John and Yoko are asked to appear live at a Rock 'n' Roll Revival concert in Toronto, scheduled for the following day. John hurriedly gathers together Eric Clapton, Klaus Voormann and Alan White to join him and Yoko in forming a makeshift Plastic Ono Band.

13 Sept.   The Plastic Ono Band fly from Heathrow to Toronto, grabbing their only chance to rehearse on board the plane. Later that night they take the stage at the Varsity Stadium and perform 'Blue Suede Shoes', 'Money', 'Dizzy Miss Lizzy', 'Yer Blues', 'Give Peace A Chance', and a new Lennon composition, 'Cold Turkey', as well as two lengthy Yoko compositions, 'Don't Worry Kyoko' and 'John, John (Let's Hope For Peace)'.

25 Sept.   After months of protracted dealings in the City, John and Paul lose control of Northern Songs and thereby the full rights to all of their past—and a good deal of their future—compositions, to Lew Grade's A.T.V. Music.

Oct.   John invites his father to his house at Tittenhurst Park for what is to be their last meeting.

12 Oct.   Yoko loses a baby expected in December—her second miscarriage—at King's College Hospital, Denmark Hill, London S.E.5.

3 Nov.   An evening of John and Yoko films at Nash House, London S.W.1. under the collective title of *Something Else*. A second such evening is held a week later, on 10 November.

7 Nov.   Apple release John and Yoko's *Wedding Album*. The luxurious package contains not only a record but a copy of their marriage certificate, various

pictures, two booklets, a poster, and a photograph of a slice of wedding cake.

13 Nov.   A group of hippies travel to Ireland to inspect a tiny uninhabited island, Dornish, off the coast of County Mayo. It is being offered to them rent free by John Lennon who bought it in 1966 at a cost of £1,500.

25 Nov.   (Announced 26 November) John returns his M.B.E. medal to Buckingham Palace 'in protest against Britain's involvement in the Nigeria–Biafra thing, against our support of America in Vietnam, and against ''Cold Turkey'' slipping down the charts.' His letter is signed 'With love, John Lennon of Bag'.

27 Nov.   Buckingham Palace reports that Mr Barry Hearn, who returned his M.B.E. medal in 1965 when the Beatles were awarded the M.B.E.s, has asked for its return following John's return of his medal. Unfortunately Buckingham Palace cannot locate it.

1 Dec.   John and Yoko offer to buy a 32-foot caravan school for gypsy children to be situated on an unofficial site at Caddington, near Luton, Bedfordshire.

3 Dec.   John is asked to play the part of Christ in the Tim Rice/Andrew Lloyd Webber musical *Jesus Christ Superstar*, to be staged in St Paul's Cathedral.

4 Dec.   Rice and Lloyd Webber withdraw their offer, stating that the part would be better suited to an unknown actor.

9 Dec.   Apple announce that John and Yoko are to make a film about James Hanratty, the convicted and executed 'A6' murderer. It would reveal facts never before disclosed, they claim.

11 Dec.   John startles a crowd of 200 people outside the Kensington Odeon, there for the première of *The Magic Christian*, which starred Ringo, by slowly carrying past a banner reading 'Britain Murdered Hanratty'.

12 Dec.   *The Plastic Ono Band—Live Peace in Toronto 1969* is released by Apple.

14 Dec.   A white sack labelled 'A Silent Protest For James Hanratty', with two anonymous wriggling occu-

pants (John and Yoko?) is taken to Speakers' Corner, Marble Arch, London W.1., where Hanratty's father calls for a public inquiry into his son's hanging. A petition is later handed in to 10 Downing Street.

15 Dec. The Plastic Ono Supergroup—John augmented by Yoko, George Harrison, Eric Clapton, Billy Preston, Keith Moon, and many more—play at a *Peace for Christmas* concert at the Lyceum Ballroom in London in aid of UNICEF.

16 Dec. Huge posters and billboards go up in various locations in eleven cities world-wide reading: 'War Is Over! If You Want It. Happy Christmas from John and Yoko.'

23 Dec. Back in Canada for the third time in seven months John and Yoko have a fifty-one-minute private conference with Prime Minister Pierre Trudeau in Ottawa. They later describe him as 'more beautiful than we expected' and add, 'If all politicians were like Trudeau there would be world peace.'

24 Dec. Back in England John and Yoko briefly join a sit-in and fast outside Rochester Cathedral in Kent to call for peace and spotlight world poverty.

29 Dec. John and Yoko fly to the small village of Aalborg in Denmark to holiday with Kyoko at the home of Anthony Cox and his new wife, Melinda.

30 Dec. I.T.V. transmit *Man Of The Decade*—a sixty-minute television programme split into three twenty-minute segments featuring John F. Kennedy, Mao Tse-Tung, and John Lennon. John's section includes a lengthy, newly recorded interview filmed at Tittenhurst Park.

1970

5 Jan. From Denmark John announces that all future proceeds from his songs and records will go towards promoting peace on earth.

15 Jan. An exhibition of fourteen John Lennon lithographs opens at the London Arts Gallery in New Bond Street, London W.1.

16 Jan.   Detectives from Scotland Yard raid the exhibition and confiscate eight of the lithographs, which are deemed to be erotic and indecent.

19 Jan.   It is reported that sales of *Bag One*, the collection of John's lithographs, have rocketed since the police raid. Three hundred sets are for sale at £550 each.

20 Jan.   Still in Denmark John and Yoko have their hair cropped in the barn of Anthony Cox's north-Jutland retreat.

22 Jan.   All fourteen John Lennon lithographs go on show at the London Gallery in Detroit, U.S.A.—to no reaction.

27 Jan.   Back in England John writes, records, and mixes his next single, 'Instant Karma!', all in one day. Phil Spector produces. It is released just ten days later.

28 Jan.   The London exhibition of John's lithographs—with only six remaining on show—comes to its scheduled end at the London Arts Gallery.

4 Feb.   John and Yoko swap their shorn hair, neatly tied up in plastic bags, for a pair of blood-stained Muhammad Ali boxing trunks in a ceremony with Michael X, the notorious Black Power leader, on the roof of X's 'Black House' in Holloway, north London. John and Yoko intend auctioning the trunks to raise money for peace.

11 Feb.   John pays the outstanding fines, totalling £1,344, imposed on ninety-six people involved in protests against the South African rugby team who played a match in Scotland in December 1969.

12 Feb.   The Plastic Ono Band appear live in the studio on the B.B.C. programme *Top Of The Pops* singing 'Instant Karma!' (The entire show was tele-recorded on 11 February.)

25 Feb.   A summons is served on the London Arts Gallery for showing John's lithographs—'an indecent exhibition contrary to the Metropolitan Police Act, 1839'.

22 Mar.   In an interview with the French magazine *L'Express*

John reveals that the Beatles smoked marijuana in the toilets at Buckingham Palace prior to their M.B.E. investiture in 1965. A Palace spokesman curtly replies: 'Obviously when people come along to an investiture toilet facilities are available.'

29 Mar. John sends a telephone message, broadcast to 8,000 people at a Campaign for Nuclear Disarmament (C.N.D.) rally in Victoria Park, Bethnal Green, east London. During his message he reveals that Yoko is expecting a baby in October. Later in the year she miscarries again.

1 April Defence lawyers in the London Arts Gallery prosecution trial compare John Lennon's works with those of Picasso.

10 April Paul McCartney announces his resignation from the Beatles.

Late April John and Yoko travel to Los Angeles to undergo four months of primal therapy under Dr Arthur Janov.

27 April The lithographs court case is dismissed in favour of the London Arts Gallery and the exhibits are returned.

13 May World première of the Beatles' *Let It Be* film in New York. None of the four attend.

1 Aug. John's first wife Cynthia re-marries, to Italian hotelier Roberto Bassanini.

8 Dec. John records a mammoth interview with *Rolling Stone* magazine.

11 Dec. *Plastic Ono Band*, John's stark and brilliant first true 'solo' album is released.

31 Dec. Paul begins proceedings in the London High Court to end the Beatles partnership.

1971

21 Jan. *Rolling Stone* publish Part One of their extensive John Lennon interview. Part Two follows on 4 February.

3 Mar. South African Broadcasting Corporation (S.A.B.C.) finally lift their ban on Beatles music implemented on 8 August 1966, although John Lennon compo-

sitions, vocals, and solo work remain blacklisted.

12 Mar. Paul wins Beatles court case in London. A receiver, James Douglas Spooner, is appointed to look after the group's business and financial affairs, superseding Allen Klein.

23 April In Palma, Majorca, John and Yoko are escorted by Spanish police to the magistrates' court and questioned over the alleged abduction of Yoko's daughter, Kyoko. Anthony Cox complained to the police after her disappearance from a playground.

3 May John and Yoko pass through Heathrow Airport on their way from Trinidad back to Majorca to see the Justices there about the custody of Kyoko.

15 May World première of two more Bag productions, *Apotheosis (Balloon)* and *Fly* at the Cannes Film Festival, attended by John and Yoko.

1 June John, in possession of a nine-month U.S. visa issued on 31 May, jets to New York with Yoko in an attempt to locate and gain custody of Kyoko.

6 June John and Yoko make a surprise appearance on stage with Frank Zappa and The Mothers of Invention at the Fillmore East in New York City.

July John records his *Imagine* album over seven days at Tittenhurst Park and two days at the Record Plant in New York.

15 July John and Yoko attend a promotion and book-signing session at Selfridges giant department store on Oxford Street, London, for the re-publication of Yoko's *Grapefruit*.

17 July John and Yoko are interviewed on the B.B.C. *Parkinson* T.V. show. It turns out to be their last public appearance before leaving the U.K. for good.

19 July John and Yoko hold a press conference at the Apple H.Q. in Savile Row to talk about *Grapefruit*. John says: 'In England I'm regarded as the guy who won the pools. She's [Yoko] regarded as the lucky Jap who married the guy who won the pools. In America we are both treated as artists.'

11–31 A programme of five John and Yoko films are shown

Aug.	at *Art Spectrum,* a potpourri exhibition of modern art held in the Great Hall at London's Alexandra Palace.
11 Aug.	More than 1,000 demonstrators, including John and Yoko, march past the Ulster Office in London. The demonstration is split between those supporting the *Oz* editors, who are being tried for publishing an obscene underground paper, and those against internment and the use of troops in Northern Ireland. John says: 'The two matters are integral and cannot be divided.'
12 Aug.	John and Yoko send £1,000 to the 'fighting fund' of the Upper Clyde [Scotland] Shipbuilding union who are refusing to stop work after being made redundant. The previous week they had sent roses.
3 Sept.	John and Yoko leave English soil for the last time and fly to New York.
9 Sept.	John on the *Dick Cavett* U.S. television show, says that the Beatles broke up 'because of Beatlemania and screaming crowds that drowned out the music, not because of Yoko Ono'.
8 Oct.	John's classic *Imagine* album is released.
9–27 Oct.	Yoko's art exhibition, with John as a guest artist, entitled *This Is Not Here,* takes place at the Everson Museum of Art in Syracuse, New York. A television special about the show is transmitted on 11 May 1972.
6 Nov.	After a day of large scale demonstrations in New York City, a benefit concert for the casualties of the Attica prison riots at the Apollo Theatre includes a surprise stage appearance by John and Yoko. (On 13 September, four days after prison camp guards had been taken hostage, 1,000 New York State troopers had invaded the prison under a pall of tear gas, killing twenty-eight prisoners and nine hostages in the process.)
11 Dec.	John and Yoko perform live at a benefit rally held in the Crisler building, Ann Arbor, Michigan, for left-wing writer John Sinclair who had been jailed for ten years in 1969 for possession of two mari-

	juana cigarettes. Fifty-five hours after the rally, on 13 December, Sinclair is freed on bail.
15 Dec.	John and Yoko attend a reception in honour of U Thant, the retiring United Nations Secretary-General.
18 Dec.	John and Yoko visit Houston, Texas to try to gain access to Kyoko.
22 Dec.	Houston, Texas. Anthony Cox is jailed for five days after refusing to allow Yoko to visit Kyoko.

1972

13 Jan.	John and Yoko appear on the U.S. television *David Frost Show*.
5 Feb.	John and Yoko, in temperatures well below freezing, are among 400 demonstrators outside the New York building of British Overseas Airways Corporation (B.O.A.C.), supporting union leaders' boycott of British exports as a protest against British policy in Northern Ireland.
14–18 Feb.	John and Yoko co-host *The Mike Douglas Show* on U.S. television in the absence of Douglas. Every night they feature interviews and music and on one show John plays live and jams with his teenage idol, Chuck Berry.
17 Feb.	John and Yoko's forty-minute colour film of the campaign for an inquiry into the Hanratty execution of 1961 is shown in the crypt of St Martin in the Fields, London.
29 Feb.	John and Yoko's U.S. visas expire. They are granted a routine fifteen-day extension in order to make a fresh application.
3 Mar.	Yoko is finally awarded custody of Kyoko but Anthony Cox flees with the child and cannot be found.
6 Mar.	The temporary extensions of John and Yoko's visas are cancelled at the instigation of the Deputy Attorney-General and the couple's four-year battle against deportation begins.
16 Mar.	John and Yoko are served with deportation orders because of his 1968 London drugs conviction. Yoko says it will cause the couple to lose the custody of

Kyoko, although both she and the child's father, Anthony Cox, are still in hiding.

22 April   John and Yoko address the crowd at the National Peace Rally in New York, protesting against the bombing of North Vietnam.

27 April   (Announced 29 April) John Lindsay, the Mayor of New York City, appeals in a letter to the Commissioner of Immigration and Naturalization in Washington, D.C., for John and Yoko's deportation order to be dropped. He says that the proceedings are 'a grave injustice' and adds that the real reason behind the order is not John's 1968 London drug conviction but because the couple 'speak out with strong and critical voices on the major issues of the day'.

11 May   John appears on *The Dick Cavett Show* and claims he is being followed by government agents and that his telephone is being tapped.

17 May   At a deportation hearing before the immigration authorities in New York, John says, 'I don't know if there is any mercy to plead for, but if so, I would like it for both us and our child.'

12 June   *Some Time In New York City*, John and Yoko's angry and heavily political album is released in America. Its anti-British content, together with copyright problems, prevents simultaneous U.K. release, which does not happen until 15 September.

2 July   John and Yoko's lawyers prepare a final brief, outlining the reasons why the couple want to stay in the U.S.A.

4 July   On American Independence Day, Lord Harlech, former British Ambassador to the U.S.A., writes to the Immigration and Naturalization Service in John's defence.

30 Aug.   The Madison Square Garden arena in New York City hosts two *One To One* concerts in aid of retarded children and adults. John and Yoko with the Elephants Memory band appear on the bill with Stevie Wonder, Roberta Flack, and Sha Na Na. A total of $1½ million is raised including $60,000

donated by the Lennons. A T.V. special recorded at the concerts is aired on 14 December 1972.

6 Sept.   John and Yoko with Elephants Memory appear live on Jerry Lewis' Muscular Dystrophy telethon.

23 Dec.   *Imagine*, a film made to accompany the album of the same name, receives its belated world première on U.S. television.

1973

22 Jan.   Northern Songs and Maclen Music of London and New York sue John for over $1 million claiming that he, with Allen Klein's encouragement, intentionally and unlawfully violated a 1965 agreement that the companies would have exclusive rights to his compositions, whether written solo or in collaboration with someone else. Five songs are in dispute, all written with Yoko and with half-copyright claimed by Ono Music Ltd. Ironically Paul McCartney had recently gone through a similar ordeal when he tried to write with *his* wife, Linda.

23 Mar.   John is ordered to leave the U.S. within sixty days but Yoko is granted permission to remain as a permanent resident. The couple are not present at the hearing but issue a statement from the West Coast: 'Having just celebrated our fourth wedding anniversary, we are not prepared to sleep in separate beds. Peace and love, John and Yoko.'

24 Mar.   John formally appeals against the sixty-day deportation order.

31 Mar.   John, George, and Ringo's management contract with Allen Klein and his company ABCKO expires and is not renewed.

28 June   Allen Klein and ABCKO Industries sue John for a total of $508,000 over allegedly unrepaid loans.

9 Sept.   Tittenhurst Park, John and Yoko's Ascot home, is put up for sale.

18 Sept.   Ringo Starr buys Tittenhurst Park.

Oct.   John and Yoko separate after four and a half years of marriage. John flees to Los Angeles.

Oct.–Dec. John records a prospective album of rock 'n' roll

standards with Phil Spector producing. The sessions eventually disintegrate into a drunken nightmare and Spector runs off with the tapes. After much wrangling John finally retrieves them in June 1974.

24 Oct. John sues the U.S. government, demanding it admit or deny whether he and/or his lawyer, Leon Wildes, have been the subject of illegal wiretapping or surveillance by the F.B.I.

2 Nov. John, George, and Ringo bring legal action in the High Court against Allen Klein and ABCKO (nicknamed grABCKO by John), claiming damages for alleged misrepresentation. Klein responds with a counteraction, suing for lost fees, commissions and expenses.

16 Nov. John's *Mind Games* album is released.

11 Dec. John sends £1,000 to the ailing British underground paper *IT* (formerly *International Times*). It eventually folds eight months later.

1974

1 Feb. It is reported that the costs of all three appeals to stop the hanging of Michael X (real name Michael Abdul Malik) have been met by John. X was found guilty of murder in Trinidad. (After many further appeals and much deliberation Malik was eventually executed on 16 May 1975.)

Mar.– Mayhem and drunkenness abound during the recording of *Pussy Cats*, a Harry Nilsson album, produced by John at the Record Plant in Los Angeles. Similar scenes are rife at the Santa Monica home they share with Keith Moon and Ringo Starr.

13 Mar. John is ejected from the Troubadour night club in West Hollywood after hurling insults and foul language at the Smothers Brothers during their act. Encouraged by his drinking pal Harry Nilsson, John tries to assault the Smothers' manager Ken Fritz, and Brenda Mary Perkins, a waitress-cum-'photographer' who tries to take a Polaroid snapshot of

John while he is being thrown out of the club.

27 Mar. The Los Angeles District Attorney dismisses a citizen's complaint filed against John by Brenda Mary Perkins who claims to have been slapped during the fracas at the Troubadour.

17 July John is again ordered to leave the U.S. within sixty days and again he lodges an appeal.

31 Aug. John claims in court what people have come to realize over the previous few months: that the Nixon administration tried to have him deported not because of his 1968 London drug conviction but because they mistakenly believed that he was one of the organizers of a possible anti-war demonstration to be held at the Republican Convention in 1972.

4 Oct. John's *Walls And Bridges* album is released.

8 Oct. John meets music publishing and record company executive, Morris Levy, to discuss an out-of-court settlement over his copyright infringement of the Levy-owned Chuck Berry composition 'You Can't Catch Me' on 'Come Together', recorded for the Beatles' *Abbey Road* album in 1969.

1 Nov. John requests a Federal judge to allow him the right to question immigration officials in connection with an alleged police vendetta led by former Attorney General, John N. Mitchell, which arose after John began supporting the Democrats in 1972.

16 Nov. John's first 'solo' U.S. number one as 'Whatever Gets You Thru The Night' tops the *Billboard* singles chart. Elton John, who had played keyboards on the recording, had made John vow that if it reached number one he would have to join him on stage some time in the future.

28 Nov. John keeps his promise and makes a surprise appearance onstage during Elton's Thanksgiving Day concert at the Madison Square Garden, New York, singing three songs.

27 Dec. John, accompanied by his son Julian, and May Pang, spends the New Year holidays at Disneyland, Los Angeles.

1975

Jan.
John returns to New York and is re-united with Yoko at the Dakota. Yoko is soon pregnant.

9 Jan.
The partnership of The Beatles and Co. is finally dissolved in the London High Court.

Mid–Jan.
David Bowie, in New York to record his *Young Americans* album, invites John to play guitar on his version of the Lennon song 'Across The Universe'. While together they also write and record 'Fame'.

8 Feb.
American T.V. advertisements appear for the semi-legal Lennon album *Roots*, available by mail order from Morris Levy's Adam VIII label.

21 Feb.
E.M.I./Capitol rush release John's *Rock 'n' Roll* album to counteract *Roots*. Litigation looms large again as Morris Levy sues for $42 million.

1 Mar.
John and Yoko make their first public appearance together since their reunion at the annual Grammy Awards ceremony in Los Angeles.

6 Mar.
John issues a statement that his eighteen-month separation from Yoko 'was not a success' and that he has returned to live with her in New York.

18 April
B.B.C. Television transmit their famous *Old Grey Whistle Test* interview with John.

13 June
U.S. Television airs a *Salute to Lew Grade* T.V. special in which John appears live, singing 'Imagine' and 'Slippin' and Slidin' ' backed by a 'two-faced' band—John's none too subtle dig at Grade. It was his last live appearance before an audience.

19 June
John sues former Attorney-General John N. Mitchell, and other U.S. law officers, for 'improper selective prosecution' arising from the deportation attempt.

13 July
John awarded a total of $144,700 by a New York court for lost royalties and damaged reputation over the *Roots* album.

23 Sept.
John's deportation order is temporarily halted on humanitarian grounds because of Yoko's pregnancy which has reached a critical stage.

7 Oct.
The New York State Supreme Court votes by a two-to-one decision to reverse the deportation or-

der, instructing the Immigration Service to re-consider John's request for resident status. The chief judge adds: 'The court cannot condone selective deportation based upon secret political grounds.'

9 Oct. At the age of forty-two and on John's thirty-fifth birthday, after three previous miscarriages, Yoko gives birth at the New York Hospital to their first child—a son—named Sean Taro Ono Lennon. 'I feel higher than the Empire State Building,' says John.

1976

5 Jan. Mal Evans, the Beatles' former road manager, aide, gofer and confidant, is shot dead by police in Los Angeles.

6 Feb. John's recording contract with E.M.I./Capitol expires and is not renewed. For the first time in nearly fifteen years John is not tied to a contract.

1 April Freddy Lennon, John's father, dies in Brighton General Hospital, England, aged sixty-three.

April During the Los Angeles recording of Ringo Starr's *Rotogravure* album John makes his last commercial studio appearance for four years, playing piano on his own composition 'Cookin' (In The Kitchen Of Love)'.

27 July John's battle to remain in the U.S. is finally over when his application to become a permanent resident is formally approved at a special hearing in New York. He is awarded his precious Green Card, number A17–597–321, and proclaims: 'It's great to be legal again.' The judge, Ira Fieldsteel, informs John that he can apply for U.S. citizenship in 1981.

20 Sept. New York promoter Sid Bernstein, the man behind the Beatles' American tours in the sixties, places a page advertisement in the *International Herald Tribune* asking the Beatles to perform a reunion concert for charity—possible revenue $230 million.

Oct. John begins his 'retirement' and house-husband period, bringing up Sean at the Dakota.

1977

10 Jan. All outstanding litigation between the Beatles/Apple Corps and Allen Klein/ABCKO is dropped after a settlement costing Apple $5 million and ABCKO $800,000.

20 Jan. John and Yoko attend Jimmy Carter's Presidential inauguration gala in Washington D.C.

June The Lennon family travel to Japan for five months.

1978

4 Feb. John and Yoko pay more than $178,000 for several plots of land in Delaware County, New York, for use as a vacation retreat and to raise Regis Holstein cows. It is also revealed that the couple are buying every apartment which becomes available at the Dakota Building.

16 June John unsuccessfully tries to prevent the London *News of the World* newspaper publishing extracts from *A Twist of Lennon*, the book written by his first wife, Cynthia.

1979

27 May John and Yoko place whole-page advertisements in the *New York Times*, the London *Sunday Times*, and a Tokyo newspaper, entitled: 'A Love Letter From John And Yoko. To People Who Ask Us What, When and Why.'

9 Sept. Sid Bernstein makes a public plea for three Beatles reunion concerts—to be held in Cairo, Jerusalem, and New York, in aid of the Vietnamese 'boat people'. Possible revenue, $500 million.

21 Sept. Kurt Waldheim, Secretary-General of the United Nations, gets in on the act and also asks the Beatles to perform a reunion concert in aid of the 'boat people'.

15 Oct. John and Yoko contribute $1,000 to a campaign to provide New York City policemen with bullet-proof vests.

31 Dec.   Bag Productions, John and Yoko's film and production company formed in 1969, is dissolved, along with several other late sixties ventures.

1980

28 Jan.   John and Yoko buy a beachside mansion in Palm Beach, Florida to add to their ever-growing list of property investments.

20 Mar.   John and Yoko celebrate their eleventh wedding anniversary in West Palm Beach, Florida. John gives Yoko a diamond heart and 500 fresh gardenias. Yoko gives John a vintage Rolls-Royce.

23 May   To gain independence and boost his confidence John goes alone to Cape Town, South Africa for a holiday.

July   John and a five-man crew sail to Bermuda on *Isis*, his 63-foot yacht. While there he begins to compose music again.

2 July   A Holstein cow owned by John and Yoko is sold for a world record $265,000 to buyer Steve Potter at an auction in New York State Fairgrounds, Syracuse, New York.

4 Aug.   John and Yoko enter the Hit Factory recording studios in Manhattan to record their first album for six years.

Sept.   Over three weeks John and Yoko record a mammoth interview for *Playboy* magazine.

22 Sept. David Geffen, former top executive with Warner Brothers and Asylum Records, signs John and Yoko to his newly formed independent record label, Geffen Records, and announces that their new album will be entitled *Double Fantasy*.

29 Sept. The first publication of a 'comeback' interview—in *Newsweek*.

9 Oct.   Yoko celebrates John's fortieth birthday and Sean's fifth, by having a message of love sky-written over Manhattan.

17 Nov.   *Double Fantasy* is released.

5 Dec.   John records an interview for *Rolling Stone*.

6 Dec.   B.B.C. disc jockey Andy Peebles flies to New York

        to record a lengthy radio interview with John and
        Yoko.
8 Dec.   John gives an interview for R.K.O. Radio.
8 Dec.   (9 December in the U.K.) John Ono Lennon is shot
           dead.

DISCOGRAPHY
1962–1966

Every commercially released song John Lennon wrote and/or sang during the period covered in this book is included in this list. It is Lennon's recording career as *he* planned it. This list does not, therefore, include the many compilations and reissues or audition tapes and live albums recorded during this period but released later: these albums were marketing operations and have no bearing on Lennon's chronological songwriting pattern, which this list also sets out to reflect. This discography aims to show the reader, at a glance, what John and the Beatles did, and when.

To this end, the listing is based on British record releases, as the Beatles themselves intended. The group always specifically recorded singles *as singles,* and album tracks likewise. In Britain these two paths crossed only rarely. But in America Capitol Records, through shrewd marketing practice and a great deal of song repetition, managed to produce considerably more singles and 'new' albums without using any additional material.

Songs either completely written or co-written by John Lennon are printed in capitals. But songs to which John contributed a few words, a line or a phrase – and there are a great many – are not ascribed to him.

Singles

October 1962   'Love Me Do'/'P.S. I Love You'

January 1963	'PLEASE PLEASE ME'/'ASK ME WHY'
April 1963	'FROM ME TO YOU'/'THANK YOU GIRL'
August 1963	'SHE LOVES YOU'/'I'LL GET YOU'
November 1963	'I WANT TO HOLD YOUR HAND'/'THIS BOY'
March 1964	'Can't Buy Me Love'/'YOU CAN'T DO THAT'
July 1964	'A HARD DAY'S NIGHT'/'Things We Said Today'
*November 1964	'I FEEL FINE'/'She's A Woman'
April 1965	'TICKET TO RIDE'/'YES IT IS'
July 1965	'HELP!'/'I'm Down'
*December 1965	'DAY TRIPPER'/'WE CAN WORK IT OUT'
June 1966	'Paperback Writer'/'RAIN'
*August 1966	'Yellow Submarine'/'ELEANOR RIGBY'

*Denotes a double A-sided record

Albums

March 1963   **Please Please Me**

'I Saw Her Standing There'; 'MISERY'; 'Anna (Go To Him)'; 'Chains'; 'Boys'; 'ASK ME WHY'; 'PLEASE PLEASE ME'.

'Love Me Do'; 'P.S. I Love You'; 'Baby It's You'; 'DO YOU WANT TO KNOW A SECRET'; 'A Taste of Honey'; 'THERE'S A PLACE'; 'Twist And Shout'.

November 1963   **With the Beatles**

'IT WON'T BE LONG'; 'ALL I'VE GOT TO DO'; 'All My Loving'; 'Don't Bother Me'; 'LITTLE CHILD'; 'Till There Was You'; 'Please Mister Postman'.

'Roll Over Beethoven'; 'Hold Me Tight'; 'You Really Got A Hold On Me'; 'I WANNA BE YOUR MAN'; 'Devil In Her Heart'; 'NOT A SECOND TIME'; 'Money (That's What I Want)'.

July 1964   **A Hard Day's Night**

'A HARD DAY'S NIGHT'; 'I SHOULD HAVE KNOWN BETTER'; 'IF I FELL'; 'I'M HAPPY JUST TO DANCE WITH YOU'; 'And I Love Her'; 'TELL ME WHY'; 'Can't Buy Me Love'.

'ANY TIME AT ALL'; 'I'LL CRY INSTEAD'; 'Things We Said Today'; 'WHEN I GET HOME'; 'YOU CAN'T DO THAT'; 'I'LL BE BACK'.

December 1964   **Beatles For Sale**

'NO REPLY'; 'I'M A LOSER'; 'BABY'S IN BLACK'; 'Rock and Roll Music'; 'I'll Follow The Sun'; 'Mr. Moonlight'; 'Kansas City/Hey-Hey-Hey-Hey!'

'EIGHT DAYS A WEEK'; 'Words Of Love'; 'Honey Don't'; 'EVERY LITTLE THING'; 'I DON'T WANT TO SPOIL THE PARTY'; 'WHAT YOU'RE DOING'; 'Everybody's Trying To Be My Baby'.

August 1965   **Help!**

'HELP!'; 'The Night Before'; 'YOU'VE GOT TO HIDE YOUR LOVE AWAY'; 'I Need You'; 'Another Girl'; 'YOU'RE GOING TO LOSE THAT GIRL'; 'TICKET TO RIDE'.

'Act Naturally'; 'IT'S ONLY LOVE'; 'You Like Me Too Much'; 'Tell Me What You See'; 'I've Just Seen A Face'; 'Yesterday'; 'Dizzy Miss Lizzy'.

December 1965   **Rubber Soul**

'DRIVE MY CAR'; 'NORWEGIAN WOOD (THIS BIRD HAS FLOWN)'; 'You Won't See Me'; 'NOWHERE MAN'; 'Think For Yourself'; 'THE WORD'.

'WHAT GOES ON'; 'GIRL'; 'I'm Looking Through You'; 'IN MY LIFE'; 'Wait'; 'If I Needed Someone'; 'RUN FOR YOUR LIFE'.

August 1966   **Revolver**

'Taxman'; 'ELEANOR RIGBY'; 'I'M ONLY SLEEPING'; 'Love You Too'; 'Here, There and Everywhere'; 'Yellow Submarine'; 'SHE SAID SHE SAID'.

'Good Day Sunshine'; 'AND YOUR BIRD CAN SING'; 'For No One'; 'DOCTOR ROBERT'; 'I Want To Tell You'; 'Got To Get You Into My Life'; 'TOMORROW NEVER KNOWS'.

MISCELLANEOUS

June 1964 **Long Tall Sally** (E.P.)

'Long Tall Sally'; 'I CALL YOUR NAME'.

'Slow Down'; 'Matchbox'.

December 1966 **A Collection Of Beatles Oldies** (L.P.)

Contains one track previously unavailable: 'Bad Boy'.

True collectors would also require two tracks from the 1961 Hamburg recording session when the Beatles were recruited mainly for backing Tony Sheridan. One is the first recorded and published John Lennon composition, co-written with George Harrison, the instrumental, 'CRY FOR A SHADOW'. The other is the Lennon lead vocal on 'Ain't She Sweet'.

Songs written or co-written by John Lennon, not commercially recorded by him but instead 'given' to other artists.

'BAD TO ME': Billy J. Kramer and the Dakotas, 1963.
'HELLO LITTLE GIRL': The Fourmost, 1963.
'I'M IN LOVE': The Fourmost, 1963.

DISCOGRAPHY
1967 — 1984

SINGLES

*February 1967   'Penny Lane'/'STRAWBERRY FIELDS FOR-
EVER' *(The Beatles)*

July 1967   'ALL YOU NEED IS LOVE'/'BABY, YOU'RE A
RICH MAN' *(The Beatles)*

November 1967   'Hello, Goodbye'/'I AM THE WALRUS' *(The
Beatles)*

March 1968   'Lady Madonna'/'The Inner Light' *(The
Beatles)*

August 1968   'Hey Jude'/'REVOLUTION' *(The Beatles)*

April 1969   'Get Back' *(The Beatles with Billy Preston)*/
'DON'T LET ME DOWN' *(The Beatles)*

May 1969   'THE BALLAD OF JOHN AND YOKO'/'Old
Brown Shoe' *(The Beatles)*

July 1969   'GIVE PEACE A CHANCE'/'Remember Love'
(Plastic Ono Band)

October 1969   'COLD TURKEY'/'Don't Worry Kyoko
(Mummy's Only Looking For Her Hand In
The Snow)' *(Plastic Ono Band)*

*October 1969   'Something'/'COME TOGETHER' *(The Bea-
tles)*

February 1970   'INSTANT KARMA!'/'Who Has Seen The
Wind?' *(Lennon/Ono with the Plastic Ono
Band)*

March 1970	'Let It Be'/'YOU KNOW MY NAME (LOOK UP THE NUMBER' *(The Beatles)*
March 1971	'POWER TO THE PEOPLE' *(John Lennon/Plastic Ono Band)*/'Open Your Box' *(Yoko Ono/Plastic Ono Band)*
†November 1972	'HAPPY XMAS (WAR IS OVER)' *(John and Yoko/The Plastic Ono Band with the Harlem Community Choir)*/'Listen, The Snow Is Falling' *(Yoko Ono and the Plastic Ono Band)*
November 1973	'MIND GAMES'/'MEAT CITY' *(John Lennon)*
October 1974	'WHATEVER GETS YOU THRU THE NIGHT' *(John Lennon with the Plastic Ono Nuclear Band)*/'BEEF JERKY' *(John Lennon with the Plastic Ono Nuclear Band/Little Big Horns and Booker Table and the Maitre D's)*
January 1975	'#9 DREAM'/'WHAT YOU GOT' *(John Lennon)*
April 1975	'STAND BY ME'/'MOVE OVER MS.L' *(John Lennon)*
October 1975	'IMAGINE'/'WORKING CLASS HERO' *(John Lennon)*
October 1980	'(JUST LIKE) STARTING OVER' *(John Lennon)*/'Kiss, Kiss, Kiss' *(Yoko Ono)*
January 1981	'WOMAN' *(John Lennon)*/'Beautiful Boys' *(Yoko Ono)*
March 1981	'WATCHING THE WHEELS' *(John Lennon)*/'I'm Your Angel' *(Yoko Ono)*
November 1982	'LOVE'/'GIVE ME SOME TRUTH' *(John Lennon)*
January 1984	'NOBODY TOLD ME' *(John Lennon)*/' "O" Sanity' *(Yoko Ono)*
March 1984	'BORROWED TIME' *(John Lennon)*/'Your Hands' *(Yoko Ono)*
July 1984	'I'M STEPPING OUT' *(John Lennon)*/'Sleepless Night' *(Yoko Ono)*
November 1984	'EVERY MAN HAS A WOMAN WHO LOVES HIM' *(John Lennon)*/'IT'S ALRIGHT' *(Sean Lennon)*

ALBUMS

June 1967   Sgt. Pepper's Lonely Hearts Club Band

'Sgt Pepper's Lonely Hearts Club Band'; 'WITH A LITTLE HELP FROM MY FRIENDS'; 'LUCY IN THE SKY WITH DIAMONDS'; 'Getting Better'; 'Fixing A Hole'; 'SHE'S LEAVING HOME'; 'BEING FOR THE BENEFIT OF MR. KITE!'.

'Within You Without You'; 'When I'm Sixty-Four'; 'Lovely Rita'; 'GOOD MORNING GOOD MORNING'; 'Sgt Pepper's Lonely Hearts Club Band' *(Reprise)*; 'A DAY IN THE LIFE'.

(The Beatles)

November 1968   The Beatles

'Back in the U.S.S.R.'; 'DEAR PRUDENCE'; 'GLASS ONION'; 'Ob-La-Di, Ob-La-Da'; 'Wild Honey Pie'; 'THE CONTINUING STORY OF BUNGALOW BILL'; 'While My Guitar Gently Weeps'; 'HAPPINESS IS A WARM GUN'.

'Martha My Dear': 'I'M SO TIRED'; 'Blackbird'; 'Piggies'; 'Rocky Racoon'; 'Don't Pass Me By'; 'Why Don't We Do It In The Road'; 'I Will'; 'JULIA'.

'Birthday'; 'YER BLUES'; 'Mother Nature's Son'; 'EVERYBODY'S GOT SOMETHING TO HIDE EXCEPT ME AND MY MONKEY'; 'SEXY SADIE'; 'Helter Skelter'; 'Long Long Long'.

'REVOLUTION 1'; 'Honey Pie'; 'Savoy Truffle'; 'CRY BABY CRY'; 'REVOLUTION 9'; 'GOOD NIGHT'.   *(The Beatles)*

November 1968   Unfinished Music No.1: Two Virgins

'TWO VIRGINS NO.1'; 'TOGETHER'; 'TWO VIRGINS NO.2'; 'TWO VIRGINS NO.3'; 'TWO VIRGINS NO.4'; 'TWO VIRGINS NO.5'; 'TWO VIRGINS NO.6'.

'HUSHABYE HUSHABYE'; 'TWO VIRGINS NO.7'; 'TWO VIRGINS NO.8'; 'TWO VIRGINS NO.9'; 'TWO VIRGINS NO.10'.

(John Lennon and Yoko Ono)

January 1969   **Yellow Submarine**

'Yellow Submarine'; 'Only A Northern Song'; 'All Together Now'; 'HEY BULLDOG'; 'It's All Too Much '; 'ALL YOU NEED IS LOVE'.

(The remainder of the album comprises original film score by George Martin.)   *(The Beatles)*

May 1969   **Unfinished Music No.2: Life With The Lions**

'CAMBRIDGE 1969'.

'NO BED FOR BEATLE JOHN'; 'BABY'S HEARTBEAT'; 'TWO MINUTES SILENCE'; 'RADIO PLAY'.   *(John Lennon and Yoko Ono)*

September 1969   **Abbey Road**

'COME TOGETHER'; 'SOMETHING'; 'Maxwell's Silver Hammer'; 'Oh! Darling'; 'Octopus's Garden'; 'I WANT YOU (SHE'S SO HEAVY'.

'Here Comes The Sun'; 'BECAUSE'; 'You Never Give Me Your Money'; 'SUN KING'; 'MEAN MR MUSTARD'; 'POLYTHENE PAM'; 'She Came In Through The Bathroom Window'; 'Golden Slumbers'; 'Carry That Weight'; 'The End'; 'Her Majesty'.

(The Beatles)

November 1969   **Wedding Album**

'JOHN AND YOKO'.

'AMSTERDAM'.   *(John and Yoko)*

December 1969   **Live Peace in Toronto 1969**

'Blue Suede Shoes'; 'Money (That's What I Want)'; 'Dizzy Miss Lizzy'; 'YER BLUES'; 'COLD TURKEY'; 'GIVE PEACE A CHANCE'.

'Don't Worry Kyoko (Mummy's Only Looking For Her Hand In The Snow)'; 'John John (Let's Hope For Peace)'.

(The Plastic Ono Band)

May 1970   **Let It Be**

'Two Of Us'; 'DIG A PONY'; 'ACROSS THE UNIVERSE'; 'I Me Mine'; 'DIG IT'; 'Let It Be'; 'MAGGIE MAE'.

'I'VE GOT A FEELING'; 'ONE AFTER 909'; 'The Long and Winding Road'; 'For You Blue'; 'Get Back'.   *(The Beatles)*

December 1970   **John Lennon/Plastic Ono Band**

'MOTHER'; 'HOLD ON'; 'I FOUND OUT'; 'WORKING CLASS HERO'; 'ISOLATION'.

'REMEMBER'; 'LOVE'; 'WELL WELL WELL'; 'LOOK AT ME'; 'GOD'; 'MY MUMMY'S DEAD'.   *(John Lennon)*

October 1971   **Imagine**

'IMAGINE'; 'CRIPPLED INSIDE'; 'JEALOUS GUY'; 'IT'S SO HARD'; 'I DON'T WANT TO BE A SOLDIER'.

'GIVE ME SOME TRUTH'; 'OH MY LOVE'; 'HOW DO YOU SLEEP?'; 'HOW?'; 'OH YOKO!'
     (John Lennon/Plastic Ono Band [with the Flux Fiddlers])

September 1972   **Some Time In New York City***

'WOMAN IS THE NIGGER OF THE WORLD'; 'Sisters, O Sisters'; 'ATTICA STATE'; 'Born In A Prison'; 'NEW YORK CITY'.

'SUNDAY BLOODY SUNDAY'; 'THE LUCK OF THE IRISH'; 'JOHN SINCLAIR'; 'ANGELA'; 'We're All Water'.
     (John and Yoko/Plastic Ono Band with Elephants Memory
                         and The Invisible Strings)

'COLD TURKEY'; 'Don't Worry Kyoko (Mummy's Only Looking For Her Hand In The Snow)'.
     (John and Yoko/Plastic Ono Band with a cast of thousands)

'Well (Baby Please Don't Go)'; 'JAMRAG'; 'SCUMBAG'; 'AU'.
(John and Yoko/Plastic Ono Band with Frank Zappa and the
                         Mothers of Invention)

*Denotes released in the U.S.A. June 1972

November 1973   **Mind Games**

'MIND GAMES'; 'TIGHT AS'; 'AISUMASEN (I'M SORRY'; 'ONE DAY (AT A TIME'; 'BRING ON THE LUCIE (FREDA PEOPLE'; 'NUTOPIAN INTERNATIONAL ANTHEM'.

'INTUITION'; 'OUT THE BLUE'; 'ONLY PEOPLE'; 'I KNOW (I KNOW)'; 'YOU ARE HERE'; 'MEAT CITY'.   (*John Lennon*)

October 1974   **Walls and Bridges**

'GOING DOWN ON LOVE'; 'WHATEVER GETS YOU THRU THE NIGHT'; 'OLD DIRT ROAD'; 'WHAT YOU GOT'; 'BLESS YOU'; 'SCARED'.

'#9 DREAM'; 'SURPRISE, SURPRISE (SWEET BIRD OF PARADOX)'; 'STEEL AND GLASS'; 'BEEF JERKY'; 'NOBODY LOVES YOU (WHEN YOU'RE DOWN AND OUT)'; 'Ya Ya'.

February 1975   **Rock 'n' Roll**

'Be-Bop-A-Lula'; 'Stand By Me'; 'Rip It Up/Ready Teddy'; 'You Can't Catch Me'; 'Ain't That A Shame'; 'Do You Want To Dance'; 'Sweet Little Sixteen'.

'Slippin' and Slidin''; 'Peggy Sue'; 'Bring It On Home To Me/ Send Me Some Lovin''; 'Bony Moronie'; 'Ya Ya'; 'Just Because'.   (*John Lennon*)

October 1975   **Shaved Fish**

'GIVE PEACE A CHANCE'; 'COLD TURKEY'; 'INSTANT KARMA!'; 'POWER TO THE PEOPLE'; 'MOTHER'; 'WOMAN IS THE NIGGER OF THE WORLD'.

'IMAGINE'; 'WHATEVER GETS YOU THRU THE NIGHT'; 'MIND GAMES'; '#9 DREAM'; 'HAPPY XMAS (WAR IS OVER)'; 'GIVE PEACE A CHANCE (live reprise)'.

(*John Lennon/Plastic Ono Band*)

November 1980   **Double Fantasy**

'(JUST LIKE) STARTING OVER'; 'Kiss Kiss Kiss'; 'CLEANUP TIME'; 'Give Me Something'; 'I'M LOSING YOU'; 'I'm Moving On'; 'BEAUTIFUL BOY (DARLING BOY)'.

'WATCHING THE WHEELS'; 'I'm Your Angel'; 'WOMAN'; 'Beautiful Boys'; 'DEAR YOKO'; 'Every Man Has A Woman Who Loves Him'; 'Hard Times Are Over'.

(John Lennon and Yoko Ono)

November 1982 **The John Lennon Collection**

'GIVE PEACE A CHANCE'; 'INSTANT KARMA!'; 'POWER TO THE PEOPLE '; 'WHATEVER GETS YOU THRU THE NIGHT'; '#9 DREAM'; 'MIND GAMES'; 'LOVE'; 'HAPPY XMAS (WAR IS OVER)'.

'IMAGINE'; 'JEALOUS GUY'; 'Stand By Me'; '(JUST LIKE) STARTING OVER'; 'WOMAN'; 'I'M LOSING YOU'; 'BEAUTIFUL BOY (DARLING BOY)'; 'WATCHING THE WHEELS'; 'DEAR YOKO'. *(John Lennon)*

December 1983 **Heart Play—Unfinished Dialogue**

(Conversation. Tracks not banded.)

(John Lennon and Yoko Ono)

January 1984 **Milk and Honey**

'I'M STEPPING OUT'; 'Sleepless Night'; 'I DON'T WANNA FACE IT'; 'Don't Be Scared'; 'NOBODY TOLD ME'; '"O" Sanity'.

'BORROWED TIME'; 'Your Hands'; '(FORGIVE ME) MY LITTLE FLOWER PRINCESS'; 'Let Me Count The Ways'; 'GROW OLD WITH ME'; 'You're The One'. *(John Lennon and Yoko Ono)*

MISCELLANEOUS

December 1967 **Magical Mystery Tour** (E.P.)

'Magical Mystery Tour'; 'Your Mother Should Know'/'I AM THE WALRUS'.

'The Fool On The Hill'; 'FLYING'/'Blue Jay Way'.

(The Beatles)

December 1969 **No One's Gonna Change Our World** (L.P.)

(Album using various artists. Contains early version of 'ACROSS THE UNIVERSE').

July 1971   **Elastic Oz Band** (single)

(B-side, 'DO THE OZ', John Lennon/Plastic Ono Band under a pseudonym)

March 1981   **Elton John/John Lennon** (single)

'I Saw Her Standing There'/'WHATEVER GETS YOU THRU THE NIGHT'; 'LUCY IN THE SKY WITH DIAMONDS'.

(Note: 'I Saw Her Standing There' was also released previously as the B-side of Elton John's 'Philadelphia Freedom' in February 1975.)

    (Elton John Band featuring John Lennon and the Muscle Shoals Horns)

Sept. 1984. *Every Man Has A Woman* (LP); an album using various artists and containing John's version of Every Man Has A Woman Who Loves Him.

Songs written or co-written by John Lennon, not commercially recorded by him but instead 'given' to other artists.

'THE BALLAD OF NEW YORK CITY' — David Peel and the Lower East Side, 1972

'COOKIN' (IN THE KITCHEN OF LOVE)' — Ringo Starr, 1976

'FAME' — David Bowie, 1975

'GOD SAVE US' — Bill Elliot and the Elastic Oz Band, 1971

'I'M THE GREATEST' — Ringo Starr, 1973

'(IT'S ALL DA-DA DOWN TO) GOODNIGHT VIENNA' — Ringo Starr, 1974

'MUCHO MUNGO' — Harry Nilsson, 1974

'ROCK AND ROLL PEOPLE' — Johnny Winter, 1974

Guest Appearances

John Lennon appeared many times as a guest on other artists' recordings. A selection of titles on which John had particular influence is given below.

David Bowie: 'ACROSS THE UNIVERSE' and 'FAME', 1975
Elephants Memory: *Elephants Memory*, 1972

Elton John: 'LUCY IN THE SKY WITH DIAMONDS' and 'ONE DAY (AT A TIME)', 1974

Harry Nilsson: *Pussy Cats*, 1974

Yoko Ono: All albums pre-1981—*Yoko Ono/Plastic Ono Band*, 1970; *Fly*, 1971; *Approximately Infinite Universe*, 1973; *Feeling The Space*, 1973. All singles, including 'Walking On Thin Ice', 1981, which John was producing on the night of his murder. David Peel and the Lower East Side: *The Pope Smokes Dope*, 1972

INDEX